THE PAPERS OF
WOODROW WILSON
VOLUME 63
SEPTEMBER 4-NOVEMBER 5, 1919

SPONSORED BY THE WOODROW WILSON
FOUNDATION
AND PRINCETON UNIVERSITY

THE PAPERS OF
WOODROW WILSON

ARTHUR S. LINK, *EDITOR*

JOHN E. LITTLE, *ASSOCIATE EDITOR*

MANFRED F. BOEMEKE, *ASSOCIATE EDITOR*

L. KATHLEEN AMON, *ASSISTANT EDITOR*

PHYLLIS MARCHAND, *INDEXER*

Volume 63
September 4-November 5, 1919

PRINCETON, NEW JERSEY
PRINCETON UNIVERSITY PRESS
1990

$55.00

INTRODUCTION

THE opening of this volume finds Wilson in Columbus, Ohio, on September 4, 1919, where he inaugurates a transcontinental speaking tour to rally public opinion in support of the ratification of the Versailles Treaty and American membership in the League of Nations. Carrying the President, Mrs. Wilson, a skeleton staff, and a large group of reporters, the special train wends its way through the Middle West, with speeches by Wilson in Columbus, St. Louis, Kansas City, Des Moines, Omaha, and St. Paul and Minneapolis. From here the presidential special makes its way across the northern Plains and Rocky Mountains, with stops in Bismarck, North Dakota, Billings and Helena in Montana, Coeur d'Alene in Idaho, and Spokane, Washington. Next comes an incursion into the Pacific Northwest and speeches in Tacoma, Seattle, and Portland. From the latter city, the train runs down the Pacific slope to San Francisco and the Bay area, and, southward, to San Diego and Los Angeles. Wilson and his party go thence to Reno, by way of Sacramento, and on to Salt Lake City, Cheyenne, Denver, and Pueblo, Colorado. In this, the most extensive speaking tour of his life, Wilson delivers thirty-two major addresses and eight short ones. Still suffering from the effects of a small stroke on July 19 when he leaves Washington, Wilson presses on in spite of mounting hypertension and its symptoms—severe headaches, asthmatic attacks, double vision, and extreme fatigue. In the early morning hours of September 26, as his train reaches the eastern plateau of Colorado, Wilson suffers such a severe stroke warning that Dr. Grayson cancels the tour that was to have taken Wilson on to Wichita, Oklahoma City, Little Rock, Memphis, and Louisville.

His physical afflictions affect Wilson's usual highly graceful and literate rhetorical style. Characteristically, Wilson writes none of his speeches in advance and falls back on his accustomed ability to memorize a speech in advance and then deliver it in elegant, well-phrased style. This once great power sometimes fails him under the impact of pounding headaches and fatigue. He cannot always see the sentences in his mind as he speaks them, and they are often ungrammatical, incomplete, disconnected, and rambling. His mind's eye also cannot see the map of Europe, and it wanders circuitously as he traces the path of Pan-Germanism from Bremen to Baghdad—in Persia, as he sees it on the map.

Even so, Wilson draws upon his ebbing physical and mental resources to accomplish the main objectives of his tour, at least for his listeners and posterity. He describes the Paris settlement as the epochal event of modern history because it restores independence to Poland and Czechoslovakia and unity to the Serbs, Croats, and Slovenes; establishes trusteeships for the peoples of the former German colonies; promotes human rights through the protection of ethnic and religious minorities in Poland and Central Europe; and creates an international labor organization to promote the welfare of working people. He defends the disarmament of Germany and imposition of reparations on that country as severe but fair punishment for the great wrong that Germany has done the world. At the same time, he holds out the hand of welcome to the new international community to a democratic, self-governed, and peaceful Germany. In all these discourses and discussions, Wilson takes the high ground of nonpartisanship in trying to speak for all Americans.

The great debate over the League of Nations is gathering force in Washington and throughout the country, and Wilson devotes most of his attention in his speeches to the Covenant of the League of Nations, the obligations of the United States under the Covenant, and the role of leadership in that organization that he covets for the American people. He paints a dark and foreboding picture of the United States outside the League, cut off from its former associates, going it alone, an armed camp set in hostility against the world. Over and over, he answers critics of the Covenant on such specific questions as the Shantung settlement, the Monroe Doctrine, the right of withdrawal from the League, the protection of national sovereignty over domestic questions, and the representation of the British Dominions in the Assembly of the League. Again, over and over, he patiently explains the peacekeeping machinery of the League and describes that machinery as a 98 per cent insurance against war in the future. And he forecasts the coming of new world catastrophe within a generation if the United States does not guarantee the maintenance of peace through the League.

On the question of reservations, Wilson is equivocal. On the one hand, he declares that he has no objection to reservations that simply further clarify what he says is already clear concerning the obligations of the United States under the Covenant. At other times, he repeats his old misunderstanding that ratification with reservations will compel renegotiation of the treaty.

The heart of the Covenant and the pledge of future world peace, Wilson says in almost every speech, is Article X, by which member states undertake to guarantee the territorial integrity and political independence of members against external aggression. Trying to mollify fears that Article X will draw the United States into countless future wars, Wilson says over and over that, under the Covenant, the League Council can only advise member states as to action to be taken in the event of war, and that, in any event, the decision for war will always rest with Congress, which alone possesses the war-making power. However, he never squarely meets the issue, much emphasized by his opponents, of the Executive's possible use of United States military forces in local, limited peacekeeping activities by the League.

During his later speeches, Wilson frequently uses Article X as the metaphor for the moral obligation of the American people to preserve the peace and stability of the world. He speaks kindly and respectfully of his senatorial critics of an unreserved Article X until near the end of his tour. Then news comes that Lodge and the so-called mild Republican reservationists in the Senate have agreed upon a reservation to Article X. It declares that the armed forces of the United States can be used to participate in any of the League's peacekeeping activities only with the explicit consent of Congress which, under the Constitution, alone possesses the power to de-clare war.

To repeat, Wilson has said the same thing in his speeches; moreover, in an "interpretive" reservation of his own, sent to Senator Hitchcock just before he left Washington, Wilson proposed to say that the advice of the League Council regarding the employment of armed force contemplated in Article X "is to be regarded only as advice and leaves each Member State free to exercise its own judgment as to whether it is wise or practicable to act upon that advice or not." Yet, at Salt Lake City on September 23, he declares that the moderate Republicans' reservation cuts out the heart of the Covenant, "is a rejection of the Covenant" and "an absolute refusal to carry any part of the same responsibility that the other members of the League carry." Is this a declaration of war against his Republican allies and supporters generally and a sign that Wilson will refuse to meet halfway senators whose votes are essential to the treaty's success in the Senate?

The impact of Wilson's speeches is problematic. Press coverage for the first two or three of them is extensive. As he moves westward, the speeches become repetitive, and reporters from the major newspapers and news services write briefer and briefer reports, which pay more attention to local receptions and events than to the substance of Wilson's speeches. Wilson probably generates some generalized support for the idea of American membership in the League. But his refusal to meet the question of reservations head-on before his speech at Salt Lake City (and even there he addresses only the proposed reservation to Article X) creates the impression that reservations are at worst redundant. Following Wilson's lead, the chief opinion makers—the editorial writers of newspapers and magazines, the spokesmen of the League to Enforce Peace and of churches and peace organizations, and so on—strongly support Wilson's generalized arguments, assume that he will compromise with the Senate on reservations, and mount no campaign whatever for ratification without reservations. As far as the Senate is concerned, the most that can be said about the impact of Wilson's speeches is that they perhaps strengthen the resolve of the Republican moderates to resist the movement for amendments to the treaty. But on the question of reservations, Wilson's campaign does not change a single mind or vote.

Wilson returns to Washington on September 28 seriously ill but still able to function at a minimal level. About 8:30 a.m. on October 2, he suffers a stroke which paralyzes the left side of his body. For several days in mid-October he is at the point of death on account of a urinary obstruction, but nature saves his life. Meanwhile, and throughout the period covered by the balance of this volume, he lies prostrate in his bedroom and sees no one but Dr. Grayson, medical specialists, his nurses, and Mrs. Wilson, who is constantly by his bedside. In his daily bulletins, Grayson, refusing to reveal that his patient has suffered a severe stroke, does not attempt to minimize the serious nature of his illness, which he attributes to neurasthenia, "nervous prostration," "nervous fatigue," "nervous breakdown," etc.

The leader is stricken, but various agencies of the government continue to operate through heads of the executive departments. A few communications from them get to the sickroom. Mrs. Wilson reads them to her husband, and he is able to return replies through her. Lansing calls the Cabinet into session on October 3 to discuss whether Wilson is disabled, within the constitutional meaning of that term, and whether to call upon the Vice-President to assume the powers of the presidency. Lansing finds no support for any such move, but he continues to call and preside over Cabinet meetings for an exchange of views. Tumulty runs the business of the Executive Office. He writes a veto of the Volstead bill for the enforcement of the Eighteenth Amendment, and he, the Attorney General, and the Secretary of Labor devise a temporary solution of a threatened nationwide strike of bituminous coal miners.

The one sphere of action in which Wilson has exercised presidential power most watchfully, directly, and zealously—the conduct of the foreign relations of the United States—is totally paralyzed. Wilson is now convinced that Lansing was disloyal at Paris and is trying to usurp the presidential power, and he refuses to communicate with his Secretary of State other than to say that he does not have the strength to answer Lansing's appeals for direction on urgent matters of any kind. In this one area of policy making, the great government of the United States is paralyzed.

We are indebted to Bert E. Park for his essay on Wilson's stroke, which we print as an Appendix to this volume. Timothy Connelly of the National Historical Publications and Records Commission continued his invaluable research for us in Washington and also supplied all the pictures for this volume. David W. Hirst worked with the Editor to produce the first versions of our transcripts of Wilson's speeches. John Milton Cooper, Jr., William H. Harbaugh, August Heckscher, Richard W. Leopold, and Betty Miller Unterberger of the Editorial Advisory Committee all read the manuscript of this volume critically and helpfully. Alice Calaprice was our editor at Princeton University Press. To all these friends and co-workers, we are deeply indebted.

THE EDITORS

Princeton, New Jersey
April 18, 1990

Postcript: We call the attention of our readers to the important new materials on Wilson's stroke of October 2, 1919, which will be printed in Volume 64. These include extensive medical records from Dr. Grayson's papers.

CONTENTS

Introduction, vii
Illustrations, xix
Abbreviations and Symbols, xxi

The Papers, September 4-November 5, 1919
Domestic Affairs

Wilson addresses, statements, and messages
  Address to the Columbus Chamber of Commerce, September 4, 1919, 7
  Remarks on board the presidential train at Richmond, Indiana, September 4, 1919, 18
  Address in the Indianapolis Coliseum, September 4, 1919, 19
  Luncheon address to the St. Louis Chamber of Commerce, September 5, 1919, 33
  Address at the St. Louis Coliseum, September 5, 1919, 43
  Address in Convention Hall in Kansas City, September 6, 1919, 66
  Address in the Coliseum in Des Moines, September 6, 1919, 76
  Address in the Auditorium in Omaha, September 8, 1919, 97
  Address in the Coliseum in Sioux Falls, September 8, 1919, 107
  Address at St. Paul to a joint session of the legislature of Minnesota, September 9, 1919, 125
  Address in the Minneapolis Armory, September 9, 1919, 131
  Address in the St. Paul Auditorium, September 9, 1919, 138
  Address at Bismarck, September 10, 1919, 153
  Address from the rear platform at Mandan, North Dakota, September 10, 1919, 162
  Address in the Billings Auditorium, September 11, 1919, 170
  Address in the Marlow Theater in Helena, September 11, 1919, 180
  Address at Coeur d'Alene, September 12, 1919, 212
  Address in the Spokane Armory, September 12, 1919, 224
  Remarks in the Tacoma Stadium, September 13, 1919, 240
  Address in the Tacoma Armory, September 13, 1919, 241
  After-dinner remarks in Seattle, September 13, 1919, 253
  Address in the Seattle Arena, September 13, 1919, 254
  Luncheon address in Portland, September 15, 1919, 277
  Address in the Portland Auditorium, September 15, 1919, 283
  Luncheon address in San Francisco, September 17, 1919, 311
  Address in the San Francisco Civic Auditorium, September 17, 1919, 323
  Luncheon address in San Francisco, September 18, 1919, 341
  Address in the Greek Theater in Berkeley, September 18, 1919, 350
  Address in the Oakland Municipal Auditorium, September 18, 1919, 352
  Address in the San Diego Stadium, September 19, 1919, 371
  After-dinner speech in San Diego, September 19, 1919, 382
  After-dinner speech in Los Angeles, September 20, 1919, 400
  Address in the Shrine Auditorium in Los Angeles, September 20, 1919, 407
  Remarks in Sacramento, September 22, 1919, 426
  Address in Reno, September 22, 1919, 428
  Remarks in Ogden, Utah, September 23, 1919, 448
  Address in the Tabernacle in Salt Lake City, September 23, 1919, 449
  Address in the Princess Theater in Cheyenne, September 24, 1919, 467

Address in the Denver Auditorium, September 25, 1919, 490

Address in the City Auditorium in Pueblo, Colorado, September 25, 1919, 500

Statement on the threatened coal miners' strike, October 25, 1919, 596 (draft), 599

Message vetoing the Volstead bill, October 27, 1919, 601

Thanksgiving Proclamation, November 4, 1919, 613

Wilson correspondence
  From Wilson to
    Newton Diehl Baker, 301
    Julius Howland Barnes, 589
    Bernard Mannes Baruch, 336
    Louis Brownlow, 302
    William Byron Colver, 301, 425
    Calvin Coolidge, 615
    Josephus Daniels, 556
    Edward Irving Edwards, 615
    Rudolph Forster, 392
    Carter Glass, 336
    Walker Downer Hines, 300
    Members of the Industrial Conference, 554, 584
    Members of the public group of the Industrial Conference, 612
    Thomas William Lamont, 388
    Franklin Knight Lane, 591
    Thomas Riley Marshall, 117
    Henry Lee Myers, 197
    George William Norris, 197
    William Phillips, 304
    Joseph Patrick Tumulty, 625, 626
    The people of Utah, 447
    The people of Wichita, 524
    William Bauchop Wilson, 593

  To Wilson from
    Newton Diehl Baker, 296
    Emmet Derby Boyle, 54
    Louis Brownlow, 264, 295
    Albert Sidney Burleson, 266, 442
    William Byron Colver, 389
    Josephus Daniels, 610, 618
    John Fitzpatrick and others, 148
    Harry Augustus Garfield, 55
    Carter Glass, 200
    Samuel Gompers and others, 29
    Walker Downer Hines, 88, 118
    Gilbert Monell Hitchcock, 482
    Thomas William Lamont, 165
    Franklin Knight Lane, 582, 611
    Robert Lansing, 337, 588
    Vance Criswell McCormick, 363
    John A. O'Connell, 268
    William Phillips, 444

William Cox Redfield, 573
Upton Beall Sinclair, 425
Joseph Patrick Tumulty, 371, 397, 399, 609, 625
Francis Patrick Walsh, 389
William Bauchop Wilson, 53, 54, 56

Collateral correspondence
Mary Anderson to Joseph Patrick Tumulty, 58
Bernard Mannes Baruch to Cary Travers Grayson, 149
Bernard Mannes Baruch to Joseph Patrick Tumulty, 149
William Joseph Hamilton Cochran to Joseph Patrick Tumulty, 198, 483
Josephus Daniels to Edith Bolling Galt Wilson, 557
Josephus Daniels to Joseph Patrick Tumulty, 610
Rudolph Forster to Joseph Patrick Tumulty, 51, 93, 150, 169, 268, 445, 483
Andrew J. Gallagher and others to Joseph Patrick Tumulty, 302
Cary Travers Grayson to Bernard Mannes Baruch, 53
Walker Downer Hines to Joseph Patrick Tumulty, 595
Franklin Knight Lane to Joseph Patrick Tumulty, 582, 591
Russell Cornell Leffingwell to Joseph Patrick Tumulty, 267
Breckinridge Long to Joseph Patrick Tumulty, 444
Guy Mason to Joseph Patrick Tumulty, 445
Vance Criswell McCormick to Joseph Patrick Tumulty, 117, 235
Michael J. McGuire to Joseph Patrick Tumulty, 296
William Phillips to Joseph Patrick Tumulty, 369
Key Pittman to Joseph Patrick Tumulty, 117
William Cox Redfield to Joseph Patrick Tumulty, 573
Joseph Patrick Tumulty to Newton Diehl Baker, 164
Joseph Patrick Tumulty to Louis Brownlow, 150, 296
Joseph Patrick Tumulty to John Fitzpatrick, 164
Joseph Patrick Tumulty to Rudolph Forster, 92, 164, 198, 447, 522 (2), 531
Joseph Patrick Tumulty to Andrew J. Gallagher, 303
Joseph Patrick Tumulty to Samuel Gompers, 52, 163
Joseph Patrick Tumulty to Walker Downer Hines, 595
Joseph Patrick Tumulty to Franklin Knight Lane, 591
Joseph Patrick Tumulty to Russell Cornell Leffingwell, 165
Joseph Patrick Tumulty to Edith Bolling Galt Wilson, 602, 609
Joseph Patrick Tumulty to William Bauchop Wilson, 554, 593
Edith Bolling Galt Wilson to Josephus Daniels, 558

Notes, reports, and memoranda
Memorandum by Harry Augustus Garfield on appointments for a joint conference of mine workers and coal operators, 56
Memorandum by Joseph Patrick Tumulty on the cost of the war to the Allies and the Central Powers, 221
Memorandum by Joseph Patrick Tumulty on themes for an address by Wilson, 222
Report by the Washington bureau of the League to Enforce Peace on the prospect of ratification of the treaty, 235
Notes by Wilson for addresses in Tacoma and San Francisco, 241, 310, 322
Memorandum by Wilson in reply to questions by the San Francisco Labor Council, 303
Extract from a speech by William McKinley, 398
Memorandum by Robert Lansing on Wilson's state of health, 618

News reports

"Wilson Begins Hard Week," September 8, 1919, 96

Wilson's definition of the fundamental principles of the peace treaty, September 10, 1919, 163

"Wilson Dropped Greatness and Showed His Weariness," September 25, 1919, 487

A description of Wilson at work, September 25, 1919, 513

"President is Ill and Cancels His Tour," September 26, 1919, 522

"Wilson Very Ill, Condition Cause of Real Anxiety," September 27, 1919, 527

"Push Reservation Wilson Scouted; Republicans Now Favor Compromise which, the President Said, 'Knifes the Treaty,' " September 27, 1919, 529

"Wilson Sleeping Better and Improving; Allowed to Give a Little Time to Work," September 30, 1919, 536

"President is Jaded Again, After Another Restless Night," October 1, 1919, 538

" 'Very Sick Man' Says Grayson of President in Late Night Bulletin," October 3, 1919, 543

"Found Wilson Cheerful, Dr. Dercum Announces," October 3, 1919, 546

"President is Improving Slightly, Late Report by Dr. Grayson Says," October 4, 1919, 549

"More Encouraging Day," October 4, 1919, 550

"Wilson Has Good Day," October 6, 1919, 552

"Wilson Still Gains," October 7, 1919, 555

"Wilson Is Improved," October 11, 1919, 560

"President Needs Long Rest," October 11, 1919, 561

"Reports Wilson Suffered Shock," October 11, 1919, 563

"Rumor Busy about Wilson," October 12, 1919, 564

"Had Slight Retinal Lesion," October 12, 1919, 567

"President's Condition is 'About the Same,' Says the Latest White House Bulletin," October 13, 1919, 568

"Wilson's Mind 'Clear' and He Can Act, but Grayson Says Cure Requires Time," October 13, 1919, 569

"Spent Restless Day," October 15, 1919, 572

"Good Day for Wilson," October 16, 1919, 574

"Wilson Told of Vote; Grayson Allows Him to Hear Shantung Clause is Beaten," October 17, 1919, 576

"President Improves after Setback; Dr. Young, Gland Specialist, Called in," October 17, 1919, 577

"Dr. H. H. Young Tells of Wilson Jesting," October 17, 1919, 580

"Wilson Has Best Day," October 19, 1919, 581

"President Better, Signs Four Bills," October 22, 1919, 586

"President Maintains His Improvement," October 23, 1919, 590

"Belgian Royalties See the President," October 30, 1919, 602

"President Interested in Election Returns," November 4, 1919, 608

Diaries

Henry Fountain Ashurst, 586

Ray Stannard Baker, 619

Josephus Daniels, 548, 552 (2), 555, 557, 559, 598, 612

Cary Travers Grayson, 3, 31, 63, 92, 93, 122, 152, 168, 210, 236, 273, 274, 300, 308, 340, 369, 396, 423, 426, 446, 467, 487, 518, 526, 532

Edward Mandell House, 585
Robert Lansing, 543, 547, 552, 554, 606
Breckinridge Long, 558

Diplomatic, Military, and Naval Affairs

Wilson correspondence
  From Wilson to
    Newton Diehl Baker, 274
    The chairman of the joint committee of Congress in charge of welcoming
      the First Division, 295
    The First Division of the United States Army, 274
    Rudolph Forster, 295
    Peter Augustus Jay, 484, 534
    Robert Lansing, 391 (2), 392
    Francesco Saverio Nitti, 484
    William Phillips, 166, 297, 421, 463, 464, 532 (2), 534
    Frank Lyon Polk, 270, 424
    Eleuthérios Kyrios Vénisélos, 391

  To Wilson from
    Newton Diehl Baker, 361
    Georges Clemenceau, 367, 393
    Georges Clemenceau, Arthur James Balfour, and André Tardieu, 60
    Georges Clemenceau and David Lloyd George, 204
    Carter Glass, 518
    Edward Mandell House, 271, 299, 421, 537
    Peter Augustus Jay, 464, 515
    Robert Lansing, 606, 616
    Francesco Saverio Nitti, 464
    John Barton Payne, 368
    William Phillips, 62, 91, 119, 204, 235, 270, 271, 297, 298, 305, 306, 307,
      364, 366, 392, 394 (2), 423, 445, 466, 485
    Frank Lyon Polk, 91, 120, 306, 364, 393, 465, 524, 525
    Tommaso Tittoni, 365

Collateral correspondence
  Newton Diehl Baker to Joseph Patrick Tumulty, 441
  Georges Clemenceau to Edward Mandell House, 271
  Rudolph Forster to Joseph Patrick Tumulty, 526
  Peter Augustus Jay to Robert Lansing, 297, 543
  Edward Fenton McGlachlin, Jr., to Peyton Conway March, 361
  William Phillips to Peter Augustus Jay, 560
  William Phillips to Robert Lansing, 119
  William Phillips to Frank Lyon Polk, 151
  Frank Lyon Polk to Edward Mandell House, 59
  Frank Lyon Polk to Robert Lansing, 59, 60 (2), 204, 306
  Frank Lyon Polk to William Phillips, 166, 235
  Joseph Patrick Tumulty to Rudolph Forster, 515
  Joseph Patrick Tumulty to Robert Lansing, 613
  Joseph Patrick Tumulty to William Phillips, 91, 270
  Joseph Patrick Tumulty to Edith Bolling Galt Wilson, 615
  Edith Bolling Galt Wilson to Robert Lansing, 617

Memoranda, reports, and aide-mémoire
  Memorandum by André Tardieu on the question of Thrace, 121
  Notes of a conversation with Wilson by William Emmanuel Rappard, 626,
    630

Personal Affairs

Wilson correspondence
  From Wilson to
    Albert Sidney Burleson, 395
    Mary Allen Hulbert, 419
    Catharine Milligan McLane, 623
    Désiré Félicien François Joseph Cardinal Mercier, 197
    John Carver Palfrey, 624
    Jessie Woodrow Wilson Sayre, 521
    Lyon Gardiner Tyler, 463
    Charles Warren, 623
    Announcement of Wilson's marriage to Edith Bolling Galt, 624

  To Wilson from
    Albert, King of the Belgians, 535
    Albert Sidney Burleson, 534
    Cleveland Hoadley Dodge, 535
    James Watson Gerard, 535
    Edward Mandell House, 536
    Désiré Félicien François Joseph Cardinal Mercier, 166, 549
    Jessie Woodrow Wilson Sayre, 166

Collateral correspondence
  Newton Diehl Baker to Edith Bolling Galt Wilson, 534
  Elisabeth, Queen of the Belgians, to Edith Bolling Galt Wilson, 548
  Pietro Cardinal Gasparri to Joseph Patrick Tumulty, 555
  Cary Travers Grayson to Harry Augustus Garfield, 538
  Cary Travers Grayson to Gilbert Monell Hitchcock, 593
  Edward Mandell House to Edith Bolling Galt Wilson, 587
  Robert Lansing to Frank Lyon Polk, 540, 571
  Alexander Mitchell Palmer to Roland Sletor Morris, 608
  William Phillips to Frank Lyon Polk, 537
  Frank Lyon Polk to William Phillips, 536
  Joseph Patrick Tumulty to Edith Bolling Galt Wilson, 539
  Edith Bolling Galt Wilson to Edward Mandell House, 592
  Edith Bolling Galt Wilson to Loulie Hunter House, 580
  Margaret Woodrow Wilson to Edith Gittings Reid, 575

Editorial Note: Wilson's Speeches on His Western Tour, 5
Appendix I: From a Memoir by Irwin Hood Hoover, 632
Appendix II: Woodrow Wilson's Stroke of October 2, 1919 (Park), 639
Index, 647

ILLUSTRATIONS

Following page 360

PICTURES FROM THE WESTERN TOUR

In St. Paul, Minnesota
Library of Congress

En route to the Theater in Bismarck, North Dakota
Library of Congress

At the Tacoma Stadium
Library of Congress

With Reporters and Others
Library of Congress

On Parade in San Francisco
Library of Congress

In the Greek Theater at Berkeley
Library of Congress

At a Reception in San Diego
Library of Congress

In Union Station on His Return to Washington
Princeton University Library

ABBREVIATIONS

ALI	autograph letter initialed
ALS	autograph letter signed
ASB	Albert Sidney Burleson
CC	carbon copy
CCL	carbon copy of letter
EAW	Ellen Axson Wilson
EBW	Edith Bolling Galt Wilson
EMH	Edward Mandell House
FLP	Frank Lyon Polk
FR	*Papers Relating to the Foreign Relations of the United States*
FR 1919, Russia	*Papers Relating to the Foreign Relations of the United States, 1919, Russia*
HCH	Herbert Clark Hoover
Hw, hw	handwritten, handwriting
JD	Josephus Daniels
JPT	Joseph Patrick Tumulty
MS, MSS	manuscript, manuscripts
NDB	Newton Diehl Baker
PPC	*Papers Relating to the Foreign Relations of the United States, The Paris Peace Conference, 1919*
RG	record group
RL	Robert Lansing
T	typed
TC	typed copy
TCL	typed copy of letter
TL	typed letter
TLS	typed letter signed
TS	typed signed
TWL	Thomas William Lamont
WBW	William Bauchop Wilson
WCR	William Cox Redfield
WP	William Phillips
WW	Woodrow Wilson
WWT	Woodrow Wilson typed
WWTLS	Woodrow Wilson typed letter signed

ABBREVIATIONS FOR COLLECTIONS AND REPOSITORIES

Following the National Union Catalog of the
Library of Congress

AzU	University of Arizona
CtY	Yale University
DLC	Library of Congress
DNA	National Archives
EBR	Executive Branch Records
MH-BA	Harvard University Graduate School of Business Administration

MHi   Massachusetts Historical Society
MnHi   Minnesota Historical Society
NjP   Princeton University
SDR   State Department Records
WC, NjP   Woodrow Wilson Collection, Princeton University
WP, DLC   Woodrow Wilson Papers, Library of Congress

SYMBOLS

[September 26, 1919]   publication date of published writing; also date of doc-
                       ument when date is not part of text
[*October 6, 1919*]   composition date when publication date differs
[[October 15, 1919]]   delivery date of speech when publication date differs
**** ***   text deleted by author of document

THE PAPERS OF

WOODROW WILSON

VOLUME 63

SEPTEMBER 4-NOVEMBER 5, 1919

THE PAPERS OF
WOODROW WILSON

From the Diary of Dr. Grayson[1]

Thursday, September 4, 1919.

The President made his first appearance on the rear platform of the car as the train halted for a few seconds at two or three of the little Ohio towns[2] en route to Columbus. The crowds were very friendly but the President made no effort to make any speeches, contenting himself with shaking hands with those who were able to get up to the rear platform.

Columbus was reached at 11:00 o'clock in the morning. It was a gray, September day and had been raining for some time, but the rain stopped just before the party reached the Ohio Capital. A combination of circumstances made the Columbus meeting very unsatisfactory. There was a street railway strike in progress, which made it impossible for the people of the out-lying sections to get down town. In addition, the President had made a number of speeches in Columbus and was pretty well known there. All of this, combined with the fact that it was Thursday morning—a bad time for any kind of a meeting—had the effect in holding down the number in attendance.[3] The President had a severe headache and was in none too good a physical condition.

When he arrived at the hall he lost no time in getting right after the opponents of the Treaty. He took occasion right here at the outset of his trip to take a position of open opposition to the statement made in a speech a few nights ago by Senator Knox, of Pennsylvania,[4] that the terms of the Treaty of Versailles were unjust—indeed they were too severe upon Germany. The President's excoriation of the German crimes which had resulted in the war and the manner in which the German Government had outraged all forms of international law and all forms of decency in warfare, made a great hit with the crowd.

The Presidential Special left Columbus at 1:00 o'clock, headed for Indianapolis, where the night meeting was to be held.

En route to Indianapolis big crowds had gathered at all of the stations through which the train passed, and at a number of points where the train halted the President went out on the rear platform and shook hands with those who could get up close to the train.[5]

It was very apparent that so far as the people themselves were concerned they were deeply interested in the President and in his mission. He took cognizance of this by telling them very plainly that he had come to the people to make a report of his stewardship and that he was more concerned that the people know all of the facts than he was of the political advantage that might accrue to any party as a result of the fight over the Treaty.

Indianapolis was reached at 6:00 o'clock but the train did not run into the station there until half an hour later, as the President was given an opportunity to have his dinner uninterrupted by the crowds that would have gathered about the train if it had been run directly into the station.

The meeting in Indianapolis was held at the Fair Grounds. A state fair was in progress at the time. The President on detraining was greeted by a non-partisan reception committee, included among the number being Governor Goodrich,[6] the Republican Governor of Indiana. Mrs. Wilson was presented with a magnificent bouquet of roses as she passed through the station by a committee of the women of the city, who had been organized for that purpose.

There was an automobile parade, headed by a band, through the principal streets of Indianapolis. Arriving at the Fair Grounds, it was found that the big auditorium, which is usually used for the display of prize produce, fancy articles and the like, was jammed to the doors. Estimates as to the number present varied from 16,000 to 20,000 people. The auditorium is not intended for speech-making. The platform had been erected in the center of the great building. There was no sounding-board, and it was a physical impossibility for any one human voice to fill this space. Governor Goodrich had been selected as the presiding officer, and when he was introduced he launched into a lengthy speech, in which he attempted to define his position as a Republican Executive, calling attention to the non-partisan character of the gathering. The crowd had not come there to hear the Governor, and in a very few moments it was out of hand. There was "booing" in some sections of the hall and jeering in others, while a score of people yelled at the Governor to "introduce the President and sit down." This was probably the first time that a Republican Governor had been jeered and hooted in a Republican State while he was endeavoring to introduce a Democratic President to an audience.

When the President finally was introduced the audience was very much excited and there was much shuffling of feet. As a result the President's voice failed to carry at the commencement and a number of people away in the far corners of the auditorium started for the doors. This caused uneasiness and confusion, so that the President finally stopped talking, and, at his request, a stentorian-voiced usher asked all who wanted to leave and who could not hear to pass out so that the others who had come to hear would be afforded an opportunity to do so. Possibly a couple of hundred went out and then the doors were closed and the President resumed. While at the outset his voice was a trifle husky, before he had been talking five minutes he had the audience under complete control, and from then on his address was listened to with the deepest of attention, and the points which he made were applauded in a very friendly manner. The meeting was a huge success. It was very plain that the people were well pleased with the arguments which the President presented, and once or twice when he touched upon subjects that had been matters of debate in the Senate, cries of "Better tell that to Harry New and Jim Watson (Senators from Indiana)" were heard.

When the President left the hall a hurried trip was made to the station and the train re-boarded, and a start made for St. Louis at 10:00 o'clock that night.

T MS (in possession of James Gordon Grayson and Cary T. Grayson, Jr.).
[1] About this diary, see n. 1 to the extract from it printed at Dec. 3, 1918, Vol. 53.
[2] Including Dennison and Newark.
[3] News reports confirm that the crowds along Wilson's route to Memorial Hall were small. However, Louis Seibold reported that 4,000 persons, admitted on a first-come, first-served basis, were seated in the hall, and that two thousand more clamored for admittance. New York *World*, Sept. 5 and 6, 1919.
[4] Actually, Knox had spoken before the Senate shortly after 11 a.m. on August 29. In the course of a lengthy attack on the Versailles Treaty, he asserted that its terms were so harsh that they could only lead to even bloodier conflicts in the future than in the recent past. He urged the Senate to reject the treaty and the House and Senate to declare hostilities at an end by concurrent resolution. *Cong. Record*, 66th Cong., 1st sess., pp. 4493-4501. Extensive quotations from his speech appear in the *New York Times*, Aug. 30, 1919, and in many other newspapers of that date.
[5] Wilson responded to several questions and comments from the crowd in Urbana, Ohio. He answered strongly in the affirmative when asked if he thought that Japan would in fact return Shantung to China. New York *World* and Columbus *Ohio State Journal*, Sept. 5, 1919. His remarks at Richmond are printed at this date. The crowd at the railroad station there was estimated at between two and three thousand persons. *Indianapolis News*, Sept. 5, 1919.
[6] James Putnam Goodrich.

EDITORIAL NOTE

WILSON'S SPEECHES ON HIS WESTERN TOUR

Charles Lee Swem accompanied Wilson on his western tour and recorded his speeches stenographically. His shorthand notebooks are in the Charles L. Swem Collection in the Princeton University Library. Swem transcribed these notes along the way; he also had a mimeograph machine with him and distributed copies of his transcripts. Immediately after Wilson's return to Washington, Swem or someone in the White House gave a complete set of these transcripts to Senator Hitchcock, who presented them to the Senate, which, on October 7, 1919, ordered them printed. They were printed by the Government Printing Office in 1919 as *Addresses of President Wilson: Addresses Delivered by President Wilson on his Western Tour, September 4 to September 25, 1919, on the League of Nations, Treaty of Peace with Germany, Industrial Conditions, High Cost of Living, Race Riots, Etc.*, 66th Cong., 1st sess., Sen. Doc. 120. Reprinted verbatim by Ray Stannard Baker and William E. Dodd, eds., *The Public Papers of Woodrow Wilson* (6 vols., New York, 1925-27), V-VI, they have to this time been regarded as the standard texts.

Transcripts of Wilson's speeches, prepared by their own reporters, were usually printed by all the newspapers of the cities in which he spoke; in addition, either full or partial texts were distributed by the national news services or printed in the newspapers which had special reporters on the tour. We have attempted to recover all versions of Wilson's speeches in all newspapers. Following our usual practice in reconstructing Wilson's speeches, we first compared Swem's transcripts to other versions. In addition, we read Swem's transcripts against his own shorthand notes. These exercises at once revealed that Swem made numerous errors of transcription. Moreover, his versions are highly critical ones, that is, he edited them extensively. He changed sentences to make them grammatical; omitted portions of speeches which, for various reasons, he thought ought not to be published; rearranged portions of speeches to make Wilson appear coherent; and expanded all contractions.

Following standard editorial method, we have regarded complete texts of Wilson's speeches as the basic texts. In several cases, Swem's texts are the only complete texts available; we have used them as the basic texts and have corrected them insofar as possible by a reading of Swem's transcripts of them against extant incomplete texts. In other cases, when complete texts, which appeared to us to be accurate renderings, were available in local newspapers, we used them as the basic texts and, whenever appropriate, have corrected them from a reading of Swem's texts and other complete or partial texts in other newspapers. Since the spelling, punctuation, capitalization, paragraphing, and so on of all these texts were those of the reporters who recorded them, we have modernized spellings, reparagraphed, and made such changes in capitalization and punctuation as seemed appropriate.

In all cases, Wilson delivered these speeches without a written text. As had been his practice since he entered public life in 1910, Wilson relied upon brief outlines to assist his memory of what he wanted to say. Also, probably at some time before he left on his western tour, Wilson typed eight pages of notes on special subjects: themes, the character and scope of the treaty, the Covenant of the League of Nations, the voting powers of the Assembly, and "Change of Policy." Either in California, or soon afterward, Wilson typed up new general outlines for speeches and extracts for quotation. All these notes are WWT MSS in WP, DLC. We do not print all of them because Wilson developed their points and subjects in his speeches repetitively.

An Address to the Columbus Chamber of Commerce

[[September 4, 1919]]

Mr. Chairman, Governor Campbell,[1] and my fellow citizens. (applause) It is with very profound pleasure that I find myself face to face with you. I have for a long time chafed at the confinement of Washington. I have for a long time wished to fulfill the purpose with which my heart was full when I returned to our beloved country, namely, to go out and report to my fellow countrymen concerning those affairs of the world which now need to be settled.

The only people I owe any report to are you and the other citizens of the United States, and it has become increasingly necessary, apparently, that I should report to you. After all the various angles at which you have heard the treaty held up, perhaps you would like to know what is in the treaty. I find it very difficult in reading some of the speeches that I have read to form any conception of that great document.

It is a document unique in the history of the world for many reasons, and I think I cannot do you a better service, or the peace of the world a better service, than by pointing out to you just what this treaty contains and what it seeks to do.

In the first place, my fellow countrymen, it seeks to punish one of the greatest wrongs ever done in history—the wrong which Germany sought to do to the world and to civilization, and there ought to be no weak purpose with regard to the application of the punishment. She attempted an intolerable thing, and she must be made to pay for the attempt.

The terms of the treaty are severe, but they are not unjust. I can testify that the men associated with me at the peace conference in Paris had it in their hearts to do justice and not wrong. But they knew, perhaps with a more vivid sense of what had happened than we could possibly know on this side of the water, the many solemn covenants which Germany had disregarded, the long preparation she had made to overwhelm her neighbors, the utter disregard which she had shown for human rights—for the rights of women and children and those who were helpless.

They had seen their lands devastated by an enemy that devoted itself not only to the effort of victory, but to the effort of terror—seeking to terrify the people whom they fought. And I wish to testify that they exercised restraint in the terms of this treaty. They did not wish to overwhelm any great nation; they acknowledged that Germany was a great nation; and they had no purpose in over-

---

[1] The chairman was William Oxley Thompson, President of Ohio State University. Campbell was James Edwin Campbell, Democrat, Governor of Ohio, 1890-1892.

whelming the German people. But they did think that it ought to be burned into the consciousness of men forever that no people ought to permit its government to do what the German government did.

In the last analysis, my fellow countrymen, as we in America would be the first to claim, a people are responsible for the acts of their government. If their government purposes things that are wrong, they ought to take measures and see to it that that purpose is not executed.

Germany was self-governed. Her rulers had not concealed the purpose that they had in mind, but they had deceived their people as to the character of the methods they were going to use. And I believe, from what I can learn, that there is an awakened consciousness in Germany itself of the deep iniquity of the thing that was attempted.

When the Austrian delegates came before the peace conference, they in so many words spoke of the origination of the war as a crime and admitted in our presence that it was a thing intolerable to contemplate. They knew in their hearts that it had done them the deepest conceivable wrong—that it had put their people and the people of Germany at the judgment seat of mankind. And throughout this treaty, every term that was applied to Germany was meant, not to humiliate Germany, but to rectify the wrong that she had done.

And if you will look even into the severe terms of reparation, for there was no indemnity—no indemnity of any sort was claimed, merely reparation, merely paying for the destruction done, merely making good the losses, so far as the losses could be made good, which she had unjustly inflicted, not upon the governments (for the reparation is not to go to the governments), but upon the people whose rights she had trodden upon with absolute absence of everything that even resembled pity. There is no indemnity in this treaty, but there is reparation, and, even in the terms of reparation, a method is devised by which the reparation shall be adjusted to Germany's ability to pay it.

I am astonished at some of the statements I see made about this treaty, and the truth is that they are made by persons who have not read the treaty or who, if they have read it, have not comprehended its meaning.

There is a method of adjustment in the treaty by which the reparation shall not be pressed beyond the point which Germany can pay, but she will be pressed to the utmost point that she can pay— which is just, which is righteous. It would be intolerable if there had been anything else. For my fellow citizens, this treaty is not meant merely to end this single war. It is meant as a notice to every government which in the future will attempt this thing that mankind will unite to inflict the same punishment.

There is no national triumph sought to be recorded in this treaty. There is no glory sought for any particular nation. The thought of the statesmen collected around that table was of their people, of the sufferings that they had gone through, of the losses they had incurred—that great throbbing heart which was so depressed, so forlorn, so sad in every memory that it had had of the five tragical years that have just gone by. Let us never forget those years, my fellow countrymen. Let us never forget the purpose—the high purpose, the disinterested purpose—with which America lent its strength, not for its own glory, but for the advance of mankind. And, as I said, this treaty was not intended merely to end this war. It was intended to prevent any similar war.

I wonder if some of the opponents of the League of Nations have forgotten the promises we made our people before we went to that peace table. We had taken by process of law the flower of our youth from every countryside, from every household, and we told those mothers and fathers and sisters and wives and sweethearts that we were taking those men to fight a war which would end business of that sort. And if we do not end it, if we do not do the best that human concert of action can do to end it, we are of all men the most unfaithful—the most unfaithful to the loving hearts who suffered in this war, the most unfaithful to those households bowed in grief, yet lifted with the feeling that the lad laid down his life for a great thing, among other things, in order that other lads might not have to do the same thing.

That is what the League of Nations is for, to end this war justly. And it is not merely to serve notice on governments which would contemplate the same things which Germany contemplated that they will do it at their peril, but also concerting the combination of power which will prove to them that they will do it at their peril. It is idle to say the world will combine against you, because it may not, but it is persuasive to say the world is combined against you, and will remain combined against any who attempt the same things that you attempted. The League of Nations is the only thing that can prevent the recurrence of this dreadful catastrophe and redeem our promises.

And the character of the League is based upon the experience of this very war. I did not meet a single public man who did not admit these things—that Germany would not have gone into this war if she had thought Great Britain was going into it, and that she most certainly would never have gone into this war if she had dreamed

America was going into it. And they have all admitted that a notice beforehand that the greatest powers of the world would combine to prevent this sort of thing would have prevented it absolutely.

When gentlemen tell you, therefore, that the League of Nations is intended for some other purpose than this, merely reply this to them: "If we do not do this thing, we have neglected the central covenant that we made to our people." And there will be no statesmen of any country who can thereafter promise his people any alleviation from the perils of war. The passions of this world are not dead. The rivalries of this world have not cooled. They have been rendered hotter than ever. The harness that is to unite nations is more necessary now than it ever was before, and, unless there is this sureness of combined action before wrong is attempted, wrong will be attempted just so soon as the most ambitious nations can recover from the financial stress of this war.

Now, look what else is in the treaty. This treaty is unique in the history of mankind, because the center of it is the redemption of weak nations. There never was a congress of nations before that considered the rights of those who could not enforce their rights. There never was a congress of nations before that did not seek to effect some balance of power brought about by means of serving the strength and interest of the strongest powers concerned, whereas this treaty builds up nations that never could have won their freedom in any other way. It builds them up by gift, by largess, not by obligation; builds them up because of the conviction of the men who wrote the treaty that the rights of people transcend the rights of governments, because of the conviction of the men who wrote that treaty that the fertile source of war is wrong.

The Austro-Hungarian Empire, for example, was held together by military force and consisted of peoples who did not want to live together, who did not have the spirit of nationality as towards each other, who were constantly chafing at the bands that held them. Hungary, though a willing partner of Austria, was willing to be her partner because she could share Austria's strength for accomplishing her own ambitions, and her own ambitions were to hold under the Jugo-Slavic peoples that lie to the south of her: Bohemia, an unhappy partner—a partner by duress, flowing in all her veins the strongest national impulse that was to be found anywhere in Europe; and, north of that, pitiful Poland, a great nation divided up among the great powers of Europe, torn asunder, kinship disregarded, natural ties treated with contempt, and an obligatory division among sovereigns imposed upon her, a part of her given to Russia, a part of her given to Austria, and a part of her given to Germany, and great bodies of Polish people never permitted to have the normal intercourse with their kinsmen for fear that that fine instinct of the heart should assert itself which binds families together.

Poland never could have won her independence. Bohemia never could have broken away from the Austro-Hungarian combination. The Slavic peoples to the south, running down into the great Balkan Peninsula, had again and again tried to assert their nationality and their independence, and had as often been crushed, not by the immediate power they were fighting, but by the combined power of Europe. The old alliances, the old balances of power, were meant to see to it that no little nation asserted its rights to the disturbance of the peace of Europe, and every time an assertion of rights was attempted they were suppressed by combined influence and force.

And this treaty tears away all that and says these people have a right to live their own lives under the governments which they themselves choose to set up. That is the American principle, and I was glad to fight for it. And when strategic considerations were urged, I said—not I alone, but it was a matter of common counsel—that strategic considerations were not in our thought, that we were not now arranging for future wars but were giving people what belonged to them.

My fellow citizens, I do not think there is any man alive who has a more tender sympathy for the great people of Italy than I have, and a very stern duty was presented to us when we had to consider some of the claims of Italy on the Adriatic, because strategically, from the point of view of future wars, Italy needed a military foothold on the other side of the Adriatic. But her people did not live there except in little spots. It was a Slavic people, and I had to say to my Italian friends that everywhere else in this treaty we have given territory to the people who lived on it, and I do not think that it is for the advantage of Italy, and I am sure it is not for the advantage of the world, to give Italy territory where other people live.

I felt the force of the argument for what they wanted, and it was the old argument that had always prevailed, namely, that they needed it from a military point of view, and I have no doubt that if there is no League of Nations, they will need it from a military point of view. But if there is a League of Nations, they will not need it from a military point of view.

If there is no League of Nations, the military point of view will prevail in every instance, and peace will be brought into contempt. But if there is a League of Nations, Italy need not fear the fact that the shores on the other side of the Adriatic tower above her lower sandy shores on her side of the sea, because there will be no threatening guns there, and the nations of the world will have concerted, not merely to see that the Slavic peoples have their rights, but that the Italian people have their rights as well. I would rather have everybody on my side than be armed to the teeth. And every settlement that is right, every settlement that is based upon the principles I have alluded to, is a safe settlement, because the sympathy of mankind will be behind it.

Some gentlemen have feared with regard to the League of Nations that we will be obliged to do things we don't want to do. If the treaty were wrong, that might be so, but if the treaty is right, we will wish to preserve right. I think I know the heart of this great people whom I, for the time being, have the high honor to represent, better than some other men that I hear talk. I have been bred, and am proud to have been bred, in the old Revolutionary stock which set this government up, when America was set up as a friend of mankind, and I know, if they do not, that America has never lost that vision or that purpose. But I haven't the slightest fear that arms will be necessary if the purpose is there. If I know that my adversary is armed and I am not, I do not press the controversy. And if any nation entertains selfish purposes set against the principles established in this treaty and is told by the rest of the world that it must withdraw its claim, it will not press them.

The heart of the treaty then, my fellow citizens, is not even that it punishes Germany. That is a temporary thing. It is that it rectifies the age-long wrongs which characterized the history of Europe. There were some of us who wished that the scope of the treaty would reach some other age-long wrongs. It was a big job, and I don't say that we wished that it were bigger. But there were other wrongs elsewhere than in Europe and of the same kind which no doubt ought to be righted, and some day will be righted, but which we could not draw into the treaty because we could deal only with the countries whom the war had engulfed and affected. But so far as the scope of our treaty went, we rectified the wrongs which have been the fertile source of war in Europe.

Have you ever reflected, my fellow countrymen, on the real source of revolutions? Men don't start revolutions in a sudden passion. Do you remember what Thomas Carlyle said about the French Revolution? He was speaking of the so-called Hundred Days' Terror, which reigned, not only in Paris, but throughout France, in the days of the French Revolution, and he reminded his readers that back of that Hundred Days of Terror lay several hundred years of agony and of wrong. The French people had been deeply and consistently wronged by their government—robbed, their human rights disregarded—and the slow agony of those hundreds of years had after a while gathered into a hot anger that could not be suppressed.

Revolutions don't spring up overnight. Revolutions gather through the ages; revolutions come from the long suppression of the human spirit. Revolutions come because men know that they have rights and that they are disregarded. And, when we think of the future of the world in connection with this treaty, we must remember that one of the chief efforts of those who made this treaty was to remove that anger from the heart of great peoples, great peoples who had always been suppressed, and always been used, who had always been the tools in the hands of governments, generally of alien governments, not their own. And the makers of the treaty knew that if these wrongs were not removed, there could be no peace in the world, because, after all, my fellow citizens, war comes from the seed of wrong and not from the seed of right. This treaty is an attempt to right the history of Europe, and, in my humble judgment, it is a measurable success.

I say "measurable," my fellow citizens, because you will realize the difficulty of this. Here are two neighboring peoples. The one people have not stopped at a sharp line, and the settlements of the other people, or their migrations, begun at that sharp line; they have intermingled. There are regions where you can't draw a national line and say there are Slavs on this side and Italians on that. There is this people there and that people there. It can't be done. You have to approximate the line. You have to come to it as near to it as you can, and then trust to the processes of history to redistribute, it may be, the people who are on the wrong side of the line. And there are many such lines drawn in this treaty and to be drawn in the Austrian treaty, and where perhaps there are more lines of that sort than in the German treaty.

When we came to draw the line between the Polish people and the German people, not the line between Germany and Poland— there wasn't any Poland, strictly speaking—the line between the German people and the Polish people, there were districts like the upper part of Silesia, or rather the eastern part of Silesia, which is called Upper Silesia because it is mountainous and the other part is not. High Silesia is chiefly Polish, and, when we came to draw a line to represent Poland, it was necessary to include High Silesia if we were really going to play fair and make Poland up of the Polish peoples wherever we found them in sufficiently close neighborhood to one another.

But it wasn't perfectly clear that Upper Silesia—that High Silesia—wanted to be part of Poland. At any rate, there were Germans in High Silesia who said that it did not, and therefore we did there what we did in many other places. We said, "Very well, then, we will let the people that live there decide. We will have a referendum within a certain length of time after the war, under the supervision of an international commission, which will have a sufficient armed force behind it to preserve order and see that nobody interferes with the elections. We will have an absolutely free vote, and High Silesia shall go either to Germany or to Poland, as the people in High Silesia prefer." And that illustrates many other cases where we provided for a referendum, or a plebiscite, as they choose to call it, and are going to leave it to the people themselves, as we should have done, what government they shall live under. It is none of my prerogative to allot peoples to this government and the other. It is nobody's right to do that allotting except the people themselves, and I want to testify that this treaty is shot through with the American principle of the choice of the governed.

Of course, at times it went further than we could make a practical policy of, because various peoples were keen upon getting back portions of their populations which were separated from them by many miles of territory, and we couldn't spot the map over with little pieces of separated states. I even had to remind my Italian colleagues that, if they were going to claim every place where there was a large Italian population, we would have to cede New York to them, because there are more Italians in New York than in any Italian city. But I believe—I hope—that the Italians in New York City are as glad to stay there as we are to have them. But I would not have you suppose that I am intimating that my Italian colleagues entered any claim for New York City.

We of all peoples in the world, my fellow citizens, ought to be able to understand the questions of this treaty, and without anybody explaining them to us, for we are made up out of all the peoples of the world. I dare say that in this audience there are representatives of practically all the peoples dealt with in this treaty. You don't have to have me explain national ambitions to you, national aspirations. You have been brought up on them. You have learned of them since you were children, and it is those national aspirations which we sought to realize, to give an outlet to in this great treaty.

But we do much more than that. This treaty contains, among other things, a Magna Carta of labor—a thing unheard of until this interesting year of grace. There is a whole section of the treaty devoted to arrangements by which the interests of those who labor with their hands all over the world—whether they be men or women or children—are all of them to be safeguarded. And next month there is to meet the first assembly under this section of the League—and let me tell you it will meet whether the treaty is ratified by that time or not. There is to meet an assembly which represents the interests of laboring men throughout the world. Not their political interests—there is nothing political about it. It is the interests of men concerning the conditions of their labor, concerning the character of labor which women shall engage in, the character of labor which children shall be permitted to engage in; the hours of labor; and, incidentally, of course, the remuneration of labor—that labor shall be remunerated in proportion, of course, to the maintenance of the standard of living, which is proper for the man who is expected to give his whole brain and intelligence and energy to a particular task. I hear very little said about this Magna Carta of labor which is embodied in this treaty. It forecasts the day, which ought to have come long ago, when statesmen will realize that no nation is fortunate which is not happy, and that no nation can be happy whose people are not contented—contented in their industry, contented in their lives, and fortunate in the circumstances of their lives.

If I were to state what seems to me to be the central idea of this treaty, it would be this—it is almost a discovery in international conferences—that nations do not consist of their government but consist of their people! That is a rudimentary idea. It seems to us to go without saying, to us in America, but, my fellow citizens, it was never the leading idea in any other international congress that I ever heard of; that is to say, any international congress made up of the representatives of governments. They were always thinking of national policy, of national advantages, of the rivalries of trade, of the advantages of territorial conquest. There is nothing of that in this treaty.

You will notice that even the territories which are taken away from Germany, like her colonies, are not given to anybody. There isn't a single act of annexation in this treaty. But territories inhabited by people not yet able to govern themselves, either because of economic or other circumstances or the stage of their development, are put under the care of powers who are to act as trustees— trustees responsible in the forum of the world at the bar of the League of Nations, and the terms upon which they are to exercise their trusteeship are outlined. They are not to use those people by way of profit and to fight their wars for them. They are not to permit any form of slavery among them, or of enforced labor. They are to see to it that there are humane conditions of labor with regard, not only to the women and the children, but the men, too. They are to establish no fortifications. They are to regulate the liquor and the opium traffic. They are to see to it, in other words, that the lives of the people whose care they assume—not sovereignty over whom they assume, but whose care they assume—are kept clean and safe and wholesome. There again the principle of the treaty comes out—that the object of the arrangement is the welfare of the people who live there, and not the advantages of the government.

It goes beyond that. And it seeks to gather under the common supervision of the League of Nations the various instrumentalities by which the world has been trying to check the evils that were in some places debasing men, like the opium traffic, like the traffic—for it was a traffic—in men, women, and children, like the traffic in other dangerous drugs, like the traffic in arms among uncivilized people, who could use arms only for their detriment, for sanitation, for the work of the Red Cross. Why, those clauses, my fellow citizens, draw the hearts of the world into league, draw the noble impulses of the world together and make a poem of them.

I used to be told that this was an age in which mind was monarch, and my comment was that, if that were true, then mind was one of those modern monarchs that reigns and does not govern. But, as a matter of fact, we were governed by a great representative assembly made up of the human passions, and that the best we could manage was that the high and fine passions should be in a majority so that they could control the baser passions, so that they could check the things that were wrong. And this treaty seeks something like that. In drawing the humane endeavors together it makes a mirror of the fine passions of the world, of its philanthropic passions, of its passion of pity, of its passion of human sympathy, of its passion of human friendliness and helpfulness–for there is such a passion. It is the passion that has lifted us along the slow road of civilization. It is the passion that has made ordered government possible. It is the passion that has made justice and established the thing in some happy part of the world.

That is the treaty. Did you ever hear of it before? Did you ever know before what was in this treaty? Did anybody before ever tell you what the treaty was intended to do? I beg, my fellow citizens, that you and the rest of those Americans with whom we are happy to be associated all over this broad land will read the treaty for themselves, or, if they won't take time to do that—for it is a technical document that is hard to read—that they will accept the interpretation of those who made it and know what the intentions were in the making of it.

I hear a great deal, my fellow citizens, about the selfishness and the selfish ambitions of other governments, but I would not be doing justice to the gifted men with whom I was associated on the other side of the water if I didn't testify that the purposes that I have outlined were their purposes. We differed as to the method very often. We had discussions as to the details, but we never had any serious discussion as to the principles. And, while we all acknowledged that the principles might perhaps in detail have been better, really we are all back of those principles. There is a concert of mind and of purpose and of policy in the world that was never in existence before.

I am not saying that by way of credit to myself or to those colleagues to whom I have alluded, because what happened to us was that we got messages from our people. We were there under instructions, whether they were written down or not, and we did not dare come home without fulfilling those instructions. If I could not have brought back the kind of treaty I brought back, I never would have come back, because I would have been an unfaithful servant, and you would have had the right to condemn me in any way that you chose to use. So that I testify that this is an American treaty, not only, but it is a treaty that expresses the heart of the peoples— of the great peoples—who were associated together in the war against Germany.

I said at the opening of this informal address, my fellow citizens, that I had come to make a report to you. I want to add to that a little bit. I have not come to debate the treaty. It speaks for itself, if you will let it. The arguments directed against it are directed against it with a radical misunderstanding of the instrument itself. Therefore, I am not going anywhere to debate the treaty. I am going to expound it, and I am going, right here, now today, to urge you, in every vocal method that you can use, to assert the spirit of the American people in support of it. Don't let them pull it down. Don't let them misrepresent it. Don't let them lead this nation away from the high purposes with which this war was inaugurated and fought. As I came through that line of youngsters in khaki a few minutes ago, I felt that I could salute it because I had done the job in the way I promised them I would do it. And when this treaty is accepted, men in khaki will not have to cross the seas again. That is the reason I believe in it.

I say "when it is accepted," for it will be accepted. I have never entertained a moment's doubt of that, and the only thing I have been impatient of has been the delay. It is not a dangerous delay, except for the temper of the peoples scattered throughout the world who are waiting. Do you realize, my fellow citizens, that the whole world is waiting on America? The only country in the world that is trusted at this moment is the United States, and they are waiting to see whether their trust is justified or not. That has been the ground of my impatience. I knew their trust was justified, but I begrudged the time that certain gentlemen oblige us to take in telling them so. We shall tell them so in a voice as authentic as any voice in history, and in the years to come men will be glad to remember that they had some part in the great struggle which brought this incomparable consummation of the hopes of mankind.

Printed in the *St. Louis Post-Dispatch*, Sept. 5, 1919; with minor corrections from the complete texts in the Columbus *Ohio State Journal*, Sept. 5, 1919, and the *New York Times*, Sept. 5, 1919.

Remarks on Board the Presidential Train at Richmond, Indiana

September 4, 1919.

I am trying to tell the people what is in the treaty. You would not know what is in it to read some of the speeches I read, and if you will be generous enough to me to read some of the things I say, I hope it will help to clarify a great many matters which have been very much obscured by some of the things which have been said. Because we have now to make the most critical choice we ever made as a nation, and it ought to be made in all soberness and without the slightest tinge of party feeling in it. I would be ashamed of myself if I discussed this great matter as a Democrat and not as an American. I am sure that every man who looks at it without party prejudice and as an American will find in that treaty more things that are genuinely American than were ever put into any similar document before.

The chief thing to notice about it, my fellow citizens, is that it is the first treaty ever made by great powers that was not made in their own favor. It is made for the protection of the weak peoples of the world and not for the aggrandizement of the strong. That is a noble achievement, and it is largely due to the influence of such great people as the people of America, who hold at their heart this principle, that nobody has the right to impose sovereignty upon anybody else; that, in disposing of the affairs of a nation, that nation or people must be its own master and make its own choice. The extraordinary achievement of this treaty is that it gives a free choice to people who never could have won it for themselves. It is for the first time in the history of international transactions an act of systematic justice and not an act of grabbing and seizing.

If you will just regard that as the heart of the treaty—for it is the heart of the treaty—then everything else about it is put in a different light. If we want to stand by that principle, then we can justify the history of America as we can in no other way, for that is the history and principle of America. That is at the heart of it. I beg that, whenever you consider this great matter, you will look at it from this point of view: shall we or shall we not sustain the first great act of international justice? The thing wears a very big aspect when you look at it that way, and all little matters seem to fall away and one seems ashamed to bring in special interests, particularly party interests. What difference does party make when mankind is involved? Parties are intended, if they are intended for any legitimate purpose, to serve mankind, and they are based upon legitimate differences of opinion, not as to whether mankind shall be served or not, but as to the way in which it shall be served; and, so far as those differences are legitimate differences, they justify the differences between parties.

Printed in *Addresses of President Wilson*, with corrections from the complete text in the *New York Times*, Sept. 5, 1919.

An Address in the Indianapolis Coliseum

[[September 4, 1919]]

Mr. President, my fellow citizens, so great a company as this tempts me to make a speech, (laughter and applause) and yet I want to say to you in all seriousness and soberness that I have not come here to make a speech in the ordinary sense of that term. I have come upon a very sober errand, indeed. I have come to report to you upon the work which the representatives of the United States attempted to do at the conference of peace on the other side of the sea, because, I realize, my fellow citizens, that my colleagues and I, in the task we attempted over there, were your servants. We went there upon a distinct errand, which it was our duty to perform in the spirit which you had displayed in the prosecution of the war and in conceiving the purposes and objects of that war.

I was in the city of Columbus this forenoon, where I was endeavoring to explain to a body of our fellow citizens there just what it was that the treaty of peace contains. For I must frankly admit that, in most of the speeches that I have heard in debate upon the treaty of peace, it would be impossible to form a definite conception of what that instrument means. I want to recall to you for the purposes of this evening the circumstances of the war and the purposes for which our men spent their lives on the other side of the sea.

You will remember that a prince of the House of Austria was

slain in one of the cities of Serbia.[1] Serbia was one of the small kingdoms of Europe. She had no strength which any of the great powers needed to fear. As we see the war now, Germany and those who conspired with her made a pretext of that assassination in order to make unconscionable demands on the weak and helpless Kingdom of Serbia, not with a view of bringing about an acquiescence in those demands, but with a view to bringing about a conflict in which their purposes, quite separate from the purposes connected with these demands, could be achieved.

I was recalling, my fellow citizens, the circumstances which began the terrible conflict that has just been concluded. So soon as the unconscionable demands of Austria were made on Serbia, the other governments of Europe sent telegraphic messages to Berlin and Vienna asking that the matter be brought into a conference, and the significant circumstance of the beginning of this war is that the Austrian and German governments did not dare to discuss the demands on Serbia or the purpose which they had in view. It is universally admitted on the other side of the water that, if they had ever gone into an international conference on the Austrian demands, the war never would have been begun. There was an insistent demand from London, for example, by the British Foreign Minister that the cabinets of Europe should be allowed time to confer with the governments at Vienna and Berlin, and the governments at Vienna and Berlin did not dare to admit time for discussion.

I am recalling these circumstances, my fellow citizens, because I want to point out to you what apparently has escaped the attention of some of the critics of the League of Nations—that the heart of the League of Nations Covenant does not lie in any of the portions which have been discussed in public debate. The great bulk of the provisions of that Covenant contain these engagements and promises on the part of the states which undertook to become members of it: that in no circumstances will they go to war without first having either submitted the question to arbitration, in which case they agree to abide by the result, or, having submitted the question to discussion by the Council of the League of Nations, in which case they will allow six months for the discussion and engage not to go to war until three months after the Council has announced its opinion upon the subject under dispute. So that the heart of the Covenant of the League is that the nations solemnly covenant not to go to war for nine months after a controversy becomes acute.

[1] Of course, Archduke Francis Ferdinand was shot in Sarajevo, Bosnia, not Serbia.

If there had been nine days' discussion, Germany would not have gone to war. If there had been nine days within which to bring to bear the opinion of the world—the judgment of mankind—upon the purposes of these governments, they never would have dared to execute those purposes. So that what it is important for us to remember is that, when we sent those boys in khaki across the sea, we promised them, we promised the world, that we would not conclude this conflict with a mere treaty of peace. We entered into solemn engagements with all the nations with whom we associated ourselves that we would bring about such a kind of settlement and such a concert of the purpose of nations that wars like this could not again occur. If the war has to be fought over again, then all our high ideals and purposes have been disappointed, for we did not go into this war merely to beat Germany. We went into this war to beat all purposes such as Germany entertained.

And you will remember how the conscience of mankind was shocked by what Germany did—not merely by the circumstances to which I have already adverted, that unconscionable demands were made upon a little nation which could not resist—but that immediately upon the beginning of the war solemn engagements of treaty were cast on one side, and the chief representative of the Imperial government of Germany said that, when national purposes were under discussion, treaties were mere scraps of paper. And immediately upon that declaration the German armies invaded the territories of Belgium, which they had engaged should be inviolate—invaded those territories with the half-avowed purpose that Belgium was necessary to be permanently retained by Germany in order that she should have a proper frontage on the sea and a proper advantage in her contest with the other nations of the world. So that that act, which was characteristic of the beginning of this war, was a violation of the territorial integrity of the Kingdom of Belgium.

We are presently, my fellow countrymen, to have the very great pleasure of welcoming on this side of the sea the Queen and King of the Belgians, (applause) and I, for one, am perfectly sure that we are going to make it clear to them that we have not forgotten the violation of Belgium, that we have not forgotten the intolerable wrongs which were put upon that suffering people.

I have seen their devastated country.[2] Where it was not actually laid in ruins, every factory was gutted of its contents. All the machinery by which it would be possible for men to go to work again

[2] About Wilson's tour of the battlefields and ruined cities of Belgium, see the news reports and documents printed at June 18-19, 1919, Vol. 61.

was taken away, and those parts of the machinery that they could not take away were destroyed by experts who knew how to destroy them. Belgium was a very successful competitor of Germany in some lines of manufacture, and the German armies were sent there to see to it that that competition was put a stop to. Their purpose was to crush the independent action of that little kingdom—not merely to use it as a gateway through which to attack France. And when they got into France, they not only fought the armies of France, but they put the coal mines of France out of commission, so that it will be a decade or more before France can supply herself with coal from her accustomed sources.

You have heard a great deal about Article X of the Covenant of the League of Nations. Article X speaks the conscience of the world. Article X is the article which goes to the heart of this whole bad business, for that article says that the members of this League—and that is intended to be all the great nations of the world—engage to respect and to preserve against all external aggression the territorial integrity and political independence of the nations concerned. That promise is necessary in order to prevent this sort of war from recurring, and we are absolutely discredited if we fought this war and then neglect the essential safeguard against it.

You have heard it said, my fellow citizens, that we are robbed of some degree of our sovereign independence of choice by articles of that sort. Every man who makes a choice to respect the rights of his neighbors deprives himself of absolute sovereignty, but he does it by promising never to do wrong, and I cannot, for one, see anything that robs me of any inherent right that I ought to retain when I promise that I will do right.

We engage in the first sentence of Article X to respect and preserve from external aggression the territorial integrity and the existing political independence, not only of the other member states, but of all states. And if any member of the League of Nations disregards that promise, then what happens? The Council of the League advises what should be done to enforce the respect for that Covenant on the part of the nation attempting to violate it, and there is no compulsion upon us to take that advice except the compulsion of our good conscience and judgment. So that it is perfectly evident that if, in the judgment of the people of the United States, the Council adjudged wrong and that this was not an occasion for the use of force, there would be no necessity on the part of the Congress of the United States to vote the use of force. But there could be no advice of the Council on any such subject without a unanimous vote, and the unanimous vote would include our own, and if we accepted the advice we would be accepting our own advice. For I need not tell you that the representatives of the government of the United States would not vote without instructions from their government at home, and that what we united in advising we could be certain that our people would desire to do. There is in that Covenant not one note of surrender of the independent judgment of the government of the United States, but an expression of it, because that independent judgment would have to join with the judgment of the rest.

But when is that judgment going to be expressed, my fellow citizens? Only after it is evident that every other resource has failed, and I want to call your attention to the central machinery of the League of Nations. If any member of that League, or any nation not a member, refuses to submit the question at issue either to arbitration or to discussion by the Council, there ensues automatically by the engagements of this Covenant an absolute economic boycott. There will be no trade with that nation by any member of the League. There will be no interchange of communication by post or telegraph. There will be no travel to or from that nation. Its borders will be closed. No citizen of any other state will be allowed to enter it, and no one of its citizens will be allowed to leave it. It will be hermetically sealed by the united action of the most powerful nations in the world. And if this economic boycott bears with unequal weight, the members of the League agree to support one another and to relieve one another in any exceptional disadvantages that may arise out of it.

And I want you to realize that this war was won not only by the armies of the world, but it was won by economic means as well. Without the economic means, the war would have been much longer continued. What happened was that Germany was shut off from the economic resources of the rest of the globe, and she could not stand it. A nation that is boycotted is a nation that is in sight of surrender. Apply this economic, peaceful, silent, deadly remedy, and there will be no need for force. It is a terrible remedy. It does not cost a life outside the nation boycotted, but it brings a pressure upon that nation which, in my judgment, no modern nation could resist.

I dare say that some of those ideas are new to you, because while it is true, as I said this forenoon in Columbus, that apparently nobody has taken the pains to say what is in this treaty, very few have taken the pains to say what is in the Covenant of the League of Nations. They have discussed three—chiefly, three, out of twenty-six articles, and the other articles contain this heart of the matter—that instead of war there shall be arbitration, instead of war there shall be discussion, instead of war there shall be the closure of intercourse, that instead of war there shall be the irresistible pressure of the opinion of all mankind. If I had done wrong, I would a great deal rather have a man shoot at me than stand me up for the judgment of my fellow men. I would a great deal rather see the muzzle of a gun than the look in their eyes. I would a great deal rather be put out of the world than live in a world boycotted and deserted. The most terrible thing is outlawry. The most formidable thing is to be absolutely isolated. And that is the kernel of this engagement. War is on the outskirts. War is a remote and secondary threat. War is a last resort. Nobody in his senses claims that the Covenant of the League of Nations is certain to stop war, but I confidently assert that it makes war violently improbable, and that, even if we cannot guarantee that it will stop war, we are bound in conscience to do our utmost in order to avoid and prevent it.

I was pointing out, my fellow citizens, this forenoon, that this Covenant is a part of a great document. I wish I had brought a copy of it along with me just to show you its bulk. It is an enormous volume, and almost all the things you hear talked about in that treaty are not the essential things. This is the first treaty in the history of civilization in which great powers have associated themselves together in order to protect the weak. I need not tell you that I speak with knowledge in this matter—knowledge of the purpose of the men with whom the men representing America were associated at the peace table. Everyone I consulted with came there with the same idea—that wars had arisen in the past because the strong had taken advantage of the weak, and that the only way to stop war was to band ourselves together to protect the weak; that this war was an example which gave us the finger pointing to the way of escape; that as Austria and Germany had tried to put upon Serbia, so we must see to it that Serbia and the Slavic nations—peoples associated with her—and the peoples of Rumania and those of Bohemia, and the peoples of Hungary and of Austria, for that matter, should feel assured in the future that the strength of the great powers was behind their liberty and their independence and was not intended to be used, and never should be used, for aggression against them.

And so when you read the Covenant, read the treaty with it. I have no doubt that in this audience there are many men who come from that ancient stock of Poland, for example, men in whose blood there is the warmth of old affections connected with that betrayed and ruined country, men whose memories run back to insufferable wrongs endured by those living in that country. And I call them to witness that Poland never could have won unity and independence by herself. Those gentlemen sitting at Paris presented Poland with a unity she could not have won and an independence which she cannot defend unless the world guarantees it to her. There is one of the most noble chapters in the history of the world—that this war was concluded in order to remedy the wrongs which had beaten so deeply into the experience of the weaker peoples of that great continent. The object of the war was to see to it that there was no more of that sort of wrong done. Now, when you have that picture in your minds—that this treaty was meant to protect those who could not protect themselves—turn the picture and look at it this way.

Those very weak nations are situated through the very tract of country—between Germany and Persia—which Germany had intended to conquer and dominate, and if the nations of the world do not maintain their concert to sustain the independence and freedom of those peoples, Germany will yet have her will upon them. And we shall witness the very interesting spectacle of having spent millions upon millions of American treasure and, what is much more precious, hundreds of thousands of American lives, to do a futile thing, to do a thing which we will then leave to be undone at the leisure of those who are masters of intrigue, at the leisure of those who are masters in combining wrong influences to overcome right influences, of those who are the masters of the very things we hate and mean always to fight.

For, my fellow citizens, if Germany should ever attempt that again, whether we are in the League of Nations or not, we will join to prevent it. We do not stand off and see murder done. We do not profess to be the champions of liberty and then consent to see liberty destroyed. We are not the friends and advocates of free government and yet willing to stand by and see free government die before our eyes. For if the power such as Germany was—but, thank God, no longer is—were to do this thing upon the fields of Europe, then America would have to look to it that she did not do it also upon the fields of the western hemisphere, and we should at last be face to face with a power which at the outset we could have crushed, and which now it is within our choice to keep within the harness of civilization.

I am not arguing this thing with you, my fellow citizens, as if I had any doubt of what the verdict of the American people would be. I haven't the slightest doubt. I just wanted to have the pleasure of pointing out to you how absolutely ignorant of the treaty and of the Covenant some of the men are who have been opposing it. If they do read the English language, they do not understand the English language as I understand it. If they have really read this treaty and this Covenant, they only amaze me by their inability to understand what is plainly expressed.

So that my errand upon this journey is not to argue these matters, but to recall you to the real issues which are involved. And one of the things that I have most at heart in this report to my fellow citizens is that they should forget what party I belong to and what party they belong to. I am making this journey as a democrat, but I am spelling it with a little "d," and I don't want anybody to remember, so far as this errand is concerned, that it is ever spelt with a big "D." I am making this journey as an American and as a champion of the rights which America believes in; and I need not tell you that, as compared with the importance of America, the importance of the Democratic party and the importance of the Republican party and the importance of every other party is absolutely negligible. Parties, my fellow citizens, are intended to embody in action different policies of government. They are not, when properly used, intended to traverse the principles which underlie government, and the principles which underlie the government of the United States have been familiar to us ever since we were children. You have been bred, I have no doubt, as I have been bred, in the Revolutionary school of American thought. I mean that school of American thought which takes its inspiration from the days of the American Revolution. There were only three million of us then, but we were ready to stand out against the world for liberty. There are more than one hundred million of us now, and we are ready to insist that everywhere men shall be champions of liberty.

I want you to notice another interesting point that has never been dilated upon in connection with the League of Nations. I am now treading upon delicate ground, and I must express myself with caution. There were a good many delegations that visited Paris wanting to be heard by the peace conference who had real causes to present, and which ought to be presented to the view of the world, but we had to point out to them that they did not happen, unfortunately, to come within the area of settlement, that their questions were not questions which were necessarily drawn into the things that we were deciding. We were sitting there with the pieces of the Austro-Hungarian Empire in our hands. It had fallen apart. It never was naturally cohesive. We were sitting there with various dispersed assets of the German Empire in our hands, and with regard to every one of them we had to determine what we were going to do, but we did not have our own dispersed assets in our hands. We did not have the assets of the nations which constituted the body of the nations associated against Germany to dispose of, and, therefore, we had often, with whatever regret, to turn

away from questions that ought to some day be discussed and settled and upon which the opinion of the world ought to be brought
to bear.

I therefore want to call your attention, if you will turn to it when
you go home, to Article XI, following Article X, of the Covenant of
the League of Nations. That Article XI, let me say, is the favorite
article in the treaty, so far as I am concerned. It says that every
matter which is likely to affect the peace of the world is everybody's
business, and that it shall be the friendly right of any nation to call
attention in the League to anything that is likely to affect the peace
of the world or the good understanding between nations, upon
which the peace of the world depends, whether that matter immediately concerns the nation drawing attention to it or not.

In other words, at present we have to mind our own business.
Under the Covenant of the League of Nations, we can mind other
peoples' business, and anything that affects the peace of the world,
whether we are parties to it or not, can by our delegates be brought
to the attention of mankind. We can force a nation on the other
side of the globe to bring to that bar of mankind any wrong that is
afoot in that part of the world which is likely to affect the peace of
the world, which is likely to affect the good understanding between
nations, and we can oblige them to show cause why it should not
be remedied.

There is not an oppressed people in the world which cannot
henceforth get a hearing at that forum, and you know, my fellow
citizens, what a hearing will mean if the cause of those people is
just. The one thing which those who have reason to dread, have
most reason to dread, is publicity and discussion, because if you
are challenged to give a reason why you are doing a wrong thing it
has to be an exceedingly good reason, and if you give a bad reason
you confess judgment, and the opinion of mankind goes against
you.

At present what is the state of international law and understanding? No nation has the right to call attention to anything that does
not directly affect its own affairs. If it does, it cannot only be told
to mind its own business, but it risks the cordial relationship between itself and the nation whose affairs it draws into discussion;
whereas under Article XI, the very sensible provision is made that
the peace of the world transcends all the susceptibilities of nations
and governments, and that they are obliged to consent to discuss
and explain anything that does affect the understanding between
nations.

Not only that, but there is another thing in this Covenant which
was one of a number of difficulties that we encountered at Paris. I

need not tell you that at every turn in these discussions we came across some secret treaty, some understanding that had never been made public before, some understanding that embarrassed the whole settlement. I think it will not be improper for me to refer to one of those matters. When we came to the settlement of the Shantung question with regard to China, we found that Great Britain and France were under specific treaty obligations to Japan that she should get exactly what she got in the treaty with Germany, and the most that we do—I mean the most that the United States could do—was to urge upon the representatives of Japan the very fatal policy that was involved in such a settlement and obtain from her the promise, which she gave, that she would not take advantage of those portions of the treaty, but would return, without qualification, the sovereignty which Germany had enjoyed in Shantung Province to the Republic of China. We have had repeated assurances since then that Japan intends to fulfill those promises in absolute good faith.

But my present point is that there stood at the very gate of that settlement a secret treaty between Japan and two of the great powers engaged in this war on our side. We could not ask them to disregard those promises. This war had been fought in part because of the refusal to observe the fidelity which is involved in a promise, in a failure to regard the sacredness of treaties. And this Covenant of the League of Nations provides that no secret treaty shall have any validity. It provides in explicit terms that every treaty, every international understanding, shall be registered with the Secretary of the League, that it shall be published as soon as possible after it is there registered, and that no treaty that is not there registered will be regarded by any of the nations engaged in the Covenant. So that we not only have the right to discuss anything, but we make everything open for discussion. And if this Covenant accomplished little more than the abolition of private arrangements between great powers, it would have gone far toward stabilizing the peace of the world and securing the justice which it has been so difficult to secure so long as nations could come to secret understandings with one another.

When you look at the Covenant of the League of Nations thus in the large, you wonder why it is a bogey to anybody. You wonder what influences have made gentlemen afraid of it. You wonder why it is not obvious to everybody, as it is to those who study it with disinterested thought, that this is the central and essential Covenant of the whole peace. As I said this forenoon, I can come through a double row of men in khaki and acknowledge their salutes with a free heart, because I kept my promise to them. I told them when they went to this war that this was a war, not only to beat Germany, but to prevent any subsequent wars of this kind. I can look all the mothers of this country in the face and all the sisters and sweethearts and say, "The boys will not have to do this again."

You would think to hear some men discuss this Covenant that it is an arrangement for sending men abroad again just as soon as possible. It is the only conceivable arrangement which will prevent our sending our men abroad again very soon. And, if I may use a very common expression, I would say, if it is not to be this arrangement, what arrangement do you suggest to secure the peace of the world? It is a case of "put up or shut up." Opposition is not going to save the world. Negations are not going to construct the policies of mankind. A great plan is the only thing that can defeat a great plan. The only triumphant ideas in this world are the ideas that are organized for battle. The only thing that equals an organized program is a better program. If this is not the way to secure peace, I beg that the way may be pointed out. If we must reject this way, then I beg that, before I am sent to ask Germany to make a new kind of peace with us, I should be given specific instructions as to what kind of peace it is to be. If the gentlemen who don't like what was done at Paris think that they can do something better, I beg that they will hold their convention soon and do it now. They cannot in conscience or good faith deprive us of this great work of peace without substituting some other that is better.

And so, my fellow citizens, I look forward with profound gratification to the time, which I believe will now not much longer be delayed, when the American people can say to their fellows in all parts of the world: "We are the friends of liberty; we have joined with the rest of mankind in securing the guarantees of liberty; we stand here with you the eternal champions of what is right, and may God keep us in the covenant that we have formed."

Printed in the *Indianapolis News*, Sept. 5, 1919, with a few corrections and additions from the text in the *St. Louis Post-Dispatch*, Sept. 5, 1919, and the T MS in WP, DLC.

From Samuel Gompers and Others

Washington D C Sept 4 1919

The executive committee representing the various international unions in the iron and steel industry met today to consider the awful situation which exists in many of the iron and steel industry centers. The coercion and the brutality employed to prevent men and unions from meeting in halls engaged upon private property in the open air, the thuggery of the corporations emissaries, the whole discharge of numbers of men for no reason than the one assigned that they have become members of the unions, has brought about a situation that it is exceedingly difficult to withhold or restrain the indignation of the men and the resistance that they declare it is their purpose to present stop The executive committee relying upon the case as presented to you last week[1] and your earnest declaration to endeavor to bring about a conference for the honorable and peaceful adjustment of the matters in controversy have thus far been enabled to prevail upon the men not to engage in a general strike stop We cannot now affirm how much longer we shall be able to exert that influence but we urge you even in the great work in which you are engaged to give prompt attention to this most vital of issues, for if the men can no longer be restrained it is impossible to foretell what the future may hold in store for an industrial crisis which may ensue and frustrate the project which you have worked at for a peaceful and honorable adjustment of industrial affairs in our country stop A meeting of all presidents of the twenty four international unions in the steel industry has been called to take place on Tuesday September ninth in Washington D C to take such action as they deem necessary stop May we not have your reply on or before that time as to whether or not a conference with the steel corporation is possible

> Samuel Gompers, John Fitzpatrick,
> D J Davis, Wm Hannon, Edw J Evans,[2]
> Wm Z Foster.

T telegram (WP, DLC).

[1] Wilson, on August 29 at 3 p.m., had met for about forty-five minutes with Gompers; John Fitzpatrick, president of the Chicago Federation of Labor; David J. Davis, secretary-treasurer of the Amalgamated Association of Iron, Steel, and Tin Workers; and William Hannon and William Zebulon Foster, both full-time organizers for the American Federation of Labor. All were members of the National Committee for Organizing Iron and Steel Workers, of which Fitzpatrick was chairman and Foster secretary-treasurer.

The committee had been established in Chicago on August 1, 1918, under the auspices of the A. F. of L., to take advantage of the gains made by organized labor during the wartime emergency in an attempt to break into the hitherto largely nonunion iron and steel industry. The committee was made up of representatives of twenty-four craft unions. Gompers was the nominal chairman, but in practice Fitzpatrick held that position and was soon given the title.

The organizational drive made good progress in the first few months, despite being seriously underfinanced. However, with the end of the war, the steel manufacturers, led by United States Steel, began to take countermeasures to halt the unionization effort. Many companies made some economic concessions to their workers and encouraged the establishment of company unions. Some discharged workers suspected of membership or involvement in national unions. Many used strong-arm tactics to prevent union organizers from holding meetings in mill towns, especially in the crucially important region in and around Pittsburgh. The basic position of the companies, and above all of United States Steel, was that they supported the open shop and would not recognize or have any dealings with national unions.

By late May 1919, the organizing committee found itself caught between its own realization that it was not yet strong enough for a confrontation with the steel companies and the rising militancy of the approximately 100,000 iron and steel workers it had organized, many of whom believed that only a nationwide strike would compel the companies to recognize and deal with the A. F. of L. unions. On June 20, Samuel Gompers sent a letter to Elbert H. Gary, chairman of the board of directors of the United States Steel Corporation, requesting that the latter meet with a committee representing the steel workers. Gary ignored the letter. The national committee decided to take a strike-authorization vote of the organized workers on July 20. When the vote of the various unions was tabulated on August 20, it was found that approximately 98 per cent of the voters had approved a strike unless the companies came to the bargaining table. On August 26, Fitzpatrick, Davis, and Foster entered the main offices of the United States Steel Corporation in New York and asked to see Gary. Gary refused to see them but said that they could state their business in a letter. The three then sent a letter requesting a conference, which Gary promptly refused. The committee sent Gary an ultimatum on August 27: either meet with them or face a strike. That same day, they went to Washington and requested Gompers and the executive committee of the A. F. of L. to ask Wilson to arrange a meeting for them with the officers of United States Steel. For a detailed account of events to this point, see David Brody, *Labor in Crisis: The Steel Strike of 1919* (Philadelphia and New York, 1965), pp. 62-103.

Gompers included in his testimony before the Senate Committee on Education and Labor on September 26, 1919, an account of the conference with Wilson on August 29. "[We] had the honor of a conference with the President," he recalled, "where we presented to him this entire situation and related to him the efforts which had been made to have a conference with Judge Gary and the inability to secure such a conference. The President expressed the belief that, in his judgment, a conference might be helpful to adjust the differences. We asked him whether he would not use his good offices to try to bring about a conference with Judge Gary and a committee of the employees of his corporation. We presented to him the thought that the subsidiary companies are under the general jurisdiction of the United States Steel Corporation, and that if the corporation, speaking for the corporation itself, as well as for its subsidiary companies, would have a conference with a committee representing the men in the various plants of the corporation, we would regard that as being proper. The President seemed to be in favor of our position that a conference should be held. I am not divulging any confidence. I would not do that if I was conscious of it, particularly in the case of the President, or in the case of any other man, but the President said that he would make an effort to try to bring about such a conference, and try to prevail upon Judge Gary to permit such a conference to take place." *Investigation of Strike in Steel Industries: Hearings Before the Committee on Education and Labor, United States Senate, Sixty-Sixth Congress, First Session* (Washington, 1919), pp. 106-107.

[2] Edward J. Evans, vice-president of the Brotherhood of Electrical Workers and also a member of the National Committee for Organizing Iron and Steel Workers.

From the Diary of Dr. Grayson

Friday, September 5, 1919.

The Presidential Special reached St. Louis at 4:00 o'clock in the morning. It was taken out to a siding at Forest Park on the outskirts of the city, and the President allowed to rest until 9:00 o'clock. There was a guard of soldiers about the train when the President awoke and a good-sized crowd of people were waiting to see him emerge. A reception committee headed by the Governor and the Mayor,[1] and including more Republicans than Democrats, arrived at 9:00 o'clock, and after shaking hands with the President he was escorted to an automobile and headed a line of machines that proceeded through the principal sections of the city to the hotel, where an opportunity was afforded both the President and Mrs. Wilson to rest for a brief time.

The President's first public appearance outside of the auto parade was at a luncheon that had been arranged in his honor by the Chamber of Commerce of St. Louis. This luncheon was an enormous success. So large was the attendance[2] that not only the roof garden of the hotel was utilized, but all of the small ante-rooms usually reserved for cloak rooms were converted into a space to allow the people to hear the President.

His luncheon address was an exceptionally brilliant one. The roof garden dining-room was most elaborately decorated in the national colors, and the President was seated at a table on a platform raised a few feet from the floor. Big bouquets of American roses were festooned on the walls. In introducing the President here the chairman of the meeting[3] made it very plain that there was no partisanship in the St. Louis welcome. He declared that a majority of the committee were Republicans; that some of them were anti-Treaty, but that all of them took the greatest pleasure in welcoming the President of the United States to their city. That was the sentiment all during the day. The people appreciated that the President and his wife were visiting them and there was no untoward demonstration of any character.

In the afternoon the President and Mrs. Wilson and myself quietly slipped away from the hotel and were taken out to one of the parks, where we were able to take a brisk walk. The President needed this exercise very much, as his headache was still troubling him somewhat.

The President and Mrs. Wilson dined alone, and at 8:00 o'clock that evening proceeded to Convention Hall, where a big night meeting had been arranged. The Convention Hall here holds 12,000 people and every inch of available space within the building was filled, while outside there were many hundreds who could not obtain admission and who remained until the meeting was over just for the opportunity of catching a fleeting glimpse of the Chief Executive and his wife as they departed from the hall.

The meeting inside was a great success. The acoustics of Convention Hall are splendid, and the President was able to make every person in the building hear his argument. The President in his night speech emphasized the fact that the nations of the world were waiting on America to show the qualities of leadership which had made it famous in the past, and he took occasion severely to criticise those Senators who wanted the League of Nations changed so that America would enjoy privileges that no other member of the League had. He sharply denounced the Senators who, he said, were so timid that they wanted to "sit on the edge of their chair near the door, ready to scuttle and run the moment something transpired in the League of Nations that they did not like." This reference to "scuttle and run" made a great hit with the audience here.

A great crowd accompanied the President to the station to see him off, and he stood beside the car for nearly ten minutes shaking hands with the committee and saying good-bye.

St. Louis was left at 11:00 o'clock, Kansas City being the next stopping point.

¹ Frederick Dozier Gardner, Democrat, Governor of Missouri, and Henry William Kiel, Republican, Mayor of St. Louis.
² The *St. Louis Post-Dispatch*, Sept. 5, 1919, reported that 1,500 seats for the luncheon had been sold for $2.00 each.
³ Jackson Johnson, shoe manufacturer and president of the St. Louis Chamber of Commerce.

A Luncheon Address to the St. Louis Chamber of Commerce

September 5, 1919.

Mr. Johnson, Your Honor, Mr. Mayor, ladies and gentlemen: It is with great pleasure that I find myself in St. Louis again, because I have always found it possible in St. Louis to discuss serious questions in a way that gets mind in contact with mind, instead of that other very less desirable thing—passion in contact with passion. I am glad to hear the Mayor say—and I believe it is true—that politics is adjourned. Politics has no place, I mean party politics has no place, my fellow citizens, in the subjects that we are now obliged to discuss and to decide. Politics in the wider sense has a great deal to do with them. The politics of the world, the policy of mankind, the concert of the methods by which the world is to be bettered, that concert of will and of action which will make every nation a nobler instrument of divine Providence—that is world politics.

I have sometimes heard gentlemen discussing the questions that are now before us with a distinction drawn between nationalism and internationalism in these matters. It is very difficult for me to follow their distinction. The greatest nationalist is the man who wants his nation to be the greatest nation, (applause) and the greatest nation is the nation which penetrates to the heart of its duty and mission among the nations of the world. (applause, cheers) With every flash of insight into the great politics of mankind, the nation that has that vision is elevated to a place of influence and power which it cannot get by arms, which it cannot get by commercial rivalry, which it can get by no other way than by that spiritual leadership which comes from a profound understanding of the problems of humanity. (applause) It is in the light of ideas of this sort that I conceive it a privilege to discuss the matters that I have come away from Washington to discuss.

I have come away from Washington to discuss them because, apparently, it is difficult to discuss them in Washington. (laughter, applause) The whole subject is surrounded with mists which it is difficult to penetrate. I brought home with me from the other side of the water a great document, a great human document, but after you hear it talked about in Washington for a while you think that it has just about three or four clauses in it. You fancy that it has a certain Article X in it, that it has something about Shantung in it, that it has something about the Monroe Doctrine in it, that it has something about quitting, withdrawing from the League, showing that you don't want to play the game. And I don't hear about anything else in it. Why, my fellow citizens, these are mere details—the incidents of a great human enterprise—and I have sought the privilege of telling you what I conceive that human enterprise to be.

The war that has just been finished was no accident. Any man who had followed the politics of the world up to that critical break must have known that that was the logical outcome of the processes that had preceded it, must have known that the nations of the world were preparing for that very thing and were expecting it.

One of the most interesting things that I realized after I got to the other side of the water was that the mental attitude of the French people with regard to the settlement of this war was largely determined by the fact that for nearly fifty years they had expected it, that for nearly fifty years they had dreaded, by the exercise of German force, the very thing that had happened. And their constant theme was: "We must devise means by which this intolerable fear will be lifted from our hearts. We cannot, we will not, live another fifty years under the cloud of that terror."

The terror had been there all the time, and the war was its flame and consummation, and it had been expected, because the politics of Europe were based upon a definite conception. That conception was that the strong had all the rights and that all that the weak could enjoy was what the strong permitted them to enjoy; that no nation had any right that could not be asserted by the exercise of force; and that the real politics of Europe consisted in determining how many of the weak elements of the European combination of families of nations should be under the influence and control of one set of nations; how many of those elements should be under the influence and control of another set of nations.

One of the centers of all the bad business was in the town of Constantinople. I don't believe that intrigue was ever anywhere else reduced to such a consummate art or practiced with such ardor and stealth as in Constantinople. And that was because Constantinople was the key to the weak part of Europe. That was where the pawns were, not the kings and the queens and the castles and the bishops and the rest of the game—of the chess game—of politics, but the little pawns. They made the openings for the heavier pieces. Their maneuvers determined the arrangement of the board, and those who controlled the pawns controlled the outcome of the whole plot to checkmate and to match, and to capture, and to take advantage. The shrewdest politicians in the diplomatic service of the several nations were put at Constantinople to run the game, which consisted in maneuvering the weak for the advantage of the strong. And every international conference that preceded the conference at Paris, which is still in process, has been intended to complete and to consummate the arrangements for that game. For the first time in the history of mankind, the recent conference at Paris was convened to destroy that system and substitute another. (applause)

I take it, my fellow citizens, that when you look at that volume that contains the treaty of peace with Germany in the light of what I have been saying to you, you will read it with greater interest than you have hitherto attached to it. It is the charter and constitution of a new system for the world, (applause) and that new system is based upon an absolute reversal of the principles of the old system. The essential object of that treaty is to establish the independence and protect the integrity of the weak peoples of the world. (applause) I hear some gentlemen, who are themselves incapable of altruistic purposes, say, "Oh, but that is altruistic. It is not our business to take care of the weak nations of the world." No, but it is our business to prevent war, and if we don't take care of the weak nations of the world, there will be war. (applause) These gentlemen assume the role of being very practical men, and they say, "We don't want to get into war to protect every little nation in the world." Very well, then, let them show me how they will keep out of war by not protecting them, (applause) and let them show me how they will prove that, having gone into an enterprise, they are not absolutely contemptible quitters if they don't see the game through. (applause) They joined all the rest of us in the profession of fine purposes when we went into the war, and what were the fine purposes that they professed? It was not merely to defeat Germany. It is not a handsome enterprise for any great nation to go into a war merely to reduce another nation to obedience. They went in, and they professed to go in, to see to it that nobody after Germany's defeat should repeat the experiment which Germany had tried. (applause) And how do they propose to do that? To leave the material that Germany was going to make her dominating empire out of helpless and at their mercy.

What was the old formula of Pan-Germanism? From Bremen to Baghdad, wasn't it? Well, look at the map. What lies between Bremen and Baghdad? After you get past the German territory, there is Poland. There is Bohemia, which we have made into Czechoslovakia. There is Hungary, which is now divided from Austria and does not share Austria's strength. There is Rumania. There is Yugoslavia. There is broken Turkey; and then Persia and Baghdad. The route is open. The route is wide open, and we have undertaken to say, "This route is closed!" It has been closed. If you do not close it, you have no choice but some day or other to enter into exactly the same sort of war that we have just gone through. Those gentlemen are dreaming. They are living in a past age which is gone and all but forgotten when they say that we can mind our own business.

Our own business? Is there any merchant present here or any manufacturer or any banker who can say that our interests are separate from the interests of the rest of the world, commercially, industrially, financially? There is not a man in any one of those professions who doesn't admit that our industrial fortunes are tied up with the industrial fortunes of the rest of the world. He knows that, and when he draws a picture to himself—if he is frank—of what some gentlemen propose, this is what he sees: America minding her own business and having no other—(laughter and applause) despised, suspected, distrusted. And on the other side of the water, the treaty and its operation—interrupted? Not at all!

We are a great nation, my fellow citizens, but the treaty is going to be applied just the same whether we take part in it or not. And part of its application—at the center of its application—stands that great problem of the rehabilitation of Germany industrially. I say the problem of her rehabilitation because unless she is rehabilitated she cannot pay the reparation. And the Reparation Commission created by the treaty was created for the purpose of seeing that Germany pays the reparation, (applause) and it was admitted in all our conferences that, in order to do that, steps must be taken to enable Germany to pay the reparation, which means her industrial and commercial rehabilitation. Not only that, but some of you gentlemen know we used to have trade with Germany. All of that trade is going to be in the hands and under the control of the Reparation Commission. I humbly asked leave to appoint a member to look after our interests, and I was rebuked for it.

I am looking after the industrial interests of the United States. I would like to see the other men who are. They are forgetting the industrial interests of the United States, and they are doing things that will cut us off, and our trade off from the normal channels, because the Reparation Commission can determine where Germany buys, what Germany buys, and how much Germany buys. The Reparation Commission can determine in what instruments of credit she temporarily expresses her debt. It can determine how those instruments of credit shall be used for the basis of the credit which must underlie international exchanges. It is going to stand at the center of the financial operations of the world. Now, is it minding our business to keep out of that? On the contrary, it is handing our business over to people who are not particularly interested in seeing that it prospers. These are facts which I can appropriately address to a chamber of commerce because they are facts which nobody can controvert and which yet seem often to be forgotten. The broader aspects of this subject are seldom brought to your attention. It is the little picayune details here and there.

That brings me, my fellow citizens, to the guarantee of this whole thing. We said that we were going to fight this war for the purpose of seeing to it that the mothers and sisters and fathers of this land, and the sweethearts and wives, did not have to send their lads over on the other side of the sea to fight any more, and so we took part in an arrangement by which justice was to be secured throughout the world. The rest of the world, partly at our suggestion, said "Yes," and said it gladly; said, "Yes, we will go into the partnership to see that justice is maintained." And then I come home and hear some gentlemen say, "But will we?" Are we interested in justice? The treaty of peace, as I have just said to you, is based upon the protection of the weak against the strong, and there is only one force that can protect the weak against the strong, and that is the universal concert of the strength of mankind. That is the League of Nations.

But I beg that you will not conceive of the League of Nations as a combination of the world for war, for that is exactly what it is not. It is a combination of the world for arbitration and discussion. I was taking the pains the other day to make a sort of table of contents of the Covenant of the League of Nations, and I found that two thirds of its provisions were devoted to setting up a system of arbitration and discussion in the world.

Why, these are the facts, my fellow citizens. The members of the League agree that no one of them will ever go to war about anything without first doing one or other of two things: without either submitting the question to arbitration, in which case they agree to abide by the decision of the arbitrators absolutely, or submitting it to discussion by the Council of the League of Nations, in which case they agree that, no matter what the opinion expressed by the Council may be, they will allow six months for the discussion, and, whether they are satisfied with the conclusion or not, will not go to war in less than three months after the rendering of the opinion. I think we can take it for granted that the preliminaries would take two or three months, in which case you have a whole year of discussion even when you do not get arbitration. And I want to call you to witness that in almost every international controversy which has been submitted to thorough canvass by the opinion of the world it has become impossible for the result to be war. War is a process of heat. Exposure is a process of cooling; and what is proposed in this is that every hot thing shall be spread out in the cooling air of the opinion of the world and, after it is thoroughly cooled off, then let the nations concerned determine whether they are going to fight about it or not.

And notice the sanction. Any member of the League which breaks these promises with regard to arbitration or discussion is to be deemed thereby to have committed an act of war against the other members of the League, not merely to have done an immoral thing, but, by refusing to obey those processes, to have committed an act of war and put itself out of court. And you know what then happens. You say, "Yes, we form an army and go to fight them." Not at all. We shut their doors and lock them in. We boycott them. Just so soon as that is done they cannot ship cargoes out or receive them shipped in. They cannot send a telegraphic message. They cannot send or receive a letter. Nobody can leave their territory and nobody can enter their territory. They are absolutely boycotted by the rest of mankind.

I don't think that after that it will be necessary to do any fighting at all. What brought Germany to her knees was not only the splendid fighting of the incomparable men who met her armies, but that her doors were locked and she could not get supplies from any part of the world. There were a few doors open, doors to some Swedish ore, for example, that she needed for making munitions, and that kept her going for a time; but the Swedish door would be shut this time. There would not be any door open, and that brings a nation to its senses just as suffocation removes from the individual all inclination to fight.

Now, that is the League of Nations—an agreement to arbitrate and discuss, and an agreement that if you do not arbitrate and discuss, you shall be absolutely boycotted and starved out. There is hardly a European nation, my fellow citizens, that is of a fighting inclination which has enough food to eat without importing food, and it will be a very persuasive argument that it has nothing to eat, because you cannot fight on an empty stomach any more than you can worship God on an empty stomach.

When we add to that some other very interesting particulars, I think the League of Nations becomes a very interesting thing indeed. You have heard of Article X, and I am going to speak about that in a minute, but read Article XI, because, really, there are other articles in the Covenant! Article XI says—I am not quoting its language, but its substance—that anything that is likely to affect the peace of the world or the good understanding upon which the peace of the world depends shall be everybody's business; that any nation, the littlest nation at the table, can stand up and challenge the right of the strongest nation there to keep on in a course of action or policy which is likely to disturb the peace of the world, and that it shall be its "friendly right" to do so. Those are the words. It cannot be regarded as an hostile or unfriendly act. It is its friendly right to do that, and if you will not give the secret away, I wrote those words myself. I wanted it to be our friendly right, and everybody's friendly right, to discuss everything that is likely to affect the peace of the world, because that is everybody's business. It is everybody's business to see that nothing happens that does disturb the peace of the world.

And there is added to this this very interesting thing: there can hereafter be no secret treaties. There were nations represented around that board—I mean the board at which the Commission on the League of Nations sat, where fourteen nations were represented—there were nations represented around that board who had entered into many a secret treaty and understanding, and they made not the least objection to promising that hereafter no secret treaty should have any validity whatever. The provision of the Covenant is that every treaty or international understanding shall be "registered," I believe the word is, with the General Secretary of the League, that the General Secretary shall publish it in full just so soon as it is possible for him to publish it, and that no treaty shall be valid which is not thus registered. It is like our arrangements with regard to mortgages on real estate, that until they are registered nobody else need pay any attention to them. So with the treaties. Until they are registered in this office of the League, nobody, not even the parties themselves, can insist upon their execution. You have cleared the deck thereby of the most dangerous thing and the most embarrassing thing that has hitherto existed in international politics.

It was very embarrassing, my fellow citizens, when you thought you were approaching an ideal solution of a momentous question, to find that some of your principal colleagues had given the whole thing away. And that leads me to speak just in passing of what has given a great many people unnatural distress. I mean the Shantung settlement, the settlement with regard to a portion of the province of Shantung in China. Great Britain and, subsequently, France, as everybody now knows, in order to make it more certain that Japan would come into the war and so assist to clear the Pacific of the German fleets, had promised that any rights that Germany had in China should, in the case of the victory of the Allies, pass to Japan. There was no qualification in the promise. She was to get exactly what Germany had, and so the only thing that was possible was to induce Japan to promise—and I want to say in all fairness, for it wouldn't be fair if I didn't say it, that Japan did very handsomely make the promises which were requested of her—that she would retain in Shantung none of the sovereign rights which Germany had enjoyed there, but would return the sovereignty without qualification to China and retain in Shantung Province only what other nationalities had already had elsewhere—economic rights with regard to the development and administration of the railroad and of certain mines which had become attached to the railway. That is her promise, and, personally, I haven't the slightest doubt that she will fulfill that promise. She cannot fulfill it right now because the thing doesn't come into operation until three months after the treaty is ratified, so that we must not be too impatient about it. But she will fulfill those promises.

And suppose that we said we wouldn't assent. England and France must assent, and if we are going to get Shantung Province back for China and those gentlemen don't want to engage in foreign wars, how are they going to get it back? Their idea of not getting into trouble seems to be to stand for the greatest possible number of unworkable propositions. It is all very well to talk about standing by China, but how are you standing by China when you withdraw from the only arrangements by which China can be assisted? If you are China's friend, but don't go into the Council where you can act as China's friend—if you are China's friend, then put her in a position where these concessions which have been made need not be carried out! If you are China's friend, scuttle and run! That is not the kind of American I am.

Now, just a word about Article X. Permit me, if you will, to recur to what I said at the opening of these somewhat disjointed remarks. I said that the treaty was intended to destroy one system and substitute another. That other system was based upon the principle that no strong power need respect the territorial integrity or the political independence of any weak power. I need not confine the phraseology to that. It was based upon the principle that no power is obliged to respect the territorial integrity or the political independence of any other power if it has the force necessary to disregard it. So that Article X cuts at the very heart, and is the only instrument that will cut to the very heart, of the old system. Remember that if this Covenant is adopted by the number of nations, which it probably will be adopted by, it means that every nation except Germany and Turkey, because we have already said we would let Austria come in (Germany has to undergo a certain period of probation to see whether she has really experienced a change of heart and effected a genuine change of constitutional provision)—it means that all the nations of the world, except one strong and one negligible one, agree that they will respect and preserve against external aggression the territorial integrity and existing political independence of the other nations of the world. You would think from some of the discussions that the emphasis is on the word "preserve."

We are partners with the rest of the world in respecting the territorial integrity and political independence of the others. They are all under solemn bond themselves to respect and preserve those things, and if they don't preserve them, if they don't respect them and preserve them, what happens? The Council of the League then advises the several members of the League what it is necessary to do. I can testify from having sat at the board where the instrument was drawn that advice means advice. I supposed it did before I returned home, but I found some gentlemen doubted it. Advice means advice, and the advice cannot be given without the concurrent vote of the representative of the United States. "Well," but somebody says, "suppose we are a party to the quarrel?" I cannot suppose that, because I know that the United States is not going to disregard the territorial integrity or political independence of any other nation. But for the sake of the argument, suppose that we are a party. Very well, then, the scrap is ours anyway. For what these gentlemen are afraid of is that we are going to get into trouble. If we are a party, we are in trouble already, and if we are not a party, we can control the advice of the Council by our vote. And, my friends, that is a little like an open and shut game! And I am not afraid of advice which we give ourselves. And yet that is the whole of the bugaboo which these gentlemen have been parading before you.

The solemn thing about Article X is the first sentence, not the second sentence. The first sentence says that we will respect and preserve against external aggression the territorial integrity and existing political independence of other nations. And let me stop a moment on the words "external aggression." Why were they put in? Because every man who sat at that board held that the right of revolution was sacred and must not be interfered with. Any kind of a row can happen inside, and it is nobody's right to interfere. The only thing that there is any right to object to or interfere with is external aggression, by some outside power undertaking to take a piece of territory or to interfere with the internal political arrangements of the country which is suffering from the aggression. Because territorial integrity does not mean that you cannot invade another country; it means that you cannot invade it and stay in it. I haven't impaired the territorial integrity of your backyard if I walk into it, but I very much impair it if I insist upon staying there and won't get out. And the impairment—the integrity contemplated in this article is the kind of integrity which is violated if there is a seizure of territory, if there is an attempted annexation, if there is an attempted continuing domination either of the territory itself or the methods of government inside of that territory.[1]

When you read Article X, therefore, you will see that it is nothing but the inevitable, logical center of the whole system of the Covenant of the League of Nations. And I stand for it absolutely. If it should ever in any important respect be impaired, I would feel like asking the Secretary of War to get the boys who went across the water to fight together on some field where I could go and see them. And I would stand up before them and say: "Boys, I told you before you went across the seas that this is a war against wars, and I did my best to fulfill the promise, but I am obliged to come to you in mortification and shame and say I have not been able to fulfill the promise. You are betrayed. You fought for something that you did not get." And the glory of the armies and the navies of the United States is gone like a dream in the night, and there ensues upon it, in the suitable darkness of the night, the nightmare of dread which lay upon the nations before this war came. And there will come some time, in the vengeful Providence of God, another struggle in which, not a few hundred thousand fine men from America will have to die, but as many millions as are necessary to accomplish the final freedom of the peoples of the world.[2]

Printed in *Addresses of President Wilson*, with corrections from the incomplete texts in the *St. Louis Globe-Democrat*, Sept. 6, 1919; the *St. Louis Post-Dispatch*, Sept. 5, 1919; the New York *World*, Sept. 6, 1919; and the *Kansas City Times*, Sept. 6, 1919.
[1] Wilson had said the same thing in briefer language in his interview with the Senate Foreign Relations Committee printed at Aug. 19, 1919, Vol. 62. See n. 38 to the transcript of this interview.
[2] There is a WWT outline of this speech in WP, DLC.

An Address in the St. Louis Coliseum

[[September 5, 1919]]

Mr. Chairman,[1] Governor Gardner, my fellow countrymen. We have met upon an occasion which is much too solemn—(a photographic bomb is discharged) this is much too solemn an occasion, my fellow countrymen, to care how we look. We ought to care how we think. (applause) And I have come here tonight to ask permission to discuss with you some of the very curious aberrations of thinking that have taken place in this country of late. I have sought—I think I have sought without prejudice—to understand the point of view of the men who have been opposing the treaty and the Covenant of the League of Nations. Many of them are men whose judgment and whose patriotic feeling I have been accustomed to admire and respect. And yet I must admit to you, my fellow countrymen, that it is very hard for me to believe that they have followed their line of thinking to its logical and necessary conclusion. Because when you reflect upon their position, it is either that we ought to reject this treaty altogether or that we ought to change it in such a way as will make it necessary to reopen negotiations with Germany and reconsider the settlements of the peace in many essential particulars. We cannot do the latter alone, and other nations will not join us in doing it. The only alternative is to reject the peace and to do what some of our fellow countrymen have been advising us to do—stand alone in the world.

I am going to take the liberty tonight of pointing out to you what this alternative means. I know the course of reasoning which is either uttered or implied in this advice when it is given us by some of the men who propose this course. They believe that the United States is so strong, so financially strong, so industrially strong, if necessary so physically strong, (scattered applause) that it can impose its will upon the world if it is necessary for it to stand out against the world. And they believe that the processes of peace can be processes of domination and antagonism, instead of processes of cooperation and good feeling. I therefore want to point out to you that only those who are ignorant of the world can believe that any nation, even so great a nation as the United States, can stand alone and play a signal part in the history of mankind. (applause)

Begin with a single circumstance, for I have not come here tonight to indulge in any kind of oratory. I have come here tonight to present to you certain hard facts which I want you to take home with you and think about. I suppose that most of you realize that

[1] James Ellwood Smith, president of the Mississippi Valley Waterways Association and chairman of the reception committee.

it is going to be very difficult for the other nations that were engaged in this war to get financially on their feet again. I dare say you read the other day the statement of Mr. Herbert Hoover's opinion—an opinion which I always greatly respect—that it will be necessary for the United States immediately to advance four or five billion dollars for the rehabilitation of credit and industry on the other side of the water, and I must say to you that I learned nothing in Paris which would lead me to doubt that conclusion. And I think the statement of the sum is a reasonable and conservative statement. If the world is going bankrupt, if credit is going to be destroyed, if the industry of the rest of the world is going to be interrupted, our market is confined to the United States. Trade will be impossible, except within our own borders. If we are to save our own markets and rehabilitate our own industries, we must save the financial situation of the world and rehabilitate the markets of the world. Very well, what do these gentlemen propose? That we should do that, for we cannot escape doing it.

Face to face with a situation of this kind, we are not, let us assume, partners in the execution of this treaty. But what is one of the central features of the execution of this treaty? It is the application of the reparation clauses. Germany can't pay for this war unless her industries are revived, and the treaty of peace sets up a great commission known as the Reparation Commission, in which it was intended that there should be a member from the United States as well as from other countries.

And the business of this commission will be in part to see that the industries of Germany are revived in order that Germany may pay this great debt which she owes to civilization. That Reparation Commission can determine the currents of trade, the conditions of credit, of international credit; it can determine how much Germany is going to buy, where it is going to buy and how it is going to pay for it. And if we must, to save ourselves, contribute to the financial rehabilitation of the world, then without being members of this partnership, we must put our money in the hands of those who want to get the markets that belong to us. That is what these gentlemen call playing a lone hand. It is indeed playing a lone hand. It is playing a hand that is frozen out! (applause) We must contribute the money which other nations are to use in order to rehabilitate their industry and credit, and we must make them our antagonists and rivals and not our partners! I put that proposition to any businessman, young or old, in the United States and ask him how he likes it, and whether he considers that a useful way for the United States to stand alone. We have got to carry this burden of reconstruction whether we will or not or be ruined, and the question is, shall we carry it and be ruined anyhow? For that is what these gentlemen propose—that at every point we shall be embarrassed by the whole financial affairs of the world being in the hands of other nations.

As I was saying at the luncheon that I had the pleasure of eating with the Chamber of Commerce today, the whole aspect of the matter is an aspect of ignorance. The men who propose these things do not understand the selfish interests of the United States, (applause) because here is the rest of the picture: hot rivalries, burning suspicions, jealousies, arrangements made everywhere if possible to shut us out, because if we won't come in as equals, we ought to be shut out. If we are going to keep out of this thing in order to prey upon the rest of the world, then I think we ought to be frozen out of it. (applause)

That is not the temper of the United States, and it is not like the United States to be ignorant enough to think any such thoughts, because we know that partners profit and enemies lose the game. (applause) But that is not all of the picture, my fellow citizens. If every nation is going to be our rival, if every nation is going to dislike and distrust us—and that will be the case—because having trusted us beyond measure the reaction will occur beyond measure. (applause) As it stands now, they trust us, they look to us, they long that we shall undertake anything for their assistance rather than that any other nation should undertake it. And if we say, "No, we are in this world to live by ourselves and get what we can out of it by any selfish processes," then the reaction will change the whole heart and attitude of the world toward this great, free, justice-loving people. And after you have changed the attitude of the world, what have you produced? Peace? Why, my fellow citizens, is there any man here or any woman, let me say is there any child here, who does not know that the seed of war in the modern world is industrial and commercial rivalry? (applause) The real reason that the war that we have just finished took place was that Germany was afraid that her commercial rivals were going to get the better of her, and the reason why some nations went into the war against Germany was that they thought that Germany would get the commercial advantage of them. The seed of the jealousy, the seed of the deep-seated hatred was hot, successful commercial and industrial rivalry.

Why, what did the Germans do when they got into Belgium? I have just seen that suffering country. Most of the Belgian factories are standing. You don't witness in Belgium what you witness in France, except upon certain battlefields—factories destroyed, whole towns wiped out. No, the factories are there, the streets are clear, the people are there. But go in the factories. Every piece of machinery that could be taken away has been taken away. If it was too big to take away, experts directed the way in which it should be injured so that it could never be used again. And that was because there were textile industries and iron industries in Belgium which the Germans hated the Belgians for having, because they were better than the Germans and outdid them in the markets of the world. This war, in its inception was a commercial and industrial war. It was not a political war. (applause)

Very well then, if we must stand apart and be the hostile rivals of the rest of the world, then we must do something else. We must be physically ready for anything to come. We must have a great standing army. We must see to it that every man in America is trained to arms. We must see to it that there are munitions and guns enough for an army that means a mobilized nation; that they are not only laid up in store, but that they are kept up to date; that they are ready to use tomorrow; that we are a nation in arms; because you can't be unfriendly to everybody without being ready that everybody shall be unfriendly to you.

And what does that mean? Reduction of taxes? No. Not only the continuation of the present taxes but the increase of the present taxes. And it means something very much more serious than that. We can stand that, so far as the expense is concerned, if we care to keep up the high cost of living and enjoy the other luxuries that we have recently enjoyed. But, what is much more serious than that is we have got to have the sort of organization which is the only kind of organization that can handle armies of that sort. We may say what we please of the German government that has been destroyed, my fellow citizens, but it was the only sort of government that could handle an armed nation. (applause) You can't handle an armed nation by vote. You can't handle an armed nation if it is democratic, because democracies don't go to war that way. (applause) You have got to have a concentrated, militaristic organization of government to run a nation of that sort. You have got to think of the President of the United States, not as the chief counselor of the nation, elected for a little while, but as the man meant constantly and every day to be the commander in chief of the armies and navy of the United States, ready to order it to any part of the world where the threat of war is a menace to his own people.

And you can't do that under free debate. You can't do that under public counsel. Plans must be kept secret. Knowledge must be accumulated by a system which we have condemned, because we have called it a spying system. The more polite call it a system of intelligence. (laughter) And you can't watch other nations with your unassisted eye. You have got to watch them by secret agencies planted everywhere.

Let me testify to this, my fellow citizens. I not only did not know it until we got into this war, but I did not believe it when I was told that it was true, that Germany was not the only country that maintained a secret service. Every country in Europe maintained it, because they had to be ready for Germany's spring upon them, and the only difference between the German secret service and the other secret services was that the German secret service found out more than the others did. (applause and laughter) And therefore Germany sprang upon the other nations at unawares, and they were not ready for it.

And you know what the effect of a military nation is upon social questions. You know how impossible it is to effect social reform if everybody must be under orders from the government. You know how impossible it is, in short, to have a free nation if it is a military nation and under military orders. You may say, "You have been on the other side of the water and got bad dreams." I have got no dreams at all. I am telling you the things, the evidence of which I have seen with wakened eyes and not with sleeping eyes. And I know that this country, if it wishes to stand alone, must stand alone as part of a world in arms. (applause) Because, ladies and gentlemen, I don't say it because I am an American and my heart is full of the same pride that fills yours with regard to the power and spirit of this great nation, but merely because it is a fact which I think everybody would admit, outside of America, as well as inside of America—the organization contemplated by the League of Nations without the United States would merely be an alliance and not a League of Nations. (applause) It would be an alliance in which the partnership would be between the more powerful European nations and Japan, and the other party to the world arrangement, the antagonist, the dissociated party, the party to be standing off and to be watched by the alliance, would be the United States of America. There can be no League of Nations in the true sense without the partnership of this great people. (applause)

And with the partnership of this great people, let us mix the selfish with the unselfish. If you don't want me to be too altruistic, let me be very practical. If we are partners, let me predict we will be the senior partner. The financial leadership will be ours. The industrial primacy will be ours. The commercial advantage will be ours. And the other countries of the world will look to us, and, shall I say, are looking to us for leadership and direction? (applause) Very well, then, if I am to compete with the critics of this League and of this treaty as a selfish American, I say I want to get in and get in as quick as I can. I want to be inside and know how the thing is run and help to run it. So that you have the alternative—armed isolation or peaceful partnership.

Can any sane man hesitate as to the choice, and can any sane man ask a question, which is the way of peace? I have heard some men say with an amazing ignorance (laughter and applause) that this was, that the Covenant of the League of Nations was, an arrangement for war. (laughter) Very well, the other arrangement—what would it be? (laughter) An arrangement for peace? For kindliness? For cooperation? Would everybody beckon us to their markets? Would everybody come to us and say, "Tell us how to use your money?" Would everybody come to us and say, "Tell us how much of your goods you want us to take; tell us how much of what Germany is producing you would like when we want it?" I cannot bring my credulity up to that point. (laughter, growing applause) I have reached years of discretion, (laughter, applause) and I have met some very young men who knew a great deal more than some very old men. (applause)

I want you, therefore, after seeing this very ugly picture that I have painted, for it is an ugly picture—it is a picture from which one turns away with distaste and disgust and says, "That isn't America; it isn't like anything we have conceived"—I want you to look at the other side. I wonder if some of the gentlemen who are commenting upon this treaty ever read it! (applause) If anybody will tell me which of them hasn't, I will send him a copy. (a great cry of "read, read," laughter) Because it is written in two languages. On this side is the English and on that side is the French, and since it is evident that some men don't understand English, I will hope that they understand French. (laughter) There are excellent French dictionaries by which they can dig out the meaning, if they cannot understand English. (laughter) It is the plainest English that you would desire, particularly the Covenant of the League of Nations. There isn't a phrase of doubtful meaning in the whole document.

And what is the meaning? It is that the Covenant of the League of Nations is a covenant of arbitration and discussion. (applause) Had anybody ever told you that before? I dare say that everybody you have heard talk about this has discussed Article X. Well, there are twenty-five other articles in it, and all of them are about something else. They discuss how soon and how quick we can get out of it. Well, I am not a quitter for one. (applause and cheering, prolonged and renewing) We can get out just so soon as we want to, but we don't want to get out just as soon as we get in. And then they talk about the Monroe Doctrine, when it expressly says that nothing in that instrument shall be construed as affecting in any way the validity of the Monroe Doctrine. It says so in so many words. And all the other things they talk about draw your attention from the essential matter. The essential matter, my fellow citizens, is this: every member of that League—and it will include all the fighting nations of the world, except Germany—the only nations that will not be admitted into it promptly are Germany and Turkey, and I take it that we needn't discuss it. (applause). We can at any rate postpone Turkey until Thanksgiving. (laughter)

All the fighting nations of the world are in it, and what do they promise? This is the center of the document. They promise that they never will go to war without first submitting the questions at issue to arbitration and absolutely abiding by the decision of the arbitrators, or, if they are not willing to submit it to arbitration, submit it to discussion by the capital Council of the League; that they will give the Council of the League six months in which to consider it, and that, if they do not like the opinion of the Council, they will wait three months after the opinion is rendered before going to war. And I tell you, my fellow citizens, that any nation that is in the wrong and waits nine months before it goes to war never will go to war. (applause)

"Ah," but somebody says, "suppose they don't abide by that?" Because all the arguments you hear are based upon the assumption that we are going to break the Covenant, that bad faith is the accepted rule. There has not been any such bad faith among nations in recent times except the flagrant bad faith of the nation we have just been fighting, (applause) and that bad faith is not likely to be repeated in the immediate future. (applause) Suppose somebody does not abide by this engagement, then what happens? War? No, not war. Something much more terrible than war—absolute boycott of the nation. (applause) The doors are closed upon her, so that she can't ship anything out or receive anything. She can't send a letter out or receive one in. No telegraphic message can cross her borders. No person can cross her borders. She is absolutely closed, (applause) and all the fighting nations of the world agree to join in that boycott. (applause) My own judgment is that war will not be necessary after that. If it is necessary, then it is perfectly evident that the nation is one of the nations that wants to run amuck, and if any nation wants to run amuck in modern civilization, we must all see that the outlaw is captured.

I was saying in one of the first speeches I made upon this little expedition of mine that I was very happy in the circumstance that there was no politics in this business. I mean no party politics, and

I invited that audience, and I invite you, to forget all about parties. Forget that I am a Democrat. Forget that some of you are Republicans. Forget all about that. That has nothing to do with it. And this afternoon a book I had forgotten all about—one of the campaign books of the last political campaign—was put in my hands, and I found in that book the platforms of the two parties. And in both those platforms they advocated just such an arrangement as the League of Nations. (applause) When I was on the other side of the water, I did not know that I was taking, obeying orders from both parties, but I was. And I am very happy in that circumstance, because I can testify to you that I did not think anything about parties when I was on the other side of the water. (applause) I am just as much in my present office the servant of my Republican fellow citizens as I am the servant of my Democratic fellow citizens. I am trying to be what some gentlemen don't know how to be—just a simple, plain-thinking, plain-speaking, out-and-out American. (applause)

Now, I want you to understand that I didn't leave Washington and come out on this trip because I doubted what was going to happen. I didn't. For one thing, I wanted to have the pleasure of leaving Washington, (applause) and for another thing I wanted to have the very much greater pleasure of feeling the inspiration that I would get from you. (applause) Things get very lonely in Washington sometimes. (applause) The real voices of the great people of America sometimes sound faint and distant in that strange city! You hear politics until you wish that both parties were smothered in their own gas. (applause) And I wanted to come out here and hear some plain Americans, hear the kind of talk that I am accustomed to talk, the only kind of talk that I can understand, and the only kind of atmosphere with which I can fill my lungs wholesomely. And, then, incidentally, there is a hint in some quarters that the American people had not forgotten how to think. (applause)

There are certain places where talk doesn't count for anything. I am inclined to think that one of those places is the fashionable dinner table. I have never heard so many things that weren't so anywhere else. In the little circles of fashion and wealth, information circulates the more freely the less true it is. For some reason, there is a preference for the things that are incredible. I admit there is a certain intellectual excitement in believing the things that you know are incredible. It is very much duller to believe only the things that you know are so. But the spicy thing, the unusual thing, the thing that runs athwart the normal and wholesome currents of society—those are the things that one can talk about with an unusual vocabulary and have a lot of fun in expounding. But they are not the things that make up the daily substance of thinking on the part of a wholesome nation like yourselves.

And this nation went into this war to see it through to the end, (applause) and the end has not come yet. This is the beginning, not of the war, but of the processes which are going to render a war like this impossible. (applause) There are no other processes than these that are proposed in this great treaty. It is a great treaty, it is a treaty of justice, of rigorous and severe justice, but don't forget that there are many other parties to this treaty than Germany and her opponents. There is rehabilitated Poland. There is rescued Bohemia. There is redeemed Yugoslavia. There is rehabilitated Rumania. All the nations that Germany meant to crush and reduce to the status of tools in her own hand have been redeemed by this war and given the guarantee of the strongest nations of the world that nobody shall invade their liberty again. (applause) If you don't want to give them that guarantee, then you make it certain that without your guarantee the attempt will be made again. And if another war starts like this one, are you going to keep out of it? If you keep out of this arrangement, that sort of war will come soon. Go into it, and it never will come. (applause)

We are in the presence, therefore, of the most solemn choice that this people was ever called upon to make. That choice is nothing less than this: shall America redeem her pledges to the world? America is made up of the peoples of the world. All the best bloods of the world flow in her veins, all the old affections, all the old and sacred traditions of peoples of every sort through the wide world circulate in her veins, and she has said to mankind at her birth: "We have come to redeem the world by giving it liberty and justice." Now we are called up before the tribunal of mankind to redeem that immortal pledge.

Printed in the *St. Louis Post-Dispatch*, Sept. 6, 1919, with corrections from the complete text in the *St. Louis Globe-Democrat*, Sept. 6, 1919.

Rudolph Forster to Joseph Patrick Tumulty

The White House Sept 5 1919

Please look out for three packages of mail at Kansas City All correspondence I have seen enthusiastic over reports of trip Gus Karger[1] tells me that there is rather severe criticism on the Hill of sentence in Presidents address that quote at present we have to mind our own business and the covenant we will mind other peoples business unquote that there is enthusiastic commendation over sentence that quote if the critics of the League have anything better to suggest they should do it at once unquote[2] He hopes this will be hammered home He tells me that mild reservationists have not been affected at all by their committee reservation on Article Ten[3] semicolon that they are standing absolutely pat period Secretary Re[d]field has admitted to correspondents that he has or is about to tender resignation[4]   Forster

T telegram (WP, DLC).
[1] That is, Gustav J. Karger.
[2] Both sentences (not quoted very accurately) occur in Wilson's address at Indianapolis, Sept. 4, 1919.
[3] The Senate Foreign Relations Committee had voted on September 4 to report the Treaty of Versailles out of committee with four reservations, to be made a part of the resolution of ratification, and thirty-eight amendments to the text. The news report in the *New York Times*, Sept. 5, 1919, includes the text of the four reservations. They are also embodied in the report of the Foreign Relations Committee presented to the Senate on September 10, 11, and 15, 1919, and printed as 66th Cong., 1st sess., *Senate Report No. 176*, as well as in *Cong. Record*, 66th Cong., 1st sess., pp. 5112-14, 5213-15, and 5356-59. The four reservations, as printed in *Senate Report No. 176*, pp. 5-6, are as follows:
"1. The United States reserves to itself the unconditional right to withdraw from the league of nations upon the notice provided in article 1 of said treaty of peace with Germany.
"2. The United States declines to assume, under the provisions of article 10, or under any other article, any obligation to preserve the territorial integrity or political independence of any other country or to interfere in controversies between other nations, members of the league or not, or to employ the military or naval forces of the United States in such controversies, or to adopt economic measures, for the protection of any other country, whether a member of the league or not, against external aggression or for the purpose of coercing any other country, or for the purpose of intervention in the internal conflicts or other controversies which may arise in any other country, and no mandate shall be accepted by the United States under article 22, Part I, of the treaty of peace with Germany, except by action of the Congress of the United States.
"3. The United States reserves to itself exclusively the right to decide what questions are within its domestic jurisdiction, and declares that all domestic and political questions relating to its affairs, including immigration, coastwise traffic, the tariff, commerce, and all other domestic questions, are solely within the jurisdiction of the United States and are not under this treaty submitted in any way either to arbitration or to the consideration of the council or of the assembly of the league of nations, or to the decision or recommendation of any other power.
"4. The United States declines to submit for arbitration or inquiry by the assembly or the council of the league of nations provided for in said treaty of peace any questions which in the judgment of the United States depend upon or relate to its long-established policy, commonly known as the Monroe doctrine; said doctrine is to be interpreted by the United States alone, and is hereby declared to be wholly outside the jurisdiction of said league of nations and entirely unaffected by any provision contained in the said treaty of peace with Germany."
[4] The Associated Press reported from Washington on September 5 that Redfield had tendered his resignation to Wilson and that it had been accepted, effective November 1, 1919. See, for example, the *St. Louis Post-Dispatch*, Sept. 5, 1919.

Joseph Patrick Tumulty to Samuel Gompers

[St. Louis] 5 September, 1919.

The President is using his utmost influence in the matter of telegraph about [telegram][1] but is a little discouraged by the results.

J. P. Tumulty

T telegram (WP, DLC).
   [1] That is, S. Gompers *et al.* to WW, Sept. 4, 1919.

Cary Travers Grayson to Bernard Mannes Baruch

[St. Louis] 5 September, 1919

The President begs that you will urge his advice upon Judge Gary as strongly as possible.   Cary T. Grayson

T telegram (WP, DLC).

From William Bauchop Wilson, with Enclosure

My dear Mr. President: Washington September 5, 1919.

I have your letter inclosing telegram from Governor Boyle of Nevada, suggesting an organized nation-wide oral interpretation of your statement to the shopmen of the country[1] by volunteer speakers who are fair and sympathetic with labor.

The idea would be an admirable one if it could be put into successful operation with a reasonable assurance that the interpreters could retain the confidence and respect of the workers. There is no other man who can command their respect as you do. There are few other men whose sincerity they would not question. You have made your statement. It has been published broadcast. The wageworkers generally have read it and understand it. To start a nation-wide campaign of interpretation, even though conducted by recognized leaders of labor, would be misunderstood. The motives of the men engaged in it would be continually questioned and the beneficial effect of your statement thereby lost. I think it is better to allow the labor leaders to go on as they are doing, with their own interpretation in their own way, seeking to calm the unrest existing throughout the country, which seems to be very rapidly abating.

I would therefore advise against putting the suggestion into effect, particularly in view of the fact that it would require the rapid building of an organization whose interpretations you would in a measure be responsible for and yet because of the rapid and temporary character of the organization you would be unable to direct and control.   Faithfully yours,   W B Wilson

TLS (WP, DLC).
   [1] Printed at Aug. 25, 1919, Vol. 62.

ENCLOSURE

Ely, Nevada, August 28, 1919.

THE PRESIDENT. Your admirable public statement in connection with shopmen's demands seems to me to sound the most timely note of counsel yet delivered. You are better informed than any of us regarding probability of strike as result of failure to secure full wage advance demanded, but it occurs to me that an organized nation wide oral interpretation of your statement to the shopmen of the country by volunteer speakers who are fair and sympathetic with labor might be the best possible insurance against such a calamity as would be precipitated by a vote to go out. I will most cheerfully organize a speakers' committee in this state to carry out our part in such a program if you approve, and doubtless others will do the same in other states. The Department of Labor, being perhaps best qualified to suggest names of organizers who I think should not be the governors in all instances.

With assurances of high esteem,

Emmet D[erby]. Boyle, Governor.

T telegram (WP, DLC).

From William Bauchop Wilson, with Enclosures

My dear Mr. President: Washington September 5, 1919.

I am in receipt of your favor of the 1st instant,[1] inclosing letter from Dr. Garfield relative to issuing a statement to the coal operators and coal miners before their joint meeting in September in line with your letter to the railway shopmen.

The two situations are entirely different. The railway shopmen are engaged in work under direct control of the Government. They have been in negotiation concerning their wage rates since last January. They had taken a strike vote, and some of them were putting the vote into effect. You are the final authority in all matters pertaining to Federal administration. You were speaking for the American people to employees working for corporations under the control of the American people.

The mine situation is different. Mining operations are not under the direct control of the Government. They are working under contract with private employers. They are seeking a change in the contract. A joint conference of operators and miners has been arranged for the purpose of considering such changes. The miners are formulating their demands, some of them startling in their nature. The operators are also formulating their propositions, although they have not as yet been given to the public. These different propositions will be submitted to the joint conference, and the experience of the past has demonstrated that there will be many and great modifications in each of them before either an agreement or a disagreement is reached.

To make any statement at this time before the final position of each side is known would be premature. The proper course to pursue, it seems to me, would be to watch closely the negotiations and if they result in a break with the probability of tying up the fuel supply, take such steps as the situation at that time would warrant.

I am returning Dr. Garfield's letter herewith.

Faithfully yours,   W B Wilson

TLS (WP, DLC).
¹ WW to WBW, Sept. 1, 1919, TLS (Letterpress Books, WP, DLC): "I would very much appreciate an indication from you of the sort of message you think I ought to send to these gatherings which Mr. Garfield mentions, and whether you think I ought to send any or not."

E N C L O S U R E   I

From Harry Augustus Garfield

Dear Mr. President: Mentor, Ohio, Aug. 29/19

I rejoice to note that your letter to the railroad shopmen, & the White House conference on the treaty have greatly strengthened your position hereabout. The belief grows that wise counsels will prevail. May I suggest a direct word to the coal operators & mine workers, before their meetings in September, in line with your letter to the railroad shopmen. Neither wages nor prices ought to be increased; but certain operators are likely to take advantage of demand now mounting above supply for the better coals—I refer to bituminous coal—, & the radicals among the mine workers plan to push for immediate increase of wages. Even the leaders, who recognize that they are bound by their promise to you until peace is promulgated, will work for a substantial increase effective when peace is proclaimed. Should this suggestion appeal to you the enclosed memorandum may be of service. I am leaving tonight for Boston & expect to reach Williamstown on the 4th of September.

Cordially & Faithfully Yours,   H. A. Garfield.

ALS (WP, DLC).

E N C L O S U R E   I I

Memorandum

The United Mine workers meet in Cleveland Sept. 9th & a conference of operators & mine workers has been called to meet in Buffalo Sept. 25th. Secretary Wilson will know whom to rely upon among the mine workers. I found John P. White[1] reliable & the ablest of them all, but he is not now in office. Among the operators, I believe J. H. Wheelwright of Baltimore,[2] former president of the National Coal Association, can be depended upon. He was & I think still is president of the Consolidation Coal Co., a Democrat & an active supporter of your administration. He is not as able as Mr. Field,[3] president of the Pittsburgh Coal Co., nor as influential as Mr. H. N. Taylor[4] of Kansas City, the present president of the National Coal Assn., but he is able & at the present juncture would be of surer service to you. I do not mean by this to reflect upon the sincerity of Mr. Field & Mr. Taylor. Mr. Thos. T. Brewster[5] of St. Louis, who will be an important factor at the Buffalo conference, has a clearer head & more of a vision than any of the others, but I do not know his political views. If he is an advocate of your policies I should put him first.   H. A. Garfield.

Aug. 29/19

Hw MS (WP, DLC).
  [1] John Philip White, president of the United Mine Workers of America, 1912-1917; labor consultant to the United States Fuel Administration, 1917-1918.
  [2] Jere Hungerford Wheelwright, chairman of the board of directors of the Consolidated Coal Co. of Baltimore.
  [3] W. K. Field.
  [4] Henry Noble Taylor, president of numerous coal companies in the Midwest.
  [5] Thomas T. Brewster, chairman of the Coal Operators Association.

From William Bauchop Wilson, with Enclosure

PERSONAL AND CONFIDENTIAL.

My dear Mr. President: Washington September 5, 1919.

I trust I have not caused you any serious uneasiness by the appointment of Miss Mary Anderson as Chief of the Women's Bureau.[1] I have known Miss Anderson for a considerable time and have always found her a level-headed woman. Of course, I have known of her association with Mrs. Robins[2] in the National Women's Trade Union League. That was carefully taken into consideration by me before I determined upon her promotion. There are three distinct groups within the League: A group of radicals, headed by Mrs. Robins; a group of extra-radicals, headed by Rose Schneidermann, which seems for the present to be in the ascendency; and a group without any definite recognized head that is much more conservative than the others. Miss Anderson has the respect of each of these groups more than any other woman, and for that reason, together with her general ability and disposition, I believe she would make the most efficient successor to Miss Van Kleeck,[3] with whom she has been associated as an Assistant since the organization of the Bureau.

I do not anticipate any serious difficulty growing out of Miss Anderson's connection with the Committee on International Relations of the League. There is no doubt that the Conference is being called for the purpose of exercising an influence upon the International Labor Conference when it meets, and it may cause some embarrassment. I stated very frankly to the representatives of the League when they called upon me that the Federal Government could not call such a Conference; that the law prevented it from doing so; that it could not be placed in the position of even seemingly calling the Conference. It was then stated that they did not ask the Government to place itself in that position, but that it would facilitate the sending of the invitation if it could be sent through the State Department. I could see no objections to sending it through the State Department if it went as a message from them, simply using the State Department as the channel of communication. It was indicated to me that the State Department was not willing to act unless I approved. Consequently I attached my approval to a memorandum to that effect, with the condition that the telegram be sent over their signatures so as not to commit the Government to the calling of the Conference. The refusal of the State Department to transmit the message on the grounds that it would not be appropriate to do so inasmuch as the proposed Conference is not being called under authorization of Congress should be considered as final and the National Women's Trade Union League advised that the Conference can only be called by themselves through the ordinarily established methods of communication.

May I add with reference to Miss Barnum[4] that she does not desire any appointment except in the Conciliation Service of the Department and that as soon as we are in a position to do so Miss Barnum will be given such appointment.

Trusting this may throw some light on the situation, I am

Faithfully yours,   W B Wilson

[1] About this matter, see Elizabeth M. Bass to WW, Aug. 5, 1919; WW to WBW, Aug. 8, 1919; Elizabeth M. Bass to WW, Aug. 15, 1919; and WW to WBW, Aug. 21, 1919; all in Vol. 62.

[2] That is, Margaret Dreier (Mrs. Raymond) Robins.

[3] That is, Mary Abby van Kleeck.

[4] That is, Gertrude Barnum.

Mary Anderson to Joseph Patrick Tumulty

My dear Mr. Tumulty: Washington, D. C. August 28, 1919.

In accordance with my conversation with you this morning, I am handing you herewith a statement of the matter concerning which I called.

The National Women's Trade Union League, by vote of its national convention in Philadelphia June 2 to 7, following conferences between the League's representatives and the representatives of the organized working women of Great Britain and France, decided to call an international congress of working women, to be held in Washington the week preceding the International Labor Conference called by the League of Nations. In order to facilitate the assembling of the women delegates, Professor James A. [T.] Shotwell suggested that the State Department be asked to transmit for the National Women's Trade Union League the cablegrams calling the congress, and during his recent visit to this country Dr. Shotwell himself took the matter up with the State Department.

When on August 12 the copy for the cablegrams was submitted to the State Department, the matter was referred to the Secretary of Labor for his endorsement, and this endorsement was given. Since that time our representatives, in arranging the details with officials of the State Department, have been led to understand that there would be no obstacle to the carrying out of our request.

On August 26 I received, by messenger, a letter from Assistant Secretary Adee[1] dated August 23, stating that "I consider that it would not be appropriate for this Department to transmit for the National Women's Trade Union League of America cablegrams calling an International Congress of Working Women, inasmuch as the proposed congress is not being called by the Department of State under authorization of Congress." This decision was naturally disappointing to our committee, both because of the serious and fruitless delay that had been incurred, and because the assistance of the State Department would have been of great value to the working women both of our own country and abroad.

Moreover, an unfortunate complication has arisen. The representatives of the National Women's Trade Union League have at no time stated or indicated that any request had been made to the State Department. They have scrupulously avoided any reference to the State Department in their published announcements of the Congress. Yesterday, however, a representative of the United Press called at our office and stated that he had information from the State Department that the Department had refused to transmit the cablegrams for the League. He intended to publish the story, he said, and called upon us for a comment to publish in that connection. We declined to make any comment. But we fear that if the story of the State Department's action goes out over the country the success of the working women's congress will be seriously endangered.

We shall appreciate your courtesy in bringing this matter to the attention of the President.

Very truly yours,   Mary Anderson
Secretary Committee on International Relations.

TLS (WP, DLC).

[1] That is, Alvey Augustus Adee, Second Assistant Secretary of State.

Frank Lyon Polk to Edward Mandell House

[Paris, Sept. 5, 1919]

Confidential and urgent for Colonel House.

Following just received from Washington QUOTE 3023, Sept 3rd, 5 p.m.[1] Your 3927 August 28th 10 p.m.[2] and 3996 September 1st 1 p.m.[3]

It is the President's view that the council of the League of Nations ought not to come into being until at least four of the great powers and a majority of the minor powers which have membership on the council have ratified the treaty. If the work of the League should be begun by a majority [minority] there would be lack of moral authority and the organization would wear the aspect of an alliance. That should be avoided until it is certainly known how many will adhere to the treaty. When it is definitely known those adhering should go forward with the organization. The President wished me to say for your information that he is confident the U. S. will join the League by ratifying the Treaty. 3023. LANSING. END QUOTE. Paragraph.

Perhaps you will think it wise to inform Drummond of the substance of this message.   Polk   Amission.

T telegram (F. L. Polk Papers, CtY).

[1] RL to FLP, Sept. 3, 1919, T telegram (SDR, RG 256, 185.111/355, DNA).

[2] FLP to RL, Aug. 27, 1919, T telegram (SDR, RG 256, 868.00/193A, DNA). Its text follows:

"In case you have reached no final decision on Thracian question, Johnson suggests that legitimate objections of France and England to a large Constantinople State which might come under dominant control of England or France respectively, in case America does not accept mandate, could be satisfied by a form of international government of the State in which both France and England would be represented. Possibly a commission government, combining certain features of the Saar, Danzig and Fiume arrangements, but properly adapted to the special conditions of the Constantinople area, would best meet the needs of a region in which both the local populations and the large vital interests are truly international in character. If necessary to appease Greek opinion, it might be conceded that Greece should have a representative on the Commission in view of the large Greek populations in parts of Eastern Thrace. If accepted, the plan would at least have the merit of removing the strongest grounds upon which France, England and Greece oppose the idea of a large international state to include both Eastern and Western Thrace."

[3] FLP to RL, Sept. 1, 1919, T telegram (SDR, RG 256, 185.111/354A, DNA). Its text follows: "In view of the fact that the President is leaving Washington, would it not be possible to get a reply to our 3921 August 27 10 P.M., inasmuch as attitude of our representatives on Commission on Execution of Treaty with Germany depends upon expression of your views?"

Frank Lyon Polk to Robert Lansing

Paris, September 5, 1919

4065 Confidential.

For the Secretary of State from Polk.

Following is translation of note handed me by Tardieu on September first with request that I forward it to President as being the views of Clemenceau, Balfour and Tardieu:

Quote. At its meeting of September 1 the Supreme Council considered the rely of President Wilson to Mr. Venizelos' letter of August 15.[1] It was unanimously decided that it was desirable to forward to President Wilson the following summary of the arguments developed by Messrs. Clemenceau, Balfour and Tardieu, President of the Bulgarian Treaty Committee. Paragraph.

Like the President, the Council is unanimous in trying to arrive at a settlement which shall eliminate future causes for war and which shall have a character of permanence. It is for the purpose of securing this result that the above mentioned members have presented the following observations: Paragraph.

1. From an ethnographic standpoint, the solution proposed by President Wilson would place in the European portion of the international state some 700,000 Greeks, namely: 28,000 in western Thrace, 306,000 in eastern Thrace, 364,000 in the vilayet of Constantinople. The number of Turks in this same territory would be about 730,000. This large Greek population, placed under non-Greek sovereignty at the very door of Greece would be a constant source of disturbance. Paragraph.

2. There are in Greece, Thrace and Asia Minor approximately 7,300,000 Greeks. The American solution would result in 37% of this population being outside of Greek territory. It is important to decrease this proportion and to apply more widely to the Greeks the principle of self-determination.

3. The international state of Constantinople had been conceived with a direct and definite object: to insure the liberty of the straits.

It was for this reason that the Council accepted as a fundamental hypothesis the determination of the boundary of the international state by the Enos-Midia line. To include in this state all of eastern Thrace and a part of western Thrace is in the first place to change its character, as well as to render its government more difficult and finally, by adding to the 364,000 Greeks of Constantinople the 335,000 Greeks of eastern and western Thrace, to give over the state to inevitable racial conflicts. Mr. Clemenceau emphasises strongly the danger of such a solution.

4. Mr. Venizelos brought about the entry of his country into the war voluntarily and unconditionally. Since the armistice he has responded to all the requests and listened to all the advice of the Powers. Since that time he has mobilized three more divisions than he had in 1918, making a total of twelve, thus holding himself in readiness to carry out the task with which the Conference has charged Greece both at Smyrna and more recently in regard to Bulgaria. It must be recognized that the American solution would put Greece, compared with the other eastern countries and notably with Roumania, in a disadvantageous position which she has not deserved and which would be the more regretable in view of the undoubtedly Greek character of the populations claimed. Paragraph.

5. The Powers have just forbidden the restoration of the Hapsburgs at Budapest.[2] They run the risk, in provoking the fall of Mr. Venizelos, of paving the way for the return of King Constantine to Greece, who, in case the American solution prevails, would have the right to say that Mr. Venizelos had failed to obtain the territories of Greek race to which he has made claim. Paragraph.

For these reasons, ethnographic, political and moral, the above mentioned members of the Supreme Council have expressed the desire that Mr. Polk should call the attention of President Wilson to the great importance in searching after, so far as this question is concerned, a solution more in accordance with fundamental principles of the peace, less unfavorable to Greece and better calculated to prevent the occurrence of unpleasant incidents in the Balkans. End quote. paragraph.

I called Tardieu's attention to the fact that he gave the President nothing definite. I will forward another note from him on this subject. Following are the observations of Doctor Johnson[3] on the statements contained in the above note: paragraph.

Paragraphs 1, 2 and 3 appeal to statistics based on Greek estimates which are in many cases grossly exaggerated. Even if we accept them, the number of Greeks in Western Thrace is insignificant. Of those in Eastern Thrace the majority are south of the

Enos-Midia line and would therefore probably come within the international state in any case. Both in the rest of Eastern Thrace and in Western Thrace the Turks constitute the majority of the population. The statement that 37% of the Greeks will be left outside the frontiers of Greece presupposes that Greece will not receive any further accessions of territory. Should she be allotted Cyprus, the Dodekannesos or any part of Asia Minor the percentage would be reduced. The percentage given is itself based on exaggerated Greek estimates, and refers to areas in which the Greek population is for the most part a minority population. Hence it is not accurate to say that the populations claimed by Greece are incontestably Greek.   Polk, Ammission.

T telegram (SDR, RG 256, 868.00/201A, DNA).
   [1] For Vénisélos' message to WW, see FLP to RL, Aug. 16, 1919, Vol. 62. Wilson's reply was RL to FLP, Aug. 28, 1919, *ibid*.
   [2] The Council of Heads of Delegations to the Paris Peace Conference had sent a telegram to the Interallied Military Mission in Budapest on August 22 demanding the resignation of the government headed by Archduke Joseph of Hapsburg (about the Archduke and his regime, see n. 1 to the memorandum by Robert Lansing printed at Aug. 20, 1919, Vol. 62). The mission transmitted the message to Archduke Joseph on the afternoon of August 23, giving him two hours in which to reply and advising him that, should he fail to resign, the message would be made public. At 8 p.m. the mission was informed that the Archduke and his government were resigning. See *PPC*, VII, 803, 855, and Francis Deák, *Hungary at the Paris Peace Conference: The Diplomatic History of the Treaty of Trianon* (New York, 1942), pp. 128-29.
   [3] That is, Douglas Wilson Johnson, also mentioned in FLP to EMH, Sept. 5, 1919, n. 2.

From William Phillips

[Washington] September 5, 7 P.M. [1919]

Mr. Polk asks whether you agree with Clemenceau's proposal that decision of the question of the admission of German and Austrian labor delegates to the forthcoming International Labor Conference at Washington should be left to that conference itself.

This proposal was made at meeting of Council on August 29th and was supported by Balfour, who wanted however to refer the question to his Government. Italians said that their Labor Confederation declared it would not send representatives or recognize International Labor Conference or its decisions unless German delegates were admitted.

Tittoni however seems to favor admission of Germans as well as Austrians.   William Phillips
                    Acting Sec'y of State.

T telegram (WP, DLC).

From the Diary of Dr. Grayson

Saturday, September 6, 1919.

The Presidential Special was halted on a siding six miles out of Kansas City at 7:00 o'clock in the morning and held there until 9:00 in order that the President might have an opportunity to enjoy his breakfast in peace. The Private Car MAYFLOWER was already jammed with flowers of every sort which had been put on board by the admirers of the President and Mrs. Wilson in St. Louis.

After breakfast the train proceeded slowly through the Kansas City yards, pulling into the big Union Station at 9:00 o'clock. It was a bright, sunshiny morning, and the President was greeted by a reception committee, the chairman of which was the Mayor of Kansas City.[1] The committee had been named by the Chamber of Commerce and was selected entirely without regard to political faith. Emerging from the station the President was escorted to a great flag-bedecked automobile, and a parade headed by a troop of cavalry and a regiment of Missouri National Guardsmen, was quickly organized. Because it had been found impossible to accommodate all of the people who wanted to hear the President, a very lengthy routed march had been selected and most of the business section of Kansas City was covered by the parade before it finally returned to the Coliseum. There were thousands and thousands of school children lined up all along the routed march. Each of them had been given a small American flag and they waved the flag and sang as the car bearing the President and Mrs. Wilson passed them. It was a really cheering sight. The children had no partisanship; in fact, they did not know why the President was there, but it was very plain that they all knew that it was the President. Their welcome was of a character that was most pleasing to every one in the party. The President and Mrs. Wilson especially were deeply interested in the children .

Arriving at the Coliseum[2] the President found that every inch of space again was occupied and that many had been turned away. The President referred almost at the outset of his speech to the children who had greeted him. He told his audience that it was for these children and those like them throughout the country that he wanted the Treaty ratified. Only ratification of the Treaty, he said, would prevent the boys he had seen from being offered a sacrifice to war. The President emphasized the fact that the world was aflame and that unless America was willing to assume the leader-

[1] James S. Cowgill, Democrat.
[2] Actually, Convention Hall. The crowd there was estimated at 20,000 persons. *Kansas City Star*, Sept. 6, 1919.

ship and lead the world back to sanity, another war must come whose toll in human lives would be far greater than the one which had just ended. The President made no direct reference in his speech here to Senator Reed's opposition to the Treaty, although this was the Senator's home. However, the President did point out that a good many of the arguments that had been produced against the Treaty could not stand the light of day. He told the audience that it did not know what was in the Treaty. He told them they had been told about Article X of the League Covenant, but that most of the other articles had never been discussed in their presence. He told them that no Senator who had spoken in opposition to the Treaty had ever told the people of the United States that this Treaty included a "Magna Charta" for labor. The President explained the Treaty at great length, telling the audience that what he wanted to do was to have them understand that the entire document was a "human measure that went to the very heart of the world itself." The audience applauded the President's telling points and his reception was very friendly and very warm.

Some of the members of the committee had expressed the fear that some of Senator Reed's followers would endeavor to heckle the President, but their fears were entirely groundless. As a matter of fact, the President could not have had a better welcome nor a more attentive and appreciative audience.[3]

At noon the Presidential Special left for Des Moines, Iowa. Enroute a brief stop was made at St. Joseph, Missouri, where a crowd of 10,000 people had gathered hoping to hear the President make a speech. Because of the tremendous strain that he was to be under during the entire trip, I was forced right at the outset to put my foot down on any rear platform speeches or on any additions to the announced itinerary. Secretary Tumulty wanted to have the President speak at every place that the train stopped, believing that he could stand the strain, but I knew far better, and, at my request, the President contented himself with shaking hands and bowing to the crowds that met the train at the junction points where halts had to be made to change engines and to take on needed supplies. As a matter of fact, although the President was very good in obeying my instructions and refraining from talking at these other stops, he was forced to waste a great deal of badly needed energy in greeting the crowds. The people were friendly—they could not have been more friendly—but with their friendship there was that amount of unreasonableness that characterizes the average American crowd. They did not think of the strain the President was un-

---

[3] After his speech, Wilson complained of the heat in the auditorium, saying: "I believe I lost at least two pounds. It was dreadfully warm up there." *Ibid.*

der. They thought of themselves. And they felt that they ought to have as much of him as was possible. Consequently, every one tried to shake him by the hand and he was forced to lean away over the railing of the private-car platform and shake hands with both hands to satisfy the demands of the crowd. This was a physical strain that was hard to measure and had a decided effect in adding to the fatigue of the trip.

Des Moines was reached at 8:00 o'clock at night. It was a terribly hot and dusty trip over the Missouri plains, and the steel cars of the special train held the heat like ovens. The President tried to rest but was unable to get very much because of the fast schedule that had to be maintained to make the evening engagement on time and the heat of the day.

The crowd in Des Moines was a revelation to the pessimists in the party. The Iowa Capital certainly did itself proud. Gathered in and about the station was a crowd so dense that it was almost impossible for the automobiles bearing the party to make their way through it.[4] A snail's pace was maintained in the automobile parade that preceded the meeting in the big Armory. The crowds surged about the President's automobile, almost overwhelming the secret service guard, and did their best to get close enough to pat the President and Mrs. Wilson on the back and to cheer them. The President stood in his car all the way from the station to the Armory,[5] where the meeting was held. He was forced to keep his hat in his hand while he bowed to the constantly increasing roar and applause. It was certainly friendly territory that he had encountered on the trip.

The Armory was filled to overflowing. The audience was a particularly attentive one, and it followed the President's arguments from start to finish, with many manifestations of approval.

It was plain that a strike in the steel industry was almost inevitable, and during the day the President had sent a telegram to Samuel Gompers, President of the American Federation of Labor, asking him to do everything in his power to prevent a walk-out of the organized employees of the great steel corporations.[6]

In his speech here the President took occasion to go on record as opposed to any employer of labor refusing to discuss with his employees the problems affecting their work. While no names were mentioned, there was no doubt that his remarks were di-

[4] The reception committee at Des Moines included, among others, William Lloyd Harding, Republican, Governor of Iowa, and Tom Patterson Fairweather, Mayor of Des Moines.

[5] Actually, the Coliseum.

[6] This telegram, which Wilson sent on September 5, not September 6, is missing. For the reply to it, see J. Fitzpatrick *et al.* to WW, Sept. 9, 1919.

rected at the head of Judge E. H. Gary, President of the United States Steel Corporation, who had refused point blank to meet a committee of the Federation of Labor that had desired to discuss with him the problems which threatened to bring about the strike.

The President in his speech also emphasized the fact that the Treaty if ratified would be a "ninety-five per cent insurance against war." He called attention to the fact that the United States already had signed some forty treaties[7]—known as the Bryan treaties— which provided for a discussion of all questions at issue between this country and other nations that might lead to war. He declared that if Germany had only discussed the questions that brought about the war for one week, the war never would have started, and he called attention to the fact that under the League of Nations Constitution nine months would necessarily elapse before any two countries that were parties to the agreement could go to war. His reference to arbitration was very sympathetically received by the audience here in Des Moines.

It was nearly 11:00 o'clock before the President ended his address and was able to go to his hotel for a much needed night's rest.

[7] Actually, thirty. About these treaties, see the index references under "Bryan, William Jennings, conciliation, or 'cooling off' treaties" in Vol. 27 and Arthur S. Link, *Wilson: The New Freedom* (Princeton, N. J., 1956), pp. 280-83.

An Address in Convention Hall in Kansas City

[[September 6, 1919]]

Mr. Chairman,[1] my fellow citizens, it is very inspiring to me to stand in the presence of so great a gathering of my fellow citizens and have the privilege of performing the duty I have come to perform. And that duty is to report to my fellow citizens concerning the work of the peace conference. And every day it seems to me to become more necessary to report, because so many people who are talking about it do not understand what it is.

I came back from Paris bringing one of the greatest documents of human history. One of the things that made it great was that it was penetrated throughout with the principles to which America has devoted her life. Let me hasten to say that one of the most delightful circumstances of the work on the other side of the water was that I discovered that what we called American principles had penetrated to the heart and to the understanding, not only of the

[1] B. A. Parsons, president of the Kansas City Chamber of Commerce.

great peoples of Europe, but to the hearts and understandings of the great men who were representing the peoples of Europe. When these principles were written into this treaty, they were written there by common consent and by common conviction. But it remains true, nevertheless, my fellow citizens, that principles were written into that treaty which were never written into any great international understanding before, and that they had their natural birth and origin in this country to which we have devoted our life and service.

I have no hesitation in saying that in spirit and essence it is an American document. And if you will bear with me—for this great subject is not a subject for oratory, it is a subject for examination and discussion—if you will bear with me, I will remind you of some of the things that we have long desired and which are at last accomplished in this treaty. I think that I can say that one of the things that America has had most at heart throughout her existence has been that there should be substituted for the brutal processes of war the friendly processes of consultation and arbitration. And that is done in the Covenant of the League of Nations.

I am very anxious that my fellow citizens should realize that that is the chief topic of the Covenant of the League of Nations—the greater part of its provisions. The whole intent and purpose of the document are expressed in provisions by which all the member states agree that they will never go to war without first having done one or the other of two things, either submit the matter in controversy to arbitration, in which case they agree to abide by the verdict, or submit it to the decision of the Council of the League of Nations. And for that purpose, they consent to allow six months for the discussion and, whether they like the opinion expressed or not, they will not go to war for three months after that opinion has been expressed. So, whether you get arbitration or not, you have nine months' discussion.

And I want to remind you that that is the central principle of some thirty treaties entered into between the United States of America and some thirty other sovereign nations, all of which were confirmed by the Senate of the United States. (applause) We have such an agreement with France. We have such an agreement with Great Britain. We have such an agreement with practically every great nation except Germany, which refused to enter into such an agreement, because, my fellow citizens, Germany knew that she intended something that did not bear discussion, and that, if she had submitted the purposes which led to this war to so much as one month's discussion, she never would have dared go into the enterprise against mankind which we finally did get into. (applause) And, therefore, I say that this principle of discussion is the principle already adopted by America.

And what is the compulsion to do this? The compulsion is this, that if any member state violates that promise to submit either to arbitration or discussion, it is thereby *ipso facto* deemed to have committed an act of war against all the rest. Then, you will ask, do we at once take up arms and fight them? No, we do something very much more terrible than that. We absolutely boycott them. It is provided in the instrument that there shall be no communication ever between them and the rest of the world. They shall receive no goods, and they shall ship no goods. They shall receive no telegraphic messages, and they shall send none. They shall receive no mail, and no mail will be received from them. The nationals, the citizens, of the member states will never enter their territory until the matter is adjusted, and their citizens cannot leave their territory. It is the most complete boycott ever conceived in a public document, and I want to say to you with confident prediction that there will be no more fighting after that.

Gentlemen talk as if the most terrible outcome of this great combination of all of the fighting peoples of the world was going to be to fight; whereas, as a matter of fact, the essence of the document is to the effect that the processes shall be peaceful, and peaceful processes are more deadly than the processes of war. Let any merchant put it to himself, that if he enters into a covenant and then breaks it and the people all around him absolutely desert his establishment and will have nothing more to do with him—ask him after that if it will be necessary to send the police. The most terrible thing that can happen to an individual, and the most conclusive thing that can happen to a nation, is to be read out of decent society. (applause)

There was another thing that we wished to accomplish which is accomplished in this document. We wanted disarmament, and this document provides in the only possible way for disarmament—by common agreement. Observe, my fellow citizens, that, as I said just now, every great fighting nation in the world is to be a member of this partnership except Germany, and inasmuch as Germany has accepted a limitation of her army to 100,000 men, I don't think for the time being she may be regarded as a great fighting nation. Here in the center of Europe a great nation of more than 60,000,000 that has agreed not to maintain an army of more than 100,000 men, and all around her the rest of the world in concerted partnership to see that no other nation attempts what she attempted, and agreeing among themselves that they will not impose this limitation of armament upon Germany merely, but they will impose it upon themselves.

And you know, my fellow citizens, what armaments mean: great standing armies and great stores of war material. They don't mean merely burdensome taxation, they don't mean merely compulsory military service, which saps the economic strength of the nation; but they mean also the building of a military class.

Again and again, my fellow citizens, in the conference at Paris we were face to face with this circumstance—that, in dealing with a particular civil government, we found that they would not dare to promise what their general staff was not willing that they should promise, and that they were dominated by the military machine which they had created, nominally for their own defense, but really, whether they willed it or not, for the provocation of war. And so soon as you have a military class, it does not make any difference what your form of government is. If you are determined to be armed to the teeth, you must obey the orders and directions of the one man who can control the great machinery of war. Elections are of minor importance, because they determine the political policy, and back of that political policy is the constant pressure of the men trained to arms, enormous bodies of disciplined men around them, unlimited supplies of military stores, and wondering if they are never going to be allowed to use their education and skill and ravage some great people with the force of arms. That is the meaning of armament. It is not merely the cost of it, although that is overwhelming, but it is the spirit of it. This country has never had and I hope, in the Providence of God, never will have, that spirit. (great applause) And there is no other way to dispense with great armaments except by the common agreement of the fighting nations of the world. And here is the agreement: they promise disarmament, and promise to agree upon a plan.

But there was something else we wanted that is accomplished by this treaty. We wanted to destroy autocratic authority everywhere in the world. We wanted to see to it that there was no place in the world where a small group of men could use their fellow citizens as pawns in a game; that there was no place in the world where a small group of men, without consulting their fellow citizens, could send their fellow citizens to battle and death in order to accomplish some dynastic scheme, some political plan that had been conceived in private, some object that had been prepared for by universal, worldwide, intrigue. That is what we wanted to accomplish.

The most startling thing that developed itself at the opening of our participation in this war was not the military preparation of Germany—we were familiar with that, though we had been dreaming that she would not use it—but her political preparation—to find that every community in the civilized world was penetrated by her intrigue. The German people did not know that, but it was known in Wilhelmstrasse, where the central offices of the German government were, and Wilhelmstrasse was the master of the German people. And this war, my fellow citizens, has emancipated the German people as well as the rest of the world. (applause) We don't want to see anything like that happen again, because we know that democracies will sooner or later have to destroy that form of government, and if we don't destroy it now the job is still to be done. And by a combination of all the great fighting peoples of the world, to see to it that the aggressive purposes of such governments cannot be realized, you cannot any longer have the situation where they will have little groups of men to contrive the downfall of civilization in private conference.

But I want to say something about that that has a different aspect, and perhaps you will regard it as a slight digression from the discussion which I am asking you to be patient enough to follow. My fellow citizens, it doesn't make any difference what kind of a minority governs you, if it is a minority, and the thing we must see to is that no minority anywhere masters the majority. That is at the heart, my fellow citizens, of the tragical things that are happening in that great country which we long to help and can find no way that is effective to help. I mean the great realm of Russia. The men who are now largely in control of the affairs of Russia represent nobody but themselves. They have again and again been challenged to call a constitutional convention. They have again and again been challenged to prove that they had some kind of a mandate, even from a single class of their fellow citizens, and they dare not attempt it. They have no mandate from anybody. There are only thirty-four of them, I am told, and there were more than thirty-four men who used to control the destinies of Europe from Wilhelmstrasse. There is a closer monopoly of power in Petrograd and Moscow than there ever was in Berlin, and the thing that is intolerable is not that the Russian people are having their way, but that another group of men more cruel than the Czar himself is controlling the destinies of that great people.

And I want to say here and now that I am against the control of any minority anywhere. Search your own economic history, and what have you been uneasy about? Now and again you have said there were small groups of capitalists who were controlling the industry and therefore the development of the United States. Seriously, my fellow citizens, if that is so, and I sometimes have feared that it was, we must break up that monopoly. I am not now saying that there is any group of our fellow citizens who are consciously doing anything of the kind, and I am saying that these allegations must be proved. But if it is proved that any class, any group, anywhere, is, without the suffrage of their fellow citizens, in control of our affairs, then I am with you to destroy the power of that group.

We have got to be frank with ourselves, however. If we don't want a minority government as they have in Germany, we must see to it that we don't have it in the United States. If you don't want little groups of selfish men to plot the future of Europe, we must not allow little groups of selfish men to plot the future of America. Any man that speaks for a class must prove that he also speaks for all his fellow citizens and for mankind, and then we will listen to him. The most difficult thing in a democracy, my fellow citizens, is to get classes, where they definitely exist, to understand one another and unite, and you have not got a great democracy until they do understand one another and unite. If we are in for seeing that there are no more Czars and no more Kaisers, then let us do a thorough job and see that nothing of that sort occurs anywhere.

Then there was another thing we wanted to do, my fellow citizens, that is done in this document. We wanted to see that helpless peoples were nowhere in the world put at the mercy of unscrupulous enemies and masters. There is one pitiful example which is in the hearts of all of us. I mean the example of Armenia. There was a Christian people, helpless, at the mercy of a Turkish government which thought it the service of God to destroy them. And at this moment, my fellow citizens, it is an open question whether the Armenian people will not, while we sit here and debate, be absolutely destroyed. When I think of words piled upon words, of debate following debate, when these unspeakable things that cannot be handled until the debate is over are happening, in these pitiful parts of the world, I wonder that men do not wake up to the moral responsibility of what they are doing. Great peoples are driven out upon a desert, where there is no food and can be none, and they are driven to die, and then men, women, and children thrown into a common grave, so imperfectly covered up that here and there is a pitiful arm stretched out to heaven, and there is no pity in the world. When shall we wake up to the moral responsibility of this great occasion?

And, so, my fellow citizens, there are other aspects to that matter. Not all the populations that are having something that is not a square deal live in Armenia. There are others, and one of the glories of the great document which I brought back with me is this, that everywhere in the area of settlement covered by the political questions involved in that treaty, people of that sort have been given their freedom and guaranteed their freedom.

But the thing does not end there, because the treaty includes the Covenant of the League of Nations. And what does that say? That says that it is the privilege of any member state to call attention to anything, anywhere, that is likely to disturb the peace of the world or the good understanding between nations upon which the peace of the world depends. And every people in the world that have not got what they think they ought to have is thereby given a world forum in which they can bring the thing to the bar of mankind. An incomparable thing, a thing that never was dreamed of before! A thing that was never conceived of, that was never possible before— that it should not be regarded as an unfriendly act on the part of the representatives of one nation to call attention to something that was being done within the confines of another empire which was disturbing the peace of the world and good understanding between nations.

There never before has been provided a world forum in which the legitimate grievances of peoples entitled to consideration can be brought to the common judgment of mankind. And if I were the advocate of any suppressed or oppressed people, I surely could not ask any better forum to stand up before the world and challenge the other party to make good its excuses for not acting in that case. That compulsion is the most tremendous moral compulsion that could be devised by organized mankind.

I think I can take it for granted that you never have realized what a scope this great treaty has. You have been asked to look at so many little spots in it with a magnifying glass that you do not know how big it is, (applause) what a great enterprise of the human spirit it is, what a thoroughly American document it is. It is the first great international agreement in the history of mankind where the principle adopted has not given power to the strong but the right to the weak. (applause)

To reject that treaty, to alter that treaty, is to impair one of the first charters of mankind. And yet there are men that deliberate the question with passion, with private passion, with party passion, who think only of some immediate advantage to themselves or to a group of their fellow countrymen, and who look at the thing with the jaundice eyes of those who have some private purpose of their own. When at last, in the annals of mankind they are gibbeted, they will regret that the gibbet is so high.

I would not have you think that I am trying to characterize those who conscientiously object to anything in this great document. I take off my hat to any man who is conscientious, and there are men who are conscientiously opposed to it, though they will pardon me if I say ignorantly opposed. (applause) I have no quarrel with them. It has been a pleasure to confer with some of them and to tell them as frankly, as I would have told my most intimate friend, the whole inside of my mind and of every other mind that I knew anything about that had been concerned with the conduct of affairs at Paris, in order that they might understand this thing and go with the rest of us in the consummation of what is necessary for the peace of the world. (applause) I have no intolerant spirit in the matter, I assure you, but I also assure you that from the bottom of my feet to the top of my head I have got a fighting spirit about it.

And if anybody dares to defeat this great experiment, then they must gather together the counselors of the world and do something better. (applause) If there is a better scheme, I, for one, will subscribe to it, (applause) but I want to say now, as I said the other night, it is a case of "put up or shut up." Negation will not save the world. Opposition constructs nothing. Opposition is the specialty of those who are Bolshevistically inclined. And again I assure you I am not comparing any of my respected colleagues to Bolsheviki; but I am merely pointing out that the Bolshevistic spirit lacks every element of constructive opposition. They have destroyed everything, and they have proposed nothing. And, while there is a common abhorrence for political Bolshevism, I hope there won't be any such a thing growing up in our country as international Bolshevism, the Bolshevism that destroys the constructive work of men who have conscientiously tried to cement the good feeling of the great peoples of the world.

The magnificent thing about the League of Nations is that it is to include the great peoples of the world, all except Germany. Germany is one of the great peoples of the world. I would be ashamed not to say that those 60,000,000 industrious and inventive and accomplished people are one of the great peoples of the world. They have been put upon. They have been misled. Their minds have been debased by a false philosophy. And they have been taught things that the human spirit ought to reject, but they will come out of that nightmare, that phantasma, and they will again be a great people. And when they are out of it, when they have got over that dream of conquest and of oppression, when they have shown that their government really is based upon new principles and upon democratic principles, then we, all of us at Paris, agreed that they should be admitted to the League of Nations.

In the meantime, her onetime partner, Austria, is to be admitted.

Hungary, I dare say, will be admitted. The only nations of any consequence outside of the League of Nations—unless we choose to stand out and get in line with Germany—are Germany and Turkey, and we are just now looking for the pieces of Turkey. She has so been thoroughly disintegrated that the process of assembling the parts is becoming exceedingly difficult, and the chief controversy is who shall attempt that very difficult and perilous job?

Is it not a great vision, my fellow citizens—this of the thoughtful world combined for peace, and this of all the great peoples of the world associated to see that justice is done, that the strong who intend wrong are restrained and that the weak who cannot defend themselves are made secure?

We have a problem ahead of us that ought to interest us in this connection. We have promised the people of the Philippine Islands that we will set them free, and it has been one of our perplexing questions how we should make them safe after we set them free. Under this arrangement, they will be safe from the outset. They will become members of the League of Nations, and every great nation in the world will be obliged to respect and preserve against external aggression from any quarter the territorial integrity and political independence of the Philippines. It simplifies one of the most perplexing problems that has faced the American public. But it does not simplify our problems merely, gentlemen. It illustrates the triumph of the American spirit. I do not want to attempt any flight of fancy, but I can fancy those men of the first generation, that so thoughtfully set this great government up—the generation of Washington, Hamilton, Jefferson, and the Adamses—I can fancy their looking on with a sort of enraptured amazement that the American spirit should have made conquest of the world.

I wish you could have seen the faces of some of the people that talked to us over there about the arrival of the American troops. At first they didn't know that we were going to be able to send so many. But they got something from the first troops that changed the whole aspect of the war. One of the most influential ladies in Paris, the wife of a member of the cabinet, told us that on the Fourth of July of last year that she and others had attended the ceremonies with very sad hearts and merely out of courtesy to the United States, because they did not believe that the arrival of the United States troops was going to be effective. But she said, "After we had been there and seen the faces of those men in khaki, seen the spirit of their swing and attitude and seen the vision that was in their eyes, we came away knowing that victory was in sight."

What Europe saw in our boys was not merely men under arms, indomitable men under arms, but men with an ideal in their eyes, men who had come a long way from home to defend other people's homes—men who had forgotten the convenience of everything that personally affected them and had turned away from the longing love of the people who were dear to them and gone across the broad sea to rescue the nations of the world from an intolerable oppression.

I tell you, my fellow citizens, the war was won by the American spirit. Orders were picked up on the battlefield, German orders, directing the commanders not to let the Americans get hold of a particular position, because you never could get them out again. (applause) And you know what one of our American wits said, that it took only half as long to train an American army as any other, because you only had to train them to go one way. (applause) And it is true that they never thought of going any other way, and when they were restrained, because they were told it was imprudent or dangerous, they were impatient. They said, "We didn't come over here to wait, we came over here to fight," and their very audacity, their very indifference to danger, changed the morale of the battlefield. They were not fighting prudently; they were fighting to get there. And America in this treaty has realized, my fellow countrymen, what those gallant boys we are so proud of fought for. The men who make this impossible or difficult will have a lifelong reckoning with the men who won the war. I have consorted with those boys. I have been proud to call myself their commander in chief. I didn't run the business. They didn't need anybody to run it. All I had to do was to turn them loose!

And now for a final word, my fellow citizens. If anything that I have said has left the impression on your mind that I have the least doubt of the result, please dismiss the impression. And if you think that I have come out on this errand to fight anybody—anybody— please dismiss that from your mind. I have not come to fight or antagonize any individual, or body of individuals. I have, let me say without the slightest affectation, the greatest respect for the Senate of the United States. But, my fellow citizens, I have come out to fight for a cause. That cause is greater than the Senate. It is greater than the government. It is as great as the cause of mankind, and I intend, in office or out, to fight that battle as long as I live. (applause) My ancestors were troublesome Scotchmen, and among them were some of that famous group that were known as the Covenanters. Very well, here is the Covenant of the League of Nations. I am a Covenanter!

Printed in the *Kansas City Star*, Sept. 6, 1919, with corrections from the complete text in the *New York Times*, Sept. 7, 1919.

An Address in the Des Moines Coliseum

[[September 6, 1919]]

Mr. Chairman[1] and fellow countrymen, you make my heart very warm with your generous welcome, and I want to express my unaffected gratitude to your chairman for having so truly struck the note of an occasion like this. He has used almost the very words that were in my thought—that the world is inflamed and profoundly disturbed, and we are met to discuss the measures by which its spirit can be quieted and its affairs turned to the right courses of human life. My fellow countrymen, the world is desperately in need of the settled conditions of peace, and it cannot wait much longer. It is waiting upon us. That is the thought, that is the burdensome thought, upon my heart tonight, that the world is waiting for the verdict of the nation to which it looked for leadership and which it thought would be the last that would ask the world to wait.

My fellow citizens, the world is not at peace. I suppose that it is difficult for one who has not had some touch of the hot passion of the other side of the sea to realize how all the passions that have been slumbering for ages have been uncovered and released by the tragedy of this war. We speak of the tragedy of this war, but the tragedy that lay back of it was greater than the war itself, because back of it lay long ages in which the legitimate freedom of men was suppressed. Back of it lay long ages of recurrent war in which little groups of men, closeted in capitals, determined whether the sons of the land over which they ruled should go out upon the field and shed their blood. For what? For liberty? No, not for liberty, but for the aggrandizement of those who ruled them. And this had been slumbering in the hearts of men. They had felt the suppression of it. They had felt the mastery of those whom they had not chosen as their masters. They had felt the oppression of laws which did not admit them to the equal exercise of human rights. And now all of this is released and uncovered and men glare at one another and say, "Now we are free, and what shall we do with our freedom?"

What happened in Russia was not a sudden and accidental thing. The people of Russia were maddened with the suppression of Czarism. When at last the chance came to throw off those chains, they threw them off, at first with hearts full of confidence and hope. And then they found out that they had been again de-

---

[1] James Bellamy Weaver, lawyer, Republican member of the Iowa House of Representatives, and president of the Des Moines Chamber of Commerce. The Rt. Rev. Harry Sherman Longley, Protestant Episcopal Coadjutor Bishop of Iowa, had given the invocation.

ceived. There was no assembly chosen to frame a constitution for them, or, rather, there was an assembly chosen to choose a constitution for them and it was suppressed and dispersed. And a little group of men just as selfish, just as ruthless, just as pitiless, as the agents of the Czar himself assumed control and exercised their power by terror and not by right.

And in other parts of Europe the poison spread—the poison of disorder, the poison of revolt, the poison of chaos. And do you honestly think, my fellow citizens, that none of that poison has got in the veins of this free people? Do you not know that the world is all now one single whispering gallery? Those antenna of the wireless telegraph are the symbols of our age. All the impulses of mankind are thrown out upon the air and reach to the ends of the earth. And quietly upon steamships, silently under the cover of the postal service, with the tongue of the wireless and the tongue of the telegraph, all the suggestions of disorder are spread through the world. And money, coming from nobody knows where, is deposited by the millions in capitals like Stockholm, to be used for the propaganda of disorder and discontent and dissolution throughout the world. And men look you calmly in the face in America and say they are for that sort of revolution, when "that sort of revolution" means government by terror, government by force, not government by vote. It is the negation of everything that is American; but it is spreading, and, so long as disorder continues, so long as the world is kept waiting for the answer to the question of the kind of peace we are going to have and what kind of guarantees are to be behind that peace, that poison will steadily spread, more and more rapidly, spread until it may be that even this beloved land of ours will be distracted and distorted by it.

That is what is concerning me, my fellow countrymen. I know the splendid steadiness of the American people, but, my fellow citizens, the whole world needs that steadiness, and the American people are the makeweight in the fortunes of mankind. How long are we going to debate into which scale we will throw that magnificent equipoise that belongs to us? How long shall we be kept waiting for the answer whether the world may trust or despise us?

They have looked to us for leadership. They have looked to us for example. They have built their peace upon the basis of our suggestions. That great volume that contains the treaty of peace is drawn along the specifications laid down by the American government, and now the world stands at amaze because an authority in America hesitates whether it will endorse an American document or not.

You know what the necessity of peace is. Why, my fellow countrymen, political liberty can exist only when there is peace. Social reform can take place only when there is peace. The settlement of every question that concerns our daily life waits for peace.

I have been receiving delegations in Washington of men engaged in the service of the government temporarily in the administration of the railways, and I have had to say to them: "My friends, I cannot tell what the railways can earn until commerce is restored to its normal courses. Until I can tell what the railroads can earn, I cannot tell what the wages that the railroads can pay will be. I cannot suggest what the increase of freight and passenger rates will be to meet these increases in wages, if the rates must be increased. I cannot tell yet whether it will be necessary to increase the rates or not, and I must ask you to wait."

But they are not the only people that have come to see me. There are all sorts of adjustments necessary in this country. I have asked representatives of capital and labor to come to Washington next month and confer—confer about the fundamental thing of our life at present, that is to say, the conditions of labor. Do you realize, my fellow citizens, that all through the world the one central question of civilization is, "What shall be the conditions of labor?" The profoundest unrest in Europe is due to the doubt prevailing as to what shall be the conditions of labor, and I need not tell you that that unrest is spreading to America.

And in the midst of the treaty of peace is a Magna Carta, a great guarantee for labor—that labor shall have the councils of the world devoted to the discussion of its conditions and of its betterment. And labor all over the world is waiting to know whether America is going to take part in those conferences or not. The confidence of the men who sat at Paris was such that they put it in the document that the first meeting of the labor conference under that part of the treaty should take place in Washington upon the invitation of the President of the United States.

I am going to issue that invitation, whether we can attend the conference or not. But think of the mortification! Think of standing by in Washington itself and seeing the world take counsel upon the fundamental matters of civilization without us. The thing is inconceivable, but it is true.

The world is waiting—waiting to see, not whether we will take part, but whether we will serve and lead, for it has expected us to lead. I want to say that the most touching and thrilling thing that ever happened to me was that which happened almost every day when I was in Paris. Delegations from all over the world came to me to solicit the friendship of America. They frankly told us that they were not sure of anybody else that they could trust, but that they did absolutely trust us to do them justice and to see that justice was done them. Why, some of them came from countries which I have, to my shame, to admit that I never heard of before, and I had to ask as privately as possible what language they spoke. Fortunately, they always had an interpreter, but I always wanted to know at least what family of languages they were speaking. But the touching thing was that from the ends of the earth, from little pocketed valleys, where I did not know that a separate people lived, there came men—men of dignity, men of intellectual parts, men entertaining in their thought and in their memories a great tradition, some of the oldest people of the world—and they came and sat at the feet of the youngest nation of the world and said, "Teach us the way to liberty."

That is the attitude of the world, and reflect, my fellow countrymen, upon the reaction, the reaction of despair, that would come if America said: "We do not want to lead you. You must do without our advice. You must shift without us."

How are you going to bring about a peace, peace for which everything waits? We cannot bring it about by doing nothing. I have been very much amazed and very much amused, if I could be amused in such criticial circumstances, to see that the statesmanship of some gentlemen consists in the very interesting proposition that we do nothing at all. I had heard of standing pat before, but I never had before heard of standpatism going to the length of saying it is none of our business, and we do not care what happens to the rest of the world.

Your chairman made a profoundly true remark just now. The isolation of the United States is at an end, not because we chose to go into the politics of the world, but because, by the sheer genius of this people and the growth of our power, we have become a determining factor in the history of mankind. And after you have become a determining factor you cannot remain isolated, whether you want to or not. Isolation ended by the processes of history, not by the processes of our independent choice, and the processes of history merely fulfilled the prediction of the men who founded our republic. Go back and read some of the immortal sentences of the men that assisted to frame this government and see how they set up a standard to which they intended that the nations of the world should rally. They said to the people of the world; "Come to us; this is the home of liberty; this is the place where mankind can learn how to govern their own affairs and straighten out their own difficulties." And the world did come to us.

Look at your neighbor. Look at the statistics of the people of your state. Look at the statistics of the people of the United States. They have come, their hearts full of hope and confidence, from practically every nation in the world, to constitute a portion of our strength and our hope and a contribution to our achievement.

Sometimes I feel like taking off my hat to some of those immigrants. I was born an American. I could not help it, but they chose to be Americans. They were not born Americans. They saw this star in the West rising over the heads of the world, and they said: "That is the star of hope and the star of salvation. We will set our footsteps toward the West and join that great body of men whom God has blessed with the vision of liberty." I honor those men. I say: "You made a deliberate choice which showed that you saw what the drift and history of mankind was."

I am very grateful, I may say in parentheses, that I did not have to make that choice. I am grateful that, ever since I can remember, I have breathed this blessed air of freedom. I am grateful that every instinct in me, every drop of blood in me, remains and stands up and shouts out the traditions of the United States. But some gentlemen are not shouting now about that. They are saying, "Yes, we made a great promise to mankind, but it will cost too much to redeem it."

My fellow citizens, that is not the spirit of America, and you cannot have peace, you cannot have even your legitimate part in the business of the world unless you are partners with the rest. If you are going to say to the world, "We will stand off and see what we can get out of this," the world will see to it that you do not get anything out of it. If it is your deliberate choice that, instead of being friends, you will be rivals and antagonists, then you will get just exactly what rivals and antagonists always get—just as little as can be grudgingly vouchsafed you.

And yet you must keep the world on its feet. Is there any businessman here who would be willing to see the world go bankrupt and the business of the world stop? Is there any man here who does not know that America is the only nation left by the war in a position to see that the world does go on with its business? And is it your idea that if we lend our money, as we must, to men whom we have bitterly disappointed, that that money will bring back to us the largesse to which we are entitled?

I do not like to argue this thing on this basis, but if you want to talk business, I am ready to talk business. If it is a matter of how much you are going to get from your money, you will not get half as much as antagonists as you will get as partners. So think that over, if you have none of that thing that is so lightly spoken of, known as altruism. And, believe me, my fellow countrymen, the only people in the world who are going to reap the harvest of the future are people who can entertain ideals, who can follow ideals to the death.

I was saying to another audience today that one of the most beautiful stories I know is the story that we heard in France about the first effect of the American soldiers when they got over there. The French did not believe at first, the British did not believe, that we could finally get 2,000,000 men over there. The most that they hoped at first was that a few American soldiers would restore their morale, for let me say that their morale was gone.

The beautiful story to which I referred is this—the testimony that all of them rendered was that they got their morale back the minute they saw the eyes of those boys. Here were not only soldiers. There was no curtain in the front of the retina of those eyes. They were American eyes. They were eyes that had seen visions. They were eyes the possessors of which had brought with them a great ardor for a supreme cause, and the reason those boys never stopped was that their eyes were lifted to the horizon. They saw a city not built with hands. They saw a citadel toward which their steps were bent where dwelt the oracles of God himself. And on the battlefield were found German orders to commanders here and there to see to it that the Americans did not get lodgment in particular places, because if they ever did you never could get them out. They had gone to Europe to go the whole way towards the realization of the teaching which their fathers had handed down to them. There never were crusaders that went to the Holy Land in the old ages that we read about that were more truly devoted to a holy cause than these gallant, incomparable sons of America.

So my fellow citizens, you have got to make up your minds, because, after all, it is you who are going to make up the minds of this country. I do not owe a report or the slightest responsibility to anybody but you. I do not mean only you in this hall, though I am free to admit that this is just as good a sample of America as you can find anywhere, and the sample looks mighty good to me. I mean you and the millions besides you—thoughtful, responsible American men and women all over this country. They are my bosses, and I am mighty glad to be their servant.

I have come out upon this journey not to fight anybody but to report to you, and I am free to predict that if you credit the report there will be no fighting. It is not only necessary that we should make peace with Germany and make peace with Austria, and see that reasonable peace is made with Turkey and Bulgaria—that is not only not all of it, but it is a very dangerous beginning if you do not add something to it.

I said just now that the peace with Germany, and the same is true of the pending peace with Austria, was made upon American specifications, not unwillingly. Do not let me leave the impression on your mind that the representatives of America in Paris had to insist and force their principles upon the rest. That is not true. Those principles were accepted before we got over there, and the men I dealt with carried them out in absolutely good faith. But they were our principles, and at the heart of them lay this, that there must be a free Poland, for example.

I wonder if you realize what that means. We had to collect the pieces of Poland. For a long time one piece had belonged to Russia, and we cannot get a clear title to that yet. Another part belonged to Austria. We got a title to that. Another part belonged to Germany, and we have settled the title to that. But we found Germany also in possession of other pieces of territory occupied predominantly or exclusively by patriotic Poles, and we said to Germany, "You will have to give that up, too; that belongs to Poland." Not because it is ground, but because those people there are Poles and want to be part of Poland, and it is not our business to force any sovereignty upon anybody who does not want to live under it. And when we had determined the boundaries of Poland, we set it up and recognized it as an independent republic. There is a Minister, a diplomatic representative of the United States, at Warsaw[2] right now in virtue of our formal recognition of the Republic of Poland.

But upon Poland center some of the dangers of the future. And south of Poland is Bohemia, which we cut away from the Austrian combination. And below Bohemia is Hungary, which can no longer rely upon the assistant strength of Austria, and below her is an enlarged Rumania. Alongside of Rumania is the new Slavic kingdom,[3] that never could have won its own independence, which had chafed under the chains of Austria-Hungary, but never could throw them off. We have said: "The fundamental wrongs of history center in these regions. These people have the right to govern their own country and control their own fortunes." That is at the heart of the treaty, but, my fellow citizens, this is at the heart of the future.

The businessmen of Germany did not want the war that we have passed through. The bankers and the manufacturers and the merchants knew that it was unspeakable folly. Why? Because Germany, by her industrial genius, was beginning to dominate the world economically, and all she had to do was to wait about two more generations when her credit, her merchandise, her enterprise, would have covered all of the parts of the world that the great

[2] Hugh Simons Gibson.
[3] He meant the new Kingdom of the Serbs, Croats and Slovenes.

fighting nations did not control. The formula of Pan-Germanism, you remember, was Bremen to Baghdad—Bremen on the North Sea to Baghdad in Persia.

These countries that we have set up as a new home of liberty lie right along that road. If we leave them there without the guarantee that the combined force of the world will assure their independence and their territorial integrity, we have only to wait a short generation, when our recent experience will be repeated. We did not let Germany dominate the world this time. Are we then? If Germany had known then that all the other fighting nations of the world would combine to prevent her action, she never would have dreamed of attempting it. If Germany had known—this is the common verdict of every man familiar with the politics of Europe—if Germany had known that England would go in, she never would have started it. If she had known that America would come in, she never would have dreamed of it. And now the only way to make it certain that there never will be another world war like that is that we should assist in guaranteeing the peace and its settlement.

It is a very interesting circumstance, my fellow countrymen, that the League of Nations will contain all the great nations of the world, and the little ones, too, except Germany, and Germany is merely put on probation. We have practically said to Germany: "If it turns out that you really have had a change of heart and have gotten the nonsense out of your system; if it really does turn out that you have substituted a genuine self-governing republic for a kingdom where a few men on Wilhelmstrasse plotted the destiny of the world, then we will let you in as partners, because you will be respectable."

And in the meantime, accepting the treaty, Germany's army is reduced to 100,000 men, and she has promised to give up all the war material over and above what is necessary for 100,000 men. For a nation of 60,000,000! She has surrendered to the world. She has said: "Our fate is in your hands. We are ready to do what you tell us to do." And the rest of the world is combined, and the interesting circumstance is that the rest of the world, excluding us, will continue combined if we do not go into it. Some gentlemen seem to think they can break up this treaty and prevent this League by not going into it. Not at all.

I can give you an interesting circumstance. There is the settlement, that you have heard so much discussed, about that rich and ancient province of Shantung in China. I do not like that settlement any better than you do, but these were the circumstances. In order to induce Japan to come into the war and clear the Pacific of the German power, England and France bound themselves without any qualification to see to it that Japan got anything in China that Germany had, and that Japan would take it away from her, upon the strength of which promise Japan proceeded to take Kiaochow and occupy the portions of Shantung Province which had been ceded by China for a term of years to Germany. And the most that could be got out of it was that, in view of the fact that America had nothing to do with it, the Japanese were ready to promise that they would give up every item of sovereignty which Germany would otherwise have enjoyed in Shantung Province and return it without restriction to China, and that they would retain in the province only the economic concessions such as other nations already had elsewhere in China—though you do not hear anything about that—concessions in the railway and the mines which had become attached to the railway for operative purposes.

But suppose that you say that is not enough. Very well, then, stay out of the treaty, and how will that accomplish anything? England and France are bound and cannot escape their obligation. Are you going to institute a war against Japan and France and England to get Shantung back for China? That is an enterprise which does not commend itself to the present generation.

I am putting it in brutal terms, my fellow citizens, but that is the fact. By disagreeing to that provision, we accomplish nothing for China. On the contrary, we stay out of the only combination of the councils of nations in which we can be of service to China. With China as a member of the League of Nations, and Japan as a member of the League of Nations, and America as a member of the League of Nations, there confronts every one of them that now famous Article X, by which every member of the League agrees to respect and preserve the territorial integrity and existing political independence of all the other member states.

Do not let anybody persuade you that you can take that article out and have a peaceful world. That cuts at the root of the German war. That cuts at the root of the outrage against Belgium. That cuts at the root of the outrage against France. That pulls that vile, unwholesome upas tree[4] of Pan-Germanism up by the roots, and it pulls all other "pans" up, too. Every land-grabbing nation is served notice: "Keep on your own territory. Mind your own business. That territory belongs to those people, and they can do with it what they please, provided they do not invade other people's rights by the use they make of it."

So my fellow citizens, the thing is going to be done whether we

[4] A tall Javanese tree of the mulberry family, which yields an intensely poisonous milky juice, used as an arrow poison. Used figuratively to describe a poisonous or harmful influence or institution.

are in it or not. If we are in it, then we are going to be the determining factor in the development of civilization. If we are out of it,
we ourselves are going to watch every other nation with suspicion,
and we will be justified, too; and we are going to be watched with
suspicion. Every movement of trade, every relationship of manufacture, every question of raw materials, every matter that affects
the intercourse of the world, will be impeded by the consciousness
that America wants to hold off and get something which she is not
willing to share with the rest of mankind. I am painting the picture
for you, because I know that it is as intolerable to you as it is to me.
But do not go away with the impression, I beg you, that I think
there is any doubt about the issue. The only thing that can be accomplished is delay. The ultimate outcome will be the triumphant
acceptance of the treaty and the League.

And let me pay the tribute which it is only just that I should pay
to some of the men who have been, I believe, misunderstood in this
business. It is only a handful of men, my fellow citizens, who are
trying to defeat the treaty or to prevent the League. The great majority, in official bodies and out, are scrutinizing it, as it is perfectly
legitimate that they should scrutinize it, to see if it is necessary
that they should qualify it in any way. And my knowledge of their
conscience, my knowledge of their public principles, makes me
certain that they will sooner or later see that it is safest, since it is
all expressed in the plainest English that the English dictionary
affords, not to qualify it—to accept it as it is. Because I have been
a student of the English language all my life, and I do not see a
single obscure sentence in the whole document. Some gentlemen
either have not read it or do not understand the English language.
But, fortunately, on the right-hand page it is printed in English,
and on the left-hand page it is printed in French. Now, if they do
not understand English, I hope they will get a French dictionary
and dig out the meaning on that side. The French is a very precise
language, more precise than the English language, I am told. I am
not on a speaking acquaintance with it, but I am told that it is the
most precise language in Europe, and that any given phrase in
French always means the same thing. That cannot be said of English. So, in order to satisfy themselves, I hope these gentlemen
will master the French version and then be reassured that there
are no lurking monsters in that document; there are no sinister
purposes; that everything is said in the frankest way.

For example, they have been very much worried at the phrase
that nothing in the document shall be taken as impairing in any
way the validity of such regional understandings as the Monroe
Doctrine. And they said: "Why put in 'such regional understand-

ings as' "? What other understandings are there? Have you got something up your sleeve? Is there going to be a Monroe Doctrine in Asia? Is there going to be a Monroe Doctrine in China? Why, my fellow citizens, the phrase was written in perfect innocence. The men that I was associated with said: "It is not wise to put a specific thing that belongs only to one nation in a document like this. We do not know of any other regional understanding like it; we never heard of any other; we never expect to hear of any other. But there might some day be some other, and so we will say 'such regional understandings as the Monroe Doctrine,' " and their phrase was intended to give right of way to the Monroe Doctrine in the western hemisphere.

I reminded the Committee on Foreign Relations of the Senate the other day that the conference I held with them was not the first conference I had held about the League of Nations. When I came back to this, our own dear country in March last, I held a conference at the White House with the Senate Committee on Foreign Relations, and they made various suggestions as to how the Covenant should be altered in phraseology. I carried those suggestions back to Paris, and every one of them was accepted. I think that is a sufficient guarantee that no mischief was intended. And the whole document is of the same plain, practical, explicit sort. And it secures peace, my fellow citizens, in the only way in which peace can be secured.

I remember, if I may illustrate a very great thing with a very trivial thing, I had two acquaintances who were very much addicted to profanity. Their friends were distressed about it. It subordinated a rich vocabulary, which they might otherwise have cultivated, and so we induced them to agree that they never would swear inside the corporate limits, that if they wanted to swear they would go out of town. The first time the passion of anger came upon them, they rather sheepishly got in a street car and went out of town to swear, and by the time they got out of town they did not want to swear.

And that very homely story illustrates in my mind the value of discussion. Let me remind you that every fighting nation in the world is going to belong to this League, because we are going to belong to it, and all the fighting nations make this solemn engagement with each other, that they will not resort to war in the case of any controversy until they have done one or other of two things—until they have either submitted the question at issue to arbitration, in which case they promise to abide by the verdict, whatever it may be, or, if they do not want to submit it to arbitration, have submitted it to discussion by the Council of the League.

They agree to give the Council six months to discuss the matter, to supply the Council with all the pertinent facts regarding it, and that, after the opinion of the Council is rendered, they will not then go to war if they are dissatisfied with the opinion until three more months have elapsed. They give nine months in which to spread the whole matter before the judgment of mankind. And if they violate this promise, if any one of them violates it, the Covenant prescribes that that violation shall in itself constitute an act of war against the other members of the League.

But it does not provide that there shall be war. On the contrary, it provides for something very much more effective than war. It provides that that nation, that covenant-breaking nation, shall be absolutely cut off from intercourse of every kind with the other nations of the world; that no merchandise shall be shipped out of it or into it; that no postal messages shall go into it or come out of it; that no telegraphic messages shall cross its borders; and that the citizens of the other member states shall not be permitted to have any intercourse or transactions whatever with its citizens or its citizens with them. There is not a single nation in Europe that can stand that boycott for six months. There is not a single nation in Europe that is self-sufficing in its resources of food or anything else that can stand that for six months. And in those circumstances we are told that this Covenant is a covenant of war. It is the most drastic covenant of peace that was ever conceived, and its processes are the processes of peace. The nation that does not abide by its covenants is taboo, is put out of the society of covenant-respecting nations.

So that this is a covenant of arbitration and discussion, of compulsory arbitration or discussion, and just so soon as you discuss matters, my fellow citizens, peace looks in at the window. Did you ever really sit down and discuss matters with your neighbor when you had a difference and come away in the same temper that you went in? One of the difficulties in our labor situation is that there are some employers who will not meet their employees face to face and talk with them. And I have never known an instance in which such a meeting and discussion took place that both sides did not come away in a softened temper and with an access of respect for the other side. The processes of frank discussion are the processes of peace not only, but the processes of settlement, and those are the processes which are set up for all the powerful nations of the world.

I want to say that this is an unparalleled achievement of thoughtful civilization. To my dying day, I shall esteem it the crowning privilege of my life to have been permitted to put my name to a document like that; and in my judgment, my fellow citizens, when passion is cooled and men take a sober, second thought, they are all going to feel that the supreme thing that America did was to help bring this about and then put her shoulder to the great chariot of justice and of peace which was going to lead men along in that slow and toilsome march—toilsome and full of the kind of agony that brings bloody sweat—but nevertheless going up a slow toilsome incline to those distant heights upon which will shine at last the serene light of justice, suffusing a whole world in blissful peace.[5]

Printed in the *Des Moines Sunday Register*, Sept. 7, 1919.
[5] There is a WWT outline of this speech in WP, DLC.

From Walker Downer Hines

Dear Mr. President: Washington September 6, 1919.

Last May when I reached the conclusion, after careful consultation with my advisors, that I could not endorse the prices which the Steel interests had fixed and the Peek Committee had approved, I called for bids for the steel rail needed by the Railroad Administration.[1] In reply to the bids the Steel interests named uniformly the prices which they had suggested to the Peek Committee and which had been approved by it (with the exception of one company which named prices $10.00 higher per ton). There seeming to be no escape from the course, I therefore purchased 200,000 tons of steel rail at the price thus uniformly specified, issuing a public statement expressing the opinion that the price was too high and that there was danger that the price would go still higher if business improved.

Recently it has become necessary to buy additional rail and I have again called for bids and the result has been the same as before. I still see no way in which the Government can secure the rail at a lower price and therefore I shall probably have to order in the next day or two from 100,000 to 200,000 tons of rail at this price ($47.00 per ton). I have discussed the matter with the Attorney General recently, in anticipation of the bids being the same as heretofore and he expressed the opinion that no other course was practicable but to buy the rail absolutely necessary at the price thus fixed.

When I was discussing the wage matter with the shopmen's representatives after you had addressed them at the White House, one of them urged the point that the Government treated the Steel interests better than it treated Labor because when the Steel interests named an excessive price the Government nevertheless paid it although nominally protesting against it; but that when Labor asked for increased wages the Government refused to pay them because it regarded the wages proposed as unreasonable. While the fact was that the prices we paid the Steel interests represented a substantial reduction from the war prices, and the wages demanded by Labor represented a substantial increase over the war wages for railroad employees, the point made is not without force and can be used with great advantage to impress upon the laboring men the view that the capitalistic interests are able to force upon the Government prices which they claim are reasonable, while the laboring men are denied a corresponding privilege.

All these considerations go to sustain the view that I expressed to you that the Federal Government ought to have a much greater control than at present over the large industrial enterprises (which could not exist at all except by the acquiescence of the Federal Government in their exercise of franchises to engage in interstate business)

I believe that legislation is highly desirable looking toward the closest supervision over the capitalization of these large enterprises, the preventing any concurrent action by them whatever in the matter of fixing prices except at meetings at which the Government is represented, perhaps the preventing of any increases in prices by them except upon filing with the Government a full statement of the reasons for the increases, and the requiring in all things of complete current publicity.

But before legislation may be practicable, I think it highly desirable to make a start by obtaining such current publicity as is possible under the Federal Trade Commission Act, and it is to this point to which I wish to direct your specific attention at the moment.

I have requested the Federal Trade Commission to obtain currently information of two sorts from the Steel interests: First, information monthly from each of the principal Steel Corporations as to the cost per ton of producing rolled steel products and Second, a full statement either monthly or quarterly from each of the principal companies as to its revenues, expenses and profits, with clear explanation as to the various confusing and dubious elements of expense such as royalties, depreciation charges and other "reserves."

I regard both of these classes of information as important. I regard the second as much more important than the first. If a corporation makes a relatively small profit per ton, the corporation by reason of its stupendous size may make an aggregate profit which may be so large as to be incompatible with the public interest or at any rate, may suggest the desirability of special restrictions.

The Commission was unwilling to obtain and publish this second class of information at all, but originally stated in a letter to me of May 19th it would undertake to obtain the monthly costs per ton. I was greatly surprised a few days ago to learn that the Commission had reconsidered this decision and had determined not to supply the information. It developed that an important element in the reasons for this re-consideration was the fact that the Counsel of one of the Steel Companies had threate[ne]d to enjoin the Trade Commission if it sought for information. The Commission felt that if it obtained the information on its own initiative, or on the initiative of the Railroad Administration, the injunction might be granted. In response to my queries I gather that the Commission feels that the prospect of success in the application for injunction would not exist if the Commission were directed to obtain the information either by the President or by Congress.

My definite recommendation therefore is that, in such form as the Department of Justice may approve, you direct or request the Commission to obtain monthly for the benefit of the various Governmental agencies the cost per ton of producing rolled steel products and in addition to obtain and publish for the information of the entire country, either monthly or quarterly, statements of the revenues, expenses and profits of the principal Steel Corporations.

I believe both these steps will be of benefit to the Government and the public and will be useful in laying the foundation for the legislation which I believe must come in the public interest in the control of these great enterprises whose success is due to the use of what are in effect Federal franchises but whose existence is due solely to charters from states wholly unable to control in the public interest the corporations they thus create.

I do not believe it would be advisable to undertake at the outset the obtaining of corresponding information from every class of big business. I think the danger in such a program would be that the task would be so difficult as to make a beginning almost impossible. My thought is to make a beginning with one highly concentrated industry and then take that as a starting point for further work.

The Steel interests already make annual reports to their stockholders, and these are generally published sometime after the end of the corporate year, but the difficulty is that the reports are made up exclusively according to the theories of the corporations, with only such explanations of the obscure items of expense as the corporations choose to give, and are necessarily practically ancient history by the time they reach the public.

Cordially yours,   Walker D Hines

TLS (WP, DLC).
  ¹ About Hines' controversy with the Industrial Board of the Department of Commerce (the "Peek Committee") over the price that the Railroad Administration should pay for steel rails, see the index references under "Industrial Board of the Department of Commerce" in Vols. 56-59.

Joseph Patrick Tumulty to William Phillips

[Kansas City] 6 September, 1919

President agrees with Clemenceau's proposal that decision of the question of the admission of German and Austrian labor delegates to the forthcoming International Labor Conference at Washington should be left to that conference itself.

J. P. Tumulty

T telegram (WP, DLC).

From William Phillips

Washington, D. C., 8 P.M., Sept. 6 [1919].

Sept. 6, 5 P.M. The following telegram from the Mission¹ is repeated for your information:

"Urgent 4050 Sept. 5, 11 a.m. Confidential. For the President and the Secretary of State. See our 3974 [3774] August 31.² On Monday, September 1st, Balfour said that he would much prefer to try to come to an understanding among ourselves rather than refer the matter to the President. After a conference with White, Bliss and Johnson on Tuesday I told the Council I was prepared to discuss the matter in secret session to see if there was a possibility of our reaching an agreement on some plan that we too could recommend to the President. It immediately developed that Tittoni's plans for Fiume were of such a character that I could not discuss them, so I stopped discussion and said that Mr. White and Dr. Johnson would see Tittoni that afternoon in order to try to reach some common ground.

"Mr. White and Dr. Johnson had a consultation with Tittoni in which Tittoni renounced claim to the Islands of Lagosta and Uglian and asked for Zara merely some form of connection with Italy without Italian sovereignty. We advised (?) Tittoni that the President could accept free State of Fiume only on basis of terms already stated by the President, which include no special status for

Fiume and a plebiscite at the end of five years. Today Johnson had a long conference with Mr. Balfour in which it developed that the British had not yet given their adhesion to the Tittoni memorandum, and it is doubtful whether they will. Johnson and Mr. Balfour are seeking solution of Fiume problem in accordance with the President's principles, which British and French may join in urging Tittoni to accept. POLK"   Phillips, Acting.

T telegram (WP, DLC).
  [1] FLP to RL, No. 4050, Sept. 5, 1919, 11 a.m., T telegram (SDR, RG 59, 763.72119/6530, DNA).
  [2] FLP to WW and RL, Aug. 31, 1919, Vol. 62.

From the Diary of Dr. Grayson

Sunday, September 7, 1919.

The President slept fairly late, and after breakfast proceeded to the Presbyterian Church,[1] where he listened to a very interesting sermon, in which no reference whatever was made to his presence or to the big problems before the country. He returned to the hotel for luncheon and in the afternoon went for a brief automobile ride.

Afterwards he received the members of the reception committee in his apartment and thanked them individually for their great work in arranging the meeting. He also told the committee that in his opinion it was necessary that every American understand the great issues before the country. The President made it very plain that so far as he was concerned political advantage had no part in his desire to present the facts concerning the Treaty to the people of the United States. "It was a problem far away beyond politics," he told the committee.

The President dined quietly in his hotel and went to the train shortly after 10:00 o'clock. Des Moines was left at midnight with Omaha, Nebraska, as the next objective.

  [1] The Central Presbyterian Church of Des Moines, whose pastor, the Rev. Dr. Frank Chalmers McKean, preached the sermon.

Joseph Patrick Tumulty to Rudolph Forster

Des Moines, Iowa, 2:39 pm., September 7, 1919.

President asks that only such mail as is absolutely essential be forwarded to him. Please ask State Department not to forward to the President dispatches but simply to put up to him such questions as need his decision.   J. P. Tumulty.

T telegram (WP, DLC).

Rudolph Forster to Joseph Patrick Tumulty

The White House [Sept.] 7th [1919]

Breckinridge Long telegraphs from York Harbor Maine requesting that following be wired to you quote Senator Norris speaking in Senate Saturday said Presidents statement in St Louis speech to the effect that England and the other Allies had promised Japan Germanys rights in China in order to get Japan into the war was erroneous stop Norris further said quote The President represented our government at the Peace Conference and he knows what was presented there and what the facts are stop It is a matter of history that Great Britain and the other Allies did not make this secret agreement with Japan till nineteen seventeen stop. At the time that agreement was made all of Germanys possessions in China had been captured and there was not a ship in the Pacific stop So the President has not got his history straight stop I challenge the President to produce evidence to substantiate what he said in St Louis unquote The facts are that England and Japan did agree in nineteen fourteen to Japanese capture and possession of German rights in China and of all the German islands north of the Equator stop The agreement was made to induce Japan to enter the war stop Japan has since declared she was not bound under the regular Anglo Japanese Alliance to enter the war on the side of England stop The secret treaties of nineteen seventeen between Japan and the Allies were made to conform [confirm?] to Japan title to and perpetuate possession of these German dominions stop

I send the above in case the President should consider the matter of sufficient importance to differentiate in some speech between the Japanese English agreement of nineteen fourteen and the secret treaties of nineteen seventeen stop I think the President['s] remarks at St Louis as reported were susceptible to the misconstruction placed upon them by Norris stop We have no positive evidence of the agreement of nineteen fourteen end quote.

Forster

T telegram (WP, DLC).

From the Diary of Dr. Grayson

Monday, September 8, 1919.

Although it was "blue Monday" morning, the President's reception in Omaha was really wonderful. It had not been expected that there would be much of a turn-out. As a matter of fact, no one in the party had expected that the Auditorium would be more than half filled, and if there had been only a few people on the streets there would have been little disappointment. Consequently, nearly every member of the party was amazed when they found after leaving the station in automobiles that the principal street was lined for blocks with a crowd six and eight deep, while all of the windows of the various mercantile establishments were filled with people anxious to see the President and cheer him. It was just exactly 9:00 o'clock as the President entered the automobile that headed the parade. A detachment of Regular Army Cavalry was on hand to act as an escort. The party proceeded to the outskirts of Omaha and turned up a side street in the residential section. There was a degree of curiosity as to the reason for this diversion from the usual program, but it soon developed that the President and Mrs. Wilson had accepted an invitation to greet Mrs. [Dietz][1] an elderly lady, the mother of the President of the Nebraska Branch of the League to Enforce Peace.[2] She has been confined to her house for a number of years but has taken a very active interest in matters of public importance, and during visits to Omaha former Presidents Roosevelt and Taft also had called to greet her. The old lady was seated in an invalid's chair on the porch of her home, and she thanked the President and Mrs. Wilson for their consideration in making the call.

The party proceeded back down the main street to the Nebraska National Guard Armory, where the meeting was held. The Republican Governor of Nebraska, [Samuel Roy McKelvie][3] presided over the meeting and introduced the President in a very brief but well-chosen address, in which he declared himself in favor of the Treaty.

This was the home State of Senator Norris, the Republican Senator, who had announced that he was in favor of the entire Treaty, with the exception of the section that settled the Shantung Province disposal. The President took advantage of this fact to explain to his audience just what was behind the Shantung settlement. He told them that Great Britain, France and Italy had pledged themselves to see that Japan secured all the Shantung Peninsula as payment for its part in the war. He recited the manner in which these secret treaties had been brought out at the Conference in Paris and declared that he had done all that he could to safeguard the rights of China and had secured promises from Japan that would greatly aid China in getting back the property that originally was stolen from her by Germany. The President referred to the fact that Germany forced the seizure of the Shantung rights as a result of the murder of two German missionaries[4] and declared the fact that this outrage against a peaceful nation had originated through a religious pretext. The President declared that regardless of what the United States might do in the matter, France, Great Britain and Italy would stand by their original promises to Japan, and he demanded of the audience whether they believed the United States should go to war with Japan, Great Britain, France and Italy to secure for China something that she herself could secure once the League of Nations Covenant was ratified. The audience shouted "No" to his query and showed itself thoroughly in sympathy with the position that he had assumed.

Omaha was left at noon, and another long tiresome ride commenced with Sioux Falls, South Dakota, as the objective. As the train passed through the Nebraska and Dakota prairies a few people could be seen gathered at the lone stations that marked the stopping places of the various trains. There were very few towns in sight but the farmers and ranchmen had driven to the railway hoping to get a sight of the President. For a good many miles the President and Mrs. Wilson rode on the rear platform of the Private Car and waved greetings to the little knots of people gathered at the various points.

Sioux Falls was not reached until 8:00 o'clock. This is a little town of about 16,000 inhabitants, and nearly the entire population, not only of the city but of the surrounding countryside, was on hand to greet the President. A guard of former soldiers, sailors and marines had been organized, and the President's car was placed in a hollow square of these men, who marched with him as far as the Armory, in which the meeting was held.

The President had now begun to reach the so-called "bolshevist" territory. North and South Dakota and Minnesota were the stamping ground of what originally was known as the Farmers' Non-partisan League.[5] This organization was very radical in its tendencies and had been characterized as unpatriotic during the war. The President recognized this fact by making a sharp reference in his address to the Russian situation. He declared that he personally never would sanction government by minority. He declared that the condition of Russia today was due to the fact that a minority ruled there, and he said that the Lenine-Trotsky government actually was composed of only about thirty men, yet they worked their will upon the millions of people of that unhappy nation. The President took occasion to declare that any government that was based upon violence or threats of violence must fail, and he declared that the government of the United States must always be found on the side of right and opposed to those who would rule by force. The President also declared that he was in no way opposed to radicalism so long as that radicalism confined its efforts to remedying conditions that were unsatisfactory although permitted by law. He said that he believed the right of protest should be safeguarded to all Americans, and in his opinion only through protest could proper government be worked out.

The party returned to the special train just before 10:00 o'clock and left at 10:00 for St. Paul—240 miles away.

[1] Leonora Antoinette Cooke (Mrs. Gould Price) Dietz.
[2] Gould Cooke Dietz, active in the lumber and coal business in Omaha and Sheridan, Wyoming.
[3] Several newspaper reports of Wilson's speech in Omaha say that he was introduced by Gurden Wallace Wattles, a banker of Omaha, also active in the League to Enforce Peace.
[4] On this affair and its results, see John E. Schrecker, *Imperialism and Chinese Nationalism: Germany in Shantung* (Cambridge, Mass., 1971), pp. 33-42.
[5] About this organization, see the index references under "Nonpartisan League" in Vols. 39 and 52.

A News Report

[*Sept. 8, 1919*]
WILSON BEGINS HARD WEEK.
Is Conserving His Strength, Avoiding Platform Speeches.

On Board President Wilson's Special Train, Sept. 8.—Carrying his appeal for acceptance of the Peace Treaty into the heart of the Northwest, President Wilson began today a week of travel that will take him to the Pacific Coast.

On the advice of his physician, Dr. Grayson, the President is conserving his strength for the three weeks of travel and speech making ahead of him. After his breathing spell in Des Moines yesterday Mr. Wilson was said to be in excellent trim, but Dr. Grayson will insist that he take things easy wherever possible. It was principally on account of a slight cold, impairing the President's voice, that Dr. Grayson advised against rear platform speeches. Although his voice is holding up well, it has broken once or twice during his addresses.

On the private car Mayflower, the President and Mrs. Wilson are well taken care of. Mrs. Wilson's maid came along and there is one of the White House cooks aboard to prepare their meals.

The rest of the train also is fitted up with a view to reducing the fatigues and inconveniences of the 10,000-mile trip. The dining car is to be carried all the way and there is a club car, which the newspaper correspondents, secret service men, and secretaries use as a lounging place.

The President and Mrs. Wilson dine privately, but Mr. Wilson strolls back into the club car occasionally for a chat with other members of the party.

One of the hardest working members of the Presidential party is Charles L. Swem, Mr. Wilson's personal stenographer, who handles single handed, the official transcripts of the President's addresses. As soon as an address is completed he transcribes it directly on the stencil of a mimeograph machine on board the train, so that official copies of the text may be available without delay.

Printed in the *New York Times*, Sept. 9, 1919.

An Address in the Auditorium in Omaha

[[September 8, 1919]]

Mr. Chairman and my fellow citizens: I never feel more comfortable in facing my fellow citizens than when I can realize that I am not representing a peculiar cause, that I am not speaking for a single group of my fellow citizens, that I am not the representative of a party, but the representative of the people of the United States. I went across the water with that happy consciousness. And in all the work that was done on the other side of the sea, where I was associated with distinguished Americans of both political parties, we all of us constantly kept at our heart the feeling that we were expressing thoughts of America, that we were working for the things that America believed in. And I have come here to testify that this treaty contains the things that America believes in.

I brought a copy of the treaty along with me, for I fancy that, in view of the criticisms that you have heard of it, you thought it consisted of only four or five clauses. Only four or five clauses out of this volume were picked out for criticism. Only four or five phrases in it are called to your attention by some of the distinguished orators who oppose its adoption. Why, my fellow citizens, this is one of the great charters of human liberty, and the man who picks flaws in it—or, rather, picks out the flaws that are in it, for there are flaws in it—forgets the magnitude of the thing, forgets the majesty of the thing, forgets that the counsels of more than twenty nations combined and were rendered unanimous in the adoption of this great instrument. Let me remind you of what everybody admits who has read the document. Everybody admits that it is a complete settlement of the matters which led to this war, and that it contains the complete machinery which provides that they shall be settled.

You know that one of the greatest difficulties in our own domestic affairs is unsettled land titles. Suppose that somebody were mischievously to tamper with the land records of the State of Nebraska, and that there should be a doubt as to the line of every farm. You know what would happen in six months. All the farmers would be sitting on their fences with shotguns. Litigation would penetrate every community, hot feeling would be generated, contests not only of lawyers, but contests of force would ensue.

Very well, one of the interesting things that this treaty does is to settle the land titles of Europe, and to settle them in this way—on the principles that every land belongs to the people that live on it. This is actually the first time in human history that that principle was ever recognized in a similar document, and yet that is the fundamental American principle. The fundamental American principle is the right of the people that live in the country to say what shall be done with that country. We have gone so far in our assertions of popular right that we not only say that the people have a right to have a government that suits them, but that they have a right to change it in any respect at any time. Very well, that principle lies at the heart of this treaty.

There are peoples in Europe who never before could say that the land they lived on was their own, and the choice that they were to make of their lives was their own choice. I know there are men in Nebraska who come from that country of tragical history, the now restored Republic of Poland. And I want to call your attention to the fact that Poland is here given her complete restitution; and not only is she given the land that formerly belonged to the Poles, but she is given the lands which were occupied by Poles, are now occupied by Poles but had been permitted to remain under other sovereignties. She is given those lands on a principle that all our hearts approve of. Take what in Europe they call High Silesia, the mountainous, the upper portions of the district of Silesia. The very great majority of the people in High Silesia are Poles. But the Germans contested the statement that most of them were Poles. We said: "Very well, then, it is none of our business; we will let them decide. We will put sufficient armed forces into High Silesia to see that nobody tampers with the processes of the election, and then we will hold a referendum there, and those people can belong to either Germany or Poland, as they prefer, and not as we prefer." And wherever there was a doubtful district we applied the same principles, that the people should decide and not the men sitting around the peace table at Paris. So that when these referendums are completed, the land titles of Europe will be settled, and every country will belong to the people that live on it to do with what they please. You seldom hear of this aspect of this treaty, my fellow citizens.

You have heard of the council that the newspapermen call the "Big Four." We had a very much bigger name for ourselves than that. We called ourselves the "Supreme Council of the Principal Allied and Associated Powers," but we had no official title, and sometimes there were five of us instead of four. But those represented, with the exception of Germany, of course, the great fighting nations of the world. They could have done anything with this treaty that they chose to do, because they had the power to do it. And they chose to do what had never been chosen before—to renounce every right of sovereignty in that settlement to which the people concerned did not assent. That is the great settlement which is represented in this volume.

And it contains, among other things, a great charter of liberty for the workingmen of the world. For the first time in history, the counsels of mankind are to be drawn together and concerted for the purpose of defending the rights and improving the conditions of working people—men, women, and children—all over the world. Such a thing as that was never dreamed of before. And what you are asked to discuss in discussing the League of Nations is the method of seeing that this thing is not interfered with. There is no other way to do it than by a universal league of nations, and what is proposed is a universal league of nations. Only two nations are for the time being left out. One of them is Germany, because we did not think that Germany was ready to come in, because we felt that she ought to go through a period of probation. She says that she made a mistake. We now want her to prove it by not trying it again. She says that she has abolished all the old forms of government by which little secret councils of men, sitting nobody knew exactly where, determined the fortunes of that great nation and, incidentally, tried to determine the fortunes of mankind. But we want her to prove that her constitution is changed and that it is going to stay changed.

And then who can, after those proofs are produced, say "No" to a great people, 60,000,000 strong, if they want to come in on equal terms with the rest of us and do justice in international affairs? I want to say that I did not find any of my colleagues in Paris disinclined to do justice to Germany. But I hear that this treaty is very hard on Germany. When an individual has committed a criminal act, the punishment is hard, but the punishment is not unjust. And this nation permitted itself, through unscrupulous governors, to commit a criminal act against mankind, and it is to undergo the punishment, not more than it can endure, but up to the point where it can pay it must pay for the wrong that it has done.

But the things prescribed in this treaty will not be fully carried out if any one of the great influences that brought that result about is withheld from its consummation. Every great fighting nation in the world is on the list of those who are to constitute the League of Nations. I say every great nation, because America is going to be included among them, and the only choice, my fellow citizens, is whether we will go in now or come in later with Germany; whether we will go in as founders of this covenant of freedom or go in as those who are admitted after they have made a mistake and re-pented.

I wish I could do what is impossible in a great company like this. I wish I could read that Covenant to you, because I do not believe, if you have not read it yourself and have only listened to certain speeches that I have read, that you know anything that is in it. Why, my fellow citizens, the heart of that Covenant is that there shall be no war.

To listen to some of the speeches that you may have listened to or read, you would think that the heart of it was that it was an arrangement for war. On the contrary, this is the heart of that treaty: the bulk of it is concerned with arrangements under which all the members of the League—that means everybody but Ger-many and dismembered Turkey—agree that they never will go to war without first having done one or the other of two things—either submitted the question at issue to arbitration, in which case they agree absolutely to abide by the verdict, or, if they do not care to submit it to arbitration, submit it to discussion by the Council of the League of Nations, in which case they must give six months for the discussion and wait three months after the rendering of the decision, whether they like it or not, before they go to war. They agree to cool off for nine months before they yield to the heat of passion which might otherwise have hurried them into war.

And if they do not do that, it is not war that ensues. It is some-thing that will interest them and engage them very much more than war. It is an absolute boycott of the nation that disregards the Covenant. The boycott is automatic, and just so soon as it applies, then this happens. No goods can be shipped out of that country; no goods can be shipped into it. No telegraphic message may pass either way across its borders. No package of postal matter—no let-ter—can cross its borders either way. No citizen of any member of the League can have any transactions of any kind with any citizen of that nation. It is the most complete isolation and boycott ever conceived, and there is not a nation in Europe that can live for six months without importing goods out of other countries. After they have thought about the matter for six months, I predict that they will have no stomach for war.

But all that you are told about in this Covenant, so far as I can learn, is that there is an Article X. I will repeat Article X to you; I think I can repeat it verbatim, the heart of it at any rate. Every member of the League promises to respect and preserve as against external aggression—not as against internal revolution—the territorial integrity and existing political independence of every other member of the League. And if it is necessary to enforce this promise—I mean, for the nations to act in concert with arms in their hands to enforce it—then the Council of the League shall advise what action is necessary. Some gentlemen who doubt the meaning of English words have thought that advice did not mean advice, but I do not know anything else that it does mean, and I have studied English most of my life and speak it with reasonable correctness. The point is this. The Council cannot give that advice without the vote of the United States, unless it is a party to the dispute. But, my fellow citizens, if you are a party to the dispute, you are in the scrap anyhow. If you are a party, then the question is not whether you are going to war or not, but merely whether you are going to war against the rest of the world or with the rest of the world.

And the object of war in that case will be to defend that central thing that I began by speaking about. That is the guarantee of the land titles of the world which have been established by this treaty. Poland, Czechoslovakia, Rumania, Yugoslavia—all those nations which never had a vision of independent liberty until now—have their liberty and independence guaranteed to them. And if we do not guarantee them, then we have this interesting choice. I hear gentlemen say that we went into the recent war because we were forced into it, and their preference now is to wait to be forced in again. They do not pretend that we can keep out; they merely pretend that we ought to keep out until we are ashamed not to go in.

And this is the Covenant of the League of Nations that you hear objected to—the only possible guarantee against war. I would consider myself recreant to every mother and father, every wife and sweetheart in this country, if I consented to the ending of this war without a guarantee that there would be no other. You say, "Is it an absolute guarantee?" No, there is no absolute guarantee against human passion; but even if it were only 10 per cent of a guarantee, wouldn't you rather have 10 per cent guarantee against war than none? If it only creates a presumption that there will not be war, wouldn't you rather have that presumption than live under the certainty that there will be war? For, I tell you, my fellow citizens, I can predict with absolute certainty that, within another generation, there will be another world war if the nations of the world—if the League of Nations—does not prevent it by concerted action.

But I didn't come here this morning, I remind myself, so much to expound upon the treaty as to talk about these interesting things that we hear about that are called reservations. A reservation is an assent with a "but" to it. We agree—but. Now, I want to call your attention to some of these buts. I will take them, as far as I can remember the order, in the order in which they deal with clauses of the League itself.

In the first article of the Covenant, it is provided that a nation can withdraw from the League on two years' notice, provided that, at the time of its withdrawal—that is to say, at the expiration of the two years—it has fulfilled all its international obligations and all its obligations under the Covenant. But some of our friends are very uneasy about that. They want to sit close to the door and with their hand on the knob, and they want to say: "We are in this thing, but we are in it with infinite timidity, and we are in it only because you overpersuaded us and wanted us to come in. But we are going to sit here and try this door every once and a while and see that it isn't locked. And just as soon as we see anything we don't like, we are going to scuttle." (laughter and applause)

Now, what is the trouble? I want you to put this to every man you know who makes this objection, what is he afraid of? Is he afraid that, when the United States wishes to withdraw, it will not have fulfilled its international obligations? Is he willing to bring that indictment against this beloved country? My fellow citizens, we never did fail to fulfill any obligation we have made; (applause) and, God guiding and helping us, we never will. I, for one, am not going to admit in any connection the slightest doubt that, if we ever choose to withdraw, we will then have fulfilled our obligations.

Because, if we make reservations, as they are called, about this, what do we do? This Covenant does not set up any tribunal to judge whether we have fulfilled our obligations at that time or not. There is only one thing to restrain us, and that is the opinion of mankind. Are these gentlemen such poor patriots that they are afraid the United States will cut a poor figure in the opinion of mankind? And do they think that they can bring this great people to withdraw from that League if at that time their withdrawal would be condemned by the opinion of mankind? We have always been at pains to earn the respect of mankind, and we shall always be at pains to retain it. (applause) I, for one, am too proud as an American to say that any doubt will ever hang upon our right to withdraw upon the condition of the fulfillment of our international obligations. (applause)

I have already adverted to the difficulties under Article X and will not return to those. That difficulty is merely as I represented it just now. They don't want to go in as partners, they want to go in as late joiners, because they all admit that in a war which imperils the just arrangements of mankind, America, the greatest, richest, freest people of the world, must take sides with the cause. We cannot live without taking sides. We devoted ourselves to justice and liberty when we were born, and we are not going to get senile and forget it. (applause)

But they don't like the way in which the Monroe Doctrine is mentioned. Well, I wouldn't stop on a question of style. The Monroe Doctrine is adopted. It is swallowed, hook, line, and sinker, (applause) and, being carefully digested into the central organism of the whole instrument, I don't care what language they use about it. The language is entirely satisfactory as far as I know, I mean as far as I understand the English language. That puzzles me, my fellow citizens. The English language seems to have gotten some new meaning in it since I studied it that bothers these gentlemen. I don't know what dictionaries they studied. But the Monroe Doctrine is expressly authenticated in this document, for the first time in history, by all the great nations of the world, and it was put there at our request. (applause) When I came back to this dear country in March, I brought the first draft—the provisional draft—of the Covenant of the League. And I submitted it to the Foreign Relations Committee of the Senate of the United States, and I explained and I discussed it with them. They made a number of suggestions, and I carried every one of those suggestions to Paris, and every one of them was adopted. (applause)

Now apparently they want me to go back to Paris and say, "I am much obliged to you, but we don't like the language used." Now I suggest that if they don't like that language there is another language in here. That page is English (illustrating); this page is French (illustrating)—it is the same thing. Now, if the English don't suit them, let them engage the services of some French scholar and see if they like the French better. It is the same thing—done in perfect good faith and nobody trying to fool anybody else. This is the genuine work of honest men. (applause)

And the fourth matter of their concern is about domestic questions, and so they want to put in a reservation enumerating certain questions as domestic questions, which everybody on both sides of the water admit are domestic questions. That seems to me, to say the least, to be the work of supererogation. It doesn't seem to me to be necessary to specify what everybody admits, but they are so careful—I believe the word used to be so "meticulous"—that they want to put in clearly what is implied in the whole instrument. "Well," you say, "why not?" Well, why not, my fellow citizens? The conference at Paris will still be sitting when the Senate of the United States has acted upon this treaty—well, perhaps I oughtn't to say that so confidently, for no man not in on the secrets of Providence can tell how long it will take the United States Senate to do anything. (laughter and applause) But I realize that, in the normal course of human fatigue, the Senate will have acted upon this treaty before the conference in Paris gets through with the Austrian treaty and Bulgarian treaty and Turkish treaty. Why, they will still be there on the job.

Now, when you take a contract—every lawyer will follow me on this—if you take a contract and change the words, even though they don't change the sense, you have to get the other parties to accept those words. Isn't that true? Therefore every reservation will have to be taken back to all the signatories of this treaty, and I want you to notice that that includes Germany. We will have to ask Germany's consent to read this treaty the way we understand it. Now I want to tell you that we didn't ask Germany's consent with regard to the meaning of any one of those terms while we were in Paris. We told her what they meant and said, "Sign here." (applause and laughter) Are there any patriotic Americans who desire the method changed? (cries of "No") Do they want me to ask the Germans if I may read the treaty to them expressed in the words the United States Senate thinks it ought to have been written in?

So, you see, reservations come down to this, that they want to change the language of the treaty without changing its meaning. And, let me say, there are indications—I am not judging from official dispatches, but from the newspapers—that people are not in as good a humor over in France now as they were when I was there, and it is going to be more difficult to get a new agreement from now on than it was before. And after dealing with some of those gentlemen, I found that they were as ingenious as any American in attaching unexpected meanings to plain words. I do not want, therefore, having gone through the mill on the existing language, to go through it again on changed language.

But I must not turn away from this great subject without attention to the Shantung clause, the provision with regard to the transfer of certain German rights in the province of Shantung, China, to Japan. I frankly said to my Japanese colleagues at the conference—therefore I can without impropriety say it here—that I was very deeply dissatisfied with that part of the treaty. But, my fellow

citizens, Japan agreed at that very time, and as part of the understanding upon which these clauses were put into the treaty, that
she would relinquish every item of sovereignty that Germany had
enjoyed to China, and that she would retain what other nations
have elsewhere in China—certain economic concessions with regard to the railways and the mines, which she was to operate under a corporation and subject to the laws of China. As I say, I wish
she could have done more. But suppose, as some have suggested,
that we dissent from that clause in the treaty. You can't sign all of
a treaty but one part, my fellow citizens. It is like the President's
veto. He can't veto provisions in a bill. He has got either to sign the
bill or veto the bill. We can't sign the treaty with the Shantung
provision out of it, and if we could, what sort of service would that
be doing China?

Let us state the facts with brutal frankness. England and France
are bound by solemn treaty, entered into before the conference at
Paris, before we entered the war, to give Japan what she gets in
this treaty in the province of Shantung. They cannot in honor withdraw from that promise. They cannot consent to a peace treaty
which does not contain these provisions with regard to Shantung.
England and France, therefore, will stand behind Japan, and if we
are not signatories to the treaty and not parties, she will get all that
Germany had in Shantung, more than she will get under the promises which she made to us. And the only way we can get it away
from her is by going to war with Japan and Great Britain and
France. Does that look like a workable proposition? Is that doing
China a service? Whereas, if we go into this treaty, we are members of the League, China is a member of the League, Japan is a
member of the League, and under Article X, Japan promises, and
we guarantee, that the territorial integrity and political independence of China will be respected and preserved. (applause) That is
the way to serve China. That is the only possible way in the circumstances to serve China.

Therefore we cannot rewrite this treaty. We must take it or leave
it, and after all the rest of the world has signed it, we will find it
very difficult to make any other kind of a treaty. As I took the occasion of saying the other night, it is a case of "put up or shut up."
The world cannot breathe in the atmosphere of negations. The
world cannot deal with nations who say, "We won't play!" The
world cannot have anything to do with an arrangement in which
every nation says, "We will take care of ourselves."

Is it possible—is it possible, for the sinister thing has been suggested to me—that there is a group of individuals in this country
who has conceived it as desirable that the United States should

exercise its power alone, should arm for the purpose, should be ready for the enterprise and undertake to dominate the world by arms? There are indications that there are groups of citizens in this country who do not find that an intolerable program. Are we going to substitute for Pan-Germanism a sinister Pan-Americanism? The thing is intolerable. It is hideous. No man dare propose that in plain words to any American audience anywhere. (applause) The heart of this people is pure. The heart of this people is true. This great people loves liberty. It loves justice. It would rather have liberty and justice than wealth and power. It is the great idealistic force of history, and the idealism of America is what has made conquest of the spirits of man.

While I was in Paris, men of every race, from every quarter of the globe, sought interviews with us in order to tell us how absolutely they believed in America, how all their thoughts, all their pleas for help, all their hope of political salvation, reached out toward America. (applause) And my heart melted within me. I said to some of the simpler sort among them: "I pray you that you will not expect the impossible. America cannot do all the things you are expecting her to do. The most I can promise is that we will do everything we can."

And we are going to redeem that promise, not because I made it, but because when I made it, I spoke the hopes and heart of the United States. If I felt that I personally in any way stood in the way of this settlement, I would be glad to die that it might be consummated, because I have a vision, my fellow citizens, that, if this thing should by some mishap not be accomplished, there would arise from that upon the fair name of this people a stain which never could be effaced, which would be intolerable to every man who knew America and was ready with stout heart to uphold it.

I said just now, before opening, that I was happy to forget on a campaign like this what party I belonged to, and I hope you will not think I am recalling what party I belong to if I say how proud I have been to stand alongside of Senator Hitchcock in this fight. I would be just as glad to stand by Senator Norris if he would let me. But I refer to Senator Hitchcock because I know this is his home town, because of my personal regard for him, because I want to be the brother, the comrade, and coworker of every man who will work for this great cause. And it heartens me when I find, as I found in Des Moines and I find here, that there are more Republicans on the committees that meet me than Democrats. That may be in proportion to the population, (laughter) but, nevertheless, I judge from what I see of these gentlemen that they are, at any rate, very favorable specimens, and that I can take it for granted, because of what I see in my dealing with them, that they do represent some of the permanent and abiding influences of great communities like this. (applause) Why, the heart of America beats in these great prairies and on these hillsides. Sometimes in Washington you seem very far away. The voices that are most audible in Washington are not voices that anybody cares to listen to for very long, (laughter) and it is refreshing to me to get out among the great body of my fellow citizens and feel the touch of the hand and contact of the shoulder and the impulse of mass movement which is going to make conquest, spiritual conquest, of the world. (applause)

Printed in the Omaha *World-Herald*, Sept. 9, 1919. There is a WWT outline of this address in WP, DLC.

An Address in the Coliseum in Sioux Falls

September 8, 1919.

Governor Norbeck[1] and my fellow citizens: I must admit that, every time I face a great audience of my fellow countrymen on this trip, I am filled with a feeling of peculiar solemnity, because I believe, my fellow countrymen, that we have come to one of the turning points in the history of the world. And what I, as an American, covet for this great country is that, on every great occasion, when mankind's fortunes are hung in the balance, America may have the distinction of leading the way. (applause)

In order to enable you to realize some part of what is my thought tonight, I am going to ask you to turn your thoughts back to the tragedy through which we have just passed. A little incident as we came along in the train today brought very close home to me the things that have been happening. A very quiet lady came up with a little crowd at a way station to shake hands with me, and she had no sooner taken my hand than she turned away and burst into tears. I asked a neighbor what was the matter, and he said that she had meant to speak to me of her son who was dead in France, but that the words would not come from her lips. And all over this country, my fellow citizens, there are women who have given up their sons, wives who have given up their husbands, young women who have given up their sweethearts, to die on the other side of the sea for a great cause which was not the peculiar cause of America, but the cause of mankind and of civilization itself. (applause)

I love to repeat what the people on the other side of the water

[1] Peter Norbeck, Republican, Governor of South Dakota.

said about those boys of ours. They told us that they didn't look like any of the other soldiers, that they didn't seem to be merely soldiers, that they seemed to be crusaders, that there was something in their eyes that they had never seen in the eyes of any other army. And I was reminded of what I had so often seen on former journeys across the seas: going over in the steerage, bright-eyed men, who had been permeated with the atmosphere of free America; coming back, among the immigrants coming from the old countries—dull-eyed men, tired-looking men, discouraged-looking men. They were all of them going both ways, men who had come from across the sea, but going out they were going with the look of America in their eyes to visit the old people at home. Coming back, they had the fatigue of Europe in their eyes and had not yet got the feeling that penetrates every American, that there is a great future for all men, that he is master of his own fortune, and that he need be governed by no man whom he does not choose as his master.

And that is what these people saw in the eyes of the American boys who carried their arms across the sea. There was America in every one of those lively eyes, and they were not looking merely at the fields of France, or merely seeking to defeat Germany, but were seeking to defeat everything that Germany's action represented, and to see to it that there never would be such a thing again. (applause)

I want to remind you, my fellow countrymen, that that war was not an accident. That war didn't just happen. That was not some sudden cause which brought on the conflagration. On the contrary, Germany had been preparing for that war for generations. Germany had been preparing every resource and perfecting every skill, developing every invention, which would enable her to master the European world and to dominate the rest of the world. Everybody had been looking on. Everybody had known. For example, it was known in every war office in Europe, and in the War Department at Washington, that the Germans not only had a vast supply of great field guns, but that they had ammunition enough for every one of those guns to wear out the guns. And yet we were living in a fool's paradise. We thought that Germany meant what she said—that she was armed for defense, and that she never would use that great store of guns against her fellow men.

Why, my friends, it was foreordained the minute Germany conceived these purposes that she should do the thing which she did in 1914. The assassination of the Austrian Crown Prince in Serbia was not what started the war. They were ready to start it and merely made that an occasion and an excuse. Before they started it, Serbia had yielded to practically every demand they made of her, and they would not let the rest of the world know that Serbia had yielded, because they did not want to miss the occasion to start the war.

They were afraid that other nations would prepare. They were afraid that they had given too much indication of what they were going to do, and they did not want to wait. What immediately happened, when the other foreign offices of Europe learned of what was going on, was that from every other foreign office, so far as I have been able to learn, messages went to Berlin instructing their representatives to suggest to the German government that the other governments be informed, and that an opportunity be obtained for a discussion, so as to see if war could not be avoided. And Germany didn't dare to discuss her purposes for twenty-four hours.

Now, I have brought back from Europe with me, my fellow citizens, a treaty in which Germany is disarmed (applause) and in which all the other nations of the world agree never to go to war (applause) without first of all having done one or other of two things, either having submitted the question in dispute to arbitration, in which case they will abide by the verdict, or, if they do not care to submit it to arbitration, having submitted it to discussion by the League of Nations; that they will allow six months for the discussion; that they will publish all the facts to all the world; and that not until three months after the expiration of the six will they go to war. (applause) There is a period of nine months of cooling off, and Germany did not dare cool off for nine days! (applause) If Germany had dreamed that anything like the greater part of the world would combine against her, she never would have begun the war, and she didn't dare to let the opinions of mankind crystallize against her by the discussion of the purposes which she had in mind.

So what I want to point out to you tonight is that we are making a fundamental choice. You have either got to have the old system, of which Germany was the perfect flower, or you have got to have a new system. You cannot have a new system unless you supply a substitute, an adequate substitute, for the old. And I want to say that when certain of our fellow citizens take the position that we do not want to go into any combination at all, but want to take care of ourselves, all I have to say to them is that that is exactly the German position.

Germany through the mouth of her Emperor, Germany through the mouths of her orators, Germany through the pens of her writers of all sorts said: "Here we stand, ready to take care of ourselves.

We will not enter into any combination. We are armed for self-defense, and no nation dares interfere with our rights."

That, it appears, is the American program in the eyes of some gentlemen. And I want to tell you that, within the last two weeks, the pro-German element in this country has lifted its head again. It is again heartened. It again has air in its lungs. It again says, "Ah, now we see a chance when America and Germany will stand outside this League and take care of themselves." Not take care of themselves as partners—I do not mean to intimate that—but where America will play the same role that Germany played, under that old order which brought us through that agony of bloody sweat, that great agony in which the whole world seemed to be caught in the throes of a crisis, when for a long time we did not know whether civilization itself was going to survive or not.

And do not believe, my fellow countrymen, that civilization is saved now. There were passions let loose upon the field of the world by that war which have not grown quiet yet, which will not grow quiet for a long time, and every element of disorder, every element of chaos, is hoping that there may be no steadying hand from a council of nations to hold the order of the world steady until we can make the final arrangements of justice and of peace. The treaty of peace with Germany is very much more than a treaty of peace with Germany. The German part of it takes a good many words, because there are a great many technical details to be arranged, but that is not the heart of the treaty. The heart of the treaty is that it undoes the injustice that Germany did; that it not only undoes the injustice that Germany did, but it enables the world to see that such injustice will in the future be impossible.

And not forgetting, but remembering with intense sympathy, the toiling mass of mankind, the conference at Paris wrote into the heart of that treaty a great charter of labor. I think that those of us who live in this happy land can have little conception of the conditions of labor in some of the European countries up to the period of the outbreak of this war. And one of the things that that treaty proposes to do is to organize the opinion of all nations to assist in the betterment and the release of the great forces of labor throughout the world. It is a laboring man's treaty in the sense that it is the average man's treaty.

Why, my fellow citizens, the thing that happened at Paris was absolutely and literally unprecedented. There never was a gathering of the leading statesmen of the world before who did not sit down to divide the spoils, to make the arrangements the most advantageous that they could devise for their own strong and powerful governments. Yet this gathering of statesmen sat themselves down to do something which a friend of mine the other day very aptly described as establishing the land titles of the world, because the principle underlying the treaty was that every land belonged to the native stock that lived in it, and that nobody has the right to impose the sovereignty of any alien government on anybody was for the first time recognized in the councils of international deliberation. In this League of Nations Covenant, which some men ask you to examine in a spot here and there with a magnifying glass, there lies at the heart of it this great principle: nobody has the right to take any territory any more.

You will see what our situation was. The Austrian Empire, for example, had gone to pieces, and here we were with the pieces on the table. The Austrian treaty is not yet completed, but it is being made on the same principle as the German, and will serve as an illustration. In the old days, they would have compacted it between armies. They did not do that this time. They said: "This piece belongs to the Poles and to nobody else. This piece belongs to the Bohemians and to nobody else. This piece belongs to Rumania, though she never could have got it for herself; we are going to turn it over to her, though other people want it. This piece belongs to the Slavs, who live in the northern Balkans—the Yugoslavs, as we have come to know them to be—and they shall have what belongs to them."

When we turned to the property of Germany, which she had been habitually misgoverning—I mean the German colonies, particularly the colonies in Africa—there were many nations who would like to have had those rich, undeveloped portions of the world. But none of them got them. We adopted the principle of trusteeship. We said: "We will put you in charge of this, that, and the other piece of territory, and you will make an annual report to us. We will deprive you of your trusteeship whenever you administer it in a way which is not approved by our judgment, and we will put upon you this primary limitation—that you shall do nothing that is to the detriment of the people who live in that territory. You shall not enforce labor on it, and you shall apply the same principles of humanity to the work of their women and children that you apply at home. You shall not allow the illicit trade in drugs and in liquors. You shall not allow men who want to make money out of powder and shot to sell arms and ammunition to those who can use them to their own disadvantage. You shall not make those people fight in your armies. The country is theirs, and you must remember that and treat it as theirs." There is no more annexation. There is no more land grabbing. There is no more extension of sovereignty. It is an absolute reversal of history, an absolute revolution in the way in which international affairs are treated. And it is all in the Covenant of the League of Nations.

The old system was, be ready. And we can be ready. I have heard gentlemen say, "America can take care of herself." Yes, she can take care of herself. Every man would have to train to arms. We would have to have a great standing army. We would have to have accumulations of military material such as Germany used to have. We would enjoy the luxuries of taxes even higher than we pay now. We could accumulate our force, and then our force would have to be directed by some kind of sufficiently vigorous central power. You would have a military government in spirit if not in form. No use having a fighting nation if there is not somebody to command it! If you want to turn your President from a representative of the civil purposes of this country, you can turn him into a commander in chief, ready to fight the world.

But if you did nobody would recognize America in those strange and altered circumstances. All the world would stand at amaze and say, "Has America forgotten everything that she ever professed?" The picture is one that every American repudiates, and I challenge any man who has that purpose at the back of his thought to avow it. If he comes and tells you that America must stand alone and take care of herself, ask him how it is going to be done. And he will not dare tell you, because you would show him the door and say, "We do not know any such American."

Yet we cannot do without force. You cannot establish land titles, as I have expressed it, and not maintain them. Suppose that the land titles of South Dakota were disturbed. Suppose the farm lines were moved, say, ten feet. You know what would happen. Along every fence line you would see farmers perching with guns on their knees. The only reason they are not perching now is that there are land deeds deposited in a particular place, and the whole majesty and force and judicial system of the State of South Dakota are behind the titles.

Very well, we have got to do something like that internationally. You cannot set up Poland, whom all the world through centuries has pitied and sympathized with, as the owner of her property and not have somebody take care that her title deeds are respected. You cannot establish freedom, my fellow citizens, without force. And the only force you can substitute for an armed mankind is the concerted force of the combined action of mankind through the instrumentality of all the enlightened governments of the world. This is the only conceivable system that you can substitute for the old order of things which brought the calamity of this war upon us and would assuredly bring the calamity of another war upon us.

Your choice is between the League of Nations and Germanism. I have told you what I mean by Germanism—taking care of yourselves, being armed and ready, having a chip on your shoulder, thinking of nothing but your own rights and never thinking of the rights of anybody else, thinking that you were put into this world to see that American might was asserted and forgetting that American might ought never to be used against the weak, ought never to be used in an unjust cause, ought never to be used for aggression, ought to be used with the heart of humanity beating behind it.

Sometimes people call me an idealist. Well, that is the way I know I am an American. America, my fellow citizens—I do not say it in disparagement of any other great people—America is the only idealistic nation in the world. When I speak practical judgments about business affairs, I can only guess whether I am speaking the voice of America or not. But when I speak the ideal purposes of history, I know that I am speaking the voice of America, because I have saturated myself since I was a boy in the records of that spirit, and everywhere in them there is this authentic tone of the love of justice and the service of humanity.

If, by any mysterious influence of error, America should not take the leading part in this new enterprise of concerted power, the world would experience one of those reversals of sentiment, one of those penetrating chills of reaction, which would lead to a universal cynicism. For if America goes back upon mankind, mankind has no other place to turn. It is the hope of nations all over the world that America will do this great thing.

Yet I find some gentlemen so nervous about doing right that their eyes rest very uneasily on the first article of the Covenant of the League of Nations, and they say, "That says that we can get out after two years' notice, if we have fulfilled all our international obligations at that time. Now, we want to make it perfectly clear that we will get out when we want to."

You cannot make it perfectly clear in the way they want it, unless you make it perfectly clear at the outset that you want to get out. You cannot choose the seat by the door and keep fumbling with the knob without creating the impression that you are going to get out in a minute; that you do not like the company you are in; that you do not like the job; that you are by constitution and disposition a scuttler!

If America goes into this thing, she is going to stay in, and she is going to stay in in order to see that justice is done. She can see to it, because if you read this Covenant of the League, nothing material can be done under that League without a unanimous vote of the Council. America can determine what action is going to be taken. No action that is against her policy or against her will can be taken, unless her judgment is rendered in some case where she is one of the disputants. But, my fellow citizens, if she is one of the disputants, she is in trouble anyhow. If the war that they are trying to avert is her war, then I do not see that she is any more benefited by being out of the League than in it. On the contrary, if she is in the League, she has at least the good offices of other friendly states to see that some accommodation is reached.

And she is doing exactly what she has done already. Some gentlemen forget that we already have nearly thirty treaties with the leading nations of the world. Yes, and to do the very thing that is in this Covenant. Only we agree to take twelve months to discuss everything, whereas the League gives nine months. The American choice would be twelve. We promise not to fight without first talking.

I want to call here a great many witnesses to this circumstance, for I am sure by looking at you that you know something about it. What is the certain way to have difficulty between capital and labor? It is to refuse to sit down in the same room and talk it over. I cannot understand why one man or set of men should refuse to discuss claims or grievances with another set of men, unless they know to begin with that they are wrong. I am very averse from discussing anything when I know I have got the wrong end. But when I think I have got either the right end or as good an end as the other fellow, then I am perfectly willing to discuss it. There is an old saying accredited to a rather cynical politician of what I hope I may regard as the older school, who said to his son, "John, do not bother your head about lies; they will take care of themselves. But if you ever hear my denying anything, you may be sure it is so." The only thing we are afraid of, the only thing we dodge, is the truth. If we see facts coming our way, it is just as well to get out of the way. Always take this attitude, my friends, toward facts: always try to see them coming first, so that they will not catch you at unawares.

So with all matters, grading up from the smallest to the greatest. Human beings can get together by discussion, and it is the business of civilization to get together by discussion and not by fighting. That is civilization. The only reason this country is civilized is because we do not let two men who have a difference fight one another. We say: "Wait a minute; we have arranged for that. Just around the corner there you will find a courthouse. On certain days the court is sitting. Go and state the matter to those men, and neither before nor after the decision shall you touch one another."

That is civilization. You have got the ordered processes of consultation and discussion. You have got to act by rule, and justice consists in applying the same rule to everybody, not one rule to the rich man and another to the poor, not one rule to the employer and another to the employee, but the same rule to the strong and to the weak.

That is exactly what is attempted in this treaty. I cannot understand the psychology of men who are resisting it. I cannot understand what they are afraid of, unless it is that they know physical force and do not understand moral force. Moral force is a great deal more powerful than physical. Govern the sentiments of mankind and you govern mankind. Govern their fears, govern their hopes, determine their fortunes, get them together in concerted masses, and the whole thing sways like a team. Once get them suspecting one another, once get them antagonizing one another, and society itself goes to pieces. We are trying to make a society instead of a set of barbarians out of the governments of the world. I sometimes think, when I wake in the night, of all the wakeful nights that anxious fathers and mothers and friends have spent during those weary years of this awful war. And I seem to hear the cry, the inarticulate cry, of mothers all over the world, millions of them on the other side of the sea and thousands of them on this side of the sea: "In God's name, give us the sensible and hopeful and peaceful processes of right and of justice!"

America can stay out, but I want to call you to witness that the peace of the world cannot be established without America. America is necessary to the peace of the world. And reverse the proposition: the peace and good will of the world are necessary to America. Disappoint the world, center its suspicion upon you, make it feel that you are hot and jealous rivals of the other nations, and do you think you are going to do as much business with them as you would otherwise do?

I do not like to put the thing on that plane, my fellow countrymen, but if you want to talk business, I can talk business. If you want to put it on the low plane of how much money you can make, you can make more money out of friendly traders than out of hostile traders. You can make more money out of men who trust you than out of men who fear you. You can bring about a state of mind where by every device possible foreign markets will be closed to you, and men will say: "No, the wheat of America tastes bitter; we will eat the wheat of Argentina; we will eat the wheat of Australia, for that is the wheat of friendship, and this is the wheat of antagonism. We do not want to wear clothes made out of American cotton; we are going to buy just as much cotton from India as we can.

We are going to develop new cotton fields. America is up to something; we do not know just what, and we are going to shut and lock every door we can against her." You can get the world in that temper. Do you think that would be profitable? Do you think there is money in that?

But I am not going to dwell upon that side of it. I am just as sure of what you are thinking as I am of what I am thinking. We are not thinking of money. We would rather retain the reputation of America than have all the money in the world. I am not ready to die for money, and neither are you. But you are ready and I am ready to die for America. A friend of mine made a very poignant remark to me one day. He said: "Did you ever see a family that hung it's son's yardstick or ledger or spade up over the mantlepiece?" But how many of you have seen the lad's rifle, his musket, hung up? Well, why? A musket is a barbarous thing. The spade and the yardstick and the ledger are the symbols of peace and steady business. Why not hang them up? Because they do not represent self-sacrifice. They do not glorify you. They do not dignify you in the same sense that the musket does, because when you took that musket at the call of your country you risked everything and knew you could not get anything. The most that you could do was to come back alive, but after you came back alive there was a halo about you. That boy was in France! That boy served his country and served a great cause! That boy risked everything to see that the weak peoples of the world were redeemed from intolerable tyranny! Here comes— ah, how I wish I were going to be in Washington on the seventeenth—here comes, do you not hear it, the tread of the First Division—those men, along with their comrades, to whom the eyes of all Europe turn! All Europe took heart when they saw that brilliant flag unfurled on French soil.

Did you ever hear that thrilling song that is being sung so much now of the blind Frenchman wishing to know if the Americans had come, bidding his son watch at the window. "Look, my lad, what are they carrying? What are the colors? Are they red stripes upon a field of white? Is there a piece of heaven in the corner? Is that piece of heaven full of stars? Ah, the Americans have come! Thank God, the Americans have come!"

That is what we have at our hearts, my fellow citizens, and we hang the musket up, or the sword, over the mantlepiece. And if the lad is gone and dead, we share the spirit of a noble lady, who said to me, without the glimmer of a tear in her eye: "I have had the honor of losing a son upon the fields of France. I have had the honor, not the pain. I have had the distinction of losing a son of mine upon the field of honor." It is that field of honor that we are going to redeem. We are not going to redeem it with blood any more, but we are going to make out of the councils of the people of the world councils of peace and of justice and of honor.[2]

Printed in *Addresses of President Wilson*, with a few corrections from the incomplete text in the Sioux Falls *Daily Argus-Leader*, Sept. 9, 1919.
    [2] There is a WWT outline of this address in WP, DLC.

To Thomas Riley Marshall

My dear Mr. Vice President: [Sioux Falls] 8 September, 1919
    I shall be greatly obliged if you will represent me at the reception to General Pershing in Washington and the parade of the First Division.   Cordially and faithfully yours,   Woodrow Wilson

CC telegram (WP, DLC).

Vance Criswell McCormick to Joseph Patrick Tumulty

Washington D C. Sept 8 1919
    Following from Vance McCormick Harrisburg Quote Glad to get your telegram Congratulate President upon excellent effect being produced by his frank explanation of the Treaty When people of the country understand fully what he was up against in Paris their sympathy and support will be overwhelmingly with him Think it most important that he keep in as close touch as possible with Senator Hitchcock I spent Friday at the Capitol stirring up some of our inactive friends I think they will be heard from later unquote.
                                                                    Forster

T telegram (WP, DLC).

Key Pittman to Joseph Patrick Tumulty

The White House, September 8, 1919
    Senator Pittman asks that following be wired you:
    "Anti-League Republican papers are whining. Say President is only dealing with vituperation and glittering generalities. Papers enthusiastic in reference to President. His supporters elated beyond expression. Astounded the way he can change his style to appeal to a people's audience. His punches are bound to tell. His explanation of Article X and his exposure of certain Senate leaders seems to appeal most strongly. People have no sympathy for the Senate. The President should expose effect of Committee reserva-

tion dealing with Section X.[1] By it all discretion of Congress removed.

"Since Lodge drew out of Irish Committee full account of their experience at Paris,[2] the President is justified in stating what he attempted to do for the Committee and how they injured the cause of Ireland. There is strong drift of conservative Irish against Dunne and Walsh. Action on Amendments first proceeding. This sure to arouse bitter fight in Republican ranks. Simmons said today that he was satisfied that the Treaty should be ratified without reservations, and that he was therefore ready to vote for reservations of an interpretative character. [Blank][3] in interview said that there were only twenty-seven senators for ratification without reservation. While many desire interpretative reservations, I do not believe that many of our people want the President to go further. With the exception of the need of a definite proposal on our side and too much talking, conditions are much brighter. Hitchcock is doing splendid work."   Forster.

T telegram (WP, DLC).
    [1] For the text of which, see R. Forster to JPT, Sept. 5, 1919, n. 3.
    [2] Francis Patrick Walsh, Michael J. Ryan, and Edward Fitzsimons Dunne had testified before the Senate Foreign Relations Committee on August 30 concerning the activities of the American Commission on Irish Independence in Paris. Walsh submitted copies of the commission's correspondence with Wilson, the other American peace commissioners, and various British officials, as well as its interview with Wilson on June 11 (about which, see the extract from the Diary of Dr. Grayson printed at June 11, 1919, Vol. 60). These documents were printed as part of the official record: *Treaty of Peace With Germany: Hearings Before the Committee on Foreign Relations United States Senate*, 66th Cong., 1st sess., Senate Document No. 106 (Washington, 1919), pp. 794-864.
    [3] The *New York Times*, Sept. 6, 1919, identified this man as "a leading Democratic Senator who declined to allow the use of his name." He made this remark on September 5. He was probably Henry Fountain Ashurst of Arizona.

From Walker Downer Hines

Dear Mr. President: Washington September 8, 1919

Since I wrote you under date of the sixth instant, I have decided that the purchase of additional steel rail can and ought to be postponed for at least three or four weeks, and I hope the postponement can safely be made somewhat longer.

I feel it would be distinctly unfortunate for the Government, in the midst of its campaign to reduce the cost of basic commodities, to pay the same excessive price for steel rail, against which protest was made so vigorously and so justly a few months ago. Steel products are so typical of prices generally that such purchase would constitute a most unfortunate governmental endorsement of a "stand pat" attitude on the part of business men.

I fear that we cannot make sufficiently effective progress with a campaign to reduce the high cost of living unless we can arouse the business interests of the country to a realization of the proposition that their own interests and the public interest call alike for a reduction in prices all along the line. If manufacturers, wholesalers, and retailers, merely hold to the existing basic prices, I do not believe we can possibly affect a reduction in the cost of living which will meet the just expectations and real needs of Labor.

I therefore submit for your consideration the question whether in connection with any conference you may arrange with the steel interests on the labor matter, it would not be highly beneficial to seek to get them to make a substantial reduction in their existing basic prices. The example to other industries and business would be of immense value and I believe the step would be highly beneficial to the steel interests themselves.

The recommendation I thus submit is not incompatible with the recommendation I submitted in my letter of the sixth instant relative to monthly statements of costs, and monthly or quarterly statements of profits.

Indeed, I think if the two recommendations be carried out each step would help the other.

Cordially yours,   Walker D. Hines.

TLS (WP, DLC).

From William Phillips

Washington, D. C. Sept. 8, 1919

Would it be agreeable to you to have the Mayflower placed at the disposal of the King and Queen of Belgium, leaving Washington at midnight October 28th, to convey them to Hampton Roads, where they will board ship for Belgium? Inasmuch as the royal party will be in Washington for a few hours on October 28th, would you care to receive them either for a small dinner at 8.30 or after dinner about 9.30, after which they could proceed directly to the Mayflower?   William Phillips, Acting Secretary of State.

T telegram (WP, DLC).

William Phillips to Robert Lansing[1]

Dear Mr. Secretary: Washington September 8, 1919.

I send you enclosed a confidential message for you from Polk, regarding the Roumanian situation,[2] together with the text of a note which the Council has presented to the Roumanian Government.[3] You will note that Polk asks your opinion on a very important matter.

I have received word from the President today that he does not wish to be bothered with any telegrams from the Mission or elsewhere which do not require his immediate decision, consequently we are from now on not sending anything to him except telegrams of that nature. I have not even transmitted to him these two telegrams. I should, however, be very grateful for an expression of your views.

I enclose a third confidential telegram from Polk to you.[4] It is a note handed in by Tardieu as being the views of Clemenceau, Balfour and Tardieu regarding Thrace. You will note (page 4) that Tardieu promises to send a further note. I am awaiting, therefore, this further note before submitting the whole matter to the President.

Sincerely yours,   William Phillips

TLS (R. Lansing Papers, DLC).
    [1] At this time on vacation in Watertown, New York.
    [2] FLP to RL, No. 4062, Sept. 5, 1919, T telegram (SDR, RG 59, 763.72119/6542, DNA). Polk wrote that the Rumanian situation was still unsatisfactory because some officials of the French and Italian governments had been encouraging Rumania in its opposition to the peace conference. "In view of the fact," Polk continued, "that defiance by Roumania would destroy the influence of the Council and cast doubts on the ability of the League of Nations to control affairs in Europe, I suggest that you send for the Roumanian Chargé, tell him how seriously we regard the situation and that it may even be necessary to break off diplomatic relations if Roumania defies Council. I would like your opinion as to whether it might not even be necessary for us to go to the extent of advocating [before] the Council a blockade of Roumanian ports on the Black Sea. Personally I do not think there is any possible chance of this being necessary, yet the Council has to assert itself, otherwise its influence, as well as that of any body succeeding it, such as Council of the League of Nations, is hopelessly destroyed. Please give me benefit of your advice."
    [3] FLP to RL, No. 4073, Sept. 6, 1919, T telegram (SDR, RG 256, 864.00/484B, DNA). This note was a scathing indictment of what it called Rumania's "plundering" of Hungary. It said that the situation was such that the Associated Powers had to ask themselves whether Rumania still counted herself among their number. Remonstrances addressed to Bucharest had remained without reply or effect. The note then put three questions directly to the Rumanian government asking whether it was prepared to cooperate with the Associated Powers. It ended by asking whether Rumania would gain by a severance of friendly relations with her western associates and demanded a prompt reply.
    [4] See FLP to RL, Sept. 5, 1919.

Frank Lyon Polk to Woodrow Wilson and Robert Lansing

Paris September 8, 1919

4104 Confidential for the information of the President and Secretary of State. In connection with my 4065, September 5, 11 p.m. and in compliance with my suggestion that the Allies should make a definite suggestion in regard to Thrace, Tardieu has sent me the following memorandum which I do not know that any of the other Powers have seen. I told him that I did not think there was any possibility of the President's going as far as he Tardieu suggested.

Quote. Suggestion of a solution relative to Thrace. Paragraph. Conforming with the note remitted to Mr. Polk on September 2nd, and with his expressed desire to receive, as conclusion to this note, a positive suggestion, the following principles are recommended for his examination: Paragraph.

1. Bulgaria should have, to Dedeagatch and on the railway lines in the Maritza Valley, a right of economic passage under the most favorable conditions and with full liberty, under the guarantee of the League of Nations. Paragraph.

2. The International State of Constantinople should have a common frontier with Bulgaria. Paragraph.

3. The territories of the two Thraces, Western and Eastern, inhabited in majority by Greeks, should be returned to Greece. Paragraph.

4. The territories of Eastern and Western Thrace ceded to Greece should receive a special regime of autonomy. Paragraph.

If Mr. Polk accepts these principles, the following solution is suggested: Paragraph.

1. That Dedeagatch be created a free city under the sovereignty of the League of Nations and under the administration of a Commissioner, assisted by three delegates with consulting power, one Greek, the other Bulgarian, and the third Turkish. Paragraph.

2. Aside from the administration of the free city, the Commissioner shall have a right of control over the railroad lines, particularly as to rates. Paragraph.

3. The Greek frontier in Thrace is fixed as follows (English map 1/1000000 scale) to the North by the line adopted by the Conference September 2nd, to a point even with Vaisal; from this point by a line to be fixed by experts following the general direction Seliolo-Havsa-Hairobolu-Hereke-Golfe de Xeros. Paragraph.

4. The territory included between this line and the Greek frontier, as it was accepted by President Wilson, shall at the same time, as it is attached to Greece, receive an autonomous constitution analogous with that accorded to the Ruthenian territories attached to Czecho-Slovakia. Paragraph.

The solution above proposed has the following advantages: Paragraph.

(a) It conforms with the right of peoples to self-determination; because it again attaches to Greece, in territories which were not included in the line proposed by President Wilson:

Greeks   146,661
Bulgarians   38,883
Turks   146,180

(b) It is inspired by the general principles already adopted by the Conference both concerning guarantees of autonomy accorded to populations, as regarding the constitution of the free city of Dedeagatch. On the first point, reference is made to the articles relative to Czecho-Slovakia, and on the second to the articles relative to Dantzig. End quote.   Polk. Ammission.

T telegram (SDR, RG 256, 868.00/205A, DNA).

From the Diary of Dr. Grayson

Tuesday, September 9, 1919.

The first real unpleasant episode of the entire trip occurred here in St. Paul. The President was scheduled to address a special session of the Minnesota Legislature, which was in session to consider the High Cost of Living. The special train arrived at the station exactly on time at 8:30. A great crowd had gathered about the station, but the reception committee was conspicuous by its absence, as were the automobiles for the party. For more than half an hour the train remained on the siding waiting, and the lame explanation was made that the party had arrived half an hour ahead of time. As a matter of fact, this was not true. Governor Burnquist[1] was chairman of the reception committee, and he not only was opposed to the Treaty but was a politician of the small town type. As a result he delayed the entire committee, holding them in the Capitol, when they should have been at the station. It was after 9:00 o'clock before the automobiles and the reception committee finally put in an appearance. The Governor did not have the graciousness even to apologize for keeping the Chief Executive of the Nation waiting, and his action brought about some very bitter comment from men who were usually extremely friendly to him. The President, however, although he realized what had taken place made no comment whatever upon it. It was one of those things which can only be experienced where small natures try to take advantage of situations to bring about personal advancement.

The President was escorted to the State Capitol by a regiment of the Minnesota National Guard. Just before the party started a quartette of men from the Red Cross gathered on a platform beyond where the MAYFLOWER was stopped and sang some patriotic songs for the benefit of the President and Mrs. Wilson.

Arriving at the Capitol the President was first escorted to the

Governor's private office, while word of his arrival was sent to the Legislature. The joint session was held in the Assembly Chamber, the larger of the two meeting rooms, and only members of the Legislature and their families were able to be present, as the room was quite small. The President took for his subject the High Cost of Living and told the Legislature that in his opinion one of the greatest necessities of the nation was to see that the market arrangements were equitable. He advocated control over all industries that had to do with the marketing of the necessities of life, and also advocated rigid control of cold storage appliances. The audience was friendly in the extreme, although the Legislature was overwhelmingly Republican. The President only referred incidentally to the Treaty of Versailles, but told the Legislature that as long as it remained unsettled there was little hope of the country returning to normal conditions.

After the formal meeting the President returned to the Governor's Room and was greeted by the members of the Legislature personally. Leaving the Capitol we proceeded to the hotel,[2] where the President rested until luncheon.

A formal luncheon had been arranged by the Governor, but there were no speeches. The day's program was so heavy that I had insisted that only the regular set addresses be delivered, and even they were a terrible strain on the President.

After luncheon the automobiles were entered and the entire party proceeded to Minneapolis, where a big rally had been arranged in the Armory. The reception in Minneapolis was the most enthusiastic and largest up to date. The crowds on the street were very dense—every window in the business section was filled with people, while grand-stands to accommodate other spectators had been erected at various points. Old-timers, who knew the Twin Cities well, said that the President's reception and welcome compared very favorably with any in the history of this territory.

The crowd in the Armory,[3] like that at all meetings to date, was appreciative and cheered the President's points as he made them. The President again called attention here to the fact that the people did not know what was in the Treaty because the document was so bulky and technical that they would not examine it themselves, while the politicians, who were opposed to it, had no desire to tell them anything about it that would influence them in favor of it. The President repeated his Shantung explanation here and elaborated upon it. He called attention to the fact that the United States had not entered any objection to the taking over of Port Arthur by Russia, or of other exactions made by European nations on Chinese territory in the past. The reason for this, the President said, was that the United States had no business to do so under international law, but, he declared, that if the United States accepted the Treaty and ratified the League Constitution, it would be possible for China to get back all of the territory that had been stolen from her.

Leaving Minneapolis the President returned to the hotel for dinner and a night meeting in St. Paul. The St. Paul crowd that night[4] was one of the largest that had ever turned out in that city. The word of the morning's fiasco engineered by the Governor had circulated throughout the city and aroused much resentment. One of those who voiced that resentment to me was Louis W. Hill,[5] of the Great Northern Railroad. He characterized it as an outrage and told me that there was not the slightest doubt that it was deliberate and premeditated. Other people had the same idea, and the Governor was the subject of sharp criticism.

The meeting in the Coliseum in St. Paul was one of the most enthusiastic the President ever addressed anywhere. The Mayor, [Laurence Curran Hodgson],[6] was in great fettle. He is well liked and the majority of the people call him by his first name. After the President had finished his address the Mayor jumped to the front of the platform and in tones that carried to every corner of the hall demanded of the audience that they go on record as to whether they supported the President. He shouted: "All those in favor of the ratification of the Treaty without a single change will vote Aye." And there was a thundering volume of Ayes that reverberated from the rafters of the big building. It seemed as though every person there had voted approval of the President's stand. When the Mayor called for the Noes, hardly twenty-five responded. The crowd was on its feet cheering when the President left the hall.

[1] Joseph Alfred Arner Burnquist, Republican, Governor of Minnesota.
[2] The Saint Paul Hotel.
[3] Estimated at 10,000 persons. *Minneapolis Morning Tribune*, Sept. 10, 1919.
[4] Estimated at 15,000 persons. *Ibid.*
[5] Louis Warren Hill, president of the Great Northern Railway and the son of its founder, James Jerome Hill.
[6] A Democrat.

An Address in St. Paul to a Joint Session
of the Legislature of Minnesota

September 9, 1919

Mr. Speaker,[1] Mr. Governor,[2] gentlemen of the legislature, ladies and gentlemen. I esteem it an unusual privilege to stand in this place today and address the members of this great body, because the errand upon which I have left Washington is so intimate a matter of the life of our own nation, as well as of the life of the world.

And yet I am conscious, standing in this presence, that perhaps the most appropriate things I could allude to are those which affect us immediately. I know that you have been called together in special session for special purposes. And one of those purposes you have already achieved, and I rejoice with you (applause) in the adoption of the suffrage amendment. Another purpose, I understand, is for you to consider the high cost of living, and the high cost of living is one of those things which is so complicated, ramifying in so many directions, that it seems that we can't do anything in particular about it without knowing how the particulars affect the whole. It is dangerous to play with a complicated piece of machinery, piece by piece, unless you know how the pieces are related to each other.

And the cost of living is a world condition. It is due to the fact that the manpower has been sacrificed on the agony of the battlefield and that all the processes of industry have either been slackened or diverted. Production of foodstuffs, production of clothing, production of all the necessaries of life has either been slackened or it has been turned into channels which are not immediately useful to the general civil population. Great factories, as I need not tell you, which in our country were devoted to the uses of peace, have recently been converted in such fashion as to serve the processes of war. And it will take a certain length of time to restore them to their old adjustments, to turn their machinery to the old uses again, to lead labor so that it will not be concentrated upon the manufacture of munitions and the other stuffs necessary for war, but will be devoted to the general processes of production so necessary to our life.

Back of all that—and I do not say this merely for an argument, but because it is true—back of that lies the fact that we have not yet learned what the basis of peace is going to be. The world is not going to settle down, my fellow citizens, until it knows what part

[1] William Ignatius Nolan, Republican.
[2] Burnquist also spoke briefly. A copy of his remarks is in the J. A. A. Burnquist Papers, MnHi.

the United States is going to play in the peace. The strain upon the finances of other governments of the world has been all but a breaking strain. I imagine it will be several generations before foreign governments can finally adjust themselves to carrying the overwhelming debts which have been accumulated in this war. The United States has accumulated a great debt, but not in proportion to those that other countries have accumulated, when you reckon our wealth as compared with theirs.

We are the only nation in the world that is likely in the immediate future to have a sufficient body of free capital to put the industrial world, here and elsewhere, on its feet again. Until the industrial world is put on its feet you cannot finally handle the question of the cost of living, because the cost of living in the last analysis depends upon the thing we are always talking about but do not know how to manage—the law of supply and demand.

It depends upon manufacture and distribution. It depends upon all the normal processes of the industrial and commercial world. It depends upon international credit. It depends upon shipping. It depends upon the multiplication of transportation facilities domestically. Our railroads at this moment are not adequate to moving the commerce of this country. Every here and there they run through a little neck—for example, the Pennsylvania System at Pittsburgh—where everything is congested and you are squeezing a great commerce through a little aperture. Terminal facilities at the ports are not adequate. The problem grows the more you think of it.

What we have to put our minds to is the international problem, first of all—to set the commerce of the world going again and the manufacturing of the world going again. And we have got to do that largely. Then we have got to see that our own production and our own methods of finance and our own commerce are quickened in every way possible, and that we, sitting in legislatures like this and in the Congress of the United States, have to see to it, if you will permit a vulgar expression, that no one monkeys with the machinery.

I understand that one of the excellent suggestions mentioned by your Governor is that you look into the cold storage. Well, there are other kinds of storage besides cold storage. There are other ways of covering the reserve stocks of goods. You do not have to keep everything cold, though you can keep the cold hand of control on it. You can manage by a contract that isn't put on paper to see that goods are doled out so as not to bring the highest prices. The communities of the United States are entitled to see that these dams are removed and that the waters that are going to fructify the world flow in their normal courses. It is not easy. It is not always pleasant. You do not like to look censoriously into the affairs of your fellow citizens too much or too often, but it is necessary to look with a very unsympathetic eye at some of the processes which are retarding distribution and the supply which is going to meet the demand.

Not only that, but we have got to realize that we are face to face with a great industrial problem which does not center in the United States. It centers elsewhere, but we share it with the other countries of the world. That is the relation between capital and labor, between those who employ and those who are employed. And we might as well sit up straight and look facts in the face, gentlemen. The laboring men of the world are not satisfied with their relations with their employers. Of course, I do not mean to say that dissatisfaction is universal dissatisfaction, because there are situations in many instances of satisfaction, but I am now speaking of the general relations between capital and labor. Everywhere there is dissatisfaction, much more on the other side of the water than on this side.

And one of the things that have to be brought about for mankind can be brought about by what we do in this country, because, as a matter of fact, if I may refer for a moment to the treaty of peace, there is a part of that treaty which sets up an international method of consultation about the conditions of labor. It is a splendid instrument locked up in that great document. I have called it frequently the Magna Carta of labor, for it is that, and the standards set up, for standards are stated, are the standards of American labor so far as they could be adopted in a general conference. The point I wish to make is that the world is looking to America to set the standards with regard to the conditions of labor and the relations between labor and capital, and it is looking to us because we have been more progressive in those matters, though sometimes we have moved very slowly and with undue caution.

As a result of our progressiveness, the ruling influences among our working men are conservative in the sense that they see that it is not in the interest of labor to break up civilization, and progressive in the sense that they see that a constructive program has to be adopted. By a progressive I do not mean a man who is ready to move, but a man who knows where he is going when he moves. A man who has got a workable program is the only progressive, because if you have not got a workable program you cannot make it good and you cannot progress.

Very well, then, we have got to have a constructive program with regard to labor. And the minute we get it we will relieve the strain all over the world, because the world will accept our standards and follow our example. I am not dogmatic about this matter. I can't presume that I know how it should be done. I know the principle upon which it should be done. The principle is that the interests of capital and the interests of labor are not different but are the same, and men of business sense ought to know how to work out an organization which will express that identity of interest. Where there is identity of interest there must be community of interest. You can't any longer regard labor as a commodity. You have got to regard it as a means of association—the association of physical skill and physical vigor with the enterprise which is managed by those who represent capital. And when you do, the production of the world is going to go forward by leaps and bounds.

Why is it that labor organizations jealously limit the amount of work that their men can do? Because they are driving hard bargains with you; they don't feel that they are your partners at all. And so long as labor and capital are antagonistic, production is going to be at its minimum. Just so soon as they are sympathetic and cooperative, it is going to bound, and that will be one of the means of bringing down the cost of living. In other words, my fellow citizens, we can do something, we can do a great deal, along the lines of your Governor's recommendation and along the lines that I took the liberty of recommending to the Congress of the United States. But we must remember that we are only beginning the push, that we are only learning the job, and that its ramifications extend into all the relationships of international credit and international industry. We ought to give our thought to this, gentlemen. America, though we do not like to admit it, has been very provincial in regard to the world's business. When we had to engage in banking transactions outside of the United States, we generally did it through English bankers or, more often, through German bankers. You did not find American banks in Shanghai and Calcutta and all around the circle of the world. You found every other bank there; you found French banks and English banks and German banks and Swedish banks. You did not find American banks. American bankers have not, as a rule, handled international exchange, and here, all of a sudden, as if by the turn of the hand, because of the sweeping winds of this war which have destroyed so many things, we are called upon to handle the bulk of international exchange. We have got to learn it, and we have got to learn it fast. We have got to have American instrumentalities in every part of the world if American money is going to rehabilitate the world, as American money must.

If you want to trade you have got to have somebody to trade with.

If you want to carry your business to the ends of the world, there must be business at the ends of the world to tie in with. And if the business of the world lags, your industries lag and your prosperity lags. We have no choice but to be the servants of the world if we would be our own servants. I do not like to put it on that ground because that is not the American ground. America is ready to help the world, whether it benefits her or not. She did not come into the world, she was not created by the great men who set her government up, in order to make money out of the rest of mankind. She was set up in order to rehabilitate the rest of mankind, and the dollar of American money spent to free those who have been enslaved is worth more than a million dollars put in any American pocket.

It is in this impersonal way that I am trying to illustrate to you how the problem that we are facing in the high cost of living is the end and the beginning and a portion of a world problem, and the great difficulty, just now, my fellow citizens, is in getting some minds adjusted to the world. One of the difficulties that are being encountered about the treaty and the League of Nations, if I may be permitted to say so—and perhaps I can say so the more freely here because I do not think this difficulty exists in the mind of either senator from this state—(applause) the difficulty is not prejudice so much but that thing which is so common and so inconvenient—just downright ignorance. Ignorance, I mean, of the state of the world and of America's relation to the state of the world.

We cannot change that relation. It is a fact. It is a fact bigger than anybody of us, and one of the advantages that the United States has it ought not to forfeit; it is made up out of all the thinking peoples of the world. We do not draw our principles from any one nation; we are made up out of all the sturdy stocks of the round world. We have gotten uneasy because some other kinds of stocks tried to come in. But the bulk remains the same. We are made up out of the hard-headed, hard-fisted, practical and yet idealistic, and forward-looking peoples of the world. And we of all people ought to have an international understanding, an ability to comprehend what the problem of the world is and what part we ought to play in that problem. We have got to play our part, and we can play it either as members of the board of directors or as outside spectators. We can play it inside or on the curb, and you know how inconvenient it is to play on the curb.

There is one thing that I respect more than any other, and that is a fact. I remember, when I was Governor of the State of New Jersey, I was very urgently pressing some measures which a particular member of the Senate of the state, whom I knew and liked very much, was opposed to. His constituents were very much in favor of it, and they sent an influential committee down personally to change his vote; and after he had voted for the measure they brought him, looking a little sheepish, into my office to be congratulated. Well, he and I kept as straight faces as we could, and I congratulated him very warmly, and then with a very heavy wink he said to me behind his hand, "Governor, they never get me if I see 'em coming first."

Now, that is not a very high political principle, but I commend that principle to you with regard to facts. Never let them get you if you see them coming first. And any man with open eyes can see the facts coming, coming in serried ranks, coming in overwhelming power, not to be resisted by the United States or any other nation. The facts are marching, and God is marching with them. You cannot resist them. You must either welcome them or subsequently, with humiliation, surrender to them. It is welcome or surrender. It is acceptance of great world conditions and great world duties or scuttle now and come back afterwards.

But I am not arguing this with you, because I do not believe it is necessary in the State of Minnesota. I am merely telling you. It is like the case of the man who met two of his fellow lawyers and asked them what they were discussing. They said, "We were discussing who is the leading member of the bar of this country," and the other said, "Why, I am." They said, "How do you prove it?" He said, "I don't have to prove it, I admit it." I think that that is the state of mind of the thoughtful persons of our country, and they, thank God, are the chief portions of it, with regard to the great crisis that we are face to face with now.

It has been a privilege, gentlemen, to be permitted in this informal way to disclose to you some part of the thought which I am carrying about with me as really a great burden, because I have seen the disturbed world on the other side of the water. I know the earnest hope and beautiful confidence with which they are looking toward us, and my heart is full of the burden of it. It is a great responsibility for us to carry. We will have to have infinite intelligence and infinite diligence in business to fulfill the expectations of the peoples of the world; and yet that is our duty, our inescapable duty, and we must concert together to perform it.

Everywhere I have been on this trip the majority of the committee that has received me has consisted of Republicans, and nothing has pleased me so much, because I should be ashamed of myself if I permitted any partisan thought to enter into this great matter. If I were a scheming politician and anybody wished to present me with the peace of the world as a campaign issue, it would be very welcome, because there could be no issue easier to win on. But everybody knows that that is not a worthy thought, everybody knows that we are all Americans. Scratch a Democrat or a Republican, and underneath it is the same stuff. And the labels rub off upon the slightest effort—not the memories, the recollections; some of them are very stubborn, but it is the principle that matters. The label does not make much difference. The principle is just the same, and the only thing we differ about is the way to carry out the principle. Back of all lies that wonderful thing, that thing which the foreigner was amazed to see in the faces of our soldiers—that incomparable American spirit which you do not see the like of anywhere; that universal brightness of expression, as if every man knows there was a future and that he had something to do with molding it, instead of that dull, expressionless face which means that there is nothing but a past and a burdensome present. You do not see that in the American face. The American face mirrors the future, and, my fellow citizens, the American purpose mirrors the future of the world.

Printed in *Addresses of President Wilson*, with minor corrections from the incomplete text in the *Minneapolis Journal*, Sept. 9, 1919.

An Address in the Minneapolis Armory

September 9, 1919.

Your Honor, your Excellency,[1] my fellow countrymen: I have come here to discuss a very solemn question, and I shall have to ask your patience while you bear with me in discussing somewhat in detail the very great matter which now lies, not only before the consideration of the people of the United States, but before the consideration of the people of the world. You have heard so many little things about the treaty that perhaps you would like to hear some big things about it.

To hear some gentlemen, you would think it was an arrangement for the inconvenience of the United States, whereas, as a matter of fact, my fellow citizens, it is a world settlement, the first ever attempted, attempted upon broad lines which were first laid down in America. For, my fellow citizens, what does not seem to me realized in this blessed country of ours is the fact that the world is in revolution. I do not mean in active revolution. I mean that it is in a state of mind which may bring about the dissolution of gov-

[1] J. Edward Meyers, Republican, Mayor of Minneapolis, who had introduced Wilson. "Your Excellency" was of course Governor Burnquist.

ernments if we do not enter into a world settlement which will really in fact and in power establish justice and right.

The old order of things the rest of the world seemed to have got in some sense used to. The old order of things was not to depend upon the general moral judgment of mankind, not to base policies upon international right, but to base policies upon international power. So there were drawn together groups of nations which stood armed, facing one another, which stood drawing their power from the vitality of people who did not wish to be subordinated to them, drawing their vitality from the energy of great peoples who did not wish to devote their energy to force, but wished to devote their energy to peace. The world thought it was inevitable. This group of nations thought that it represented another set of principles, and that the best that could be accomplished in the world was this thing that they used to call the balance of power.

Notice the phrase. Not the balance that you try to maintain in a court of justice, not the scales of justice, but the scales of force— one great force balanced against another force. Every bit of the policy of the world, internationally speaking, was made in the interest of some national advantage on the part of the stronger nations of the world. It was either the advantage of Germany or the advantage of Great Britain or the advantage of Italy or the advantage of Japan. I am glad to say that I am not justified in adding that the policy of the world was ever conceived by us upon the basis of the advantage of America. We wished always to be the mediators of justice and of right, but we thought that the cool spaces of the ocean to the east and the west of us would keep us from the infections that came, arising like miasmatic mists out of that arrangement of power and of suspicion and of dread.

I believe, my fellow countrymen, that the only people in Europe who instinctively realized what was going to happen and what did happen in 1914 was the French people. It has been my privilege to come into somewhat intimate contact with that interesting and delightful people, and I realize now that, for nearly fifty years, ever since the settlement which took Alsace-Lorraine away from them in 1871, they have been living under the constant dread of the catastrophe which at last came. And their thought throughout this conference was that they must concert some measure, must draw together some kind of cooperative force, which would take this intolerable dread from their hearts, that they could not live another fifty years expecting what would come at last.

But the other nations took it lightly. There were wise men in Great Britain, there were wise men in the United States, who pointed out to us not only what they suspected, but what we all knew with regard to the preparations for the use of force in Europe. Nobody was ignorant of what Germany was doing. What we shut our eyes against deliberately was the probability that she would make the use of her preparation that she did finally make of it. Her military men published books and told us what they were going to do with it, but we dismissed them. We said: "The thing is a nightmare. The man is a crank. It cannot be that he speaks for a great government. The thing is inconceivable and cannot happen." Very well, could not it happen? Did not it happen? Are we satisfied now what the balance of power means? It means that the stronger force will sometimes be exercised or an attempt be made to exercise it to crush the other powers.

The great nations of the world have been asleep, but, God knows, the other nations have not been asleep. I have seen representatives of peoples over there who for generations through, in the dumbness of unutterable suffering, have known what the weight of those armaments and the weight of that power meant. The great Slavic people, the great Rumanian people, the people who were constantly under the pressure of that power, the great Polish people—they all knew, but they were inarticulate; there was no place in the world where they dared speak out. Now the catastrophe has come. Blood has been spilt in rivers, the flower of the European nations has been destroyed, and at last, the voiceless multitudes of men are awake, and they have made up their minds that rather than have this happen again, if the governments cannot get together, they will destroy the governments.

I am not speaking revolution, my friends. I believe that the most disastrous thing that can happen to the under man, to the man who is suffering, to the man who has not had his rights, is to destroy public order, for that makes it certain he never can get his rights. I am far from intimating that, but I am intimating this: that the people of the world are tired of every other kind of experiment except the one we are going to try. I have called it an experiment; I frankly admit that it is, but it is a very promising experiment, because there is not a statesman in the world who does not know that his people demand it. He is not going to change his mind. He is not going to change his direction. He is not speaking what he wants, it may be, but he is speaking what he knows he must speak, and that there is no turning back, that the world has turned a corner that it will never turn again. The old order is gone, and nobody can build it up again.

In the meantime, what are men doing? I want you to reflect upon this, my fellow countrymen, because this is not a speech-making occasion; this is a conference. I want you men to reflect upon what I am about to call your attention to. The object of the war was to destroy autocratic power; that is to say, to make it impossible that there should be anywhere, as there was on Wilhelmstrasse, in Berlin, a little group of military men who could brush aside the bankers, brush aside the merchants, brush aside the manufacturers, brush aside the Emperor himself, and say: "We have perfected a machine with which we can conquer the world. Now stand out of the way, we are going to conquer the world." There must not be that possibility any more. There must not be men anywhere in any private place who can plot the mastery of civilization.

But in the meantime look at the pitiful things that are happening. There is not a day goes by, my fellow citizens, that my heart is not heavy to think of our fellow beings in that great, pitiful Kingdom of Russia, without form, without order, without government. Look what they have done. They have permitted a little handful of men—I am told there are only thirty-four of them constituting the real Bolshevist government—to set up a minority government just as autocratic and just as cruelly unmerciful as the government of the Czar ever was. The danger to the world, my fellow citizens, against which we must absolutely lock the door in this country, is that some governments of minorities may be set up here as elsewhere. We will brook the control of no minority in the United States. For my own part, I would as leave live under one autocracy as another; I would as leave obey one group as another; I would as leave be the servant of one minority as another. But I do not intend to be the servant of any minority. As I have told you, the mass of men are awake. They are not going to let the world sink back into that old slough of misused authority again.

Very well, then, what are we discussing? What are we debating in the United States? Whether we will take part in guiding and steadying the world or not. And some men hesitate. It is the only country in the world whose leadership and guidance will be accepted. If we do not give it, we may look forward, my fellow citizens, to something like a generation of doubt and of disorder, which it will be impossible to pass through without the wreckage of a very considerable part of our slowly constructed civilization. America and her determinations now constitute the balance of moral force in the world, and if we do not use that moral force we will be of all peoples the most derelict. We are in the presence of this great choice, in the presence of this fundamental choice, whether we will stand by the mass of our own people and the mass of mankind.

Pick up the great volume of the treaty. It is a great volume. It is as thick as that (illustrating). You would think it just had three or four articles in it to hear some men talk about it. It is a thick volume, containing the charter of the new order of the world. I took the pains to write down here some of the things that it provides for, and if you will be patient I will read them, because I can make it more brief that way.

It provides for the destruction of autocratic power as an instrument of international control, admitting only self-governing nations to the League of Nations. Had you ever been told that before? No nation is admitted to the League of Nations whose people do not control its government. That is the reason that we are making Germany wait. She says that henceforth her people are going to control her government, but we have got to wait and see. If they do control it, she is as welcome to the League as anybody else, because we are not holding nations off. We are holding selfish groups of men off. We are not saying to peoples, "We do not want to be your comrades and serve you along with the rest of our fellow beings," but we are saying: "It depends upon your attitude. If you take charge of your own affairs, then come into the game and welcome." The League of Nations sends autocratic governments to Coventry. This is the first point.

It provides for the substitution of publicity, discussion, and arbitration for war. That is the supreme thing that it does. I will not go into details now, but every member of the League promises not to go to war until there has been a discussion and a cooling off of nine months. And, as I have frequently said on this tour, if Germany had submitted to discussion for nine days she never would have dared to go to war. Though every foreign office in Europe begged her to do so, she would not grant twenty-four hours for a meeting of the representatives of the governments of the world to ask what it was all about, because she did not dare tell what it was all about.

Nine months' cooling off is a very valuable institution in the affairs of mankind. And you have got to have a very good cause if you are willing that all your fellow men should know the whole case, for that is provided for, and talk about it for nine months. Nothing is more valuable, if you think your friend is a fool, than to induce him to hire a hall. If you think he is a fool the only way to prove it is to let him address a mass of his fellow citizens and see how they like his ideas. If they like them and you do not, it may be that you are the fools! The proof is presented at any rate.

Instead of using force after the period of discussion, something very much more effective than force is proposed, namely, an absolute boycott of the nation that does not keep its covenant. And when I say an absolute boycott, I mean an absolute boycott. There cannot be any kind of intercourse with that nation. It cannot sell or buy goods. It cannot receive or send messages or letters. It cannot have any transactions with the citizens of any member of the League. And when you consider that the League is going to consist of every considerable nation in the world, except Germany, you can see what that boycott will mean. There is not a nation in the world, except this one, that can live without importing goods for nine months, and it does not make any difference to us whether we can or not, because we always fulfill our obligations, and there will never be a boycott for us.

It provides for placing the peace of the world under constant international oversight, in recognition of the principle that the peace of the world is the legitimate and immediate interest of every nation. Why, as it stands at present, my fellow citizens, if there is likely to be trouble between two nations other than the United States, it is considered an unfriendly and hostile act for the United States to intervene. This Covenant is the right of the United States, and not the right of the United States merely, but the right of the weakest nation in the world, to bring anything that the most powerful nation in the world is doing that is likely to disturb the peace of the world under the scrutiny of mankind. (Voice in audience, "And that is right!") My friend in the audience says that is right, and it undoubtedly is, because the peace of the world is everybody's business. Yet this is the first document that ever recognized that principle.

This is an effective Covenant. It is carried out by the attitude of the Irishman who went into one of those antique institutions known as the saloon and saw two men fighting in the corner. He went up to the bartender and he said, "Is this a private fight, or can everybody get in?"

Now, in the true Irish spirit, we are abolishing private fights, and we are making it the law of mankind that it is everybody's business and everybody can get in. The consequence is that there will be no attempt at private fights.

It provides for disarmament on the part of the great fighting nations of the world.

It provides in detail for the rehabilitation of oppressed peoples, and that will remove most of the causes of war.

It provides that there shall be no more annexations of territory anywhere, but that those territories whose people are not ready to govern themselves shall be entrusted to the trusteeship of the nations that can take care of them, the trustee nation to be responsible in annual reports to the League of Nations; that is to say, to mankind in general, subject to removal and restricted in respect to anything that might be done to that population which would be to the detriment of the population itself. So that you cannot go into darkest Africa and make slaves of those poor people, as some governments at times have done.

It abolishes enforced labor. It takes the same care of the women and children of those unschooled races that we try to take of the women and children of ours. Why, my fellow citizens, this is the great human document of all time.

It provides that every secret treaty shall be invalid. It sweeps the table of all private understandings and enforces the principle that there shall be no private understandings of any kind that anybody is bound to respect. One of the difficulties in framing this treaty was that, after we got over there private—secret—treaties were springing up on all sides like a noxious growth. You had to guard your breathing apparatus against the miasma that arose from some of them. But they were treaties, and the war had been fought on the principle of the sacredness of treaties. We could not propose that solemn obligations, however unwisely undertaken, should be disregarded. But we could do the best that was possible in the presence of those understandings and then say, "No more of this; no more secret understandings." And the representative of every great nation in the world assented without demur—without the slightest difficulty.

I do not think you realize what a change of mind has come over the world. As we used to say in the old days, some men that never got it before have got religion.

It provides for the protection of dependent peoples.

It provides that high standards of labor, such as are observed in the United States, shall be extended to the workingman everywhere in the world.

It provides that all the great human instrumentalities, like the Red Cross, like the conventions against the opium trade, like the regulation of the liquor traffic with debased and ignorant people, like the prohibition of the selling of arms and ammunition to people who can use them only to their own detriment, shall be under the common direction and control of the League of Nations. Now, did you ever hear of all these things before? That is the treaty, my fellow citizens, and I can only conjecture that some of the men who are fighting the treaty either never read it themselves or are taking it for granted that you will not read it. I say without hesitation that no international agreement has ever before been drawn up along those lines—of the universal consideration of right and the interest of humanity.

Now, it is said that that is all very well, but we need not go in. Well, of course we need not. There is perfect freedom of the will. I am perfectly free to go to the top of this building and jump off, but if I do I will not take very much interest in human affairs. The nation is at liberty in one sense to do anything it pleases to discredit itself; but this is absolutely as certain as I stand here, that it never will do anything to discredit itself. Our choice in this great enterprise of mankind that I have tried to outline to you is only this: shall we go in and assist as trusted partners or shall we stay out and act as suspected rivals?

We have got to do one or the other. We have got to be either provincials or statesmen. We have got to be either ostriches or eagles. The ostrich act I see being done all around me. I see gentlemen burying their heads in something and thinking that nobody sees that they have submerged their thinking apparatus. That is what I mean by being ostriches. What I mean by being eagles I need not describe to you. I mean leaving the mists that lie close along the ground, getting upon strong wing into those upper spaces of the air where you can see with clear eyes the affairs of mankind, see how the affairs of America are linked with the affairs of men everywhere, see how the whole world turns with outstretched hands to this blessed country of ours and says, "If you will lead, we will follow." God helping us, my fellow countrymen, we will lead when they follow. The march is still long and toilsome to those heights upon which there rests nothing but the pure light of the justice of God, but the whole incline of affairs is toward those distant heights. And this great nation, in serried ranks, millions strong—presently hundreds of millions strong—will march at the fore of the great procession, breasting those heights with its eyes always lifted to the eternal goal![2]

Printed in *Addresses of President Wilson*, with corrections from the incomplete text in the *New York Times*, Sept. 10, 1919.
    [2] There is a WWT outline of this address in WP, DLC, and a WWT MS entitled "THE TREATY PROVIDES" in the T. W. Brahany Coll.

An Address in the St. Paul Auditorium

September 9, 1919.

Mr. Chairman,[1] my fellow countrymen, I am very happy that the Mayor sounded the note that he has just sounded, because by some sort of divination he realized what was in my heart tonight. I do not feel since I have left Washington this time that I am on an

    [1] That is, Laurence Curran Hodgson.

ordinary errand. I do not feel that I am on a political errand, even in the broad sense of that term. I feel rather that I am going about to hold counsel with my fellow countrymen concerning the most honorable and distinguished course which our great country can take at this turning point in the history of the world. And the Mayor was quite right when he said that this is a conference concerning the true interpretation of the American spirit. I believe, I hope without an undue touch of national pride, that it is only the American spirit that can be the true mediator of peace.

The theme that I find uppermost in my thought tonight is this: we are all actuated, my fellow countrymen, by an intense consciousness and love of America. I do not think that it is fancy on my part; it is based upon long experience that in every part of the world I can recognize an American the minute I see him. And yet that is not because we are all of one stock. We have more people of various origin than any people in the world. We come from all the great Caucasian races of the world. We are made up out of all the nations and peoples who have stood from time to time at the center of civilization. In this part of the country, it is doubtful whether in some of our great cities 50 per cent of the people come from parents born in America. One of the somewhat serious jests which I allowed myself to indulge on the other side of the water was with my Italian colleagues when they were claiming the city of Fiume upon the Adriatic because of its Italian population, and other cities scattered here and there whose surrounding population was not Italian but in whom an Italian element played an important part. I said: "That is not a sufficient argument for the extension of Italian sovereignty to these people, because there are more Italians in New York City than in any city in Italy, and I doubt if you would feel justified in suggesting that the sovereignty of Italy be extended over the city of New York." I advert to this, my fellow citizens, merely as one illustration, that could be multiplied a hundredfold, of the singular makeup of this great nation.

I do not know how it happens that we are all Americans, we are so different in origin, we are so different in memories. The memory of America does not go very far back as measured by the distances of history, and a great many millions of our people carry in their hearts the traditions of other peoples, the traditions of races never bred in America. And yet we are all unmistakably and even in appearance American, and nothing else. And there is only one possible explanation for that, my fellow citizens, and that is that there is in the practice and in the tradition of this country a set of principles which, however imperfectly, get into the consciousness of every man who lives in this country.

One of the chief elements that make an American is this, that in almost every other country there is some class that dominates, or some governmental authority that determines the course of policy, or some ancient system of land laws that limits the freedom of land tenure, or some ancient custom which puts a man into a particular groove in the land in which he lives. And there is none of that in America. Every man in America, if he behaves himself, knows that he stands on the same footing as every other man in America, and, thank goodness, we are in sight of the time when every woman will know that she stands upon the same footing. We do not have to ask anybody's leave what we shall think or what we shall do or how we shall vote. We do not have to get the approval of a class as to our behavior. We do not have to square ourselves with standards that have been followed ever since our great-grandfathers. We are much more interested in becoming great-grandfathers than in having had great-grandfathers, because our view is to the future. America does not march, as so many other peoples march, looking back over its shoulder. It marches with its eyes not only forward, but with its eyes lifted to the distances of history, to the great events which are slowly culminating, in the providence of God, in the lifting of civilization to new levels and new achievements. That is what make us Americans.

And yet I was mistaken a moment ago when I said we are nothing else, because there are a great many hyphens left in America. For my part, I think the most un-American thing in the world is a hyphen. I don't care what it is that comes before the word "American." It may be a German-American, or it may be an Italian-American, or a Swedish-American, or an Anglo-American, or an Irish-American. It don't make any difference what comes before the "American," it ought not to be there, and every man that comes to take counsel with me with a hyphen in his conversation, I take no interest in whatever. The entrance examination, to use my own parlance, into my confidence is: "Do you put America into your thoughts?" If you put it first, always first, unquestionably first, then we can sit down together and talk, but not otherwise.

Now, I want you distinctly to understand that I am not quarreling with the affectionate memories of the people who have drawn their origin from other countries. I no more blame a man for dwelling with fond affection upon the traditions of some great race not bred in America than I blame a man for remembering with reverence his mother and father and his forebears that bred him and that gave him a chance in the world. I am not quarreling with those affections; I am talking about purposes. Every purpose is for the future, and the future must be for America.

We have got to choose now, my fellow citizens, what kind of future it is going to be for America. I think that what I have said justifies me in adding that this nation was created to be the mediator of peace, because it draws its blood from every civilized stock in the world and is ready by sympathy and understanding to understand the peoples of the world—their interests, their rights, their hopes, their destiny. America is the only nation in the world that has that equipment. Every other nation is set in the mold of a particular breeding. We are set in no mold at all. Every other nation has certain prepossessions which run back through all the ramifications of an ancient history. We have nothing of the kind. We know what all peoples are thinking, and yet we, by a fine alchemy of our own, combine that thinking into an American plan and an American purpose. America is the only nation which can sympathetically lead the world in organizing peace.

Constantly, when I was on the other side of the water, delegations representing this, that, and the other peoples of Europe or of Asia came to visit me to solicit the interest of America in their fortunes. And, without exception, they were able to tell me that they had kinsmen in America. Some of them, I am ashamed to say, came from countries I had never heard of before, and yet even they were able to point, not to a handful, not to a few hundreds, but to several thousand kinsmen in America. I never before knew that they came, but they are here, and they are our interpreters—the interpreters on our behalf of the interests of the people from whom they spring.

They came to America as sort of advanced couriers of those people. They came in search of the Golden West. They came in search of the liberty that they understood reigned among that free and happy people. They were drawn by the lure of justice, by the lure of freedom, out of lands where they were oppressed, suppressed, where life was made impossible for them upon the free plane that their hearts had conceived. They said, "Yonder is our star in the West," and then the word went home: "We have found the land. They are a free people that are capable of understanding us. You go to their representatives in Paris and put your case before them, and they will understand." What a splendid thing that is, my fellow countrymen! I want you to keep this in your minds as a conception of the question that we are now called upon to decide.

You hear some men talk about the League of Nations, and you would suppose it was a trap set for America. You would suppose it was an arrangement whereby we entered into an alliance with other great powers of Europe to make war some time. But it bears no resemblance to any such description. It is a great method of

common counsel with regard for the common interests of mankind. We shall not be drawn into war; we shall be drawn into consultation, and we will be the most trusted adviser in the whole
group. Consultation, discussion, is written all over the whole face
of the Covenant of the League of Nations. For the heart of it is that
nations promise not to go to war until they have consulted, until
they have discussed, until all the facts in the controversy have
been laid before the court which represents the common opinion
of mankind.

That is the League of Nations. Nothing can be discussed there
that concerns our domestic affairs. Nothing can be discussed there
that concerns the domestic affairs of any other people, unless
something is occurring in some nation which is likely to disturb
the peace of the world. And any time any question arises which is
likely to disturb the peace of the world, then the Covenant makes
it the right of any member, strong or weak, big or little, of that
universal council of nations to bring that matter up for clarification
and discussion.

Can you imagine anything more calculated to put war off, not
only to put if off, but to make it violently improbale? When a man
wants to fight he doesn't go and discuss the matter with the other
fellow. He goes and hits him, and then somebody else has to come
in and either join the fight or break it up.

I used a very homely illustration the other night, which perhaps
it may not be amiss for me to use again. I had two friends who
were becoming more and more habitually profane. Their friends
did not like it. They not only had the fundamental scruple that it
was wrong, but they also thought, as I heard a very refined lady
say, "It was not only wrong but, what was worse, it was vulgar."
They did not like to see their friends adjourning all the rest of their
vocabulary and using only those words. So they made them enter
into a solemn agreement—I ought to say they lived in a large city—
that they would not swear inside the corporate limits; that if they
got in a state of mind which made it necessary to explode in profanity they would get out of town and swear.

The first time the passion came upon them, they recalled their
promise and they got sheepishly on a streetcar and made for the
town limits, and I need hardly tell you that, when they got there,
they no longer wanted to swear. They had cooled off. The long
spaces of the town, the people going about their ordinary business,
nobody paying any attention to them, the world seeming to be at
peace when they were at war, all brought them to a realization of
the smallness of the whole business, and they turned around and
came into town again.

Comparing great things with small, that will suffice as a picture of the advantage of discussion in international matters as well as in individual matters, because it was universally agreed on the other side of the water that if Germany had allowed the other governments to confer with her twenty-four hours about the recent war, it could not have taken place. We know why. It was an unconscionable war. She did not dare discuss it. You cannot afford to discuss a thing when you are in the wrong, and the minute you feel that the whole judgment of the world is against you, you have a different temper in affairs altogether.

This is a great process of discussion that we are entering into, and my point tonight—it is the point I want to leave with you—is that we are the people of all people in the world intelligently to discuss the difficulties of the nations which we represent, although we are Americans. We are the predestined mediators of mankind. I am not saying this in any kind of national pride or vanity. I believe that is mere historic truth, and I try to interpret circumstances in some intelligent way. If that is the kind of people we are, it must have been intended that we should make some use of the opportunities and powers that we have.

Really, then, when I hear gentlemen saying we must keep out of this thing and take care of ourselves, I think to myself: "Take care of ourselves? Where did we come from? Is there nobody else in the world that we care for? Have we no sympathies that do not run out into the great field of human experience everywhere? Is that what America is, with her mixture of blood?" Why, my fellow citizens, that is a fundamental misconception of what it is to be an American, and these gentlemen are doing a harm which they do not realize.

I want to testify to you here tonight, my fellow countrymen, because I have the means of information, that, since it has seemed to be uncertain whether we are going to play this part of leadership in the world—this part of leadership in accommodation—the old intrigues have started up in this country again. That intrigue which we universally condemn—that hyphen which looked to us like a snake, the hyphen between "German" and "American"—has reared its head again. And you hear the "his-s-s" of its purpose, and what is that purpose? It is to keep America out of the concert of nations, in order that America and Germany, being out of that concert, may some time, in their mistaken dream, unite to dominate the world, or at any rate, the one to assist the other in holding the nations of the world off while its ambitions are realized.

There is no conjecture about this, my fellow citizens. We know the former purposes of German intrigue in the country, and they are being revived. Why? We haven't reduced very materially the number of the German people, Germany remains the great power of Central Europe. She has more than 60,000,000 people now (she had nearly 70,000,000 before Poland and other provinces were taken away). She has now more than 60,000,000 people. You cannot change the temper and expectations of a people by five years of war, particularly by five years of war in which they are not conscious of the wrong they did or the wrong way in which they did it. And they are expecting the time of the revival of their power, and, along with the revival of their power goes their extraordinary capacity, their unparalleled education, their great capacity in commerce and finance and manufacture.

The German bankers and the German merchants and the German manufacturers did not want this war. They were making conquest of the world without it. They knew that it would spoil their plans, not advance them. And it has spoiled their plans, but they are there yet with their capacity, with their conception of what it is to serve the world materially and so subdue the world psychologically. All of that is still there, my fellow countrymen, and, if America stays out, then the rest of the world will have to watch Germany and watch America, and when there are two dissociated powers there is danger that they will have the same purposes.

There can be but one intelligible reason for America staying out of this, and that is that she does not want peace, that she wants war some time and the advantage which war will bring to her. And I want to say now and here that the men who think that by that thought they are interpreting America are making the sort of mistake upon which it will be useful for them to reflect in obscurity for the rest of their lives.

This is a peaceful people. This is a liberty-loving people, and liberty is suffocated by war. Free institutions cannot survive the strain of prolonged military administration. In order to live tolerable lives, you must lift the fear of war and the practice of war from the lives of nations. America is evidence of the fact that no great democracy ever entered upon an aggressive international policy. I want you to know, if you will be kind enough to read the Covenant of the League of Nations—most of the people that are arguing against it are taking it for granted that you have never read it—take the pains to read it, and you will find that no nation is admitted to the League of Nations that cannot show that it has the institutions which we call free. Nobody is admitted except the self-governing nations, because it was the instinctive judgment of every man who sat around that board that only a nation whose government was its servant and not its master could be trusted to preserve the peace of the world. There are not going to be many other kinds of nations long, my fellow citizens. The people of this world—not merely the people of America, for they did the job long ago—have determined that there shall be no more autocratic governments.

And in their haste to get rid of one of them, they set up another. I mean in pitiable Russia. I wish we could learn the lesson of Russia so that it would be burned into the consciousness of every man and woman in America. And that lesson is that nobody can be free where there is not public order and authority. What has happened in Russia is that an old and distinguished and skillful autocracy has had put in its place an amateur autocracy—a little handful of men exercising without the slightest compunction of mercy or pity the bloody terror that characterized the worst days of the Czar.

That is what must happen if you knock things to pieces. Liberty is a thing of slow construction. Liberty is a thing of universal co-operation. Liberty is a thing which you must build up by habit. Liberty is a thing which is rooted and grounded in character. And the reason I am so certain that the leadership of the world, in respect of order and progress, belongs to America is that I know that these principles are rooted and grounded in the American character.

It isn't our intellectual capacity, my fellow citizens, that has given us our place in the world, though I rate that as high as the intellectual capacity of any other people that ever lived, but it is the heart that lies back of the mind that makes America. (applause)

Ask this question to yourselves. I have no doubt this room is full of mothers and fathers and wives and sweethearts who sent their loved young men to France. What did you send them there for? What made you proud that they were going? What made you willing that they should go? Did you think they were seeking to aggrandize America some way? Did you think they were going to take something for America that had belonged to somebody else? Did you think they were going into a quarrel which they had provoked and must maintain?

The question answers itself. You were proud that they should go because they were going on an errand of self-sacrifice, in the interests of mankind. Ah, when these youngsters grow old who have come back from the fields of France, what a halo there will be about their brows! They saved the world! They are of the same stuff as those old veterans of the Civil War! They saved a nation.

Now mind you, I was born and bred in the South, but I can pay that tribute with all my heart to the men who saved the Union. It ought to have been saved. It was the greatest thing that men had conceived up to that time. Now we come to a greater thing—to the union of great nations in conference upon the interests of peace. That is the fruitage, the fine and appropriate fruitage, of what these men achieved upon the fields of France.

I saw many fine sights in Paris, many gallant sights, many sights that quickened the pulse; but my pulse never beat so fast as when I saw groups of our boys swinging along the street. They looked as if they owned something, and they did. They owned the finest thing in the world—the thing that we are going to bring to the others. They owned the ideals and conceptions that will govern the world. And on this errand that I am going about on, I feel that I am doing what I can to complete what they so gallantly began. I should feel recreant, my fellow citizens, if I did not do all that is in my power to do to complete the ideal work which those youngsters so gallantly began.

This was a war to make similar wars impossible, and merely to win this war and stop at that is to make it certain that we shall have to fight another and a final one. I hear opponents of the League of Nations say that this does not guarantee peace. No, nothing guarantees us against human passion and error. But I would like to put this business proposition to you: if it increases the probability of peace by, let us say, 10 per cent, don't you think it is worthwhile? ("Yes," cheers) And in my judgment, it increases it about 90 per cent. Henceforth the genius of the world will be devoted to accommodating the counsels of mankind and not confusing them; not supplying heat but supplying light; not putting friction into the machine, but easing the friction off and combining the parts of the great machinery of civilization so that they will run in smooth harmony and perfection.

My fellow citizens, the tasks of peace that are ahead of us are the most difficult tasks to which the human genius has ever been devoted. I will state the fundamental task, for it is the fundamental task. It is the relationship between those who toil with their hands and those who direct that toil. I will not say the relationship between capital and labor; that means something slightly different. I say the relationship between those who organize enterprise and those who make enterprise go by the skill and labor of their hands.

There is at present, to say the least, a most unsatisfactory relationship between those two, and we must devote our national genius to working out a method of association between the two which will make this nation the nation to solve triumphantly and for all time the fundamental problem of peaceful production.

You ask, "What has that got to do with the League of Nations?" I dare say that you do not know because I have never heard anybody tell you that the great charter, the new international charter, of labor is in the treaty of peace and associated with the League of Nations. A great machinery of consultation is set up there, not merely about international political affairs, but about standards of labor, about the relationships between managers and employees, about the standards of life and the conditions of labor, about the labor of women and of children, about the humane side and the business side of the whole labor problem.

And the first conference is going to sit in Washington next month; not the conference which some of you might have heard of, which I have just called of our own people, but an international conference to consider the interests of labor all over the world. I don't know—nobody knows—whether the Senate will have stopped debating by that time or not. I heard a member of the Senate say that nobody knew except God Almighty! But whether it has finished or not, the conference is going to sit, and if it has not finished, the only question that will be left unsettled is whether we are going to sit inside of it or outside of it. The conference at Paris voted, in their confidence in the American people, that the first meeting should be held in Washington and should be called by the President of the United States. They supposed in their innocence that the President of the United States represented the people of the United States. And in calling this conference, as I have called it, I am confident that I am representing the people of the United States. After I have bidden the delegates welcome, perhaps I can have a chair just outside the door and listen.

I am jesting, my fellow citizens, but there is a little sadness in the jest. Why do we wait to do a great thing? Why do we wait to fulfill the destiny of America? Why do we make it possible that anybody should think we are not coming in now, but are going to wait until later and come in with Germany? I suppose there is a certain intellectual excitement and pleasure in debate, but I do not experience any when great issues like this are pending, and I would be very sad, indeed, if I did not have an absolutely unclouded confidence in the result.

I had the great good fortune to be born an American; I have saturated myself in the traditions of our country; I have read all the great literature that interprets the spirit of our country; and, when I read my own heart with regard to these great purposes, I feel confident that it is a sample American heart. Therefore I have the most unbounded confidence in the result. All that is needed is that you should be vocal and audible. I know what you want. Say it and get it. I am your servant; all the men elected to go to Washington are your servants. It is not our privilege to follow our private convictions. It is our duty to represent your convictions and execute your purposes, and therefore all that is needed is a consciousness. Tell me that you do not want to do what I am urging and I will go home. (Cries of "No" and "Go to it." The crowd rose and cheered.) But tell me, as your faces and your voices tell me, that you do want what I want, and I will be heartened for the rest of my journey. And I will say to the folks all the way from here to the Pacific, "Minnesota is up and on her tiptoes and behind you. Let's all of us get in the great team which is to redeem the destinies of mankind."

Our fathers of the Revolutionary age had a vision, my fellow citizens. There were only 3,000,000 Americans then, in a little strip of settlements on the Atlantic coast. Now the great body of American citizens extends from ocean to ocean, more than a hundred millions strong. These are the people of whom the founders of the republic were dreaming—those great hosts of free men and women who should come in the future and who should say to all the world: "Here are the testaments of liberty. Here are the principles of freedom. Here are the things which we must do in order that mankind may be released from the intolerable things of the past."

And there came a day at Paris when representatives of all the great governments of the world accepted the American specifications upon which the terms of the treaty of peace were drawn. Shall we have our treaty, or shall we have somebody else's? (shouts of "ours!" "ours") Shall we keep the primacy of the world, or shall we abandon it?[2]

Printed in *Addresses of President Wilson*, with corrections from the incomplete texts in the *New York Times*, Sept. 10, 1919; the *Minneapolis Journal*, Sept. 10, 1919; and the *Minneapolis Morning Tribune*, Sept. 10, 1919.
    [2] There is a WWT outline of this address in WP, DLC.

From John Fitzpatrick and Others

Washington D C 715 PM Sept 9 1919

Secretary Tumultys telegram of September fifth to Samuel Gompers was read today at the meeting of the presidents of the twenty four international unions in the steel industry and given the most careful consideration stop After a long and earnest discussion of it the undersigned were instructed to wire you requesting a more definite statement as to the possibility of an early conference being arranged by your efforts between the heads of the United States Steel Corporation and of the unions involved stop The conditions in the industry are steadily growing worse with large numbers of union men being discharged and otherwise discriminated against and abused and it will be impossible to hold our men much longer from defending themselves by striking unless some genuine relief of [is] vouchsafed them stop Our meeting will remain in session here for forty eight hours awaiting your reply before taking final action stop Please send answer to John Fitzpatrick Chairman of National Committee American Federation of Labor Building Washington D C

John Fitzpatrick, M F Tighe, Wm Hannon, Wm Z Foster

T telegram (WP, DLC).

Bernard Mannes Baruch to Cary Travers Grayson

From Baruch, for Dr. Grayson: The White House, Sept. 9, 1919

I have seen Gary, who says he regrets more than he can say that he is unable to change his position and he regrets it more because the request comes from a man for whom he has such great respect. He furthermore stated that if the President knew all the facts, he would be in agreement.[1]

If Gary persists in this attitude, and I think he will, a most embarrassing position might result, because it would bring acutely to the front at this time a new issue which our enemies would use to embarrass the League of Nations fight. I am wondering whether the President could not say to the workers that in view of the coming conference[2] only about two weeks off and the truce he has asked for, that the matter be deferred until after the forthcoming conference where it is hoped that a solution may be found for problems of this very character. The President can take this position in all similar cases of which doubtless there will be others.

T telegram (WP, DLC).
    [1] There are no documents or other materials in the B. M. Baruch Papers, NjP, relating to this meeting.
    [2] That is, the Industrial Conference scheduled to meet on October 6. See WBW to WW, Aug. 30, 1919 (first letter of that date), and WW to S. Gompers, Sept. 3, 1919, both in Vol. 62.

Bernard Mannes Baruch to Joseph Patrick Tumulty

The White House, Sept. 9, 1919

Baruch telephones following from New York:

"Have had long conference with Gompers this morning. We discussed at length police situation in Washington, which I understand is as follows:

"American Federation of Labor gave notice a short time ago that the Federation would give Police organizations charter. They have had about thirty-five applications, of which one was from the Washington police force. I understand this was given with the proviso that there should be no strike and that they would obey the commands of the Police Department in protecting life and property. The District Commissioners have ruled that all members have to resign from organizations with Labor Federation charter or lose positions. Injunction has been asked by the Police Organization and is to be argued Thursday. Not aware of the Commissioners' side of the story; therefore cannot give full facts. Would it be possible for District Commissioners to await result of conference and keep things in status quo until after conference. Gompers says, if this is done, and Labor is asked to hold in abeyance all disputes, including steel matter, until conference is held, he will use influence to have all differences held over until that time. This appears wise and would postpone all discussion until after the conference, when it is possible that a broad solution may be found to cover all such questions. This is in line with my telegram of today. Gompers' attitude is not in the least threatening, and I feel he wants to be helpful, but he is alarmed at police situation in Washington."

Forster

T telegram (WP, DLC).

Joseph Patrick Tumulty to Louis Brownlow[1]

[St. Paul, Sept. 9, 1919]

The President suggests the great advisability of postponing any issue regarding the police situation until after the forthcoming conference at Washington, and hopes that the postponement can be effected.   J. P. Tumulty

T telegram (WP, DLC).
    [1] District commissioner in charge of the police.

Rudolph Forster to Joseph Patrick Tumulty

The White House, Sept. 9, 1919

Gus Karger asks me to send the following:

"Lodge is trying to make it appear that his reservation X differs but little from the mild reservation offered by the McCumber group.[1] Chairman Hays[2] seems to be aiding him by his statement that it is unanimously supported by the Republicans. The situation, however, is unchanged. McCumber, McNary, Colt, Nelson,

Kellogg and Lenroot are standing firm. I hope nothing will be said which may tend to offend any of the mild reservationists. More Democrats are turning to the mild reservations, and whenever the proper moment arrives and the word is given, a compromise seems inevitable. All amendments, I am advised, are sure to be beaten; also that the treaty, without mild reservations, does not command enough votes."

Billy Cochran[3] advises that a Democratic editor from Utah tells him that the principal cause of criticism of the League in the West is the thought that Great Britain has six votes to one for the United States, and suggests that the President either in Utah or before reaching there answer that criticism. Thinks such answer will have fine effect throughout the West.   Forster.

T telegram (WP, DLC).
    [1] For the text of which, see the news report printed at Aug. 2, 1919, Vol. 62.
    [2] That is, Will H. Hays.
    [3] William Joseph Hamilton Cochran, at this time Washington correspondent for the *St. Louis Republic*. He had worked for the Democratic National Committee in 1916 and became its Director of Publicity in 1920.

William Phillips to Frank Lyon Polk

Washington September 9, 1919.

VERY URGENT. RUSH.

3068 Personal for Polk from Phillips.

Your 3975, August 31, 11 p.m.,[1] 4065, September 5, 11 p.m.[2] and 4104, September 8, 6 p.m.[3] bring up the whole Thracian question.

The President has indicated that while on his trip he does not wish to have submitted to him any matters that do not require an immediate decision.

You will appreciate the great burden which would be imposed upon the President if he is required to consider this question while travelling, particularly in view of the absence of maps which can only be supplied to him by courier.

Under these circumstances and in view of Item Four of your 4102, September 8, 5 p.m.[4] quoting Section 3, Article 48 of the Treaty with Bulgaria, do you think it possible that the consideration by the President of the Thracian question might be deferred until his return from his trip at the end of this month?

If possible an immediate reply is requested as pending your reply I am deferring communication with the President on this subject.

Phillips Acting.

TS telegram (SDR, RG 59, 763.72119/6453, DNA).

[1] FLP to RL, Aug. 31, 1919, Vol. 62.
[2] FLP to RL, Sept. 5, 1919.
[3] FLP to WW and RL, Sept. 8, 1919.
[4] "4. The Council approved the following article for insertion in the Treaty with Bulgaria (Section III, Article 48):

"Quote Bulgaria renounces, in favor of the Principal Allied and Associated Powers, all her rights and titles in the territory of Thrace which belongs to the Bulgarian Monarchy and which, situated beyond the new frontiers of Bulgaria as they are described in Articles 27-30, part II (Frontiers of Bulgaria) are at present assigned to no country.

"Bulgaria undertakes to recognize the provisions that the Principal Allied and Associated Powers shall make concerning this territory, notably concerning the nationality of the inhabitants.

"The Principal Allied and Associated Powers undertake that the freedom of the economic outlets of Bulgaria to the Aegean Sea be guaranteed.

"The conditions of this guarantee shall be fixed later. unquote" FLP to RL, Sept. 8, 1919, T telegram (SDR, RG 256, 180.03501/48, DNA).

From the Diary of Dr. Grayson

Wednesday, September 10, 1919.

Leaving St. Paul at 10:00 o'clock last night, the Presidential Special wound its way across North Dakota's prairies until 11:00 o'clock, when Bismarck, the Capital, was reached. The trip was uneventful. Very few houses could be seen from the car windows, and miles and miles of wheat land stretched away in an unchanged vista. The President spent most of the time trying to rest. He was very tired as the result of his exertions of yesterday, and, in addition, he had again suffered from a recurrence of the headache which has been troubling him for some little time.

Bismarck was reached at 11:00 o'clock, and a brief street parade was held prior to the regular meeting. The meeting place was the Bismarck Theatre, and although it was a fairly large auditorium, it was far too small to accommodate the crowd that wanted to see and hear the President.[1] This was the home of the radical Farmers' Non-Partisan League, and the President devoted a good part of his speech to a characterization of the right and the wrong kinds of radicalism. He again referred to the situation in Russia and declared that the people of the United States could do nothing for that unfortunate nation until it had purged itself of the leaders who were far worse than the Czar ever had been.

After the meeting the President was taken to the Country Club, where he could get a sight of the prairies. The Country Club is situated on a little hill just outside of the city of Bismarck and from it the President was able to see the old fort[2] from which General Custer started on the last expedition which had its unhappy termination in the massacre of the Little Big Horn. The sluggish headwaters of the Missouri River were pointed out to the President and he was told that the River was lower then than it had ever been in the memory of man. A number of former well-known frontiers-men were in the party that greeted the President here, including several Indian chiefs.

After leaving the Country Club, the party proceeded to the State Capitol, where the log cabin formerly occupied by Colonel Theodore Roosevelt at Medora[3] has been erected. This was pointed out to the President, as was the figure-head taken from the Cruiser NORTH DAKOTA[4] that has been mounted on a big slab of marble and placed as a permanent monument just outside of the Capitol grounds.

The President returned to the train shortly before 1:00 o'clock, leaving at 1:00 o'clock for Billings, Montana.

[1] The *New York Times*, Sept. 11, 1919, reported that the auditorium held about 1,500 persons and that there were possibly 15,000 people from Bismarck and surrounding districts who had come to the city to see Wilson.

[2] Fort Abraham Lincoln.

[3] Roosevelt had spent a part of each year from 1884 to 1887 at a cattle ranch called Maltese Cross or Chimney Butte, in which he had a sizable financial investment, located near the village of Medora, in the present Billings County, North Dakota.

[4] Actually a battleship, launched in 1908 and commissioned in 1910, which remained in service until decommissioned in 1923.

An Address at Bismarck

September 10, 1919.

Governor Frazier,[1] my fellow countrymen: I esteem it a great privilege to stand in your presence and to continue the discussion that I have been attempting in other parts of the country of the great matter which is pending for our determination. I say it is pending for our determination, because, after all, it is a question for the men and women of the United States. I believe that the gentlemen at Washington are trying to assess the opinion of the United States and trying to express it.

It seems very strange from day to day, as I go about, that I should be discussing the question of peace. It seems very strange that, after six months spent in Paris, where the minds of more than twenty nations were brought together and where, after the most profound consideration of every question and every angle of every question concerned, an extraordinary agreement should have been reached, an extraordinary concurrence of minds should have been reached, and that, while every other country concerned has stopped debating the thing, America is debating it.

It seems very strange to me, my fellow countrymen, because, as

[1] Lynn Joseph Frazier, Governor of North Dakota, supported by both the Republican party and the Nonpartisan League.

a matter of fact, we are debating the question of peace or war. There is only one way to have peace, and that is to have it by the concurrence of the minds of the world. America can't bring about peace by herself. No other nation can bring about peace by itself. The agreement of a small group of nations cannot bring about peace.

The world is not at peace. It is not, except in certain disturbed quarters, actually using military means of war, but the mind of the world is not at peace. The mind of the world is waiting for the verdict, and the verdict they are waiting for is this: shall we have in the future the same dangers, the same suspicions, the same distractions, and shall we expect that, out of these dangers and distractions, armed conflict will arise? Or shall we expect that the world will be willing to sit down at the conference table to talk the thing over; to delay all use of force until the world is willing to express its judgment on the matter at issue? Because if this be not the solution, if the world is not to substitute discussion for war, then the world is not now in a state of mind to have peace, even for the time being.

While victory has been won, my fellow countrymen, it is won only over the force of a particular group of nations. It has not been won over the passions of those nations, but over the passions of the nations that were set against us. This treaty, which I have brought back with me, is a great world settlement, and it tries to deal with some of the elements of passion which were likely at any time to blaze out in the world, and now have blazed out and set the world on fire.

The trouble was at the heart of Europe. At the heart of Europe there were suffering peoples, inarticulate but with hearts on fire against the iniquities practiced against them; held in the grip of military power, submitting to nothing but force; their spirits insurgent. And so long as that condition existed, there could not be the expectation of continued peace. And this great settlement at Paris for the first time in the world considered the cry of the people and did not listen to the pleas of governments. It did not listen to dynastic claims. It did not read over the whole story of rival territorial ambitions, but it said: "The door is closed on that. These lands belong to the stocks, the ancient stocks, of people that live upon them. We are going to give them to those people. The land always should have been yours; it is now yours, and you can govern it as you please."

That is the principle that is at the heart of this treaty, but if that principle cannot be maintained, then there will ensue from the passions in the hearts of those peoples a despair which will bring

about universal chaos. Men in despair do not construct governments. Men in despair destroy governments. Men whose whole affairs are so upset, whose whole systems of living are so disrupted
that they cannot get food, that they cannot get clothing, that they
cannot turn to any authority that can give them anything certain—
they cannot construct governments. There are words of a preacher
that interested me very deeply, on the sequence of the petitions in
the Lord's Prayer. He called attention to the fact that the first petition was, "Give us this day our daily bread," and he pointed out
that our Saviour probably knew better than anybody else that a
man cannot serve God or his fellow men on an empty stomach,
that he has got to be physically sustained. When a man has got an
empty stomach, most of all when those he loves are starving, he is
not going to serve anybody, he is going to serve himself by the
quickest way he can find.

Now you say, "What has this got to do with the adoption by the
United States Senate of the treaty of peace?" It has this to do with
it, my fellow citizens, that the whole world is waiting upon us, and
if we stay out of it, if we qualify our assent in any essential way,
the world will say, "Then there can be no peace, for that great nation in the West is the only makeweight which will hold these
scales steady." I hear counsels of selfishness uttered. I hear men
say, "Very well, let us stay out and take care of ourselves and let
the rest of the world take care of itself." I do not agree with that
from the point of view of sentiment. I would be ashamed to agree
with it from the point of view of sentiment, and I think I have intelligence enough to know that it would not work, even if I wanted
it to work.

Are we disconnected from the rest of the world? Take a single
item. If Europe is disordered, who is going to buy wheat? There is
more wheat produced in this country than we can consume and
more foodstuffs, and there will be no market that anybody can
count upon until there is a settled peace. Men are not going to buy
until they know what is going to happen tomorrow, for the reason
that they cannot get any money amidst a disordered organization
of industry and in the absence of those processes of credit which
keep business going.

We have managed in the process of civilization, my fellow citizens, to make a world that cannot be taken to pieces. The pieces
are intricately dovetailed and fitted with one another, and unless
you assemble them as you do, the intricate parts of a great machine, the pieces won't work. I believe that, with the exception of
the United States, there is not a country in the world that could
live without imports. There are only one or two countries that can

live without importing foodstuffs. There are no countries that I know of that can live in their ordinary way without importing manufactured goods and raw materials—raw materials of many kinds.

Take that great kingdom, for example, for which I have the greatest admiration—the great Kingdom of Italy. There are great factories there, but they have to get all the raw material that they manufacture from the outside. There is no coal in Italy, no fuel. They have to get all their coal from outside. And, at the present moment, because the world is holding its breath and waiting, the great coal fields of Central Europe are not producing except to about 40 per cent of their capacity. So that the coal in Silesia and the coal in Bohemia is not being shipped out, and industries are checked and chilled and drawn in, and starvation comes nearer, unemployment becomes more and more universal.

At this moment there is nothing brought to my attention more often at Washington than the necessity for shipping out our fuel and our raw materials to start the world again. If we do not start the world again, then we check and stop to that extent our own industries and our exports, of course. You cannot disentangle the United States from the rest of the world. If the rest of the world goes bankrupt, the business of the United States is in a way to be ruined.

I do not like to put the thing upon this basis, my fellow citizens, because this is not the American basis. America was not founded to make money; it was founded to lead the world on the way to liberty, and now, while we debate, all the rest of the world is saying: "Why does America hesitate? We want to follow her. We shall not know which way to go unless she leads. We want the direction of her business genius. We want the suggestion of her experience, and she hesitates. She does not know whether she wants to go in or not." Oh, while she does, my fellow citizens, some among us do not know whether we must go in or not.

But we know. (applause) There is no more danger of the American people staying out of this great thing than there is of our reversing all the precedents of our history, forgetting all the blood that has been spilled, so much precious blood, to the state. But, in the meantime, the delay is endangering the whole world and us, of course, along with the rest, because we are a very big and, in my opinion, an extremely important part of the world.

I have told many times, but I must tell you again, of the experience that I had in Paris. Almost every day of the week that I was not imperatively engaged otherwise I was receiving delegations. Delegations from where? Not merely groups of men from France and other nearby regions, but groups of men from all over the world, as I have several times admitted, from some parts of the world that I never heard the names of before. I do not think they were in my geography when I was in school. If they were, I had forgotten them. Did you ever hear of Azerbaijan, for example? A very dignified group of fine-looking men came in from Azerbaijan. I did not dare ask them where it was, but I looked it up secretly afterwards and found that it was a very prosperous valley region lying south of the Caucasus and that it had a great and ancient civilization.

I knew from what these men said to me that they knew what they were talking about, though I did not know anything about their affairs. They knew, above all things else, what America stood for. And they had come to me, figuratively speaking, with outstretched hands and said, "We want the guidance and the help and the advice of America." And they all said that, until my heart grew fearful, and I said to one group of them: "I beg that you will not expect the impossible. America cannot do the things that you are asking her to do. We will do the best we can. We will stand as your friends. We will give you every sort of aid that we can give you, but please do not expect the impossible." They believe that America can work miracles merely by being America and asserting the principles of America throughout the globe. And that kind of assertion, my fellow citizens, is the process of peace, and that is the only possible process of peace.

When I say, therefore, that I have come here this morning actually to discuss the question with you whether we shall have peace or war, you may say, "There is no war; the war is over." The fighting is over, but there is not peace, and there cannot be peace without the assistance of America. The assistance of America comes just at the center of the whole thing that was planned in Paris. You have heard some men talk about separating the Covenant of the League of Nations from the treaty.

I intended to bring a copy of the treaty with me. It is a volume as thick as that, and the very first thing in it is the League of Nations Covenant. By common consent, that was put first, because by common consent that is the only thing that will make the rest of the volume work. That was not the opinion at the beginning of the conference. There were a great many cynics on that side of the water who smiled indulgently when you spoke hopefully of drawing the nations together in a common concert of action, but before we got through there was not a man who hadn't come, as a hard, practical judgment, to the conclusion that we couldn't do without it, that you couldn't make a world settlement without setting up an organization that would see that it was carried out, and that you couldn't compose the mind of the world unless that settlement included an arrangement by which discussion should be substituted for war.

If the war we have just had had been preceded by discussion, it never would have happened. Every foreign office in Europe urged through its Minister at Berlin that no action should be taken until there should be an international conference of other governments and learn what if any processes of mediation they might propose. And Germany did not dare delay it for twenty-four hours. If she had, she never would have gone into it. You daren't lay a bad case before mankind. You daren't kill the young men of the world for a dishonest purpose. And we have let thousands of our lads go to their death in order to convince, not Germany merely, but any other nation that may have in the back of its thought a similar enterprise, that the world doesn't mean to permit any iniquity of that sort. And if it had been displayed as an iniquity in open conference for not less than nine months, as the Covenant of the League of Nations provides, it never could have happened.

And when your attention is called to certain features of this treaty—the only features to which your attention ever is called by those who are opposed to it—you are left with the impression that it is an arrangement by which war is just on the hair trigger. You are constantly told about Article X. Now, Article X has no operative force in it unless we vote that it shall operate. I will tell you what Article X is—I think I can repeat it almost verbatim. Under Article X every member of the League undertakes to respect and preserve the territorial integrity—to protect and preserve as against external aggression—the territorial integrity and the existing political independence of the other members of the League. So far so good. The second sentence provides that, in case of necessity, the Council of the League shall advise what steps are necessary to carry out the obligations of that promise; that is to say, what force is necessary, if any. Now the Council cannot give that advice without a unanimous vote. It can't give the advice, therefore, without the affirmative vote of the United States, unless the United States is a party to the controversy in question.

Let us see what that means. Do you think that the United States is likely to seize somebody else's territory? Do you think that the United States is likely to disregard the first sentence of the article? And if she is not likely to begin an aggression of that sort, who is likely to begin it against her? Is Mexico going to invade us and appropriate Texas? Is Canada going to come down with her nine or ten millions and overwhelm the hundred millions of the United States? Who is going to grab our territory, and, above all things else, who is going to propose, who is going to entertain the idea, after the rest of the world has said, "No; we are all pledged to see that you don't do that."

But suppose that somebody does attempt to grab our territory, or that we do attempt to grab somebody else's territory? Then the war is ours anyhow. So what difference does it make what advice the Council gives? So that unless it is our war, we can't be dragged into a war without our own consent. If that is not an open and shut security, I don't know of any. And yet that is Article X.

I don't recognize this Covenant when I hear some other men talking about it. I spent hours and hours in the presence of the representatives of thirteen other nations examining every sentence of it, up and down and crosswise, and tried to keep out of it anything that interfered with the essential sovereignty of any member of the League. I carried over with me in March all the suggestions made by the Foreign Relations Committee of the Senate, and they were all accepted. And yet I come back and find that I don't understand what the document means. And I am told that plain sentences, which I thought were written in unmistakable language, mean something that I never heard of and that nobody else ever entertained as a purpose.

But whatever you may think of Article X, my fellow citizens, it is the heart of the treaty. You either have got to take it or you have got to throw the world back into that old contest over land titles, which would upset the state of North Dakota or any other part of the world.

Suppose there were no guarantee of any land titles in North Dakota! I can fancy how every farmer and every man with a city lot would go armed. He would hire somebody, if he was too sleepy to sit up all night, to see that nobody trespassed and took squatter's possession of his unsecured land.

And we have been trying to do something analogous to that with the territories of Europe—to fix land titles, and, then having fixed them, we have got to have Article X. Under Article X these titles are established, and we all join to guarantee their maintenance. There is no other way to quiet the world, and if the world is not quieted, then America is sooner or later involved in the maelstrom. My fellow citizens, we sometimes forget what a powerful nation the United States is. Do you suppose we can ask the other nations of the world to forget that we are out of the arrangement? Do you suppose that we can stay out of the arrangement without being suspected and intrigued against and hated by all the rest of them? And do you think that that is an advantageous basis for international transactions? Any way you take this question, you are led straight around to this alternative—either this treaty with this Covenant or a disturbed world and certain war. There is no escape from it.

America recalls, I am sure, all the assurances that she has given to the world in the years past. Some of the very men who are now opposing this peace Covenant were most eloquent in support of an international government which would be carried to the point where the exercise of independent sovereignty would be almost stopped. They put it into measures of Congress. Last November, in the naval appropriation bill, by unanimous vote of the committee, they put in the provision that, after the building program had been authorized by Congress, the President could cancel any of it the moment he had been able to induce the other governments of the world to set up an international tribunal which would settle international difficulties.[2] They actually had the matter so definitely in mind that they authorized the President not to carry out an act of Congress with regard to the building of great ships if he could get an arrangement similar to the arrangement which I have now laid before them, because their instinctive judgment is, my instinctive judgment and yours is, that we have no choice, if we want to stop war but to take the steps that are necessary to stop it.

And if we don't enter into this Covenant, what is our situation? Our situation is exactly the situation of Germany herself, except that we are not disarmed and Germany is disarmed. We have joined with the rest of the world to defeat the purpose that Germany had in mind. We now hesitate to sign the treaty that is supposed to disarm Germany. She is disarmed, nevertheless, because the other nations will enter into it. And there is planted in their heart, planted in the hearts of those 60,000,000 people, maybe the thought that, some day, by gathering their forces and a change of circumstances, they may have another chance. And the only other nation that they can look to is the United States. The United States has repudiated the treaty. The United States has said: "Yes, we sent 2,000,000 men over there to accomplish this, but we do not like it now and we will not guarantee it. We are going to set up such a situation that some day we may send 2,000,000 more men over there. We promised the mothers and the fathers and the wives and the sweethearts that those men were fighting there that these

[2] Actually, the House Naval Affairs Committee had voted on January 31, 1919, to report a naval appropriation bill which included the provision that Wilson referred to. See JD to WW, Jan. 31, 1919, n. 1, Vol. 54. The naval appropriation bill of 1918 died with the expiration of the Sixty-fifth Congress on March 3, 1919. The provision just mentioned repeated, with some minor changes, the one included in the Naval Appropriation Act of 1916. For the text of this earlier version, see R. Forster to JPT, Sept. 11, 1919.

things should not happen again, but we are going to arrange it so that it may happen again." And so the two nations that will stand and play a lone hand in the world would be Germany and the United States.

I am not saying this to you, my fellow citizens, because I believe it is likely. I know it is not. I am not in the least troubled about that, but I do want you to share fully with me the thought that I have brought back from Europe. I know what I am talking about when I say that America is the only nation whose guarantee will suffice to substitute discussion for war, and I rejoice in the circumstance. I rejoice that the time has come when America can fulfill her destiny. Her destiny was expressed much more in her open doors when she said to the oppressed all over the world: "Come and join us. We will give you freedom. We will give you opportunity. We have no governments that can act as your masters. Come and join us to conduct a free government which is our own." And they came in thronging millions, and their genius was added to ours; their sturdy capacity multiplied and increased the capacity of the United States. And now, with the blood of every great people in our veins, we turn to the rest of the world and say: "We still stand ready to redeem our promise. We still believe in liberty. We still mean to exercise every force that we have and, if need be, spend every dollar that is ours to vindicate the standards of justice and of right."

It is a noble purpose. It is a noble principle. My pulses quicken at the thought of it. I am glad to have lived in a day when America can redeem her pledges to the world, when America can prove that her leadership is the leadership that leads out of these age-long troubles, these age-long miseries, into which the world will not sink back, but which, without our assistance, it may struggle out of only through a long period of bloody revolution.

The peoples of Europe are in a revolutionary frame of mind. They do not believe in the things that have been practiced upon them in the past, and they mean to have new things practiced.

In the meantime, they are, some of them, like pitiful Russia, in danger of doing a most extraordinary thing—substituting one kind of autocracy for another. Russia repudiated the Czar, who was cruel at times, and set up her present masters, who are cruel all the time and pity nobody, who seize everybody's property and feed only the soldiers that are fighting for them. And now, according to the papers, they are likely to brand every one of those soldiers so that he may not easily, at any rate, escape their clutches and desert. Branding their servants and making slaves of a great and lovable people! There is no people in the world fuller of the naive sentiments of good will and of fellowship than the people of Russia, and they are in the grip of a cruel autocracy that, in spite of the challenge of every friendly government of Europe to do so, they dare not have an election and assemble a constituent assembly. They dare not appeal to the people. They know that their mastery would end the minute the people took charge of their own affairs.

Do not let us expose any of the rest of the world to the necessity of going through any such terrible experiences as that, my fellow citizens. We are at present helpless to assist Russia, because there are no responsible channels through which we can assist her. Our heart goes out to her, but the world is in disorder, and while it is in disorder—here we debate![3]

Printed in *Addresses of President Wilson*, with a few corrections from the complete text in the *Bismarck Daily Tribune*, Sept. 11, 1919, and the incomplete text in the *New York Times*, Sept. 11, 1919.

[3] There is a WWT outline of this address in WP, DLC.

An Address from the Rear Platform at Mandan, North Dakota

[[September 10, 1919]]

I am glad to get out to see the real folks, to feel the touch of their hands, and know, as I have come to know, how the nation stands together in the common purpose to complete what the boys did who carried their guns with them over the sea. We may think that they finished that job, but they will tell you they did not; that unless we see to it that peace is made secure, they will have the job to do over again, and we, in the meantime, will rest under a constant apprehension that we may have to sacrifice the flower of our youth again. The whole country has made up its mind that it shall not happen. And presently, after a reasonable time is allowed for unnecessary debate, we will get out of this period of doubt and unite the whole force and influence of the United States to steady the world in the lines of peace. And it will be the proudest thing and finest thing that America ever did. She was born to do these things, and now she is going to do them.

I am very much obliged to you for coming out.

Printed in the *Billings*, Mont., *Gazette*, Sept. 11, 1919.

A News Report

[*Sept. 10, 1919*]

On Board President Wilson's Special Train, Sept. 10. Ten points in the peace treaty were defined by President Wilson tonight as the fundamental principles on which he is asking its acceptance by the United States.

Riding westward into Montana at the end of the first week of his speech-making tour, the president made no stop for a night address, but instead made known through the newspaper correspondents the platform he desires to place before the people in his plea for the treaty's acceptance.

A few hours earlier he told a crowd at Mandan, N. D., that his week of travel had convinced him that the people were for the treaty. The 10 points on which he epitomises the treaty provisons are as follows:

One—The destruction of autocratic power as an instrument of international control admitting only self-gover[n]ing nations to the league.

Two—The substitution of public discussion and arbitration for war, using the boycott rather than arms.

Three—Placing the peace of the world under constant international oversight in recognition of the principle that the peace of the world is the legitimate immediate interest of every state.

Four—Disarmament.

Five—The liberation of oppressed peoples.

Six—The discontinuance of annexation and the substitution of trusteeship with responsibility to the opinion of mankind.

Seven—The invalidation of all secret treaties.

Eight—The protection of dependent peoples.

Nine—High standards of labor under international sanction.

Ten—The international co-ordi[n]ation of humane reform and regulation.

Printed in the *Billings*, Mont., *Gazette*, Sept. 11, 1919.

Joseph Patrick Tumulty to Samuel Gompers

[Bismarck, ? Sept. 10, 1919]

In view of the difficulty of arranging any present satisfactory mediation with regard to the steel situation, the President desires to urge upon the steel men, through you, the wisdom and desirability of postponing action of any kind until after the forthcoming industrial conference at Washington.   (Signed)   J. P. Tumulty.

Printed in the *New York Times*, Sept. 11, 1919.

Joseph Patrick Tumulty to John Fitzpatrick

[Bismarck ?] September 10, 1919.

The President has not as yet received any final word in the matter to which you refer.[1] He is still hoping it will be favorable.

J. P. Tumulty.

T telegram (WP, DLC).
[1] See J. Fitzpatrick *et al.* to WW, Sept. 9, 1919.

Joseph Patrick Tumulty to Rudolph Forster

Dickinson N Dak [Sept. 10, 1919]

Please wire if provision in naval act approved August 29th 1916 declaring it to be the policy of the United States to settle international disputes through arbitration and providing for calling of conference to consider disarmament was continued in naval bills of 1917 1918 or 1919. If not has Congress enacted any similar provision since 1916? And if so when. If so please send text. Impossible to tell until we reach San Francisco whether President can motor to San Jose. Will have to consider time and how greatly he is fatigued. We will motor about fourteen miles from Rathdrum to Coeur d'Alene. Railroad officials advise tracks wont carry this heavy train. Fine meeting at St Paul last night. Everything satisfactory.   J P Tumulty.

T telegram (WP, DLC).

Joseph Patrick Tumulty to Newton Diehl Baker

[Bismarck ?] September 10, 1919.

Can you send me for use in President's speeches approximate figures of cost of war to allies and entente powers and the United States, approximate figures as to dead and wounded on both sides. I recall a speech you made some months ago which contains a statement about the cost of war. Please send me by telegraph any information you have touching upon these matters. We are having great meetings. What is your reaction on President's speeches.

J. P. Tumulty.

T telegram (WP, DLC).

Joseph Patrick Tumulty to Russell Cornell Leffingwell

[Bismarck ?] 10 September 1919.

Will appreciate any advice or suggestions you have on trip. What is your reaction on it?   J P Tumulty.

T telegram (WP, DLC).

From Thomas William Lamont

Dear Mr. President   North Haven, Maine. Sept. 10 [1919]

For your information, I attach herewith copy of my statement (which you were good enough to approve)[1] as it finally appeared in the press. I have already begun to receive a large number of letters from known and unknown correspondents, warmly approving the statement.

The New York Tribune, as you may have noted, is beginning to hedge very strongly in its support of the Lodge type. In fact, it is against him, as witness the enclosed editorial from a recent issue.

Let me congratulate you upon the series of speeches which you are delivering. They must have their effect upon the country & thus upon the Senate. Though facts seem to have little impression upon some of our Senators.

Sometime after your return to Washington I should be privileged if I could claim a few moments of your time to follow up the talk that we had on the George Washington in reference to Mexico. With the conciliatory disposition which Carranza seems now to be showing, it seems to me that the great investment interests of America, Great Britain & France ought to be able to unite on a policy that would assist Carranza & minimize the pressure for intervention which is coming from some quarters.

Please give cordial regards from Mrs Lamont & me to Mrs. Wilson & the other members of your family. Always with deep regard,
Very Sincerely Yours   Thomas W. Lamont

ALS (WP, DLC).
[1] See T. W. Lamont to WW, Aug. 25, 1919, and WW to TWL, Aug. 29, 1919, both in Vol. 62. Lamont released his statement to the press on September 7. It is printed in the *New York Times*, Sept. 8, 1919.

To William Phillips

[Bismarck ?] 10 September, 1919

Very glad to accord to the King and Queen of Belgium the use of the Mayflower as suggested.[1] Will postpone decision with regard to other question in your message until after my return to Washington.   Woodrow Wilson

T telegram (WP, DLC).
[1] Wilson was replying to W. Phillips to WW, Sept. 8, 1919.

From Désiré Félicien François Joseph Cardinal Mercier

New York, Sept. 10 [1919].

Remembering your kind visit Malines beg to express you my respectful and cordial greetings on landing on American soil.
                                Cardinal Mercier.

T telegram (WP, DLC).

Frank Lyon Polk to William Phillips

Paris September 10, 1919

URGENT 4142 Confidential for Phillips from Polk. Your 3068, Sept. 9, 5 p.m.

Did President see my 3975, August 31,[1] before leaving? In view of Venizelos' message to him think he should send some message of regret and appreciation to Venizelos.

My 4065, September 5, and 4104, September 8, can wait. Believe the President should be informed, however, that in drawing the line for the Bulgarian Treaty it was necessary to make some changes from line indicated by him in your 2981, August 28, 4 p.m.[2] This will be explained in a telegram which is now being prepared and should be sent to him for his information.
                                Polk, Ammission.

T telegram (SDR, RG 256, 868.00/207, DNA).
[1] It is printed at that date in Vol. 62.
[2] Also printed at that date in Vol. 62.

From Jessie Woodrow Wilson Sayre

Dearest Father,   Vineyard Haven Mass Sept. 10, 1919

Your dear beautiful letter arrived on my birthday![1] The Davis's[2] and we, the children included, had been on a wonderful picnic on the surf-side of the island, a perfect day all white and gold and blue and when we came back there was your letter and a telegram from Nell[3] waiting for me to make the day quite perfect.

Dear, dear Father, thank you so much for your generous present to me. I don't see, these days, with so *much* to do how you can spare so much! *I* have already spent it on a beautiful rug, a real oriental, for our new house. And it will probably lie in the hallway to greet you and welcome you, some day in the dim distance when you can come and see our new nest. We are having great fun getting it in order for ourselves though it is dragging out so long now that we are getting anxious to get in.

We have postponed the christening indefinitely. I am not superstitious enough to think it can hurt the baby[4] to wait till a more propitious time, and he would be—later on—so sad to think you had not been there. So there is no hurry at all we can even wait if need be till the four years are over and you are a free man again.

Meanwhile he is flourishing at last, under Dr. Davis' wonderful care and really looks like a baby again and not a poor little plucked chicken. He is beautiful now, all golden and pink and looks *very* much like you. Yes, he does! His blue eyes and his hands and the shape of his head, but then—I can hardly hope to convince you!

Needless to say we have been following your trip with breathless interest and we feel it is all counting tremendously for you and your cause. That old Reed[5] is here in Boston tonight to speak. The Police are all on strike and there has been rioting all day.[6] I *can't* wish that he may escape a *few* jolts and bruises. I hope the building is stampeded![7]

Please thank Edith for her little note and good wishes

With ever devoted love from all your loved ones here

Your loving daughter   Jessie

ALS (WP, DLC).
    [1] WW to Jessie W. W. Sayre, Aug. 26, 1919, Vol. 62. Her birthday was August 28.
    [2] That is, the Edward Parker Davises.
    [3] That is, Eleanor Wilson McAdoo.
    [4] That is, Woodrow Wilson Sayre, born February 23, 1919.
    [5] That is, Senator James Alexander Reed of Missouri.
    [6] Many members of the Boston police force had gone on strike at the evening roll call at 5:45 p.m. on September 9. The immediate issues were the recognition of their recently organized union and its affiliation with the American Federation of Labor and the reinstatement of nineteen patrolmen who had been suspended by the Boston Police Commissioner, Edwin Upton Curtis, for their union-organizing activities. Ultimately, 1,117 of the city's 1,544 policemen went out on strike. The patrolmen who remained on duty were unable to cope with the widespread mob violence and looting which occurred on the night of September 9-10. Mayor Andrew James Peters, acting under a state law of 1917, called up approximately 1,000 members of the State Guard located within the city limits on September 10, and Governor Calvin Coolidge, at the mayor's request, called out an additional 3,000 guardsmen on the same day. A second night of rioting left five persons dead. The State Guard was in control of the city by the morning of September 11. It was only then that Coolidge issued a proclamation in which he took command of the State Guard and the police force in the emergency. Police Commis-

sioner Curtis announced on September 13 that none of the striking policemen would be allowed to return to the force, and that he would fill the vacancies with new men.

The most detailed study of the background, events, and aftermath of the Boston police strike is Francis Russell, *A City in Terror, 1919: The Boston Police Strike* (New York, 1955). See also Richard L. Lyons, "The Boston Police Strike of 1919," *New England Quarterly*, XX (June 1947), 147-68; Robert K. Murray, *Red Scare: A Study in National Hysteria, 1919-1920* (Minneapolis, 1955), pp. 122-34; and Donald R. McCoy, *Calvin Coolidge: The Quiet President* (New York and London, 1967), pp. 83-94.

[7] The meeting in opposition to the League of Nations at which Reed was to speak, sponsored by William Randolph Hearst and to be held at Symphony Hall, was canceled because of the police strike.

From the Diary of Dr. Grayson

Thursday, September 11, 1919.

The Presidential Special was stopped a few miles outside of Billings[1] at 4:00 o'clock in the morning and remained there until 9:00 that morning.

Arriving at Billings the President was greeted by a reception committee, which included a number of the leading cattlemen of that district. The party proceeded in automobiles to the Fair Grounds, where the meeting was held in a big auditorium[2] that has been erected there especially for meetings of this character. The Mayor of Billings[3] introduced the President in a very brief address, in which he said: "I want to introduce you to a man that is all man, a regular he-man." The Mayor's daughter[4] presented Mrs. Wilson with a magnificent basket of flowers, which had been secured for her by the ladies of the city.

The President's address here was characterized by an analysis of the labor clauses of the Treaty. He referred to the growing unrest throughout the world and said that the United States must do its part in placing labor on a suitable basis. Women and children, he said, could not expect to secure their rights unless the United States took its part in carrying out the suggestions that had been incorporated in the Treaty by the Labor Conference that met in Paris.

Among those who heard the President were a large number of Indians who had come into Billings from the reservations near that city.

Leaving Billings at 11:00 o'clock a quick run was made to Helena, the Capital, which was reached at 7:30 that night. Helena is a typical mining city, and the crowd that greeted the President here differed materially from any that he had seen up to the present time. There was a great percentage of miners in the crowd and a large number of radicals were there. However, they were extremely friendly to the President. I noticed that in the cities where the radical sentiment was reported to be the strongest, the crowds seemed perfectly willing to accept the President as a fair-minded Executive, who would give every one a square deal.

The meeting was held in the Helena Theatre,[5] and the President was introduced by the Governor.[6]

Just before the meeting the President received word that the Boston Police had gone on strike and that the situation in that city was very serious. Mobs of thugs and thieves were roaming about unchecked, and the President was urged to send Federal troops to assist in restoring order.

The President took occasion in his address bitterly to denounce the action of the Boston Police in going on strike. He compared them to soldiers who had deserted their posts on the eve of battle. The President's speech was sharp and when it was telegraphed back to Boston it had a very salutary effect in forcing the Governor of Massachusetts to act in aiding Mayor Peters and the Boston city authorities to control the mob and restore order.

Before the train left Helena, Governor [Stewart] placed on board the Special a forty-five pound rainbow trout that he personally had caught that day in the mountains.

The Governor and his wife[7] accompanied the President and Mrs. Wilson and myself to the Special and expressed his appreciation of the visit to the Capital.

Helena was left at 10:00 o'clock that night.

[1] At Worden, twenty-five miles east of Billings.
[2] Nearly 9,000 persons crowded the building to its capacity to hear Wilson. *Billings, Mont., Gazette*, Sept. 12, 1919.
[3] William Lee Mains, Republican. George Washington Pierson, lawyer and chairman of the Democratic committee of Yellowstone County, also spoke briefly. Their remarks are printed in *ibid*.
[4] Lillian Mains.
[5] There was no estimate of the number of persons who heard Wilson in Helena. The *Helena, Mont., Independent*, September 12, 1919, stated that Wilson spoke to "an audience which packed the Marlow theater to the dome, occupying every inch of available space in the structure."
[6] Samuel Vernon Stewart, Democrat.
[7] Stella Baker Stewart.

Rudolph Forster to Joseph Patrick Tumulty

The White House [Sept. 11, 1919]

Telegram received Provision in question reads as follows quote It is hereby declared to be the policy of the United States to adjust and settle its international disputes through mediation or arbitration to the end that war may be honorably averted. It looks with apprehension and disfavor upon a general increase of armament through[ou]t the world but it realizes that no single nation can disarm and that without a common agreement upon the subject every considerable power must maintain a relative standing in military strength. In view of the premises the President is authorized and requested to invite at an appropriate time not later than the close of the war in Europe all the great governments of the world to send representatives to a conference which shall be charged with the duty of formulating a plan for a court of arbitration or other tribunal to which disputed questions between nations shall be referred for adjudication and peaceful settlement and to consider the question of disarmament and submit their recommendation to their respective governments for approval. The President is hereby authorized to appoint nine citizens of the United States who in his judgment shall be qualified for the mission by eminence in the law and by devotion to the cause of peace to be representatives of the United States. In such a conference the President shall fix the compensation of said representatives and such secretaries and other employees as may be needed. Two hundred thousand dollars or so much thereof as may be necessary is hereby appropriated and set aside and placed at the disposal of the President to carry into effect the provisions of this paragraph unquote This is continuing provision still in force according to Judge Advocate General of Navy. No reference to it in any subsequent laws.   Forster.

T telegram (WP, DLC).

An Address in the Billings Auditorium

September 11, 1919.

Mr. Mayor, Judge Pierson, my fellow countrymen, it is with genuine pleasure that I face this company and realize that I am in the great state of Montana. I have long wanted to visit this great state and come in contact with its free and vigorous population, and I want to thank Judge Pierson for the happy word that he used in speaking about my errand. He said that I had come to consult with you. That is exactly what I have come to do. I have come to consult with you in the light of certain circumstances which I want to explain to you—circumstances which affect not only this great nation, which we love, and of which we try to constitute an honorable part, but also affect the whole world. I wonder when we speak of the whole world whether we have a true conception of the fact that the human heart beats everywhere the same.

Nothing impressed me so much on the other side of the water as the sort of longing for sympathy which those people exhibited.

The people of France, following the misery and terror they have suffered at the hands of the enemy, are never so happy as when they realize that we across the sea, at a great distance, feel with them the keen arrows of sorrow that have penetrated their hearts, and they are glad that our boys went over there and helped rescue them from the terror that lay upon them day and night.

And what I have come to say to you today, my friends, is this: we are debating the treaty of peace with Germany, and we are making a mistake, I take the liberty of saying, in debating it as if it were an ordinary treaty with some particular country, a treaty we could ourselves modify without conflicting with the affairs of the world; whereas, as matters are, it is not merely a treaty with Germany. Matters were drawn into this treaty which affected the peace and happiness of the whole continent of Europe, and not of the continent of Europe merely, but of the farthermost populations in Africa, people we hardly know about in the usual affairs of our country, where the influence of German policy had existed, and everywhere that influence had to be guarded, had to be rejected, had to be altered. What I want to impress upon you today is that it is the treaty of nations. And it is this treaty or no treaty. It is this treaty because there can be no other.

Consider the circumstances. For the first time in the world some twenty nations sent men—thoughtful and responsible men—to consult together at the capital of France to effect a settlement of the affairs of the world. And I want to render my testimony that these gentlemen entered upon their deliberations with great openness of mind. Their discussions were characterized by the utmost candor. And they realized, my fellow citizens, what, as a student of history I venture to say, no similar body ever acknowledged before—that they were nobody's masters. They did not have the right to vary a line to any nation's advantage in determining on the settlements and the basis of peace, but that they were the servants of their people and the servants of the people of the world. This settlement, my fellow citizens, is the first international settlement intended for the happiness and safety of men and women throughout the world. This is indeed and in truth a people's treaty. It is the first people's treaty. And I venture to say that no parliament or congress will attempt to alter it. (applause)

It is a people's treaty, notwithstanding the fact that it is also a treaty with Germany. And while it is a treaty with Germany, in no sense is it an unjust treaty, as some have characterized it. My fellow citizens, Germany tried to commit a crime against civilization, and this treaty is justified as a measure to make Germany pay for the crime up to her full capacity for payment. (applause) Some of the very gentlemen who are now characterizing this treaty as harsh are the same men who less than twelve months ago were criticizing the administration at Washington, in the fear that we would compromise with Germany and let her off from the payment of the utmost that she could pay in retribution for what she had done. They were pitiless then; they are pitiful now. (applause)

It is meet, my fellow citizens, that we should not forget what this war means. I am amazed at the indications that we are forgetting what we went through. There are some indications that, on the other side of the water, they are about to forget what they went through. I venture to say that there are thousands of parents—fathers, mothers, wives, sisters, and sweethearts in this country who are never going to forget what they went through. Thousands of our gallant youth lie buried in France.

Buried for what? For the protection of America? America was not directly attacked. For the salvation of mankind everywhere, and not alone for the salvation of America. It is the noblest errand that troops ever went on. I appeared once in the presence of a little handful of men whom I revere, who fought in the Civil War. And it seems to me that they fought for the greatest principle of their day, and now with what reverence we look upon those men who fought for the safety of the nation! I say this although I was born below the Mason and Dixon Line. We revere the men who saved the Union.

We are not going to deny those sentiments to the boys who were in this war. Don't you think that when they are old men, a halo will seem to be about them, because they were crusaders for the liberty of the civilized world?

One of the hardest things for me to do during this war, as for many another man in this country, was merely to try to advise and direct and not take a gun and go myself. When I feel the pride that I often have felt in having been the commander in chief of these gallant armies and those splendid boys at sea, I think, "Ah, that is fine, but, oh, to have been one of them and to have accomplished this great thing which has been accomplished!"

The fundamental feature of this treaty is—and a fundamental feature never before acknowledged—the principle that had its birth and growth in this country—that the countries of the world belong to the people who live in them, (applause) and that they have a right to determine their own affairs, their own form of government, their own polity, and that no body of statesmen, sitting anywhere in the world, no matter whether they represent the overwhelming physical force of the world or not, has the right to assign any great people to a sovereignty under which it does not care to live.

This is the great treaty which is being debated. This is the treaty which is being examined with a microscope. This is the treaty which is being pulled about and about which suggestions are made as to changes of phraseology. Why, my friends, are you going to be narrow-minded enough and near-sighted enough as to look that way at a great charter of human liberty?

The thing is impossible. Then you can never have any treaty, because you can never get together again the elements which made it up. You cannot do it by dealing with separate governments. You cannot assemble the forces again that were back of it. You cannot bring the agreement upon which it rests into force again. It was the laborious work of many, many months of the most intimate conference. It has very, very few compromises in it and is, most of it, laid down in straight lines according to American specifications. The choice is either to accept this treaty or play a lone hand.

What does that mean? To play a lone hand now means that we must always be ready to play by ourselves. It means that we must always be armed, that we must always be ready to mobilize the man strength and the manufacturing resources of the country. That means that we must continue to live under, not diminishing, but increasing taxes. It means that we shall devote our thought and the organization of our government to being strong enough to beat any nation in the world. An absolute reversal of all the ideals of American history!

If you are going to play a lone hand, the hand that you play must be upon the handle of the sword. You cannot play a lone hand and do your civil business except with the other hand—one hand incidental for the business of peace, the other hand constantly for the assertion of force. It is either this treaty or a lone hand, and the lone hand must have a weapon in it. The weapon must be all the young men of the country trained to arms, and the business of the country must pay the piper, must pay for the whole armament, the arms and the men. That is the choice.

And do you suppose, my fellow citizens, that any nation is going to stand for that? We are not the only people who are sick of war. We are not the only people who have made up our minds that our government must devote its attention to peace and to justice and to right. The people all over the world have made up their minds as to that. We need peace more than we ever needed it before. We need ordered peace, calm peace, settled peace, assured peace—for what have we to do? We have to reregulate the fortunes of men. I mean that we have to reconstruct the machinery of civilization. I use the words deliberately—we have to reconstruct the machinery of civilization.

The central fact of the modern world is universal unrest, and the unrest is not due merely to the excitement of a recent war. The unrest is not due merely to the fact of recent extraordinary circumstances. It is due to a universal conviction that the conditions under which men live and labor are not satisfactory. It is a conviction all over the world that there is no use talking about political democracy unless you have also industrial democracy.

You know what this war interrupted in the United States. We were searching our own hearts; we were looking closely at our own methods of doing business. A great many were convinced that the control of the business of this country was in too few hands. Some were convinced that the credit of the country was controlled by small groups of men, and the great Federal Reserve Act and the great Land Bank Act were passed in order to release the resources of the country on a broader and more generous scale. We had not finished dealing with monopolies. We have not finished dealing with monopolies. With monopolies there can be no industrial democracy. With the control of the few, of whatever kind or class, there can be no democracy of any sort. The world is finding that out, in some portions of it in blood and terror.

Look what has happened in Russia, my fellow citizens. I find, wherever I go in America, that my fellow citizens feel as I do—an infinite pity for that great people, an infinite longing to be of some service to them. Everybody who has mixed with the Russian people tells me that they are among the most lovable people in the world—a very gentle people, a very friendly people, a very simple people, and in their local life a very democratic people, people who easily trust you, and who expect you to be trustworthy as they are. And yet this people is delivered into the hands of an intolerable tyranny. It came out of one tyranny to get into a worse. A little group of some thirty or forty men are the masters of that people at present. Nobody elected them. They chose themselves. They maintain their power by the sword, and they maintain the sword by seizing all the food of the country and letting only those who will fight for them eat, and the rest of them can starve. And because they can command no loyalty, we are told by the newspapers that they are about to brand the men under arms for them, so that they will be forever marked as their servants and slaves. That is what pitiful Russia has got in for, and there will be many a bloody year, I am afraid, before she finds herself again.

I speak of Russia. Have you seen no symptoms of the spread of that sort of chaotic spirit into other countries? If you had been across the sea with me, you would know that the dread in the mind of every thoughtful man in Europe is that that distemper will spread to their countries, that before there will be settled order, there will be tragical disorder. Have you heard nothing of the propaganda of that sort of belief in the United States? That poison is running through the veins of the world, and we have made the methods of communication throughout the world such that all the veins of the world are open and the poison can circulate. The wireless throws it out upon the air. The cable whispers it underneath the sea. Men talk about it in little groups, men talk about it openly in great groups, not only in Europe, but here also in the United States. There are disciples of Lenin in our own midst. To be a disciple of Lenin means to be a disciple of night, chaos, and disorder. There must be no discord or disorganization. Our immediate duty, therefore, my fellow countrymen, is to see that no minority, no class, no special interest, no matter how respectable, how rich or how poor, shall get control of the affairs of the United States.

The singular thing about the sort of disorder that prevails in Russia is that, while every man is, so to say, invited to take what he can get, he cannot keep it when he gets it, because, even if you had leave to steal it, which is the leave very generously given in Russia at present, you would have to go and get somebody to help you to keep it. Without organization you cannot get any help, so the only thing you can do is to dig a hole and find a cave somewhere. Disordered society is dissolved society. There is no society when there is not settled and calculable order. When you do not know what is going to happen to you tomorrow, you do not much care what is going to happen to you today. These are the things that confront us. The world must be satisfied of justice. The conditions of civilized life must be purified and perfected, and, if we do not have peace, that is impossible. We must clear the decks of this matter we are now discussing. This is the best treaty that can possibly be gotten, and, in my judgment, it is a mighty good treaty, for it has justice, the attempt at justice at any rate, at the heart of it.

Suppose that you were feeling that there was a danger of a general conflagration in your part of the country. I mean a literal fire. Which would you rather have, no insurance at all or 10 per cent insurance? Don't you think some insurance is better than none at all? Put the security obtained by this treaty at its minimum, and it is a great deal better than no security at all. And without it there is no security at all, and no man can be sure what his business will be from month to month, or what his life will be from year to year. The leisureliness of some of the debate creates the impression on my mind that some men think there is leisure. There is no leisure in the world, my fellow citizens, with regard to the reform of the conditions under which men live. There is no time for any talk before getting down to the business of what we are going to do.

I dare say that many of you know that I have called a conference to sit in Washington the first week of next month—a conference of men in the habit of managing business and of men engaged in manual labor, what we generally call employers and employees. And I have called them together for the sake of getting their minds together, getting their purposes together, getting them to look at the picture of our life at the same time and in the same light and from the same angles, so that they can see the things that ought to be done. I am trying to apply there what is applied and in a degree covered by the Covenant of the League of Nations—that if there is any trouble, the thing to do is not to fight, but to sit around the table and talk it over. (applause)

The League of Nations substitutes discussion for fighting, and without discussion there will be fighting. One of the greatest difficulties that we have been through in the past is in getting men to understand that fundamental thing.

There is a very interesting story, and a very charming story, told of a great English writer of a past generation. He was a man who stuttered a little bit, and he stuttered out some very acid comment on some man who was not present. One of his friends said, "Why, Charles, I didn't know you knew him." "Oh, n-n-no," he said, "I-I d-d-don't k-know him; I-I c-c-an't hate a m-man I-I know." How much truth there is in that, my fellow countrymen! You cannot hate a fellow you know. I know some crooks that I cannot help liking. I can judge them in cool blood and correctly only when they are not there. They are extremely fetching and attractive fellows; indeed, I suspect that a disagreeable fellow cannot be a successful crook.

But, to speak seriously, conference is the healing influence of civilization, and the real difficulty between classes, when a country is unfortunate enough to have classes, is that they do not understand one another. I myself think that the real barriers in life are the barriers of taste, that some people like one way of doing things and that other people do not like that way of doing things; that one sort of people are not comfortable unless the people they are with are dressed the way they are. I think that goes so much deeper than people realize. It is the absence of the ability to get at the point of view and look through the eyes of the persons with whom you are not accustomed to deal. In order, therefore, to straighten out the affairs of America, in order to calm and correct the ways of the world, the first and immediate requisite is peace, and it is an immediate requisite. We cannot wait. It is not wise to wait, because we ought to devote our best thoughts, the best impulses of our hearts, the clearest thinking of our brains, to correcting the things that are wrong everywhere.

I know, my fellow citizens—at least I have been told—that this western part of the country is particularly pervaded with what is called radicalism. There is only one way to meet radicalism, and that is to deprive it of food, and wherever there is any wrong, there is an abundance of food for radicalism. The only way to keep men from agitating against grievances is to remove the grievances, and as long as things are wrong I do not intend to ask men to stop agitating. I intend to beg that they will agitate in an orderly fashion; I intend to beg that they will use the orderly methods of counsel, and, it may be, the slow processes of correction, which can be accomplished in a self-governing people through political means. Otherwise we will have chaos. But so long as there is something to correct, I say Godspeed to the men who are trying to correct it. That is the only way to meet radicalism. Radicalism means cutting up by the roots. Well, remove the noxious growth, and there will be no cutting up by the roots. Then there will be the wholesome fruitage of an honest life from one end of this country to the other.

In looking over some papers the other day, I was reminded of a very interesting thing. The difficulty which is being found with the League of Nations is that apparently the gentlemen who are discussing it unfavorably are afraid that we will be bound to do something we do not want to do. Now, the only way in which you can have an impartial determination in this world is by consenting to something you don't want to do. Every time you have a case in court, one or the other of the parties has to consent to do something he does not want to do. There is not a case in court, and there are thousands of cases in the courts, hundreds of thousands every year, in which one of the parties is not disappointed. Yet we regard that as the foundation of civilization—that we will not fight about these things and that when we lose in court we will take our medicine. Very well; I find that the two houses of Congress suggested that there be an international court, and suggested that they were willing to take their medicine. They put it in a place where you would not expect it. They put it in the naval appropriation bill. (applause) And, not satisfied with putting it there once, they put it there several times; I mean in successive years. This is the form of it.

"It is hereby declared to be the policy of the United States to adjust and settle its international disputes through mediation or arbitration (that is, the League of Nations), to the end that war may be honorably avoided. It looks with apprehension and disfavor upon a general increase of armament throughout the world, but it realizes that no single nation can disarm, and that, without a common agreement upon the subject, every considerable power must maintain a relative standing in military strength. In view of the premises, the President is authorized and requested to invite at an appropriate time, no later than the close of the war in Europe (this immediately preceded our entry into the war), all the great governments of the world to send representatives to a conference which shall be charged with the duty of formulating a plan for a court of arbitration or other tribunal to which disputed questions between nations shall be referred for adjudication and peaceful settlement, and to consider the question of disarmament and submit their recommendations to their respective governments for approval. (We now have the League of Nations.) The President is hereby authorized to appoint," etc. A provision for an appropriation to pay the expenses is also embodied.

Now that they have got it, they do not like it. (laughter, applause) They also provided in this legislation that, if there could be such an assemblage, if there could be such an agreement, the President was authorized to cancel the naval building program authorized by the bill, or so much of it as he thought was wise in the circumstances. They looked forward to it with such a practical eye that they contemplated the possibility of its coming soon enough to stop the building program of that bill. It came much sooner than they expected (applause) and apparently has taken them so much by surprise as to confuse their minds. I suppose that this would be a very dull world if everybody were consistent, but consistency, my fellow citizens, in the sober, fundamental, underlying principles of civilization, is a very serious thing indeed.

If we are, indeed, headed towards peace with the real purpose of our hearts engaged, then we must take the necessary steps to secure it, and we must make the sacrifices necessary to secure it, and not only to discuss it. I repudiate the suggestion, which underlies some of the suggestions I have heard, that the other nations of the world are acting in bad faith, and that only the United States is acting in good faith. (applause) That is not true. I can testify that I was occupied with honorable men on the other side of the water, and I challenge anybody to show where, in recent years, while the opinion of mankind has been effective, there has been the repudiation of an international obligation by France or Italy or Great Britain or by Japan. Japan has kept her engagements, and Japan here engages to unite with the rest of the world in maintaining justice and a peace based upon justice. There can be cited no instances where these governments have been dishonorable, and I need not add that there is, of course, no instance where the United States has not kept faith.

When gentlemen discuss the right to withdraw from the League of Nations and look suspiciously upon the clause which says that we can withdraw upon two years' notice, if at that time we have fulfilled our international obligations, I am inclined to ask: "What are you worried about? Are you afraid that we will not have fulfilled our international obligations?" I am too proud an American to believe anything of the kind. We never have failed to fulfill our international obligations, and we never will, and our international obligations will always look towards the fulfillment of the highest purposes of civilization. When we came into existence as a nation we promised ourselves and promised the world that we would serve liberty everywhere. We were only 3,000,000 strong then, and shall we, when more than a hundred million strong, now fail to fulfill the promises we made when we were weak? We have served mankind, and we shall continue to serve mankind, for I believe, my fellow men, that we are the flower of mankind so far as civilization is concerned.

But please do not let me leave the impression on your mind that I am arguing with you. I am not arguing this case; I am merely expounding it. I am just as sure what the verdict of this nation is going to be as if already rendered, and what has touched me and convinced me of this, my fellow citizens, is not what big men have told me, not what men of large affairs have said to me—I value their counsel and seek to be guided by it—but by what plain people have said to me, particularly by what women have said to me. When I see a woman plainly dressed, with the marks of labor upon her, and she takes my hand and says, "God bless you, Mr. President; God bless the League of Nations," I know that the League of Nations has gone to the hearts of those people. (applause)

A woman came up to me the other day and grasped my hand and said, "God bless you, Mr. President!" and then turned away in tears. I asked a neighbor, "What is the matter?" and he said, "She intended to say something to you, Sir, but she lost a son in France." That woman did not take my hand with a feeling that her son ought not to have been sent to France. I sent her son to France, and she took my hand and blessed me, but she could not say anything more, because the whole well of spirit in her came up into her throat and the thing was unutterable. Down deep in it was the love of her boy, the feeling of what he had done, the justice and the dignity and the majesty of it, and then the hope that through such a poor instrumentality as men like myself could offer, no other woman's son would ever be called upon to lay his life down for the same thing.

I tell you, my fellow citizens, the whole world is now in the state where you can fancy that there are hot tears upon every cheek, and those hot tears are tears of sorrow. But they are also tears of hope. It is amazing how, through all the sorrows of mankind and all the unspeakable terrors and injustices that have been inflicted upon men, hope springs eternal in the human breast. God knows that men, and governments in particular, have done everything they knew how to kill hope in the human heart, but it has not died. It is the one conquering force in the history of mankind. What I am pleading for, therefore—not with you, for I anticipate your verdict—but what I am pleading for with the Senate of the United States is to be done with debate and release and satisfy the hope of the world.[1]

Printed in *Addresses of President Wilson,* with corrections from the complete text in the *Billings,* Mont., *Gazette,* Sept. 12, 1919, and a few corrections from the incomplete text in the *New York Times,* Sept. 12, 1919.
[1] There is a WWT outline of this address in WP, DLC.

An Address in the Marlow Theater in Helena

September 11, 1919.

Governor Stewart and my fellow countrymen: I very heartily echo what Governor Stewart has just said. I am very glad that an occasion has arisen which has given me the opportunity and the pleasure of coming thus face to face, at any rate, with some of the people of the great State of Montana. (applause) I make haste to say to you that I have not come from Washington so much to advise you as to get in touch with you, as to get the feeling of the purposes which are moving you, because, my fellow citizens, I may tell you, as a secret, that some people in Washington lose that touch. They don't know what the great purposes are that are running through the hearts and minds of the people of this great country. (applause) And, if one stays in Washington too long, one is apt to catch that same remove and numbness which seems to characterize others that are there. (laughter and applause) I like to come out and feel once more the thing that is the only real thing in public affairs, and that is the great movement of public opinion in the United States. (laughter and applause)

And I want to put the case very simply to you tonight, for with all its complexities, with all its many aspects, there is a very simple question when you get to the heart of it. That question is nothing more nor less than this: shall the great sacrifice that we made in this war be in vain, or shall it not? I want to say to you very solemnly that, notwithstanding the splendid achievement of our boys on the other side of the sea—who, I don't hesitate to say, saved the world—(applause) notwithstanding the noble things they did, their task is only half done, and it remains for us to complete it. I want to explain that to you. I want to explain to you why, if we left the thing where it is and did not carry out the program of the treaty of peace in all its fullness, (applause) men like these would have to die to do the work over again and convince provincial statesmen that the world is one, and that only by an organization of the world can you save the young men of the world. (applause)

As I think upon this theme, there is a picture very distinctly in my mind. On last Memorial Day I stood in an American cemetery in France, just outside Paris, on the slopes of Suresnes.[1] The hills slope steeply to a little plain. And when I went out there all the slope of the hill was covered with men in the American uniform, standing, but rising tier on tier as if in a great witness stand. Then below, over a little level space, were simple crosses that marked the resting place of the American dead.

And just by the stand where I spoke was a group of French women who had lost their own sons, but, just because they had lost their own sons and because their hearts went out in thought and sympathy to the mothers on this side of the sea, they had made themselves, so to say, mothers of those graves, and every day had gone to take care of them, every day had strewn them with flowers. And they stood there, their cheeks wetted with tears, while I spoke, not of the French dead, but of the American boys who had died in the common cause.

They seemed to be thrown together on that day in that little spot with the hearts of the world. And I took occasion to say on that day that those who stood in the way of completing the task that those men had died for would some day look back upon it as those have looked back upon the days when they tried to divide this Union and prevent it from being a single nation, united in a single form of liberty. For the completion of the work of those men is this— that the thing that they fought to stop shall never be attempted again.

I call to your minds that we did not go into this war willingly. I was in a position to know. In the Providence of God, the leadership of this nation was entrusted to me during those early years of the war when we were not in it. I was aware through many subtle

[1] Wilson's speech at Suresnes is printed at May 30, 1919, Vol. 59; for a description, see the extract from the Grayson Diary printed at the same date.

channels of the movement of opinion in this country. And I know that the thing that this country chiefly desired—that you out here in the West chiefly desired and the thing that of course every living woman had at her heart—was that we should keep out of the war. And we tried to persuade ourselves that European business was not our business. We tried to convince ourselves that, no matter what happened on the other side of the sea, no obligation of duty rested upon us.

And finally we found the currents of humanity too strong for us. We found that a great consciousness was welling up in us that this was not a local cause, this was not a struggle which was to be confined to Europe, or confined to Asia, to which it had spread, but that it was something that involved the very fate of civilization. And there was one great nation in the world that couldn't afford to stay out. (applause) And now there are gentlemen opposing the ratification of this treaty who, at that time, taunted the administration of the United States that it had lost touch with its international consciousness. They were eager to go in, and now that they have got in, and are caught in the whole network of human consciousness, they want to break out and stay out.

We were caught in this thing by the action of a nation utterly unlike ourselves. What I mean to say is that the German nation— the German people—had no choice whatever as to whether it was to go into that war or not, did not know that it was going into it until its men were summoned to the colors. I remember, not once, but often, sitting at the cabinet table in Washington, and I asked my colleagues what their impression was of the opinion of the country before we went into the war. And I remember one day one of my colleagues said to me, "Mr. President, I think the people of the country would take your advice and do whatever you suggested." "But," I said, "that is not what I am waiting for; that is not enough. If they can't go in with a whoop, there is no use going in. I don't want them to wait on me. I am waiting on them. I want to know what the conscience of this country is saying. I want to know what ideas are arising in the minds of the people of this country with regard to this war situation." When I thought I heard this voice, it was then I proposed to the Congress of the United States that we should include ourselves in the challenge that Germany was making to mankind.

We fought Germany in order that there should be a world fit to live in. But the world is not fit to live in, my fellow citizens, if one great government is in a position to do what the German government did—secretly plot war and begin it with the whole strength of its people, without so much as consulting its own people.

A great war cannot begin with public deliberations. A great war can begin only by private plotting, because the peoples of this world are not asleep, as they used to be. The German people is a great, educated people. All the thoughtful men in Germany, so far as I have been able to learn, who were following peaceful pursuits—the bankers and the merchants and the manufacturers—did not want to go into that war. They said so then, and they have said so since. They have said that they were not consulted. But the masters of Germany were the general military staff. Not even the members of the Reichstag were consulted by the General Staff. And it was these men who nearly brought a complete catastrophe upon civilization itself.

Very well then, it stands to reason, if we would permit anything of that sort to happen again, we are recreant to the men we sent across the seas to fight this war. We are deliberately guilty then of preparing a situation which will inevitably lead to what? What shall I call it? The final war? Alas, my fellow citizens, it might be the final arrest, though I pray only the temporary arrest, of civilization itself.

And America has, if I may take the liberty of saying so, a greater interest in the prevention of that war than any other nation. America is less exhausted by war—she is not exhausted at all. America has paid for the war that has gone by less heavily, in proportion to her wealth, than other nations. America still has capital, capital enough for its own industries and for the industries of the other countries that have to build their industries anew. And the next war would have to be paid for in American blood and American money. The nation of all nations that is most interested to prevent the recurrence of what has already happened is the nation which would assuredly have to bear the brunt of that great catastrophe—(applause) either have to bear it, or stop where we are.

Who is going to take care of the growth of this nation? Who is going to shape the accumulation of physical power of this nation—if you choose to put it in that form? Who is going to reduce the natural resources of this country? Who is going to change the circumstance that we largely feed the rest of the world? Who is going to change the circumstance that many of our resources are unique and indispensable? America is going to grow more and more powerful; and the more powerful she is, the more inevitable it is that she should be entrusted with the peace of the world. (applause)

And now, at last, a miracle has happened. I dare say many of you have in mind the very short course of American history. You remember how, when this nation was born and we were just a little group of 3,000,000 people on the Atlantic coast, how the nations on the other side of the water, the statesmen of that day, regarded us with a certain condescension—looked upon us as a sort of group of hopeful children, pleased for the time being with the conception of absolute freedom and political liberty, far in advance of the other peoples of the world because less experienced than they, less aware of the difficulties of the great task that confronted them. And as the years have gone by, they have watched the growth of this nation with astonishment and for a long time with dismay.

They watched it with dismay until a very interesting and significant thing happened. When we fought Cuba's battle for her, then they said: "Ah, it is the beginning of what we predicted. She will seize Cuba and, after Cuba, what she pleases to the south of her. It is the beginning of the history we have gone through ourselves." They ought to have known; they set us the example! And when we actually fulfilled to the letter our promise that we would set helpless Cuba up as an independent government and guarantee her independence, when we carried out that great policy, we astounded and converted the world.

Then began—let me repeat the word began—the confidence of the world in America. And I want to say to you tonight that nothing was more overpowering to me and my colleagues in Paris than the evidence of the absolutely unquestioning confidence of the peoples of the world in the people of America. (applause) We were touched by it, not only touched by it, but I must admit we were frightened by it, because we knew that they were expecting things of us that we could not accomplish. We knew that they were hoping for some miracle of justice, which would set them forward the same hundred years that we have traveled on the progress towards free government. And we knew that it was a slow road. We knew that you could not suddenly transform a people from a people of subjects into a people of self-governing units. I tried—and I perhaps returned a little to my old profession of teacher—to point out to them that some of the things they were expecting of us could not be done now. But they refused to be disabused of their absolute confidence that America could and would do anything that was right for the other peoples of the world. An amazing thing!

And what was more interesting still, my fellow citizens, was this: you know that it happened—I will explain in a moment what I mean by the word "happened"—it happened that America laid down the specifications for the peace. It happened that America proposed the principles upon which the peace with Germany should be built. I used the word "happened" because I have found, and everybody who has looked into the hearts of the people of this country and some of the people on the other side of the water, have found, that the people on the other side of the water, whatever may be said about their governments, have learned their lesson from America before, and they believed in those principles before we promulgated them.

And their statesmen, knowing that their people believed in them, accepted them, accepted them before the American representatives crossed the sea. So that we found them ready to lay down the foundations of that peace along the lines that America had suggested, and all of Europe was aware that what was being done was building up American principle. In such circumstances, we were under a big compulsion to carry the work to the point which had filled our convictions from the first.

Where did the suggestion first come from? Where did the idea first spread that there should be a society of nations? It was first suggested, or it first spread in the United States, and some gentlemen were the chief proponents of it who are now objecting to the adoption of the Covenant of the League of Nations. They went further, some of them, than any portion of that Covenant goes. And now, for some reason, which I must admit is inscrutable to me, they are opposing the very thing into which they put their heart and their genius in building up a great organization to convert the people of the United States, as if they needed conversion, to the great underlying idea. And so all people knew we were doing an American thing when we put the Covenant of the League of Nations at the beginning of the treaty.

One of the most interesting things that happened over there was our dealing with some of the most cynical men I had to deal with— and there were some cynics over there—men who believed in what has come to be known as the late Darwinian idea of "the survival of the fittest." They said: "In nature, the strong eats up the weak, and in politics, the strong overcomes and dominates the weak. It has always been so, and it is always going to be so."

When I first got to Paris, they talked about the League of Nations indulgently in my presence and politely. I think some of them had the idea, "Oh, well, we must humor Wilson along so that he won't make a public fuss about it." And some of these very men, before our conferences were over, suggested more often than anybody else that some of the most difficult and delicate tasks in carrying out this peace should be left to the League of Nations. (applause) They all admitted that the League of Nations, which they had deemed an ideal dream, was a demonstrable and practical necessity. (applause) This treaty cannot be carried out without the League of Nations.

I have several times said, and perhaps I may say again, that one of the principal things about this treaty is that it establishes the land titles of the world. It says, for example, that Bohemia shall belong to the Bohemians and not to the Austrians or to the Hungarians; that if the Bohemians do not want to live in a monarchy, dual or single, it is their business and not ours, and that they can do what they please with their own government. We have said that the Austrian territories south of Austria and Hungary, occupied by the Yugoslavs, never did belong to Austrians. They always belonged to Slavs, and the Slavs shall have them for their own, and we will guarantee the title.

I have several times asked, "Suppose that the land titles of Montana were clearly enough stated and somewhere recorded, but yet there was no way of enforcing them?" Do you know what would happen? Every one of you would enforce his own land titles. You used to go armed out here long ago. (applause) If this is a poor speech, I hope none of you do tonight. (applause) And you would resume the habit if there was nobody to guarantee your legal titles. You would have to resort to the habit if society should not guarantee them. You have got to see to it that others respect them for your own protection. And that was the condition of Europe and will be the condition of Europe again if these settled land titles which we have laid out are not guaranteed by organized society, and the only organized society that can guarantee them is a society of nations.

But it was not easy to draw the line. It was not a surveyor's task. There were no well-known points from which to start and to which to go, because we were trying to give the Bohemians, for example, the lines where the Bohemians lived, but the Bohemians did not stop at a straight line. If you will pardon the expression, they slopped over. And the Germans slopped over into Poland, and in some places there was an almost inextricable mixture of two or more populations. And everybody said that the statistics lied. Because the German statistics with regard to High Silesia, for example, were not true, because the Germans wanted to make it appear that the Germans were in the majority, and the Poles declared that the Poles were in the majority.

And we said: "This is a difficult business. Sitting in Paris, we cannot tell by count how many Poles there are in High Silesia, or how many Germans. And if we could count them, we cannot tell from Paris what they want. High Silesia does not belong to us, it does not belong to anybody but the people who live in it. We'll do this: we'll put that territory under the care of the League of Nations for a limited period; we will establish a small armed force there, made up of contingents from the different Allied nations so that none of them will be in control. And then we will hold a referendum, and Upper Silesia shall belong either to Germany or Poland, as the people in Upper Silesia desire." (applause)

And that is only one case out of half a dozen. The League of Nations is to see to it in regions where the makeup of the populations is doubtful and the desire of the population is as yet uncertain, the League of Nations is to be the instrumentality by which the territories of those various countries are to be delivered to the people to whom they belong. (applause)

No other international conference ever conceived such a purpose, and no earlier conference of that sort would have been willing to carry out such objects. Up to the time of this war, my fellow citizens, it was the firm and fixed conviction of statesmen in Europe that the greater nations ought to dominate, guide, and determine the destiny of the weaker nations. The American principle was rejected. The American principle is that the justice of the weak man is the same as that of the strong; that the weak man has the same legal rights that the strong man has; the justice of the poor man shall be the same as that of the rich, although I am sorry to say the poor man does not always get his rights. (applause) So as between nations the principle of equality is the only principle of justice, and the weak nations have just as many rights and just the same rights as stronger nations. If you do not establish that principle, then this war is going to come again, because this war came by reason of a grievance against a weak nation.

What happened, my fellow citizens? Don't you remember? The Crown Prince of Austria was assassinated in Serbia. Not assassinated by anybody according to order from the government of Serbia or anybody over whom the government of Serbia had any control, but assassinated by some man who had at his heart the memory of something that was intolerable to him, something that had been done to the people he belonged to. And the Austrian government acted, not immediately, but by suggestion from Berlin, where it is whispered: "We are ready for the World War, and this is a good chance to begin it. The other nations do not believe we are going to begin it. We will begin it and overwhelm France, first of all, before the others can come to their aid." They sent an ultimatum to Serbia practically demanding that she surrender her sovereign rights, and gave her twenty-four hours to decide. Poor Serbia, in her sudden terror, with the memory of things that had occurred in the past, practically yielded to every demand, but, with regard to a little portion of it, said she would like to talk it over with them, but they did not dare wait. They knew that, if the world ever had the facts of that dispute laid before them, the nations of mankind would overwhelm anybody that undertook to inflict such a grievance against Serbia in such circumstances. But they always chose this little nation. They had always chosen the Balkans as the ground of their entry into war. German agents were planted all through the land, so that when Germany got ready she could use the Balkan states as a base in her game.

And what does the treaty of peace do? The treaty of peace sets all of these nations up in independence again; gives Serbia back what had been torn away from her; sets up the Yugoslav states, or what is known as Jugo-Slavokia—I wish it was—(laughter) and the Bohemian states under the name of Czechoslovakia. And if you leave it at that, you leave those nations just as weak as they were before. By giving them their land titles, you do not make them any stronger. You make them stronger in spirit but not in number. But physically they are no stronger. They may be full of a new enthusiasm, but their love of country cannot now express itself in action. And physically they are no stronger than they were before.

That road that we heard so much of—from Bremen to Baghdad—was wide open. The Germans were traveling that road. Their General Staff uninterruptedly came through there. Merchants and manufacturers and the bankers of Germany were making a conquest of the world. All they had to do was to wait a little while longer, and a German net would have been spread or stretched all through that country, which never could have been withdrawn or broken. But the war spoiled the game of German intrigue which was penetrating all of these countries and controlling them. The dirty center of the entire German net—dirty in every respect—was Constantinople, and from there ramified all the threads that made this web, in the center of which was the venomous spider.

If you leave that road open, if you leave those nations to take care of themselves, knowing that they cannot take care of themselves, then you have committed the unpardonable sin of undoing the victory which our boys won. (applause) You say, "What have we got to do with it?" Let us answer that question, and not from a sentimental point of view at all. Suppose we did not have any hearts under our jackets. Suppose we did not care for these people. Care for them? Why, their kinsmen are everywhere in the communities of the United States; people who love people over there are everywhere in the United States. We are made up out of mankind; we cannot tear our hearts away from them. Our hearts are theirs. But suppose they were not. Suppose we had forgotten everything except the material, commercial, monetary interests of the United States. You cannot get those markets away from Germany if you let her reestablish her old influence there. The 300,000,000 people between the Rhine and the Ural Mountains will be in such a condition that they cannot buy anything, their industries cannot start, unless they surrender themselves to the bankers of *Mittel-Europa*, that you used to hear about. And the peoples of Italy and France and Belgium, some 80,000,000 strong, who are your natural customers, cannot buy anything in disturbed and bankrupt Europe. If you are going to trade with them, you have got to go partners with them.

When I hear gentlemen talk about America standing for herself, I wonder where they have been living. Has America disconnected herself from the rest of the world? Her ambition has been to connect herself with all the rest of the world commercially, and she is bankrupt unless she does. Look at the actual situation right now, my fellow citizens. The war was a very great stimulation to some of the greatest of the manufacturing industries of this country, and a very interesting thing has been going on. You remember, some of you perhaps painfully remember, that the Congress of the United States put a very heavy tax on excess profits, and a great many men who were making large excess profits said: "All right, we can manage this. These will not be profits; we will spend these in enlarging our plants, advertising, increasing our facilities, spreading our agencies."

They have got ready for a bigger business than they can do unless they have the world to do it in, and if they have not the world to do it in, there will be a recession of prosperity in this country; there will be unemployment; there will be bankruptcy in some cases. The giant is so big that he will burst his jacket. The rest of the world is necessary to us, if you want to put it on that basis. I do not like to put it on that basis. That is not the American basis. America does not want to feed upon the rest of the world. She wants to feed it and serve it. America, if I may say it without offense to great peoples for whom I have a profound admiration on the other side of the water, is the only national idealistic force in the world, and idealism is going to save the world. Selfishness will embroil it. Narrow selfishness will tie things up into ugly knots that you cannot get open except with a sword. All the human passions, if aroused on the wrong side, will do the world an eternal disservice.

I remember somebody said to me one day, using a familiar phrase, that this was an age in which mind was monarch, and my reply was: "Well, if that is true, mind is one of those modern monarchs that reign and do not govern. As a matter of fact, we are governed by a great popular assembly made up of the passions, and the best that we can manage is that the handsome passions shall be in the majority." That is the task of mankind—that the handsome passions, the handsome sentiments, the handsome purposes, shall always have a dominating and working majority, so that they will always be able to outvote the baser passions, to defeat all the cupidities and meannesses and criminalities of the world. That is the program of civilization.

The basis of the program of civilization, I want to say with all the emphasis that I am capable of, is Christian and not pagan, and in the presence of this inevitable partnership with the rest of the world, these gentlemen say, "We will not sign the articles of co-partnership." Well, why not? You have heard, I dare say, only about four things in the Covenant of the League of Nations. I have not heard them talk about anything else. It is a very wonderful document, and you would think there were only four things in it. The things that they talk about are the chance to get out, the dangers of Article X, the Monroe Doctrine, and the risk that other nations may interfere in our domestic affairs. Those are the things that keep them awake at night, and I want very briefly to take those things in their sequence.

I do not like to discuss some of them. If I go to do a thing, I do not say at the beginning, "My chief interest in this thing is how I am going to get out." I will not be a very trusted or revered partner if it is evident that my fear is that I will continue to be a partner. But we will take that risk. We will sit by the door with our hand on the knob, and sit on the edge of our chair. There is nothing in the Covenant to prevent our going out whenever we please, with the single limitation that we give two years' notice. The gentlemen who discuss this thing do not object to the two years' notice. They say, "It says that you can get out after two years' notice if at that time you have fulfilled your international obligations," and they are afraid somebody will have the right to say that they have not. That right cannot belong to anybody unless you give it to somebody, and the Covenant of the League does not give it to anybody. It is absolutely left to the conscience of this nation, as to the conscience of every other member of the League, to determine whether at the time of its withdrawal it has fulfilled its international obligations or not. And, inasmuch as the United States always has fulfilled its international obligations, I wonder what these gentlemen are afraid of! There is only one thing to restrain us from getting out, and that is the opinion of our fellow men, and that will not restrain us in any conceivable circumstance if we have followed the honorable course which we always have followed. I would be ashamed as an American to be afraid that, when we wanted to get out, we should not have fulfilled our international obligations.

Then comes Article X, for I am taking the questions in the order in which they come in the Covenant itself. Let me repeat to you Article X nearly verbatim; I am not trying to repeat it exactly as it is written in the Covenant. Every member of the League agrees to respect and preserve as against external aggression the territorial integrity and existing political independence of the other members of the League. There is the guarantee of the land titles. Without that clause, there is no guarantee of the land titles. Without that clause, the heart of the recent war is not cut out. The heart of the recent war was an absolute disregard of the territorial integrity and political independence of the smaller nations. If you do not cut the heart of the war out, that heart is going to live and beat and grow stronger, and we will have the cataclysm again.

Then the article adds that it shall be the duty of the Council of the League to advise the members of the League what steps may be necessary from time to time to carry out this agreement—to advise, not to direct. The Congress of the United States is just as free under that article to refuse to declare war as it is now; and it is very much safer than it is now. The opinion of the world and of the United States bade it to declare war in April 1917. It would have been shamed before all mankind if it had not declared war then. It was not given audible advice by anybody but its own people, but it knew that the whole world was waiting for it to fulfill a manifest moral obligation.

This advice cannot be given, my fellow citizens, without the vote of the United States. The advice cannot be given without a unanimous vote of the Council of the League. The member of the Council representing the United States has to vote aye before the United States or any other country can be advised to go to war under that agreement, unless the United States is herself a party.

What does that mean, unless the United States is going to seize somebody else's territory or somebody else is going to seize the territory of the United States. I do not contemplate it as a likely contingency that we are going to steal somebody else's territory. I dismiss that as not a serious probability, and I do not see anybody within reach who is going to take any of ours. But suppose we should turn highwayman, or that some other nation should turn highwayman and stretch its hands out for what belongs to us. Then what difference does it make what advice the Council gives? We are in the scrap anyhow. In those circumstances, Congress is not going to wait to hear what the Council of the League says to determine whether it is going to war or not. The war will be its war.

So that any way you turn Article X, it does not alter in the least degree the freedom and independence of the United States with regard to its action in respect of war. All of that is stated in such plain language that I cannot for the life of me understand how anybody reads it any other way. I know perfectly well that the men who wrote it read it the way I am interpreting it. I know that it is intended to be written that way, and if I am any judge of the English language, they succeeded in writing it that way.

Then they are anxious about the Monroe Doctrine. The Covenant says in so many words that nothing in that document shall be taken as invalidating the Monroe Doctrine. I do not see what more you could say. While the matter was under debate in what was called the Commission on the League of Nations, the body that drew the Covenant up, in which were representatives of fourteen nations, I tried to think of some other language that could state it more unqualifiedly, and I could not think of any other. Can you? Nothing in that document should be taken as invalidating the Monroe Doctrine—I cannot say it any plainer than that—and yet by a peculiar particularity of anxiety these gentlemen cannot believe their eyes; and from one point of view it is not strange, my fellow citizens.

The rest of the world always looked askance on the Monroe Doctrine. It is true, though some people have forgotten it, that President Monroe uttered that doctrine at the suggestion of the British cabinet, and in its initiation, in its birth, it came from Mr. Canning, who was Prime Minister of England[2] and who wanted the aid of the United States in checking the ambition of some of the European countries to establish their power in South America.

Notwithstanding that, Great Britain did not like the Monroe Doctrine as we grew so big. It was one thing to have our assistance and another thing for us not to need her assistance. And the rest of the world had studiously avoided on all sorts of interesting occasions anything that could be interpreted as an acknowledgment of the Monroe Doctrine. So I am not altogether surprised that these gentlemen cannot believe their eyes. Here the nations of Europe say that they are entering into an arrrangement no part of which shall be interpreted as invalidating the Monroe Doctrine. I do not have to say anything more about that. To my mind, that is eminently satisfactory, and as long as I am President I shall feel an added freedom in applying, when I think fit, the Monroe Doctrine.

---

[2] George Canning was Foreign Secretary in 1823; he did not become Prime Minister until 1827.

I am very much interested in it, and I foresee occasions when it might be appropriately applied.

In the next place they are afraid that other nations will interfere in our domestic questions. There, again, the Covenant of the League distinctly says that if any dispute arises which is found to relate to an exclusively domestic question, the Council shall take no action with regard to it and make no report concerning it. And the questions that these gentlemen most often mention, namely the questions of the tariff and of immigration and of naturalization, are acknowledged by every authoritative student of international law without exception to be as, of course, domestic questions.

These gentlemen want us to make an obvious thing painfully obvious by making a list of the domestic questions, and I object to making the list for this reason—that if you make a list you may leave something out. I remind all students of law within the sound of my voice of the old principle of the law that the mention of one thing is the exclusion of other things; that if you meant everything, you ought to have said everything; that if you said a few things, you did not have the rest in mind. I object to making a list of domestic questions, because a domestic question may come up which I did not think of. In every such case the United States would be just as secure in her independent handling of the question as she is now.

Then, outside the Covenant is the question of Shantung. Some gentlemen want to make a reservation or something that they clothe with a handsome name with regard to the Shantung provision, which is that the rights which Germany illicitly got—for she got it by duress—from China shall pass to Japan. While the war was in progress, Great Britain and France expressly, in a written treaty, though a secret treaty, entered into an engagement with Japan that she should have all that Germany had in the province of Shantung. If we repudiate this treaty in that matter, Great Britain and France cannot repudiate the other treaty, and they cannot repudiate this treaty inasmuch as it confirms the other. Therefore, in order to take away from Japan—for she is in physical possession of it now—what Germany had in China, we shall have to fight Japan and Great Britain and France; and at the same time do China no service, because one of the things that is known to everybody is that, when the United States consented, because of this promise of Great Britain and France, to putting that provision in the treaty, Japan agreed that she would not take all of what was given to her in the treaty; that, on the contrary, she would, just as soon as possible, after the treaty was carried out, return every sovereign right or right resembling a sovereign right that Germany had enjoyed in

Shantung to the government of China, and that she would retain at Shantung only those economic rights with regard to the administration of the railway and the exploitation of certain mines that other countries enjoy elsewhere in China.

It is not an exceptional arrangement—a very unfortunate arrangement, I think, elsewhere as there, for China—but not an exceptional arrangement. Under it, Japan will enjoy privileges exactly similar and concessions exactly similar to what other nations enjoy elsewhere in China, and nothing more. In addition to that, if the treaty is entered into by the United States, China will for the first time in her history have a forum to which to bring every wrong that is intended against her or that has been committed against her.

When you are studying Article X, my fellow citizens, I beg of you that you will read Article XI. I do not hear that very often referred to. Article XI—I am not going to quote the words of it—makes it the right of any member of the League to call attention to anything, anywhere, that is likely to disturb the peace of the world or the good understanding between nations upon which the peace of the world depends. Every aspiring people, every oppressed people, every people whose hearts can no longer stand the strain of the tyranny that has been put upon them, can find a champion to speak for it in the forum of the world.

Until that Covenant is adopted, what is the international law? International law is that, no matter how deeply the United States is interested in something in some other part of the world that she believes is going to set the world on fire or disturb the friendly relations between two great nations, she cannot speak of it unless she can show that her own interests are directly involved. It is a hostile and unfriendly act to call attention to it, and Article XI says, in so many words, that it shall be the friendly right of every nation to call attention to any such matter anywhere; so that if anybody contemplates anything that is an encroachment upon the rights of China, he can be summoned to the bar of the world. I do not know when any nation that could not take care of itself, as unfortunately China cannot, ever had such a human advantage accorded it before. It is not only we, my fellow citizens, who are caught in all the implications of the affairs of the world; everybody is caught in it now, and it is right that anything that affects the world should be made everybody's business.

The heart of the Covenant of the League of Nations is this: every member of the League promises never to go to war without first having done one or other of two things—either having submitted the matter to arbitration, in which case it agrees absolutely to abide by the award, or having submitted it to discussion by the Council of the League of Nations. If it submits it for discussion by the Council, it agrees to allow six months for the discussion and to lay all the documents and facts in its possession before the Council, which is authorized to publish them. And even if it is not satisfied with the opinion rendered by the Council, it agrees that it will not go to war within less than three months after the publication of that judgment. There are nine months in which the whole matter is before the bar of mankind, and, my fellow citizens, I make this confident prediction—that no nation will dare submit a bad case to that jury. I believe that this covenant is better than 95 per cent insurance against war. Suppose it was only 5 per cent insurance; would not you want it? I ask any mother, any father, any brother, anybody with a heart, "Do not you want some insurance against war, no matter how little?"

And the experience of mankind, from the conferences between employers and employees, is that if people get together and talk things over, it becomes more and more difficult to fight the longer they talk. There is not any subject that has not two sides to it, and the reason most men won't enter into discussion with antagonists is they are afraid that the other fellows' side will be stronger than theirs. The only thing that you are afraid of, my fellow citizens, is the truth.

A cynical old politician once said to his son, "John, do not bother your head about lies; they will take care of themselves, but if you ever hear me denying anything you may make up your mind it is so." The only thing that is formidable is the truth. I learned what I know about Mexico, which is not as much as I should desire, by hearing a large number of liars tell me all about it. At first, I was very much confused, because the narrative did not tally. And then one day, when I had a lucid interval, it occurred to me that that was because what was told me was not true. The truth always matches; it is the lies that don't match. I also observed that, back of all these confusing contradictions, there was a general mass of facts which they all stated, and I knew that that was the region into which their lying capacity did not extend. They had not had time to make up any lies about that, and the correspondences in their narratives constituted the truth. The differences could be forgotten. So I learned a great deal about Mexico by listening to a sufficiently large number of liars. And the truth is the regnant and triumphant thing in this world. You may trample it under foot, you may blind its eyes with blood, but you cannot kill it, and sooner or later it rises up and seeks and gets its revenge.

It behooves us to remember, my fellow citizens, in these radical days, the men who want to cure the wrongs of government by destroying government are going to be destroyed themselves—destroyed, I mean, by the chaos that they had created by removing the organism of society. And, even if you are strong enough to take anything that you want, you are not, of course, smart enough to keep it. And the next stronger fellow will take it away from you, and the strongest and most audacious group among you will make slaves and tools of you. That is the truth that is going to master society and in any other place that tries Russia's unhappy example.

I hope you won't think it inappropriate if I stop here to express my shame as an American citizen at the race riots that have occurred at some places in this country, where men have forgot humanity and justice and orderly society and have run amuck. That constitutes a man, not only the enemy of society, but his own enemy, and the enemy of justice.

I want to say this, too, that a strike of the policemen in a great city, leaving that city at the mercy of an army of thugs, is a crime against civilization. In my judgment, the obligation of a policeman is as sacred as the obligation of a soldier. He is a public servant, not a private employee, and the whole honor and safety of the community is in his hands. He has no right to prefer any private advantage to the public safety. I hope that that lesson will be burned in so that it will never again be forgotten, because the pride of America is that she can exercise self-control. That is what a self-governing nation is—not merely a nation that elects people to do its job for it, but a nation that can keep its head, concert its purposes, and find out how those purposes can be executed.

One of the noblest sentences ever uttered was uttered by Mr. Garfield before he became President. He was a member of Congress, as I remember it, at the time of Mr. Lincoln's assassination. He happened to be in New York City, and Madison Square was filled with a surging mass of deeply excited people when the news of the murder came. Mr. Garfield was at the old Fifth Avenue Hotel, which had a balcony out over the entrance, and they begged him to go out and say something to the people. He went out and, after he had attracted their attention, he said this beautiful thing: "My fellow citizens, the President is dead, but the government lives and God Omnipotent reigns."[3]

America is the place where you cannot kill your government by killing the men who conduct it. The only way you can kill government in America is by making the men and women of America forget how to govern, and nobody can do that. They sometimes

[3] For a much earlier use of this apocryphal story by Wilson, see his address to the Commercial Club of Chicago printed at Nov. 29, 1902, Vol. 14.

find the team a little difficult to drive, but they sooner or later whip it into the harness. And, my fellow citizens, the underlying thought of what I have tried to say to you tonight is the organization of the world for order and peace. Our fortunes are directly involved, and my mind reverts to that scene that I painted for you at the outset— that slope at Suresnes, those voiceless graves, those weeping women—and I say: "My fellow citizens, the pledge that speaks from those graves is demanded of us. We must see to it that those boys did not die in vain. We must fulfill the great mission upon which they crossed the sea."[4]

Printed in *Addresses of President Wilson*, with numerous corrections and additions from the incomplete texts in the *Helena, Mont., Independent*, Sept. 12, 1919, and the *New York Times*, Sept. 12, 1919.
    [4] There is a WWT outline of this address, dated Sept. 10, 1919, in WP, DLC.

To George William Norris

Garrison Mont [Sept. 11, 1919]

I thank you for correcting an unintentional inaccuracy in one of my recent speeches[1]   Woodrow Wilson.

T telegram (G. W. Norris Papers, DLC).
    [1] See R. Forster to JPT, Sept. 7, 1919.

To Henry Lee Myers

[En route, c. Sept. 11, 1919]

Our reception in Montana was wonderful and reflected in the most convincing way the generous support you and Senator Walsh[1] are giving the League.   Woodrow Wilson

WWT telegram (T. W. Brahany Coll.).
    [1] That is, Thomas J. Walsh, like Myers, a Democratic senator from Montana.

To Désiré Félicien François Joseph Cardinal Mercier

[Helena ? Sept. 11, 1919]

May I not bid you a most cordial welcome and extend to you my warm personal regards stop. I shall look forward with the greatest pleasure to greeting you in person stop.   Woodrow Wilson.

T telegram (WP, DLC).

Joseph Patrick Tumulty to Rudolph Forster

Helena Mont [Sept. 11, 1919]

In speech four[1] we have sent you on page eight change sentence quote Great Britain and France as everybody knows in order to make it more certain that Japan would come into the war etc unquote to read quote Great Britain and subsequently France as everybody knows in order to make it more certain that Japan would cooperate in the war etc unquote   J P Tumulty.

T telegram (WP, DLC).
[1] That is, the address to the St. Louis Chamber of Commerce printed at Sept. 5, 1919.

William Joseph Hamilton Cochran to Joseph Patrick Tumulty

The White House, 1919 Sept. 11, 8 P.M.

Answering your message, on the whole reaction is favorable. Opponents of Treaty in Senate evidently worried over President's speeches and are desperately seeking to combat them. Hitchcock and Pittman both optimistic today. Generally conceded all amendments will be beaten and that our position strategically will be strengthened as result when fight comes on reservations. Fact is being driven home to opposition as result of publicity given President's tour that people will not tolerate alteration in treaty that will force its return to the Peace Conference. Opposition will make big amendment fight on proposal to equalize British and American voting strength in League. Seek to create impression that this change would not necessitate sanction by Germany. Hitchcock minority report on treaty filed today with Senate refutes this claim.[1] Hope you see Hitchcock's report as it is clear exposition of Administration position. Feeling among friends at Capitol that President should take up in more detail American questions relating to treaty, such as the Monroe Doctrine, immigration, etc., and disprove contentions of opposition in this regard, thus discounting the attempts to raise the nationalism issue. Hitchcock report to Senate today makes big point of material gains that will come to America through domestic ratification of treaty. Only unfavorable reaction here has come from Shields'[2] defection and from announcements by Simmons and Pomerene[3] that they would support reservations rather than see treaty defeated, and from Kenyon's[4] stand in favor of reservations.   Cochran

T telegram (WP, DLC).
[1] The minority report was signed by six of the seven Democratic members of the Senate Foreign Relations Committee: Gilbert Monell Hitchcock, John Sharp Williams,

Claude Augustus Swanson, Atlee Pomerene, Marcus Aurelius Smith, and Key Pittman. Only John Knight Shields declined to sign (see n. 2 below). The signers urged "the early ratification of the pending treaty of peace without amendments and without reservations." "We deplore," they continued, "the long and unnecessary delay to which the treaty has been subjected while locked up in the committee whose majority decisions and recommendations were from the start a foregone conclusion. They could have been made in July as well as in September and would have been the same."

The Democratic senators discussed the stagnation of American and world trade caused by the delay in ratification. They also condemned the majority's amendments to the text of the treaty: "In our opinion they have no merit, but whether they be good, bad, or indifferent their adoption by the Senate can have no possible effect except to defeat the participation of the United States in the treaty. None of them could by any possibility be accepted even by the great nations associated with the United States in the war, and none of them could by any possibility be dictated to Germany. To adopt any one of them, therefore, is equivalent to rejecting the treaty." The argument put forward by the majority report that the peace conference was still sitting in Paris and, hence, could consider amendments to the treaty and that German representatives could be brought to Paris for the same purpose indicated "a total misconception of the situation." "The peace conference," the minority report continued, "has acted finally upon this treaty. Great Britain has ratified it, France is about to do so, and with the action of one other power it will in all human probability be in actual operation even before the Senate of the United States reaches a decision. Moreover, the peace conference possesses no further power to 'bring German representatives to Paris.' The power of compulsion has been exhausted. Germany was told where to sign and when to sign and when to ratify, and Germany has closed the chapter by signing and by ratifying. Germany can not be compelled to do anything more or different with regard to this treaty by being confronted with an amended treaty whether once a month, day, or week. . . . If an amended treaty is not signed by Germany then it is in none of its parts binding on her." The minority report then listed twelve important "concessions" by Germany in the peace treaty, the benefit of which the United States would lose by adopting amendments to the treaty or rejecting it outright.

The minority report bluntly condemned the reservations to the Covenant of the League of Nations proposed in the majority report. "The reservations," it said, "proposed by the majority of this committee are of such a character as at once betray their authorship. They are the work of Senators organized for the purpose of destroying the league and if possible defeating this treaty. Their phraseology is such as make this purpose plain. They are in no sense interpretative reservations to be used to make clear language in the treaty that might be considered doubtful, but they are so framed as to receive the support of Senators who desire the defeat of the treaty. While masquerading in the guise of reservations they are in fact alterations of the treaty. They have all the vices of amendments and the additional vice of pretending to be what they are not. Presented as parts of the resolution to ratify the treaty they would in fact, if adopted, result in its defeat." Finally, the report listed the important advantages for world peace that would be secured by the adoption of the League Covenant.

The minority report is printed as Part 2 of 66th Cong., 1st sess., *Senate Report No. 176*. It is printed also in *Cong. Record*, 66th Cong., 1st sess., pp. 5213-15.

² The *New York Times*, Aug. 26, 1919, reported that Shields had stated in an interview in Knoxville that he was not in favor of the Covenant of the League of Nations as embodied in the peace treaty. "I oppose any covenant," he was reported to have said, "that will involve the United States in every broil and engage it in every war that may be waged throughout the world." He was also reported to favor reservations to the Covenant but had specified none.

³ That is, Senators Simmons of North Carolina and Pomerene of Ohio. Simmons made the following statement on the floor of the Senate on September 8:

"I am in favor of and would gladly vote for the treaty and the league covenant as it was originally presented to the Senate by the President, without amendment or reservation. I agree with the President's interpretation of the controverted provisions of that document, and I do not believe it contains anything which would jeopardize American interests. I also believe it is of the highest importance to this country and the world that it should be ratified without further delay.

"However, after a thorough study of the situation in the Senate, I am convinced that some concessions in the way of reservations will have to be made to secure its ratification, and, so believing, I have recently discussed with a number of my colleagues the advisability of reaching some compromise between those who favor the treaty without reservation and those who are in favor of it with conservative reservations of an interpretative nature.

"I am utterly opposed, however, to the reservations proposed by the Foreign Relations Committee. Some of these reservations are, in substance and essence, amendments which would radically change the scope and character of the instrument, emasculating some of the main provisions of the league, and which would call for reconsideration by the peace conference." *Cong. Record*, 66th Cong., 1st sess., p. 5015.

Pomerene, in an interview on or about September 9, made the following comment: "While I favor having the treaty ratified without change, I would accept reservations if I thought that their defeat would mean the rejection of the treaty." He indicated that this did not mean that he would definitely vote for reservations, but rather that he would decide on his course of action as the Senate debate proceeded. *New York Times*, Sept. 10, 1919.

4 Senator William Squire Kenyon, Republican of Iowa, who had been considered one of the "middle-ground reservationists" (according to the *New York Times*, Sept. 11, 1919), made an impassioned speech in the Senate on September 10 in which he announced that he would support the four reservations to the League Covenant just reported by the Foreign Relations Committee and strongly attacked Wilson both for his conduct of the peace negotiations and for his speeches on his western tour. *Cong. Record*, 66th Cong., 1st sess., pp. 5149-55.

From Carter Glass

Dear Mr. President: Washington September 11, 1919.

In view of the general importance of and interest in a solution of the international financial situation, I deem it advisable that the present position relative to foreign financing, and the general policy of the Treasury concerning this vital problem should be fully stated.

Since the armistice the United States has advanced to the Governments of the allies, as of the close of business August 15, 1919, the sum of $2,141,996,211.55, and there remained on August 15 an unexpended balance of $780,889,038.45 from the total loans of $10,000,000,000 authorized under the Liberty Loan Acts. The Treasury sees no need of an additional appropriation for government loans, though, it may later have occasion to ask the Congress to make some further modification of the terms under which the existing appropriation is available.

The Treasury asked and obtained power for the War Finance Corporation to make advances up to the amount of $1,000,000,000 for non-war purposes and the War Finance Corporation is prepared to make such advances.

The Secretary of War is authorized to sell his surplus stores on credit.

The United States Wheat Director is authorized to sell wheat to Europe on credit.

The power which at present exists in the Government or Governmental agencies to assist in meeting Europe's financial needs is, therefore, considerable. This power must, of course, be exercised with extreme caution and with the most careful regard for the urgent needs of our own people for an ample supply of foodstuffs and other necessities of life at reasonable prices.

The Treasury is prepared, at the convenience of the Governments of the Allies, to take up with their representatives the funding of the demand obligations which the United States holds, into long-time obligations, and at the same time the funding during the reconstruction period, or say for a period of two or three years, of the interest on the obligations of foreign Governments acquired by the United States under the Liberty Loan Acts.

The Treasury believes that the need of Europe for financial assistance, very great and very real though it is, has been much exaggerated both here and abroad. Our hearts have been so touched by the suffering which the war left in its train, and our experience is so recent of the financial conditions which existed during the war (when men were devoting themselves to the business of destruction) that we are prone to overlook the vast recuperative power inherent in any country which, though devastated, has not been depopulated, and the people of which are not starved afterwards. We must all feel deep sympathy for the suffering in Europe today, but we must not allow our sympathy to warp our judgment and, by exaggerating Europe's financial needs, make it more difficult to fill them.

Men must go back to work in Europe, must contribute to increase production. The industries of Europe, of course, cannot be set to work without raw materials, machinery, etc., and, to the extent that these are to be secured from the United States, the problem of financing the restoration of Europe belongs primarily to our exporters. Governmental financial assistance in the past and talk of plans for future government or banking aid to finance exports has apparently led our industrial concerns to the erroneous expectation that their war profits, based so largely on exports, will continue indefinitely without effort or risk on their part. To them will fall the profits of the exports and upon them will fall the consequences of failure to make the exports. So soon as domestic stocks, which were very low at the time of the armistice, have been replenished, those industries which have been developed to meet a demand for great exports, paid for out of government war loans, will be forced to close plants and forego dividends unless they maintain and develop an outlet abroad. The industries of the country must be brought to a realization of the gravity of this problem, must go out and seek markets abroad, must reduce prices at home and abroad to a reasonable level, and create or cooperate in creating the means of financing export business.

Since armistice day, the consistent policy of the Treasury has been, so far as possible, to restore private initiative and remove governmental controls and interferences. It has been the view of the

Treasury that only thus can the prompt restoration of healthy economic life be gained. The embargoes on gold and silver and control of foreign exchange have been removed, as well as the voluntary and informal control of call money and the stock exchange loan account. The control exercised by the Capital Issues Committee[1] over capital issues has been discontinued. Thus the financial markets of the United States have been opened to the whole world and all restrictions removed that might have hindered America's capital and credit resources, as well as its great gold reserve, from being available in aid of the world's commerce and Europe's need.

There are those who believe that the dollar should be kept at par—no more, no less—in the market of foreign exchange. If effective action were taken to carry out such a policy, it could only be done by drawing gold out of the United States when the dollar would otherwise be at a discount, and by inflating credit when the dollar would otherwise be at a premium.

The dollar is now at a premium almost everywhere in the world. Its artificial reduction and maintenance at the gold par of exchange in all currencies is quite unthinkable unless we propose to level all differences in the relative credit of nations and to substitute for our gold reserve, a reserve consisting of the promises to pay of any nation that chooses to become our debtor. Inequalities of exchange reflect not only the trade and financial balance between two countries, but, particularly after a great war such as that we have been through, the inequalities of domestic finance. The United States has met a greater proportion of the cost of the war from taxes and bond issues than any other country. Largely as a consequence of this policy, the buying power of the dollar at home has been better sustained than has the buying power at home of the currency of any European belligerent. For the United States to determine by governmental action to depress the dollar as measured in terms of foreign exchange and to improve the position of other currencies as measured in terms of dollars would be to shift to the American people the tax and loan burdens of foreign countries. This shifted burden would be measured by the taxes to be imposed and the further loans to be absorbed by our people as a consequence, and by increased domestic prices.

United States Government action at this time to prevent in respect to foreign exchange the ordinary operation of the law of supply and demand, which automatically sets in action corrective causes, and to prevent the dollar from going to a premium when its natural tendency is to do so, would artificially stimulate our ex-

---

[1] About which, see R. L. Owen to WW, July 18, 1918, Vol. 49.

ports, and, through the competition of export demand with domestic demand, maintain or increase domestic prices.

The view of the Governments of the Allies, I take it, is that had they, after the war control of their imports had been relaxed, attempted to continue to "peg" their exchanges here at an artificial level by Government borrowing, the effect would be to stimulate their imports and discourage their exports, thus aggravating their already unfavorable international balances.

The Treasury approves the Bill of Senator Edge (S. 2472)[2] to authorize the organization under Federal law of corporations to engage in the business of foreign banking and financing exports, of which corporations the Government would not be a stockholder, and the Bill (S. 2395) to permit national banks, to a limited extent, to be stockholders in such corporations.

The Treasury approves the Senate Joint Resolution No. 31, introduced by Senator Owen, to amend the War Finance Corporation Act, among other things, to remove the fixed minimum on the interest rate charged by it.[3]

It is essential to discriminate between plans, on the one hand, to support exchange by direct action of the United States Government and plans, on the other hand, to facilitate the extension of private credit and the investment of private capital in Europe. To the former the Treasury is utterly opposed. Of the latter the Treasury heartily approves.

It is not, of course, to be expected that the breach left by the withdrawal of Governmental support of exchange can be filled by private initiative until the ratification of the Treaty of Peace has given reasonable assurance against the political risk which, rather than any commercial or credit risk, now deters private lenders. Some progress has already been made in placing here through private channels the loans of Allied and neutral European countries and municipalities. The Treasury favors the making, in our markets, of such loans, which contribute to relieve the exchanges. I am sure that when Peace is consummated, and the political risk measurably removed, American exporters and European importers will lay the basis of credit in sound business transactions, and I know that American bankers will not fail then to devise means of financing the needs of the situation, nor American investors to respond to Europe's demand for capital, on a sound investment basis.

Meanwhile, it is well to remember the silent factors, which are

[2] About which, see also R. L. Owen to WW, July 16, 1919, and n. 4 thereto, Vol. 61, and C. Glass to WW, Aug. 25 (second letter of that date), 1919, Vol. 62.

[3] Again, see C. Glass to WW, Aug. 25, 1919. S. J. Res. 31 never emerged from the Senate Committee on Finance.

always at work towards a solution of the problem. Immigrants' remittances to Europe are, and will continue to be a very large item in rectifying the exchanges. As soon as Peace is concluded, foreign travel will be a further item. Another very important factor is the purchase of European securities and repurchase of foreign held American securities by American investors. But the principal factor in Europe's favor is the inevitable curtailment of her imports and expansion of her exports. These processes, of course, are stimulated by the very position of the exchanges which they tend to correct.   Faithfully yours,   Carter Glass

TLS (WP, DLC).

From William Phillips

Washington, D. C., Sept. 11, 1919

Sept. 11, 8 P.M. In view of the urgent request of Mr. Polk, and the possibility which his telegram appears to present, of a final settlement of the Adriatic question, I repeat the following telegram just received with the hope that, if possible, it may receive your attention and that you may be able to indicate a reply to be sent to Mr. Polk:

"Urgent 4143, Sept. 10, 10 P.M. Confidential. For the Secretary of State, from Polk.

Met Clemenceau and Lloyd George Saturday. The following draft[1] of a telegram which they planned to send to (the President) on the subject of the Adriatic:

'The attitude adopted by Signor Tittoni since his arrival in Paris is distinctly different from that of Signor Orlando and Sonnino. He has shown the most conciliatory disposition and a spirit of close solidarity with the Allies.

On one hand, instead of invoking, as did his predecessor, the Treaty of London (while claiming its violation Fiume) Signor Tittoni has taken his stand on the general principles of the conference (ethnographic and economic).

On the other hand, on this same basis, he has consequently, since the beginning of our conversations with him, consented to important sacrifices as compared with his first demands.

We (know) the keen desire that you showed during your stay in

[1] Drafts, both in English and French, of the following Clemenceau-Lloyd George proposal are in SDR, RG 256, 186.3411/790 and 793, DNA. Our corrections and additions are from those versions.

Paris to assist in a just (settlement) of the Adriatic problem. Only the obstinacy of Signor Orlando and Sonnino prevented us from succeeding.

From the point of view of the Peace negotiations, it is urgent to carry matters to a conclusion in the two-fold interest of the local calm in these regions, of the general peace of Europe, and of necessary solidarity of the countries founding the (League) of Nations. For these reasons we recommend urgently to your approval the following solution.

Part 1. Line of President Wilson

Italy accepts as Eastern frontier the line of President Wilson. She only demands that to the north of Albona this line shall join the sea South of [the] Chersano Fianona, thus leaving to Italy the city of Albona which is essentially Italian and whence there have come numerous Italian volunteers.

Part 2.

For Fiume two solutions are suggested.

First Solution. The city and district of Fiume (corpus separatum) shall be placed under the sovereignty of Italy. In this hypothesis, there will be no independent State of Fiume. Jugoslavia will receive all the territories comprising [comprised in] this state, according to the line of President Wilson (including the Island of Cherso, and excepting only Albona).

On the other hand, all the territories in question, that is, those that were to have formed part of the independent state, will be demilitarized [permanently]. Still in the same hypothesis, the Port of Fiume will be handed over with all facilities for its development as well as for that of the railway[s] terminating there, to the League of Nations which will make such arrangements as it may see fit for the country for which that port is the outlet as well as for the city of Fiume itself.

Second Solution. Fiume shall be constituted an independent state within the boundaries fixed by President Wilson (with the single rectification of Albona). This state shall be placed under the sovereignty of the League of Nations which shall (oversee) [assure] its administration under a [commission of] government which [and] shall control the port and railroads as much in the interest of the countries of which they are the outlet as in the interest of the state itself. All facilities shall be furnished for the development of the port and railways terminating there.

A special statute protecting the Italianity of the corpus separatum of Fiume shall be established by the commission of government.

In both cases the rights of ethnical minorities shall be guarded [guaranteed].

Part 3. Dalmatia.

All Dalmatia to the Jugoslavs except the city of Zara and the island of Uglian immediately neighbor of Zara, which shall be submitted to a (garbled group) special commission [regime]. The strong [Their] Italian character shall be dealt with [protected] by constituting Zara a free and autonomous city under the [guarantee of the] League of Nations, which shall recognize and encourage its intimate connection with the Italian State and Italian culture. (Every facility shall be furnished to the commerce of the hinterland.) The economic interests of Italy which existed [exist] in Dalmatia and the Italian [blank] [minority] rights shall be guaranteed.

Part 4. Islands.

The only Italian islands would be Lussin, Unie, Lissa, and Pelagosa.

Part 5. Albania.

Mandate to Italians.

Part 6. Valona.

Italian sovereignty over the city, with the hinterland strictly necessary to its economic life and to its security.

Part 7. Railroads.

Concerning the Asseling [Assling] railroad, [Italy] no longer presents territorial demands but only asks for precise guarantees for the use of the line in Jugoslav territory. As a counter, no territorial cessation [cession] shall be granted the Jugoslavs in the Drin Valley, but there [they] shall be accorded a reciprocal use of the railroad to be constructed, and the same guarantees which would be given to Italy regarding the Asseling railroad.

Part 8. Neutralization.

Italy proposes the general neutrality [neutralization] of [all] the coast and the islands from the south point of Istria as far as and including Cattaro.

Part 9. Resumé.

Italy [therefore] makes the following concessions:

(A) She withdraws her territorial demands concerning the Asseling triangle.

(B) She accepts the Line of President Wilson from Idria as far as the north of Albona.

(C) She accepts that the Cherso Island constitute either a part of the independent state or of Jugoslavia.

(D) She abandons all Dalmatia.

(E) She accepts general neutralization.'

(End of the joint telegram of Clemenceau and Lloyd George.)

I wrote a personal letter to Clemenceau and Balfour on the advice of Johnson and the (commissioners),[2] saying that I was convinced your reply would certainly be negative unless certain indispensable changes were made. The changes we urged were the following:

Part 2. First Solution.

Change first sentence to read "The city and district of Fiume (that is, the corpus separatum) will constitute a free and independent city-state under the permanent protection of the League of Nations." Change last sentence to read "Still under the same hypothesis, the port and port facilities, including the railways within the city-state, will be placed under control of the [League of Nations, which will lease them for a term of years to the State of the] Serbs, Croats, and Slovenes, under a charter guaranteeing the free development of the city and of all the hinterland states for which the port is the natural outlet." This last provision seems essential to get Jugoslav government aid for the costly port improvements.

Part 2. Second Solution.

The free state must have right of plebiscite in five years, the state to vote as a whole and not by parts, with no special status for Fiume. We have throughout maintained a firm stand that any settlement for Fiume must involve rights [right] of plebiscite as provided in the President's former declaration [formula], if there is a large free state; but that if there is to be permanent independence [imposed] without a plebiscite, only the corpus separatum of Fiume itself must be involved. I emphasized the fact that America cannot consent to forcing 200,000 Jugoslavs of the larger state to remain apart from the rest of their nation unless they themselves consent by plebiscite to such permanent separation. Tittoni wants large permanent [free] state without right of plebiscite, saying frankly that plebiscite would result in union with Jugoslavia. Balfour and Lloyd George both approve American position [attitude] but feel under obligations to Tittoni to send his proposed formal declaration [formula] to the President.

Part 3.

Omit reference to Island of Uglian, and change second sentence to read: "The Italian character of the town of Zara will be recognized and safeguarded by making it an autonomous city under [blank] [permanent] guarantee of the League of Nations [blank] [The modality of this self-government] and its relation to the gov-

[2] An undated copy of this letter, drafted by Johnson, is in SDR, RG 256, 186.3411/788B, DNA. This letter paraphased "Johnson Modifications of Final Proposal of Clemenceau and Lloyd George on Adriatic Settlement," T MS, SDR, RG 256, 186.3411/789, DNA. Corrections are from this copy.

ernment of the State of Serbs, Croats and Slovenes will be determined by Zara itself through its properly authorized organization
[representatives], in conference with the representatives of the
State of the Serbs, Croats and Slovenes. In case of disagreement,
the League of Nations shall decide the points at issue." Regarding
Zara we have maintained that there must be no solution separating
the city from the Jugoslav nation, with which it has all its natural,
geographic, political, and economic connections, and upon which
it depends for its future prosperity. It is the consummation [capital]
of Dalmatia, and to sever its political ties with the province would
be disastrous. The island of Uglian has 8,000 Jugoslavs and only
24 Italians. We have therefore refused to consider Italy's claims to
this island, and Tittoni has agreed that he will withdraw his claim,
although he wants the telegram to go to the President, thus [with-
out] making the concession in advance. Balfour supports our views
in regard to Zara.

Part 4.

Change to read as follows: "The only Italian islands will be Lussin, Unie, Lissa, and [the] smaller islands to the West of [and] the
Pelagosa group. The Slav populations of the Lissa group will be
given complete local autonomy under Italian sovereignty." Tittoni
abandoned claim to Lagosta in return for small outer islands west
of Lissa. Omission of these smaller islands from text of telegram[3]
is an error.

Part 7.

Omit second sentence, as this is a special problem to be considered on its merits when arranging terms of mandate for Albania. It
is understood that use of lines [line] across Asseling triangle means
guarantees of unhampered transit.

Part 8.

Principle of navigation convention [neutralization] accepted, but
southward limit of neutralization to be determined in consultation
with naval authorities of the principal Allied and Associated Powers.

Tittoni,[4] Balfour, and Tardieu called on me yesterday and said
that in view of my letter, they suggested that I should send to you
informally their proposal, and at the same time, the substance of
the letter referred to above, which I wrote Balfour and Clemenceau; their idea being that it would be better to have the case
(placed) before the President in that way rather than make a per-

[3] FLP to WW and RL, Aug. 31, 1919, Vol. 62.
[4] At this point, Polk begins to write. All corrections in the following paragraph are
from W. Phillips to WW, Sept. 11, 1919, T telegram (SDR, RG 59, 763.72119/6669,
DNA).

sonal appeal to him, and have signified hope that the President could give them an answer which would be his final word on the subject of the Adriatic question. I told them that they must realize that if the President made any concessions, the whole Adriatic question must be treated as a [blank] [whole] and that if they did not accept his [this] proposal, all likelihood that[5] concessions made by him lapsed. I pointed out in regard to the Albanian mandate that the President had always thought [felt] this question should not be settled at this time. They all said that as that question was important to Italy, they hoped some decision could be reached.

Regarding[6] the Albanian mandate, we have discussed the question at some length with the French and British. The commissioners, and experts, including Johnson and Coolidge, are unanimously of the opinion that a single mandate over a united Adriatic [Albania] is far wiser than any solution involving division of that country among the [blank] [Jugoslavs], Greeks, and Italians, as foreseen in the Treaty of London, or the establishment of three spheres of influence or three different mandates in the territory. Italy can never agree to a French mandate, and the British say that they cannot accept the mandate. If, as seems probable, an American mandate is out of the question, we are of the opinion that the only practical solution is an Italian mandate, and that in the absence of a better solution, we should not oppose the desire of the British and French to accord this mandate to Italy, but should use our entire influence in so circumscribing and limiting the terms of the mandate as to prevent Italian colonization, militarization, and exploitation of the country. If the president will approve this point of view, Clemenceau and Lloyd George believe that they can induce Tittoni to accept all the modifications for Italy [of his proposal] which are contained in my letter quoted above.[7] We would then be in a position to enter upon [get] an immediate settlement of the entire Adriatic controversy which would contain nothing that the Jugoslavs could not reasonably be expected to accept. We earnestly hope, therefore, that the President will authorize amending and accepting [the accepting of] the entire proposed settlement on the understanding that the modifications suggested in this telegram are made, and that the Albanian mandate is to be so limited as to prevent colonization, and provide neutralization or a military sterilization of the territory outside of Veipona [Vallona], and to guarantee to Jugoslavia the right to consolidate [construct] and op-

[5] "likelihood that" not in the telegram cited in n. 4 above.
[6] At this point, Polk resumes quoting from Johnson's memorandum cited above. All corrections in the following paragraph are from it.
[7] "in my letter quoted above" is Polk's change.

erate a railway across the northern part of the territory and to improve and develop the Boyana river, which serves as the outlet of the basin of Montenegro [blank] [Scutari] most of which lies in Montenegro. This last on condition that Montenegro joins the Jugoslav State.

I may add[8] that this solution has been carefully worked out by Johnson and has his full approval, also that Tittoni is ready to make concessions after the President urges their necessity, and take such steps.[9] [that] Clemenceau and Balfour expect Tittoni to accept the modifications proposed. As Tittoni is to speak before the Chamber next Tuesday, it is decidedly useful to know by that date whether the President will accept solution as modified. For that reason, this message should be sent to the President without a moment's delay, in the hope that he can give us an answer immediately, as it will assist Nitti and Tittoni in their fight to have the treaty ratified in Italy, if they can know the President's decision. [Polk]"   William Phillips

T telegram (WP, DLC).
   [8] Here Polk resumes writing.
   [9] "take such steps" is not in the telegram cited in n. 4 above.

From the Diary of Dr. Grayson

Friday, September 12, 1919.

It had been intended that the Special train would leave the Great Northern tracks and proceed to Coeur d'Alene, Idaho, via the Inland Empire Route. However, as a result of the war, the Inland Empire tracks had deteriorated somewhat and the officials did not want to take the chances of having a very heavy train run over the line. In consequence, the train was halted at Wallace,[1] Idaho, and Coeur d'Alene was reached by an automobile ride of twenty-five miles. It had rained during the night—the first rain for many months—and it was still cloudy when the President left the train. The run through the country was very pleasant, and when Coeur d'Alene was reached a good crowd was on hand to greet the President.

The meeting here was held in a big circus tent that had been erected on the shores of Coeur d'Alene Lake.[2] There was no auditorium in the city, but because Idaho was the home of Senator Borah, the chief opponent of the Treaty of Versailles, it had been felt essential that the President should make an address in the city.

Governor [David William Davis] presided at the meeting. He is a Republican but he declared himself as favorable to the Treaty in general. He and Mrs. [Davis][3] had been compelled to go all the way to Spokane, Washington, from Boise in order to reach Coeur d'Alene and preside at the meeting. But he told the President that he considered the time well spent.

The President again repeated his strictures on the Boston Police for their strike, and also attacked all radicalism that savored of violence.

Returning to the train[4] a start was made for Spokane at 12:00 o'clock, and the latter city was reached at 2:00 in the afternoon. The 21st Infantry of the Regular Army acted as the President's escort through the streets of Spokane. It was somewhat of a coincidence that this particular organization should be on duty here inasmuch as in the days just before the Spanish American War this regiment was stationed at Plattsburgh, New York, and was known throughout the service as "The President's Own," because of the interest that President McKinley took in it. After a lapse of twenty-one years, the regiment, which had been "The President's Own" near the Atlantic, was the president's Guard near the Pacific.

The President was escorted to the National Guard Armory, where he delivered an address, in which he followed rather closely the lines of his Coeur d'Alene speech. The crowd,[5] as usual, was demonstrative and apparently well pleased with his arguments.

Spokane was left at 4:00 o'clock for a night run to Tacoma, Washington.[6]

[1] Actually, Wilson's party both left the train and returned to it at the village of Rathdrum, Idaho, approximately twelve miles northwest of Coeur d'Alene. *Coeur d'Alene Evening Press*, Sept. 12, 1919, and *Seattle Post-Intelligencer*, Sept. 13, 1919.

[2] The *Seattle Post-Intelligencer* reported that Wilson spoke before an audience of "less than 2,000 persons . . . although the seating capacity was much larger." *Ibid.*

[3] Nellie Johnson Davis.

[4] Wilson briefly addressed a crowd from the rear platform of the train at Rathdrum. Spokane *Spokesman-Review*, Sept. 13, 1919.

[5] "The Armory was comfortably filled, the number of people seated and standing be [was] estimated at 4,500." The same reporter also commented: "It was remarked that his voice lacked resonance, and there was a suggestion of a man very much fatigued in his delivery." *Seattle Post-Intelligencer*, Sept. 13, 1919.

[6] The *New York Times*, Sept. 14, 1919, reported that Wilson's train stopped briefly at Pasco, Washington, shortly after 9 p.m. on September 12. Wilson came out of his private car to shake hands and exchange greetings with a large crowd. "After telling several stories," the account continued, "he wound up by making a short speech, in which he said that the war was unfinished until the United States had assumed responsibility for its pledges that future wars should be made impossible."

An Address at Coeur d'Alene

September 12, 1919.

Governor Davis, my fellow citizens, it is with the very greatest pleasure that I find myself facing an audience in this great state. I echo the wish of the Governor that it might be our privilege to stay a long time in Idaho and know something more than her fame— know her people, come in contact with her industries, and see the things that we have all so long read about and admired from a distance. But, unfortunately, it is necessary for us to go back to Washington as soon as we can, though it was a great pleasure to escape from Washington. (laughter and applause) Washington is a very interesting place, but it is a very lonely place. (laughter) The people of the United States do not live there, and in order to know what the people of the United States are thinking about and talking about, it is necessary to come and find out for yourself. And that really is my errand.

I have taken pains since I was a boy so to saturate myself in the traditions of America that I generally feel a good deal of confidence that the impulses which I find in myself are American impulses. But no matter how thoroughly American a man may be, he needs constantly to renew his touch with all parts of America and to be sure that his mind is guided, if he be in public station, by the thoughts and purposes of his fellow countrymen. And it was, therefore, with the most earnest desire to get in touch with you and the rest of my fellow countrymen that I undertook this trip, for, my fellow countrymen, we are facing a decision now in which we cannot afford to make a mistake. We must not let ourselves be deceived as to the gravity of that decision or as to the implications of that decision. It will mean a great deal now, but it will mean infinitely more in the future. And America has today, at this moment, nothing less than to prove to the world whether she has meant what she said in the past. (applause)

I must confess that I have been amazed that there are some men in responsible positions who are opposed to the ratification of the treaty of peace with Germany altogether. It is natural that so great a document, full of so many particular provisions, should draw criticisms upon itself for this, that, or the other provision. It is natural that a world settlement—for it is nothing less—should give occasion for a great many differences of opinion with regard to particular features of it. But I must admit that it amazes me that there should be any who should propose that the arrangement should be rejected altogether.

Because, my fellow citizens, this is the issue: we went into this

Great War from which we have just issued with certain assurances given ourselves and given to the world, and those assurances cannot be fulfilled unless this treaty is adopted. We told the world, and we assured ourselves, that we went into this war in order to see to it that the kind of purpose represented by Germany in this war should never be permitted to be accomplished by Germany or anybody else. (applause)

Do not let your thoughts dwell too constantly upon Germany. Germany attempted this outrageous thing, but Germany was not the only country that had ever entertained the purpose of subjecting the peoples of the world to its will. And when we went into this war, we said that we sent our soldiers across the sea, not because we thought this was an American fight in particular, but because we knew that the purpose of Germany was against liberty, and that when anybody was fighting liberty it was our duty to go into the contest. (applause) We set this nation up with the profession then that we wanted to set an example of liberty, not only, but to lead the world in the paths of liberty and justice and of right. And, at last, after long reflection, after long hesitation, after trying to persuade ourselves that this was a European war and nothing more, we suddenly looked our own consciences in the face and said: "This is not merely a European war. This is a war which imperils the very principles for which this government was set up, and it is our duty to lend all the force that we have, whether of men or of resources, to the resistance of these designs."

And it was America—never let anybody forget this—it was America that saved the world, (applause) and those who propose the rejection of the treaty propose that, after having redeemed the world, we should desert the world, for it would be nothing less.

The settlements of this treaty cannot be maintained without the concerted action of all the great governments of the world. I asked you just now not to think exclusively about Germany, but turn your thoughts back to what it was that Germany purposed. Germany did direct her first offense against France and against Belgium, but you know that it was not her purpose to remain in France, although it was part of her purpose to remain in Belgium. She was using her arms against these people so that they could not prevent what she intended elsewhere, and what she intended elsewhere was to make an open line of dominion between her and the Far East. The formula that she adopted was Bremen to Baghdad, the North Sea to Persia—to crush not only little Serbia, whom she first started to crush, but all the Balkan states, get Turkey in her grasp, take all the Turkish and Arabian lands beyond, penetrate the wealthy realms of Persia, open the gates of India, and, by dominating the central trade routes of the world, dominate the world itself.

That was her plan; and what does the treaty of peace do? For I want you to remember, my fellow countrymen, that this treaty is not going to stand by itself. The treaty with Austria has now been signed. It will presently be sent over, and I shall lay that before the Senate of the United States. It will be laid down along exactly the same lines as the treaty with Germany. And the lines of the treaty with Germany suggest this—that we are setting up the very states which Germany and Austria intended to dominate as independent, self-governing units. We are giving them what they never could have got with their own strength, what they could have got only by the united strength of the armies of the world, and which was the only thing that will prevent German domination, which was at first intended. But we have not made them strong by making them independent. We have given them what I have called their land titles. We have said: "These lands that others have tried to dominate and exploit for their own uses belong to you, and we cede them to you in fee simple. They never did belong to anybody else. They were loot. It was brigandage to take them. We give them to you in fee simple." But what is the use of setting up the titles if we do not guarantee them? (applause) And that guarantee is the only guarantee against the repetition of the war we have gone through just so soon as that great nation, the German nation, 60,000,000 strong, can again recover its strength and its spirit, for east of Germany lie the fertile fields of intrigue and power. At this moment the only people who are dealing with the Bolshevist government in Russia are the Germans. They are fraternizing with the few who exercise control in that distracted country. They are making all their plans that the finances of Russia and the commerce of Russia and the development of Russia shall be as soon as possible in the hands of Germans. And just so soon as she can command that great power, that is also her road to the East and to the domination of the world. If you do not guarantee the titles that you are setting up in these treaties, you leave the whole ground fallow in which again to sow the dragon's teeth with the harvest of armed men.

That, my fellow citizens, is what Article X, that you hear so much talked about in the Covenant of the League of Nations, does. It guarantees the land titles of the world; and if you do not guarantee the land titles of the world, there cannot be the ordered society in which men can live. (applause) Off here in this beloved continent, with its great free stretches and great free people, we have not realized the cloud of dread and terror under which the people of Europe have lived. I have heard men over there say: "It is intolerable. We would rather die now than live another fifty years under the cloud that has hung over us ever since the Franco-Prussian War of 1870-1871. Because we have known that this force was gathering, we have known what the purpose was ultimately to be, we have known that dread and terror lay ahead of us, and we cannot and will not live under that cloud any more."

And America, my fellow citizens, is necessary to the peace of the world. America is absolutely necessary to the peace of the world. Germany realizes that, and I want to tell you now and here—I wish I could proclaim it in tones so loud that they would reach the world—Germany wants us to stay out of this treaty. (applause) Not under any delusion. Not under the delusion that we will turn in sympathy toward her. Not under the delusion that we would seek in any direct or conscious way to serve Germany, but with the knowledge that the guarantees will not be sufficient without America, and that, inasmuch as Germany is out of the arrangement, it will be very useful to Germany to have America out of the arrangement.

Because Germany knows that if America is out of the arrangement, America will lose the confidence and cooperation of all the other nations in the world, and, fearing America's strength, she wants to see America alienated from the peoples from whom she has been alienated. It is a perfectly reasonable program. She wants to see America isolated. She is isolated. She wants to see one great nation left out of this combination which she never would again dare face. (applause) Evidence is not lacking—nay, evidence is abounding—that the pro-German propaganda has started up in this country coincidently with the opposition to the adoption of this treaty. I want those who have any kind of sympathy with the purposes with which we went into the war now to reflect upon this proposition: are we going to prove the enemy of the rest of the world just when we have proved their savior? The thing is intolerable. The thing is impossible. America has never been unfaithful, and she never will be unfaithful. (applause)

And don't let anybody delude you, my fellow citizens, with the pose of being an American. If I am an American, I want at least to be an intelligent American. If I am a true American, I will study the true interests of America. If I am a true American, I will have the world vision that America has always had—drawing her blood, drawing her genius, as she has drawn her people, out of all the great constructive peoples of the world. A true American conceives America in the atmosphere and the whole setting of her fortune and her destiny. And America needs the confidence of the rest of the world just as much as other nations do. America needs the cooperation of the rest of the world to release her resources, to make her markets, above all things else to link together the spirits of men who mean to redeem the race from the wrongs that it has suffered.

This is the country par excellence, I mean this western country is par excellence the country of progressivism. I am not now using it with a big "P." It does not make any difference whether you belong to the Progressive party or not; you belong to the progressive thought, (applause) as I hope every intelligent man belongs to the progressive thought. It is the only thought that the world is going to tolerate. And if you believe in progress, if you believe in progressive reform, if you believe in making the lot of men better, if you believe in purifying politics and enlarging the purposes of public policy, then you have got to have a world in which that will be possible. And if America does not enter with all her soul into this new world arrangement, progressives might as well go out of business, because there is going to be universal disorder, as there is now universal unrest.

Don't mistake the signs of the times, my fellow countrymen, and don't think that America is immune. The poison that has spread all through that pitiful nation of Russia is spreading all through Europe. There is not a statesman in Europe who does not dread the infection of it. And just so certainly as those people are disconcerted, thrown back upon their own resources, disheartened, rendered cynical by the withdrawal of the only people in the world they trust, just so certainly there will be universal upsetting of order in Europe.

And if the order of Europe is upset, do you think America is going to be quiet? Have you not been reading in the papers of the intolerable thing that has just happened in Boston? When the police of a great city walk out and leave that city to be looted they have committed an intolerable crime against civilization. (loud and long applause) And if that spirit is going to prevail, where is your program? How can you carry a program out when every man is taking what he can get? How can you carry a program out when there is no authority upon which to base it? How can you carry a program out when every man is looking out for his own selfish interests and refuses to be bound by any law that regards the interests of others? There will be no reform in this world for a generation if the conditions of the world are not now brought to settled order, and they cannot be brought to settled order without the cooperation of America. (applause)

I am not speaking with conjecture, my fellow citizens. I would be ashamed of myself if, upon a theme so great as this, I should seek to mislead you by overstatement of any kind. I know what I am talking about. I spent six months amidst those disturbed peoples on the other side of the water, and I can tell you, now and here, that the only people they depend upon to bring the world to settled conditions are the people of America. (applause) A chill will go to their hearts, a discouragement will come down upon them, a cynicism will take possession of them, which will make progress impossible, if we do not take part, not only, but do not take part with all our might and with all our genius. Everybody who loves justice and who hopes for programs of reform must support the unqualified adoption of this treaty. (applause)

I send this challenge out to the conscience of every man in America—that if he knows anything of the conditions of the world, if he knows anything of the present state of society throughout the world and really loves justice and purposes just reform, he must support the treaty with Germany. I do not want to say that and have it proved by tragedy, for if this treaty should be rejected, if it should be impaired, then, amidst the tragedy of the things that would follow, every man would be converted to the opinion that I am now uttering. But I do not want to see that sort of conversion. I do not want to see an era of blood and chaos to convert men to the only practicable methods of justice.

My fellow citizens, there are a great many things needing to be reformed in America. We are not exempt from those very subtle influences which lead to all sorts of incidental injustices. We ourselves are in danger at this present moment of minorities trying to control our affairs. And, whenever a minority tries to control the affairs of a country, it is fighting against the interest of that country just as much as if it were trying to upset the government. (applause) If you think that you can afford to live in a chaotic world, then speak words of encouragement to the men who are opposing this treaty. But if you want to have your own fortunes held steady, realize that the fortunes of the world must be held steady; that if you want to keep your own boys at home after this terrible experience, you will see that boys elsewhere are kept at home. Because America is not going to refuse, when the other catastrophe comes, again to attempt to save the world, and, having given this proof once, I pray God we may not be given occasion to prove it again!

We went into this war promising every loving heart in this country who had parted with a beloved youngster that we were going to fight a war which would make that sacrifice unnecessary again, and we must redeem that promise or be of all men the most unfaithful. (applause) If I did not go on this errand through the United States, if I did not do everything that was within my power that is honorable to get this treaty adopted, and adopted without qualifications, I never could look another mother in the face upon whose cheeks there were the tears of sorrowful memory with regard to the boy buried across the sea. The moral compulsion laid upon America now is a compelling compulsion and cannot be escaped. And so, my fellow countrymen, because it is a moral issue, because it is an issue in which is mixed up every sort of interest in America, I am not in the least uneasy about the results.

If you put it on the lowest level, you cannot trade with a world disordered, and if you do not trade you draw your own industries within a narrower and narrower limit. This great state, with its untold natural resources, with its great undeveloped resources, will have to stand for a long generation stagnant because there are no distant markets calling for these things. All America will have to wait a long, anxious generation through to see the normal courses of her life restored. And so, if I were putting it upon the lowest conceivable basis of the amount of money we could make, I would say: "We have got to assist in the restoration of order and the maintenance of order throughout the world by the maintenance of the morale of the world."

You will say, "How? By arms?" That, I suspect, is what most of the opponents of the League of Nations, at any rate, try to lead you to believe, that this is a league of arms. Why, my fellow citizens, it is a league to bring about the things that America has been advocating ever since I was born. It is a league to bring it about that there shall not be war, but that there shall be substituted for it arbitration and the calm settlements of discussion. (applause) That is the heart of the League. The heart of the League is this: every member of the League—and that will mean every fighting nation in the world except Germany—every member of the League agrees that it will never go to war without first having done one or the other of two things—either having submitted the matter in dispute to arbitration, in which case it agrees absolutely to abide by the result, or, having submitted it to consideration by the Council of the League of Nations, in which case it promises to lay all the documents, all the facts, in its possession before the Council and to wait and to give the Council six months in which to consider the matter. And, if it does not like the opinion of the Council at the end of the six months, still to wait three months more before it resorts to arms. (applause)

Why, that is what America has been striving for. That is what the Congress of the United States directed me to bring about. (slight applause) Perhaps you do not know where. It was in an unexpected place—in the naval appropriations bill. (laughter) Congress, authorizing a great building program of ships and the expenditure of vast sums of money to make our navy one of the strongest in the world, paused a moment and declared, in the midst of the appropriation bill, that it was the policy of the United States to bring about disarmament, and that for that purpose it was the policy of the United States to cooperate in the creation of a great international tribunal to which should be submitted questions of international difference and controversy. (slight applause) And it directed the President of the United States, not later than the close of this war, to call together an international conference for that purpose. It even went so far as to make an appropriation to pay the expenses for the conduct of such a conference in the city of Washington. And that is a continuing provision of the naval appropriations bill. When I came back with this Covenant of the League of Nations, I had fulfilled the mandate of the Congress of the United States. (applause) And now they don't like it. (laughter)

There is only one conceivable reason for not liking it, my fellow citizens, and to me as an American it is not a conceivable reason, and that is that we should wish to do some nation some great wrong. If there is any nation in the world that can afford to submit its purposes to discussion, it is the American nation. (applause) If I belonged to some other nation, there are some things that I know I would not like to see submitted to the discussion of mankind. (laughter) But I do not know anything in the present purposes of the United States that I would not be perfectly willing to lay upon any table of council in the world. And so, in carrying out the mandate of the Congress, I was serving the age-long purpose of this great people, which purpose centers in justice and in peace.

You will say, "Well, why not go in with reservations?" I wonder if you know what that means. If the Senate of the United States passes a resolution of ratification and says that it ratifies on condition that so and so and so and so is understood, that will have to be resubmitted to every signatory of the treaty, and what gravels me is that it will have to be submitted to the German Assembly at Weimar. And that goes against my digestion. (applause) We cannot honorably put anything in that treaty, which Germany has signed and ratified, without Germany's consent, whereas it is perfectly feasible, my fellow countrymen, if we put interpretations upon that treaty which its language clearly warrants, to notify the other governments of the world that we do understand the treaty in that sense. It is perfectly feasible to do that, and perfectly honorable to do that, because, mark you, nothing can be done under this treaty through the instrumentality of the Council of the League of Nations except by a unanimous vote. The vote of the United States will always be necessary, and it is perfectly legitimate for the United States to notify the other governments beforehand that its vote in the Council of the League of Nations will be based upon such and such an understanding of the provisions of the treaty.

And the treaty is not susceptible of misunderstanding. I do not object to painting the rose or refining fine gold. There isn't any phrase in the Covenant of the League of Nations that can legitimately be said to be of doubtful meaning. But if the Congress of the United States wants to state the meaning over again in other words and say to the other nations of the world, "We understand the treaty to mean what it says," I think that is a work of supererogation, but I do not see any moral objection to it. (laughter and applause)

But anything that qualifies the treaty, anything that is a condition to our ratification of it, must be submitted to all the others, and we must go over this process again—this process which took six months of intensive labor, which took six months of very difficult adjustment and arrangement, which quieted jealousies, which allayed suspicions, which set aside controversies, which brought about the most extraordinary union of minds that was ever brought about in so miscellaneous an assembly, divided by so many interests. All that must be gone over again, and in the meantime the world must wait and its unrest grow deeper, and all the pulses of life go slower, waiting to see what is going to happen—all because the United States asks the other governments of the world to accept what they have already accepted in different language.

That is all that it amounts to, I mean all that the reasonable reservations amount to. Some of them amount to staying out altogether, some of them amount to a radical change of the spirit of the instrument, but I am speaking now of those which some men of high conscience and of high public purpose are seriously pressing in order that there may be no misunderstanding. You can avoid any misunderstanding without changing the document. You can avoid a misunderstanding without qualifying the terms of the document, because, as I have said and shall say again and again, America is at liberty as one of the voting members of the partnership to state how she understands the articles of copartnership.

I beg that these things may sink in your thoughts, my fellow countrymen, because we are at a turning point in the fortunes of the world. Out upon these quiet hills and in these great valleys it is difficult sometimes for me to remember the turmoil of the world in which I have been mixing on the other side of the sea. It is difficult for me to remember the surging passions which moved upon the face of the other continents of the world. It is difficult for me to remember the infinite suffering that obtained even in this beloved country. It is difficult for me to remember the delegations from weak peoples that came to me in Paris, figuratively speaking, with outstretched hands, pleading that America should lead the world out of the darkness into the light. It is difficult out here in this great place for anybody, even, I dare say, for these fine fellows in khaki who were over there and saw something of it, to remember the hot strain and terror of the thing. But we must remember it, my fellow citizens, and we must see to it that this strain and terror never come upon the world again. It is with this solemn thought—that we are at a turning point in the destinies of mankind and that America is the makeweight of mankind—that I, with perfect confidence, leave this great question to your unbiased judgment. (applause)[1]

Printed in *Addresses of President Wilson*, with corrections from the complete text in the Spokane *Spokesman-Review*, Sept. 13, 1919.
[1] There is a WWT outline of this address in WP, DLC.

Two Memoranda by Joseph Patrick Tumulty

[En route] September 12, 1919.

Memo for the President[1] is as follows:

War cost to allies, exclusive of normal expenses and loans to one another, as follows:

Great Britain and Dominions,	$ 38,000,000,000;
France	26,000,000,000;
United States	22,000,000,000;
Russia	18,000,000,000;
Italy	13,000,000,000.
Total (including Belgium, Japan and smaller countries)	123,000,000,000;
Central powers:	
Germany	39,000,000,000;
Austria-Hungary	21,000,000,000;
Turkey and Bulgaria	3,000,000,000;
Total	63,000,000,000;
GRAND TOTAL (direct war cost)	186,000,000,000.

The expenditures of the United States was at the rate of one million dollars an hour for two years.

Battle deaths during the whole war, as follows:

Russia	1,700,000;
Germany	1,600,000;

France	1,385,000;
Great Britain	900,000;
Austria	800,000;
Italy	364,000;
United States	50,300;
Total for all belligerents including above	7,450,200.

Totals for wounded not obtainable. Total wounded for United States army 230,000, excluding killed, for which figures given above.

The total of all battle deaths in all the wars of the world, from the year 1793 to 1914, was something under 6,000,000 men.

The battle deaths in this war alone exceeded those of the previous hundred years by one and a half million men.

[1] The following memorandum is based on information transmitted in NDB to JPT, Sept. 12, 1919, T telegram (WP, DLC).

Memorandum for the President: [En route] 12 September 1919.

Suggestions for Speech

Answer the question, "Is there to be a big standing army in Europe to back up our mandatories?"

What we fought for. (See President's speech to Congress on April 2, 1917—page 197 of attached volume.)

"We shall fight for the things which we have always carried nearest our hearts,—for democracy, for the right of those who submit to authority to have a voice in their own governments, for the rights and liberties of small nations, for a universal dominion of right by such a concert of free peoples as shall bring peace and safety to all nations and make the world itself at last free. To such a task we can dedicate our lives and our fortunes, everything that we are and everything that we have, with the pride of those who know that the day has come when America is privileged to spend her blood and her might for the principles that gave her birth and happiness and the peace which she has treasured."

The President might read this to his audiences.

Reavowal of those prinicples in the Fourteen Points. Their acceptance by the leading newspapers and Republican statesmen of the country.

Argument: The League of Nations, a non-partisan instrumentality. The result of agitation of years. Backed by Republicans throughout the country, as well as leaders of opinion. Call attention to Mr. Taft and Mr. Wickersham; call attention to peculiar character of Mr.

Wickersham's support—originally an opponent, but after his visit to Europe, an enthusiastic supporter.[1]

It substitutes arbitration and investigation for war. Mr. Roosevelt in his last article appearing in the Metropolitan Magazine,[2] advocated arbitration treaties with all nations making every question, even those affecting national honor, arbitral.

Result of nations violating terms of League—economic isolation, black list.

The world has drawn the sword of public opinion against war. The issue is one of peace or war. The President should read to the audience the figures in Secretary Baker's telegram giving the cost of the war in money, and in deaths and wounded. The President could in an eloquent way call attention to what these figures mean. Something like the following: "These figures are cold but it is the tragedy that lies behind those figures which calls forth our emotion and our interest and even our pity. They speak of broken hearts, desolated homes and ravaged fields. They speak of mothers bereft of their sons whom they freely gave to the Nation to vindicate the splendid conceptions of liberty and freedom which the genius of America typefies. They speak of wives in despair and of sweethearts whose tender hopes were cut asunder. They speak of the flower of European and American youth going out to die that the world may be free. Do not these figures carry home a lesson to you all? What do you think these boys died for? What do you think these mothers who freely gave up their sons wished for down in the depths of their very hearts and souls? These boys died like crusaders that men might be free, that their children might be free. No mother ever gave up her son to war who did not in her heart of hearts pray that statesmen might develop some instrumentality which might make these horrible things forever impossible. No man who visited Europe and who witnessed the wreck and ruin wrought by this monster of war did not pray God that out of this maelstrom of blood and tears might come a League of Nations that might make this thing of war impossible in the future."

T MSS (WP, DLC).

[1] George Woodward Wickersham, Attorney General in the Taft cabinet, had expressed doubts about a league of nations in a speech in New York before the Council on Foreign Relations on November 26, 1918. He declared that the association of nations proposed by Wilson in his Fourteen Points Address (printed at Jan. 8, 1918, Vol. 45) was "nothing more or less than an offensive and defensive alliance of all the nations," which would "embrace great and small States, and secure to them their territorial integrity." Such a proposal raised an "infinite number of questions." What nations would belong to the league? Were great and small nations to have an equal voice in its deliberations and decisions? Would there be any limits on the questions that might be brought before it? The American people and the United States Senate, he said, would have a great deal to say about any concrete project for such an organization. *New York Times*, Nov. 27, 1918.

However, by March 1919, after his return from a trip to Europe to observe the peace conference as a special correspondent for the *New York Tribune*, Wickersham had become a strong supporter of the League of Nations Covenant. In a speech before the Japan Society in New York on March 14, he said that the United States had an obligation to help restore order in the world. The Covenant established an organization that could do so. "That document," he continued, "is not perfect. It should be amended in several particulars. Doubtless it will be so amended. It has the merit of simplicity of conception and structure. If there is to be a League its constitution hardly could contain less than does that document. It contains provisions for growth." *New York Times,* March 15, 1919. He clarified his thought in an address in Boston four days later: "If there is to be any League of the Nations responsible for the overthrow of the Teuton powers, to preserve the fruits of victory, and to prevent unnecessary and preventable war in the future, it could be vested with no less power than is conferred in this instrument." *Ibid.,* March 19, 1919.

In June, Wickersham contributed a lengthy article to the *New York Times* in which he refuted point by point the criticisms of the League made not only by senators such as Lodge, Knox, Borah, and Johnson but also by such moderate Republican leaders as Root, Taft, and Hughes. "WICKERSHAM ANSWERS LEAGUE OBSTRUCTIONISTS," *ibid.,* June 22, 1919, Sect. III, p. 2. Finally, in a statement issued by the League to Enforce Peace in Washington on August 15, Wickersham called for immediate Senate approval of the peace treaty and the League, with the understanding that the Covenant could be amended later to remedy its defects, just as the Constitution had been ratified with the understanding that a Bill of Rights would soon be added. *Ibid.,* Aug. 17, 1919.

See also Ruhl J. Bartlett, *The League to Enforce Peace* (Chapel Hill, N. C., 1944), pp. 129, 133, 153.

² Tumulty was in error here. Roosevelt's last article in the *Metropolitan* made no reference to arbitration of any kind. T. Roosevelt, "The League of Nations," *Metropolitan,* XLIX (Jan. 1919), 9, 70. What Tumulty had probably read and was paraphrasing was Roosevelt's editorial in the *Kansas City Star,* November 17, 1918 (reprinted in *Roosevelt in the Kansas City Star: War-Time Editorials by Theodore Roosevelt, with an Introduction by Ralph Stout* [Boston and New York, 1921], pp. 261-65), entitled "The League of Nations." In this editorial, Roosevelt said that it "would be perfectly safe to enter into universal arbitration treaties with the British empire, for example. . . ."

An Address in the Spokane Armory

[[September 12, 1919]]

Mr. Mayor,¹ my fellow countrymen, I esteem it a real privilege to stand face to face with a representative audience of this great city, because I have come away from Washington, my fellow countrymen, not to make speeches, but to get into contact with just such bodies of men and women as this and feel that I have exchanged ideas with them with the utmost frankness of which I was capable. I have not come to paint pictures of fancy. I have come to disclose to you what I understand to be facts, and I want so much as possible to get down to the very essence and marrow of the things that we are now talking about.

I don't think I need tell you, my fellow citizens, that America and the world have come to the point where they must make one of the most critical choices ever made by great bodies of men and nations. They have now to determine whether they will act on the one chance that has ever been offered to insure the peace of the world. (applause) I call it frankly a chance to insure the peace of

¹ Charles Marvin Fassett, Republican.

the world. Nobody can guarantee the world against the ugly passions that sometimes get abroad. Nobody can engage that the
world will not again go mad with blood, but I want to put it frankly
to you, though the chance should be poor, isn't it worth taking a
chance? (applause) Let men discount the proposed arrangement
as much as they will; let us regard it as an insurance policy. If you
can get 10 per cent insurance of your fortunes in respect of peace,
wouldn't you rather take it than no insurance at all? (cries of "Yes"
and "Of course") As a matter of fact, I believe, after having sat in
conference with men all over the world and finding the attitude of
their minds, the character of their purposes, that this is a 98 per
cent insurance against war. If the nations of the world will in deed
and in truth accept this great Covenant of a League of Nations and
agree to put arbitration and discussion always first and war always
last, I say that we have an immense insurance against war, and
that is exactly what this great Covenant does.

I have found it necessary upon this trip, my fellow citizens—I
have actually found it necessary—to tell great audiences what the
treaty of peace contains. You never could divine it from the discussion of the men who are opposed to it. (applause) Let me tell you
some of the things this treaty does, apart from the Covenant of the
League of Nations, which stands by common consent of those who
framed it at the beginning of it. Quite apart from the League of
Nations, it is the first attempt ever made by an international congress to substitute justice for national advantage. It is the first attempt ever made to settle the affairs of the world according to the
wishes of the people in the parts of the world that were being dealt
with. It is a treaty that deals with peoples and nations, and not with
dynasties and governments. (applause)

Every representative of every great government I met on the
other side of the sea acknowledged, as I, of course, acknowledge,
that he was master of nobody, that he was the servant of the people
whom he represented, and that the people he represented wanted
what the people of the United States wanted. They wanted a just,
a reasonable, a permanent settlement, and that is what this treaty
tried to give them. It substitutes for the aggression, which always
was the beginning of war, a settled title on the part of the weak
nations, along with the strong, to their own territories—a settled
right to determine their own policies, a settled right to realize the
national hopes so long suppressed, to free themselves from the
oppression so long endured. Europe was full of people under the
iron and relentless hand of military power, and that hand has been
removed and crushed. This treaty is the means of doing it.

And the guarantee of this treaty is the part of the covenant of

nations which you have heard most criticized. I mean the celebrated, the now celebrated, Article X. Article X is an engagement
of the most extraordinary kind in history. It is an engagement by
all the fighting nations of the world never to fight upon the plan
on which they always fought before. They—all of them—agree to
respect and preserve against external aggression the territorial integrity and existing political independence of the others, and they
agree that, if there should be any breach of that Covenant, the
Council of the League shall advise what steps shall be taken to
make the promise good. That is the Covenant with which you have
been frightened. Frightened, my fellow citizens? Why, it is the
only possible or conceivable guarantee against the wars that have
ravaged the world, because those wars have habitually begun by
territorial aggression, by the seizure of territory that didn't belong
to the power that was effecting the seizure.

How did this great war begin? It began by the invasion of Belgium, and it was admitted by all German statesmen that they never
meant to get out of Belgium. By guaranteeing the territorial integrity of a country, you don't mean that you guarantee it against invasion. You guarantee it against the invader staying there and
keeping the spoils. The integrity is the title, the ownership. You
agree never to take territory away from the people to whom it belongs, and you agree never to interfere with the political independence of the people living in the territories whose titles are now
made clear by a universal international guarantee.

I therefore want to discuss with you, very frankly indeed, just as
frankly as I know how, the difficulty that has been suggested, because I say, not in the spirit of criticism, but in a spirit of intended
fairness, that not one of the qualifications which has been suggested in this discussion is justified by the language of the instrument. Let me take them one by one.

In the first article of the Covenant of the League, it is provided
that any member state may withdraw from the League upon two
years' notice, provided that, at the time of withdrawal, it has fulfilled its international obligations and its obligations under the Covenant. And gentlemen object that it is not said who shall determine
whether it has fulfilled its international obligations and its obligations under the Covenant or not. Having sat at the table where the
instrument was drawn, I know that that was not done accidentally,
because that is a matter upon which no nation can sit in judgment
upon another. That is left to the conscience and to the independent
determination of the nation that is withdrawing, and there is only
one jury that it need fear, and that is the great embodied jury expressing the opinion of mankind. (applause)

I want to differentiate myself, particularly, from the men who are afraid of this clause, because I want to record my feelings in the matter that, as an American, I am never afraid that the United States will fail to perform its international obligations. (applause) And, being certain that it will never fail, I have nothing to fear that an occasion will arise when we need be sensitive to the opinion of mankind. (applause) That is the only jury set up in the case, and I am ready to go before that jury at any time. (applause) These gentlemen want to say what the instrument itself says—that we can withdraw when we please. The instrument does not say it in these words. It says it in effect, and the only limitation upon it is that we should not please unless we have done our duty. We never will please, God helping us, to neglect our duty. (applause)

The second difficulty—taking them in the order in which they come in the Covenant itself—is the article I was a moment ago discussing, Article X. Article X says that if the promise to respect and preserve as against external aggression—I left those words out inadvertently—if the promise to respect and preserve against external aggression the territorial integrity and existing political independence of the member states is broken, then the Council shall advise what is to be done. I do not know any but one meaning for the word "advise," and I have been very curious and interested to learn how many other meanings have been put into it. In my surprise, I have looked in the dictionary to be sure that I was not mistaken, and, so far as I can find out, "advise" means "advise." And more than that, and more interesting than that, the advice cannot be given without the affirmative vote of the United States. (applause) There must be a unanimous vote of the Council before there is advice, and the United States is a member of the Council by the constitution of the Council, by the constitution of the League itself, a member now and always a member, so that neither the United States nor any other country can be advised to go to war for the redemption of that promise without the concurrent affirmative vote of the United States. (applause)

And yet I hear gentlemen say that this is an invasion of our sovereignty. Why, my fellow citizens, if it is anything, it is an exaggeration of our sovereignty, because it puts our sovereignty in a way to put a veto on that advice being given to anybody. Our present sovereignty merely extends to making choice as to whether we will go to war or not, but this extends our sovereignty to saying whether other nations shall go to war or not. (applause)

If that does not constitute a very considerable insurance against war, I would like somebody to write a provision which would; because, at every point, my fellow citizens, the opposition of these gentlemen who criticize this instrument is either that they do not understand the Covenant or that they can suggest something better. In fact, I have never heard any of them suggest anything better. In fact, I have never heard any of them suggest anything. (loud applause and cheers) If the world is going to be at peace, it must be this or something better, and I want to say again and again, it is a case of "put up or shut up." (applause)

And let me make a slight digression here, if I may, to speak about a matter of some delicacy. I have had a great many men say to me, "I am a Republican, but I am in favor of the League of Nations." Why the "but"? (laughter) So far as I remember, every meeting I have spoken at on this trip has been presided over by a Republican. (applause) And I want to tell you, my fellow citizens, that there is one element in this whole discussion which ought not to be in it. There is, though I say it myself, an element of personal bitterness. And one would suppose that this Covenant of the League of Nations was first thought of, and first invented, and first written by a man named Wilson. (laughter) Now, I wish it were. (laughter) If I had done that, I would be willing to have it recorded that I had done that and nothing else. (applause) But I didn't do it. And I got the idea twenty years ago. I do not mean I alone, but thousands of my fellow countrymen got the idea years ago, chiefly from Republican public men. (applause) Take men like ex-Senator Burton of Ohio.[2] He has been preaching a league of nations for twenty years. Go through the list. I don't want to mention names, because I do not want to record a gentlemen against himself. (loud applause and continued laughter) But go through the list and you will find most of the leading, thinking minds on the Republican side in favor of this very kind of thing. (applause) And I want to remind every Republican of the criticism that he and his comrades have usually made of the Democratic party and the boast that they have generally made of their party. They said that the Democratic party was a party of negations and not a party of constructive policies, and that the Republican party was a party of constructive policies.

Very well, then, why that "but"? "I am a Republican," but—"I am in favor of the greatest constructive thing that has ever been suggested!" (laughter and applause) If I were a Republican, I would say, "I am a Republican and therefore I am in favor of a League of Nations." (applause) But my present point is to dissociate the League of Nations from the present speaker. I did not originate it. It is not my handiwork. It has originated out of the

[2] That is, Theodore Elijah Burton.

consciences and thought of men who wanted justice and peace for generations. And my relation to it is just what my relation ought to be to every public question—the relationship which a man bears to his fellow citizens when he tries to interpret their thought and their consciences. That is what I conceive to be my part in the League of Nations. I did have a part in some of the phraseology, and every time I did, it was to carry out the ideas that these gentlemen are fighting for.

For example, there is one part of the Covenant—the principal part of it—where it speaks of arbitration and where it provides that any member state failing to keep these covenants—these particular covenants—shall be regarded as thereby *ipso facto* to have committed an act of war against the other members. The way it originally read was, "Shall thereby *ipso facto* be deemed at war with the other nations." And I said: "No, I cannot agree to that. That provision would put the United States at war without the consent of the Congress of the United States, and I have no right in this part of the Covenant or any other to assent to a provision which would deprive the Congress of the United States of its free choice whether it makes war or not." (applause) There, and at every other point in the Covenant where it was necessary to do so, I insisted upon language which would leave the Congress of the United States free, and yet these gentlemen say that the Congress of the United States is deprived of its privilege. (laughter) I fought that battle and won it. It is not necessary for them to fight it over again. (applause and cheers) I have finished about Article X.

You will say, "It is all very well what you say about the word of the United States being necesary to the advice, provided the United States is not one of the parties to the dispute. In that case it cannot vote." That is very true. But in that case it has got the fight on its hands anyhow, because if it is one of the parties to the dispute, the war belongs to it. It does not have to go into it. Therefore it cannot be forced by the vote into the war. The only thing the vote can do is to force it out of the war.

And I want to ask you to think what it means when it is suggested that the United States may be a party. A party to what? A party to seizing somebody else's territory? A party to infringing some other country's political independence? Is any man willing to stand on this platform and say that the United States is likely to do either of those things? I challenge any man to stand up before an American audience and say that that is the danger. "Ah, but somebody else may seek to seize our territory or impair our political independence." Well, who? Who has an arm long enough, who has an audacity great enough to try to take a single inch of American

territory (applause and cheers) or to seek to interfere for one moment with the political independence of the United States? These
gentlemen are dreaming of things that can't happen, (laughter and
applause) and I cannot bring myself to feel uneasy about things
that I know are not so. The great difficulty in this discussion, as in
so many others, is the number of things that men know that are
not so. (laughter)

"But the Monroe Doctrine?" I must admit to you, my fellow citizens, I don't know how the Monroe Doctrine could be any more
explicitly accepted than it is in the Covenant of the League of Nations. It says that nothing in the Covenant shall be interpreted as
impairing the validity of the Monroe Doctrine. What more could
you say? I did try while I was in Paris to define the Monroe Doctrine and get it written into the document, but I will confess to you
in confidence that, when I tried to define it, I found that it escaped
analysis, (laughter) and that all that you could say was that it was
a principle with regard to the interference of foreign powers in the
politics of the western hemisphere which the United States is at
liberty to apply in any circumstances where it thought it pertinent.
Now, that is not a definition. That means that the United States
means to play big brother to the western hemisphere in any circumstances where it thinks it wise to play big brother. And therefore, inasmuch as you cannot or would not define the Monroe Doctrine—at least I would not, because I do not know how much we
may want to extend it—inasmuch as we do not want to define it,
what more could you say than that nothing in that instrument
shall impair the validity of the Monroe Doctrine?

I tell you, my fellow citizens, that is the most extraordinary sentence in that treaty, for this reason: up to that time, there was not
a nation in the world that was willing to admit the validity of the
Monroe Doctrine. (applause) I have made a great many speeches
in my life—perhaps too many—but I do not think that I ever put
so much of what I hope is the best in me as I put in the speech in
the conference on the League of Nations in favor of the Monroe
Doctrine.[3] And it was upon that occasion that it was embodied, and
we have this extraordinary spectacle, of the world recognizing the
validity of the Monroe Doctrine. (applause) Yet these gentlemen
seem to want something more. What more could you get? Shall we
get them to express their belief in the deity of the Monroe Doctrine? (laughter) They accepted it for the first time in the history
of the world, and they say that they will do nothing that will inter-

[3] See Wilson's remarks printed at April 11, 1919, Vol. 57.

fere with it. And I must submit that it is absolutely irrational to ask for anything more.

But there is the question of domestics—of their interfering with domestic policies—immigration, naturalization, tariffs—matters of that sort. There, again, I can't understand or feel the weight of the difficulty, because the Covenant says that the Council of the League of Nations, if any international difficulty is brought under discussion, if one of the parties claims and the Council finds that it is a matter of domestic jurisdiction, shall cease to discuss it and shall make no report about it. And the only way you could make the document more clear would be by enumerating domestic questions which you have in mind. Very well. I ask any lawyer here if that would be safe. Mightn't you be in danger of leaving out something? Mightn't you be in danger of not mentioning something that would afterwards become important? The danger of making a list is that the mention of the things you mention constitutes the exclusion of the things you do not mention. And, therefore, inasmuch as there is no dispute among any authoritative students of international law that these matters that we are most concerned about—immigration, naturalization, tariffs, and the like—are domestic questions, it is inconceivable that the Council should ever seek to interfere with or to discuss such questions, unless we had ourselves deliberately made them matters of international agreement, when even the opponents of the League admit they would be suitable and proper subjects for discussion.

Those are the matters upon which they are talking about reservations. And the only reservations that I can imagine are reservations which say over again what the Covenant itself says in plain language, and make it necessary that we should go back to Paris and discuss in new language the things which we all will have to admit, if we were more frank or honest, are already in the document. (applause)

But there is another matter. I have forgotten who it was that said it, but I wouldn't mention his name if I remembered it, (laughter) that this Covenant was an arrangement for the dominance of Great Britain, and he based that upon the fact that in the Assembly of the League there are six representatives of the various parts of the British Empire. Well, I mean there are more than that, because every member of the Assembly has three representatives, but six units of the British Empire are represented, whereas the United States is represented as only one unit. Now let me be didactic for a moment and tell you how the League is constituted. There is an Assembly made up of three members from each of the constituent states, and there is a Council. The Council is the only part of the organization that can take effective action. No powers of action rest with the Assembly at all, but it is only in the Assembly that the British Empire is represented as consisting of six units—for brevity's sake I will say as having six votes. There is only one occasion when the Assembly can vote at all, and that is when the Council refers a matter in dispute to the Assembly, in which case the Assembly can decide a matter by a majority, provided all the representatives of the nations represented in the Council vote on the side of the majority. So that, alike in the Assembly and in the Council, the one vote of the United States is an absolute veto.

I have said that there was only one occasion upon which the Assembly could vote, and that is literally true. The Council of the League is made up of one representative from each of the five principal Allied and Associated Powers, that is to say, the United States, Great Britain, France, Italy, and Japan, and four other nations selected by the Assembly of the League, four as against five. The present members are Spain, Brazil, Belgium—I am afraid I am at a loss for the other. And in the Council is vested all the active powers of the League. Everything that is done by the League emanates, is formulated and passed by the Council, and a unanimous vote is required.

Indeed, my fellow citizens, that is the only thing that seems to me weak about the League. I am afraid that a unanimous vote will sometimes be very difficult to get. And the danger is not action, but inaction. The danger is not that they will do something that we do not like, but that, upon some critical occasion, they won't do anything. If there is any weakness in it, it is the safeguard that is thrown around the power of the members of the Council. If a matter in controversy arises and one of the parties demands that it shall be taken out of the Council and put into the Assembly, the Council is obliged so to refer it. But in the final vote in the Assembly, the affirmative action is not valid unless all the states represented in the Council shall also in the Assembly vote in the affirmative. So if we can always veto, always offset with our vote the British six votes, I must say that I look with perfect philosophy upon the difference in number.

The justification for the representation of more than one part of the British Empire is that the British Empire is made up of semi-independent provinces, as no other empire in the world is. You know how Canada, for example, passes her own tariff laws, does what she pleases to inconvenience the trade of the mother country. And her voice in the Assembly is merely a debating voice. The Assembly is a great discussing body. It is a body in which some of the most valuable things that the League is going to do can be done.

And I want to ask of you, after you have read Article X again, to read Article XI. Article XI makes it the right of any member of the League, however weak and small, to call attention to anything, anywhere, that is likely to disturb the peace of the world and draw it into debate, draw it into the open, draw it where everybody can know the facts and talk about it. It is the only time, my fellow countrymen, in the history of the world when the weak and oppressed and restive people have been given a hearing. (applause) Nothing is going to keep this world fit to live in like exposing in public debate every crooked thing that is going on. (applause) If you suspect your friend of being a fool, the best way you can prove it or disprove it is by advising him to hire a hall. Then your judgment will be confirmed or reversed by the popular verdict. (applause and laughter) If you think a policy is good, you will want to talk about it. If you think it is bad, you won't consent to talk about it. The League of Nations takes everything into public. It makes every secret agreement of every kind invalid; it provides that no treaty hereafter shall be valid unless registered with the Secretary of the League and published. And, after bringing everything into the open, it authorizes the Assembly to discuss anything that is likely to affect the peace and happiness of any part of the world. (applause) So that in every direction where you look, the safeguards of this treaty are thrown around those who are oppressed.

And, my fellow citizens, unless America takes part in that, the world is going to lose heart.

I cannot too often repeat to you how deep the impression made upon me on the other side of the water was that this was the nation upon which the whole world depended to hold the scales of justice even. (applause) If we fail them, God help the world, for then despair will ensue. Despair is just at the door on the other side of the water now. Men do not hope in Europe, as they do in America. They hope tremblingly. They hope fearfully. They do not hope with confidence and self-reliance, as we do on this side of the water. And everywhere in Europe there is that poison of disorder and distress, and shall we take away from this unsteady world the only thing that reassures it?

If we do, then where is the boasted independence of America? Are we indeed independent in our life of the rest of the world? Then why did we go into the war? Germany had not directed her efforts directly, immediately against us. We went in because we were partners with mankind to see that an iniquity was not practiced upon it. (applause) You know how we regard the men who fought the Civil War. They did the greatest thing that was to be done in their day. And now, these boys here, (indicating soldiers) and others like them, (applause) have done the greatest thing that it was possible to do in our day. (applause) As their fathers saved the Union, they saved the world. (loud applause) And we sit and debate whether we will keep true and finish the job or not! Why, my friends, that debate can't last one minute longer than the moment when this country realizes what it means. It means that, having sent these men to risk their lives and having sent some, whose mothers' hearts can count, to die in France, in order to redeem the world, we, in cool debate, in distant assemblies, say we will not consent that the world should reap the fruits of their victory! Nothing less than that hangs in the balance. I am ready to fight from now until all the fight has been taken out of me by death to redeem the faith and promise of your action. (long and continued applause)

I leave the verdict with you, and I beg my fellow citizens, my Republican fellow citizens, (laughter and applause) that you will not allow yourselves for one moment, as I do not allow myself for one moment, as God knows my conscience, to think of 1920 when thinking about the redemption of the world. (applause) And I beg that you will cut that "but" out of your sentences, and that you will stand up, as you are entitled to stand up by the history of your party, and say, "I am a Republican and therefore I am for the League of Nations." I do not admit the indictment, which has been brought against the Democratic party, but I do admit the distinguished history of the Republican party. I do admit that it has been the creator of great constructive policies, and I should be very sorry to see it lose the prestige which it has earned by such policies. I should be very sorry to have any man feel that there was any embarrassment in supporting a great world policy because he belonged to a great constructive party, and that party an American party, the constructive force in the world, the people who have done the most advanced thinking in the world, and the people who, God helping them, will lead and save the world. (applause)

Printed in the Spokane *Spokesman-Review*, Sept. 13, 1919, with corrections from the complete text in *Addresses of President Wilson* and from the incomplete text in the *Seattle Post-Intelligencer*, Sept. 13, 1919.

Vance Criswell McCormick to Joseph Patrick Tumulty

[The White House] 1919 Sept. 12

Vance McCormick asks me to forward following: "Have just received the following report from League Publicity Bureau, Washington.[1] 'Treaty is going to be ratified; is not going to be amended; there will be reservations in ratifying resolution. Doubt possibility of getting two thirds vote for ratification otherwise. The President's efforts up to this time no effect except perhaps to stiffen opposition. Several Democratic Senators do not think the President's attacks on the Senate help. Hope cumulative effect of the President's speeches will be to bring great pressure to bear on the Senate from folks at home. As to how drastic the reservations will be will depend a whole lot on the ability of Democratic Senators as poker players and how ably they are led. Some Democratic senators are not going to follow the President any further than they have to, to preserve their party standing. Judgment is that if a vote were taken today, there would be a safe majority for reservations, approximately those of Lodge, and leave a good margin over one third who would refuse to ratify without reservations. Believe Republicans can be forced to concede much less drastic Article X reservation than one reported by Lodge. This will depend upon the courage and ability of the Democrats. Frankly, would feel much better about things if had more faith in the enterprise and loyalty of the Democrats.' (End of report.) My personal observations largely confirm this report, but I look for good results from an aroused public. President should fully explain to the people his responsibility under the Constitution in making treaties. Opposition Senators have made some headway due to misunderstanding of the question."

Forster.

T telegram (WP, DLC).
  [1] That is, the Washington bureau of the League to Enforce Peace, which was in charge of publicity for that organization.

From William Phillips

[Washington] 5.59 P.M., Sept. 12, 1919

Sept. 12, 6 P.M. At my request Mr. Polk has arranged that your consideration of the Thracian question may be deferred until your return, when various telegrams on the subject will be submitted to you. In the meantime, at Mr. Polk's special request, the following telegram is repeated for your information:

"No. 4153, Sept. 11, 5 P.M. Confidential. For Phillips from Polk. Referring my 4142, Sept. 10, 6 P.M. The line proposed by the President in your 2981,[1] for the railway from Constantinople to Dedea-gatch, both of which places are in the International State as proposed by the President, would pass through a small section of Bulgarian territory. Furthermore, Adrianople would be in the International state, but would have no railway connections within the limits of that state. A considerable portion of the territory to the West of Adrianople, left in Bulgaria by the line in question, contains many Greeks and no Bulgarians. The view which [blank] [we][2] have maintained is that if Bulgaria is pledged [keeps] her territorial access to the sea, the territory in the vicinity of Adrianople which she secured from Turkey in 1915 should remain with Bulgaria, on the ground that it is useless to give her a territorial access to the sea, if such access is blocked further inland by foreign territory extending across the only railway to Dedeagatch and the Maritza river, which is Bulgaria's natural outlet to the Aegean. This argument loses its force if the Dedeagatch region is placed within the International State, and it is consistent for us to admit that if this outlet is in international territory the approaches to this outlet should likewise be in international territory. The other powers object to rewarding Bulgaria by granting to her territory which she received as a bribe for entering the war on the side of our enemies, and we cannot successfully combat this point of view if they stand on our own arguments and hold that this non-Bulgarian district should have the same disposition as the Dedeagatch area, with which it is [blank] [geographically] and economically connected.

For the various reasons above stated, we have tentatively accepted a rectification of the line proposed by the President, which puts [leaves] in the International state the corner of easterly Thrace situated to the West of Adrianople instead of leaving this territory to Bulgaria. POLK"

William Phillips, Acting Sec'y of State.

T telegram (WP, DLC).
  [1] RL to FLP, Aug. 28, 1919, Vol. 62.
  [2] Additions and corrections from FLP to W. Phillips, No. 4153, Sept. 10, 1919, T telegram (SDR, RG 256, 868.00/209A, DNA).

From the Diary of Dr. Grayson

Saturday, September 13, 1919.

The President's Special followed the regular itinerary and was halted for two hours outside of Tacoma, while the President breakfasted in peace and away from the crowd. Reentering the city, automobiles were boarded and a run through the principal business section was started. Following this the President was taken for a long ride around the shores of the Bay and through the outlying park section, of which Tacoma is so proud. Just why this long trip was inflicted upon the President, I could not find out, but I did not like it at all, inasmuch as the President needed the rest far more than he needed an opportunity to look over parks and real estate developments that were of no particular interest to him. It was manifest that—at least some of the members of the party suggested that it was—a majority of the members of the reception committee planned the trip so that they could bring the procession past their own houses and give their families a chance to look at their visitors.

Returning to the city the party proceeded to the State Armory, where the meeting was to be held. After the Armory was reached, it was found that some one had locked the door to the side-entrance, and the President and party were compelled to stand on the side-walk for a few minutes while a searching party went after the keys, finally locating them.

The meeting itself, however, made up for any little discomfitures that might have been encountered. The building was filled to overflowing, and the crowd was with the President from his first utterance. Because the Japanese question is such a great problem on the Pacific Coast, the President devoted a considerable part of his address to an explanation of the Shantung settlement. He took occasion to denounce secret treaties and declared that most of the responsibility for the present war grew out of the fact that so many nations had participated in secret treaties. Ratification of the Treaty of Versailles, the President declared, would absolutely eliminate all secret treaties in the future, as under the League of Nations Covenant treaties must be arrived at in the open and recorded with the Secretary-General of the League before they can become effective.

The President left Tacoma at noon for Seattle, Washington. His reception in Seattle admittedly was the greatest and warmest ever accorded to any individual visiting that city. There were two reasons for this: In the first place, the President's popularity was such that the State of Washington had gone on record as favoring the unqualified ratification of the Treaty. Then again, the Pacific fleet, which had been cruising from port to port along the Coast, had been massed in Puget Sound in order that the President could review it. For the last couple of days it had been impossible to secure hotel accommodations in the city, and on the eve of the President's arrival it was estimated that more than five thousand people were compelled to sleep in the parks, not being able to secure accommodations anywhere. Churches had been thrown open to accom-

modate as many people as possible, while public halls were utilized
for the same purpose. This was especially the case with the headquarters of the Industrial Workers of the World, who had been
nicknamed in the Pacific Northwest as the "Wobblies." Because of
the large number of these men, all of them advocates of violence
and direct action, fears had been entertained for the safety of the
President, and the most extraordinary precautions had been taken
to guard him. However, even the radicals recognized his natural
fairness, and he was not only warmly welcomed but at no time was
there any untoward demonstration.

Arriving in Seattle the President headed a procession of automobiles that proceeded through the principal streets to the Government Dock at the Naval Station. The crowds that filled the streets,
the windows of the buildings and the rooftops equaled those which
greeted the President in Rome and in Paris. Despite the most
strenuous efforts of the police it was almost impossible to force a
way through the crowd with the automobiles. In fact, had the Boy
Scouts not been on the job, assisting the police, there might have
been a number of serious accidents. As it was, these little fellows,
uniformed, would clasp hands, and, with their scout staffs
stretched in front of them, push the crowd back. The contrast between boys of ten and fifteen years old and grown men and women
was so great that it pleased the crowd and made an appeal to their
consideration with the result that invariably when the police had
failed in opening the lanes and in keeping the crowd back, the boys
were able to do so.

All the way along the principal streets the party was deluged
with confetti and flowers, thrown from the roof-tops. The President
stood erect in his automobile from the time it left the station until
it reached the Naval Dock.

Those of the I.W.W.'s who lined the route wore badges on their
breasts on which was inscribed: "We demand the release of all political prisoners." The President noted this but made no comment
at the time. Strange as it may seem, the I.W.W.'s led the cheering
and the applause for the President.[1]

[1] Several newspapers gave a different view of the activities of the Industrial Workers
of the World in Seattle. The *New York Times*, September 14, 1919, reported as follows:
"The demonstration had at some points a sinister note, for there were present in the
crowd thousands of members of the Industrial Workers of the World, which is strong in
Seattle. As a hatband each member of this organization wore a ribbon bearing the words
'Release Political Prisoners.' They have been agitating for the release of Eugene Debs
and other radicals convicted of seditious utterances.
"Not a few of the men who wore these hatbands had themselves defied the law and
served sentences. They were found in greatest number in the Woodley district, a section
of the city through which the President first passed soon after leaving his train. They
were for the most part men of foreign extraction, sullen of face, and undemonstrative.
For several blocks along Second Avenue they held positions on the curb. Some had

Secretary of the Navy Daniels was on hand to welcome the President, and as soon as the Naval Dock was reached a launch was boarded and the party proceeded to the old Battleship OREGON, which had been selected as the vessel from which the review was to take place. In order to expedite matters, because time was very valuable, the battle-fleet, with its attending destroyers and craft of every description, was drawn up in parallel lines, and the OREGON passed along the line. The review was hurried through as much as possible, and the President returned to land and was hurriedly driven to the hotel, where he rested until dinner.

The night meeting was held in what is known as the Seattle Coliseum,[2] which seats about 9,000 people. The police estimated that there were fully 11,000 inside when the doors were closed. Because of some mix up, however, there was a portion of the auditorium that was not occupied, and when word of this got out to the enormous crowd that was outside of the Coliseum, it attempted to break down the doors to get in. It took some time before the police, aided by the soldiers especially detailed for the work, managed to get the crowd under control and drove it back.

Prior to the opening of the meeting in the big auditorium, the President and Mrs. Wilson, accompanied by myself, were guests at a "popular" dinner that had been arranged for by the Seattle Chamber of Commerce, and which was held in a restaurant[3] di-

---

literature which they distributed among the crowd. As a rule these men and the women with them did not join the throngs that attempted to storm the President's automobile.

"There are no fewer than 5,000 I.W.W.s living in Seattle, and more than that number in addition flocked in from the lumber camps and mines. They were dressed roughly and had no coats or neckties. They did not attempt any anti-Wilson demonstration. It would probably be incorrect to picture them as bitterly antagonistic to the President, but they wished him to know their strength in this section. Not a few of their leaders boasted that such was their purpose."

David Lawrence, in a news report in the New York *Evening Post*, September 15, 1919, also reported on the silent members of the I.W.W. The report in the *New York Tribune*, September 14, 1919, suggested that the demonstration had been planned in advance.

Louis Adamic later supported this account in "The 'Assassin' of Wilson," *American Mercury*, XXI (Oct. 1930), 138-46. Adamic had had several conversations in 1923 with a longshoreman and I.W.W. leader named Jack Kipps and apparently took extensive notes. Kipps claimed that he had originated the idea of a silent demonstration by I.W.W. members along Wilson's route through Seattle on behalf of imprisoned labor leaders. He said that he and his fellows had nothing against Wilson personally; aside from the demonstration on behalf of political prisoners, they chiefly wanted to embarrass former Mayor Ole Hanson and his followers. Kipps gave a detailed account of the scene. Some 5,000 members of the I.W.W. were arrayed along both sides of the street for five blocks, all silent and staring straight past Wilson. He said that Wilson was quite visibly shaken by the demonstration and looked physically stricken. The affair became part of I.W.W. folklore and hence, in light of Wilson's physical collapse less than two weeks after the event, Kipps came to be called "the guy who assassinated Wilson."

[2] Actually, the Arena.

[3] A large hall called the Hippodrome. Actually, 1,600 persons were at the dinner. Secretary and Mrs. Daniels, Admiral Hugh Rodman, commander of the Pacific Fleet, and other dignitaries were present.

rectly across from the auditorium. Fully 5,000 people had paid three dollars a piece for the privilege of eating and seeing the President, inasmuch as he did not make any address at this place.

The President's night address touched on the Shantung settlement, and he also dwelt on the labor clauses of the Treaty. He declared that the industrial questions confronting the United States were the most momentous in its history, and he insisted that the Treaty should be ratified with an unqualified endorsement of the labor clauses, inasmuch as they proposed to carry out the principles of industrial justice. The President was not feeling very well—the tremendous strain of the last few days being evident—but his spirit carried him through the night, and his address was wonderfully well received.

The suggestion had been made that after the President had finished his night speech, he re-board the Special Train and proceed to Mount Rainier for a Sunday and Monday rest. There was no question but that he needed this rest. The terrific strain which he had been under for more than a year was telling, and his exertions which were a necessary accompaniment of the present trip were sapping up his vitality very fast. I had done all that I possibly could to spare him and had insisted, and continued to insist, that there be no deviation from the original program, and that he be not compelled to make any additional speeches. However, here in Seattle the situation that encountered us was rather serious. A delegation of labor leaders, among them several of the radicals in the labor movement, had demanded that they be afforded opportunity personally to appeal to the President for executive pardon for a number of I.W.W. and radical leaders, who were serving sentences under the Federal Espionage Act. When the President was told that these men demanded to see him, he vetoed the proposition of a Sunday rest and agreed that he would meet the men after church the following day.

Remarks in the Tacoma Stadium[1]

September 13, 1919.

My friends, I am delighted to visit you in this beautiful spot, and I am thrilled with the welcome you have given me. I can make no regular address at the present time, but I can say from my heart how glad I am to see you, and how profoundly touched I am by your welcome. What impresses me most is this charming circle of school children, which is the more important as all our thoughts in America recently are to bring about conditions which mean more for our children. Our work now is to care for the future, so that the world may be a better place for our children, and to this factor we have given much thought in our plans for peace. I again thank you with all my heart for your reception.

Printed in the *Tacoma Ledger*, Sept. 13, 1919.
    [1] Wilson made a brief visit to the stadium during his automobile ride through the Tacoma area before his major speech in the Armory.

The First Page of Notes for an Address

TACOMA.

WHAT WE FOUGHT FOR.

"We shall fight for the things which we have always carried nearest our hearts,—for democracy, for the right of those who submit to authority to have a voice in their own governments, for the rights and liberties of small nations, for a universal dominion of right by such a concert of free peoples as shall bring peace and safety to all nations and make the world itself at last free. To such a task we can dedicate our lives and our fortunes, everything that we are and everything that we have, with the pride of those who know that the day has come when America is privileged to spend her blood and her might for the principles that gave her birth and happiness and the peace which she has treasured. God helping her, she can do no other."

What the war cost (Baker's figures)

What we have sought to substitute: arbitration, discussion, economic boycott, a universal guarantee against aggression.

A non-partisan product, supported by both parties.

Without such a substitute, let mothers weep

over

WWT MS (WP, DLC).

An Address in the Tacoma Armory

September 13, 1919.

Mr. Mayor, Mr. Chairman, Your Excellency,[1] my fellow countrymen: It is with very great pleasure that I find myself in your presence. I have long wanted to get away from Washington in order to

    [1] Crockett Morgan Riddell, Democrat; Noah Beery Coffman, Republican, banker of Chehalis, Wash., president of the Washington State branch of the League to Enforce Peace; and Governor Louis Folwell Hart, Republican.

get into touch with the great body of my fellow citizens. Because I feel, as I am sure you feel, that we have reached one of the most critical periods in the history of the United States. The shadow of the war is not yet lifted from us, my fellow countrymen, and we have just come out of the depths of the valley of death. I thought that it might be useful this morning if I reminded you of a few things, lest we forget. It is so easy, with the strong tides of our life, to be swept away from one situation into another, to forget the real depths of meaning which lie underneath the things that we are merely touching the surface of. Therefore I thought it would not be impertinent on my part if I asked permission to read you the concluding passage of the address in which I requested the government of the United States to accept Germany's challenge of war:

"We shall fight," I said, "for the things which we have always carried nearest our hearts,—for democracy, for the right of those who submit to authority to have a voice in their own governments, for the rights and liberties of small nations, for a universal dominion of right by such a concert of free peoples as shall bring peace and safety to all nations and make the world itself at last free. To such a task we can dedicate our lives and our fortunes, everything that we are and everything that we have, with the pride of those who know that the day has come when America is privileged to spend her blood and her might for the principles that gave her birth and happiness and the peace which she has treasured. God helping her, she can do no other."

That is the program we started out on. (applause) That is the program which all America adopted without respect of party. And shall we now hesitate to carry it out? Shall we now falter at the very critical moment when we are finally to write our name to the standing pledge which we then took? (cries of "No! No!")

I want to remind you, my fellow citizens, that many other nations were put under a deeper temptation than we. It would have been possible for little helpless Belgium at any time to make terms with the enemy. Belgium was not prepared to resist. Belgium knew that resistance was useless. Belgium knew that she could get any terms of advantage from Germany that she pleased if she would only submit. And, at the cost of everything that she had, Belgium did nothing less than underwrite civilization. (prolonged applause) I do not know anywhere in history of a more inspiring fact than that. I have seen the fields of Belgium. I have seen great spaces swept of cities and towns as clean as if there had never been anything there except piles of stone. And, further in, in that beautiful country—the factories standing, all the houses there—but everything that could be useful taken out of the factories; the machinery taken out and taken to Germany, because this was a commercial war in part—on Germany's part—and she feared the competition of the skillful Belgians. She took all of her machinery away. And where it was too bulky to take away, it was all destroyed under the direction of experts—not blown to pieces, but the very part that made it impossible to use without it absolutely destroyed. I have been through great plants there that seemed to the eye to have much of the substantial machinery left, but experts showed me that it could never work again. And Belgium lies prostrate because she fulfilled her pledge to civilization.

Italy could have had her terms at the hands of Austria at almost any period of the war, particularly just before she made her final stand at the Piave River, but she would not compound with the enemy. She, too, had underwritten civilization. And my friends, this passage which I have read to you, which the whole country accepted as its pledge, is but an underwriting of civilization. (applause)

But in order to let you remember what the thing cost, just let me read you a few figures. If I did not have them on official authority, I would deem them incredible. Here is what the war cost those who were engaged against Germany.

It cost Great Britain and her dominions $38,000,000,000. These figures do not include what the different powers loaned each other; they are direct war costs. Great Britain and her dominions, $38,000,000,000; France, $26,000,000,000; the United States, $22,000,000,000; Russia, $18,000,000,000; Italy, $13,000,000,000; and the total, including Belgium, Japan, and other smaller countries, $123,000,000,000. It cost the Central Powers: Germany, $39,000,000,000; Austria-Hungary, $21,000,000,000; Turkey and Bulgaria, $3,000,000,000—a total of $63,000,000,000. A grand total of direct war costs of $186,000,000,000—an incredible sum— to save civilization. Now the question is, are we going to keep it safe? The expenditures of the United States were at the rate of $1,000,000 an hour for two years, $1,000,000 an hour, including the nighttime, for two years.

Battle deaths—and this is the cost that touches our hearts— the battle deaths were Russia, 1,700,000; Germany, 1,600,000; France, 1,385,000; Great Britain, 900,000; Austria, 800,000; Italy, 364,000; the United States, 50,300 dead—a total for all belligerents of 7,450,200 men dead on the field of battle! Seven and a half million! The totals for the wounded are not obtainable at present, but the total wounded for the United States Army was 230,000, excluding those, of course, those who were killed.

The total of all battle deaths in all the wars of the world from the year 1793 to 1914 were something under 6,000,000; so that, in all the wars of the world for more than 100 years, fewer men died than have been killed upon the field of battle in the last five years. These are terrible facts, my fellow citizens, and we ought never to forget them. We went into this war to do a thing that was fundamental for the world, and what I have come out upon this journey for is to ascertain whether the country has forgotten it or not. I have found out already. (applause) The country has not forgotten it and never will permit any man who stands in the way of the fulfillment of these great pledges ever to forget the sorrowful day when he made the attempt. (applause)

I read you these figures in order to emphasize and set it in a higher light, if I may, a substitute which is offered—a substitute for war, a substitute for turmoil, a substitute for sorrow and de- spair. That substitute is offered in the Covenant of the League of Nations. (applause) America alone cannot underwrite civilization. All the great free peoples of the world must underwrite it, and only the free peoples of the world can join the League of Nations. The membership is open only to self-governing nations. Germany is for the present excluded, because she must prove that she is self-gov- erning; she must prove that she has changed the processes of her constitution and the purposes of her policy. But when she has proved these things, she can become one of the partners, guaran- teeing that civilization shall not suffer again these intolerable things. It is not only a union of free peoples to guarantee civiliza- tion; it is something much more than that. It is a League of Na- tions to advance civilization by substituting something that will make the improvement of civilization possible.

I call you to witness, my fellow citizens, that our civilization is not satisfactory. It is an industrial civilization, and at the heart of it is antagonism between those who labor with their hands and those who direct labor. You cannot compose those differences in the midst of war, and you cannot advance civilization unless you have a peace of which you make the peaceful and fullest use of bringing these elements of civilization together into a common partnership, in which every man will have the same interest in the work of his community that those have who direct the work of the community. (applause)

We have got to have leisure and freedom of mind to settle these things. This was a war against autocracy, and if you have disor- dered, if you have disquieted populations, if you have insurgent elements in your populations, you are going to have autocracy, be- cause the stronger is going to seize the power, as it has seized it in

Russia. I want to declare that I am an enemy of the rulership of any minority, however constituted. (applause) Minorities have often been right, majorities wrong, but minorities cease to be right when they use the wrong means to make their opinions prevail. We must have peaceful means; we must have discussion; we must have frank discussion: we must have friendly discussion. And these are the very things that are offered to us among the nations of the world by the Covenant of the League of Nations. (applause)

I cannot too often remind my fellow citizens of what the real heart and center of that Covenant is. It lies in the provision by which every member of the League—mind you, that means every great nation in the world, except, for the time being, Germany—every member of the League solemnly engages never to go to war without first having either submitted the subject to arbitration, in which case it agrees to abide absolutely by the verdict, or having submitted it for discussion to the Council of the League of Nations, laying all the documents, all the facts, before the Council, and consenting that the Council shall publish all the facts, so as to take the world into its confidence for the formation of a correct judgment concerning it. It agrees that it will allow six months at least for the deliberations of the Council upon the facts, and that, after these deliberations are concluded, if the advice of the Council is not acceptable, they will still not go to war for three months after the rendering of that decision.

In other words, we have the pledge of all the nations of the world that they will sit down and talk everything over that is apt to make trouble amongst them, and that they will talk it over in public, so that the whole illuminating process of public knowledge and public discussion may penetrate every part of the country. And I believe, for my part, that that is a 98 per cent insurance against war. (applause) I take it you want some insurance against war rather than none, and if it is not 98 per cent, I dare say you would rather like 10 per cent. (applause) You would like some insurance rather than none at all, and the experience of the world demonstrates that this is an almost complete insurance.

My fellow citizens, imagine what would have happened if there had been a League of Nations in 1914. What did happen was this: some time after the Crown Prince of Austria had been assassinated in Serbia, after the world had begun to forget even so tragical an incident, the Austrian government was prompted by the government at Berlin to make that the occasion for war. Their thought was: "We are ready. The others are not. Before they can mobilize, before they can bring this matter even under discussion, we will be at their gates. Belgium cannot resist. We solemnly promised not to cross her territories, but promises are scraps of paper. We will get across her territories into France before France can mobilize." Making a pretense, they therefore made unconscionable demands against Serbia, and notwithstanding the fact that Serbia, with her sense of helplessness, practically yielded to all these demands. They would not even tell the world that she had yielded; they went on with the war. In the meantime, every foreign office was telegraphing to its representative at Berlin, begging that there might be an international conference to see if a settlement could not be effected, but Germany did not dare sit down in conference. It is the common judgment of every statesman I met on the other side of the water that, if this thing had been delayed and discussed, not six months, but six days, it never could have happened.

Here we have all the governments of the world agreeing to discuss anything that is likely to bring about war, because, after the famous Article X there is an Article XI—there are twenty-six articles altogether, although you are not told about any of them except Article X—and Article XI says that it shall be the friendly right of any member of the League, big or little, to bring to the attention of the League—and, therefore, to the attention of the world—anything, anywhere, which is likely to disturb the peace of the world or to disturb the good understanding between nations upon which the peace of the world depends.

Wherever there are oppressed nations, wherever there are suffering populations, wherever there is a smoldering flame, the trouble can be uncovered and brought to the bar of mankind, and the whole influence of public opinion the world over will be brought to bear upon it. It is the greatest process of international conference and of international discussion ever conceived, and that is what we are trying to substitute for war. That is what we must substitute for war.

Then, not in immediate connection with the League of Nations Covenant, but in a later part of the treaty, there is what I have ventured to call the Magna Carta of labor. There is the provision for the constant regular international discussion of labor problems, no matter where they arise in the world, for the purpose of lifting the whole level of labor conditions; for the purpose of safeguarding the health of women and of children; for the sake of bringing about those international comities with regard to labor upon which the happiness of mankind so much depends. There is a heart in the midst of the treaty. It is not only made by prudent men, but it is made by men with hearts under their jackets.

I have seen the light of this thing in the eyes of some men whom the world deemed cynical. I have seen men over there, whose emotions are not often touched, with suffused eyes when they spoke of the purposes of this conference, because they realized that, for the first time in the history of mankind, statesmen had got together, not in order to lay plans for the aggrandizement of governments, but in order to lay plans for the liberation of peoples.

And what I want everybody in every American audience to understand is this: the first effective impulse toward this sort of thing came from America. And I want to call your attention to the fact that it came from some of the very men who are now opposing its consummation. They dreamed the dream that has now been realized. They saw the vision twenty, twenty-five, thirty years ago which all mankind are now permitted to see. It is of particular importance to remember, my fellow citizens, at this moment, when some men have dared to introduce party passion into this question, that some of the leading spirits, perhaps I may say the leading spirits, in the conception of this great idea were the leading figures of the great Republican party.

I do not like to mention parties in this discussion. I hope that there is not a real thoughtful, conscientious person in the United States who will determine his or her opinion about this matter with any thought that there is an election in the year 1920. And, just because I want you to realize how absolutely nonpartisan this thing is, I want you to forget, if you please, that I had anything to do with it. I had the great privilege of being the spokesman of this splendid nation at this critical period of her history. But I was her spokesman, not my own, and when I advocated the things that are in this League of Nations, I had the full and proud consciousness that I was only expressing the best thought and the best conscience of my beloved fellow countrymen.

The only things that I have any special personal connection with in the League of Nations Covenant are things that I was careful to have put in there because of the very considerations which are now being urged. I brought the first draft of the Covenant of the League of Nations over to this country in March last. I then held a conference of the frankest sort with the Foreign Relations Committee of the Senate. They made a number of suggestions as to alterations and additions. I then took all of those suggestions back to Paris, and every one of them, without exception, was embodied in the Covenant. I had one or two hard fights to get them in.

You are told, my fellow citizens—it is amazing that anybody should say it—that the Covenant does not satisfactorily recognize the Monroe Doctrine. It says in so many words that nothing in that Covenant shall be construed as impairing the validity of the Monroe Doctrine. The point is that, up to that conference, there was not a nation in the world that could be induced to give official recognition to the Monroe Doctrine, and here, in this great turn of the tides of the world, all the great nations of the world are united in recognizing the Monroe Doctrine. It not only is not impaired, but is has the backing of the world. And, at every point where suggestions were made, they were accepted; and the suggestions came for the most part from the Republican side of the committee. I say that because I am particularly interested, my fellow citizens, to have you realize that there is no politics in this business, except that profoundly important politics—the politics of civilization. I have the honor today of speaking under a chairman who, I understand, is a member of the Republican party, and every meeting that I have spoken at on this trip, so far as I remember, has been presided over by a Republican. I am saying these things merely because I want to read the riot act to anybody who tries to introduce politics.

Some very interesting things happened while we were on the other side of the water. One of the most distinguished lawyers in the United States, Mr. Wickersham, of New York, who was the Attorney General in Mr. Taft's cabinet, came over to Europe, I am told—I did not see him while he was over there—to oppose the things that he understood the American peace commission was trying to accomplish, and what happened to Mr. Wickersham? He was absolutely converted, above all things else, to the necessity for a league of nations not only, but for this League of Nations. He came back to the United States and has ever since, in season and out of season, been preaching in public advocacy of this Covenant. I need not tell you of the conspicuously fine work which his chief, Mr. Taft, has been doing in the same cause.

I am very proud, my fellow citizens, to be associated with these gentlemen. I am very proud to forget party lines, because there is one thing that is so much greater than being a Republican or a Democrat that those names ought never to be mentioned in connection with, and that is being an American. There is only one way to be an American, and that is to fulfill the pledges that we gave the world at our birth, that we have given the world at every turn in our history, and that we have just now sealed with the blood of some of our best young men.

Ah, my fellow citizens, do not forget the aching hearts that are behind discussions like this. Do not forget the forlorn homes from which those boys went and to which they never came back. I have in my heart that if we do not do this great thing now, every woman ought to weep because of the child in her arms. If she has a boy at her breast, she may be sure that, when he comes to manhood, this terrible task will have to be done once more. Everywhere we go, the train when it stops is surrounded with little children, and I look at them almost with tears in my eyes, because I feel my mission is to save them. These glad youngsters with flags in their hands—I pray God that they may never have to carry those flags into battle!

There have been, if I may make a slight digression, some very amusing incidents on this journey. The small boys call me "Woody." I don't object to the name at all unless it is intended as a description. They shout their little greetings to "Woody," their friend, and sometimes they give me things. At Billings, one small boy with a flag proudly gave his banner to me. His little pal had no flag, and he looked very uneasy for a moment. Then he put his hand in his pocket, brought forth a dime, and, with a happy smile, presented me with that. I think about that dime as one might the widow's mite. Others gave something, but he gave me all he had. After all, though that is merely a passing incident, it is illustrative of the spirit of this country, my fellow citizens.

There is something in this country that is not anywhere else in the world. There is a confident looking forward to better times. There is a confidence that we can work out the most difficult problems. There is none of that heavy leaden discouragement that rests upon some other countries. Have you never crossed the sea in times of peace and noticed the immigrants who were going back to visit their folks, and then, on the return voyage, the immigrants who were coming in for the first time—the extraordinary contrast in the appearance of the two groups? The group going out, having felt the atmosphere of America, their faces bright, a sort of a sense of initiative about it, having been freed to be men and individuals; and those coming back, bearing all sorts of queer bundles, looking a bit anxious, just a little doubtful of the hope with which they are looking forward to the new country. It is the alchemy, the miracle of America, and it is the only country in the world, so far as my observation goes, where that miracle is wrought, and the rest of the world knows that.

The rest of the world implores America's aid—not her material aid; they are not looking for our dollars; they are not looking for our guns. They are saying, "Show us the road that led you out of the wilderness and made you great, for we are seeking that road." Now that the great treaty of peace has established the oppressed peoples of the world who were affected by this treaty on their own territory, given them their own freedom, given them command of their own affairs, they are looking to America to show them how to use that new liberty and that new power.

When I was at that wonderful stadium of yours a few minutes

ago, a little child, a little girl in white, came and presented me with some kind of a paper—I have not had time to read it yet—from the Poles.[2] I dare say that it is of the sort that I have received a great many of—just an expression of a sort of childlike and pitiful thanks that America assisted to free Poland.

Poland never could have freed herself. We not only tore Germany's hands away from where she meant to make ravage of the rights of the others, but we took those old peoples who had been under her power before and said: "You could not free yourselves, but we believe in liberty. Here is your own land to do with as you please." I wish that some of the men who are opposing this treaty could get the vision in their hearts of all it has done. It has liberated great populations. It has set up the standards of right and of liberty for the first time, where they were never unfurled before, and then has placed back of them this splendid power of the nations combined.

For without the League of Nations the whole thing is a house of cards. Just a breath of power will blow it down, whereas with the League of Nations it is as strong as Gibraltar. Let them catch this vision; let them take in this conception; let them take counsel of weeping mothers; let them take counsel of bereaved fathers who used to have their sons at their sides and are now alone; let them take counsel of the lonely farms where there used to be a boy to help the old man and now he cannot even get a hired man to help him, and yet he is trying to feed the world; let them realize that the world is hungry, that the world is naked, that the world is suffering, and that none of these things can be remedied until the minds of men are reassured. That is the fundamental fact, my fellow citizens.

If I wanted to have a joint debate with some man who wanted to put our part in this business down on the lowest possible level of how much money we were going to make out of it, I could silence him by showing that, so long as the world was not reassured, its industries will not begin again, that unless its industries begin again, there will be nothing to pay for anything with, that unless its industries begin again there will be no market for the goods of America, and that we will have to rest content with our domestic markets at the very time when we had enlarged our enterprises in order to make peaceful conquest of the world. The very processes of war have driven our industries to a point of expansion where they will be chilled and ruined if they do not presently get a foreign

---

[2] Cora Budziszewski, ten years old, on behalf of the citizens of Tacoma of Polish descent. *Tacoma Ledger*, Sept. 13, 1919.

outlet. Therefore, on the lowest basis, you have got to guarantee and underwrite civilization, or you have ruined the United States.

But I do not like to talk about that side of it. I believe in my heart that there is hardly a man in America, if you get really back of his superficial thoughts, who is not man enough to be willing to make the sacrifice to underwrite civilization. It is only sacrifice that tells. Don't you remember what we used to cry during the Liberty loans, "Lend until it hurts. Give until it hurts." When I heard, in some western states, that people drew their savings out of banks that were giving them 4 per cent on the savings and invested them in the first Liberty loan that was to yield them 3½ per cent, I said to myself, "That is America." They were helping the government at a sacrifice. They were not thinking of dollars. They were thinking of the dignity and might and majesty and destiny of the United States, and it is only that vision, my fellow citizens, that will ever lift us out of the slough in which men now are wading.

It is a pitiful spectacle that the great bodies of our fellow citizens should be arrayed against each other. One of the most startling things that I ever realized was months and months ago, when I was trying to moderate and assist in settling some of the difficulties between the railroads and their employees.[3] I asked the representatives of the railway brotherhoods to come to the White House, and I asked the presidents of the great railway systems to come to the White House. And I found that each side had a profound suspicion of the other, that the railway presidents were not willing to trust what their men said and the men were not willing to trust what the railway presidents said. When I took over the railroads in the name of the government, I said to a group of fine-spirited men—a group of railway presidents, who were trying to unify the administration of the railroads for the purposes of the war—I said, smilingly, but with a little sadness, "Well, at any rate, gentlemen, these men will trust me, and they do not trust you." I did not say it with pride; I said it with sorrow. I did not know whether I could justify their trust or not. But I did know that I was willing to talk things over with them whenever anything was the matter, and that if we were equally intelligent and equally conscientious we could get together whenever anything went wrong. I could not help suspecting that this distrust, this mutual distrust, was the wedge that was being driven into society, and society cannot live with a great wedge at the heart of it.

Society cannot get on industrially or socially with any such

[3] Wilson here referred to his activities during the railroad crisis of 1916, about which see the index references in Vol. 38 to "railroad crisis of 1916" and the Adamson Act.

wedge driven into its heart. We must see that the processes of peace, the processes of discussion, the processes of fairness, the processes of equity, the processes of sympathy penetrate all our affairs. I have never known anybody who had a good cause who was unwilling to discuss it. Whenever I find a man standing out stiffly against consulting with the other side, I know his case is bad. The only unconquerable thing in the world is the truth, and a man who has the truth on his side need not be afraid of anybody.

You know what witty and eloquent old Dr. Oliver Wendell Holmes once said. He said, "You needn't fear to handle the truth roughly; she is no invalid." The truth is the most robust and indestructible and formidable thing in the world. There is a very amusing story of a distinguished lawyer at Charleston, South Carolina, of a very much older generation than ours, who was followed out of the court one day after losing a civil suit by his client, who abused him. He called him a thief and a liar and everything that was disagreeable, and Mr. Petigru paid not the slightest attention to him, until he called him a Federalist, and then he knocked him down. And a friend said to him: "Why, Mr. Petigru, why did you knock him down for that? That was the least offensive thing he said." "Yes, damn him," Petigru said, "But it was the only true thing he said."[4]

Now the nations of the world have declared that they are not afraid of the truth, that they are willing to have all their affairs that are likely to lead to international complications brought into the open. One of the things that this treaty incidentally does is absolutely to invalidate all secret treaties. Everything is to be open. Everything is to be upon the table around which sit the representatives of all the world, to be looked at from the point of view of everybody—the Asiatic, the African, the American, the European. That is the promise of the future; that is the security of the future. I hope that no attempts will be made to qualify or embarrass the great process which is inevitable, and I confidently predict that some day we shall look back with surprise upon the fact that men in America, above all places, should ever have hesitated to do this great thing.

It has been a privilege, my fellow citizens, to make this simple presentation of a great theme to you, and I am happy in carrying away with me recollections of the generous response you have made to a plea which I can only characterize as a plea which has come from the heart of a true American.

Printed in *Addresses of President Wilson*, with corrections from the incomplete text in the *Tacoma News Tribune*, Sept. 13, 1919.

4 Wilson had told this story many times. "Mr. Petigru" was James Louis Petigru.

After-Dinner Remarks in Seattle

[[September 13, 1919]]

Mr. Spangler,[1] ladies and gentlemen, it was agreed that I should make no address on this occasion, and I am not going to inflict upon you anything that could bear so dignified a name. But when Mr. Spangler asked me if I would extend a word of greeting to the audience, I at once thought of the wonderful greeting that you and your fellow citizens have extended to me. And the fact I have been so warmed in my heart by that greeting would make it indeed ungracious if I did not say how much I have appreciated your welcome and how delightful it is to be associated with you, even for a few hours in this great city of Seattle.

I have been in Seattle before, when I attracted less attention.[2] I admired the city then, as I admire it still, and I could see it better then than I have seen it today. Today I have had too much of an escort to be really able to see the new features of the city with which I was not acquainted. I was reminded of some of our experiences on the other side of the water, when we had to be particular not to let anybody know we were going to a particular place for fear we would be escorted by so many persons that we would not see the place. And I have found in Washington that I am not to see the interesting things in Washington until my term is over, because all the officials in any public building feel it necessary to escort me all over the building, and either I will see the things I did not go to see, or I see nothing.

But, jesting aside, my fellow citizens, it was very delightful to see so many friendly faces on these beautiful streets. What I liked about it was not so much the cheers as the facial expressions that accompanied the cheers. They made me feel really welcome, and I could only fancy and hope that it was a reflection in their faces of the way I felt towards them. I suppose that a man in public life must renew himself by direct contact with his fellow citizens to get the feel of the great power of opinion and sentiment that exists, and nothing else heartened me so much as I have crossed the country as to feel the uniformity of sentiment from one ocean to the other.

There is no essential division in the thought or purpose of the American people, and the interesting thing to me is their steadiness. No amount of debate will set them off their balance in their thinking, because their thinking is based upon fundamental impulses of right. What they want to know is not the difficulties, but the duties ahead. If you point the duties out to them, they have a contempt for the difficulties. It is that consciousness we found in moving from one part of this beloved country to another that makes me so profoundly proud to be an American. It was not, indeed, my choice to be an American, because I was born in it, and I suppose that I can't ascribe any credit to myself for being an American. But I do claim the profoundest pleasure in sharing the sentiments and in having had the privilege for a few short years of trying to express the sentiment of this free nation, to which all the world looks for inspiration and guidance.

That is the dominating thought I had—I won't say the dominating thought—it is the controlling knowledge that I have. For I learned on the other side of the water that all the world was looking to us for its inspiration, and we will not deny it to them.

Printed in the *Seattle Times*, Sept. 14, 1919.
[1] James Williams Spangler, vice-president of the Seattle National Bank and of the Seattle Chamber of Commerce.
[2] About Wilson's earlier visit to and speeches in Seattle, see Vol. 23, pp. 76-80.

An Address in the Seattle Arena

[[September 13, 1919]]

Mr. Chairman,[1] my fellow countrymen, I esteem it a great privilege to have the occasion to stand before this great audience and expound some part of the great question that is now holding the attention of America and the attention of the world.

I was led to an unpleasant consciousness today of the way in which the debate that is going on in America has attracted the attention of the world. I read in today's papers the comments of one of the men[2] who was recently connected with the Imperial Government of Germany, saying that some aspects of this debate seemed to him like the red that precedes a great dawn. He saw in it the rise of a certain renewed sympathy with Germany. He saw in it an opportunity to separate America from the governments and peoples with whom she had associated in the war against German aggression.

And all over this country, my fellow citizens, it is becoming more and more evident that those who were the partisans of Germany are the ones who are principally pleased by some of the aspects of the debate that is now going on. The world outside of America is asking itself the question, "Is America going to stand by us now, or is it at this moment of final crisis going to draw apart and desert us?"

[1] Cecil Bernard Fitzgerald, Mayor of Seattle.
[2] Robert Richard von Scheller-Steinwartz, a former diplomat. He spoke in Berlin on September 6. *New York Times*, Sept. 8, 1919.

I can answer that question here and now. It is not going to draw apart, and it is not going to desert the nations of the world. (applause) America responds to nothing so quickly or unanimously as a great moral challenge. It is today more ready to carry through new lines before it than it was even to carry through what it had before it when we took up arms in behalf of the freedom of the world. America is unaccustomed to military tasks, but America is accustomed to fulfilling its pledges and following its visions. (applause) The only thing that causes me uneasiness, my fellow countrymen, is not the ultimate outcome, but the impressions that may be created in the meantime by the perplexed delay. The rest of the world believes absolutely in America and is ready to follow it anywhere, and it is now a little chilled. It now asks: "Is America hesitating to lead? We are ready to give ourselves to her leadership here. Will she not accept the gift?"

And so, my fellow citizens, I think that it is my duty, as I go about the country, not to make speeches in the ordinary acceptance of that word, not to appeal either to the imagination or to the emotions of my fellow citizens, but to undertake everywhere what I want to undertake tonight, and I must ask you to be patient while I undertake it. I want to analyze for you what it is that it is proposed that we should do. Generalities will not penetrate to the heart of this great question. It is not enough to speak of the general purposes of the peace. (applause outside of building) This applause was acceptable but inopportune. Perhaps I might devise some signal when they should cheer on the outside, but if you won't mind the sounds without, I think we can make some progress toward the heart of the great matter that I want to discuss with you.

I want you to realize just what the Covenant of the League of Nations means. I find that everywhere I go it is desirable that I should dwell upon this great theme, because in so many parts of the country men are drawing attention to little details in a way that destroys the great perspective of the great plan in a way that concentrates attention upon certain particulars which are incidental and not central. And I am going to take the liberty of reading you a list of the things which the nations adhering to the Covenant of the League of Nations undertake. I want to say by way of preface that it seems to me, and I am sure it will seem to you, not only an extraordinarily impressive list, but a list which was never proposed for the councils of the world before.

In the first place, every nation that joins the League, and that in prospect means every great fighting nation in the world, agrees to submit all controversies which are likely to lead to war either to arbitration or to thorough discussion by an authoritative body—the

Council of the League of Nations. These great nations, all the most ambitious nations in the world except Germany, all the most powerful nations in the world, as well as the weak ones, all the nations which we have supposed had imperialistic designs, say that they will do either one or the other of two things in case a controversy arises that cannot be settled by ordinary diplomatic correspondence. They will either frankly submit it to arbitration and absolutely abide by the arbitral verdict, or they will submit all the facts, all the documents, and the Council of the League of Nations will be given six months in which to discuss the whole matter and leave to publish the whole matter. And, at the end of six months, will still refrain for three months more from going to war, whether they like the opinion of the Council or not.

In other words, they agree to do a thing which would have made the recent war with Germany absolutely impossible. If there had been a League of Nations in 1914, whether Germany belonged to it or not, Germany would never have dared to attempt the aggressions which she did attempt, because she would have been called to the bar of the opinion of mankind and would have known that, if she did not satisfy that opinion, mankind would unite against her. You had only to expose the German case to public discussion to make it certain that the German case would fail; Germany would not dare attempt to act upon it. It was the universal opinion on the other side of the water when I was over there that, that if Germany had thought that England would have aided France and Russia, she never would have gone in. And if she had dreamed that America would throw her mighty weight into the scale, it would have been inconceivable. The only thing that reassured the deluded German people after we entered the war was the lying statement of her public men that we could not get our troops across the sea, because Germany knew if America ever got within striking distance, the story was done. (great applause and shouts) And here all the nations of the world, except Germany, for the time being at any rate, give notice that they will unite against any nation that has a bad case, and they agree that in their own case they will submit to prolonged discussion.

And there is nothing so chilling as discussion to a hot temper. (laughter and applause) If you are fighting mad and yet I can induce you to talk it over for half an hour, you won't be fighting mad at the end of the half hour. I know a very wise schoolmaster in North Carolina[3] who said that, if any boy in that school fought another, except according to the rules, he would be expelled. There

---

[3] Robert Bingham, headmaster of the Bingham School, at this time located in Asheville.

would not be any great investigation; the fact that he had fought would be enough; he would go home; but that if he was so mad that he had to fight, all he had to do was to come to the headmaster and tell him that he wanted to fight. The headmaster would arrange the ring, would see that the fight was conducted according to the Marquess of Queensberry's rules, with an umpire and a referee, and that the thing was fought to a finish. And the consequence was that there were no fights in that school. (laughter and applause) The whole arrangement was too cold-blooded. By the time all the arrangements had been made, all the fighting audacity had gone out of the contestants.

And that little thing illustrates a great thing. Discussion is destructive when wrong is intended, and all the nations of the world agree to put their case before the judgment of mankind. Why, my fellow citizens, that has been the dream of thoughtful reformers for generation after generation. (applause) Somebody seems to have conceived the notion that I originated the idea of a league of nations. I wish I had. I would be a very proud man if I had. But I did not. I was expressing the avowed aspirations of the American people, avowed by nobody so loudly, so intelligently, or so constantly as the greater leaders of the Republican party. (great applause) When the Republicans take that road, I take off my hat and follow; I don't care whether I lead or not. I want the great result which I know is at the heart of the people that I am trying to serve.

In the second place, all of these great nations agree to boycott any nation that does not submit a perilous question either to arbitration or to discussion, and to support each other in the boycott. There is no "if" or "but" about that in the Covenant. It is agreed that, just so soon as any member state, or any outside state, for that matter, refuses to submit its case to the public opinion of the world, its doors shall be locked; that no country shall trade with it, no telegraphic message shall leave it or enter it, no letter shall cross its borders either way; there shall be no transactions of any kind between the citizens of the members of the League and the Covenant-breaking state. (applause)

That is the remedy that thoughtful men have advocated for several generations. They have thought, and thought truly, that war was barbarous and that a nation that resorted to war when its cause was unjust was unworthy of being consorted with by free people anywhere. And the boycott is an infinitely more terrible instrument than war. (applause) Excepting our own singularly fortunate country, I cannot think of any other country that can live upon its own resources. And the minute you lock the door, then the pinch of the thing becomes intolerable—not only the physical pinch, not only the fact that you cannot get raw materials and must stop your factories, not only the fact that you cannot get food and your people must begin to starve, not only the fact that your credit is stopped, that your assets are useless—but the still greater pinch that comes when a nation knows that it is sent to Coventry and despised.

The most terrible punishment that ever happened to a condemned man is not that he is put in jail. But if he knows that he was justly condemned, what penetrates his heart is the look in other men's eyes. It is the soul that is wounded much more poignantly than the body. And one of the things that the German nation has not been able to comprehend is that it has lost for the time being the respect of mankind. And, as Germans, when the doors of truth were opened to them after the war had begun, they began to look aghast at the probable fortunes of Germany. For if the world does not trust them, if the world does not respect them, if the world does not want Germans to come as immigrants any more, what is Germany to do? Germany's worst punishment, my fellow citizens, is not in the treaty. It is in her relations with the rest of mankind for the next generation. (applause)

And the boycott is what is substituted for war.

In the third place, all the members of this great association pledge themselves to respect and preserve as against external aggression the territorial integrity and existing political independence of the other member states. That is the famous Article X that you hear so much about. And Article X, my fellow citizens, whether you want to assume the responsibility of it or not, is the heart of the pledge that we have made to the other nations of the world. Only by Article X can we be said to have underwritten civilization. (applause)

The wars that threaten mankind begin by that kind of aggression. For every other nation than Germany, in 1914, treaties stood as solemn and respected covenants. For Germany they were scraps of paper, and when she entered, when her first soldiers were upon the soil of Belgium, her honor was forfeited. That act of aggression, that failure to respect the territorial integrity of a nation whose territory she was especially bound to respect, pointed the hand along that road that is strewn with graves since the beginning of history, that road made red and ugly with the strife of men—the strife behind which lies savage cupidity, the strife behind which lies a disregard for the rights of others, and the thought concentrated upon what we want and mean to get. That is the history of war, and, unless you accept Article X, you do not cut the heart of war out of civilization.

Belgium did not hesitate to underwrite civilization. (applause) Belgium could have had safety on her own terms if only she had not resisted the German arms—little Belgium, helpless Belgium, ravaged Belgium. Ah, my fellow citizens, I have seen some of the fields of Belgium. I rode with her fine, democratic King over some of those fields. He would say to me, "This is the village of so and so," and there was no village there—just scattered stones all over the plain, and the plain dug deep every few feet with the holes made by exploding shells. You could not tell whether it was the earth thrown up or the house thrown down from the debris that covered the desert which the war had made.

And then we rode farther in, farther to the east, where there had been no fighting, no active campaigning, and there we saw beautiful green slopes, fields that had once been cultivated, and towns with their factories standing, but standing empty; not empty of workers merely, but empty of machinery. Every piece of machinery in Belgium that they could put on freight cars, they had taken away, and what they could not carry with them they had destroyed, under the devilishly intelligent direction of experts—great bodies of heavy machinery that never could be used again, because somebody had known where the heart of the machine lay, where to put the dynamite. The Belgians there, their buildings there, but nothing to work with, nothing to start life with again. And in the face of all that, Belgium did not flinch for a moment to underwrite the interests of mankind by saying to Germany, "We will not be bought." (applause)

Italy could have had more by compounding with Austria in the later stages of the war than she is going to get out of the peace settlement now, but she would not compound. She, also, was a trustee for civilization, and she would not sell the birthright of mankind for any sort of material advantage. She underwrote civilization. (applause) And Serbia, the first of the helpless nations to be struck down, her armies driven from her own soil, maintained her armies on other soils, and the armies of Serbia were never dispersed. Whether they could be on their own soil or not, they were fighting for their rights and, through their rights, for the rights of civilized man. (applause) And I believe that America is going to be more willing than any other nation in the world, when it gets its voice heard, to do this same thing that those little nations did.

Why, my fellow citizens, we have been talking constantly about the rights of little nations. There is only one way to maintain the rights of little nations, and that is by the strength of great nations. (applause) And, having begun this great task, we are no quitters; we are going to see it through. (applause and cheers) The red that this German counselor of state saw upon the horizon was not the red of any dawn that will reassure the people who checked the wrong that Germany did. It was the first red glare of the fire that is going to consume the wrong in the world. (applause) And as that moral fire comes creeping on, it is going to purify every field of blood upon which men sacrificed their lives. It is going to redeem France; it is going to redeem Belgium; it is going to redeem devastated Serbia; it is going to redeem the fair land to the north of Italy, and set men on their feet again, to look fate in the face and have again that hope which is the only thing that leads men forward. So this covenant is the heart of the League.

In the next place, every nation agrees to join in advising what shall be done in case one of the members fails to keep that promise. There is where you have been misled, my fellow countrymen. You have been led to believe that the Council of the League of Nations could say to the Congress of the United States, "Here is a war, and here is where you come in." Nothing of the sort is true. The Council of the League of Nations is to advise what is to be done, and I have not been able to find in the dictionary any meaning of the word "advise," except "advise." (laughter and applause) But let us suppose that it means something else; let us suppose there is some legal compulsion upon the advice. The advice can't be given except by a unanimous vote of the Council and an affirmative vote of the United States. We are a permanent member, or will be a permanent member, of the Council of the League of Nations, and no such advice is ever going to be given unless the United States votes "aye," with one exception. If we are parties to the dispute, we cannot vote. But, my fellow citizens, I want to remind you, if we are parties to the dispute, we are in the war anyhow—forced into war by the vote of the Council. We are forced into war by our quarrel with the other party, as we would be in any case.

There is no sacrifice in the slightest degree of the independent choice of the Congress of the United States whether it will declare war or not. (applause)

There is a peculiar impression on the part of some persons in this country that the United States is more jealous of its sovereignty than other countries. That provision was not put in there because it was necessary to safeguard the sovereignty of the United States. All the other nations wanted it, were just as keen for their veto as we were keen for ours. So there is not the slightest danger that they will misunderstand that article of the Covenant. There is only danger that some of us who are too credulous will be led to misunderstand it. (applause)

All the nations agree to join in devising a plan for disarmament, general disarmament. You have heard that this Covenant was a plan for bringing on war, but it is going to bring on war by means of disarmament, by establishing a permanent court of international justice. (applause) When I voted for that, I was obeying the mandate of the Congress of the United States. In a very unexpected place, namely, in a naval appropriation bill passed in 1916, it was provided—it was declared—to be the policy of the United States to bring about a general disarmament by common agreement. And the President of the United States was requested to call a conference not later than the close of the then present war for the purpose of consulting and agreeing upon a plan for a permanent court of international justice. And he was authorized, in case such an agreement should be reached, to stop the building program provided for by that naval appropriation bill. So that the Congress of the United States deliberately accepted, not only accepted but directed the President to promote an agreement of this sort for disarmament and a permanent court of international justice. You know what a permanent court of international justice is. You cannot set up a court without respecting its decrees. You cannot make a toy of it. You cannot make a mockery of it. If, indeed, you want a court, then you must abide by the judgments of the court. And we have declared already that we are willing to abide by the judgments of a court of international justice.

All the nations agree to register their treaties and agree that no treaty that is not registered and published shall be valid. Private agreements and secret treaties are swept from the table, and one of the most dangerous instruments of international intrigue and disturbance is abolished.

They agree to join in the supervision of the government of helpless and dependent people. They agree that no nation shall hereafter have the right to annex any territory merely because people that live on it cannot prevent it, and that, instead of annexation, there shall be trusteeship; under which these territories shall be administered under the supervision of the associated nations of the world. They lay down rules for the protection of dependent persons of that sort, so that they shall not have enforced labor put upon them, so that their women and children shall be protected from unwholesome and destructive forms of labor, that they shall be kept away from the opium traffic and the traffic in arms, and agree that they will never levy armies there. They agree, in other words, to do what no nation ever agreed to do before—to treat subject nations like human beings. (applause)

They agree also to accord and maintain fair and humane conditions of labor for men, women, and children, both in their own countries and in all other countries to which their commercial and industrial relations extend. And, for that purpose, they agree to join in establishing and maintaining the necessary international organization. This great treaty, which we are hesitating to ratify, contains the organization by which the united councils of mankind shall attempt to lift the levels of labor and to see that men who are working with their hands are everywhere treated as they ought to be treated—upon principles of justice and equality. How many laboring men dreamed, when this war began, that four years later it would be possible for all the great nations of the world to enter into a covenant like that?

They agree to entrust the League with the general supervision of all international agreements with regard to traffic in women and children, traffic in opium and other dangerous drugs. They agree to entrust the League with general supervision of the trade in arms and ammunition with the countries in which the control of this traffic is necessary in the common interest. They agree to join in obtaining and maintaining freedom of communications and transit and equitable treatment for commerce in respect of all the members of the League. They agree to cooperate in an endeavor to take steps for the control and the prevention of disease. They agree to encourage and promote the establishment and cooperation of duly authorized voluntary national Red Cross organizations for the improvement of health, the prevention of disease, and mitigation of suffering throughout the world.

I ask you, my fellow citizens, is that not a great peace document and a great humane document? (applause) Is it conceivable that America, the most progressive and humane nation in the world, should refuse to take the same responsibility upon herself that all the other great nations take in supporting this great Covenant?

You say: "It isn't likely that the treaty will be rejected. It is only likely that there will be certain reservations." Very well, I want very frankly to tell you what I think about that. If the reservations do not change the treaty, then it is not necessary to make them part of the resolution of ratification. If all that you desire is to say what you understand the treaty to mean, no harm can be done by saying it. But if you want to change the treaty, if you want to alter the phraseology so that the meaning is altered, if you want to put in reservations which give the United States a position of special privilege or a special exemption from responsibility among the members of the League, then it will be necessary to take the treaty back to the conference table.

And, my fellow citizens, the world is not in a temper to discuss this treaty over again. (applause) The world is just now more profoundly disturbed by social and economic conditions than it ever was before. And the world demands that we shall come to some sort of settlement which will let us get down to business and purify and rectify our affairs. (applause) This is not only the best treaty that can be obtained, but I want to say—because I played only a small part in framing it—that it is a sound and good treaty. (applause) And America, above all nations, should not be the nation that puts obstacles in the way of the peace of nations and the peace of mind of the world.

The world hasn't anywhere at this moment, my fellow countrymen, peace of mind. Nothing has struck me so much in recent months as the unaccustomed anxiety on the faces of the people. I am aware that men do not know what is going to happen, and that they know that it is just as important to them what happens in the rest of the world, almost, as what happens in America. America not only has connections with all the rest of the world, but she has necessary dealings with all the rest of the world. And no man is fatuous enough to suppose that if the rest of the world is disturbed and disordered, the disturbance and disorder are not going to extend to the United States.

The center of our anxiety, my fellow citizens, is in that pitiful country to which our hearts go out—that great mass of mankind whom we call the Russians. (applause) I never had the good fortune to be in Russia, but I know many persons who know that lovable people intimately. They all tell me that there is not a people in the world more generous, more simple, more kind, more naturally addicted to friendship, more passionately attached to peace than the Russian people. And yet, because the grip of terror that the autocratic power of the Czar had upon them, they were unable to bear it and threw it off. And they have come under a terror even greater than that. They have come under the terror of the power of men whom nobody knows how to find. One or two names everybody knows, but the rest—intrigue, terror, informing, spying, military power, the seizure of all the food obtainable in order that the fighting men may be fed and the rest go starved. And these men have been appealed to again and again by the civilized governments of the world to call a constituent assembly and let the Russian people say what sort of government they want to have, and they will not, they dare not, do it.

And that picture is before the eyes of every nation. Shall we get into the clutch of another sort of minority? My fellow citizens, I am going to devote every influence I have and all the authority I have from this time on to see to it that no minority commands the United States. (long and continuous applause and shouts)

It heartens me, but it does not surprise me, to know that that is the verdict of every man and woman here. But, my fellow citizens, there is no use passing that verdict unless we are going to take part, and a great part, a leading part, in steadying the councils of the world. (applause) Not that we are afraid of anything except the spread of moral defection, and moral defection cannot come except where men have lost faith, lost hope, have lost confidence. And, having seen the attitude of the other peoples of the world towards America, I know that the whole world will lose heart unless America consents to show the way.

It was pitiful, on the other side of the sea, to have delegation after delegation from peoples all over the world come to the house I was living in in Paris and seek conference with me to beg that America would show the way. It was touching. It made me very proud, but it made me very sad—proud that I was the representative of a nation so regarded, but very sad to feel how little of all the things that they had dreamed we could accomplish for them. But we can pledge this, my fellow citizens: we can, having taken a pledge to be faithful to them, redeem the pledge. (applause) And we shall redeem the pledge. (applause)

I look forward to the day when all this debate will seem in our recollection like a strange mist that came over the minds of men here and there in the nation, like a groping in the fog, having lost the way, the plain way, the beaten way, that America had made for itself for generations together. And we shall then know that of a sudden, upon the assertion of the real spirit of the American people, we came to the edge of the mist, and outside lay the sunny country where every question of duty lay plain and clear and where the great tramp, tramp of the American people sounded in the ears of the whole world, and they knew that the armies of God were on their way. (applause)

Printed in the *Seattle Post-Intelligencer*, Sept. 14, 1919.

From Louis Brownlow

The White House 1919 Sep 13

Brownlow asks that following be sent for information of the President.

"Certain conditions have arisen in connection with the police union matter that I deem it my duty to lay before you for your information in accordance with your suggestion as telegraphed to me by Mr Tumulty.[1] The Commissioners Thursday asked Judge Gould[2] to postpone the hearing in the case[3] until after the meeting of the industrial conference. He granted the request and set the hearing for November 7. In the meantime the commissioners order of September 2[4] stands but the temporary injunction restraining us from executing the order also stands. Thus, so far as the commissioners are concerned, the status quo is preserved. Unfortunately some members of Congress interpreted your request to mean a repudiation of the action of the commissioners—an interpretation to which they were assisted by the Washington Post and the Washington Herald on Wednesday morning. The Star and Times pointed out Wednesday afternoon the similarity in the phraseology of the telegram sent to me and that to Mr Gompers with respect to the steel men[5] and did not follow the lead of the two morning papers. Friday morning the Post contained a very brief extract from your speech at Helena concerning the Boston situation. This was followed Friday afternoon by a dispatch in the Star from David Lawrence which materially helped matters. Senator Myers[6] has introduced a resolution which forbids the commissioners to pay any money out of any funds appropriated by Congress to any policeman who is a member of any union affiliated with any other labor organization. The Senate District Committee will consider and I am informed will report favorably this resolution next Monday. Vice President Marshall Friday afternoon told me that the Myers resolution will undoubtedly pass the Senate probably on next Monday. Later on Friday afternoon I was summoned to the Capitol by Mr. Mapes[7] Chairman of the House Committee on the District of Columbia. He said to me that members of the House were planning legislation along the lines of the Myers resolution or its equivalent, they believing that the commissioners action had met with your disapproval. By that time fortunately more complete report of your Helena speech was in the Star together with a dispatch from Mr Lawrence which enabled me to counsel delay. I told him that I did not think legislation was necessary at this time, that the commissioners were advised by competent counsel, that they had full legal authority to deal with the situation, and that I was sure, although I had no advices from you, that there was a reason of national importance behind your request for a postponement of the issue here in Washington. He agreed at any rate to take no action without further consulting me. However from what the Vice President and others have said to me I believe that there is real danger that some action may be taken by Congress which may precipitate the police union issue here before you return and before of course the industrial conference meets. Believing that such action might interfere with plans you have in mind I thought I should acquaint you with the facts." Forster.

T telegram (WP, DLC).
 ¹ JPT to L. Brownlow, Sept. 9, 1919.
 ² Ashley Mulgrave Gould, Associate Justice of the Supreme Court of the District of Columbia.
 ³ About which, see B. M. Baruch to JPT, Sept. 9, 1919.
 ⁴ See *ibid.*
 ⁵ JPT to S. Gompers, Sept. 10, 1919.
 ⁶ That is, Henry Lee Myers.
 ⁷ Carl Edgar Mapes, Republican of Michigan.

From Albert Sidney Burleson

[Washington] Sept. 13, 1919

Upon my return from Canada I find situation less favorable than when I left. Certain steps can be taken that would very probably bring the recalcitrant Senators from the South back in line. Because of the cotton situation at this time and the fact that the market for about three million bales of cotton will continue closed until the treaty is ratified affords a lever that should be utilized.¹ Steps can be taken without knowledge of where the motif emanates to start the movement on this issue. Do not think this should be touched upon by you before you reach some point in the South. This would give time to start movement in South before you allude to it. The Senators with whom I confer [still]² believe that all reservations and amendments can probably be defeated, but they cannot know when the voting will begin. In the event reservations should be adopted, friendly Senators desire to know your wishes as to how they should finally vote, on the adoption of the Treaty. If an adverse vote should be had, a motion for reconsideration, if desired, could be promptly entered and negotiations could then be entered upon, looking toward mild reservations.

Congratulations on the speeches. They are proving effective.

Burleson

T telegram (WP, DLC).
 ¹ Burleson was in error. The blockade upon commerce with Germany had been lifted effective July 12, 1919. On the previous day, the Department of State had announced that all restrictions on trade with Germany would be immediately removed and blanket license given permitting such trade, excepting only in dyes, potash, and chemicals. See *PPC*, VII, 101-102, and FLP to Ammission, July 11, 1919, Vol. 61.
 The chief limitation upon the export trade to Germany at this time was the inability of German businessmen, etc., to pay for needed imports or to obtain credits to finance them.
 ² Addition from the ASBhw "original" of this telegram, written on White House stationery, in EBR, RG 130, White House Staff Files, 1900-1935, DNA.

Russell Cornell Leffingwell to Joseph Patrick Tumulty

Washington DC Sept 13 19

Telegram received stop You have better means of judging than I stop My personal reaction is something like this stop The speeches are splendid but may intensify antagonism on Hill stop Believe country is with us already and that ratification with moderate interpretations could be negotiated now that matter is out of committee stop If this were done with reasonable promptness it would be better than complete victory delayed until the world is prostrate stop Fear further protracted delay may prove fatal to Europe and perilous here stop Think unrest serious and Boston symptomatic stop I should be glad to see return expedited stop Referring to two special matters first Helena speech about policemans duty was magnificent and has done much to counteract impression for weakening resulting from telegram to Brownlow[1] stop Policeman who strikes should be treated like soldier who deserts stop Policemen should not be allowed to join any general federation of labor stop Divided allegiance on part of those sworn to protect society cannot be tolerated stop Following is quotation from New York World editorial September twelve quote Any professions on the contrary notwithstanding when the Boston police organized their force into a union affiliated with the American Federation of Labor they could have had no other object than to command the help of that great body in any measures they might resort to either to overawe or subvert the public authority as they are now trying to do stop And when the Federation accepts such an affiliation of public employees it virtually promises the help expected stop This obligation is now recognized by the Boston unions in the Federation stop This help they promise to extend by way of a general strike stop This mutiny against the public authority on the part of the police would expand into rebellion against the whole community stop What do these Boston labor unions expect to gain for themselves by such a course stop Their rebellion will be against their own people first and chiefest of all stop The rich can take care of themselves stop They are taking ample care of themselves in the police mutiny stop They have not been without armed protection for a moment stop It is for the honest poor without means to protect themselves that the authorities are exceeding themselves by calls upon the states militia unquote stop Second stop Reference in St Louis speech to Hoovers estimate that four or five billion dollars would have to be provided by United States immediately for rehabilitation of Europe has unfortunately been misunderstood erroneous impression having been gained that Government loans were meant stop This has caused dismay on Hill stop We all including [Norman H.] Davis think Hoovers estimate grossly exaggerated and that use of these big figures tends to scare off capital and prevent establishment of necessary credits   Leffingwell

T telegram (WP, DLC).
  [1] JPT to L. Brownlow, Sept. 9, 1919.

Rudolph Forster to Joseph Patrick Tumulty

The White House Washington D C Sept 13 1919

Dr Waldron Dr Brown and Professor Hawkins[1] as committee from National Race Congress called to urge that the President appoint two representatives of the colored race as delegates to industrial conference to represent more especially unorganized colored labor. This committee intimated that strong efforts were being made to induce this colored labor to affiliate with IWW and kindred organizations and that there was grave danger of success of these efforts. They urged that if the race had representatives in conference who could explain situation of unorganized colored labor much could be done to bring about a better feeling and offset sinister influences now at work.   Forster

T telegram (WP, DLC).
  [1] The Rev. Dr. John Milton Waldron, pastor of Shiloh Baptist Church in Washington; the Rev. Dr. William Cornelius Brown, a clergyman of the African Methodist Episcopal Zion Church; and John Russell Hawkins, former professor at and president of Kittrell College in Kittrell, N. C., at this time the financial secretary of the African Methodist Episcopal Church and executive secretary of the National Race Congress. The congress had been founded in 1915 to promote racial justice in the United States. Over 600 delegates attended its third annual meeting in Washington in October 1919.

From John A. O'Connell and Others

San Francisco Calif Sept 13 1919

The San Francisco Labor Council by unanimous vote on September fifth 1919 adopted resolutions quoted below and appointed the undersigned committee to request a personal meeting or conference with you at San Francisco at your convenience but before your mass meeting Wednesday night September 17th here The intention of organized labor here in appointing this committee and in requesting this meeting with you was for the purpose of seeing to it that an opportunity be afforded you to if possible clear up disputed questions in connection with the League of Nations raised by members of organized labor We are forwarding resolutions by wire[1] so that you may familiarize yourself with same and be prepared to meet committee prior to your mass meeting of Wednesday night next and answer questions as quoted below

Resolutions are as follows quote Whereas President Wilson is on a tour of the United States for the purpose of explaining to the American people the provisions of the peace treaty and the Covenant of the League of Nations with a view to secure popular approval of the same and whereas there are millions of American citizens who would gladly consent to these propositions for the sake of abolishing future wars and secure the settlement of all disputes between nations upon principles of international law and justice if they can be assured by proper reasoning and authority that by entering the League of Nations our government and people do not abandon the immortal principles of the Declaration of Independence and bind themselves thereafter to keep in perpetual subjection under the heel of the conqueror those people who of right and in the interest of humanity and civilization ought to be free and independent or assume a station in accordance with the principle of self-determination therefore be it resolved by the San Francisco Labor Council in regular meeting assembled this 5th day of September 1919 that upon his visit to San Francisco the President be and is hereby requested to make a public explanation and declaration regarding the provisions of the Covenant on the following points

1 Under the Covenant does the nation obligate itself to assist any member of the League in putting down a rebellion of its subject or conquered people

2 Under the Covenant can this nation independently recognize a government whose people seek to achieve or have achieved their independence from a member of the League

3 Under the Covenant are those subject nations or peoples only that are mentioned in the peace treaty entitled to the right of self-determination or does the League possess the right to accord a similar privilege to other subject nations or people

4 Why was the case of Ireland not heard at the peace conference and what is your position on the subject of self-determination for Ireland unquote

Respectfully submitted John P McLaughlin
B B Rosenthal
Andrew J Gallagher
Timothy A Reardon
Michael Casey
M[ichael] J McGuire
John A O'Connell Secty San Francisco Labor
Council

Please wire reply to John A O'Connell Labor Temple 16th and Capp Streets San Francisco

T telegram (WP, DLC).
¹ They were also sent in J. A. O'Connell to WW, Sept. 6, 1919, TLS (WP, DLC).

From William Phillips

Washington, September 13, [1919].

Urgent. Sept. 13, 3 P.M. CONFIDENTIAL. I have just received a confidential cablegram from the Embassy at Rome¹ saying the King sent full particulars² to Mr. Jay³ on the 11th and informed him that contrary to all precedents he was going to ask Mr. Jay to telegraph a long personal appeal to you to consent to the proposals being put forward by Tittoni in regard to the Italian claims. The King dwelt upon the sacrifices of blood and treasure made by Italy in the common cause, and upon her renunciation of much she felt she was entitled to. The King asked that this be brought immediately to your attention, as the decision is expected at any moment.

The message from Rome was received in a very badly garbled condition, but I am sending you this brief resumé pending the receipt of a repetition of the whole message which I have requested. I shall then telegraph you more in detail the nature of the King's appeal.⁴　　　　　　　　　　　　　　　　　William Phillips

T telegram (WP, DLC).
¹ P. A. Jay to SecState, No. 3136, Sept. 12, 1919, T telegram (SDR, RG 59, 763.72119/6709, DNA).
² "full particulars" not in the telegram sent: W. Phillips to WW, Sept. 13, 1919, T telegram (SDR, RG 59, 763.72119/6709, DNA).
³ That is, Vittorio Emanuele III and Peter Augustus Jay.
⁴ See W. Phillips to WW, Sept. 15, 1919 (first telegram of that date).

Joseph Patrick Tumulty to William Phillips¹

[Seattle] 13 September, 1919

The President requests that you forward the following at once to Polk in Paris, and hopes that it will not be necessary to decode and recode it, inasmuch as time is of the essence: quote

"For Polk from the President: I am quite willing to accept the proposed Adriatic settlement as modified by you and Johnson, taking the second of the two proposals with regard to Fiume and the free state, not the first, and consenting to the Italian mandate in Albania, with the understanding that such restrictions as you propose will be accepted by Italy. I also stipulate that the eastern coast of Istria be neutralized all the way down to where the American line ended. Please read the above as taking for granted at each point the modifications and formulation proposed by you and Johnson in your letter to Clemenceau and in your cable to me."[2]

J. P. Tumulty

T telegram (WP, DLC).
   [1] This telegram was received in the State Department at 7:25 a.m., Sept. 14, 1919. The received telegram is JPT to W. Phillips, Sept. 13, 1919, T telegram (SDR, RG 59, 763.72119/6706, DNA).
   [2] For both of which, see W. Phillips to WW, Sept. 11, 1919. Wilson's message was sent to Polk in W. Phillips to FLP, Sept. 14, 1919, No. 3123, T telegram (SDR, RG 256, 186.3411/808, DNA).

From William Phillips

Washington, D. C., Sept. 13, 1919

The following telegram has been received for you from Colonel House, through the American Embassy at London:

"September 12, 3 P.M. For the President, from Colonel House. I have received the following letter from Clemenceau. It indicates a growing enthusiasm for the League. I think there is now general agreement that the meeting of the Assembly should be held in Washington just as soon after the Senate ratifies the Treaty as possible. I think, too, that only a mere pro forma meeting of the Council, to put in effect that clause of the treaty relating to the Saar Valley, should be held over here. The real meeting of the Council should be held at Washington.

"Translation of letter from M. Clemenceau to Colonel House:

"Sept. 4th. I hope that I shall soon have the pleasure of seeing you in Paris, before your departure for America. But as our friend Tardieu tells me that the date is not certain, it seems to me that I ought to communicate to you immediately the reflections which are suggested to me by the possibility of decisions to be made with reference to the League of Nations.

"It seems to me, first of all, that there will be urgent need for convening the first assembly of the League as soon as possible in Washington, to be presided over by your President. In view of the hopes to which the League has given rise, and in order to facilitate the solution of the international problems with which all nations are now grappling, I would suggest that this meeting should take place during November. I would at the time propose to invite the greatest possible number of statesmen whose names have been associated with the creation of the League of Nations.

"Doubtless [in November][1] there will be only a small amount of current business to transact, but the meeting will have at least the capital advantage of setting the League in motion, whereas it now exists only on paper.

This seems to be of prime importance: (It will not succeed) in the execution of effective measures, unless preceded by a moral preparation of the people which will furnish both the condition and the sanction of the necessary results.

Moreover, in the near future [midst of] the thousand difficulties which are appearing or have already appeared to all the governments, make it [it is] necessary in my opinion that the League [of Nations] be endowed with recognized powers, should be able to recommend and enforce all solutions of "fair play" in the current order of life. In case of a crisis, it is important that it should make itself heard with a firm voice.

[Finally] Do you not think that it would be a great advantage if the rightful members of the League were put in a position to exchange their ideas upon the question of the general direction of action to be taken? No man is better qualified than President Wilson to protect the Peace Treaty of [or] have [for] the settling of the problems which the treaty does not solve and which nevertheless resulted from the war. It will then be clear to everyone that the League exists in its full moral force.

It is true that the execution of the treaty is entrusted to a certain number of commissions or experts who will necessarily be led to consult their governments. But there are many clauses [articles] of the treaty which involve the Council of the League of Nations itself, and in this connection the [all] Nations ought to have the impression that this Council is ready to function as soon as it is called upon.

On the other hand, I am sure that you agree with me that in these matters neither the action of the governments nor even that of the League of Nations can be advantageous to the nations upon the opening of the first assembly; that the League of Nations will have prestige and influence during peace time only if it succeeds in maintaining the feeling of international solicitude [solidarity, which it is hoped] for which it was brought to light during the war, upon the call of the President. For my part, I should be happy to second him in this task." End quote.

William Phillips, Acting Secretary of State.

T telegram (WP, DLC).
  [1] Corrections and additions from W. Phillips to WW, Sept. 13, 1919, TS telegram (SDR, RG 59, 763.72119/6697, DNA).

From the Diary of Dr. Grayson

Sunday, September 14, 1919.

After breakfast the President and Mrs. Wilson and myself attended services in the Presbyterian Church here.[1] For the first time in my experience I witnessed a church service interrupted while the congregation applauded a visitor. As the President entered, the audience applauded him, and they applauded him again on his departure from the sacred edifice. The fact that the Pacific Northwest was solidly for the policies that President Wilson advocated was demonstrated not only in the church but at every point where the President appeared in public during his stay in Seattle.

Returning to the hotel for luncheon, the President conferred with the labor leaders in the afternoon.[2] He told them very frankly that as far as he was concerned he would not countenance anything that savored of violence and repeated to them in substance what he had already said on this subject in public.

After the conference with the labor people, the President met the members of the Seattle reception committee and shook hands with them, telling them how much he appreciated the warmth of his welcome in the Puget Sound City.

The party left Seattle at 10:00 o'clock that night en route to Portland.

[1] The First Presbyterian Church of Seattle, the Rev. Dr. Mark Allison Matthews, pastor. Dr. Matthews, Wilson's old friend, preached on "Precious Moments With Jesus." *Seattle Post-Intelligencer*, Sept. 15, 1919.

[2] Wilson met for over an hour with James A. Duncan, secretary of the Central Labor Council of Seattle; L. W. Buck, secretary and acting president of the Washington State Federation of Labor; and C. R. Cottrell, or Cotterell, secretary of a so-called "Triple Alliance" of railroad workers, other labor groups, and farmers. The three union leaders at first refused to speak to reporters as they left the conference. Finally, Duncan was induced to say a few words. "Everybody knows that what we came here to discuss was the question of social unrest. We won't have anything to say now. We'll give the President until tomorrow morning to make a statement. I think we ought to do that, but if the President doesn't make a statement by that time, we will." *New York Times*, Sept. 15, 1919. We have found no evidence that either Wilson or the three leaders ever made any such statement. However, the newspapers reported that the conferees dealt with so-called political prisoners, that is, labor leaders such as Tom Mooney and Eugene V. Debs, as well as Seattle labor figures, who had been imprisoned for sedition and other crimes. Wilson and the three men also discussed other causes of labor unrest and the forthcoming conference of representatives of capital and labor to be held in Washington on October 6.

The New York *World*, September 15, 1919, reported on Wilson's reaction to the comments of the union leaders as follows: "The President listened very patiently and then bluntly told his callers that he did not propose to countenance the control of Government affairs by any special interest, whether it was labor or capital. He promised to look into the special cases cited by the labor leaders, but told them the Government had already moved to clear up any uncertainties there might exist as to the guilt of Mooney. He advised against a strike and suggested that all labor grievances be held in abeyance until after the industrial conference called by him to meet at Washington on October 6, as that event was intended to provide a clearing house for all differences between labor and capital. The President further told his callers that he had been greatly impressed by the radical influences that seemed to have taken hold of labor in the West and that he hoped the industrial conference would find a solution for the causes that had contributed to the growth of it."

Other brief accounts of the meeting are in the *New York Herald, New York Tribune,* and *Washington Post,* all Sept. 15, 1919. Jack Kipps, about whom see n. 2 to the extract from the Grayson Diary printed at September 13, 1919, claimed that he, too, was present at the conference and gave a detailed account of what took place. Louis Adamic, "The 'Assassin' of Wilson," pp. 142-44. However, none of the contemporary newspaper accounts mentions him or his presence at all.

To Newton Diehl Baker

[Seattle, Sept. 14, 1919]

Will you not be kind enough to communicate the following message to the First Division on the occasion of its review in Washington?   Woodrow Wilson.

Message to the First Division,
through the Secretary of War.

It is a matter of deep regret to me that I cannot be in Washington to review you and bid you a welcome in person. The whole country has followed your record in the great war with pride. It is impossible justly to assess the achievements of one Division where all acquitted themselves with such valour and distinction, but it is possible to see how each has won for itself a peculiar glory and I am sure that I speak for the whole country when I praise you alike with my heart and with my judgment for the laurels you have added to the records of American steadfastness, valour, dash, and inconquerable capacity. We welcome you with praise and with thanksgiving that our beloved country has produced such men, such champions of her own rights and of the rights of free men everywhere. It is an added pleasure that, in welcoming you home we may at the same time welcome your gallant and distinguished commander.[1] Your work is done, gallantly and nobly done. It now remains for us who gave you occasion to see that what you did is made forever complete by the concert of all the nations who love peace and pursue justice.[2]

WWT MS (T. W. Brahany Coll.).

[1] Maj. Gen. Edward Fenton McGlachlin, Jr., was the commander of the First Division. However, Wilson's comment referred to Gen. Pershing, who led the parade of the First Division in Washington on September 17. *Washington Post,* Sept. 18, 1919.

[2] The received copy of this telegram is WW to NDB, Sept. 14, 1919, T telegram (N. D. Baker Papers, DLC).

From the Diary of Dr. Grayson

Monday, September 15, 1919.

The Presidential Special arrived in the Portland station at 9:00 o'clock, and the party was greeted by a reception committee headed by Governor [Olcott][1] and C. S. Jackson,[2] publisher of the OREGON JOURNAL. The President had had a rather bad night and his cough was extremely troublesome, interfering materially with his rest. In consequence he had a headache when Portland was reached.

The program here was one that might well be criticised, as it resulted in the death of one of the members of the Presidential party and the serious injury to two others. After a ride through the principal streets, the automobiles continued for a distance of sixty miles along Portland's public thoroughfare—The Columbia Drive. This is a macadam road that skirts the Columbia River chasm for many miles and is a beautiful drive inasmuch as the entire pictur-esque river and mountain scenery is in view at all times. However, because of the crowded program, which included a luncheon and a night meeting, it was necessary that speed limits be disregarded in order that the trip could be made. All the way out to the Half-way Point on the drive, the automobiles ran at a rate of speed in excess of forty miles an hour. I tried on several occasions to have the guide-car, which was controlled by the Mayor of Portland,[3] slackened up but was unable to get my message properly delivered. As soon as we reached the Half-way Point, I went directly to the Mayor and demanded that he issue orders that on the trip back the speed do not exceed twenty-five miles an hour. He promised that he would do so. The party left the cars and looked up and down the Columbia River for ten minutes, after which the return trip to the city began.

We went directly to the hotel, where a luncheon had been ar-ranged by Mr. C. S. Jackson. However, on the way in a slight de-tour was made and the President and party passed around the race-track at the Multnomah County Fair Grounds, where the state fair was in progress. Some members of the party had promised that the President would deliver an address here, but I put my foot down sharply and refused point blank to allow him to attempt to strain his vocal chords in the open air in such circumstances. It was well that I did so because the grounds were very dusty and the trip very uncomfortable.

Just before the luncheon began I received word that one of the automobiles in which the newspaper men were riding had been in a collision outside of the city limits and that Ben F. Allen, the cor-respondent of the Cleveland PLAIN DEALER, had been killed out-right, and Stanley M. Reynolds and Robert T. Small[4] were badly hurt. I had the secret service men get in touch with the authorities and a few minutes later received word that Small had been taken to the train. I had him brought to the hotel, where I made a com-plete examination of him and found that he was suffering from severe contusions and from shock to his nervous system but that no bones were broken. I had him put to bed, and then got an automobile and proceeded to the Samaritan Hospital, where I found Reynolds had been taken. He had a fracture of the shoulder and was otherwise badly hurt. I gave directions that he should have all possible care, and upon my return to the hotel directed the secret service to make arrangements for sending the body of Mr. Allen back to his old home in Cleveland. News of the accident had reached the President and he was greatly depressed. He told the luncheon audience[5] that because of the injury to the members of his party—he did not know then that Allen had been killed—he could not make a very long speech, and he contented himself with a brief appeal to the audience to use their efforts to have the Treaty ratified.

The night meeting in the auditorium was an immense success.[6] The audience cheered for Mrs. Wilson on her arrival until she was forced to stand up and bow her greetings. She was presented with a beautiful basket of flowers on behalf of the Women's Clubs of the City.

The President made a splendid address dwelling particularly upon the arbitration features of the League of Nations Constitution. He told several stories that were apropos of his subject. One story that moved a good part of the audience to tears was of a woman who came up to him and shook hands with him, and then bursting into tears was forced to turn aside. When he asked a companion the cause of her emotion, he was told that her son had given his life for his country on the battlefields in France. The President said that this typified the spirit of the women of America; that they were willing to sacrifice their best for the cause of liberty; and that this woman and no other woman had blamed him because he in his capacity as Commander-in-Chief of the Army had sent their sons overseas to fight for the liberty of the world. The President told the audience that he would be recreant to his duty if he did not do everything in his power to have the Peace Treaty ratified so that other mothers would not have to sacrifice their loved ones in a final war for world liberty.

Portland was left at 11:00 o'clock that night. For half an hour before the train pulled out the President and I walked up and down the platform.[7] He stopped for a few moments in the compartment where Small was lying and expressed his personal sympathy and his hope for a speedy recovery.

The strain of the trip was showing on the President, and it required all of my skill to keep him fit so that he could meet the engagements before him.

[1] Ben Wilson Olcott, Republican.

[2] Charles Samuel Jackson, Wilson's old friend and supporter.

[3] George Luis Baker, Republican.

[4] Ben Farwell Allen; Stanley Meade Reynolds, of the Baltimore *Sun*; and Robert T. Small, of the Philadelphia *Public Ledger*. The driver of their car, James R. Patterson, was also killed. Later in the day, Wilson sent the following telegram to Allen's wife: "Our hearts go out to you in deepest sympathy in the tragical death of your husband, whom we all esteemed and trusted. He will be missed as a true friend and a man who always intelligently sought to do his duty." *New York Times*, Sept. 16, 1919.

[5] Two hundred invited guests were present at the luncheon. For this and other details of Wilson's visit to Portland, see Clifford W. Trow, " 'Something Desperate In His Face': Woodrow Wilson in Portland at the 'Very Crisis of his Career,' " *Oregon Historical Quarterly*, LXXXII (Spring 1981), 41-64.

[6] The audience for Wilson's address was 6,690 persons: 3,720 seated and 2,970 standing. *Ibid.*, p. 55, n. 47.

[7] It was at this time that Fred Lockley, a reporter for the *Oregon Daily Journal*, had a brief interview with Wilson, which appeared in that newspaper on September 16, 1919. "From what you have seen and heard," Lockley asked, "do you think Oregon is for the League of Nations?" "I certainly do," Wilson answered. "I believe Oregon is almost unanimously in its favor. Did you notice the audience at The Auditorium tonight? It was a very unusual one. It was the type of audience I love to address. There was very little applause. They had no time to applaud. They paid me the vastly greater compliment of eager attention. I watched their faces. I saw not only interest but agreement." "Is the West stronger for the league than the East?" Lockley inquired. "Here in the West we are more adventurous—more willing to take a chance. Are we not more willing to adventure in peace as well as in war, than the East?" "The West is more demonstrative, more outspoken than the East," Wilson replied, "but I believe the sentiment is as strongly in favor of the League of Nations in the East as it is in the West. . . . I believe in the people. I believe they will not be swayed from the path of duty or justice. When you appeal to the heart, the soul, the conscience of the people as well as to their intellect, you will be justified in your faith in their will to deal justly. I am confident that I shall not appeal in vain to the conscience of the American people. East and West, North and South, they are for the League of Nations."

A Luncheon Address in Portland

[[September 15, 1919]]

Mr. Jackson, ladies and gentlemen: I suppose that you have all heard of the accident to which Mr. Jackson has just alluded. One of the cars carrying some of the newspaper correspondents, who were accompanying my party, met with a very serious accident, and I am afraid the results were rather tragic. That naturally makes me feel somewhat depressed, because I have got to know the fine men who were injured and shall feel that, if I leave them behind, wounded, I shall leave very good friends and very estimable men behind. But I am sure that they would not wish me to omit to say how happy I am to be in the presence of a company like this.

As I return to Portland,[1] I can't help remembering that I learned a great deal in Oregon. I used to prove, when I was a teacher, to my satisfaction—I don't know whether it was to the satisfaction of my classes or not—that the initiative and referendum would not work. I came to Oregon to find that they did work, (laughter) and

[1] About Wilson's earlier visit to Portland, see the documents printed at May 19-20, 1911, Vol. 23.

have ever since been apologizing for my earlier opinion. Because I have always taken this attitude toward facts—that I never let them get me if I see them coming first. (laughter) There is nothing I respect so much as a fact. There is nothing that is so formidable as a fact. And the real difficulty in all political reform is to know whether you can translate your theories into facts or not, whether you can safely pick out the operative ideas and leave aside the inoperative ideas. For I think you will all agree with me that the whole progress of human affairs is the progress of ideas—not the ideas in the abstract form, but the ideas in the operative form—certain conceptions of justice and of freedom and of right that have got into men's natures and led those natures to insist upon the realization of those ideas in experience and in action.

And the whole trouble about our civilization, as it looks to me, is that it has grown complex faster than we have adjusted the simpler ideas to the existing circumstances. So that there was a time when men would do in their business what they would not do as individuals. There was a time when they submerged their individual consciences in a corporation and persuaded themselves that it was legitimate for a corporation to do what they individually never would have dreamed of doing. That is what I mean by saying that the organization has become complex faster than our adjustment of the simpler ideas of justice and right to the developing circumstances of our civilization.

Now, I say that because the errand that I am on concerns a subject that lies at the heart of all progress. I think we are all now convinced that we have not reached the right and final organization of our industrial society; that there are many features of our social life that ought to undergo correction; that while we call ourselves democrats—with a little "d," I mean—while we believe in democratic government, we have not seen yet the successful way of making our life in fact democratic; that we have allowed classes to disclose themselves. We have allowed lines of cleavage to be run through our communities, so that there are antagonisms set up that breed heat, because they breed friction. And the world must have leisure and order in which to see that these things are set right, and the world cannot have leisure and order unless it has a guaranteed peace.

For example, if the United States should conceivably—I think it inconceivable—but if it should conceivably stay out of the League of Nations, it would stay out at this cost: we would have to see that, since we were not going to join our force with other nations, our force was formidable enough to be respected by other nations. We would have to maintain a great army and a great navy. We would have to do something more than that: we would have to concentrate authority sufficiently to be able to use the physical force of the nation quickly upon occasion. All of that is absolutely antidemocratic in its influence. All of that means that we should not be giving ourselves the leisure of thought or the release of material resources necessary to work out our own methods of civilization, our own methods of industrial organization and production and distribution; and our problems are exactly the problems of the rest of the world.

I am more and more convinced, as I come in contact with the men who are trying to think for other countries, as we are trying to think for this one, that our problems are identical, only there is this—I was about to say temporary difference. I hope it will be a permanent difference. The peoples of other countries have lost confidence in their governments. Some of them have lost confidence in their form of government. That point, I hope and believe, has not been reached in the United States. We have not lost confidence in our government. I am not now speaking of our administration. (laughter) I am not thinking of that but of our method of government. We believe that we can manage our own affairs and that we have the machinery through which we can manage our own affairs, and that no clique or special interest is powerful enough to run away with it. And the other countries of the world believe that. They believe that we are successfully organized for justice, and they want to follow the lead. And if we don't take the lead, then we throw them back upon things in which they have no confidence and in danger of universal disorder and discontent in the midst of which it will be impossible to govern our own affairs with successful and with constant achievement.

So that, whether you will or not, our fortunes are tied in with the rest of the world. And the choice that we have to make now is whether we will receive the influences of the rest of the world and be affected by them, or dominate the influences of the world and lead it. (applause) That is a tremendous choice to make, but it is exactly that tremendous choice that we have to make. And I deeply regret the suggestions which I hear made on some sides that we should take advantage of the present situation in the world, but should not shoulder any of the responsibilities. Do you know of any business or undertaking in which you can get the advantage without assuming the responsibility? What are you going to be? Boys running around the circus tent and peeping under the canvas? Men declining to pay the admission and sitting on the roof and looking in on the game? Or are you going to play your responsible part in the game, knowing that you are trusted as a leader and umpire both? (applause)

Nothing has impressed me more, or impressed me more painfully, if I may say so, than the degree in which the rest of the world trusts us and looks to us. I say "painfully" because I am conscious that they are expecting more than we can perform. They are expecting miracles to be wrought by the influence of the American spirit on the affairs of the world, and miracles cannot be wrought. I have again and again recited to my fellow citizens on this journey how deputations from peoples of every kind and every color and every fortune, from all over the world, thronged to the house in which I was living in Paris to ask the guidance and assistance of the United States. They did not send similar delegations to anybody else, and they did not send them to me except because they thought they had heard in what I had been saying the spirit of the American people uttered. (applause)

Moreover, you must not forget this, almost all of them had kinsmen in America. You must not forget that America is made up out of the world and that there is hardly a race of any influence in the world, hardly a Caucasian race, that has not scores of hundreds, and sometimes millions, of people living in America with whom they are in correspondence, from whom they receive the subtle suggestions of what is going on in American life, and the ideals of American life. Therefore, they feel that they know America from this contact they have had with them, and they want America to be the leading force in the world.

Why, I received delegations there speaking in tongues that I didn't know anything about. I didn't know what family they belonged to—what family of languages they belonged to. Fortunately for me they always brought an interpreter along who could speak English. And one of the significant facts was that the interpreter almost always was some rather young man who had lived in America. He didn't talk English to me; he talked American to me. (laughter and applause) And there are subtle differences, which are distinguishable to me. (laughter) And so there always seemed to be a little link of some sort tying them up with us, tying them up with us in fact, in relationship, in blood, as well as in life, and the world will be turned back to cynicism if America goes back on it.

We daren't go back on it, because, I ask you even as a business proposition, whether it is most useful to trade with a cynic or an optimist. I don't like to trade with a man with a grouch. I don't like to trade with a man who begins with not believing anything that I am telling him. I like to begin with a man who is more or less susceptible to the eloquence which I address to him. (laughter and applause) And a salesman has a much longer job if he approaches a grouch than if he approaches a friend.

This trivial illustration illustrates, my fellow citizens, our relations to the rest of the world. If we don't do what the rest of the world expects of us, all the rest of the world will have a grouch towards America. You will find it a hard job to reestablish your credit in the world, and back of financial credit lies mental credit. There is not a bit of credit that hasn't got an element of assessment of character. You don't limit your credits to men who can put up the collateral, who have the assets. You extend it also to men in whose characters and abilities you can speculate—you think they are going to make good. Your credit is sort of a bet on their capacity, and that is the largest element in the kind of credit that expands enterprise. The credit that merely continues enterprise is based upon assets and past accomplishment, but the credit that expands enterprise is based upon your assessments of character. Now, if you are going to put into the world this germ, I shall call it, of American enterprise and American faith and American vision, then you must be the principal partners in the new partnership which the world is forming. (applause)

I take leave to say, without intending the least disrespect to anybody, that a man who opposes that proposition either has no imagination or no knowledge, or is a quitter. (great applause) America has put her hand to this great enterprise already, in the men she sent overseas, and their part was the negative part merely. They were sent over there to see that a malign influence did not interfere with the just fortunes of the world. They stopped her, but they did not accomplish anything constructive, and what is the use clearing the table if you are going to put nothing on it? What is the use clearing the ground if you are not going to erect any building? What is the use of going to the pains that we went to, to draw up the specifications of the new building and then saying, "We will have nothing to do with its erection?"

For the specifications of this treaty were American specifications, and we have got not only to be the architects, drawing up the specifications, but we have got to be the contractors, too. (laughter and applause) Isn't it a job that is worthwhile? Isn't it worthwhile, now that the chance has at last come, in the Providence of God, that we should show the world, demonstrate to the world, that America is what she claimed that she was? (applause) Every drop of blood I have in me gets up and shouts when I think of the opportunity that America has.

I come of a race that, being bred on barren hills and unfertile plains in Scotland, being obliged to work where work was hard, somehow has the best zest in what it does when the job is hard. (applause) And I was saying the other night—what I find my friend, Mr. Jackson, was kind enough to read—I never take the liberty of assuming that people have read what I have said, (laughter) but Mr. Jackson was kind enough to read what I said about my ancestry and about the implications of it. I come of a certain stock that raised Cain in the northern part of the island of Great Britain (laughter) under the name of the Covenanters. They met in a churchyard—they were church people, and they had a convention out of doors—and on the top of a flat tombstone they signed an immortal document called the "Solemn League and Covenant," which meant that they were going to stand by their religious principles in spite of the crown of England and the force of England and every other influence—whether of men or the devil, so long as any of them lived. (applause)

Now, I have seen men of all nations sit around a table in Paris and sign a solemn league and covenant. They have become Covenanters, and I remain a Covenanter. (great applause and cheers) We are going to see this job through no matter what influences of evil withstand it. (applause) Nothing has heartened me more on this journey than to feel that that is really the judgment of our fellow citizens.

America is made up, as I have just said, out of all sorts and elements, and it is singularly a homogeneous people, after all—homogeneous in its ideals, not in its blood; homogeneous in its infection which it has caught from a common light; homogeneous in its purpose. Every man has a sort of consciousness that America is put into the world for a purpose that is different in some respects from the purposes conceived by any other national organization.

And so throughout America you have got a conducting medium. You don't put forth an American idea and find it halted by this man and that and the other, except he be particularly asleep or cantankerous, but it spreads, it spreads by the natural contact of similar ideas and similar ambitions and similar hopes. For, my fellow citizens, the only thing that lifts the world is hope. The only thing that can save the world is such arrangements as will convince the world that hope is not altogether without foundation. It is the spirit that is in us that is unconquerable. You can kill the bodies of insurgent men who are fighting for liberty, but the more of them that you kill, the more you seem to strengthen the spirit that springs up out of the bloody ground where they fell. The only thing in the world that is unconquerable is the thought of men.

So that, when one looks back to that legendary story of the Middle Ages, of certain men fighting under the semisavage chiefs of that obscure time, who refused to obey the order of their chief because they considered it inconsistent with the traditions of their tribe, he said, "Don't you know that I have the power to kill you?" They said, "Yes, and don't you know that we have the power to die cursing you? You can't cut our spirits in two. You can't do anything but lay our bodies low and helpless. And if you do, there will spring, like dragon's teeth out of the earth, armed forces which will overcome you."

And this is the field of the spirit here in America. This is the field of the single unconquerable force that there is in the world. And when the world learns, as it will learn, that America has put her whole force into the common harness of civilization, then they will know that the wheels are going to turn, the loads are going to be drawn, men are going to begin to ascend those difficult heights of hope which have sometimes seemed so inaccessible. (applause) I am glad for one to have lived to see this day. I have lived to see a day in which, after saturating myself most of my life in the history and traditions of America, I seem suddenly to see a culmination of American hope and history—all the orators seeing their dreams realized, if their spirits are looking on; all the men who spoke the noblest sentiments for America heartened with the sight of a great nation responding to and acting upon those dreams, saying, "At last, the world knows America as the savior of the world!" (great applause and cheers)

Printed in the Portland *Morning Oregonian*, Sept. 16, 1919.

An Address in the Portland Auditorium

[[September 15, 1919]]

Mr. Chairman, Mr. Irvine,[1] my fellow countrymen: Mr. Irvine has very eloquently stated exactly the errand upon which I have come. I have come to confer, face to face, with you on one of the most solemn occasions that has ever confronted this nation. As I have come along through the country and stopped at station after station, the first to crowd around the train have almost always been little children—bright-eyed little boys, excited little girls, children all seeming sometimes of the same generation. And I thought, as I

[1] Benjamin Franklin Irvine, editor of the Portland *Oregon Daily Journal*, introduced Wilson. The news report in the *New York Times*, September 16, 1919, states that Irvine was the "presiding officer." Mayor Baker and Governor Olcott were also on the platform.

looked upon them from the car platform, that, after all, it was they to whom I had come to report.

I had come to report with regard to the safety and honor of subsequent generations of America. And I felt that, if I could not fulfill the task to which I had set my hand, I would have to say to mothers with boy babies at their breasts: "You have occasion to weep. You have occasion to fear the past as only a prediction of the future, and all this terrible thing that your brothers and husbands and sweethearts have been through may have to be gone through with again." Because, as I was saying to some of your fellow citizens today, the task—that great and gallant task—which our soldiers performed is only half finished. They prevented a great wrong. They prevented it with a spirit and courage and with an ability that will always be written on the brightest pages of our record of gallantry and of force.

I do not know when I have been so proud, as an American, as when I have seen our boys deploy on the other side of the sea. On Christmas Day last, on an open stretch of country, I saw a great division march past me,[2] with all the arms of the service, walking with that swing which is so familiar to our eyes, with that sense of power and confidence and audacity which is so characteristic of America. And I seemed to see the force that had saved the world. But they merely prevented something. They merely prevented a particular nation from doing a particular, unspeakable thing to civilization. And their task is not complete only we see to it that it has not to be done over again, unless we fulfill the promise which we made to them and to ourselves. This was not only a war to defeat Germany, but a war to prevent the recurrence of any such wrong as Germany had attempted; it was a war to put an end to the wars of aggression forever.

There is only one means of doing that, my fellow citizens. I found quoted in one of your papers the other day a passage so apposite that I do not know that I can do better than read it as the particular thing that it is found necessary to do:

"Nations must unite as men unite in order to preserve peace and order. The great nations must be so united as to be able to say to any single country, 'You must not go to war,' and they can say that effectively when the country desiring war knows that the force which the united nations apply behind peace is irresistible. In differences between individuals, the decision of a court is final, because in the last resort the entire force of the community is behind the court decision. In differences between nations which go be-

---

[2] About this review and Wilson's speech on that occasion, see the extract from the Diary of Dr. Grayson and Wilson's remarks printed at Dec. 25, 1918, Vol. 53.

yond the limited range of arbitral questions, peace can only be maintained by putting behind it the force of united nations determined to uphold it and prevent war."

That is a quotation from an address said to have been delivered at Union College in June 1915, a year after the war began, by Mr. Henry Cabot Lodge, of Massachusetts. (laughter and applause) I entirely concur in Senator Lodge's conclusion, and I hope I shall have his cooperation in bringing about the desired result. (laughter and applause) In other words, the only way we can prevent the unspeakable thing from happening again is that the nations of the world should unite and put an irresistible force behind peace and order. There is only one conceivable way to do that, and that is by means of a league of nations. The very description is a definition of a league of nations, and the only thing that we can debate now is whether the nations of the world, having met in a universal congress and formulated a covenant as the basis for a league of nations, we are going to accept that or insist upon another. I don't find any man anywhere rash or bold enough to say that he does not desire a league of nations. I only find men here and there saying that they do not desire this League of Nations, and I want to ask you to reflect upon what that means. And in order to do that I want to draw a picture for you, if you will be patient with me, of what occurred in Paris.

In Paris were gathered the representatives of nearly thirty nations from all over the civilized globe, and even from some parts of the globe which in our ignorance of it we have not been in the habit of regarding as civilized. And out of that great body were chosen the representatives of fourteen nations, representing all parts of the great stretches of people of the world which the conference as a whole represented. The representatives of those fourteen nations were constituted a Commission on the League of Nations. The first resolution passed by the conference of peace in Paris was a resolution in favor of a league of nations, setting up a commission to formulate a league of nations. It was the thought foremost in the mind of every statesman there, who knew that his errand was in vain in Paris if he went away without achieving the formation of a league of nations, that he dared not go back and face his people unless he could report that the efforts in that direction had been successful.

That commission sat day after day, evening after evening. I had the good fortune to be a member of the commission, and I want to testify to the extraordinary good temper in which the discussions were conducted. I want to testify that there was a universal endeavor to subordinate as much as possible international rivalry and conflicting international interests and come out upon a common ground of agreement in the interest of the world. I want to testify that there were many compromises, but no compromises that sacrificed the principle, and that, although the instrument as a whole represented certain mutual concessions, it is a constructive instrument and not a negative instrument. I shall never lose, so long as I live, the impression of generous, high-minded, statesmanlike cooperation which was manifested in that interesting body. It included representatives of the most powerful nations, as well as the representatives of some of those that were less powerful.

I could not help thinking, as I sat there with the representatives of Italy, speaking, as it were in the tones of the long tradition of Rome, that we heard the great Latin people who had fought, fought, fought through generation after generation of strife down to this critical moment, speaking now in the councils of peace. And there sat the Prime Minister of Greece—of the ancient Greek people—lending his singular intelligence, his singular high-minded and comprehensive counsel, to the general results. There were representatives also of France, our ancient comrade in the strife for liberty. And there were the representatives of Great Britain, supposed to be most ambitious, the most desirous of ruling the world of any of the nations of the world, cooperating with a peculiar interest in the result, with a constant and manifestly sincere profession that they wanted to subordinate the interests of the British Empire, which extended over the world, to the common interests of mankind and of peace. (applause) The representatives of Great Britain I might stop and speak of for a moment. There were two of them. One of them was Lord Robert Cecil, who belonged to an ancient family in Great Britain, some of the members of which—particularly Lord Salisbury of a past generation—had always been reputed as men particularly keen to seek and maintain the advantage of the British Empire. And yet I never heard a man speak whose heart was evidently more in the task of the humane redemption of the world than Lord Robert Cecil. (applause) And alongside of him sat General Smuts, the South African Boer, the man who had fought Great Britain, the man who had fought Great Britain so successfully that, after the war was over and the Boers nominally defeated, Great Britain saw that the wisest thing she could do was to hand the government of the country over to the Boers themselves. General Botha and General Smuts were both members of the peace conference; both had been successful generals in fighting British armies. Nobody in the conference was more outspoken in criticizing some of the aspects of British policy than General Botha and General Smuts, and General Smuts was of the same mind with Sir Robert Cecil—they were both serving the common interests of every people everywhere.

You seem to see a sort of epitome of the history of the world in that conference. There were nations that had long been subordinate and suffering. There were nations that had been indomitably free but, nevertheless, not so free that they could really accomplish the peace that they had always held dear. And I want you to realize that this conference, made up of many minds and many nations and of many traditions, came to the same conclusion with a unanimity, an enthusiasm, and a spirit which speaks volumes for the future hopes of mankind. (applause)

Not only that, but when this Covenant was drawn up in its first form, I had the occasion—for me a very happy occasion—to return for a few weeks to this country in March last. I brought the covenant in its first shape. I submitted it in intimate conference to the Foreign Relations Committee of the Senate of the United States or, rather, to the two committees of the two houses—the Foreign Relations Committee of the Senate and the Committee on Foreign Affairs of the House. We discussed all parts of the document. Many suggestions were made. I took all of those suggestions with me back to Paris, and the conference on the League of Nations adopted every one of the suggestions made. (applause) No counsels were listened to more carefully or yielded to more willingly in that conference than the counsels of the United States. (applause) Some things were put into the Covenant which, personally, I did not think necessary, which seemed to me to go without saying, but which they had no objection to putting in explicitly.

For example, take the Monroe Doctrine. As a matter of fact, the Covenant sets up for the world a Monroe Doctrine. (applause) What is the Monroe Doctrine? The Monroe Doctrine is that no nation shall come to the western hemisphere and try to establish its power or interfere with the self-government of people in this hemisphere; that no power shall extend its governing and controlling influence in any form to either of the Americas.

Very well; that is the doctrine of the Covenant. No nation shall anywhere extend its power or seek to interfere with the political independence of the peoples of the world. (applause) And, inasmuch as the Monroe Doctrine had been made the universal doctrine, I did not think that it was necessary to mention it particularly. But when I suggested that it was the desire of the United States that it should be explicitly recognized, it was explicitly recognized, for it is written in there that nothing in the Covenant shall be interpreted as affecting the validity of the Monroe Doctrine. (applause) The Monroe Doctrine is left intact, and the United States is left free to enforce it. (applause)

But that is only an example. The members of the Foreign Relations Committee and the Committee on Foreign Affairs did not see it anywhere stated explicitly in the Covenant that a member of the League could withdraw. I told them that the matter had been discussed in the Commission on the League and that it had been the universal opinion that, since it was a combination of sovereigns, any of the sovereigns had the right to withdraw from it. But when I suggested that that could be explicitly put in, no objection was made whatever, and, at the suggestion of the United States, it was explicitly provided that any member of the League could withdraw. Provision was made that two years' notice should be given, which I think everybody will recognize as perfectly fair, so that no nation is at liberty suddenly to break down this thing upon which the hope of mankind rests. But, with that limitation and with the provision that when they withdraw they shall have fulfilled all their international obligations, they are perfectly free to withdraw. And when gentlemen dwell upon that provision—that we must have fulfilled all our international obligations—I answer all their anxieties by asking them another question: "When did America ever fail to fulfill her international obligations?" (applause) There is no judge in the matter set up in the Covenant, except the conscience of the withdrawing nation and the opinion of mankind. And I, for one, am proud enough American to dismiss from my mind all fear of at any time going before the judgment of mankind on the conduct of the United States, knowing that we will go with clean hands and righteous purpose. (applause)

But I am merely illustrating now the provisions that were put in at the suggestion of the United States. Without exception, the suggestions of the United States were adopted, and I want to say, because it may interest you, that most of these suggestions came from Republican sources. (applause) I say that, my fellow citizens, not because it seems to me to make the least difference among Americans in a great matter like this which party such things came from, but because I want to emphasize in every discussion of this matter the absolutely nonpartisan character of the Covenant and the treaty. (great applause and cheers) I am not in favor of the ratification of this treaty, including the Covenant of the League of Nations, because I am a Democrat. I am in favor of it because I am an American and a lover of humanity. (applause) And, if it will relieve anybody's mind, let me add that it is not my work, that practically every portion of the Covenant of the League of Nations emanates from counsels running back ten, twenty, thirty years, among the most thoughtful men in America, and that it is the fulfillment of a dream which five years ago, when the war began, would have been deemed unattainable. So that what we are discussing ought not to be disfigured, ought not to be tinged, with the least thought of domestic politics. If anybody in this audience allows himself, when thinking of this matter, to think of the elections of 1920, I want to declare that I separate myself from him. (applause)

I draw all this picture of the care with which the Covenant was drawn—every phrase scrutinized, every interest considered, the other nations at the board just as jealous of their sovereignty as we could possibly be of ours, yet willing to harness all these sovereignties in a single great enterprise of peace, and how the whole thing was not the original idea of any man in the conference, but had grown out of the counsels of hopeful and thoughtful and righteous men all over the world—because, just as there was in America a League to Enforce Peace, which even formulated a constitution for the league of peace before the conference met, before the conference was thought of, before the war began, so there were in Great Britain and in France and in Italy and, I believe, even in Germany similar associations of equally influential men, whose ideal was some time there might come an occasion when men would be sane enough and right enough to get together to do a thing of this great sort.

I draw that picture in order to show you the other side of what is going on, and I want to preface this part by saying that I hope you will not construe anything I say as indicating the least lack of respect for the men who are criticizing any portion of this treaty. I must frankly say I haven't any respect at all for some of them, (laughter, applause and cheers) but for others, and for most of them, I have reason to have respect, for I have come into close contact and consultation with them. They are just as good Americans as I am, or as I claim to be. They are just as thoughtful of the interests of America as I try to be. They are just as intelligent as anybody who could address his mind to this thing. And my contest with them is a contest of interpretation, not a contest of intention.

All I have to urge with those men is that they are looking at this thing with too critical an eye as to the mere phraseology, without remembering the purpose that everybody knows to have been in the minds of those who framed it, and that if they go very far in attempting to interpret it by resolutions of the Senate they may, in appearance at any rate, sufficiently alter the meaning of the document to make it necessary to take it back to the council board.

And taking it back to the council board means, among other things, taking it back to Germany. And I frankly tell you, my fellow citizens, it would set very ill upon my stomach to take it back to Germany. (laughter and applause) Germany, at our request—I may say almost at our dictation—signed the treaty and has ratified it. It is a contract, so far as her part in it is concerned. I can testify that we tried to be just to Germany. When we had heard her arguments and examined every portion of the counterproposals that she made, we wrote the treaty in its final form and then said, "Sign here." (applause and cheers)

What else did our brave boys die for? Did they die in order that we might ask Germany's leave to complete our victory? They died in order that we might say to Germany what the terms of victory were in the interest of justice and peace, (applause) and we were entitled to take the course that we did take. And I can only beg these gentlemen in their criticism of the treaty and in their action in the Senate not to go so far as to make it necessary to ask the consent of other nations to the interpretations which they are putting upon the treaty. I have said in all frankness that I do not see a single phrase in the Covenant of the League of Nations which is of doubtful meaning. But if they want to say what that undoubted meaning is, in other words that don't change the undoubted meaning, I have no objection. (laughter) If they change the meaning of it, then all the other signatories have to consent. And what has been evident in the last week or two is that, on the part of some men—I believe a very few—the desire is to change the treaty, and particularly the Covenant, in a way to give America an exceptional footing.

Now, my fellow countrymen, the principle that America went into this war for was the principle of the equality of sovereign nations. (applause) I am just as much opposed to class legislation in international matters as in domestic matters. (applause) I do not, I tell you plainly, believe that any one nation should be allowed to dominate—even this beloved nation of our own—(applause) and it does not desire to dominate. I said in a speech the other night in another connection that, so far as my influence and power as President of the United States went, I was going to fight every attempt to set up a minority government. (applause)

And I was asked afterwards whom I was hitting at, what minority I was thinking of. I said: "Never mind what minority I may have been thinking of at the moment; it does not make any difference with me which minority it is, whether it is capital or labor. No sort of privilege will ever be permitted in this country." (applause) It is a partnership or it is a mockery. It is a democracy, where the majority are the masters of its hopes and purposes, or the men who founded this government have been defeated and forgotten. And I am for the same principle in international affairs.

One of the things that gave the world a new and founding hope was that the great United States had said that it was fighting for the little nations as well as the great; that it regarded the rights of the little nations as equal to its own rights; that it would make no distinction between free men anywhere; that it was not fighting for a special advantage for the United States, but for an equal advantage for all free men everywhere. (applause)

Let gentlemen beware, therefore, how they disappoint the world. Let gentlemen beware how they betray the immemorial principles of the United States. Let men not make the mistake of claiming a position of privilege for the United States which gives it all the advantages of the League of Nations and none of the risks and responsibilities. (applause) The principle of equity everywhere is that, along with a right goes a duty; that if you claim a right for yourself, you must be ready to support that right for somebody else. And if you claim to be a member in a society of any sort, you must not claim the right to dodge the responsibilities and avoid the burden, but you must carry the weight of the enterprise along with the hope of the enterprise. That is the spirit of free men everywhere, and that I know to be the spirit of the United States.

Our decision, therefore, my fellow citizens, rests upon this: if we want a league of nations, we must take this League of Nations, (applause) because there is no conceivable way in which any other league of nations is obtainable. We must leave it or take it. I should be very sorry to have the United States indirectly defeat this great enterprise by asking for something—some position of privilege—which other nations in their pride cannot grant. I had a great deal rather we should say flatly, "We won't go into the enterprise at all."

And that, my fellow citizens, is exactly what Germany is hoping and beginning to dare to expect. I am not uttering a conjecture. I am speaking of knowledge, from things that are said in the German newspapers and by German public men. They are taking heart because the United States, they hope, is not going to stand with the other free nations of the world to guarantee the peace that has been forced upon them. They see the hope that there will be two nations standing outside the League—Germany and the United States. Germany because she must; the United States because she will. She knows that that will turn the hostility and enmity of all the other nations of the world against the United States, as their hostility is already directed against her. They do not expect that now the United States will in any way align themselves with

Germany. They do not expect the sympathy of the United States to go out to them now. But they do expect the isolation of the United States to bring about an alienation between the United States and the other free nations of the world, which will make it impossible for the world ever to combine again against such enterprises as she was defeated in attempting. And all over this world, pro-German propaganda is beginning to be active again, beginning to try to add to the force of the arguments against the League in particular and against the treaty and the several items of the treaty. And the poison of failure is being injected into the whole fine body politic of the united world—a sort of paralysis, a sort of fear, as we should say.

What have we created? A great power which will bring peace. Will that power be amiable to us? Can we control that power? We can control it for anybody's proper purpose—the purpose of righteousness and peace. But for that purpose we are invited to control it by the opinion of mankind, for all over the world peoples are looking to us with confidence, our rivals along with the weaker nations. They believe in the honesty of purpose and the indomitable rectitude of purpose of the United States, and they are willing to have us lead.

And I pray God that the gentlemen who are delaying this thing may presently see it in a different light. (applause) I fain would appeal to their hearts. I wonder if they have forgotten what this war meant. I wonder if they have had mothers who lost their sons take them by the hand, as they have taken mine, and looked things that their hearts were too full to speak, praying me to do all in my power to save the sons of other mothers from this terrible thing. And I have had some fine women come to me and say, as steadily as if they were saying a commonplace, "I had the honor to lose a son in the war." How fine that is—"I had the honor to sacrifice a son for the redemption of mankind!" And yet there is a sob back of the statement, there is a tear brushed hastily away from the cheek.

A woman came up to the train the other day and seized my hand and was about to say something but turned away in a flood of tears. And I asked a stander-by what was the matter, and he said, "Why, Sir, she lost a son in France." Now, mind you, she didn't turn away first. I ordered her son overseas. I advised the Congress of the United States to sacrifice that son. She came to me as a friend. She had nothing in her heart except the hope that I could save other sons, though she had given hers gladly. (applause) And, God help me, I will save other sons. (applause) Through evil report and good report, through resistance and misrepresentation and every other vile thing, I shall fight my way to that goal.

I call upon the men to whom I have referred—the honest, patriotic, intelligent men, who have been too particularly concerned in criticizing the details of that treaty—to forget the details, to remember the great enterprise, to stand with me to fulfill the hopes and traditions of the United States. (applause)

My fellow citizens, there is only one conquering force in the world. There is only one thing you can't kill, and that is the spirit of free men. (applause) I was telling some friends today of a legendary story of the Middle Ages, of a chieftain of one of the half-civilized peoples that overran Europe commanding some of his men to do a certain thing which they believed to be against the traditions of their tribe. They refused, and he blazed out upon them, "Don't you know that I can put you to death?" "Yes," they said, "and don't you know that we can die cursing you?" He could not kill their spirits; and they knew perfectly well that if he unjustly slew them the whole spirit of their tribe would curse him. They knew that, if he did an unjust thing, out of the blood that they spilled would spring up, as it were, armed men, like dragons' teeth, to overwhelm him. Because the thing that is vindicated in the long run is the right, and the only thing that is unconquerable is the truth. And America is believed in throughout the world because she has put spirit before material ambition. She has said that she is willing to sacrifice everything that she is and everything that she has, not only that her people may be free, but that freedom may reign throughout the world. (applause)

I hear men say—how often I heard it said on the other side of the water!—how amazing it was that America went into this war. I tell you, my fellow citizens, and I tell it with sorrow, it was universally believed on the other side of the water that we would not go into the war because we were making money out of it, and loved the money better than we loved justice. They all believed that. And when we went over there, they greeted us with amazement. They said: "These men didn't have to come. Their territories are not invaded. Their independence is not directly threatened. Their interests were not immediately attacked, only indirectly. They were getting a great prosperity out of this calamity of ours. We were told that they worshiped the almighty dollar, and here come tramping, tramping, tramping these gallant fellows with something in their faces we never saw before, eyes lifted to the horizon, a dash that knows no discouragement, knowledge only of how to go forward, no thought of how to go backward, (great applause) 3,000 miles from home. What are they fighting for? Look at their faces and you will see the answer. They see a vision. They see a call. They see mankind redeemed. They see a great force which would wreck civilization. They love something they have never touched. They love the things that emanate from the throne of justice. They have come here to fight with us and for us, and they are our comrades."

We were told by certain people in France that they went to the Fourth of July celebration last calendar year in Paris with sinking hearts. Our men had come over in numbers. They didn't expect they would come soon enough or fast enough to save them. They went out of curiosity; and before the day was over, having merely been in the presence of these boys, they knew that Europe was saved, because they had seen what that blind man saw in the song.

You have heard that spirited song of the blind Frenchman, his boy at the window, music in the streets, the marching of troops, and he says to the lad: "See what it is. Do you see, lad? What are the colors? What are the men? Is there a banner with red and white stripes upon it? Is there a bit of heaven in the corner? Are there stars in that piece of the firmament? Ah, thank God, the Americans have come!" (applause)

It was the revelation to Europe of the heart of a great nation. They believe in that heart now. You never hear the old sneers. You never hear that we will seek our interests and not our honor. You never hear the old fear that we shall not stand by free men else-where who make common cause with us for justice to mankind. You hear, on the other hand, confident predictions, confident ex-pectations, confident hope that the whole world will be steadied by the magnificent purpose and force of the United States. (applause) If I was proud as an American before I went over there—and I hope my pride has just foundation—I was infinitely more proud when I came back to feel—(applause) to feel that I could bring you this message.

And now, my fellow citizens, let us—every one of us—bind our-selves in a solemn league and covenant of our own that we will redeem this expectation of the world, that we will not allow any man to stand in the way of it, that the world shall hereafter bless and not curse us, that the world hereafter shall follow us and not turn aside from us, and that in leading we will not lead along the paths of private advantage, we will not lead along the paths of na-tional ambition, but we will be proud and happy to lead along the paths of right, so that men shall always say that American soldiers saved Europe and American citizens saved the world. (applause)

Printed in the Portland *Oregon Daily Journal*, Sept. 16, 1919.

To Rudolph Forster

Portland, Oregon 15 September, 1919

Please convey the following to the Chairman of the Joint Committee of Congress to arrange the welcome to General Pershing: quote

Allow me to acknowledge with sincere appreciation your kind invitation to be present at the joint session of Congress to be held in the hall of the House of Representatives at two o'clock on the afternoon of Thursday, September eighteenth, 1919, to welcome General John J. Pershing, and to say how deeply I regret that it is impossible for me to be there. I have already expressed to General Pershing and to the soldiers of the First Division[1] what I am sure is the heartfelt welcome and admiration of the whole people, but it is a matter of special regret to me that I was not able to be present in New York and cannot be present with the Congress in extending to him the greetings and the praise he deserves. end quote.

Woodrow Wilson

T telegram (WP, DLC).
    [1] See WW to NDB, Sept. 14, 1919.

From Louis Brownlow

The White House 1919 Sep 15

Senate Committee on District of Columbia Senator Sherman[1] Chairman has summoned me to appear at eleven a.m. Tuesday the sixteenth to take my testimony on Myers Resolution which forbids commissioners to pay salaries to any policeman who is a member of a union affiliated with the American Federation of Labor or other Labor organization. The court injunction restrains us specifically from asking any member of police force if he belongs to such a union. Senators will so I am informed ask me if I consulted with you and if I consider the proposed legislation necessary to enable the commissioners to proceed on my own responsibility. I will say the whole matter should go over until after industrial conference. Senators will endeavor to have me state your position. I regard my conversations with you on the subject as confidential and I cannot quote you. Would greatly appreciate any advice you may have for me in the premises.   Louis Brownlow.

T telegram (WP, DLC).
    [1] That is, Lawrence Yates Sherman, Republican of Illinois.

Joseph Patrick Tumulty to Louis Brownlow

Portland, Oregon, Sept. 15, 1919

Telegram received. The president hopes you will feel free to state his position as he explained it to you.   J. P. Tumulty

T telegram (WP, DLC).

From Newton Diehl Baker

[Washington] Sept. 15, 11 A.M. [1919]

Confidential. For the President. Senator Pomerene came to me today deeply concerned because he learns that the mild reservationists, McCumber, Kellogg, Spencer, Colt, and others have worked out a program which has the personal acceptance of Lodge, but not his formal approval until he has taken it up with Borah and others. Pomerene says he fears agreement among them will result in the passage of reservations by a majority vote, consultation of precedents showing the practice of the Senate to recognize majority vote as adequate therefor. This, Pomerene feels, will put the friends of the treaty in a situation where they will have to vote to reject the treaty or else to accept it with more hurtful reservations than could be worked out if the friends of the Treaty sought to negotiate agreement with the mild reservationists. Pomerene is anxious to have his view placed before you, and his judgment that it would be wiser now for friends of the treaty to make an effort to secure agreement upon a few interpretative reservations and so secure accessions enough to control the vote on amendments and ratification. I have told him that I would deliver message, and felt that you would probably communicate with Senator Hitchcock rather than through me, if you had suggestions to offer.   Baker

T telegram (WP, DLC).

Michael J. McGuire to Joseph Patrick Tumulty

San Francisco Calif [Sept.] 15 [1919]

Have received no answer to our telegram delivered to you yesterday in Seattle at 8:55 morning regarding meeting between President Wilson and committee of San Francisco Labor Council here. Will you please advise us at once what time President will meet

committee here. Wire answer to Andrew J Gallagher Olympic Club
San Francisco   Michael J McGuire Vice President
                   San Francisco Labor Council Committee.

T telegram (WP, DLC).

To William Phillips

Portland, Oregon, 15 September, 1919

Please say to the British Chargé d'Affaires[1] that November 11th
will be entirely agreeable as the date to receive the Prince of Wales
in Washington.[2]   Woodrow Wilson

T telegram (WP, DLC).
    [1] That is, Ronald Charles Lindsay.
    [2] Wilson was replying to W. Phillips to WW, Sept. 12, 1919, T telegram (WP, DLC):
"British Chargé d'Affaires called today to inquire on behalf of his Government whether
November 11th would be agreeable for you to receive the Prince of Wales in Washing-
ton."

Two Telegrams from William Phillips

Washington, September 15, 1919.

Referring to my confidential message to you of September 13, 3
P.M., I am now forwarding the following paraphrase of a message
received from Mr. Jay at the American Embassy, Rome: QUOTE:
Rush. 3136, September 12, 11 p.m. Most confidential for the Secretary of State, or, in his absence for the Acting Secretary of State:
PARAGRAPH. I was sent for this afternoon by the King of Italy, and
he explained that although he was a rigidly constitutional monarch
and as such left all such matters to his Prime Minister, he felt that
he should, as an Italian, break all precedents, in this present publication [crisis][1], and do a thing that he had never before done:
Namely, owing to his having no private cipher, ask me to telegraph
to the President an appeal coming directly from him, to consent to
the proposals in regard to the Italian claims, being put forward by
Tittoni. PARAGRAPH. Owing to his having had the pleasure of knowing the President personally and whose intelligence he admired
greatly, His Majesty desired me to preface my telegram by saying
that that is the reason for his taking this unusual action. The sacrifices of blood and treasure made by Italy in the common cause
and her renunciation of much that she felt she was entitled to, was
dwelt upon by the King. By the decisions at present contemplated,
he pointed out that Idria, with its mines, which were invaluable to

her, would be lost to Italy; that such a town as Albona, which he personally knew to be purely Italian, with the division of Istria, would fall into the hands of the Jugo-Slavs and this was a matter which actually brought tears to his eyes; that Trieste would be menaced by the new arrangement and that Pola would be under the range of modern artillery, all of which would require Italy to maintain a large and expensive army, though desperately poor. His Majesty explained that while he could not speak officially, owing to the fact that relations outwardly were cordial with the Jugo-Slav Government, he wished me privately to know that, although it was unfortunate, he felt very sure that once the Jugo-Slavs were in free and full control over the Italian population across the Adriatic, the Italians would be treated by them with great cruelty. His Majesty made, in this connection, of which he presumed our government was well aware, reference to the present conduct of the Serbs in Montenegro. I was asked by His Majesty how the American people would appreciate the American colonies on the border being handed over to the arbitrary rule of the Government of Mexico. PARAGRAPH. That the final decision as to the future of Italy lies now in the hands of the President entirely, was the impression given me by the King as to the feeling of himself and of the Italian people, and that if an unfavorable decision is given, relations between the two countries which the King has labored so hard to develop, would be very materially strained. PARAGRAPH. The above is a summary of the salient points of the long conversation between the King and myself; the King was deeply emotional and his conversation contained much irrelevant matter. PARAGRAPH. The most important impression I received of this audience was that it was the wish of the King that this be his personal appeal to the President. Because of the fact that the decision is expected by His Majesty at any moment, he especially requested me to telegraph this tonight to the President. Accordingly, I request that the above be immediately brought to the President's personal attention. PARAGRAPH. American Mission not informed, as matter most personal and confidential for the President. UNQUOTE.

William Phillips Acting Secretary of State

TS telegram (SDR, RG 59, 763.72119/6709, DNA).
  [1] Correction from P. A. Jay to SecState, Sept. 12, 1919, T telegram (SDR, RG 59, 763.72119/6709, DNA).

Washington, D. C., Sept. 15 [1919].

The Italian Ambassador[1] asked me to inform you that Premier Nitti has taken a strong position disapproving the recent mutiny at Fiume;[2] that he has announced before Parliament his complete solidarity with the Allies; that energetic measures based on the military penal code will be taken to repress mutiny; and that a big majority of the House, including the Official Socialists, are warmly supporting Nitti in this position.

William Phillips Acting Secretary of State.[3]

T telegram (WP, DLC).
   [1] That is, Count Vincenzo Macchi di Cellere.
   [2] Gabriele D'Annunzio had invaded Fiume with a small force of volunteers on the morning of September 12. Units of the Italian army stationed near the city, with orders to prevent just such a coup, failed to do so, and many of their men joined the invading group. In the evening of the same day, D'Annunzio, in an outdoor speech before an enthusiastic crowd, proclaimed the annexation of Fiume to Italy. See Michael A. Ledeen, *The First Duce: D'Annunzio at Fiume* (Baltimore and London, 1977), pp. 58-77.
   [3] This was sent as W. Phillips to WW, Sept. 15, 1919, TS telegram (SDR, RG 59, 763.72119/6830a, DNA).

From Edward Mandell House

Dear Governor—   Paris, September 15, 1919.

I arrived here yesterday. The Peace Conference is practically a thing of the past. We have four Commissioners now here and the British have none other than Milner who will reamin [remain] for only a short while. My judgment is that the sooner the Conference is wound up the better it will be for the situation at home. I notice that the republican senators say that the Conference will be in session for another six months and that the Treaty can easily be amended.

If the Conference adjourns leaving someone to sign the Bulgarian and Hungarian Treaties it would be the best solution. The Turkish Treaty will have to be taken up separately and at some more distant date.

Lloyd George wanted the Conference to adjourn immediately but Clemenceau and Polk disagreed with him. Polk thinks that within ten days it ought to adjourn temporarily until the Bulgarian and Hungarian Treaties are ready for signature. I strongly advise, therefore, that you give direction to bring matters to as speedy a conclusion as the situation admits.

There is nothing in life I would dislike more than being called before the Senate Committee. I have never had any experience in such matters. However, I am convinced that it would serve the cause well if I could be there and tell a different story from any that I have read as having been told. I could certainly put your position and your attitude while in Paris in a better light. I feel somehow that you have been crucified by your friends, perhaps not consciously but nevertheless it is a fact.

I am counting now on sailing October 8th unless you indicate a wish that I come sooner. I follow you from day to day and my heart was never so responsive to your efforts in behalf of mankind.

Affectionately yours,   E. M. House

TLS (WP, DLC).

From the Diary of Dr. Grayson

Tuesday, September 16, 1919.

All today was spent travelling towards San Francisco. The trip was a beautiful one, running through the picturesque Oregon and California territory. Two deer and a large quantity of fruit of all kinds were put on board the special train at points along the road. The crowds gathered everywhere to greet the President and to cheer him. En route he announced the appointment of the Industrial Commission that was to meet in Washington on October 6th and endeavor to bring about some arrangement whereby industrial chaos in the United States might be prevented.[1]

---

[1] The *New York Times*, September 18, 1919, says that Wilson announced the appointment of the twenty-two public members of the Industrial Conference in San Francisco on September 17. They were B. M. Baruch; Oscar Edwin Bradfute, chairman of the Ohio Farm Bureau Federation; Robert Somers Brookings, businessman and philanthropist of St. Louis; Ward Burgess, businessman of Omaha; Fuller Earle Callaway, cotton manufacturer of Georgia; Thomas Lincoln Chadbourne, Jr., lawyer of New York; Charles Gates Dawes, banker of Chicago; Charles William Eliot; Henry Bradford Endicott, shoe manufacturer of Milton, Mass.; Paul Louis Feiss, clothing manufacturer of Cleveland; E. H. Gary; Edwin Francis Gay, Dean of the Harvard Graduate School of Business Administration; George Roosa James, businessman of Memphis; Thomas Davies Jones, businessman of Chicago and Wilson's old friend; Archer A. Landon, manufacturer of Buffalo; Edwin Thomas Meredith, agricultural publisher of Des Moines; Gavin McNab of San Francisco; John Davison Rockefeller, Jr.; Charles Edward Russell; John Spargo; Louis Dennison Sweet, large-scale potato producer and businessman of Denver; and Louis Titus, lawyer and businessman of San Francisco and Washington, D. C. Wilson sent the same invitation to each person. See, for example, WW to B. M. Baruch, Sept. 17, 1919.

Wilson had sent invitations on September 3 to various special interest groups, asking them to name their own representatives to the Industrial Conference. See WW to S. Gompers, Sept. 3, 1919, and n. 1 thereto, Vol. 62.

To Walker Downer Hines

On Board the President's Train,

My dear Hines: 16 September, 1919

In reply to your letter of September 8th, may I not suggest that you get into conference with Baruch who, I believe, is frequently in Washington now, in order to concert with him some method of conference with the steel men which may bring about the results which I agree with you in thinking are imperatively necessary in the matter of prices.

I am writing today to the Federal Trade Commission about the inquiries that you suggest.

                Cordially and sincerely yours,   [Woodrow Wilson]

CCL (WP, DLC).

To William Byron Colver

                                    On Board the President's Train,
My dear Mr. Chairman: 16 September, 1919

Acting upon the suggestion of the Director General of Railroads, I am going to take the liberty of suggesting that the Federal Trade Commission, acting in such form as the Department of Justice may approve, seek to obtain monthly for the benefit of the various governmental agencies, the cost per ton of producing rolled steel products, and that in addition the Commission obtain and publish either monthly or quarterly statements of revenue, expenses, and profits of the principal steel corporations.

Mr. Baruch is frequently in Washington now, I understand, and I would be very much obliged if you would obtain his opinion with regard to this matter.

I assume that it will take some time for you to make the plans for doing this, and perhaps by the time I reach Washington the thing will be in readiness for action. I can then consult with you, and we can make the final decision.

                Cordially and sincerely yours   [Woodrow Wilson]

CCL (WP, DLC).

To Newton Diehl Baker

                                    On Board the President's Train,
My dear Baker: 16 September, 1919

I would be very much obliged if you would read the enclosed letter[1] and, if you approve of Mr. Wallace's suggestion, I would be very glad to have you say to the appropriate leaders in Congress, in my name, that I hope they will favorably consider a resolution of the Congress of the sort suggested.[2] It occurs to me that nobody could draw it up better than yourself.

                Cordially and faithfully yours,   Woodrow Wilson

TLS (N. D. Baker Papers, DLC).
    ¹ H. C. Wallace to WW, Aug. 23, 1919, TLS (N. D. Baker Papers, DLC). Ambassador
Wallace called Wilson's attention to the honors which the British government had conferred on Marshal Ferdinand Foch: he had been awarded the Order of Merit by King
George V in person in Paris and, more recently, he had been made a British Field Marshal, "a distinction never before conferred on any foreigner not a crowned head." Furthermore, Wallace asserted, the British government had "delicately intimated" to the
French government in the spring of 1918 that it would be glad to pay Foch the same
salary he received from France. It was now rumored that the British government would
present a sword to him. In view of all this, Wallace suggested to Wilson "how fitting it
would be if the thanks of Congress were expressed to the Marshal and how agreeable
it doubtless would be to the French Government and people if this honor were bestowed
upon him."
    ² No such resolution was introduced during the remainder of the Sixty-sixth Con-
gress and the Wilson administration.

To Louis Brownlow

[En route] 16 September, 1919

I hope that you understood my brief telegram of the other day.¹
I am quite willing that you should tell the Senate Committee that
my position in my conversations with you was exactly the same as
I have expressed recently in speeches here in the West, and of
course I am desirous, as you are, of dealing with the police force in
the most just and generous way, but that I think that any association of the police force of the capitol city or of any great city, whose
object is to bring pressure upon the public or the community such
as will endanger the public peace or embarrass the maintenance
of order, should in no case be countenanced or permitted.

Woodrow Wilson

T telegram (WP, DLC).
    ¹ That is, JPT to L. Brownlow, Sept. 15, 1919.

Andrew J. Gallagher and Others to Joseph Patrick Tumulty

San Francisco Calif Sept 16 1919

Telegram received¹ Stop I am directed by the authorized committee of the San Francisco Labor Council appointed to seek a personal interview with the President on the subject of the League of
Nations Covenant and the question of Ireland to say that they are
aware of the great task in the Presidents hands Stop Nevertheless
they feel that if the President knows that the representatives of a
hundred thousand working men and women have requested this
conference he will not decline Stop There has already been wired
you and your Secretary Bramas² has acknowledged receipt of and
there has also been sent through the mails to Seattle copies of the

resolutions and questions which the San Francisco Labor Council by unanimous vote insists on being answered at the mass meeting tomorrow night[3] Stop I cannot but respectfully urge that the President grant a conference to these representatives whose duty it is to place these resolutions and questions in his hands with the request from all the organized workers in San Francisco that he clear up these disputed points Stop Please wire me care Olympic Club San Francisco as to whether or not the President cannot be induced to grant a mite of his valuable time to the workers who have been so faithful to the cause of democracy and who wish to act on the proposition of the League of Nations Covenant so that the most good for all the peoples of the world might be accomplished Stop Signed for the San Francisco Labor Council committee.

> Andrew J Gallagher
> Secretary Attest John A OConnell
> Secretary San Francisco Labor Council
> William T Bonsor President

T telegram (WP, DLC).
    [1] It is missing.
    [2] That is, Thomas W. Brahany.
    [3] To rcpcat, the resolutions sent by mail to Seattle, which Wilson and Tumulty did not see before they left that city, are enclosed in J. A. O'Connell to WW, Sept. 6, 1919, TLS (WP, DLC). The resolutions are repeated in J. A. O'Connell to WW, Sept. 13, 1919.

Joseph Patrick Tumulty to Andrew J. Gallagher

[En route] Sept. 16, 1919.

I have your telegram, and the resolutions to which you refer. These resolutions have been answered by the President and if you will call on me in San Francisco tomorrow I shall hand you the answers.   J. P. Tumulty.

T telegram (WP, DLC).

A Memorandum

[Sept. 16, 1919]

ANSWERS OF THE PRESIDENT TO QUESTIONS ASKED
BY THE SAN FRANCISCO LABOR COUNCIL

1. Under the Covenant, does this nation obligate itself to assist any member of the League in putting down a rebellion of its subject or conquered peoples?

Answer. It does not.

2. Under the Covenant, can this nation independently recognize

a government whose people seek to achieve or have achieved their independence from a member of the League?

Answer. The independent action of the Government of the United States in a matter of this kind is in no way limited or affected by the Covenant of the League of Nations.

3. Under the covenant, are those subject nations or peoples only that are mentioned in the Peace Treaty entitled to the right of self-determination or does the League possess the right to accord a similar privilege to other subject nations or peoples?

Answer. It was not possible for the Peace Conference to act with regard to the self-determination of any territories except those which had belonged to the defeated empires, but in the Covenant of the League of Nations it has set up for the first time, in Article XI, a forum to which all claims of self-determination which are likely to disturb the peace of the world or the good understanding between nations upon which the peace of the world depends, can be brought.

4. Why was the case of Ireland not heard at the peace conference? And what is your position on the subject of self-determination for Ireland?

Answer. The case of Ireland was not heard at the Peace Conference because the Peace Conference had no jurisdiction over any question of that sort which did not affect territories which belonged to the defeated empires. My position on the subject of self-determination for Ireland is expressed in Article XI of the Covenant in which, I may say, I was particularly interested because it seemed to me necessary for the peace and freedom of the world that a forum should be created, to which all peoples could bring any matter which was likely to affect the peace and freedom of the world.

T MS (WP, DLC).

To William Phillips

[En route] 16 September, 1919

I would be pleased if you would get into communication with Senator Williams and, through him, with the appropriate committees of Congress with regard to our being authorized to send troops to Armenia.[1] I am heartily in favor of such a course if the Congress will authorize it, but of course am still willing to defer to the French, if they are sending a sufficient number, or to join with them if they are willing to accept joint military action, and we can get the authority of Congress.   Woodrow Wilson

T telegram (WP, DLC).

¹ If Wilson was replying to a letter or telegram from John Sharp Williams, that document is missing. Williams, a long-time supporter of aid to the Armenians and a member of the executive board of the American Committee for the Independence of Armenia, had sponsored S.J. Res. 106, introduced for him by Senator Hitchcock on September 9, which called for the independence of Russian and Turkish Armenia as a unified republic and authorized the President "to use such military and naval forces of the United States as in his opinion may seem expedient for the maintenance of peace and tranquility in Armenia until the settlement of the affairs of that country has been completed by treaty between the nations." *Cong. Record,* 66th Cong., 1st sess., p. 5067, and Richard G. Hovannisian, *The Republic of Armenia* (2 vols. to date, Berkeley, Los Angeles, and London, 1971-82), II, 374-75. The resolution had been altered almost beyond recognition (it omitted any mention of the use of American forces to maintain peace, for example) when it was finally accepted by the Senate on May 13, 1920. For a detailed history of the resolution, see *ibid.*, 372-90.

Three Telegrams from William Phillips

Washington, D. C., Sept. 16, 1919

Sept. 16, 7 P.M. In a message 3974 [3975]¹ Mr. Polk referred to our 2981,² which contained at length the settlement suggested by the President as to Thrace, and asked: "Does the President intend to send any personal message [for me] to transmit to Venizelos in reply to Venizelos's plan submitted in my 3704, Aug. 15, 8 P.M.?³ I think it would help if he would. Polk."

The Venizelos plan contained in 3704 was a letter to Mr. Polk which supported the Tardieu proposal of internationalizing Dedeagatch, and argued for [against] an international state containing the Eastern half of Western Thrace, and particularly against including any part of Northern Thrace in Bulgaria. The argument proceeds on the basis of the comparative total Greek and Bulgarian populations, and ends "And what I ask on the part of Greece is not that she should be favored because she waged a just war on the side of the Allies, but that she should not be treated with less consideration and with a state [spirit] of lesser justice than that with which Bulgaria is being treated, which latter country deliberately waged an unjust war."

Since that time Mr. Polk has telegraphed in "Urgent 4142, Sept. 10, 6 P.M.⁴ Did the President see my 3975 August 31st before leaving? In view of Venizelos's message to him, think he should send some message of regret and appreciation to Venizelos," and further in 4220,⁵ Sept. 15, 10 P.M., "Possibly the President had forgotten that he received a communication from Venizelos. In view of the fact that he thought very highly of Venizelos, he would probably wish to make some reply, as Venizelos is very much distressed over the situation."

While, as I telegraphed you on September 12th,⁶ the Thracian question is deferred until you return, you might wish to transmit a personal message to Venizelos, in view of what Mr. Polk has said.

William Phillips.

¹ See FLP to RL, Aug. 31, 1919, Vol. 62. All corrections are from W. Phillips to WW, Sept. 16, 1919, T telegram (SDR, RG 59, 763.72119/6453, DNA).
² RL to FLP, Aug. 28, 1919, Vol. 62.
³ FLP to RL, Aug. 16, 1919, *ibid*.
⁴ FLP to WP, Sept. 10, 1919.
⁵ FLP to WP, Sept. 15, 1919, T telegram (SDR, RG 59, 868.00/211, DNA).
⁶ WP to WW, Sept. 12, 1919.

Washington, D. C., Sept. 16, 1919

Sept. 16, 6 P.M. The following telegrams from the Mission are repeated for your information:

(First telegram) 4126, Confidential, September 9, 7 P.M.¹ For the Secretary of State from Polk. Last week Balfour announced that as soon as the Austrian Treaty was signed, and the Bulgarian treaty delivered, he would leave, and as he saw no necessity for the Council continuing to sit, no one would come to take his place. Clemenceau objected strongly. I told Balfour and Philip Kerr, Lloyd George's Secretary, that while I thought the Council was mixing up with a great [good]² many things that really belonged to the Foreign Offices, yet an adjournment at this time would be entirely misconstrued, as the Roumanian question is unsettled, the Silesian question, and a number of other matters that could not be left up in the air. I pointed out the impression on Roumania and Hungary especially [would be extremely bad]. Balfour was firm, as he is thoroughly tired out. He leaves Thursday, but Philip Kerr has persuaded Lloyd George to come here the end of this week, and he will sit through next week. In case matters are not cleared up then, I think he will send Bonar Law or Curzon.

I feel however, that it is a mistake to continue to sit in the Quai d'Orsay [as we are] surrounded by a number of the permanent French Foreign Office officials, and thus [they are able] to create an impression in the minds of the small powers frequently not in line with the views expressed by the delegates. If we continue to sit, I will take this up. Will cable you again on this subject after I see Lloyd George on Friday. Polk.

(Second Telegram) Urgent. September 15, 5 [3] P.M.³ 4126 [*sic*], Confidential. For the President and Secretary of State. Lloyd George told me Friday night in the course of the [general] discussion that he wanted to clear up everything immediately that could be cleared up, and adjourn the conference. He said he was leaving town Monday night, that no Cabinet Officer was willing to stay here, and therefore he expected to do what could be done on Monday and then adjourn. I explained [He said] that the Italian question should be settled, and he was in favor of letting the Italians have Fiume. As to Fiume, I said [told him] that, as he knew, a compromise had been submitted to President Wilson,[4] and pending an answer from him, I did not see that any discussion could be of any use, but that, as he was aware, the United States Government could not consent to any such arrangement named in connection with the adjournment of the Conference. I saw him on Saturday afternoon and told him that while I agreed with him that the Conference should be hurried up, he must remember the delay was not our fault, and that there were many matters pending which must be settled, in my opinion, before any adjournment could be taken. I specified particularly the Roumanian and Galician [and other] pending matters. I told him that it was necessary to undertake [deliver] the Bulgarian Treaty and to complete the Hungarian Treaty, and that some organization should be kept here for the purpose of watching the Hungarian and Roumanian situations; that these might be cleared [cleaned] up this week; but that in any event I did not think the British Government had the right to issue an ultimatum and close the conference, when we were ready and willing to dispose of subjects still pending. He finally said that he agreed with me, and promised to have someone stay here after he left, and suggested Sir Eyre Crowe. I told him that in my opinion he should be one of the regular Plenipotentiaries or a Cabinet Officer; that the appearance of a British withdrawal at this time would be extremely bad. He said he would try to see what he could do to persuade Millner or Bonar Law to stay here for this week.

I will report further after our conference this morning. Polk
                                                William Phillips.

[1] The telegram received in the State Department was FLP to RL, No. 4126, Sept. 9, 1919, T telegram (SDR, RG 59, 763.72119/6617, DNA).
[2] Corrections and additions from the copy cited in n. 1.
[3] All following corrections and additions from WP to WW, Sept. 16, 1919, T telegram (SDR, RG 59, 763.72119/6617, DNA).
[4] See WP to WW, Sept. 11, 1919, and, for Wilson's conditional acceptance thereof, JPT to WP, Sept. 13, 1919.

                                   Washington, D. C., Sept. 16, 1919

Sept. 16, 7 P.M. The American Chargé at Brussels[1] advises that during his visit to the United States the King would like to bestow the Order of Leopold and other decorations upon the President, the Secretary of State, and other American officials. In order to avoid the embarrassment that would be caused by having an offer tendered and refused, Mr. Armour asks to be advised as soon as possible what your wishes are in the matter. I should be very grateful if you could indicate the nature of the reply I may send to Brussels, before the King leaves for the United States.

Mr. Armour states that nothing our Government could do would mean more to the King than to bestow upon him the Distinguished Service Medal, it being distinctly understood that the decoration was given him, not as King of the Belgians, but as Commander in Chief of the Belgian Army in the field. I have discussed this last suggestion with the Secretary of War, and he regards it with favor, but asked me to submit it to you for your information.

William Phillips

T telegrams (WP, DLC).
¹ Norman Armour.

From the Diary of Dr. Grayson

Wednesday, September 17, 1919.

Oakland was reached at 8:00 o'clock in the morning, and the President was greeted here by the reception committee from San Francisco, headed by the Governor and the Mayor.¹ A special ferry boat was waiting in the mole and the party was conveyed across to the foot of Market Street, San Francisco. Despite the early hour of arrival the streets were thronged with men and women—all anxious to cheer the Chief Executive. Market Street was a blaze of colors from the Ferry all the way to the top of the hill, and as the Presidential party passed up the crowd cheered loudly. At the Civic Center all of the school children of the city had been gathered, and they occupied special stands that had been erected for them. The President and Mrs. Wilson left their automobile here and went out to a small stand that had been constructed, from which both of them waved a greeting to the assembled children. The children were armed with American flags, which they waved while they cheered lustily their welcome to the distinguished visitors.

The party then proceeded to the St. Francis Hotel, where headquarters had been established for the two days' stay in the city. The President was allowed to rest until 1:00 o'clock, when the automobiles were reentered and he proceeded to the Palace Hotel, where a luncheon in his honor had been arranged by the Associated Women's Clubs of the city of San Francisco. There were 3,000 women and very few men present when the President entered. The President was not feeling well. He had had a splitting headache all the morning and for a time there was doubt whether he would be able to make his address. However, he insisted on carrying out the program, and I had done everything possible to relieve his pain. He drank a cup of coffee while waiting for the luncheon to terminate, and then made a splendid address, in which he appealed directly to the women for their support. He referred indirectly to the opposition led by Senator Johnson and carried his audience with him when he declared that he could not conceive how public men could wilfully misconstrue the facts concerning the Treaty. He told the audience that in the framing of the Treaty concessions had been made by all concerned, but that at no time had anyone been forced to sacrifice any principles. His address was one of the best of the entire trip and it fairly electrified the crowd of women who listened to it.

Arrangements had been made for a long automobile ride in the afternoon, but I refused to allow the President to take it. He needed rest and I was doing everything possible to prevent a breakdown and to keep him in shape so that he could carry out the program. In consequence he spent the afternoon in his apartments with Mrs. Wilson resting for the night meeting.

The night meeting was a very demonstrative one.[2] For a time it seemed that the crowd had gotten beyond the control of the presiding officer[3] and there was noise, cheering and confusion. There was apprehension on the part of Gavin McNab and the others who had arranged for the meeting that the crowd would not listen to the President and fifteen minutes was consumed in endeavoring to restore order. However, when the President himself started to speak there was a prompt checking of the enthusiasm and he was well received. As he proceeded with his address the entire crowd warmed up and he was cheered for fully five minutes after he ended his speech.

The major portion of the address was devoted to replying to allegations by Senator Johnson and others that the United States had not been sufficiently safeguarded, especially in the Covenant of the League of Nations. Senator Johnson had directly charged that the League of Nations gave six votes to Great Britain and only one to the United States. The President explained this allegation by demonstrating that the British Dominions were given a vote in the Assembly of the League of Nations, but that in the Council, which was the supreme over-all body, Great Britain had the same vote as the United States—one. The Assembly, the President told the audience, was merely the machinery for bringing to the attention of the Council matters which it must consider, and the decisions of the Council, he said, must be unanimous before they could be accepted. Because of this, the President said, the one vote of the United States counted for as much at all times as the six of Great Britain. The President also told the audience that the reason why it had not been possible for the Paris Conference to consider the claims of Ireland for independence was because it was not a matter directly affected by the war. He pointed out that the Conference had agreed that nothing could be considered by it except with unanimous consent, and inasmuch as the British representatives were opposed to any injection of the Irish question into the deliberations, it was utterly impossible for him, even if he had desired to do so, to plead the cause of Ireland in Paris. This direct answer to the Johnson charges made a great hit with the people of San Francisco.

The President returned to the hotel late at night immediately after the meeting.

[1] William Dennison Stephens and James Rolph, Jr., both Republicans.

[2] The newspaper reports of the evening meeting all agree that President and Mrs. Wilson were greeted by a prolonged ovation from the audience of over 12,000 persons packed into the Civic Auditorium and that it was difficult for Wilson to begin his address. Most accounts agree also that scattered talking or shouting persisted well into the course of the speech. The reporters for the *New York Times* and the New York *World* suggested that pro-Irish demonstrators were responsible for this later noise. All accounts agree that the noise gradually abated until finally almost total silence prevailed. Edward H. Hamilton of the *San Francisco Examiner* provided the most detailed account of the scene. He said nothing of agitators, Irish or otherwise, but pointed out that the audience had been jammed into the very warm auditorium for well over an hour before Wilson and his party arrived and asserted that most of those present (including himself) simply could not hear much, if anything, that Wilson said. See the *San Francisco Examiner*, the *New York Times*, the New York *World*, and the *New York Tribune*, all Sept. 18, 1919.

[3] Chester Harvey Rowell, editor of the *Fresno Republican*, a leader of both the Progressive and the Republican parties, and a close friend and adviser of Hiram W. Johnson, whose elections both as Governor of California and United States senator he had engineered.

Notes for an Address

LUNCH, San Francisco, 17 Sept., 1919.

The compulsion of honour. We cannot draw out of the concert of civilized nations by which the terror was defeated, because if we do draw out the task is not completed, but must be done all over again.

The compulsion of interest. Isolation will mean suspicion, new combinations of European nations (economic as well as political), and enlarged armaments,—no proper leisure to effect the reforms upon which our peaceful economic life depends.

The compulsion of humanity. The hopes, the fate of all the nations of the world depend upon the consummation of this great plan; of the weaker nations (upon whom the whole burden of the misery of the world has always fallen) most of all, but of the greater nations also, if they are to [be] thrown back on the old order.

***

WWT MS (WP, DLC).

A Luncheon Address in San Francisco

[[September 17, 1919]]

Mrs. Mott[1] and my fellow citizens: Mrs. Mott has very happily interpreted the feeling with which I face this great audience. I have come to get the consciousness of your support and of your sympathy at a time in the history of the world, I take leave to say, more critical than has ever been known during the history of the United States.

I have felt a certain burden of responsibility as I have mixed with my fellow countrymen across the continent, because I feared at times that there were those amongst us who did not realize just what the heart of this question is. I have been afraid that their thoughts were lingering in the past days, when the calculation was always of national advantage, and that they had not come to see the light of the new day in which men are thinking of the common advantage and safety of mankind. Because the issue is nothing else. Either we must stand apart, and in the phrase of some gentlemen, take care of ourselves, which means to antagonize others, or we must join hands with the other great nations of the world and with the weak nations of the world in seeing that justice is everywhere maintained.

And quite apart from the merits of any particular question which may arise about the treaty itself, I think we are under a certain moral compulsion to accept this treaty.

In the first place, my fellow citizens, it was laid down according to American specifications. The initial suggestions upon which this treaty is based emanated from America. I would not have you understand me as meaning that they were ideas confined to America, because the promptness with which they were accepted, the joy with which they were acclaimed in some parts of the world, the readiness of the leaders of nations that were supposed to be seeking chiefly their own interest in adopting these principles as the principles of the treaty, show that they were listening to the coun-

[1] Sara Maude Robinson (Mrs. Ernest J.) Mott, president of an organization of collegiate alumnae in the San Francisco area, who presided and introduced Wilson. Wilson spoke before approximately 1,600 women of the Associated Women's Clubs of San Francisco at the Palace Hotel. There is no news report of Mrs. Mott's remarks.

sels of their own people, they were listening to them and knew the critical character of the new age and the necessity we were under to take any measures for the peace of the world.

Because the thing that had happened was intolerable. The thing that Germany attempted, if it had succeeded, would have set the civilization of the world back a hundred years. We have prevented it, but prevention is not enough. We have shown Germany that upon occasion—and not Germany only, but the world—that upon occasion the great peoples of the world will combine to prevent an iniquity. But we have not shown how that is going to be done in the future with a certainty that will make every other nation know that a similar enterprise must not be attempted.

Again and again, as I have crossed the continent, generous women, women I did not know, have taken me by the hand and said, "God bless you, Mr. President." Some of them, like many of you, had lost sons and husbands and brothers. Why should they bless me? I advised Congress to declare war. I advised Congress to send their sons to their death. As commander in chief of the army, I sent them over the seas, and they were killed. Why should they bless me? Because in the generosity of their hearts, they want the sons of other women saved henceforth. And they believe that the methods proposed, at any rate, merit a very hopeful expectation that similar wars will be prevented, and that other armies will not have to go from the United States to die upon distant fields of battle. And so the moral compulsion among us, among us who at the critical stage of the world saved the world and who threw in our fortunes with all the forward-looking peoples of the world—the moral compulsion upon us to stand by and see it through is overwhelming. We cannot now turn back. We made the choice in April 1917. We cannot with honor reverse it now.

And not only is there the compulsion of honor, but there is the compulsion of interest. I never like to speak of that, because, notwithstanding the reputation that we had throughout the world before we made the great sacrifice of this war, this nation does love its honor better than it loves its interest. It does yield to moral compulsion more readily than to material compulsion. That is the glory of America. That is the spirit in which she was conceived and born. That is the mission which she has in the world. And she always has lived up to it, and, God helping her, she always will live up to it.

But if you want, as some of our fellow countrymen insist, to dwell upon the material side of it and our interest in the matter— our commercial interest—draw the picture for yourselves. The other great nations of the world are drawing together. We, who suggested that they should draw together in this new partnership, stand aside. We at once draw their suspicion upon us. We at once draw their intense hostility upon us. We at once renew the thing that had begun to be done before we went into the war. There was a conference in Paris[2] not many months before we went into the war in which the nations then engaged against Germany attempted to draw together in an exclusive economic combination, where they should serve one another's interest and exclude those who had not participated in the war from sharing in that interest. And just so certainly as we stay out, every market that can possibly be closed against us will be closed. So that if you merely look at it from the material point of view, of the material prosperity of the United States, we are under compulsion to stay in the partnership.

I was putting it to some gentlemen the other day who were engaged in commerce of various sorts, and I asked them, "Can you sell more easily to a man who trusts you or to a man who distrusts you?" There can be but one answer to that question. Can you sell most easily to a man who takes your goods because he cannot do without them or because he wants them and believes them the best? The thing demonstrates itself. You make all the lines of trade lines of resistance unless you prove true to the interests you have attempted.

And, then, there is a deeper compulsion even than that—the compulsion of humanity. If there is one thing that America ought to have learned more promptly than any other country, it is that, being made up out of all the ranks of humanity, in serving itself it must serve the whole human race.

Because I suppose I could not command the words which would exaggerate the present expectations of the world with regard to the United States. Nothing more thrilling, nothing more touching, happened to me on the other side of the water than the daily evidence that, not the weak peoples merely, not the peoples of countries that had been allowed to shift for themselves and had always borne the chief burden of the world's sufferings, but the great peoples as well, the people of France as well as the people of Serbia, the people of all the nations that had looked this terror in the face, were turning to the United States and saying: "We depend on you to take the lead, to direct us and get us out of this wilderness of doubt and fear and terror." We cannot desert humanity. We are the trustees of humanity, and we must see that we redeem the pledges which are always implicit in so great a trusteeship.

And so, feeling those compulsions—the compulsion of honor,

[2] About this, the Allied Economic Conference of Paris of June 1916, see RL to WW, June 23, 1916, Vol. 37.

the compulsion of interest, and the compulsion of humanity—I wonder what it is that is holding some minds back from acquiescence in this great enterprise of peace. I must admit to you, my fellow citizens, that I have been very much puzzled. I cannot conceive a motive adequate to hold men off from this thing. And when I examine the objections which they make to the treaty, I can but wonder if they are really thinking, or if, on the other hand, there is some emotion coming from fountains that I don't know of which are obliging them to take this course.

Let me take the point in which my initial sympathy is most with them—the matter of the cession to Japan of the interests of Germany in Shantung, in China. I have said, I said to my Japanese colleagues on the other side of the sea, and therefore I am at liberty to say it in public, that I am not satisfied with this settlement. I think it ought to be different. But when gentlemen propose to cure it by striking that clause out of the treaty or by ourselves withholding our adherence to the treaty, they propose an irrational thing.

Let me remind you of some of the history of this business. It was in 1898 that China ceded these rights and concessions to Germany. The pretext was that some German missionaries had been killed. My heart aches, I must say, when I think how we have made an excuse of religion sometimes to work a deep wrong. The central government of China had done all it could to protect those German missionaries; their death was due to local disturbances, to local passions, to local antipathy against the foreigner. There was nothing that the Chinese government as a whole could justly be held responsible for. But suppose there had been? Two Christian missionaries are killed, and therefore one great nation robs another nation and does a thing which is fundamentally un-Christian and heathen! For there was no adequate excuse for what Germany exacted of China. I read again only the other day the phrases in which poor China was made to make the concession. She was made to make that in words dictated by Germany, in view of her gratitude for Germany for certain services rendered—the deepest hypocrisy conceivable! She was obliged to do so by force.

Then, what happened, my fellow citizens? Then Russia came in and obliged China to cede to her Port Arthur and Talien-Wan,[3] not for quite so long a period, but upon substantially the same terms. Then England must needs have Weihaiwei as an equivalent concession to that which had been made to Germany. And presently certain ports and territory back of them were ceded upon similar principles to France. Everybody got in, except the United

---

[3] That is, Dairen.

States, and said, "If Germany is going to get something, we will get something." Why? No one of them was entitled to it; no one of them had any business in there on such terms.

And then, when the Japanese-Russian war came, Japan did what she has done in this war—she attacked Port Arthur and captured Port Arthur, and Port Arthur was ceded to her as a consequence of the war. Not one voice was raised in the United States against that cession—I mean, official voice. No protest was made. No protest was made by the government of the United States against the original concession of this Shantung territory to Germany. One of the highest minded men of our history was President at that time—I mean Mr. McKinley. One of the ablest men we ever had as Secretary of State, Mr. John Hay, occupied that great office. And in the message of Mr. McKinley about this transaction, he says—and I am not quoting his language—that, inasmuch as the powers that had taken these territories had agreed to keep the doors open there for our commerce, there was no reason why we should object. Just so we could trade with these stolen territories, we were willing to let them be stolen. Which of these gentlemen who are not objecting to the cession of the German rights in Shantung in China were prominently protesting against the original cession, or any one of those original cessions? It makes my heart burn when some men are so late in doing justice.

Now, in the meantime, before we got into this war, but after the war had begun, because they deemed the assistance of Japan in the Pacific absolutely indispensable, Great Britain and France both agreed that if Japan would enter the war, she could do the same thing with regard to Shantung that she had done with regard to Port Arthur, that is, she would take what Germany had in Shantung, she could keep it. She took it. She has it now—her troops are there—as spoils of war. Observe, my fellow citizens, we are not taking this thing away from China; we are taking it from Germany. China had ceded it for ninety-nine years, and, if my reckoning is correct,[4] there are eighty-three of those ninety-nine to run yet.

It was Germany's rights in Shantung, and not Chinese, that we conceded by the treaty to Japan, but with a condition—a condition which never occurred in any of these other cases—a condition which was not insisted upon at the cession of Port Arthur—upon a condition that no other nation in doing similar things in China has ever yielded to. Japan is under solemn promise to forego all sovereign rights in the province of Shantung and to retain only what private corporations have elsewhere in China—the right of conces-

[4] His reckoning was incorrect. The lease had seventy-eight years to run. Wilson corrected himself in his next address.

sionaires with regard to the operation of the railway and exploitation of the mines. Scores of foreign corporations have that right in other parts of China.

But it doesn't stop there. Coupled with this arrangement is the League of Nations, under which Japan solemnly undertakes, with the rest of us, to respect and protect the territorial integrity of China, along with the territorial integrity of other countries of the world. And back of her promise is likewise the similar promise of every other nation—that nowhere will there come a disregard for the territorial integrity or the political independence of that great helpless people, lying there hitherto as an object of prey in the great Orient. It is the first time in the history of the world that anything has been done for China. And, sitting around our council board in Paris, I put this question: "May I expect that this will be the beginning of the retrocession to China of the exceptional rights which other governments have enjoyed there?" And the responsible representatives of the other great governments said, "Yes; you may expect it."

Expect it? Why, of course I expect it. Your attention is constantly drawn to Article X, and that is the article—the heart of the Covenant—which guarantees the political integrity, not only of China, but of other countries more helpless even than China. But besides Article X, there is Article XI, which makes it the right of every member of the League, big or little, influential or not influential, to draw attention to anything, anywhere, that is likely to disturb the peace of the world or the good understanding between nations upon which the peace of the world depends.

Whenever formerly anything was done in detriment of the interests of China, we had to approach the government that did it with apologies. We had to say, as it were, "This is none of our business, but we would like to suggest that this is not in the interests of China." I am repeating, not the words but the purport, of notes that I have myself signed to Japan, in which I was obliged to use all the genuflections of apology and say, "The United States Government believes that this is wrong in principle and suggest to the Japanese government that the matter be reconsidered."

Now, when you have the treaty and the League of Nations, the representative of the United States has the right to stand up and say, "This is against the covenant of peace; it can't be done." And if occasion arises, we can add, "It shall not be done."

The weak and oppressed and wronged peoples of the world have never before had a forum made for them to which they could summon their enemies in the presence of the judgment of mankind. And if there is one tribunal that the wrongdoer ought to dread more than any other, it is that tribunal of the opinion of mankind. Some nations keep their international promises only because they wish to obtain the respect of mankind. You remember those immortal words in the opening part of the Declaration of Independence. I wish I could quote them literally, but they run this way, that, out of respect for the opinion of mankind, the leaders of the American Revolution now state the causes which have led them to separate themselves from Great Britain. America was the first to set that example, the first to admit that right and justice and even the basis of revolution are a matter upon which mankind are entitled to form a judgment.

If we do not take part in this thing, what happens? France and England are absolutely bound to it without any qualification. The alternative, therefore, is to defend China in the future, to begin with, or else let the world go back to its old methods of rapacity, or else take up arms against France and England and Japan, and begin the shedding of blood over again, almost a fratricidal blood. Does that sound like a practical program? Does that sound like doing China a service? Does that sound like anything that is rational?

Now, to go to other matters with which I have less patience, other objections to the League.

I have spoken of Article X. Those who object to Article X object to entering the League with any responsibility whatever. They want to make it a matter of opinion merely, and not a matter of action. And they know just as well as I do that there is nothing in Article X that can oblige the Congress of the United States to declare war if it does not deem it wise to declare war. We engage with the other nations of the world to respect and preserve as against external aggression—not as against internal revolution—the territorial integrity and the independence of the other members of the League. And then, in the next sentence, it is said that the Council of the League of Nations shall advise with regard to measures which may be necessary to carry out those promises on the part of the members. And, as I have said several times in my speeches, I have in vain searched the dictionary to find any other meaning for the word "advise" than "advise."

These gentlemen would have you believe that our armies can be ordered abroad by some other powers or by a combination of powers. They are thinking in an airtight compartment. America is not the only proud nation in the world. I can testify from my part in the councils on the other side of the sea that the other nations are just as jealous of their sovereignty as we are of ours. They would no more agree to give us the right to order out their armies than we would agree to give them the right to order out our army. And the advice can come from the Council only if the United States representative votes in the affirmative.

We have an absolute veto on the thing, unless we are parties to the dispute. And I want again, for I have done it several times, to call your attention to what that means. That means unless we want to seize somebody's territory or invade somebody's political independence. Or unless somebody else wants to seize our territory and invade our political independence. Now, I regard either of those contingencies as so remote that they are not troubling me in the least. I know the people of this country know that we will not be the aggressors in trying to execute a wrong, and, in looking about me, I don't see anybody else that would think it wise to try it on us.

But suppose we are parties. Then is it the Council of the League that is forcing war upon us? The war is ours anyhow. We are in circumstances where it is necessary for Congress, if it wants to steal somebody's territory or prevent somebody from stealing our territory, to go to war. So it is not the Council of the League that brings us into war at that time.

In such circumstances, it is the unfortunate circumstances which have arisen in some matter of aggression. And I want to say again that Article X is the very heart of the Covenant of the League, because all the great wrongs of the world have had their root in the seizure of territory or the control of the political independence of other people. And I believe that I speak the feeling of the people of the United States when I say that, having seen one great wrong like that attempted and having prevented it, we are ready to prevent it again.

Those are the two principal criticisms—that we do not do the impossible with regard to Shantung, and that we may be obliged to go to war. And that is all there is in either of them.

But they say, "We want the Monroe Doctrine more distinctly acknowledged." Well, if I could have found language that was more distinct than that used, I should have been very happy to suggest it. When it is said in so many words that nothing in that document shall be construed as affecting the validity of the Monroe Doctrine, I don't see what more it can say. But, as I say, if the clear can be clarified, I have no objection to its being clarified. The meaning is too obvious to admit of discussion. And I want you to realize how extraordinary that is—I mean, how extraordinary the provision is. Every nation in the world has been jealous of the Monroe Doctrine and studiously avoided doing or saying anything that would admit its validity. And yet here all the great nations of the world sign a document which admits its validity. That constitutes nothing less than a moral revolution in the attitude of the rest of the world towards America.

What does the Monroe Doctrine mean in that Covenant? It means that, with regard to aggressions upon the western hemisphere, we are at liberty to act without waiting for other nations to act. That is the Monroe Doctrine. For the Monroe Doctrine says that, if anybody tries to interfere with force in the western hemisphere, it will be regarded as an unfriendly act to the United States—not the rest of the world. And that means that the United States will look after it and won't ask the permission of anybody else to look after it. And the document says, "Nothing in this document must be construed as interfering with that."

So I dismiss the objections to the Monroe Doctrine, and I do so all the more because this is what happened. I brought the first draft of the Covenant to this country in March last. I then invited the Foreign Affairs Committee of the House and the Foreign Relations Committee of the Senate to the White House to dinner, and after dinner we had the frankest possible conference with regard to this draft. And when I got back to Paris I carried every suggestion that was made in that conference to the conference of peace itself, or rather to the Commission on the League of Nations, which consisted of representatives of fourteen nations. And every one of the suggestions of those committees of our Senate and House was embodied in the document.

I suppose it is a pride of style. I suppose that, although the substance was embodied, they would rather write it differently. But, after all, that is a literary matter. After all, that is a question of pride in the command of the English language. And I must say that there were a great many men on that Commission on the League of Nations who seemed perfectly to understand the English language and who wished to express, not only in the English text, but in its French equivalent, exactly what we wanted to say.

One of the suggestions I carried over was that we should have a right to withdraw. I must say that I did not want to say to them, "We will go into this if you will promise us that we can scuttle the ship whenever we want to." That did not seem a very handsome thing to propose, and I told the conference at the White House, when they raised the question, that it had been raised in the conference on the League of Nations, and that it was the unanimous opinion of the international lawyers who constituted that body that, insasmuch as this was an association of sovereigns, they had the right to withdraw. But I conceded that if that right was admitted there could be no harm in stating it. And so in the present draft of the Covenant it is stated that any member may withdraw upon two years' notice, which, I think, is not an unreasonable length of time, provided that at the end of two years all the international obligations of that power under the Covenant shall have been fulfilled.

Would you wish any other conditions? Would you wish the United States to withdraw without fulfilling its obligations? Is that the kind of people we are? Moreover, have we ever failed to fulfill our international obligations? It is a point of principle with me, my fellow citizens, not to debate this question. I will not debate it with anybody—whether the United States is likely to withdraw without fulfilling its obligations. And if other gentlemen entertain that possibility and expectation, I separate myself from them.

But there is another matter of pride. They say that Great Britain—the British Empire—has six votes and we have only one. Well, it happens that our one is as big as the six, and that suits me entirely. Let me explain what I mean. There is only one thing, and that is in the Assembly, wherein the British Empire has six votes. That is not true in the Council. And there is only one thing that the Assembly votes on in which it can decide a matter without the concurrence of all the states represented upon the Council, and that is the admission of new members to the League of Nations. With regard to every other matter, for example, an amendment to the Covenant, with regard to cases referred out of the Council to the Assembly, it is provided that, if a majority of the Assembly and the representatives of all the states represented on the Council concur, that the vote shall be valid and conclusive, which means that the affirmative vote of the United States is in every instance just as powerful as the six votes of the British Empire.

I took the pains yesterday, I believe it was, on the train, to go through the Covenant again, almost sentence by sentence, to find if there was any case other than the one which I have mentioned in which that is not true, and there is no other case in which that is not true.

Of course, you will understand that, wherever the United States is a party to a quarrel and that quarrel is carried to the Assembly, we cannot vote. But, similarly, if the British Empire is a party her six representatives cannot vote. So it is an even break any way you take it, and I would rather count six as one person than six as six persons. So far as I can see, it makes me a bigger man. But the point to remember is that the energy of the League of Nations resides in the Council, not in the Assembly, and that in the Council there is a perfect equality of votes. That settles that matter, and even some of my fellow countrymen who insist upon keeping a hyphen in the middle of their names should be satisfied with that, though I must admit that I don't care to argue anything with a hyphen. A man that puts anything else before the word "American" is no comrade of mine. And yet I am willing to discomfort him with the statement of a fact.

Those are the objections to yielding to these compulsions of honor, interest, and humanity. And it is because of the nature of these objections—their flimsiness, the impossibility of supporting them with conclusive argument—that I am profoundly puzzled to know what is back of the opposition to the League of Nations. I know one of the results, and that is to raise the hope in the minds of the German people that, after all, they can separate us from those who were our associates in the war. I know that the pro-German propaganda, which had heretofore not dared to raise its head again, has now boldly raised its head and is active all over the United States. These are disturbing and illuminating circumstances.

Pray understand me. I am not accusing some of the honorable men whose objections I am trying to answer with trying to draw near to Germany. That is not my point. But I am saying that what they are attempting to do is exactly what Germany desires, and that it would touch the honor of the United States very much if, at the end of this great struggle, we should seek to take the position which our enemies desire and our friends deplore.

But I am arguing the matter only because I am a very patient man. I haven't the slightest doubt as to what the result is going to be. I have felt the temper and high purpose of this great people as I have crossed this wonderful land of ours. And one of the things that make it most delightful to stand here is to remember that the people of the Pacific Coast were the first to see the new duty in its entirety. It is a remarkable circumstance that you people, who were farthest from the field of conflict, most remote from the conflict of interests which stirred so many peoples, yet outdid the rest of the country in volunteering for service and volunteering your money.

As I came through that wonderful mountain country to the north of us it occurred to me one day that the aspiring lines, those wonderful lines of the mountains, must lead people's eyes to be drawn upwards, to look into the blue serene and see things apart from the confusions of affairs, to see the real, pure vision of the interests of humanity; and that, after all, the spirit of America is best expressed where people withdraw their thoughts from the entangling interests of everyday life, purify their motives from all that are selfish and groveling and animal, based upon the desire to seize and get, and turn their thoughts to those things that are worth living for.

The only thing that makes the world inhabitable is that it is sometimes ruled by its purest spirits. I want to leave this illustration, which I have often used, in your minds as containing what I mean. Some years ago, someone said to me that the modern world was a world in which the mind was monarch. And my reply was that, if that was true, it must be one of those modern monarchs that reigned and did not govern, and that, as a matter of fact, the world was governed by a great popular assembly made up of the passions, and that the constant struggle of civilization was to see that the handsome passions had a working majority. That is the problem of civilization—that the things that engage the best impulses of the human spirit should be the prevailing things, the conquering things, the things that one can do comfortably after achieving. How do men ever go to sleep that have conceived wrong? How do men ever get their own consent to laugh who have not looked the right in the face and extended their hands to it? And if America can in the future look the rest of the world in the face, it will be because she has been the champion of justice and of right.

Printed in the *San Francisco Examiner*, Sept. 18, 1919, with two additions from the text in *Addresses of President Wilson*.

Notes for an Address

CLEAR THE TABLE.   San Francisco, 17 Sept., '19

Preface: Though farthest from the scene of conflict and from direct contact with the effect of Prussian aggression, the West led the nation in voluntary action. A wide and clear world vision.

The League born of the Conscience and wisdom of forward-looking, just men of all parties, creeds, and peoples. I acted only as spokesman and trustee of the conscience and purpose of America, the most advanced of all nations and the clearest in prevision.

Opponents are in effect, if not in purpose, defendants and advocates of the past; offer nothing but the old alliances of the strong and dominion of the weak.

What did they do for China under the old regime? But of that later.

Let us examine what they base their opposition upon and clear the table:
Withdrawal
The Monroe Doctrine

Domestic questions
Britain's six votes
Article TEN
Shantung
The right of self-determination of peoples not included in the
  scope of the treaty.

This arrangement,—or what? Changes cannot now be made in
it without renewing the whole process by which it was produced,
and renewing it under radically different conditions.

No alternative suggested except the intolerable alternative of a
separate treaty with Germany, which could change nothing in this
treaty and could accomplish nothing except our disgrace as deserters.

NOTE: March, 1898, China ceded to Germany (after certain Ger-
man missionaries had been killed) a ninety-nine year lease over
Kiao Chiao etc.
   The same month, Port Arthur to Russia With Talien-wan, rail-
ways, etc.
   Soon after Wei-hai-wai to Great Britain for same period as Port
A. and a port and territory to France for 99 yrs.

WWT MS (WP, DLC).

An Address in the San Francisco Civic Auditorium

[[September 17, 1919]]

Mr. Chairman, Mr. Rolph,[1] my fellow countrymen, you have
given me a very royal welcome, and I am profoundly appreciative
of the greeting that you have given me. It is a matter of great gratification to be permitted to speak to this great audience, representing, as it does, one of the most forward-looking states of the Union,
representing, as it does, a great body of people who are accustomed
to look and plan for the future.
   As I picture to myself the history of this great country which we
love, I remember the surging tides of humanity moving always
westward, from the eastern mountains and the plains, deploying
upon the great further slopes of the Rockies, then traveling into
these beautiful and fertile valleys by the Pacific. And that is a picture to me of the constant, forward, hopeful movement of the

[1] That is, Chester H. Rowell and Mayor Rolph.

American people. So that I feel that it is not without significance that this was the portion of the country which responded with the most extraordinary spirit to the call to arms, responded with the utmost spontaneity and generosity to the call for the money to be loaned to the government for the conduct of the Great War, responded to all these impulses with the purpose of freedom which underlay the great struggle which we have just passed through.

You have made me feel, as I have passed through the streets today, and in the many other communities north and east of you, how the spirit of the American people is coming to a single vision, how the thought of the American people is back of a single purpose. I have come to you, my fellow citizens, to discuss a very serious theme to which it is necessary that we should give our very thoughtful attention, and I would be very much obliged if my fellow countrymen near the door would devote a little more thought to it and a little less noise to it.

While in ordinary circumstances, I can hope that my voice will reach a considerable number of persons, I cannot compete against several hundred voices, and I am particularly anxious that you should give me your attention tonight, in order that I may analyze, for those of you who may care to listen, the very important issue with which this nation is now face to face. It is by far the most important question that has ever come before this people for decision, and the reason I have come out upon this long journey is that I am conscious that it is the people, their purpose, their wish, which is to decide this thing, and not the thought of those who have any private purpose of their own.

What I want to call to your attention, my fellow citizens, is this. You know that the debate in which we are engaged centers first of all upon the League of Nations, and there seems to have arisen an idea in some quarters that the League of Nations is an idea recently conceived by a small number of persons, somehow originated by the American representatives at the council table in Paris. Nothing could be further from the truth than that. I would not feel the confidence that I feel in the League of Nations if I felt that it was so recent and novel a growth as that. On the contrary, it is the fruit of many generations of thoughtful, forward-looking men, not only in this country, but in the other countries of the world, which have been able to look forward to the combined fates of mankind. I would be ashamed of myself, as I am frankly ashamed of any fellow countryman of mine, who discusses this great question with any portion of his thought devoted to the contest of the parties and the elections of next year. Some of the great spirits, some of the most instructed minds of both parties, have been devoted to this great idea for more than a generation. It has come up before the Paris conference in the stage of ideal conception. But long before that it began to assume the shape of a definite program and plan for the concert and cooperation of the nations in the interest of the peace of the world. And when I went to Paris, I was conscious that I was carrying there no plan which was novel either to America or to Europe, but a plan which all statesmen, who realized the real interests of their people, had long ago hoped might be realized in some way when the world would realize what the peace of the world meant and what were its necessary foundations.

So that when I got to Paris, I felt that I was merely the spokesman of thoughtful minds and hopeful spirits in America, not representing anything that had not been long considered. I was not putting forward any purpose of my own. So that I beg you will dismiss any personal appearance or personal relationship which this great plan may bear. I would indeed be a very proud man if I had personally conceived this very great idea, but I can claim no such honor. I can only claim the privilege of having been the obedient servant of the great ideals and purposes of beloved America.

And I want you to realize, my fellow countrymen, that those Americans who are opposing this plan of the League of Nations offer no substitute. They offer nothing that they pretend will accomplish the same object. On the contrary, they are apparently willing to go back to that old and evil order which prevailed before this war began and which furnished a ready and fertile soil for those seeds of envy which sprang up like dragon's teeth out of the bloody soil of Europe. They are ready to go back to that old and ugly plan of armed nations, of alliances, of watchful jealousy, of rabid antagonisms, of purposes concealed, running by the subtle channels of intrigue through the veins of people who do not dream what poison is being injected into their systems. They are willing to have the United States stand alone, withdraw from the concert of nations.

And what does that mean, my fellow citizens? It means that we shall arm as Germany was armed, that we shall submit our young men to the kind of constant military service that the young men of Germany were subjected to. It means that we shall pay, not lighter, but heavier taxes. It means that we shall trade in a world in which we are suspected and watched and disliked, instead of in a world which is now ready to trust us, ready to follow our leadership, ready to receive our traders, along with our political representatives, as friends, as men who are welcome, as men who bring goods and ideas for which the world is ready and for which the world has been waiting. That is the alternative which they offer.

It was my purpose, my fellow citizens, to analyze the objections which are made to this great League, and I dare say I must be very brief. In the first place, you know that one of the difficulties which has been experienced by those who are objecting to this League is that they do not think that there is a wide enough door open for us to get out. For my own part, I am not one of those who, when I go into a generous enterprise, think first of all how I am going to turn away from those with whom I am associated. I am not one of those who, when he goes into a concert for the peace of the world, wants to sit close to the door with his hand on the knob and constantly try the door to be sure that it is not locked.

If we want to go into this thing—and we do want to go into it—we will go into it with our whole hearts, with settled purpose to stand by the great enterprise to the end. But nevertheless, you will remember—some of you, I dare say—that, when I came home in March for an all too brief visit to this country, which seems to me the fairest and dearest in the world, I brought back with me the first draft of the Covenant of the League of Nations. I called into consultation the committees on foreign relations of the House and Senate of the United States. I laid the draft of the Covenant before them. One of the things that they proposed was that it should be explicitly stated that any member of the League should have the right to withdraw. I carried that suggestion back to Paris, and without the slightest hesitation it was accepted and acted upon. And their suggestion, which was made in that conference at the White House, was accepted by the peace conference in Paris. There is not a feature of the Covenant, except one now under debate, upon which suggestions were not made at that time, and there is not one of those suggestions that was not adopted by the conference of peace.

These gentlemen say: "You have laid a limitation upon the right to withdraw. You have said that we can withdraw upon two years' notice, if at that time we shall have fulfilled all our international obligations and all our obligations under the Covenant." "Yes," I reply. "Is it characteristic of the United States not to fulfill her international obligations? Is there any fear that we shall wish to withdraw dishonorably? Are gentlemen willing to stand up and say that they want to get out, whether they have the moral right to get out or not?" I for one am too proud as an American to debate the subject on that basis. The United States has always fulfilled its international obligations, and, God helping her, she always will. And there is nothing in the Covenant to prevent her acting upon her own judgment with regard to that matter. The only thing she has to fear, the only thing she has to regard, is the public opinion of mankind. And, inasmuch as we have always scrupulously satisfied the public opinion of mankind with regard to justice and right, I for my part am not afraid at any time to go before that jury. It is a jury that might condemn us if we did wrong, but it is not a jury that could oblige us to stay in the League, so that there is absolutely no limitation upon our right to withdraw.

One of the other suggestions I carried to Paris was that the committees of the two houses did not find the Monroe Doctrine safeguarded in the Covenant of the League of Nations. I suggested that to the conference in Paris, and they at once inserted the provision which is now there that nothing in that Covenant shall be construed as affecting the validity of the Monroe Doctrine. What is the validity of the Monroe Doctrine? The Monroe Doctrine means that, if any outside power, any power outside this hemisphere, tries to impose its will upon any portion of the western hemisphere, the United States is at liberty to act independently and alone in repelling the aggression; that it does not have to wait for the action of the League of Nations; that it does not have to wait for anything but the action of its own administration and its own Congress. This is the first time in the history of international diplomacy that any great nation has acknowledged the validity of the Monroe Doctrine. And now, for the first time, all the great fighting powers of the world except Germany, which for the time being has ceased to be a great fighting power, acknowledge the validity of the Monroe Doctrine and accept it as part of the international practice of the world.

But they are nervous about domestic questions. They say, "It is intolerable to think that the League of Nations should interfere with domestic questions." And, whenever they begin to specify, they speak of the question of immigration, of the question of naturalization, of the question of the tariff. My fellow citizens, no competent or authoritative student of international law would dream of maintaining that these were anything but exclusively domestic questions. And the Covenant of the League expressly provides that the League can take no action whatever about matters which are in the practice of international law regarded as domestic questions. We did not undertake to enumerate examples of domestic questions for the very good reason, which will occur to any lawyer, that if you made a list it would be inferred that what you left out was not included. Nobody with a thoughtful knowledge of international practice has the least doubt as to what are domestic questions. And there is no obscurity whatever in this Covenant with regard to the safeguarding of the United States, along with other sovereign countries, in the control of domestic questions. I beg that you will not fancy, my fellow citizens, that the United States is the only country that is jealous of its sovereignty. Throughout these conferences, it was necessary at every turn to safeguard the sovereign independence of the several nations who were taking part in the conference, and they were just as keen to protect themselves against outside intervention in domestic matters as we were. Therefore the wholeheartedness of their concurrent opinion runs with this safeguarding of domestic questions.

But it is objected that the Empire of Great Britain has six votes and we have one. The answer to that is that it is most carefully arranged that our one vote equals the six votes of the British Empire. Anybody who will take pains to read the Covenant of the League of Nations will find out that the Assembly—and it is only in the Assembly that the British Empire has six votes—will find that the Assembly is not a voting body. There is a very limited number of subjects upon which it can act at all. And I have taken the pains to write them down here, after again and again going through the Covenant for the purpose of making sure that I had not omitted anything, in order that I may give you an explicit account of this thing.

There are two things which a majority of the Assembly may do without the concurrent vote of the United States. A majority of the Assembly can admit a new member to the League of Nations. A majority of the Assembly can recommend to any nation a member of the League a reconsideration of such treaties as are apparently in conflict with the provisions of the Covenant itself. It can advise any member of the League to seek a reconsideration of any international obligation which seems to conflict with the Covenant itself. But it has no means whatever of obliging it to reconsider even so important a matter as that, which is obviously a moral duty on the part of any member of the League.

All the action, all the energy, all the initiative, of the League of Nations is resident in the Council, and in the Council a unanimous vote is necessary for action, and no action is possible without the concurrent vote of the United States. I would rather, personally, as one man, count for six than be six men. And by one vote, the United States can offset six votes. Here are the cases. When a matter in dispute is referred by the Council to the Assembly, its action must be taken by a majority vote of the Assembly, concurred in by the representatives of all the governments represented in the Council, so that the concurrence of the vote of the United States is absolutely necessary to an affirmative vote of the Assembly itself. In the case of an amendment to the Covenant, it is necessary that there should be a unanimous vote of the representatives of the nations which are represented in the Council, in addition to a majority vote of the Assembly itself. And there is all the voting that the Assembly does.

Not a single affirmative act or negative decision upon a matter of action taken by the League of Nations can be validated without the vote of the United States of America. We can dismiss from our dreams the six votes of the British Empire. The real underlying conception of the Assembly of the League of Nations is that it is the forum of opinion, not of action. It is the debating body; it is the body where the thought of the little nation, along with the thought of the big nation, is brought to bear upon those matters which affect the peace of the world, is brought to bear upon those matters which affect the good understanding between nations upon which the peace of the world depends. It is the body where this stifled voice of humanity is at last to be heard, where nations that have borne the unspeakable sufferings of the ages—it must have seemed to them like aeons—will find voice and expression, where the moral judgment of mankind can sway the opinion of the world. That is the function of the Assembly. The Assembly is the voice of mankind. And the Council, where unanimous action is necessary, is the only means through which that voice can accomplish action.

But you say, "We have heard a great deal about Article X." I just now said, while some of you were not listening, that the only substitute for the League of Nations which is offered by the opponents of the League is a return to the old system. What was the old system? That the strong had all the rights and never did pay any regard to the rights of the weak; that if a great powerful nation would say that what it wanted, it had the right to go and take, that the weak nations could cry out and cry out as they pleased, and there would be no harking ear anywhere to their rights.

I want to bring in another subject connected with this treaty, but not with the League of Nations, to illustrate what I am talking about. You have heard a great deal about the cession to Japan of the rights which Germany had acquired in Shantung Province in China. What happened under the old order of things, my fellow citizens? The story began in 1898. Two German missionaries were killed in China by parties over whom the central government of China was unable to exercise control. It was one of those outbreaks, like the pitiful Boxer Rebellion, where a sudden hatred of foreigners wells up in the heart of a nation uninformed, aware of danger, aware of wrong, but not knowing just how to remedy it, not knowing just what was the instrumentality of right. And, my fellow citizens, why should not a Chinaman hate the foreigner? The foreigner has always taken from him everything that he could get. And when, by irresponsible persons, these German mission-aries were murdered, the German government insisted that a great part of the fair province of Shantung should be turned over to them for exploitation. They insisted that Kiaochow Bay, an accessible part of it, a part where trade entered and left these rich regions, should be delivered over to them for sovereign control for ninety-nine years, and that they should be given a concession for a railway into the interior and for the right to exploit mines in the rich min-eral country for thirty miles on either side of the railroad.

This was not unprecedented, my fellow countrymen. Other civ-ilized nations had done the same thing to China, and at that time what did the government of the United States do? I want to speak with the utmost respect for the administration of that time, and the respect is unaffected. That very lovable and honest gentleman, William McKinley, was President of the United States. His Secre-tary of State was one of the most honorable of the long series of our Secretaries of State, the Honorable John Hay. I ought to pause to say that I believe Mr. Hay, if he had seen any way to accomplish more than he did accomplish, would have attempted to accomplish it. But this is all that the administration of Mr. McKinley accom-plished: they did not even protest against this compulsory granting to Germany of the best port of her rich province of a helpless coun-try, but only stipulated that the Germans should keep it open to the trade of the United States. They did not make the least efforts to save the rights of China; they only tried to save the commercial advantages of the United States.

There immediately followed upon that cession to Germany a ces-sion to Russia of Port Arthur and the region called Talien-Wan for twenty-five years, with the privilege of renewing it for a similar period. And when, soon afterwards, Japan and Russia came to blows, you remember what happened. Russia was obliged to turn over to Japan Port Arthur and Talien-Wan, just exactly as she is now allowed to take over the German rights in Shantung. And this government, though the conference which determined those things was held on our own soil, did not, so far as I have been able to learn, make the slightest intimation of objecting.

At that very same time, England came in and said that, since Germany was getting a piece of Shantung and Russia was getting Port Arthur and Talien-Wan, they insisted on having their slice of China, and the region of Weihaiwei was ceded to them. Imme-diately after that, France got into the unhandsome game, and there was ceded to France for ninety-nine years one of the ports of China with the region lying behind it. In all of these transactions there was not a single attempt made by the government of the United

States to do anything except keep those regions open to our traders.

You now have the historic setting of the settlement about Shantung. What I want to call to your attention is that the treaty of peace does not take Shantung from China; it takes it from Germany. There are seventy-eight years of the ninety-nine of that lease still to run, and not only do we not take it from China, but Japan agrees in an agreement which is formally recorded—which is acknowledged by the Japanese government—to return all the sovereign rights which Germany enjoyed in Shantung without qualification to China, and to retain nothing except what foreign corporations have throughout China—the right to run a railroad and to exploit those mines.

There is not a great commercial and industrial nation in Europe that does not enjoy privileges of that sort in China, and some of them enjoy them at the expense of the sovereignty of China. And Japan has promised to release everything that savors of sovereignty and return it to China itself. She will have no right to put armed men anywhere into that portion of China. She will have no right to interfere with the civil administration of that portion of China. She will have no rights but economic and commercial rights. Now, if we choose to say that we will not assent to the Shantung provision, what do we do for China? Absolutely nothing. Japan has what Germany had in China in her commercial possession now. She has the promise of Great Britain and France that, so far as they are concerned, she can have it without qualification. And the only way we can take it away from Japan is by going to war with Japan and Great Britain and France.

The League of Nations for the first time provides a tribunal in which not only the sovereign rights of Germany and of Japan in China, but the sovereign rights of other nations can be curtailed, because every member of the League solemnly covenants to respect and preserve the territorial integrity and existing political independence of the other members, and China is to be a member. Never before, my fellow citizens, has there been a tribunal to which people like those of China could carry the intolerable aggravations to which they have been subjected. Now a great tribunal has been set up in which the pressure of the whole judgment of the world will be exercised in her behalf.

That is the significance of Article X. Article X is the heart of the whole promise of peace, because it cuts out of the transactions of nations all attempts to impair the territorial integrity or invade the political independence of the weak as well as of the strong. Why did not Mr. Hay protest the acquisition of those rights in Shantung by Germany? Why did he not protest what England got, and what France got, and what Russia got? Because under international law, as it then stood, that would have been a hostile act toward those governments. The law of the world was actually such that if you mentioned anybody else's wrong but your own, you spoke as an enemy. After you have read Article X, read Article XI. Article XI says that it shall be the right, the friendly right, of any member of the League, strong or weak, to call the attention of the League to any matter, anywhere, that affects the peace of the world or the good understanding between nations upon which the peace of the world depends. So that for the first time it affords fine spirits like Mr. McKinley and Mr. John Hay the right to stand up before mankind and protest, and to say, "The rights of China shall be as sacred as the rights of those nations that are able to take care of themselves by arms." It is the most hopeful change in the law of the world that has ever been suggested or adopted.

But there is another subject upon which some of our fellow citizens are particularly sensitive. They say, "What does the League of Nations do for the right of self-determination?" I think I can answer that question, if not satisfactorily, at any rate very specifically. It was not within the privilege of the conference of peace to act upon the right of self-determination of any peoples except those which had been included within the territories of the defeated empires—that is to say, it was not then within their power. But the moment the Covenant of the League of Nations is adopted, it becomes their right. If the desire for self-determination of any people in the world is likely to affect the peace of the world or the good understanding between nations, it becomes the business of the League, it becomes the right of any member of the League, to call attention to it. It becomes the function of the League to bring the whole pressure of the combined world to bear upon that very matter.

Where before, and when before, may I ask some of my fellow countrymen who want a forum upon which to conduct a hopeful agitation, were they ever offered the opportunity to bring their case to the judgment of mankind? If they are not satisfied with that, their case is not good. The only case that you ought to bring with diffidence before the great jury of men throughout the world is the case that you cannot establish. The only thing I shall ever be afraid to see the League of Nations discuss, if the United States is concerned, is a case which I can hardly imagine, where the United States is wrong, because I have the hopeful and confident expectation that, whenever a case in which the United States is affected is brought to the consideration of that great body, we would naturally feel no nervousness as to the themes of the argument, so far as we were concerned. Because the glory of the United States is that it never claimed anything to which it was not justly entitled.

Indeed, my fellow citizens, I look forward with a quickened pulse to the conditions that lie ahead of us as a member of the League of Nations—for we shall be a member of the League of Nations—I look forward with confidence and with exalted hope to the time when we can indeed legitimately and constantly be the champions and friends of those who are struggling for right anywhere in the world.

And no nation is likely to forget, my fellow citizens, that behind the moral judgment of the United States resides the overwhelming force of the United States. We were respected in those old Revolutionary days when there were three millions of us. We are, it happens, very much more respected now that there are more than a hundred millions of us and now that we command some of the most important resources of the world.

Back of the majesty of the United States lies the strength of the United States. If Germany had ever dreamed, when she conceived her great ungodly enterprise, that the United States would have come into the war, she never would have dared to attempt it.

But now, my fellow citizens, the hope of Germany has revived. It has revived, because, in the debates now taking place in the United States, she sees a hope of at least doing what her arms could not do—dividing the United States from the great nations with which it was associated in the war. Here is a quotation from a recent utterance of one of her Counselors of State:[2]

"All humanity, Germany particularly, is tensely awaiting the decision of the American Senate on the peace treaty," ex-Minister Von Scheller-Steinwartz said today. "Apparently Senator"[3]—out of respect for him, I won't mention the name he mentions—"apparently Senator [pause] is the soul of the opposition. The Senator is no German hater. He hates all non-Americans equally, and he is absolutely a just man of almost anchor-like moral strength."

How delightful to receive such praise from such a source! "When he and other important Senators fight the peace treaty, their course means that the treaty displeases them because of the excessive enslavement of Germany, for which America would be forever responsible. They see grave danger of future complications. That course is thus to be hailed as the morning red of a new dawn." A new dawn for the world? Oh, no; a new dawn for Ger-

[2] That is, Robert Richard von Scheller-Steinwartz.
[3] According to the news report, Scheller-Steinwartz said Henry Cabot Lodge. *New York Times*, Sept. 8, 1919.

many. "And there is promise of a still better realization of the conditions in the prospect that America, in all seriousness, may express the wish for a separate peace with the Central Empires."

A separate peace with the Central Empires could accomplish nothing but our eternal disgrace. And I would like, if my voice could reach him, to let this German Counselor know that the red he sees upon the horizon is not the red of a new dawn, but the red of a consuming fire which will consume everything like the recent purposes of the Central Powers. It is not without significance, my fellow citizens, that coincidentally with this debate with regard to the adoption of this treaty, the old pro-German propaganda has shown its head all over the United States.

I would not have you understand me to mean that the men who are opposing the adoption of the treaty are consciously encouraging the pro-German propaganda. I have no right to say that or think it, but I do say that what they are doing is encouraging a pro-German propaganda, and that it is bringing about a hope in the minds of those whom we have just spent our precious blood to defeat that they separate us from the rest of the world and produce this interesting spectacle—only two nations standing aside from the great concert and guarantee of peace: beaten Germany and triumphant America.

See what can be accomplished by that. By that the attitude of the rest of the world towards America will be exactly what its recent attitude was towards Germany. We will be in the position, absolutely alien to every American conception, of playing a lone hand in the world for our selfish advantage and aggrandizement. The thing is inconceivable. The thing is intolerable. The thing can and will never happen.

I speak of these things in order that you may realize, my fellow citizens, the solemnity and the significance of this debate in which we are engaged; its solemnity because it involves the honor of the United States and the peace of humanity; its significance because, whether gentlemen plan it or not, not only refusal on our part, but long hesitation on our part to cast our fortunes permanently in with the fortunes of those that love right and liberty will be to bring mankind again into the shadow of that valley of death from which we have just emerged.

I was saying to some of your fellow citizens today how touching it had been to me, as I came across the continent, to have women, who I subsequently learned had lost their sons or their husbands, come and take my hand and say, "God bless you, Mr. President." Why should they say "God bless" me? I advised the Congress of the United States to take the action which sent their sons to their death. As commander in chief of the army and navy, I ordered their sons to their death. Why should they take my hand and with tears upon their cheeks say, "God bless you"? Because they understood, as I understood, they understood as their sons who are dead upon the fields of France understood, that they had gone there to fight for a great cause, and, above all else, they had gone there to see that, in subsequent generations, women should not have to mourn their dead. And as little children have gathered at every station in playful lightheartedness about the train upon which I was traveling, I have felt as if I were trustee for them. I have felt that this errand that I am going about upon was to save them the infinite sorrows through which the world has just passed, and that, if by any evil counsel or unhappy mischance, this great enterprise for which we fought should fail, then women with boys at their breasts ought now to weep, because, when those lads come to maturity, the great battle will have to be fought over again.

But my fellow citizens, there is another battle upon which we are now on the eve. That is the battle for the right organization of industrial society. I do not need to tell an audience of this great progressive state what I mean by that. But we cannot work out justice in our communities if the world is to continue under arms and ready for war. We must have peace, we must have leisure of mind and detachment of purpose, if we are going to work out the great reforms for which mankind is everywhere waiting. And I pray God that normal times will not much longer be withheld from us.

The world is profoundly stirred. The masses of men are stirred by thoughts which never moved them before. We must not again go into the camp. We must sit down at the council table and, like men and brethren, lovers of liberty and justice, see that the right is done to those who bear the heat and burden of the day, as well as to those who direct the labor of mankind.

I am not a partisan of any party to any of these contests. And I am not an enemy of anybody, except the minority that tries to control. And I do not care where the minority is drawn from. I do not care how influential or how insignificant. I do not care which side of the labor question it has been on. If the power of the United States under my direction can prevent the domination of a minority, it will be prevented.

Because, there again, I am a champion of that sort of peace, that sort of order, that sort of common counsel out of which, and out of which alone, can come the satisfactory solutions of the problems of society. You cannot solve the problems of society amidst chaos, disorder, and strife. We can only solve them when men have agreed to be calm, agreed to be just, agreed to be conciliatory, agreed that the right of the weak is as majestic as the right of the strong. And when we have come to that mind in the counsels of nations, we can the more readily come to that mind in our domestic counsels, upon which the happiness and prosperity of our own beloved people so intimately and directly depend.

I beg, my fellow citizens, that you will carry this question home with you, not in little pieces, not with this, that, and the other at the front of your mind, but as a great picture, including the whole of the nation and the whole of humanity, and know that now is the golden hour when America can at last prove that what she promised in the day of her birth was no dream, but a thing which she saw in its concrete reality—the rights of man, the prosperity of nations, the majesty of justice, and the sacredness of peace.

Printed in the *San Francisco Examiner*, Sept. 18, 1919, with a few corrections and additions from the text in the *San Francisco Chronicle*, Sept. 18, 1919.

To Bernard Mannes Baruch

San Francisco Sept 17 1919

I have called a conference at Washington for October 6th for the purpose of discussing the labor situation in the country and the possibility of formulating plans for the development of a new relationship between capital and labor. I beg that you will accept appointment as one of the representatives of the general public in that conference. There will be twenty-two representatives of the public and an equivalent number of representatives of various bodies of organized labor and organized employers. I sincerely hope that it will be possible for you to undertake this very important service.   Woodrow Wilson

T telegram (B. M. Baruch Papers, NjP).

To Carter Glass

[San Francisco, Sept. 17, 1919]

Please send the following telegram to Secretary Carter Glass, Treasury Department:

Your letter of eleventh received. While I am in entire accord with it there are some parts of it which I would like to make suggestions about which it is very difficult to make by mail or telegraph. Do you deem it absolutely necessary to publish such a statement before my return?   Woodrow Wilson.

WWT MS (WP, DLC).

From Robert Lansing

Washington, D. C., September 17, 1919.

For the President from the Secretary of State:

"After several days of being out of touch with news I have returned to my office to find much excitement over Bullitt's statement to the Foreign Relations Committee.[1] I am greatly distressed over the situation because of the way Bullitt gave out a most confidential interview.

As near as I can recall the facts they are as follows: On May 17 Bullitt resigned by letter[2] giving his reason with which you are familiar. I replied by letter on the 18th without any comments on his reasons. Bullitt on the 19th asked to see me to say good-bye, and I saw him. He elaborated on the reasons for his resignation and said that he could not conscientiously give countenance to a treaty which was based on injustice. I told him that I would say nothing against his resigning since he put it on conscientious grounds, and that I recognized that certain features of the treaty were bad as I presumed most every one did, but that was probably unavoidable in view of (conflicting) claims and that nothing ought to be done to prevent the speedy restoration of peace by signing the treaty. Bullitt then discussed the numerous European commissions provided for by the treaty on which the United States was to be represented. I told him that I was disturbed by this fact because I was (afraid) the Senate and possibly the people, if they understood this, would refuse ratification, and that I was sure Senator Knox would refuse ratification, and that I was sure Senator Knox would understand it and Senator Lodge would use it politically, and that anything which was an obstacle (preventing) ratification was unfortunate because we ought to have peace as soon as possible.

The foregoing is the substance of the important part of our conversation. I have not yet received the text of Bullitt's hearing. His conduct is most despicable and outrageous and shows that from his failure to arrange matters with the Bolsheviks, he has intended to use his opportunity to (omission) information in order to be revenged for our failure to accept his report on Russia.[3]

I have made no comment on the Bullitt statement believing that it would only introduce a controversy. Through the department Senator Hitchcock approved of this course. I sent to Hitchcock through the department a repetition of what he could use if determined, saying that I was for the ratification of the treaty without reservations.

In view of my account of the conversation with Bullitt which is of course from memory, do you think it would be wise for me to make a statement after I have the printed report on B. hearing. I wish to do everything I can to help in the ratification of the treaty and most deeply regret that I ever had any conversation with the disloyal young man who is seeking notoriety at the expense of the respect of all honorable men." Lansing.[4]   Phillips, Acting.

T telegram (WP, DLC).

[1] Lansing was being a bit disingenuous here. Newspaper reporters did reach him in Watertown, New York, on September 12 to ask for comment on William C. Bullitt's testimony before the Senate Foreign Relations Committee that morning. Lansing refused to make any comment. *New York Times*, Sept. 13, 1919.

The only senators present to hear Bullitt's testimony were Lodge, Brandegee, Fall, Knox, Harding, and New.

Following brief introductory remarks, in which Bullitt explained his activities during the war and at the peace conference, the senators questioned him closely as to what he knew of the drafting of the Covenant of the League of Nations. Bullitt's principal response was to produce copies of various drafts of the Covenant which were in his possession, all of which were later transcribed in the printed minutes of his testimony. These included Lord Robert Cecil's memorandum of December 17, 1918 (printed at that date in Vol. 53 of this series); two versions, one printed and one typed, in Bullitt's possession, of the first Paris draft of the Covenant (printed at Jan. 8, 1919, in *ibid.*); a lengthy commentary on the first Paris draft, with suggestions for changes, by David Hunter Miller (printed in his *The Drafting of the Covenant* [2 vols., New York and London, 1928], II, 65-93); two versions, one printed and one a WWT in Bullitt's possession, of the second Paris draft of the Covenant (printed at Jan. 18, 1919, Vol. 54); and the Hurst-Miller draft of the Covenant (printed at Feb. 2, 1919, *ibid.*).

Bullitt professed to know little more about the creation of the League of Nations than these drafts revealed. He did assert that Wilson had opposed proposals to provide for the representation of national parliaments and congresses in the Assembly of the League of Nations. On this point, see Miller, *Drafting of the Covenant*, I, 272-75. When asked what he considered to be Wilson's major contribution to the Covenant, he responded: "So far as I know, in the final form of the league the only proposal of the president which remains more or less intact is article 10." *Treaty of Peace with Germany: Hearings before the Committee on Foreign Relations, United States Senate*, 66th Cong., 1st sess., Sen. Doc. No. 106 (Washington, 1919), p. 1233. Regarding the American presence in the peace conference in general, Bullitt declared that Wilson had "conducted all the negotiations himself, all the actual—practically all the actual—negotiations." *Ibid.*

Bullitt then gave a lengthy account of his mission to Russia (about which, see n. 3 below) and presented numerous documents which were later printed in the minutes. Lodge and Knox questioned Bullitt as to the whereabouts of the minutes of the Council of Ten and the Council of Four. Bullitt said that detailed records of the meetings of both had been kept and added, incorrectly, that printed copies had been distributed to the American delegates and their staff. He also said that copies were probably among Lansing's papers in the State Department.

It was in response to several questions from Lodge near the end of the session that Bullitt made the remarks which prompted Lansing to write the above telegram. Lodge asked whether any member of the American delegation had expressed opinions to Bullitt about "the general character of the Treaty." Bullitt responded: "Well, Mr. Lansing, Col. House, Gen. Bliss, and Mr. White had all expressed to me very vigorously their opinions on the subject." Lodge: "Were they enthusiastically in favor of it?" Bullitt: "I regret to say, not. . . . It is no secret that Mr. Lansing, Gen. Bliss, and Mr. Henry White objected very vigorously to the numerous provisions of the treaty." Lodge commented that it was public knowledge that they objected to the provisions on Shantung but that he was not aware of any other objections. To this Bullitt replied: "I do not think that Secretary Lansing is at all enthusiastic about the league of nations as it stands at present." In support of this assertion, Bullitt read aloud a portion of his memorandum of a conversation that he had had with Lansing on May 19. He quoted it as follows:

"Mr. Lansing then said that he personally would have strengthened greatly the judicial clauses of the league of nations covenant, making arbitration compulsory. He also said that he was absolutely opposed to the United States taking a mandate in either Armenia or Constantinople; that he thought that Constantinople should be placed under a local government, the chief members of which were appointed by an international committee.

"Mr. Lansing then said that he, too, considered many parts of the treaty thoroughly bad, particularly those dealing with Shantung and the league of nations. He said: 'I consider that the league of nations at present is entirely useless. The great powers have simply gone ahead and arranged the world to suit themselves. England and France in particular have gotten out of the treaty everything that they wanted; and the league of nations can do nothing to alter any of the unjust clauses of the treaty except by unanimous consent of the members of the league, and the great powers will never give their consent to changes in the interests of weaker peoples.'

"We then talked about the possibility of ratification by the Senate. Mr. Lansing said: 'I believe that if the Senate could only understand what this treaty means, and if the American people could really understand, it would unquestionably be defeated, but I wonder if they will ever understand what it lets them in for.' He expressed the opinion that Mr. Knox would probably understand the treaty and that Mr. Lodge would; but that Mr. Lodge's position would become purely political, and therefore ineffective. He thought, however, that Mr. Knox might instruct America in the real meaning of it." *Ibid.*, pp. 1276-77.

The full text of Bullitt's testimony, together with the texts of the numerous documents he presented or quoted from, is printed in *ibid.*, pp. 1161-1297. Bullitt reprinted that portion of the text and documents dealing with his mission to Russia, together with the concluding remarks quoted in part above, in William C. Bullitt, *The Bullitt Mission to Russia: Testimony Before the Committee on Foreign Relations, United States Senate* (New York, 1919). The reports in the newspapers of September 12-13 quoted primarily Bullitt's remarks concerning Lansing. See, for example, the *New York Times*, Sept. 13, 1919.

[2] See W. C. Bullitt to WW, May 17, 1919, and RL to WW, May 20, 1919 (second letter of that date), both in Vol. 59.

[3] For Bullitt's mission to Russia, his report, and its fate, see the index references under "Bullitt, William Christian" in Vols. 55, 56, and 57 of this series.

[4] Lansing sent his message in code to the State Department, where it had to be put into the code in Wilson's possession. It was sent from the State Department in this form at 9 a.m. on September 17, when Wilson was in San Francisco.

Breckinridge Long, in a memoir on what he called "the Lansing Incident" (T MS, dated Washington, 1924, B. Long Papers, DLC), says that Dr. Grayson told him that Wilson read Lansing's telegram in Los Angeles on Sunday morning, September 21, and described Wilson's reaction as he read it: "On that same morning, Cary noticed the first physical signs of the break in Mr. Wilson. Little drops of saliva appeared at the corners of Mr. Wilson's mouth. His lips trembled slightly. The saliva continued. His pallor increased." Dr. Grayson, Long added, "was much alarmed, began scheming to cancel the balance of the trip, tried to amuse the President, interest him in other things, divert his mind."

Tumulty (*Woodrow Wilson As I Know Him* [Garden City, N. Y., 1921], pp. 441-43) tells the story as follows:

"The press representatives aboard the train called Mr. Bullitt's testimony to the President's attention. He made no comment, but it was plain from his attitude that he was incensed and distressed beyond measure. Here he was in the heart of the West, advancing the cause so dear to his heart, steadily making gains against what appeared to be insurmountable odds, and now his intimate associate, Mr. Lansing, was engaged in sniping and attacking him from behind. . . .

"When the President received this explanation [the telegram] from Mr. Lansing, he sent for me to visit with him in his compartment. At the time I arrived he was seated in his little study, engaged in preparing his speech for the night's meeting. Turning to me, with a deep show of feeling, he said: 'Read that, and tell me what you think of a man who was my associate on the other side and who confidentially expressed himself to an outsider in such a fashion? Were I in Washington I would at once demand his resignation! That kind of disloyalty must not be permitted to go unchallenged for a single minute. The testimony of Bullitt is a confirmation of the suspicions I have had with reference to this individual. I found the same attitude of mind on the part of Lansing on the other side. I could find his trail everywhere I went, but they were only suspicions and it would not be fair for me to act upon them. But here in his own statement is a verification at last of everything I have suspected. Think of it! This from a man whom I raised from the level of a subordinate to the great office of Secretary of State of the United States. My God! I did not think it was possible for Lansing to act in this way. When we were in Paris I found that Lansing and others were constantly giving out statements that did not agree with my viewpoint. When I had arranged a settlement, there would appear from some source I could not locate unofficial statements telling the correspondents not to take things too seriously; that a compromise would be made, and this news, or rather news of this kind, was harmful to the settlement I had already obtained and quite naturally gave the Conference the impression that Lansing and his kind were speaking for me, and then the French would say that I was bluffing.'

"I am convinced that only the President's illness a few days later prevented an immediate demand on his part for the resignation of Mr. Lansing."

Wilson never acknowledged Lansing's telegram, and Lansing never issued a statement.

From the Diary of Dr. Grayson

Thursday, September 18, 1919.

The President's headache was still with him when he arose this morning, but he was very much cheered over the warmth of his reception in the home stamping ground of Senator Johnson. He conferred briefly with Gavin McNab and the San Francisco reception committee during the morning, thanking them for the manner in which they had made their arrangements.

At noon he again was the guest of honor at a luncheon at the Palace Hotel, which had been arranged by the Chamber of Commerce of San Francisco. This luncheon was in distinct contrast to that of the day before when practically all of his hearers had been women. Today they were men—business men of the community[1]—who followed his argument with the deepest interest. The President again took up the so-called British argument and hammered it home to his audience.

Following the luncheon the Presidential party proceeded down Market Street to a ferry and went to Oakland. On arriving at Oakland the President proceeded in his automobile to the campus of Stanford University, where he made a brief address to the assembled students.[2] He then returned to the Oakland Hotel, where he had dinner.[3]

A night meeting had been arranged in Oakland, and once more the auditorium was found far too small[4] to accommodate those who wanted to see and hear the President. He referred in his speech here again to the fact that the women of the country were even more vitally interested than the men in the ending for all time of wars. He referred to the Treaty of Versailles and the League of Nations Covenant as a ninety-five per cent insurance against war.

Following the meeting the President returned to his train and Oakland was left at 10:00 o'clock that night for San Diego.

[1] About 1,500 members of the Associated Business Men's Clubs of San Francisco attended.

[2] Actually, Wilson spoke at the Greek theater at the University of California, Berkeley. One reporter estimated the crowd in the amphitheater at 10,000 persons. Wilson was reported to have spoken for about ten minutes, "against the express orders of his physician," under a hot sun that turned the theater into "an oven." *Oakland Tribune*, Sept. 19, 1919.

³ The Wilsons dined with his sister-in-law, Margaret Randolph Axson Elliott, and her husband, Edward Graham Elliott, a former professor, dean, and protegé of Wilson's at Princeton University, who was at this time Professor of Politics and International Law at the University of California, Berkeley.

⁴ The report in the *New York Times*, Sept. 19, 1919, says that the Oakland Civic Auditorium held about 12,000 persons.

A Luncheon Address in San Francisco

[[September 18, 1919]]

Mr. Toastmaster[1] and fellow citizens: I stood here yesterday, but before a very different audience, an audience that it was very delightful to address. But it is no less delightful to find myself face to face with this thoughtful group of citizens of one of the most progressive states in the Union. Because, after all, my fellow citizens, our thought must be of the present and the future. The men who do not look forward now are of no further service to the nation. But the immediate need of this country and of the world is peace, a settled peace—peace upon a definite and well-understood foundation, supported by such covenants as men can depend upon, supported by such purposes as will permit of a concert of action throughout all the free peoples of the world.

The very interesting remarks of your toastmaster have afforded me the opportunity to pay the tribute which they earn to the gentlemen with whom I was associated on the other side of the water. I don't believe that we even now stop to consider how remarkable the peace conference in Paris has been. It is the first great international conference which did not meet to consider the interests and advantages of the strong nations. It is the first international conference that did not convene in order to make the arrangements which would establish the control of the strong. And I want to testify that the whole spirit of the conference was the spirit of men who do not regard themselves as the masters of anybody, but as the servants of the people whom they represent. I found them quick with sympathy for the peoples who had been through all those dolorous times imposed upon, on whom the whole yoke of civilization seemed to have been fastened so that it never could be taken off again.

And the heart of this treaty is that it gives liberty and independence to people who never could have got it for themselves, because the men who constituted that conference realized that the basis of wars was the imposition of the might of strong nations

¹ Reuben Brooks Hale, proprietor of department stores in San Francisco, Oakland, Sacramento, and San Jose; civic leader of San Francisco.

upon those who could not resist. You must settle the difficulties which gave occasion to the war or you must expect war again.

You have only to take the formula of the war in order to see what was the matter. The formula of Pan-Germanism was Bremen to Baghdad. What is the line from Bremen to Baghdad? It leads through partitioned Poland, through prostrate Rumania, through subjugated Slavonia, down through disordered Turkey, and on into distressed Persia. Every foot of the line is a line of political weakness. Germany was looking for the line of least resistance to establish her power, and, unless, gentlemen, the world makes that a line of absolute resistance, this war will have to be fought over. You must settle the difficulties which gave occasion to the war, or you must expect war again.

You know what had happened all through that territory. Almost everywhere there were German princes planted on thrones where they did not belong, where they were aliens, of a different tradition and a different people—mere agents of a political plan, the seething center of which was that unhappy city of Constantinople, where, I dare say, there was more intrigue to the square inch than there has ever been anywhere else in the world, and where not only the most honest minds, but generally the most corrupt minds, were sent to play upon the cupidity of the Turkish authorities and upon the helplessness of the people in order to make a field for German aggression. I am not saying that Germany was the only aggressor and intriguer, but I am saying that there was the field where lay the danger of the world in regard to peace. Every statesman in the world knew it, and at last it dawned upon them that the remedy was not the balance of power, but liberty and right.

An illumination of profound understanding of human affairs shines upon the deliberations of the conference that never shone upon the deliberations of any other international conference in the world. And, therefore, it is a very happy circumstance to me to be afforded the opportunity to say how delightful it was to find that these gentlemen had not accepted the American specifications for the peace—for you remember they were American specifications—because America had come in and assisted them, and because America was powerful and they desired her assistance, but they accepted them because they already believed in them. When we uttered our principles—the principles for which we were fighting—they had only to examine the thoughts of their own people to find that those were also the principles for which their people were fighting, as well as the people of the United States. And the delightful enthusiasm which showed itself in accomplishing some of the most disinterested tasks was a notable circumstance of the whole conference.

I was glad, after I inaugurated it, that I drew together the little body that was called the Big Four. We didn't call it the Big Four; we called it something very much bigger than that—the Supreme Council of the Allied and Associated Powers. We had to have some name, and the more dramatic it was the better; but it was a very simple council of friends. The intimacies of that little room were the center of the whole peace conference, and they were the intimacies of men who believed the same things and thought the same thoughts. The hearts of Clemenceau and Lloyd George and the heart of Orlando beat with the people of the world, as well as with the people of their own countries. They know that there is only one way to work out peace, and that is to work it out right.

Now, the peace of the world is absolutely indispensable to us, and immediately indispensable to us. There is not a single domestic problem that can be worked out in the right temper or opportunely and in time unless we have conditions that we can count on. I don't need to tell businessmen that they cannot conduct their business if they don't know what is going to happen tomorrow. You cannot make plans unless you have certain elements in the future upon which you can depend. You cannot seek markets unless you know whether you are going to seek them among people who suspect you or people who believe in you. If the United States is going to stand off and play truant in this great enterprise of justice and right, then you must expect to be looked upon with suspicion and hostile rivalry everywhere in the world. They will say, "These men are not intending to assist us; they are intending to exploit us." You know that there was a conference just a few months before we went into the war of the principal Allied powers held in Paris for the purpose of concerting a sort of economic league in which they would manage their purchasing as well as their selling in a way which would redound to their advantage and make use of the rest of the world. That was because they then thought what they will be obliged to think again, if we do not continue our partnership with them—that we were standing off to get what we could out of them, and they were making a defensive economic arrangement. Very well, they will do that again. Almost by instinct they will do it again, not out of a deliberate hostility to the United States, but by an instinctive impulse of their own business interests. And therefore we cannot arrange a single element of our business until we have settled peace and know whether we are going to deal with a friendly world or an unfriendly world.

We cannot determine our own economic reforms until then, and there must be some very fundamental economic reforms in this country. There must be a reconsideration of the structure of our economic society. Whether we will or no, the majority of mankind demand it, in America as well as elsewhere. We have got to sit down in the peace chamber passive and, in time of quiet, in time that will permit of consideration and determine what we are going to do. We cannot do it until we have peace. We cannot release the great industrial and economic power of America and let it run free until there are right channels in which it can run. And the channels of business are mental channels as well as physical channels. In an open market, men's minds must be open.

It has been said so often that it is a very trite saying, but it remains nevertheless true, that a financial panic is a mere state of mind. There are no fewer resources in the country at the time of a panic than there were on the day before the panic. But something has frightened everybody and caused them to draw in their credits, and everybody builds a fence around himself and is careful to keep behind the fence and waits to see what is going to happen. So a panic is a waiting in fear of something that is going to happen. It doesn't usually happen. Slowly they draw their breath and see that the world looks just the same as it did, and say to each other, "We had better go to work again." As a friend of mine described it at the time of one of our panics some twenty-five years ago, he met a man and in talking said, "Business was not looking up." The reply was: "Yes, it is so flat on its back it can't look any other way." But even if it is flat on its back, it can see the world. It is not lying on its face. But while the whole world is in doubt what to expect, the whole world is under the special apprehension that is characteristic of a panic. You do not know what is safe to do with your money now. You have got to know what the world of tomorrow is going to be. You won't know until we settle this great matter of peace.

And I want to remind you how the permanency of peace is at the heart of this treaty. This is not merely a treaty of peace with Germany. It is a world settlement, not affecting those parts of the world, of course, which were not involved in the war, because the conference had no jurisdiction over them. But the war did extend to most parts of the world, and the scattered, dismembered assets of the Central Empires and of Turkey gave us plenty to do and cover the greater part of the distressed populations of the world. So that it is nothing less than a world settlement, and at the center of it stands this covenant for the future which we call the Covenant of the League of Nations. Without it, the treaty cannot be worked, and without it, it is a mere temporary arrangement with Germany. The Covenant of the League of Nations is the instrumentality for the maintenance of peace.

And how does it propose to maintain it? By the means that all forward-looking and thoughtful men have desired for generations together—by substituting arbitration and discussion for war. To hear some gentlemen talk, you would think that the Council of the League of Nations is to spend its time considering when to advise other people to fight. That is what comes of a constant concentration of attention upon Article X. Article X ought to have been somewhere further down in the Covenant, because it is in the background; it is not in the foreground. At the heart of the Covenant— as I am going to take the liberty of expounding to you, though I presume you have all read the Covenant—at the heart of the Covenant are these words. Every member of the League solemnly agrees—and that means every fighting nation in the world, because, with the present limit of an army of 100,000, Germany is not a fighting nation—every fighting nation is in this Covenant or will be—they all solemnly agree that they will never go to war without first having done one or the other of two things, without either submitting the matter of dispute to arbitration, in which case they promise absolutely to abide by the verdict, or, if they do not agree to submit it to arbitration, submit it to discussion by the Council of the League of Nations, in which case they promise to lay all the documents and all the pertinent facts before that Council. They consent that that Council shall publish all the documents and all the pertinent facts, so that all the world shall know them, that it shall be allowed six months in which to consider the matter. And even at the end of six months, if the conclusions they come to are not unanimously arrived at, or not accepted, they will still not go to war for three months following the rendering of the decision. So that, even allowing no time for the preliminaries, there are nine months of cooling off, nine months of discussion, and not of private discussion, not of discussion between those who are heated, but of discussion between those who are distinterested, except in the maintenance of the peace of the world—when the whole purifying and rectifying influence of the public opinion of mankind is brought to bear upon the conference.

If anything approaching that had been the arrangement of the world in 1914, the war would have been impossible. And I confidently predict that there is not an aggressive people in the world who would dare bring a wrongful purpose to that jury. It is the most formidable jury in the world. Personally, I have never, so far as I know, been in danger of going to jail, but I would a great deal rather go to jail than do wrong and be punished merely by the look in the eyes of the men among whom I circulated. I had rather go to jail than be sent to Coventry. I would rather go to jail than be conscious every day that I was despised and distrusted. After all, the only effective force in the world is the force of opinion.

And if any member of the League ignores these promises with regard to arbitration and discussion, what happens? War? No, not war, but something more tremendous, I take leave to say, than war. An absolute isolation and boycott. It is provided in the Covenant that any nation that disregards these solemn promises with regard to arbitration and discussion shall be thereby deemed *ipso facto* to have committed an act of war against the other members of the League, and that there shall thereupon follow an absolute exclusion of that nation from communication of any kind with the members of the League. No goods can be shipped in or out; no telegraphic messages can be obtained, except through the elusive wireless, perhaps; there would be no communication of any kind between the people of that nation and the peoples of other nations. And there isn't a nation in Europe that can stand that for six months.

Germany could have faced the armies of the world more readily than she faced the boycott of the world. Germany felt the pinch of the blockade more than she felt the stress of the blow. There is not, so far as I know, a single European country—and I say European because I think our own country is exceptional—which is not dependent upon some other part of the world for some of the necessaries of its life. Some of them are absolutely dependent. Some of them are without raw materials, practically, of any kind. Some of them are absolutely without fuel of any kind, either coal or oil. Almost all of them are without that variety of supplies of war which are necessary to modern industry and necessary to the manufacture of the munitions of war. When you apply that boycott, you have got your hand upon the throat of the offending nation, and it is a proper punishment—that is, an exclusion from civilized society.

Inasmuch as I have sometimes been said to have been very, very disregardful of the constitutional rights of Congress, may I not stop to speak just for a moment of a small matter that I was punctilious to attend to in regard to that article? You will notice the language is that any member of the League that makes breach of these covenants shall be regarded as thereby *ipso facto* to have committed an act of war. In the original draft it read, shall *ipso facto* be regarded as at war with the other nations of the world, or words to that effect. I said, "No, I can't subscribe to that, because I am bound to safeguard the right of Congress to determine whether it is at war or not. I consent to its being an act of war by the party committing it, but whether Congress takes up the gage that is thrown down or not is another matter which I cannot participate in determining in a document of this sort."

Germany committed several acts of war against us before we accepted the inevitable and took up her challenge. And it was only because of a sort of accumulation of evidence that Germany's design was not merely to sink American ships and injure American citizens, but that that was incidental to her design—her design being to destroy free political society—that war was finally determined to exist. I remember saying to Congress, before we went into war, that, if Germany committed some act of war against us that was intolerable, I might have to give Congress different advice, and I remember a newspaper correspondent asked me what I thought would constitute such an act. I said: "I don't know, but I am perfectly certain I will know it when I see it. I cannot hypothetically define it, but it will be perfectly obvious when it occurs." And if Congress regards this act by some other member of the League as such an act of war against it as necessitates the maintenance of the honor of the United States, then it may in those circumstances declare war. But it is not bound to declare war under the engagement of the Covenant. So that what I am emphasizing, my fellow citizens, is this: that the heart of this Covenant is arbitration and discussion, and that that is the only possible basis for peace in the future.

It is a basis for something better than peace. Really, civilization proceeds on the principle of understanding one another. You know how peace between those who employ labor and those who labor depends upon conference and mutual understanding. If you don't get together with the other side, it will be hostility to the end. And, after you have heard the case of the other fellow, it sometimes becomes a little awkward for you to insist upon the whole of your case, because the human mind does have this fine quality—that it finds it embarrassing to face the truth and deny it.

Moreover, the basis of friendship is intercourse. I know I am very fond of a very large number of men whom I know to be crooks. They are engaging fellows. When I form a judgment against them, I have to be in another room—that's all there is about it. I cannot, because of my personal attitude toward them, form a harsh judgment. Indeed, I suppose the very thing that gives some men a chance to be crooks is their fascinating personality—they put it over on one. But you remember that very charming remark of Charles Lamb. One night, in company with some friends, they were speaking of some person, and Lamb, in his stuttering fashion, said, "I hate that fellow." And someone said, "Why, Charles, I didn't know you knew him." "Oh, I don't," he said. "I c-c-can't hate a fellow I know"—one of the most genial utterances of the human spirit I have ever read, and one of the truest. It is mighty hard to hate a fellow you know, and it is mighty hard to hate a nation you know. If you intermingle, as I have had the good fortune to mingle, with scores of people of other nations in recent months, you would have the same feeling that I do that, after you got over superficial differences of language and some differences of manner, they are the same kinds of folks.

As I have said to a number of audiences on this trip, the most thrilling thing that happened to me over there was the constant intercourse I was having with delegations of people representing nations from all over the globe, some of which, I had shamefacedly to admit, I never heard of. Do you know where Azerbaijan is? Well, one day there came in a very dignified and interesting group of gentlemen who were from Azerbaijan. I didn't have time until they were gone to find out where they came from. But I did find this out immediately—that I was talking to men who talked the same language that I did in respect of ideas, in respect of conceptions of liberty, in respect of conceptions of right and justice. And I did find this out, that they, with all of the other delegations that came to see me, were, metaphorically speaking, holding their hands out to America, saying: "You are the disciples and leaders of the free peoples of the world. Can't you come and help us?" Until we went into this war, my fellow citizens, it was the almost universal impression of the world that our idealism was a mere matter of words; that what we were interested in was getting on in the world and making as much as we could out of it. That was the sum and substance of the usual opinion of us outside of America. In the short space that we were in this war, that opinion was absolutely reversed.

Consider what they saw. The flower of our youth sent three and four thousand miles away from their homes, homes which could not be directly touched by the flames of that war, sent to foreign fields to mix with foreign and alien armies to fight for the cause which they recognized as the common cause of mankind, and not the peculiar cause of America. It caused a revulsion of feeling, a revulsion of attitude which, I dare say, has never been paralleled in history. And at this moment, unless the cynical counsels of some of our acquaintances should prevail—which God forbid—they are expecting us to lead the civilized world, because they trust us—they really and truly trust us. They would not believe, no matter where we sent an army to be of assistance to them, that we would ever use that army for any purpose but to assist them. They know that when we say, as we said when we sent men to Siberia, we are sending them to assist in the distribution of food and clothing and shoes so that brigands won't seize them, and that for the rest we are ready to render any assistance which they want us to render, and will interfere in absolutely nothing that concerns their affairs, they believe us.

There isn't a place in this world now, unless we wait a little longer, where America's political ambitions are looked upon with suspicion. That was frankly admitted in the conference that I have spoken of. Not one of those gentlemen thought that America had any ulterior designs whatever. They were constantly near us, consulting our economic experts, consulting our geographic experts; they were constantly turning to America to act as umpire. And nine times out of ten, just because America was disinterested and could look at the thing without any other purpose than that of reaching a practical solution, it was the American solution that was accepted.

In order that we may not forget, I have brought with me the figures as to what this war meant to the world. This is a body of businessmen, and you will understand these figures. They are too big for the imagination of men who do not handle big things. Here is the cost of the war in money, exclusive of what we loaned one another, the direct costs of the war: Great Britain and her Dominions, $38,000,000,000; France, $26,000,000,000; the United States, $22,000,000,000 (this is the direct cost of our operations); Russia, $18,000,000,000; Italy, $13,000,000,000; and the total, including Belgium, Japan, and other countries, $123,000,000,000. This is what it cost the Central Powers: Germany, $39,000,000,000, the biggest single item; Austria-Hungary, $21,000,000,000; Turkey and Bulgaria, $3,000,000,000—a total of $63,000,000,000. And the grand total of direct war costs is thus $186,000,000,000—almost the capital of the world. The expenditures of the United States were at the rate of $1,000,000 an hour for two years, including nighttime with daytime. That is the biggest advertising item I have ever heard of!

The record of dead during the war is as follows: Russia lost in dead 1,700,000 men—poor Russia, that got nothing but terror and despair out of it all; Germany lost 1,600,000 men; France, 1,385,000 men; Great Britain, 900,000 men; Austria, 800,000 men; Italy, 364,000 men; the United States, 50,300 in dead—a total for all the belligerents of 7,450,300 men—just about seven and a half million men killed because we could not have arbitration and discussion, because the world had never had the courage to propose the conciliatory methods which some of us are now doubting whether we ought to accept. The totals for the wounded are not obtainable, except our own. Our own wounded were 230,000, excluding those who were killed.

The total of all battle deaths in all the wars in the world from the year 1793 to the year 1914 was something under 6,000,000 men, so that about a million and a half more men were killed in this war than in all the wars of something more than 100 preceding years.

We can hardly realize that. Those of us who lost sons or brothers can realize it. We know what it meant. The women who have little children crowding about their knees know what it means. They know that the world has hitherto been devoted to brutal methods of settlement. And every time a war occurs, it is the flower of the manhood of the belligerents that is destroyed. It is not so much the present generation as the next generation that goes off the stage, goes maimed off the stage, or is laid away in obscure graves upon some battlefield. And the great nations are impaired in their vitality for two generations to come, and all their lives are embittered by a method of settlement for which we could find, and have now found, a substitute.

My fellow citizens, I believe in divine Providence. If I did not, I would go crazy. If I thought the direction of the disordered affairs of this world depended upon our finite endeavor, I should not know how to reason my way to sanity. But I do not believe there is any body of men, however they concert their power or their influence, that can defeat this great enterprise, which is the enterprise of divine mercy and peace and goodwill.[2]

Printed in the *San Francisco Chronicle*, Sept. 19, 1919, with a few minor corrections from the complete text printed in the *San Francisco Examiner*, Sept. 19, 1919.

[2] There is an undated WWT outline of this address in WP, DLC.

An Address in the Greek Theater in Berkeley

[[September 18, 1919]]

Mr. Chairman,[1] Mr. Mayor,[2] ladies and gentlemen. I feel an old feeling coming over me as I stand in this presence. My great danger and temptation is to revert to type and talk to you as college men from a college man.

I was reminded as I received your very generous welcome of a story of Mr. Oliver Herford, a very delightful wit and artist. He was one day seated in his club, and a man came up who did not know him very well, but took many liberties and slapped him on the back and said, "Hello, Ollie, old boy, how are you?" Herford writhed a little, naturally, looked at him a little coldly, and said: "I don't know your name; I don't know your face; but your manners are very familiar."

I think also of an admonition I used often to address to my classes—perhaps I should not call it an admonition so much as a rebuke. I used to say that the trouble about the college youth of America was that they had refused to grow up; that the men and women alike continued to be schoolboys and schoolgirls. I used to remind them that, on the continent of Europe, revolutions were often made in the universities, and statesmen were nervous of nothing so much as a concerted movement of opinion at the centers of learning. And I asked them what cabinet at Washington ever cared a peppercorn of what they were thinking about.

It is your refusal, my fellow students, to grow up, that I am glad of. And one reason that I am glad to see the boys who have been to the front come back is that they have grown up. They have seen the world, seen it at its worst, but nevertheless seen it in action; seen it with its savage and its liberal passions in action. They have come back, and now they are preparing for but one kind of work, not to do physical fighting, but to do the kind of thinking that is better than fighting—the kind of thinking that makes men conscious of their duties, the kind of thinking that purifies the impulses of the world and leads it on to better things.

The burden upon my heart as I go about this errand is that men are hesitating to give us the chance. We cannot do any effective thinking for the world until we know that there is a settled peace. We cannot make any long plans for the betterment of mankind until these initial plans are made, until we know that there is going to be an opportunity to make plans that will last and become effective. That is the ground of my impatience with the debate.

I admit that there are debatable things, but I do not admit that they need to be debated so long. Not only that, but I do insist that they should be debated more fairly. I overheard a remark, or rather a remark was repeated to me which was made after the address I made in San Francisco last night. Some man said, after hearing an exposition of what was in the treaty, he was puzzled. He wondered what the debate was about. It all seemed so simple. The fault was not, I need not assure you, because I was misleading anybody or stating what was not in the treaty, but because the men he had heard debate it, and some of the newspapers he had heard debate it, had not told him what was in the treaty. This great document of human rights, this great settlement of the world, had been represented to this man as containing little traps for the United States. Men had been going about dwelling upon this, that, and the other feature and distorting those features and saying that was what the treaty proposed. They are responsible for some of the most serious mistakes that have ever been made in the history of this country; they are responsible for misleading the opinion of the United States. And it is a very distressing circumstance to me to find that, when I recite the mere facts, they are novel to some of my fellow citizens.

Young gentlemen and young ladies, what we have to do is to see that that very thing cannot happen. We must know what the truth is and insist that everybody else shall know what the truth is. And, above all things else, we must see that the United States is not defeated of its destiny, for its destiny is to lead the world in freedom and in truth.

Printed in the *Berkeley Daily Gazette*, Sept. 19, 1919.
  [1] William Carey Jones, Professor and Director of the School of Jurisprudence and Dean of the Graduate Division, University of California, Berkeley.
  [2] Louis Bartlett, Democratic Mayor of Berkeley and lawyer of San Francisco, who also spoke briefly. Reports of his remarks appear in the *Berkeley Daily Gazette*, Sept. 18, 1919, and in the *Oakland Tribune*, Sept. 19, 1919.

An Address in the Oakland Municipal Auditorium

[[September 18, 1919]]

Dr. Reinhardt[1] and my fellow countrymen: You have indeed warmed my heart with your splendid welcome, and I esteem it a great privilege to stand here before you tonight and look at some of the serious aspects of the great turning point in the history of this nation and the history of the world which affairs have brought us to. Dr. Reinhardt expressed my own feeling when she said that in my own consciousness those great ranks of little children seemed to be my real clients, seemed to be that part of my fellow citizens for whom I am pleading. It is not likely, my fellow citizens, that, with the depleted resources of the great fighting nations of Europe, there will be another war soon. But unless we concert measures and prevent it, there will be another and a final war, just about the time these children come to maturity. And it is our duty to look in the face the real circumstances of the world in order that we may not be unfaithful to the great duty which America undertook in the hour and day of her birth.

One thing has been impressed upon me more than any other as I have crossed the continent, and that is that the people of the United States have been singularly and, I sometimes fear, deliberately, misled as to the character and contents of the treaty of peace. Someone told me that, after an address I delivered in San Francisco last night, one of the men who had been present, a very thoughtful man, I was told, said that, after listening to what I had said, he wondered what the debate was about—it all seemed so simple, so obvious, so natural. And I was at once led to reflect that

  [1] Aurelia Isabel Henry (Mrs. George Frederick) Reinhardt, President of Mills College in Oakland, who introduced Wilson. John Leslie Davie, the Mayor of Oakland, presided.

that was not because of any gift of exposition that I have, but because I had told that audience what the real character and purpose of the covenant of nations is. And they had been led to look at certain incidental features of it, either on the assumption that they had not read the document or in the hope that they would not read it and would not realize what the real contents of it were.

I have not come out from Washington, my fellow citizens, on a speech-making tour. I don't see how anybody could get his own consent to think of the way in which he was saying the things that it is necessary for him to say. I should think that every man's consciousness would be fixed, as mine is, upon the critical destiny of the world which hangs upon the decision of America. I am confident what that decision is going to be, because I can see the tide of sentiment, the tide of conviction rising in this country in such might that any man who tries to withstand it will be overwhelmed. But we are an intelligent and thoughtful people. We want to know just what it is that we are about. And, if you will be patient with me, I am going to try to point out some of the things I did not dwell upon last night that are the salient and outstanding characteristics of the treaty.

I am not going to speak tonight particularly of the Covenant of the League of Nations, but I am going to point out to you what the treaty as a whole is. In the first place, of course, that treaty imposes upon Germany the proper penalty for the crime she attempted to commit. It is a just treaty in spite of its severity. It is a treaty made by men who had no intention of crushing the German people, but who did mean to have it burnt into the consciousness of the German people, and through their consciousness, into the apprehension of the world, that no people could afford to live under a government which was not controlled by their purpose and will, but which was at liberty to impose secret ambitions upon the civilization of the world. It was intended as notice to all mankind that any government that attempted what Germany attempted would meet with the same concerted opposition of mankind and would have meted out to it the same just retribution.

All that this treaty amounts to, so far as Germany is concerned, is that she shall be obliged to pay every dollar that she can afford to pay to repair the damage that she did. And except for the territorial arrangements which it includes, that is practically the whole of the treaty so far as it concerns Germany. What has not been borne in upon the consciousness of some of our people is that, although most of the words of the treaty are devoted to the settlement with Germany, the greater part of the meaning of its provisions is devoted to the settlement with the world.

For the treaty begins with the Covenant of the League of Nations, which is intended to operate as a partnership—a permanent partnership—of the great free self-governing peoples of the world to stand sponsor for the right and for civilization. So that notice is given in the very first articles of the treaty that hereafter it will not be a matter of conjecture whether the other great nations of the world will combine against a wrongdoer, but a matter of certainty that hereafter nations contemplating what the government of Germany contemplated will not have to conjecture whether Great Britain and France and Italy and the great United States will join hands against them, but will know that mankind, in serried ranks, will defend to the last the rights of human beings wherever they are.

And it is the rights of human beings. This is the first treaty ever framed by such an international convention, whose object was not to serve and defend governments but to serve and defend peoples. This is the first people's treaty in the history of international dealing. Every member of that great convention of peace was poignantly aware that at last the people of the world were awake, that at last the people of the world were aware of what wrong had been wrought by irresponsible and autocratic government, that at last all the peoples of the world have seen the vision of liberty, have seen the majesty of justice, have seen the doors thrown open to the aspirations of men and women and the fortunes of children everywhere. They did not dare assume that they were the masters of the fortunes of any people, but knew that in any settlement they must act as the servants, not only of their own people, but of the people who were waiting to be liberated, the people who could not win their own liberty, the people who had suffered for centuries together the intolerable wrongs of misgovernment. So that this is a treaty, not merely for the peoples who were represented at the peace table, but for the people who were the subjects of the governments whose wrongs were forever ended by the victory on the fields of France.

My fellow citizens, you know and you hear it said every day, you read it in the newspapers, you hear it in the conversation of your friends, that there is unrest all over the world. You hear that in every part of the world, not excluding our own beloved country, there are men who feel that society has been shaken to its foundations, and that it ought to have been shaken to its foundations, in order that men might awaken to the wrongs that had been done and that continue to be done.

And when you look into the history, not of our own free and fortunate continent, happily, but of the rest of the world, you will find that the hand of pitiless power has been upon the shoulders of the great mass of mankind since time began, and that only with that little glimmer of light which came at Calvary, that first dawn which came with the Christian era, did men begin to awake to the dignity and right of the human soul, and that, in spite of professions of Christianity, in spite of purposes of reform, in spite of theories of right and of justice, the great body of our fellow beings have been kept under the will of men who exploited them and did not give them the full right to live and realize the purposes that God had meant them to realize.

There is little for the great part of the history of the world except the bitter tears of pity and the hot tears of wrath. And, when you look, as we were permitted to look in Paris, into some of the particular wrongs which the peoples of Central Europe, the peoples upon whom the first foundations of the new German power were to be built, had suffered for generations together, you wonder why they lay so long quiet, you wonder why statesmen, men who pretended to have an outlook upon the world, waited so long to deliver them. And this great treaty is the first attempt to deliver them.

The characteristic of the treaty is that it gives liberty to peoples who never could have won it for themselves. By giving them liberty, it limits the ambitions and defeats the hopes of all imperialistic governments in the world. Governments which had theretofore been considered to desire dominion, here in this document foreswore dominion, renounced it, said: "The fundamental principle upon which we are going to act is this, that every great territory of the world belongs to the people who live in it, and that it is their right, and not our right, to determine the sovereignty they shall live under and the form of government they shall maintain." It is astonishing that this great document did not come as a shock upon the world. If the world had not already been rent by the great struggle which preceded this settlement, men would have stood at amaze at such a document as this. But there is a subtle consciousness throughout the world now that this is an end of governing people who do not desire the government that is over them.

Going further than that, the makers of the treaty proceeded to arrange those things which had always been arranged upon a competitive basis, upon a cooperative basis. I want to mention a very practical thing, which most of you, I dare say, never thought about. Most of the rivers of Europe traverse the territory of several nations, and up to that time there had been certain historic rights and certain treaty rights over certain parts of the courses of those rivers which had embarrassed the people who lived higher up upon the streams, just as if the great Mississippi, for example, passed through half a dozen states and the people down at New Orleans lived under a government which could control the navigation of the lower part of the Mississippi and so hamper the commerce of the states above them to the north who wished to pass to the sea by the course of the Mississippi.

There were abundant instances of that sort in Europe, and this treaty undertakes to internationalize all the great water highways of that continent, to see to it that their several portions are taken out of national control and put under international control, so that the stream that passes through one nation shall be just as free in all its length to the sea as if they owned the whole of it, and nobody shall have the right to put a restriction upon their passage to the sea. I mention this in order to illustrate the heart of this treaty, which is to cut out national privileges and give to every people the full right attaching to the territory in which they live.

Then the treaty did something more than that. You have heard of the Covenant of the League of Nations until, I dare say, you have supposed that is the only thing in the treaty. On the contrary, there is a document almost as extensive in the latter part of the treaty, which is nothing less than a great charter of liberty for the working men and women. One of the most striking and useful provisions of the Covenant of the League of Nations is that every member of the League undertakes to advance the humane conditions of labor for men, women, and children, to consider the interests of labor under its own jurisdiction, and to try to extend to every nation with which it has any dealings the standards of labor upon which it itself insists. So that America, which has by no means yet reached the standards in those matters which we must and shall reach, nevertheless is the most advanced nation in the world in respect of the conditions of labor, undertakes to bring all the influences it can legitimately bear upon every nation with which it has any dealings to see that labor there is put upon as good a footing as labor in America.

Perhaps some of you have not kept in mind the Seamen's Act,[2] which was passed at a recent session of Congress. Under the law before that Act, seamen could be bound to the service of their ship in such fashion that, when they came to the ports of the United States, if they tried to leave their ship, the government of the United States was bound to arrest them and send them back to their ships. And the Seamen's Act abrogates that law and practically makes it necessary for every ship that would take away from the United States the crew that it brings to it shall pay American wages to get it.

Before this treaty was entered into, the United States had en-

---

[2] About which, see the index references under "seamen's bill" in Vol. 39 of this series.

tered upon the business of trying to extend to laboring men elsewhere the advantages which laboring men in the United States
enjoyed, and, supplementing that promise in the Covenant of the
League, there is an elaborate arrangement for a continuing, that is
to say, a periodic international conference in the interest of labor.
It provides that that conference shall be called next month in the
City of Washington by the President of the United States, and the
President of the United States has already called it. We are waiting
to learn from the Senate of the United States whether we can attend it or not. We can at least sit and listen and wonder how long
we are going to be kept out of membership of this great humane
endeavor to see that working men and women and children everywhere in the world are regarded as human and taken care of as
they ought to be taken care of.

This treaty does not stop there. It attempts to coordinate all the
great humane endeavors of the world. It tries to bring under international cooperation every effort to check international crime. I
mean like that unspeakable traffic in women, like that almost
equally unspeakable traffic in children. It undertakes to control the
dealing in deadly drugs like opium. It organizes a new method of
cooperation among all the great Red Cross societies of the world. I
tell you, my fellow citizens, that the simple red cross has come to
mean to the world more than it ever meant before. Everywhere—
in the remotest recesses of the world—there are people who wear
that symbol. And every time I look at it, I feel like taking off my
hat, as if I had seen a symbol of the world's heart.

So that this treaty is nothing else than an organization of liberty
and mercy for the world. I wish you would get a copy of it and read
it. A good deal of it is technical, and you could skip that part, but
read all of it that you do not need an expert to advise you with
regard to the meaning of. The economic and financial clauses,
which particularly affect the settlements with Germany, are, I dare
say, almost unintelligible to most people. But you do not have to
understand them; they are going to be worked out by experts. The
rest of it is going to be worked out by the experience of free self-
governed peoples.

One of the interesting provisions of the Covenant of the League
of Nations is that no nation can be a member of that League which
is not a self-governing nation. No autocratic government can come
into its membership, no government which is not controlled by the
will and vote of its people. So that it is a league of free, independent
peoples all over the world. And when that great arrangement is
consummated, there is not going to be a ruler in the world that
does not take his advice from his people.

Germany for the present is excluded, but she is excluded only in order that she may undergo a period of probation, during which she shall prove two things—first, that she has really changed her constitution permanently, and, secondly, that she intends to administer that constitution in the spirit of its terms.

You read in the newspapers that there are intrigues going on in Germany for the restoration of something like the old government, perhaps for the restoration of the throne and placing upon it some member of the family of Hohenzollern. Very well, if that should be accomplished, Germany is forever excluded from the League of Nations. It is not our business to say to the German people what sort of government they shall have; it is our fundamental principle that that is their business and not ours. But it is our business to say who we will keep company with, and if Germany wishes to live in respectable society she will never have another Hohenzollern.

The other day, you will notice, Hungary for a little while put one of the Austrian princes upon her throne, and the peace conference, still sitting in Paris, sent word that they could not deal with a government which had one of the Hapsburgs at its head. The Hapsburgs and the Hohenzollerns are permanently out of business. I dare say that they personally, from what I can learn, feel antiquated and out of date. But they are out of date because, my fellow citizens, this treaty, or, rather, this great war, with its triumphant issue, characterized a new day in the history of the world.

There can no more be any such attempts as Germany made if the great leading free people of the world lends its countenance and leadership to the enterprise.

I say if, but it is a mere rhetorical if. There is not the least danger that Americans, after a treaty has been drawn up exactly along the specifications supplied by America, will desert its associates. We are a people that redeem its honor. We are not, and never will be quitters.

You notice that one of the grounds of anxiety of a small, small group of our fellow citizens is whether they get out of the League if they ever get in. So they want to have the key put in their pockets. They want to be assigned a seat right by the door. They want to sit on the edge of their chairs and say, "If anything happens in this meeting I am in the least sensitive about, I leave." That, my fellow citizens, is not the spirit of America. What is going to happen is this. We are not going to sit by the door. We are going to sit in the high seats, and if the present attitude of the peoples of the world towards America is any index of what it will continue to be, the counsels of the United States will be the prevailing counsels of the League. If we should humbly at the outset take a seat by the door, we would be invited to go up and take the chair. I, for one, do not want to be put in the attitude of children who, when the game goes against them, won't play, because I have such an unbounded confidence in the rectitude of the purpose of the United States that I am not afraid she will ever be caught proposing something which the other nations will defeat. She did not propose anything in Paris which the other nations defeated. The only obstacles, the only insuperable obstacles, met there were obstacles which were contained in treaties of which she had had no notice, in secret treaties which certain great nations were bound in honor to respect. And the Covenant of the League of Nations abolishes secret treaties.

From this time forth, all the world is going to know what all the agreements between nations are. It is going to know, not their general character merely, but their exact language and contents, because the provision of the League is that no treaty shall be valid which is not registered with the General Secretary of the League, and the General Secretary of the League is instructed to publish it in all its terms at the earliest possible moment. So that just as you go to the county courthouse and see all the mortgages on all the real estate in your county, you can go to the general secretariat of the League of Nations and find all the mortgages on all the nations. This treaty, in short, is a great clearance. It is very little short of a canceling of the past and an insurance of the future.

Men have asked me, "Do you think that the League of Nations is an absolute guarantee against war?" Of course it is not; no human arrangement can give you an absolute guarantee against human passions. But I answer that question with another: "If you thought you had 30 per cent insurance against war, wouldn't you take it? If you thought you had even 10 per cent insurance against war, wouldn't you think it better than nothing? Whereas, in my judgment, this is 98 per cent insurance.

Because the only thing that a wrong cause cannot stand is exposure. If you think you have a friend who is a fool, encourage him to hire a hall. And the particular things that this treaty provides in the Covenant of the League of Nations is that every cause shall be deliberately exposed to the judgment of mankind. It substitutes what the whole world has been longing for, namely, arbitration and discussion for war. In other words, all the great fighting nations of the world—for Germany at the time being, at any rate, is not a great fighting nation—it is a promise by all of the great fighting nations of the world to lay their case, whatever it may be, before the whole jury of humanity. If there had been any arrangement comparable with this in 1914, the calamitous war through which we were just passed would have been inconceivable.

Look what happened. An Austrian Crown Prince was assassi-

nated inside the Austrian dominions, in Bosnia, which was under
the empire of Austria-Hungary, though it didn't belong to it, and it
had no business to have it. And, because it was suspected that the
assassination was connected with certain groups of agitators and
certain revolutionary societies in Serbia, war was made on Serbia,
because the Austrian Crown Prince was assassinated in Austria! It
was just as if some great personage were to be assassinated, let us
say, in Great Britain, and because that individual was found to
have certain society connections—I mean certain connections with
a society that had an active membership in the United States—
Great Britain should declare war on the United States. That is a
violently improbable supposition, but I am merely using it as an
illustration.

Every foreign office in Europe, when it got sudden news of what
was afoot, sent messages to its representative in Berlin asking the
German government to hold an international conference to see if
the matter could not be adjusted, and the German government
would not wait twenty-four hours. Under the treaty of the League
of Nations, every fighting nation is bound to wait at least nine
months, and to lay all the facts pertaining to the case before the
whole world.

There is nothing so overpowering and irresistible, my fellow citizens, as the opinion of mankind. When this great republic was set
up, one of the most interesting and, I think, in one way, one of the
most moving sentences in the great Declaration of Independence,
is one of the opening sentences in which it is said that, out of respect to the opinion of mankind, the causes which have led the
people of the American colonies to declare their independence are
here set forth. America was the first country in the world which
laid before all mankind the reason why it went to war. And this
treaty is the exaltation and permanent establishment of the American principle of warfare and of right.

Why, therefore, do we hesitate to redeem the destiny of America? Why do we hesitate to support the most American thing that
has ever been attempted? Why do we debate details when the
heart of the thing is sound? And the beauty of it, my fellow citizens, is that the heart of America is sound.

We sent our boys across the sea to beat Germany, but that was
only the beginning. We sent them across the sea to assure the
world that nothing such as Germany attempted should ever happen again. That is the halo that is going to be about the brows of
those fine boys that have come back from overseas. That is the
light that is going to rest upon the graves overseas of the boys we
could not bring back. That is the glory that is going to attach to the

In St. Paul, Minnesota

En route to the Theater in Bismarck, North Dakota

At the Tacoma Stadium

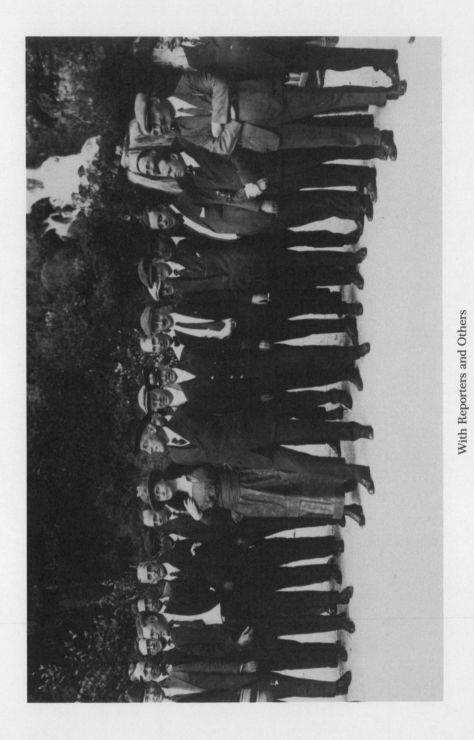

With Reporters and Others

On Parade in San Francisco

In the Greek Theater at Berkeley

At a Reception in San Diego

In Union Station on His Return to Washington

memories of that great American army, that had made the conquest of the armies of Germany, not only, but made conquest of peace for the world—greater armies than sought the Holy Grail, greater armies than sought to redeem the Holy Sepulchre, greater than fought under that visionary and wonderful girl, Joan of Arc, greater armies than sought to redeem the Holy Sepulcher, greater redeem us from the unjust rule of Britain, greater even than the armies of our Civil War which saved the Union, will be this noble army of Americans who saved the world!

Printed in the *Oakland Tribune*, Sept. 19, 1919.

From Newton Diehl Baker, with Enclosure

My dear Mr. President: Washington. September 18, 1919.

I beg leave to hand you for your files, a letter from General McGlachlin,[1] Commanding General of the First Division, to whom I presented your telegram of welcome and congratulation.[2] This letter, of course, will need no acknowledgment from you as it will not come into your hands until after the present First Division has been demobilized. I have taken the liberty of thanking General McGlachlin by letter for his message of appreciation to you, explaining your absence and telling him of the formal transmission of the message to you.

Respectfully yours, Newton D Baker

TLS (WP, DLC).
[1] That is, Edward Fenton McGlachlin, Jr.
[2] WW to NDB, Sept. 14, 1919.

ENCLOSURE

Edward Fenton McGlachlin, Jr., to Peyton Conway March

Washington, D. C. 16 September 1919.

From: Commanding General, 1st Division.
To: The Chief of Staff, U. S. Army.
Subject: Telegram from the President.

1. The rank and file of the First Division appreciate with very great pride the telegram of welcome and commendation from The President received by me at the hands of the Secretary of War on the afternoon of September fifteenth. It has been published in a General Order of the Division, which will be read to each of its

units at the points of assembly for the review in Washington and a copy will be presented to each officer and enlisted man.

2. Because I assumed command of the First Division after the Armistice and am about to leave it for other duty, I may be permitted to speak of it perhaps more freely than otherwise would appear proper.

3. Under Sibert in its period of organization and training, under Bullard, Summerall and Parker[1] in its defensive and offensive operations, the First Division established an unsurpassed reputation throughout the American Expeditionary Forces for reaching always its objectives at the prescribed hour, for holding every foot of ground that it had gained. From bottom to top it was moved by a spirit of unflinching determination to accomplish the missions assigned to it, by devotion to the beloved Country whence it came and by unswerving loyalty to the President, to the Commander in Chief and to their subordinate and its superior commanders. Its reputation was evidenced by the testimony of its brothers in arms of all other divisions and services and it was often praised in orders by its superior commanders, French and American.

4. During its march through Germany and its occupation of German territory among a hostile population it has been just, severe and efficient. Its fame has been untarnished by loss of morale or by indiscipline or by diminution of interest in its duties. I believe it to be today the best fighting division in the world, faithful to the gallant deeds of its dead, true to American ideals and the example of its leaders, confident in its own power, respectful of the high worthiness of other divisions. A particular characteristic of the Division is the mutual trust in which the infantry, artillery, engineers, signal, machine gun, medical and train units and the staff hold each other.

5. The personnel of the First Division will in a few days be scattered to all the States and possessions. It feels that the President's cordially welcoming words do it a high honor peculiarly gratifying at this time of the last appearance of its veterans in the organization of the Division as a whole.

6. The First Division asks that its gratitude for his thoughtfulness be communicated by the Secretary of War to the President with assurance that its personnel will continue their endeavor in or out of the service, to conform to the highest principles of American citizenship.   E F McGlachlin Jr

TS MS (WP, DLC).
    [1] Maj. Gen. William Luther Sibert, commander of the First Division, June-December 1917, at this time director of the Chemical Warfare Service, U.S.A.; Maj. Gen. Robert Lee Bullard, commander of the First Division, Dec. 14, 1917-July 14, 1918, most re-

cently commander of the Second Army; Maj. Gen. Charles Pelot Summerall, commander of the First Division, July 17-Oct. 11, 1918, most recently a member of the Inter-Allied Military Commission at Fiume; and Brig. Gen. Frank Parker, commander of the First Division, Oct. 17-Nov. 19, 1918.

From Vance Criswell McCormick

The White House, Washington, D. C. Sept. 18, 1919

RUSH. Most Confidential. For the President. Have been informed that semi-officially announced[1] McCumber, Kellogg, and Lenroot have prepared the following reservation, which Senator Lodge, I understand, accepts, and has agreed to secure the support of other Republican Senators. Reservation is as follows:

"The United States assumes no obligation under the provisions of Article X, to preserve the territorial integrity or political independence of any other nation or to interfere in controversies between other nations, members of the League or not, or to employ the military and naval forces of the United States under any article of the treaty for any purpose, unless such obligation shall in any particular case be assumed by Act or Joint Resolution of the Congress of the United States, which, under the Constitution, has sole jurisdiction to employ the military and naval forces, and no mandate shall be accepted by the United States under Article 22 (?), Part I, of the treaty of peace with Germany, except by the Act or Joint Resolution of the Congress of the United States."

Have also received confidentially the comments of Taft upon the above: "First, Is the statement true? Second, Do the words 'under the provisions of Article X' limit the words 'interfere in controversies between other nations.' If they do not, then the substitute is as bad as the original[2] in destroying the obligation for a boycott under Article 16 and Article 17. If the order could be changed so as to transpose and insert the following words 'under any article of the treaty for any purpose' after the word 'or' and before the words 'to employ,' the meaning would be clearer and confine the first two limitations to Article X. It will be vastly better to strike out now altogether the clause 'or to interfere in controversies between, etc.' The evident purpose of Lodge is to [destroy our duty] under Article 16 to aid in a universal boycott. I sincerely hope that McCumber and his associates will not consent thus to weaken the treaty."

This action indicates the Republican Senators are getting together. My informant advises me that the reservation is of such confidential nature that it has not yet been shown to Senator Hitchcock. Felt it important that you have this confidential information.   Vance C. McCormick.

T telegram (WP, DLC).

[1] "semi-officially announced" not in the copy of this telegram retained at the White House: V. C. McCormick to WW, Sept. 18, 1919, T telegram (EBR, RG 130, White House Staff Files, 1900-1935, DNA). The addition in square brackets below from the retained copy.

[2] For the text of which, see R. Forster, to JPT, Sept. 5, 1919, n. 3.

From William Phillips

Washington, D. C., Sept. 18, 1919

Following telegram has been received from Mr. Polk relating to the Italian situation, and is forwarded for your information:

"4247, Sept. 17, 11 P.M. Confidential. For the President and Secretary of State. In connection with the Italian matter, as I telegraphed you, Lloyd George told me [Friday][1] that he was in favor of giving Fiume to the Italians, stating reasons.[2] On Monday, at the meeting of the Five he repeated the statement, and he and Clemenceau said that they would send a message to the President, urging him, for political and other reasons, to consent to giving the town of Fiume to Italy. He said that they would provide that the port, docks, and railroad should be excepted and put under the control of the League of Nations, and the town neutralized. I at once told them I was sure this would not be satisfactory to you, and further, that there was already a plan before you, awaiting your decision. I refer to my 4143, Sept. 14, 10 P.M.[3] Lloyd George immediately said that they should await your decision, and then take up the question with you. Your telegram, 3123, Sept. 14, 8 P.M. [A.M.],[4] had [then] arrived that afternoon, but in view of the fact that Tittoni was trying to change the terms, I decided not to tell him of your answer and your concession as to Albania, but did tell him that I felt that if he would at once accept the modified plan, approved by your 3123, it might be possible for us to overcome your objection to giving the [an] Italian mandate for Albania. He frankly was very much distressed and told me he could not accept the modified plan, and begged me to send a personal appeal from him to you, urging the acceptance of Fiume as an Italian city, neutralized and with guarantees as to protection for the port, the railroads, and docks. I told him that was quite useless, but of course if he wished to send you a personal message, I could not decline to forward it.

I feel genuinely sorry for Tittoni, as Lloyd George and Clemenceau [have] upset him by their favorable attitude and, further than that, the acceptance at this moment of any plan which would deprive Italy of Fiume would be political suicide for him, in view of the occupation of Fiume by D'Annunzio.[5] When I said that a com-

munication to you meant further delay, he seemed to be rather relieved, and I feel that he would prefer not to have the matter
pressed at this moment, unless he can get some Italian sovereignty
of the town of Fiume.

In regard to the D'Annunzio movement, we have taken the position here that this is an Italian mutiny, and it is their obligation
to put it down promptly and firmly. Tittoni is anxious to stick to
this policy, and promises to push it vigorously. The British and
French troops have been withdrawn from Fiume, and it is agreed
for the moment that international ships shall be used only for the
purpose of [the] blockade. It was feared that the use of British,
French and American forces might cause irritation in Italy and encourage the Jugo-Slavs to get into action. We would [could] have a
war between those countries.

We are all handicapped in handling the Dalmatian question now,
as Johnson has left and we have no experts. I have just received
[today] the following personal appeal to the President from Tittoni,
who left for Italy last night. He asked me to say that in addition to
the arguments he advanced, any concession at this time which he
could announce to this Parliament would mean the ratification of
the treaty by Italy at once:

"In his replies, President Wilson after stating that of the two solutions proposed for Fiume, he prefers the one which would make
Fiume a free city within the free state, adds that he wishes to have
a plebiscite within five years. Much to my regret, I would be quite
unable to accept this addition to the primitive proposal, because
the great majority of the population of the suggested free state
would be Slav and five years of intense and pitiless work of dena-
tionalization would certainly be undertaken against the Italian
population of the city of Fiume (corpus separatum). The city (corpus separatum) is Italian by an immense majority. Its annexation
to Italy is not in the least a question of territorial aggrandizement
or of politics. To have or not to have a city of fifty thousand inhabitants is immaterial to Italy. For the Italian people, who have always been idealists, it is a question of sentiment, and this sentiment is deeply rooted in all classes of the population, so much so
that a favorable solution of this question could induce the Italians
to bear the sacrifices of other aspirations which is requested of
them. In any other case it would be difficult, not to say impossible,
to induce the Italian nation to bear with resignation the renounce-
ment of the advantages she expected of the war. I am animated by
the most conciliating spirit, and have come to Paris with the most
sincere wish of reaching an agreement with President Wilson. It
was a great disappointment to me to have just missed meeting

him, and to have been unable to explain to him that in order to make the much reduced peace conditions suggested for Italy acceptable to the Italian people, it was necessary to appease at least their sentiment. I beg President Wilson to consider that what I ask is a very small matter indeed. The free zone which was to constitute the free state would be entirely assigned to the Jugoslavs, the port and the railway would be free and administered by the League of Nations, which would appoint its own special commissioner. The Italian Government would have no interference whatever in these matters, and Italy would only have the sovereignty of the mere city of Fiume (corpus separatum), that is to say, a satisfaction of a purely moral character."   William Phillips

T telegram (WP, DLC).
    ¹ Additions and corrections from the telegram sent: W. Phillips to WW, Sept. 18, 1919, T telegram (SDR, RG 59, 763.72119/6799, DNA).
    ² "stating reasons" not in telegram sent.
    ³ See WP to WW, Sept. 11, 1919.
    ⁴ See JPT to WP, Sept. 13, 1919, n. 2.
    ⁵ See WP to WW, Sept. 15, 1919 (second telegram of that date), n. 2.

From William Phillips, with Enclosures

Dear Mr. President: Washington September 18, 1919.

The French Ambassador has handed me the enclosed personal message from Clemenceau to you, with the request that it be forwarded to you as an urgent matter.

I took the liberty, however, before transmitting Clemenceau's note to communicate it to the Shipping Board and attach hereto Judge Payne's reply, which is addressed to you.

Mr. Jusserand, in handing me this message, presented a very strong argument urging favorable consideration and stated that failure now to carry out Mr. Hurley's engagement with the French Government would never be understood by the Government or the people since it had been definitely announced that the matter was an accomplished fact.

I am venturing to forward the communications to you in case you feel that you wish to send an answer to Clemenceau before your return to Washington.

          Faithfully yours,   William Phillips

TLS (WP, DLC).

From Georges Clemenceau

"Paris, September 5th, 1919.

"The President of the Shipping Board has just informed the French Services in New York that he does not intend to put in force the engagement taken by his predecessor, Mr. Hurley, to hand over to France the twenty-six steel ships ordered from American shipyards by the French Government in 1917, and soon after commandeered by the Federal Government.

"The engagement taken by Mr. Hurley was unconditional. It was only, moreover, the confirmation of promises given by him in Washington and in Paris. We were only awaiting, before taking possession of the ships, the final settlement of accounts which, for two months, the Shipping Board had been promising us from week to week.

"The attitude taken by Mr. Payne is therefore a complete surprise for us. It also puts us in such a grave and awkward position that I feel it my duty to address you in view of obtaining the fulfilment of Mr. Hurley's promises.

"Not only are these ships indispensable to us in the present terrible situation of our merchant marine, but besides, on the strength of Mr. Hurley's promises, we have officially announced the agreement as concluded and asked Parliament for the necessary appropriations.

"If, under these circumstances, the ships were not handed over to us, we would find ourselves in a grave situation as regards transportation. I would also fear very unfavorable impression on the mind of the Chambers and of the Public.

"The only argument given by Mr. Payne is that, were the Shipping Board to give us back these ships, they would be obliged to do the same in favor of England for the ships ordered in the United States by the British Government or shipowners.

"This argument seems to me inadmissible. For, on the one side, Mr. Hurley, who knew the situation well, had not been stopped by that objection; on another side, only an unimportant tonnage is involved (198.000 tons) while the English orders reach one million and a half tons; then, England now has a merchant fleet of twenty million tons deadweight, whereas, France, on the contrary, has only two million, and mostly old ships.

"For these reasons, I make a personal and pressing appeal to your spirit of justice so that, in the present case when we have given full confidence to American promises, the solution announced by Mr. Hurley take place in the briefest possible delay. I have faith in your decision and take this opportunity of renewing the expression of my sentiments of sincere friendship."

(Signed) Clemenceau

T MS (WP, DLC).

ENCLOSURE II

From John Barton Payne

My dear Mr. President: [Washington] September 12, 1919.

Apropos of the telegram of Premier Clemenceau:

There is no record in this office, nor is there any one here who has knowledge, of such an agreement as he mentions.

In the case of Great Britain we had insisted on settling in money for ships requisitioned in a similar way.

The twenty-six ships requisitioned from France had been barely started as only four keels were laid. In addition to the difficulty of treating France differently from Great Britain, there are definite physical obstacles in the way of returning the particular ships requisitioned from France. These ships were not special, but were of the same class and type which we were building for ourselves.

My position has been that we reach an agreement as to the amount due and settle in ships at the present schedule of prices. If you desire, and they are prepared to pay, we could sell them enough ships so that they will have twenty-six, class for class, and ton for ton, and of type according to those requisitioned. It is my belief that on this plan the cost will be less to them than if we should return the particular ships requisitioned and require them to pay the cost of completing same.

I am afraid the real difficulty is that the French think that our prices are too high and they believe that by insisting on the return of the requisitioned ships they would get them at substantially the same price as was mentioned in the original contract. They should not have this belief because we have settled with them for four requisitioned ships and they have paid the cost.

They submitted a letter since the receipt of Premier Clemenceau's telegram making alternative suggestions, stating that the price they were willing to pay was $150 per ton, whereas our price for the same ship is $210, which as near as we can estimate is approximately our cost.

My belief, therefore, is that the difference between us is not so much a question of requisitioned ships as the question of cost.

Please indicate what course you desire taken.

Yours very truly,   John Barton Payne

TCL (WP, DLC).

William Phillips to Joseph Patrick Tumulty

Washington, September 18, 1919.

Your telegram September 17.[1]

I appreciate how you are fixed. There are, however, certain urgent matters in connection with the mission in Paris which I would not be justified in sending plain nor would it be proper for me to hold them until the President's return. I am keeping back everything that it is not essential to forward.

William Phillips

TS telegram (SDR, RG 59, 763.72119/6830b, DNA).
[1] It is missing.

From the Diary of Dr. Grayson

Friday, September 19, 1919

The train ran south on the Santa Fe during the morning, and stops were made at Oxnard and one or two other points, where the President made a rear-platform appearance and shook hands with the crowd that had gathered there. San Diego was reached at 3:30 o'clock in the afternoon, and the President was driven directly to the hotel, where he was given a public reception. He then proceeded to the big stadium, which had been transformed into an auditorium for the meeting. The first real test of the "voice phone," an electrical device designed to spread the human voice broadcast, was made at the stadium here. Thirty thousand people were gathered in the great bowl to hear the President. A speakers' stand had been erected at one end and a room, glass-enclosed, constructed there. This room was about twenty feet square with the front entirely open. A table had been erected in front of the speakers' stand and megaphones installed, to which were affixed electrical wires that carried the voice to resonators at all points in the big stand outside. The President did not relish this experience. He said afterwards that it was the most difficult speech he had ever tried to deliver in his life. He could not be free and natural because it was necessary that he remain at one spot talking so that his voice carried directly into the megaphones in front of him. However, the audience heard every word that he said with the exception of the one spot directly opposite him at the far end of the stadium. Here the electrical connection apparently did not overcome the distance and a couple of thousand people were deeply disappointed by failing to hear the address.

The audience was extremely sympathetic, and the President got them right from the start when he declared that he had not come to participate in any controversy with any Senator or anyone else, but that he was in California to tell the people of the State just what the Treaty of Versailles actually meant. He spoke for an hour and ten minutes, and then returned to the hotel for a brief rest prior to a dinner that had been arranged in his honor by the Mayor of the City.[1] At the dinner the President was introduced by former Secretary of the Treasury Lyman J. Gage,[2] a staunch life-long Republican. Former Secretary Gage electrified the entire assembly when he told it that he believed if William McKinley still were alive he would endorse everything that the President had done and would say to him: "God bless you, Woodrow Wilson." This reference very deeply touched the President, and he in his address pointed out that President McKinley had been one of the earliest advocates of the principle of a League of Nations and of arbitration to prevent war. The President paid high tribute to McKinley's statesmanship and read extracts from his addresses which showed that Mr. McKinley had always been an ardent advocate of arbitration to settle all international disputes.

San Diego was left at 10:00 o'clock, and the train was run out to a small siding directly on the ocean, where the President was allowed a night of uninterrupted rest. Originally, it had been intended that he should go to Santa Catalina Island and spend the night there, but I had vetoed this because he would have to get up so very early in the morning, and the dampness of the air might not do his throat any too much good. It developed afterwards that this was a very wise precaution, as the entire island was shrouded in a heavy fog.

[1] Louis J. Wilde.
[2] Lyman Judson Gage, banker of Chicago and New York, United States Secretary of the Treasury, 1897-1902, now living in retirement in San Diego. His remarks at the dinner meeting on September 19 were quoted at some length by Louis Seibold in the New York *World*, Sept. 21, 1919.

From Joseph Patrick Tumulty

Dear Governor: [San Diego] 19 September 1919.

I think it would be well to use these excerpts from a speech by Senator Lodge, and an interview by Mr. Roosevelt. You could use them in connection with the statement you make in your speeches that the League of Nations is not a Wilsonian theory by any means. Using these excerpts in this territory would embarrass Johnson and his crowd very much.   Sincerely yours,   Tumulty

TLS (WP, DLC).

An Address in the San Diego Stadium

[[September 19, 1919]]

Mr. Mayor, my fellow countrymen: As you know, I have come from Washington on a very serious errand, indeed, and I need not tell you with what a thrill the sight of this great body of my fellow citizens fills my heart, because I believe that one of the most important verdicts of history is now to be rendered by the great people of the United States. I believe that this is a choice from which we cannot turn back. Whether it be a choice of honor or dishonor, it will be a final choice which we will make in this court of our history.

One of the unexpected things I have found on my journey is that the people of the United States have not been informed as to the real character and scope and contents of the great treaty of peace with Germany. Whether by omission or by intention, they have been directed in all of the speeches that I have read to certain points of the treaty which are incidental, and not central. Their vision has been drawn away from the real meaning of this great human document.

For that, my fellow citizens, is just what it is. It not only concludes a peace with Germany and imposes upon Germany the proper penalties for the outrages she attempted upon mankind, but it also concludes the peace in the spirit in which the war was undertaken by the nations opposed to Germany. That challenge of war was accepted by them, not with the purpose of crushing the German people, but for the purpose of putting an end, once and for all, to such plots against the free nations of the world as had been conceived in Wilhelmstrasse, in Berlin, unknown to the people of Germany, not by their advice, but by little groups of men who had the military power to carry out private ambition.

We went into this war not only to see that power of that sort never threatened the world again, but we went into it for even larger purposes than that.

Other autocratic powers may spring up, but there is only one soil in which they can spring up—that is the wrongs done to free peoples of the world. And the heart and center of this treaty is that it sets at liberty people all over Europe and in Asia who have hitherto been enslaved by powers which were not their rightful sovereigns and masters.

So long as wrongs like that exist in the world, you cannot bring permanent peace to the world. I would go further than that. So long as wrongs of that sort exist, you ought not to bring permanent peace to the world, because those wrongs ought to be righted, and enslaved peoples ought to be freed to right them.

For my part, I will not take any part in composing difficulties that ought not to be composed, and a difficulty between an enslaved people and its autocratic rulers ought not to be composed.

We in America have stood from the day of our birth for the emancipation of people throughout the world who were living unwillingly under governments which were not of their choice. The thing that we have held more sacred than any other is that all just government rests upon the consent of the governed. All over the world that principle has been disregarded by the strong, and only the weak have suffered.

The heart and center of this treaty is the principle adopted, not only in this treaty, but put into effect in the treaty also with Austria, in the treaty with Hungary, in the treaty with Bulgaria, in the treaty with Turkey—that every great territory in the world belongs to the people who are living on it, (applause) and that it is not the privilege of any authority anywhere—certainly not the privilege of the peace conference at Paris—to impose upon those people any government which they accept unwillingly and not of their own choice.

So that nations that never before saw the gleam of hope have been liberated by this great document. Pitiable Poland, divided up as spoil among half a dozen nations, is by this document united and set free. And similarly, in the treaty with Austria, the Austrian power is taken off of every people over whom they have no right to reign. You know that great portions of Bosnia and Herzegovina, which lay between Austria and the Balkan Peninsula, were unjustly under the power of the Austro-Hungarian Empire, and it was in a city of Bosnia that the Crown Prince of Austria was assassinated—Bosnia, which was under the power of Austria. Though it was part of Austrian territory, Austria had the audacity to hold Serbia, an outside neighbor, responsible for the act of the assassin.

And this war was started because an Austrian prince was assassinated in Austrian territory, and the Austrian government chose to believe that certain societies with which it connected the assassin, societies active in Serbia, had planned and executed the assassination.

And so the world was deluged in blood, and 7,400,000 men lie dead, not to speak of the pitiable wounded, not to speak of the blind, not to speak of those with distracted brain, not to speak of all the pitiful, shattered nerves of millions of men all over the world—because of an insurgent feeling in a great population which was ruled over by rulers not of their own choice. And the peace conference at Paris knew that it would not go to the root of this business unless it destroyed power of that kind. This treaty sets those great people free. (applause)

But it does not stop with that. In the heart of the treaty, you will find a new charter for those who labor—men, women, and children all over the world. The heart of the world is depressed, my fellow citizens, the heart of the world is uneasy. The heart of the world is a little despairful of its future, because the economic arrangements of the world have not been just, and the people having unjust conditions imposed upon them are, of course, not content to live under them. When the whole world is at unrest, you may be sure that there is some real cause for the unrest. It is not whimsical. Men do not disturb the foundation of their lives just to satisfy a sudden impulse.

All these troubles, whatever shape they take, whether the action taken is just or unjust, have their root in age-long wrongs, which ought to be, must be, and will be righted. (applause)

And this great treaty makes a beginning in that great enterprise of humanity. For it provides an arrangement for recurrent and periodic international conferences, the main and sole object of which will be to improve the conditions of labor, safeguard the lives and the health of women and children who work and whose lives would otherwise be impaired or whose health rendered subject to all the inroads of disease.

So that the heart of humanity beats in this document. It is not a statesman's arrangement. It is a liberation of the peoples and the human forces of the world, and yet I never hear the slightest hint of any of these great features in the speeches of the gentlemen who are opposing this treaty. They never tell you what is really in this treaty. If they did, your enthusiasm would sweep them off their feet. If they did, they would know it was an audacity, which they had better not risk, to impair the peace and humane conditions of mankind.

And at the front of the treaty, at the very front of and part of the treaty, is the part which is most criticized, namely, the great Covenant for a League of Nations. This treaty could not be executed without such a powerful instrumentality. Unless all the right-thinking nations of the world are going to concert their purposes and their power, this treaty is not worth the paper it is written on, because it is a treaty where peace rests upon the right of the weak, and only the power of the strong can maintain the right of the weak.

If we as a nation indeed mean what we have always said—that we are the champions of human right—now is the time when we shall be brought to the test, the acid test, as to whether we mean what we said or not. I am not saying that because I have the least doubt as to the verdict. I am just as sure of it as if it had been rendered already. I know this great people among whom I was born and brought up and whom I have had the signal honor to serve, whose mouthpiece it has been my privilege to be on both sides of the sea. I know it is your consciousness that it is the duty of America which will be assumed and performed.

And you have been allowed to believe that the Covenant of the League of Nations is in some sense a private invention. It is not always said by whom, and I need not mention who is suspected. It is supposed that, out of some sort of personal ambition or party intention, some advantage of distinction and authorship, an origination is sought. Why, my fellow countrymen, I wish that I could claim the great distinction of having invented this great idea. But it is a great idea which has been growing in the minds of all generous men for several generations. Several generations? Why, it has been the dream of the friends of humanity through all the ages. And, now for the first time, a great body of practical statesmen, immersed in the business of guiding nations, gets together and realizes the dream of honest men.

I wish that I could claim some originative part in so great an enterprise, but I cannot. I was the spokesman in this matter, so far as I was influential at all, of all sorts and kinds of Americans and of all parties and factions in America. I would be ashamed, my fellow countrymen, if I treated a matter of this sort with a single thought of so small a matter as the national elections of 1920. If anybody discusses this question on the basis of party advantage, I repudiate him as a fellow American. (applause) And in order to validate what I have said, I want to make one or two quotations from representatives of a party to which I do not belong. The first I shall make from a man who has for a long time been a member of the United States Senate. In May 1916, just about two years after the Great War began, this Senator, at a banquet at which I was myself present,[1] uttered the following:

"I know of no one that would know better than one who has served long in the Senate, which is charged with the great responsibility of the ratification and confirmation of treaties, no one, I think, can feel more deeply than I do the difficulties which confront us in the work which this league—that great association extending throughout the country known as the League to Enforce Peace—which this league undertakes, but the difficulties cannot be overcome unless we try to overcome them. I believe it can be done. Probably it will be impossible to stop all wars, but it certainly will be possible to stop some wars, and thus diminish their number. The way in which this problem is to be worked out must be left to this league and to those who are giving this great question the study which it deserves, and which some gentlemen have not given. I know the obstacles. I know how squarely we shall be met with the statement this is a dangerous question which you are putting into this agreement, that no nation can submit to the judgment of other nations, and we must be careful at the beginning not to attempt too much. I know the difficulties which arise when we speak of anything which seems to involve an alliance, but I do not believe that when Washington warned us against entangling alliances he meant for one moment that we should not join with the other civilized nations of the world if a method could be found to diminish war and encourage peace. (applause)

"It was a year ago, while delivering the Chancellor's address at Union College, I made an argument on this theory, that if we want to promote international peace at the close of the present terrible war, if we are to restore international law as it must be restored, that men find some way in which the united forces of the nations could be put behind the cause of peace and law. I said then that my hearers might think I was picturing a Utopia, but it is in the search for Utopias that great discoveries have been made. This league certainly has the highest of all ambitions for the benefit of humanity, and because the pathway is sown with difficulties is no reason that we should turn from it."

That quotation is from the Honorable Henry Cabot Lodge. An-

[1] The closing banquet of the first annual national meeting of the League to Enforce Peace, held at the Willard Hotel in Washington on May 27, 1916, at which both Wilson and Henry Cabot Lodge spoke. Wilson's address is printed at that date in Vol. 37. For a complete text of Lodge's speech, only part of which is quoted below, see *Enforced Peace: Proceedings of the First Annual National Assemblage of the League to Enforce Peace, Washington, May 26-27, 1916* (New York, [1916]), pp. 164-67.

other quotation from one of the most energetic, frank, and distinguished leaders of the Republican party, which was in an article
published in the *New York Times* in October 1914:

"The only permanent move for obtaining peace which has not
been suggested with any reasonable chance of obtaining its object
is by an agreement among the great powers, in which each should
pledge itself not only to abide by the decision of a common tribunal, but to back with force the decision of that common tribunal.
The great civilized nations of the world which do not possess force,
actually or immediately, potentially should combine by solemn
agreement in a great world league for peace and righteousness."

A very worthy utterance by Theodore Roosevelt.[2] (applause) I
am glad to align myself with such utterances as that. I subscribe
to every word of it. And here in concrete form is the fulfillment of
the plan which they advocate. We cannot in reason, we cannot as
lovers of liberty, we cannot as supporters of right turn away from
it.

And those who advise us to turn away from it, what are they
afraid of? In the first place, they are afraid that it impairs in some
way that long traditional policy of the United States which was embodied in the Monroe Doctrine. But how they can fear that I cannot conceive, for the document expressly says, in words which I
am now quoting, that nothing in this Covenant shall be held to
affect the validity of the Monroe Doctrine. (applause) The phrase
was inserted under my own eye—not the phrase, but the principle—at the suggestion of the foreign relations committees of both
houses of Congress. I think I am justified in dismissing all fear that
the Monroe Doctrine is in the least impaired.

And what is the Monroe Doctrine? It is that no outside power
shall attempt to impose its will in any form upon the western hemisphere, and if it does the United States, acting upon its own initiative and alone, if it chooses, can resist and will resist the attempt.
(applause) Could anything leave the United States freer as a champion of the independence of the western hemisphere than this
world acknowledgment of the validity and competency of the Monroe Doctrine? (applause)

But they are afraid that the League will in some way deal with
our domestic affairs. The Covenant expressly says it will have no
right to deal with the domestic affairs of any member of the
League, and I cannot imagine anything more definite and satisfactory than that. There is no ambiguity about any part of this Covenant, for the matter of that, but there is certainly no ambiguity

[2] In the *New York Times*, Oct. 18, 1914, Sect. 5, p. 1.

about the statement regarding domestic affairs. For it is provided that if any matter brought before the Council is found to be a matter which, under international law, lies within the exclusive jurisdiction of the state making the claim, that the Council shall dismiss consideration of it and shall not even make a report about it.

The subjects which are giving these gentlemen the most concern are agreed by all students of international law to be domestic questions; for example, immigration, naturalization, or the tariff—these are the subjects most frequently spoken of. No one of these can be dealt with by the League of Nations, so far as the sovereignty of the United States is concerned. We have a perfectly clear field there, as we have in regard to the Monroe Doctrine.

But it is feared that our delegates will be outvoted, because I am constantly hearing it said that the British Empire has six votes and we have one. I am perfectly content to have only one vote when the one counts six, (applause) and that is exactly the arrangement under the League. But let us examine that matter a little more particularly. Besides the vote of Great Britain herself, the other five votes are the votes of Canada, of South Africa, of Australia and New Zealand, and of India. We ourselves were champions and advocates of giving a vote to Panama, of giving a vote to Cuba—both of them under the direction and directorate of the United States. And if a vote was given to Panama and to Cuba, could it reasonably be denied to the great Dominion of Canada? Could it be denied to that republic in South Africa, that is now living under a nation which did, indeed, overcome it at one time, but which did not dare retain its government in its hands, but turned it over to the very men whom it had fought? Could it be denied to Australia, that independent republic in the Pacific, which has led the world in so many liberal reforms? Could we deny it to New Zealand? Could we deny it to the hundreds of millions who live in India?

But, having given the six votes, what are the facts? The League can take no active step without the unanimous vote of all the nations represented on the Council, added to a vote of the majority in the Assembly itself. These six votes are in the Assembly, not in the Council. The Assembly is not a voting body, except upon a limited number of questions. And whenever those questions are questions of action, the affirmative votes of every nation represented on the Council is needed, and the United States is represented on the Council.

So that the six votes that you hear about can do nothing without the consent of the United States. (applause) I mean nothing in the way of action. There are two matters in which the Assembly can act, but I do not think we will be jealous of it. A majority of the

Assembly can admit new members into the League. A majority of the Assembly can advise a member of the League to reconsider any treaty which, in the opinion of the Assembly of the League, is apt to conflict with the operations of the League itself. But that is advice. It can be disregarded. It has no validity and action in it, it has no compulsion and law in it.

So that, with the single exception of admitting new members to the League, there is no energy in the six votes which is not offset by the energy in the one vote of the United States. (applause) And I am more satisfied to be one and count six than to be six and count six. This thing that has been talked about is a delusion. The United States is not easily frightened, and I dare say it is less easily frightened by things that are not true.

It is also feared that causes in which we are interested will be defeated. Well, the United States is interested in a great many causes, for a very interesting and compelling reason—that the United States is made up out of all the civilized peoples of the world.

There is not a national cause, my fellow citizens, which has not quickened the heartbeat of men in America. There is not a national cause which men in America do not understand, because they come of the same people, they come of the same traditions, they recollect through long tradition the wrongs of their peoples, the hopes of their peoples, the passions of their people. And everywhere in America there are men to stand up and speak words of sympathy for great causes. And for the first time in the history of the world, the League of Nations presents a forum, a world forum, where any one of these ambitions or aspirations can be brought to the consideration of mankind. Never before has this been possible. Never before has there been a jury of mankind to which the nations could take their causes, whether they were weak or strong.

You have heard a great deal about Article X of the Covenant. Very well, after you have read it, please read Article XI. Article XI provides that it shall be the right of any member of the League, big or little, strong or weak, to call attention to anything, anywhere, which is likely to disturb the peace of the world or the good understanding between nations upon which the peace of the world depends. And when any of our kinsmen in America are done wrong by any foreign government, it is likely to disturb the good understanding between nations upon which the peace of the world rests. And any one of the causes represented in the hearts of the American people can be brought to the attention of the whole world.

And one of the most effective means of winning a good cause is to bring it before a great jury. A bad cause will fare ill, but a good cause is bound to be triumphant in such a forum. And until this, international law made it an unfriendly act for any nation to call attention to any matter which did not immediately affect its own fortunes and its own rights. I am amazed that they do not see the extraordinary change which this will bring in the transaction of human affairs. I am amazed that they do not see that now, for the first time, not selfish national policies, but the general judgment of the world as a right is going to determine the fortunes of the peoples, whether they be weak or whether they be strong. (applause)

I myself glory in the provisions of Article XI more than I glory in any other part of the Covenant, for it draws all men together in a single friendly court, where they may discuss their own affair and determine the issues of justice—just exactly what was desired in the hearts of the men from whom I have read extracts of opinion.

But what disturbs me, perhaps, and the only thing that disturbs me, my fellow countrymen, about the form which the opposition to the League is taking is this. Certain reservations, as they are called, are perhaps in effect—I am not going to offer an opinion as to whether that is the intention or not; I have no right to judge the intention of a man who has not stated what his intention is—but in effect some of these reservations amount to this—that the United States is unwilling to assume the same obligations under the Covenant of the League that are assumed by the other members of the League. The United States wants to disclaim any part in the responsibilities which the other members of the League are assuming. And I want to say with all the emphasis of which I am capable that that is unworthy of the honor of the United States. (applause)

The principle of justice, the principle of right, the principle of international amity is this—that there is not only an imaginary but a real equality of standing and right among all the civilized peoples of the world. I do not care to advocate the rights of a people if I must regard them as my inferior, if I must do so with condescension, if I must do so because I am strong and they are weak.

You know the men, and the women, too, I dare say, who are respectful only to those whom they regard as their social equals or their industrial equals and of whom they are more or less afraid, and who will not exercise the same amenities and the same consideration for those whom they deem beneath them. Such people do not belong to democratic society, for one thing, (applause) and, for another, their whole point of view is perverted. They are incapable of justice, because the foundation of justice is that the weakest has the same rights as the strongest.

I must admit, my fellow citizens, and you cannot deny—and I

admit it with a certain profound regret, not only, but with a touch of shame—that, while that is the theory of democratic institutions, it is not always the practice. The weak do not always fare as well as the strong, the poor do not always get the same advantage and justice that the rich get. But that is due to passions and imperfections of human nature. But the foundation of the law is—the glory of the law is—that the weakest is equal to the strongest in the matter of right and privilege. (applause) And the glory about which we are constantly though stumblingly and with mistakes striving to go forward is the glory of actual justice, on the basis of equality and right, and unless you are going to establish all nations upon the actual foundation of equality, unless the United States is going to assume the same responsibility, and just as much responsibility as the other nations, we ought not to permit the mockery of going into the arrangement at all.

I will not join in claiming under the name of justice an unjust position of privilege for the country which I love and honor. (applause) Neither am I afraid of responsibility. Neither will I scuttle. Neither will I be a little American. America, in her makeup, in her purposes, in her principles, is the biggest thing in the world, and she must measure up to the measure of the world. (applause)

Why, if we were to decline to go into this great humane arrangement, we would be declining the invitation which all the world extends to us to lead them in the enterprise of liberty and of justice. I, for one, will not decline that invitation. I, for one, believe more profoundly than in anything else human in the destiny of the United States. (applause) I believe that she has a superior energy in her which no other nation can contribute to the liberation of mankind. I know that the heart of America is stronger than her business calculations.

That is what the world found out when we went into the war. When we went into the war, there was not a nation in the world that did not believe we were more interested in making money out of it than in saving the cause of liberty. And when we went in, in those few months, the whole world stood at amaze. They now believe that America will stand by anybody that is fighting for justice and for right. (applause) And we shall not disappoint her.

The age is opening, my fellow citizens, upon a new era. We are substituting in this Covenant—and this is the main purpose of it—arbitration and discussion for war. Senator Lodge says if we can stop some war, it is worthwhile. If you want insurance against war, I take it you would rather have 10 per cent insurance than none; I take it you would be delighted with 50 per cent insurance; and here I verily believe is 98 per cent insurance against war. (applause) Because all the great fighting nations of the world, without exception—because for the time being Germany is not a great fighting nation—all the great fighting nations of the world solemnly covenant with one another that they will never go to war without first having either submitted the matter in dispute to arbitration and bound themselves to abide by the verdict, or, having submitted it to discussion by the Council of the League of Nations, in which case they will lay all the facts and documents before the League and, by publication, before the world, wait six months for the opinion of the Council, and if they are dissatisfied with that opinion—they are not bound by it—they will wait another three months before they go to war. There is a period of nine months of the process which is absolutely destructive of unrighteous causes—exposure to public opinion. (applause) When I find a man who in a public matter will not state his side of the case, and state it fully, I know that his side of the case is the losing side, that he dare not state it.

And at the heart of most of our industrial difficulties, my fellow citizens—and most of you are a witness to this—lies the unwillingness of men to get together and talk it over. Half of the temper which now exists between those who perform labor and those who direct labor is due to the fact that those who direct labor won't talk differences over with the men whom they employ. (applause) I am in every such instance convinced that they are wrong and dare not talk it over. (applause) Not only that, but every time the two sides do get together and talk it together, they come out of the conference in a different temper from that with which they went in. There is nothing that softens the attitude of men like really, frankly, laying their minds alongside each other and their characters alongside each other and making a fair and manly and open comparison. And that is what all the great fighting nations of the world agree to do with every matter of difference between them—that they will either put it before a jury by whom they are bound, or before a jury which will publish all the facts to mankind and express a frank opinion in regard to it.

And so you have here what the world must have—what America went into this war to obtain. You have here an estoppel of the brutal, sudden impulse of war. You have a restraint upon the passions of ambitious nations. You have here a safeguard of the liberty of weak nations, and the world is at last ready to stand up in council and discuss the fortunes of men and women and children everywhere.

Why, my fellow citizens, nothing brings a lump into my throat quicker on this journey that I am taking than to see the thronging children that are everywhere the first, just out of their curiosity and no doubt of glee, to crowd up to the train when it stops. Because I know, if by chance, we should not win this great fight for the League of Nations, it would be their death warrant.

They belong to the generation which would then have to fight the final war, and in that final war there would not be merely seven and a half million men slain. The very existence of civilization would be in the balance. And I, for one, dare not face the responsibility of defeating the very purpose for which we sent our gallant men overseas. Every mother knows that her pride in the son that she lost is due to the fact, not that he helped to beat Germany, but that he helped to save the world. And there was in that light in the eyes of the boys that went over there that light as of men who have caught the gleam of inspiration of a great cause. The armies of the United States seemed to those people on the other side of the sea like bodies of crusaders come out of a free nation to give freedom to their fellows, ready to sacrifice their lives for an idea, for an ideal, for the only thing that is worth living for—the spiritual purpose of redemption that rests in the hearts of mankind. (applause)[3]

Printed in the San Diego *Evening Tribune*, Sept. 20, 1919.
[3] There is a WWT outline of this speech in WP, DLC.

An After-Dinner Speech in San Diego

September 19, 1919.

Mr. Mayor, ladies, and gentlemen: I am sure I may take it for granted that I have Mrs. Wilson's permission to explain about the asparagus. You will be amused, perhaps, at the origin of her advising the honorable Mayor. When we went across the water as simple republicans, we were naturally not accustomed to entertaining royalty, and when we were in Rome we gave a dinner at the American embassy, which was American territory, of course, to the King and Queen of Italy. And, not knowing the order of procedure upon such occasions and being the host, I asked instructions from the American Minister there[1] as to when I was to propose the King's health, and he said "After the asparagus."

I watchfully waited for the appearance of the asparagus. The Ambassador had spoken without consulting Mrs. Page,[2] and we learned from Mrs. Page afterwards that she had intended to have

[1] That is, Ambassador Thomas Nelson Page. About this incident, which occurred at a luncheon, not a dinner, see the extract from the Diary of Dr. Grayson printed at Jan. 4, 1919, Vol. 53.
[2] Florence Lathrop Field (Mrs. Thomas Nelson) Page.

asparagus but could not get any, and therefore I was very much embarrassed and had to choose my own moment to get up and propose the health of the King. That is the reason we are always watching for the asparagus.

It is very agreeable to have been indirectly introduced by my friend, Mr. Gage, for whom I have so affectionate a regard. I know he will not mind my saying that I first met him when we were both "lame ducks." I had just come out of the hospital after an operation,[3] and he had one arm out of commission from neuritis. And we met sitting, rather helplessly and perhaps hopelessly, on one of the broad piazzas of one of the hotels at Palm Beach. Being fellow sufferers and comrades in misery, we were drawn toward each other and drawn into confidences which I greatly enjoyed, and which I now recall with peculiar pleasure in seeing Mr. Gage without his hand bound up and in the sort of health I would wish to see him in.

What he has said has reminded me of one of the thoughts which has been prominent in my mind of late. He has spoken of our dealings with the Philippine Islands. One of the perplexities under which we have suffered is that, although we are leading the Philippine Islands towards independence, we were in doubt of what would happen to them when they obtained their independence. Before this conference at Paris, the only thing that could be suggested was that we should get a common guarantee from all the nations of the world that the Philippines should be regarded as neutral, just as Belgium was once regarded as neutral, and that they should guarantee her inviolability, because it was certainly to be expected that she would not be powerful enough to take care of herself against those who might wish to commit aggression against her.

That serves as a very useful illustration of one of the purposes for which the League of Nations has been established, for do you not observe that the moment we are ready to give independence to the Philippines, her independence is already guaranteed, because all the great nations of the world are under engagement of the most solemn sort to respect and preserve her territorial integrity and her existing political independence as against external aggression?

Those words "external aggression" are sometimes left out of the exposition of Article X. There was not a member of that peace con-

[3] About Wilson's operation and his visit to Palm Beach, Florida, see WW to R. Bridges, Dec. 9, 1904, n. 1; the two news items printed at Jan. 7, 1905; and the news item printed at Jan. 21, 1905, all in Vol. 15; the news item printed at Feb. 18, 1905, and EAW to Anna Harris, March 11, 1905, both in Vol. 16.

ference with whom I conferred who did not hold the same opinion that I hold as to the sacred right of self-determination and did not hold the principle which all Americans hold—that it was not the right of any nation to dictate to another nation what sort of government it should have or under what sort of sovereignty it would live.

For us, the problem of the future of the Philippines is solved by the League of Nations. It is the first time that the world has come to this mind about matters of that sort. And what brought it to that mind? The breakdown of the neutrality of Belgium. You know you cannot establish civil society if anybody is going to be a neutral with regard to the maintenance of the law. We are all bound in conscience, and all public officers are bound in oath, not to remain neutral with regard to the maintenance of the law and the vindication of the right. And one of the things that occurred in this conference, as a sort of practical joke on myself, was this. One of the principles that I went to Paris most insisting on was the freedom of the seas. Now, the freedom of the seas means the definition of the right of neutrals to use the seas when other nations are at war. But under the League of Nations there are no neutrals. And, therefore, what I have called the practical joke on myself was that, by the very thing that I was advocating, it became unnecessary to define the freedom of the seas. All nations are engaged to maintain the right, and in that sense no nation can be neutral when the right is invaded. And, all being comrades and partners in a common cause, we all have an equal right to use the seas. To my mind it is a much better solution than had occurred to me, or than had occurred to anyone else with regard to that single definition of right.

We have no choice, my fellow citizens, in this matter except between these alternatives: we must go forward with this concert of nations, or we must go back to the old arrangement, because the guarantees of peace will not be sufficient without the United States. And those who oppose this Covenant are driven to the necessity of advocating the old order of balances of power. If you do not have this universal concert, you have what we have always avoided—necessary alignment of this nation with one other nation or with some other group of nations.

What has disturbed me most about the present debate—not because I doubt its issue, but because I regret its length—is that it is heartening the representatives of Germany to believe that at last they are going to do in this way what they were not able to do by arms—separate us in interest and purpose from our associates in the war. I am not suggesting, I have no right to suggest, that the men who are opposing this Covenant have any thought of assisting

Germany in their minds. But my point is that, by doing what they are doing, they are assisting Germany, whether they want to do so or not. And it is not without significance, my fellow countrymen, that, coincidentally with this debate, there has been a revival of pro-German propaganda all over the United States. For this is Germany's calculation—that, inasmuch as she is obliged to stand apart and be for the time suspected and have other nations come slowly to accommodation with her, if we hold off, other nations will be similarly alienated from us, as they will be, and that there will be, whether we design it or not, a community of interest between the two isolated nations. It is an inevitable psychological result. So we must join this arrangement to complete the psychology of it.

And the psychology of this war is so that any nation that attempts to do what Germany did will certainly have the world combined against her. Germany not only did not know she would have the world combined against her, but she never dreamed she would. Germany confidently expected that Great Britain would not go into the war. She never dreamed that America would go into the war. And, in order not absolutely to dishearten her people, she had continuously to lie to them and tell them that the submarine warfare was so effective that American troops could not be sent to Europe. Friends of mine who, before we went into the war, conversed with Germans on the other side and told them that they had come over since the submarine warfare began, were not believed. The Germans said, "Why, you cannot cross the sea." The body of the German people actually thought that the sea was closed, and that we could send 2,000,000 men over there without losing any of them, except on a single transport, was incredible to them. If they had ever dreamed that that would happen, they never would have ventured upon so foolish an attack upon the liberties of mankind.

So that what is impressed upon my mind by my stay on the other side of the water, more than any one thing, is that, while old rivalries and old jealousies and while all the intricate threads of history woven in unhappy patterns have made the other nations of the world suspect one another, nobody doubts or suspects America. That is the amazing and delightful discovery I made on the other side of the water. If there was any place in our discussion where they wanted troops sent, they always begged that American troops be sent, because they said none of the other associated powers would suspect them of ulterior designs, and the people of the country would know they had not come there to keep anything they took, that they didn't come to interfere in their internal affairs; that they had come, not as exploiters, but as friends. That is the reputation of American soldiers throughout Europe, and it is their reputation because it is true. That is the beautiful background of it. That is the temper in which they go. That is the principle upon which they go and upon which the government back of them goes, and the great people whom that government represents. So that there is something more than choosing between peace and armed isolation, for that is one aspect of the choice. We are choosing between a doubtful peace and an assured peace, guided and led by the United States of America.

I was very much interested to scan the names on a very beautifully engrossed communication that was put in my hands today by Mr. Gage, a communication from the representatives of the League to Enforce Peace. I found upon it the names of many of the principal and most representative citizens and professional men of San Diego, and it happened, I believe, unless I am misinformed, that practically all the signers were Republicans.

There is one thing against which I want to enter a protest. I have had, I do not know how many, men come to me and say, "Mr. President, I am a Republican, but I am for the League of Nations." Why "but"? For as a Democrat, you will permit me to remind you who are Republicans that you have always boasted that your party is the party of constructive programs. Here is the most constructive, the greatest constructive, program ever proposed. Why should you say "but"? If I were in your place and had at my heart the pride which you very properly entertain because of the accomplishments of your party, I would say, "I am a Republican, and for that reason I am in favor of the League of Nations."

But I am not going to say that I am a Democrat, and for that reason I am in favor of the League of Nations, because I am not in favor of it because I am a Democrat. I am in favor of it because I am an American and a believer in humanity. And I believe in my heart that if the people in this country, as I am going about now, were to suspect that I had political designs, they would give me evident indication that they wanted me to go back to Washington right away. They would not give me the splendid and delightful welcomes that they are giving me. Men and women would not come to me, as they are doing now, and take my hand in theirs and say, "Mr. President, God bless you!"

I wonder if you realize, as I have tried to realize, what that gracious prayer means. I have had women who had lost their dearest in the war come up to me with tears upon their cheeks and say, "God bless you!" Why did they bless me? I advised the Congress to go into this war and to send their sons to their death. As commander in chief of the army and navy, I sent their sons to their death, and they died, and their mothers come and say "God bless you!" There can be only one explanation. They are proud of the cause in which their sons died. And, oh, my friends, since we all have to die, the way those fellows died is the best way after all. There was nothing in it for them, no possible personal gain—nothing but the noble performance of a disinterested duty, and that is the highest distinction that any man can achieve.

I remember years ago reading an essay which left a permanent impression on my mind. It was entitled "Christmas: Its Unfinished Business."[4] And it was a discourse upon what was then a very common occurrence—the meeting of assemblies to promote peace. You know, we always used to be having conventions to promote peace, and most of the men who sat on the platforms were men who were doing everything they could to bring on war by unjustly exploiting other countries and taking advantages they ought not to take, that were sure to exasperate the feeling of people elsewhere. But they didn't realize that they were really bringing on war; in their minds, they were trying to bring on peace, and the writer of the essay called attention to this.

His thesis was, "There will be peace when peace is as handsome as war." He hurried to explain that what he meant was this, that, leaving aside the men who had unjustly and iniquitously plotted war—like the General Staff in Germany—the men in the ranks gave everything that they had, their lives included, for their country, and that while you would always hang the boy's musket or his sword over the mantelpiece, you would never hang his ledger or his yardstick or his spade; not that civic implements are dishonorable, but that they are centered upon yourself, whereas the sword and the gun meant that you had forgotten yourself and remembered only the call of your country. And therefore, there was a certain sacredness about that implement that could not attach to any implement of civil life. "Now," said my essayist, "when men are devoted to the purpose of peace with the same self-forgetfulness and the same thought for the interest of their country and the cause that they are devoted to that they display under arms in war, then there will be no more war. When the motives of peace are as disinterested and as handsome as the motives of war for the common soldier, then we will all be soldiers in an army of peace, and there will be no more wars."

Now, that comes about when there is a common conception of peace, and the heart of this covenant of peace is to bring nations together into consultation so that they will see which of their ob-

<hr />

[4] Samuel McChord Crothers, "Christmas: Its Unfinished Business," *Atlantic Monthly*, XCIV (Dec. 1904), 721-27. For Wilson's earlier references to this article, see the addresses printed at Sept. 10, 1912, n. 3, Vol. 25, and Dec. 11, 1915, n. 3, Vol. 35.

jects are common, so that they will discuss how they can accommodate their interests, so that their chief object will be conciliation and not alienation. And when they understand one another, they will cooperate with one another in promoting the general interest and the common peace.

It is a parliament of nations at last, where everyone is under covenant himself to do right, to respect and preserve the territorial integrity and existing political independence of the others, and where they are engaged with one another never to go to war without first trying to settle the matter by the slow, cooling, disinterested processes of discussion.

It is what we have been striving for for generation after generation, and now some men hesitate to accept it when the golden thing is placed in their hands. It would be incredible to me, if I didn't understand some of them, but it is not permitted to one occupying my present office to make personal remarks. And, after all, personal remarks are neither here nor there. What does any one of us matter in so great a thing as this? What difference does it make whether one man rises and another falls, whether all go down or up together? We have got to serve humanity. We have got to redeem the honor of the United States. We have got to see this thing through to its great end of justice and peace.

Printed in *Addresses of President Wilson*, with an addition and corrections from the incomplete text in the San Diego *Evening Tribune*, Sept. 20, 1919.

To Thomas William Lamont

My dear Lamont: San Diego, California, 19 September, 1919

The statement was peculiarly generous of you, and I appreciate it most sincerely.[1] It ought to do, and I am sure will do, a real service in clarifying matters which I cannot help believing have been deliberately misrepresented and which I find very universally [mis]understood. The most prominent feeling, so far as I can gather it here in California, is one of resentment on the part of the public that they have been so misinformed and so misled as to the real character and purposes of the treaty and the covenant.

I note what you say of the opportunity to do something in Mexico, and will be very happy to have a talk with you after I get back to Washington and have got the Industrial Conference well started.

Mrs. Wilson joins me in most cordial messages to Mrs. Lamont[2] and yourself. We all have the most delightful recollections of our association on the "George Washington."[3]

Cordially and sincerely yours,   Woodrow Wilson

TLS (T. W. Lamont Papers, MH-BA).
  [1] Wilson was replying to T. W. Lamont to WW, Sept. 10, 1919.
  [2] That is, Florence Haskell Corliss Lamont.
  [3] That is, on the return from France, June 29 to July 8, 1919.

From Francis Patrick Walsh

New York N. Y. 1919 Sep 19

The Executive Committee of the Irish Race Convention in session here has directed me to wire you the following question: Is Ireland included in the territorial integrity of Great Britain proposed to be guaranteed by Article Ten of the Covenant of the League of Nations? They instruct me to say that a definite answer upon this point will clarify the minds of millions of our fellow American citizens. An answer addressed to me at 2142 Woolworth Building New York City will be promptly transmitted to the Committee which again meet at New York on Monday September 22 at 10 A.M.

Frank P Walsh Chairman American Commission on
Irish Independence.[1]

T telegram (WP, DLC).
  [1] On the verso of p. 2 of this telegram is the following handwritten note: "Article ten refers only to external aggression. The people of Ireland will be as secure as the people of England and the people of the United States against invasion or attack by any outside power."

From William Byron Colver

The White House, Sept. 19, 1919

On August second the Senate passed a resolution[1] requiring the Federal Trade Commission to answer whether or not it had reported to the President before July 1st, 1918 on the reasonableness of the packers' profits under the regulations of the Food Administration, and to furnish the Senate with a copy of such report if one had been made. The words "if not incompatible with the public service" did not appear in the resolution. We had hoped to be able to delay answering until after your return, but it does not seem to be feasible. The report in question was in the form of a four-page report made to you on June 28th, supported by three detailed reports, one by the expert accountants of the Commission, one by an independent certified public accounting firm, and the third signed by all the signers of the first two.[2] At that time the Commissioners' report was submitted to Hoover for his observations, and he wrote you a reply.[3]

The Commission's report was never written with the idea that it was to be made public, but Hoover raised some question as to whether or not it would be made public, and requested of you that if the Federal Trade Commission report were made public, the Hoover reply should be published at the same time. Judge Glasgow,[4] of Philadelphia, acting for Hoover, requested the Commission, if it acceded to the Senate request for its report, to include also the Hoover report, and this would seem to be a reasonable request, and it would seem that the Hoover document may properly be included in the reply of the Commission to the Senate. The Hoover reply is dated July 8th. On July 20th there was prepared by the Commission a rejoinder to the Hoover reply.[5] It was not controversial but was intended to clear up some points raised by Hoover's reply, and becomes an integral part of the discussion. The Commission's letter of July 20th was not then sent to you for the reason that it seemed to be understood that neither the Commission's report nor Hoover's reply would be made public, and for the further reason that the points made in the Commission's memorandum had practically all been covered orally with you in conferences and the Commission felt that the whole matter was closed and did not wish to burden you.

Before making reply to the Senate, and such reply it seems will of necessity be made rather presently, would welcome any suggestion which you may care to make. We have engaged ourselves to Judge Glasgow to advise him if the Commission sends to the Senate its original letter only and without accompanying it with Hoover's reply. This we believe is in order that the Food Administration may publish its reply independently. From the beginning the Commission has sought earnestly to avoid any appearance of an interdepartmental disagreement. In fact and in truth, there never was any such situation. You asked us to examine and report on certain matters, and we did so, not in the spirit of controversy but in the desire to serve your wishes.

The situation today is, therefore, that: First, we may send to the Senate only the Commission's original report, in which case the Food Administration will doubtless publish separately its reply; and Second, we may send the Commission's original report and the Hoover reply, which leaves the matter unfinished; and Third, we may send to the Senate the original report, the Hoover reply, and the Commission's memorandum. These documents will disclose an honest difference of opinion between the Commission and the Food Administration, but one which has in no wise disturbed the cordial relations between the two agencies. It would seem best, perhaps, to make the report one bite of the cherry and send the whole thing in. We shall welcome any suggestion that you may care to make. In the meanwhile, will prepare responses in alternative form, but which will be amended to fit in with any wish you may indicate. The foregoing represents the opinion of Murdock, Thompson, and myself, Governor Fort being absent.[6]

Colver.

T telegram (WP, DLC).

[1] Actually, S. Res. 177 was introduced by George W. Norris and passed by the Senate on September 3. *Cong. Record*, 66th Cong., 1st sess., p. 4650.

[2] The "four-page report" of June 28, 1918, is printed as the Enclosure with J. F. Fort to WW, July 30, 1918, Vol. 49. The "three detailed reports" by Stuart Chase, an accountant for the Federal Trade Commission; by the accounting firm of Perley Morse & Co. of New York; and by Chase, Perley Morse & Co. and Walter Y. Durand, a member of the staff of the F. T. C., are printed in 66th Cong., 1st sess., Sen. Doc. No. 110 (Washington, 1919), pp. 11-37. As indicated in the above letter, these reports furnished the detailed data on which the report of June 28 was based.

[3] See HCH to WW, July 8, 1918, n. 1, Vol. 48.

[4] William Anderson Glasgow, Jr., lawyer of Philadelphia and former counsel for the Food Administration.

[5] The commission's "rejoinder" to Hoover, cast in the form of a letter from Colver to Wilson, dated July 20, 1918, is printed in 66th Cong., 1st sess., Sen. Doc. No. 110, pp. 8-10.

[6] That is, Victor Murdock, Samuel Huston Thompson, Jr., and John Franklin Fort, the current members of the Federal Trade Commission, of which Colver was chairman.

Three Telegrams to Robert Lansing

[San Diego, Sept. 19, 1919]

Polk is taking exactly the right position with regard to the continuance of the conference,[1] and I hope you will give him our strong backing in the matter. It would be very nearly fatal to the whole state of mind of the world, if the British were to withdraw and break up the conference.[2]

[San Diego, Sept. 19, 1919]

I would appreciate it if you would ask Polk to give the following message to Venizelos. You will remember that I already sent him a message, which seems not to have reached him.[3] I would be obliged if you would explain this. quote

"My dear Mr. Venizelos: I greatly regret to learn that a previous message which I attempted to send you did not reach you. I want you to know that there is no man in the conference whom I have more respected or more wished to serve than yourself, and that if I am differing with you in any degree in regard to the Thracian settlement, it is only because I believe that the suggestions I have made will better serve the peace of that part of Europe than a cession of the territories in question to a single nation when no nation has a clear ethnical preponderance. I want to express my very

warm regard and my earnest desire to show in every way possible
my warm friendship for you and for Greece. I have heard nothing
recently of the Dodecanese Islands. Surely they are going to
Greece.   W.W.[4]

[San Diego, Sept. 19, 1919]

With regard to the desire of the King of Belgium to bestow upon
you and me and other American officials the Order of Leopold,[5] I
think it ought to be explained to him that it is against the constitutional tradition of the United States for its civil officers to receive
foreign decorations of any kind, at the same time expressing our
deep appreciation. I like Mr. Phillips suggestion, however, that we
should bestow upon the King himself our Distinguished Service
Medal, as Commander in chief of the Belgian army in the field.
                                                          W.W.

T MSS (WP, DLC).
  [1] Wilson was replying to W. Phillips to WW, Sept. 16, 1919 (second telegram of that
date).
  [2] This telegram was received in the State Department on September 19, 1919: WW
to RL, n.d., T telegram (SDR, RG 59, 763.72119/6823, DNA).
  [3] Wilson was replying to W. Phillips to WW, Sept. 16, 1919 (first telegram of that
date). Wilson undoubtedly was thinking of the message, which was not addressed personally to Vénisélos, in RL to FLP, Aug. 28, 1919, Vol. 62.
  [4] This telegram was received as WW to RL, Sept. 19, 1919, T telegram (SDR, RG 59,
763.72119/6820, DNA).
  [5] Wilson was replying to W. Phillips to WW, Sept. 16, 1919 (third telegram of that
date).

To Rudolph Forster

[San Diego, Sept. 19, 1919]

Please communicate to Senator Hitchcock confidential information received from Vance McCormick[1] and say to him that I should
regard any such reservation as a practical rejection of the Covenant.   W.W.[2]

T MS (WP, DLC).
  [1] See V. C. McCormick to JPT, Sept. 18, 1919.
  [2] The received copy of this telegram is in EBR, RG 130, White House Staff Files,
1900-1935, DNA.

Three Telegrams from William Phillips

Washington, D. C., Sept. 19, 1919

With reference to my telegram of yesterday with regard to the
Italian situation,[1] I forward the following telegram just received
from Mr. Polk:

"4265. Sept. 18, 8 P.M. Confidential. For the President and Secretary of State. Yesterday, September 17th, Scialoja, the Italian representative on the Council of Five, asked me if I would approve the message Tittoni addressed to you and sent in my 4247, September 17, 11 P.M. I told him I would not; that one proposition was before you, which I had recommended, and that I could not change every time they did. He then said that Clemenceau would support it this morning. [This morning]² I saw Clemenceau at his request, and he asked me to forward to you a message on the subject of Fiume. Following is a translation of his message.

'At the [this] time when Italy is also passing through a serious crisis, and taking into consideration the general situation [existing] between the Allies resulting from their [our] long discussion, which in my opinion it is time to bring to an end, I beg [take the liberty], Mr. President, respectfully to call your benevolent attention to the last telegram from Mr. Tittoni, regarding the question of Fiume, which has been sent you by Mr. Polk.

'I earnestly beg you to believe that I would hesitate to intervene with a personal telegram [personally] in this delicate matter, if I did not [sincerely] believe [that a capital interest of] the future of Italy and of other European countries will be touched by [attached to] your decision.

'As I have known for a long time that this question was principally a matter of sentiment for the Italian people, I suggested to Mr. Tittoni a solution making Fiume Italian, with the ports, docks, and railway internationalized and no free state. For reasons unknown to me, Mr. Tittoni was at first favorably inclined to the solution of a free state. Today events have shown him that the only solution is to give Italy a purely moral satisfaction, and to leave the Slavs the immediate territories which would have had to wait five years for a plebiscite, which I must admit Italy is not in a position to accept.

'I once more apologize for intervening in this matter at a time when so many matters engage your attention and when you are so nobly fighting for the great cause to which you have dedicated yourself. After a conversation with Tittoni and myself, Lloyd George has agreed with this idea. If you should give your consent, today the whole of the Adriatic question would be finally settled, and this would be a great relief to Europe, for I am not without anxiety with regard to the interior situation in Italy.

'With renewed apologies and with expressions [my sentiments] of respectful friendship, I am [beg to remain], Very truly yours, G. Clemenceau.' "   William Phillips.

¹ That is, W. Phillips to WW, Sept. 18, 1919, which repeated FLP to W. Phillips, No. 4247, Sept. 17, 1919.
² Corrections and additions from W. Phillips to WW, Sept. 19, 1919, T telegram (SDR, RG 59, 763.72119/6814, DNA).

Washington DC 1919 Sep 19

Referring to the exchange of notes between yourself and the other heads of governments at Paris and Admiral Kolchak at Omsk.¹ The British are reported to be supplying all clothing and equipment necessary for Denikin, the French for Czecks and anti-Bolshevik forces in western border countries, while Kolchak relies for similar equipment upon the United States. Latest reports show that unless Kolchaks forces are provided with clothing at an early date they will face the rigors of a Siberian winter unequipped and will scarcely survive the ordeal. As the United States has joined in undertaking to do its share in supplying Kolchak and his associates with munitions food and supplies to the best of its ability, I urgently recommend that you authorize the Secretary of War to sell to the Russian Ambassador² or other Russian representative in this country for shipment to Kolchak on a credit basis shoes underclothing cloth surplus overcoats especially such materials as may not find an advantageous or ready market in this country. I would not urge this upon your attention at such a time did I not believe it one of pressing importance. I am much impressed with the fact that our failure to render this assistance will not be understood in Russia and will not only weaken Kolchak but also affect unfavorably our own position to the immediate and possibly permanent advantage of Japan. The latest reports we have from Siberia dated September 11 indicate Kolchaks forces have resumed the offensive and are driving the Bolsheviki back towards the Urals.

William Phillips.³

¹ For which, see Appendix I to the minutes of the Council of Four printed at May 27, 1919, 4 p.m., Vol. 59; and A. V. Kolchak to G. Clemenceau, June 4, 1919, and the extract from the Diary of Dr. Grayson printed at June 12, 1919, both in Vol. 60.
² That is, Boris Aleksandrovich Bakhmet'ev.
³ The telegram sent was W. Phillips to WW, Sept. 19, 1919, T telegram (SDR, RG 59, 861.24/181B, DNA).

Washington DC 1919 Sep 19

I have received a cable from Mr Polk¹ emphasizing the very urgent necessity for immediate measures to repatriate the Czechoslovak forces now in Siberia. First, because they look with despair upon the possibility of another winter in Siberia and in these circumstances their retention might prove a source of danger rather than a protection. Second, because their return has become a burning political question in Czechoslovakia upon which the over-throw of the government is possible if not probable. The department for some months has been in correspondence upon this subject because it has considered the [that][2] beginning with our sending of troops to Siberia we have had a definite moral obligation in regard to the Czechoslovak armies of Siberia. Accordingly I have today written the Secretary of the Treasury urging him to advance additional credits to the Czechoslovak government up to $12,000,000 which is the estimated cost of repatriating 50,000 men. I have informed Mr Glass that if such a credit is granted I will if you so desire urge Mr Polk to insist that Great Britain and France each bear one fourth of such a loan in view of the burden assumed by the United States in general relief measures in Europe and also because of the special interest which Great Britain and France have in maintaining stable conditions in Czechoslovakia. If the additional credit to which I refer is approved I would also urgently request your authorization to have the Shipping Board set aside the tonnage necessary for this movement, it being understood that economy of tonnage will have every consideration. In conclusion, allow me to add that the importance of repatriating the Czechoslovak forces has been brought to the attention of the department from various sources and has been very particularly emphasized by Ambassador Morris in his reports from Siberia. I believe considerations of very great weight urge our starting this movement and hope you will see your way clear to authorizing the necessary credits and tonnage. Allow me to add in regard to the question of tonnage that while there is urgent demand on commercial routes for the vessels which have been engaged in returning our troops from France, I believe the political and moral considerations in this particular instance are paramount.

William Phillips.

T telegrams (WP, DLC).

[1] FLP to W. Phillips, No. 4253, Sept. 17, 1919, T telegram (SDR, RG 59, 861.00/5229, DNA), printed in *FR 1919, Russia*, pp. 296-97.

[2] Corrections and additions from W. Phillips to WW, Sept. 19, 1919, T telegram (SDR, RG 59, 861.00/5229, DNA).

To Arthur James Balfour

My dear Mr. Balfour: San Diego, California, 19 September, 1919

I greatly appreciate it that you should have undertaken to convey the request of the Glasgow University Unionist and Liberal Clubs that I accept nomination as their joint candidate for the Lord Rectorship of the University of Glasgow.[1] If I were free to accept such appointments, there is none that it would give me greater gratification to accept, but I foresee only too plainly that I cannot be confident of carrying out any private plans for the next three years, and I would be misleading the kind friends who entertain this desire, if I were to hold out the expectation that I could perform the single duty involved in the acceptance of the Rectorship. It would be very delightful to go to Glasgow again and have the honor of delivering the Rectorial Address, but alas, I am doing what I must and not what I would.

Will you not convey to the gentlemen of the University Unionist and Liberal Clubs a very warm expression of my appreciation and of my keen regret that I cannot enjoy an honor which would be so acceptable to me?

May I not add a word to say how pleasant it was to hear from you, and with what great satisfaction I look back upon our association in Paris?

Cordially and sincerely yours,   Woodrow Wilson

TLS (Letterpress Books, WP, DLC).
[1] Wilson was replying to A. J. Balfour to WW, Aug. 16, 1919, Vol. 62.

From the Diary of Dr. Grayson

Saturday, September 20, 1919.

Los Angeles was reached at 9:00 o'clock in the morning. It had originally been intended that the party would not get there until noon but a big crowd was assembled at the station to greet the President. He was not yet awake when the train pulled into the station, so I had the railway authorities pull his car back down into the yard so that he could finish his rest and breakfast before leaving the train.

Shortly after 10:00 o'clock the President proceeded to the Alexandria Hotel, where he rested until noon. In order that the original program might be carried out as closely as possible, we proceeded back to the station and the automobile procession started from there.

Los Angeles did itself proud in its reception to the President. It was estimated that more than 200,000 people were congregated along the principal streets to see and to hear him. The cheering was deafening, and it required all of the energy of the police guard to keep the crowd from overwhelming the automobile in an effort to shake the President by the hand.

Returning to the hotel after the procession through the streets, the President was given an opportunity to rest until 6:00 o'clock, when he was the guest of honor at a dinner arranged by the Commercial Club of the city. The President took advantage of the dinner to deliver an address directed to the business interests of the country. He declared that under no circumstance would it be possible for the business men of the country to expect normal conditions until after the Treaty had been disposed of. He pointed out that until the Treaty was ratified by the Senate, the business interests of the United States would be handicapped while their rivals in England and France would have a distinct advantage. England and France were already endeavoring to capture the trade of the Central Empires, the President said, and America could do nothing to meet this situation until a state of peace had been restored between it and those countries.

The President went directly from the dinner to the Mystic Shrine Temple, the largest auditorium in Los Angeles, where he addressed a night meeting. This meeting was another enthusiastic one. The crowd was very friendly and cheered his remarks to the echo. He reviewed the League compact, again pointing out that the United States had surrendered none of its prerogatives to Great Britain or any other nation, and he also went back over the ground of the Shantung settlement to show that throughout the United States had acted as China's true friend. He called attention to the fact that President McKinley had not interposed any objection while President to the partition of certain portions of China between France and Great Britain and Germany, and explained that this was because the President had no authority under international law to do so at that time. Ratification of the Treaty and the creation of the League of Nations, however, would allow the United States to act as the friend of all small nations in the future, the President said.

He returned to the hotel late at night and went right to bed. He was still suffering from headaches and was very tired.

From Joseph Patrick Tumulty, with Enclosure

Dear Governor: Los Angeles, California 20 September 1919.

The issues that are acute in this part of the country are the following: Shantung; Great Britain; isolation.

In the matter of isolation, I understand there is feeling here that we should keep separate and apart from European embroilments. I beg to call your attention to Senator Johnson's speech which is attached.[1] It will give you an idea of the line of his attack.

I also attach an editorial from the Seattle Times,—a Republican paper which is supporting us. And an editorial from the Los Angeles Examiner,—a Hearst paper.[2]

I am sending up to the Public Library for a copy of Mr. McKinley's speech made before the day he was assassinated, in which he discussed Americanism, and said the age of isolation was past. It might be well to call attention to this address in this part of the country. I think we ought to impress the fact upon the people that provincialism on the part of America means playing the game alone. It means increased taxation and a nation in arms. I think you also ought to show the possibilities of aerial attacks on America in connection with the idea of provincialism.

Sincerely yours,   Tumulty

TLS (WP, DLC).

[1] It is missing, but Tumulty referred to Johnson's speech at Sioux Falls, South Dakota, on September 16 (see Tumulty's second letter of this date for a quotation from the speech). Johnson charged that the League of Nations would in effect supersede the American Constitution and system of government with an "overlordship of eight foreign nations" or "a super-government in which our voice will be but one of nine." He denied the need for haste in ratification of the Versailles Treaty. Moreover, Johnson said, American ratification of the treaty meant the legitimation of the "land grabs" of the great powers made in secret treaties and at the Paris Peace Conference, as well as those yet to come in secret meetings of the League of Nations. The most complete report of Johnson's speech is in the *Los Angeles Times*, Sept. 17, 1919.

[2] The clippings from the *Seattle Times* and the *Los Angeles Examiner* are missing.

E N C L O S U R E

EXTRACTS FROM PRESIDENT MCKINLEY'S LAST
SPEECH, AT BUFFALO, NEW YORK. SEPT. 5, 1901.

"After all, how near one to the other is every part of the world. Modern inventions have brought into close relation widely separated peoples and made them better acquainted. Geographic and political divisions will continue to exist, but distances have been effaced. Swift ships and swift trains are becoming cosmopolitan. They invade fields which a few years ago were impenetrable. The world's products are exchanged as never before, and with increasing transportation facilities come increasing knowledge and larger trade. Prices are fixed with mathematical precision by supply and demand. The world's selling prices are regulated by market and crop reports.

"We travel greater distances in a shorter space of time and with more ease than was ever dreamed of by the fathers. Isolation is no longer possible or desirable. The same important news is read, though in different languages, the same day in all christendom. The telegraph keeps us advised of what is occurring everywhere, and the press foreshadows, with more or less accuracy, the plans and purposes of the nations."

"At the beginning of the nineteenth century there was not a mile of steam railroad on the globe. Now there are enough miles to make its circuit many times. Then there was not a line of electric telegraph; now we have a vast mileage traversing all lands and seas. God and man have linked the nations together. No nation can longer be indifferent to any other. And as we are brought more and more in touch with each other the less occasion there is for misunderstandings and the stronger the disposition, when we have differences, to adjust them in the court of arbitration, which is the noblest forum for the settlement of international disputes."

"We have a vast and intricate business, built up through years of toil and struggle, in which every part of the country has its stake, and will not permit of either neglect or of undue selfishness. No narrow, sordid policy will subserve it."

"Only a broad and enlightened policy will keep what we have."

T MS (WP, DLC).

From Joseph Patrick Tumulty

Dear Governor: Los Angeles, California 20 September 1919.

We ought to try from this time on by indirection to answer the criticisms of our opponents. For instance, the Chicago Evening Post, a Republican paper, calls attention to this statement appearing in Senator Johnson's speech: "We are the one going, solvent, national concern in the world that is attempting to enter into a world partnership with four bankrupts."

The Post retaliates in this way: " 'Bankrupt,' Mr. Johnson? And why are they bankrupt? Because they fought the noble fight, which we eventually had to fight, for almost three years before we entered it. Could anything be more ignoble, more ungenerous than this taunt? Could anything be more unfaithful to the fine ideals of common loyalty which the war taught us?"

Could you not show that the object of these criticisms is to bring about a separation of interest between us and our associates? No matter what may be said about our associates, for three years they fought to serve civilization. If they are bankrupt in money, it is because they expended it and their precious blood to save the world.   Tumulty

TLS (WP, DLC).

An After-Dinner Speech in Los Angeles[1]

September 20, 1919.

Mr. Toastmaster and ladies, and gentlemen: May I not first thank you, Mr. Toastmaster, for your very generous introduction, which has been in the same delightful tone of welcome that I have heard in the voices on the street. But I do not take that all to myself—the praise that you have so generously bestowed upon me. I nevertheless do recognize that you have set just the right note for the discussion that I want to indulge in for a few moments.

There is only one thing that has troubled me in this affair. My father used to say, "You cannot reason out of a man what reason did not put in him." (laughter) May I not say that much of the argument offered directly against the League of Nations is not based on reason. I might say I have sometimes been discouraged, because it is true that there is a great constructive plan, and no man in the presence of the present critical situation of mankind has the right to oppose any constructive plan except by a better constructive plan. (applause) I will say now that I am ready to take ship again and carry back to Paris any constructive proposals which will be a suitable and better substitute than those which have been made. (applause)

And there is a peculiarity about this constructive plan which ought, I think, to facilitate our acceptance of it. It is laid out in every part upon American principles. Everybody knows that the principles of peace proposed by America were adopted, were adopted as the basis of armistice and eventually acted upon as the basis of the peace.

And there is a circumstance about these American principles which gives me absolute confidence in them. They were not the principles which I originated. They would have none of the strength that they have if they had been of individual origination. I remember how anxiously I watched the movements of opinion in this country during the months immediately preceding our entrance into the war. Again and again, I put this question to the men around the Cabinet table. They represented different parts of the

---

[1] The *Los Angeles Sunday Times*, Sept. 21, 1919, reported that Wilson spoke before 515 persons at the dinner held in the Hotel Alexandria. He was introduced by Henry Stewart McKee, vice-president of the Merchant's National Bank of Los Angeles.

country; they were in touch with different portions of the nation. I said to them, "How do you think the people feel with regard to our relation to this war?" I remember one of them said, "Why, Mr. President, I think they are ready to do anything that you suggest." I said: "That is not what I have waited for. That is not enough. If they don't go in of their own impulse, no impulse that I will supply will suffice. I must wait until I know I am their spokesman. Then I will know that I have an irresistible power behind." (applause)

That is not wholly appreciated abroad or was not at that time. They wondered, wondered why we did not come in and came to the conclusion that we did not come in because we were making money out of the war and did not want to spoil a profitable game. Then at last they saw what we were waiting for. We were waiting in order that we might see the intrigue of what had penetrated our own life, how the poison was spreading, and how it was nothing less than a design against the freedom of the world. They knew that when America once saw that she would throw her power in with those who were going to redeem the world. And at every point of the discussion, I was attempting to be the mouthpiece of what I understood right-thinking and forward-thinking and just-thinking men, without regard to party or section in the United States, to be purposing and conceiving.

And it was the consciousness in Europe that that was the case that made it possible to construct the peace upon American principles. The American principles were not only accepted, they were acted upon. And when I came back to this country with that plan I think you will bear me out that the nation was prepared to accept it. I have no doubt, and I have not met anybody who had reason to doubt, that, if immediate action could have been secured upon the treaty at that time, only a negligible percentage of our people would have objected to its acceptance, without a single change in either wording or punctuation.

But then something intervened, my fellow citizens. I am not only not going to try to analyze what that was, I am not going to allow my own judgment to be formed as regards what it was. I don't understand it, but there is a certain part of it I do understand. It is to the immediate interest of Germany to separate us from our associates in the war, (applause) and I know that the opposition to the treaty is most acceptable in those quarters of the country where the pro-German sentiment was strongest. I know that all over the country German propaganda had lifted its hideous head again, and I hear the hiss of it on every side.

When gentlemen speak of isolation, they forget we would have a companion. There would be another isolated nation, and that is

Germany. They forget that we would be in the judgment of the world in the same class and at the same disadvantage as Germany. I mean sentimental disadvantage. We would be regarded as having withdrawn our cooperation from that concerted purpose of mankind, which was originally conceived and exercised for the liberation of mankind, and Germany would be the only nation in the world to profit by it.

I have no doubt there are scores of businessmen present. Do you think we would profit materially by isolating ourselves and centering upon ourselves the hostility and suspicion and resistance of all the liberal minds in the world? Do you think that if, after having won the absolute confidence of the world and excited the hope of the world, we should turn away from them and say: "No, we do not care to be associated with you any longer; we are looking after ourselves; we are going to play a lone hand; we are going to play it for our single advantage?" Is that good psychology for the establishment of friendly relations? Is that psychology for the establishment of credit? Do you think that throws foreign markets open?

Do you remember what happened just before we went into the war? There was a conference in Paris, the object of which was to unite the people fighting against Germany in an economic combination which would be exclusively for their own benefit. It is possible now for those powers to organize a combine in respect of the purchase of raw materials, and if the foreign market for our raw materials is united, we will have to sell at the price that they are willing to pay or not sell at all. Unless you go into the market and make a partnership with the world, you will have the rest of the world in a combine against you. But if you bring the thing down to this lowest of all bases—the basis of material self-interest—you lose your game, you do not win, and, for my part, I will say you ought to lose. (applause)

We are told that we are strong and they are weak; that we still have the economic advantage and they have not. Why, my fellow citizens, what does that mean? That means that when they went into the redemption of the freedom of the world, they went in to give everything that they had. They said, or thought, that, because we did not go in so soon or lose so much, we would make a profit out of the redemption. The thing is ridiculous. The thing is unworthy of every tradition of America. I speak of it, not because I think that sort of thing takes the least hold upon the consciousness or the purpose of America, but because it is a pleasure to condemn so ugly a thing. When we look at the objections which these gentlemen make, I have found in going about the country that the result has been that, in the greater part of the United States, the people do not know what is in that treaty. They do not know what the treaty is. To my great surprise, I have had to stand up and explain the treaty and tell them what is in it. I have had many men say: "Why, we never dreamed those things were in the treaty. We never heard anything about that, never heard anything about the greatness of the enterprise. We only heard about some of the alleged defects of the methods by which it was to be carried out." That is all they have heard.

You remember hearing it said that this was a people's war and it must be a people's peace. And that is exactly what it must be. For the first time in the history of civilized society, a great international convention, made up of the leading statesmen of the world, has proposed a settlement which is for the benefit of the weak and not for the benefit of the strong. It is for the benefit of the people who could not have liberty themselves, whose weakness was profitable to the ambitious, whose weakness had been traded on by every Cabinet in Europe. And yet these very Cabinets represented at the table in Paris were united in the opinion that the people's day had come, and that it was not their right to dispose of the fortunes of the people without the consent of those people.

At the front of this great settlement they put the only thing that will preserve it. You cannot establish independence for weak peoples and then leave them to shift for themselves. You cannot give those people rights which they never enjoyed before and say, "Now, keep them if you can." That is an Indian gift, a gift which cannot be kept. You will have to say, "This is the settlement, and we guarantee its continuance." (applause)

There is only one honorable course when you have won a cause—to see that it stays won, to see that nobody interferes with or disturbs the result. And that is the purpose of the much-discussed Article X of the Covenant of the League of Nations. It is the Monroe Doctrine applied to the world. We have, ever since Mr. Monroe uttered his famous doctrine, said to the world, "We will respect and preserve as against external aggression the territorial integrity and political independence of every state in the western hemisphere." Those are practically the words of Article X.

Under Article X, all the members of the League engage to respect and preserve as against external aggression the territorial integrity and political independence of the other member states. And if that guarantee is not forthcoming, the whole structure of peace will crumble, because you cannot point out a great war that has not begun by a violation of that principle; that has not begun by the intention to impair the territorial integrity or interfere with the political independence of some body of people or some nation.

It was the heart of the Pan-German plan. It is the heart of every imperialistic plan, because imperialism is the design to control the destinies of people who did not choose you to control them. It is the principle of domination. It is the opposite extreme of self-deter-mination, self-government. And in that same Covenant of the League of Nations is the provision that only self-governing nations shall be admitted to the League, only those who are in sympathy with self-determination shall be in it. It embodies that ancient and noble principle that underlies our institutions—that all just gov-ernment depends on the consent of the governed. (applause)

And you have no choice, my fellow citizens, because the peoples of the world, even those that slept, are awake. There is not a coun-try in the world where the great mass of mankind is not now aware of its rights and determined to have them at any cost. The present universal unrest in the world renders a return to normal conditions impossible so long as it continues. The present unrest will not stop until men are assured of some arrangement they can believe in, something which will assure them that their rights will be pro-tected, that they can go about the normal production of the neces-saries of life again and enjoy the ordinary pleasures and privileges of life without a constant shadow of some cloud of terror over them, some threat of injustice, some tyranny of control.

Men are not going to stand it. If you are going to quiet the world, you have got to reassure the world. And the only way to reassure the world is to let it know that all the great fighting powers of the world are a unit, and that they are to be used and directed to pro-tect. And every great fighting nation in the world will be in the League, because Germany for the time being is not a great fighting power. (applause) That great nation of over 60,000,000 people has consented in the treaty to reduce its armed forces to 100,000 men and to give up all the war material over and above what is neces-sary to maintain an army of 100,000 men.

So, for the time being, we may exclude Germany from the list of the fighting nations of the world and say that the whole power of the world is now offered to mankind for the maintenance of peace, and for the maintenance of peace by the very processes we have all professed to believe in by substituting arbitration and discussion for war, by substituting the judgment of mankind for the force of arms.

I say without qualification that every nation that is not afraid of the judgment of mankind will go into this League of Nations. (ap-plause) There is nothing for any nation to lose whose purposes are right and whose cause is just. The only nations that need fear to go into it are those that have designs that are illegitimate, those which have designs that are inconsistent with justice and are the opposite of peace.

So that the whole freedom of the world, not only, but the whole peace of mind of the world, depends upon the choice of America, because without America in this arrangement, the world will not be reassured.

I can testify to that. I can testify that no impression was borne in deeper on me on the other side of the water than that no great free people suspected the United States of ulterior designs, and that every nation, the weakest among them, felt that its fortunes would be safe if entrusted to the guidance of America, that America would not impose upon them. And at the peace table one of the reasons why American advice constantly prevailed—as it did—was that our experts—our financial experts and our economic experts, for you must remember that the work of the conference was not done exclusively by the men whose names you have read about every day; it was done with the most intensive labor of experts of every sort who sat down together and got down to the hardpan of every subject that they had to deal with—and in nine cases out of ten, after a long series of debates and interchanges of views and counterproposals, it was usually the American proposal that was adopted. (applause)

And that was because American experts came at last into this position of advantage—they convinced everybody they were not trying to work anything, that they were not thinking of something that they did not disclose, that they wanted all the cards on the table, and that they wanted to deal with nothing but facts. They were not dealing with national ambitions, they were not trying to disappoint anybody, and they were not trying to stack the cards for anybody. It was that conviction, and that only, which led to the success of American counsel in Paris.

Isn't that a worthy heritage for people who set up a great free nation on this continent in order to lead men in the ways of justice and of liberty? My heart is filled with a profound pride when I realize how America was regarded, and my only fear was that we would not have the wisdom to play the part—I mean we, who were over there. Delegations from literally all parts of the world came to seek interviews with me as the spokesman of America, and there was always a plea that America should lead, that America should suggest. And I remember saying to one of the delegations, which seemed to me more childlike in its confidence than the rest: "I beg that you gentlemen will not expect the impossible. But America will do everything that she can, but she cannot do some of the things that you are expecting of her. My chief fear is to disappoint, because you are expecting what cannot be realized." My fear was not that America would not prove true to herself, but that the things expected of her were so ideal that, in this practical world, full of obstacles, it would be impossible to realize the expectations. There was in the background the infinite gratification at the reputation and confidence that this country had won.

The world is in that situation industrially, economically, politically. The world will be absolutely in despair if America deserts it. But the thing is inconceivable. America is not going to desert it. (applause) The people of America are not going to desert it. The job is to get that into the consciousness of men who do not understand it. The job is to restore some of our fellow citizens to that large sort of sanity which makes a man bigger than himself.

We have had a great many successful men in America, my fellow citizens, but we seldom erect a statue to a man who has only been successful in a business way. Almost all the statues of America, almost all the memorials, are erected to men who forgot themselves and worked for other people. They may not have been rich, they may not have been successful in a worldly sense, they may have been deemed in their generation dreamers and idealists, but when they were dead America remembered that they loved mankind, America remembered that they embodied in their dreamy ideals of theirs the visions that America had had, and it remembered that they had a great surplus of character that they spent, not upon themselves, but upon the enterprises of mankind. And a man who has not got that surplus capital of character that he spends upon the great enterprises of communities and of nations will sink into a deserved oblivion. The only danger is that, in his concentration upon his own ambitions, in his centering of everything that he spends on himself, he will lead others astray and work a disservice to great communities which he ought to have served.

So that there is now an enterprise of infection ahead of us—shall I call it? We have got to infect these men with the spirit of the nation itself. We have got to make them aware that we will not be led, that we will not be controlled, that we will not be restrained by those who are not like ourselves; and that America is now in the presence of the realization of the destiny which we have awaited.

You know, you have been told, that Washington advised us against entangling alliances, and that is used as an argument against the League of Nations. What Washington had in mind was exactly what these gentlemen want to lead us back to. The day we left behind us was the day of alliances. It was a day of balances of power. It was a day of every nation taking care of itself and making a partnership with a nation or group of nations to hold the peace of the world steady or dominate the weaker portions of the world. Those were the days of alliances.

This process of the League of Nations is a process of disentanglement. I was reading only this morning what a friend of mine reminded me of—a speech that President McKinley made the day before he was assassinated. And in several passages of that speech, you see the dawn of this expectation in his mind. His whole thought was against isolation. His whole thought was that we had, by process of the circumstances, to become the partners of the rest of the world. His thought was that the world had grown little by quickened methods of intercommunication. His whole thought was that the better we knew each other and the closer we grew together, the more certain the processes of arbitration and the better the processes of arbitration. Men would not fight but would talk things over; they would realize their community of interest. And shot all through the speech, you see the morning light of just such a day as this. It would look as if the man had been given a vision just before he died—one of the sweetest and most humane souls that has been prominent in our affairs, a man who thought with his head and with his heart. And this new day was dawning upon his heart, and his intelligence was beginning to draw the lines of the new picture which has now been completed and sketched in a constructive document which we shall adopt (continued applause) and that, having adopted it, we shall finally reflect a new glory upon the things we did.

Then what significance will attach to the boy's gun or sword over the mantlepiece—not merely that he beat Germany, but that he redeemed the world. (continued applause)

Printed in *Addresses of President Wilson*, with many corrections from the nearly complete text in the *Los Angeles Sunday Times*, Sept. 21, 1919.

An Address in the Shrine Auditorium in Los Angeles[1]

September 20, 1919.

Mr. Mayor, Mrs. Cowles, my fellow citizens and countrymen: I esteem it a great privilege to stand before this great audience,[2] and I esteem it one of the most interesting occasions that I have had to expound a theme so great that I am always afraid that I am inade-

[1] Meredith Pinxton Snyder, the Democratic Mayor of Los Angeles, presided at the meeting, and Ione Virginia Hill (Mrs. Josiah Evans) Cowles, president of the General Federation of Women's Clubs, introduced Wilson.
[2] The *Los Angeles Sunday Times*, Sept. 21, 1919, estimated the size of the audience at between 6,000 and 7,000 persons.

quate to its exposition. I esteem it a privilege to be in the presence that I find myself in—on the stage with this committee of gentlemen representing the nations with whom we have been associated in the war—with these men who saved the Union and these men who saved the world. (applause)

And I feel that there is a certain sense in which I am rendering my account to the soldiers and sailors whose commander in chief I have been, for I sent them across the sea believing that their errand was not only to defeat Germany, but also to redeem the world from the danger to which Germany had exposed it, to make the world a place in which arbitration, discussion, the processes of peace, the processes of justice should stand in place of the brutal processes of war. (applause)

And I came back from the other side proud that I was bringing with me a document which contained a great constructive plan to accomplish that very thing. It is a matter of unaffected amazement on my part, my fellow citizens, that there should be men in high station to oppose its adoption. It is a matter of amazement that they should devote their scrutiny to certain details and forget the majesty of the plan, (applause) that they should actually have made it necessary that I should go through the country telling the people of the United States what is in the treaty of peace. For they have not told you. They have given you no conception of its scope. They have not expounded its object. They have not told you how it is to accomplish its purposes. They have not shown you how it is a people's and not a statesmen's peace. They have not shown you how in its heart lies the liberation of nations. They have not shown you that in it is the redemption of our promise that we were fighting for the right of the weak and not for the power of the strong. (applause)

These promises are redeemed in that great document, these hopes are realized, and the only buttress for that great structure is the League of Nations. (applause) If that should fail, there is no guarantee that any part of the settlement will stand. If that should fail, nations will once more sink back into that slough of despond in which they formerly struggled—suspecting one another, rivaling one another in preparation of war, intriguing against one another, plotting against the weak in order to supplement the power of the strong.

And they would do more than that, because mankind is now aware that the rights of the greater portion of mankind have not been safeguarded and regarded. Don't for a moment suppose that the universal unrest in the world at the present time, my fellow citizens, is due to any whim, to any newborn passion, to any newly discovered ambition. It is due to the fact—the sad, the tragic fact—that great bodies of men have throughout the ages been denied their rights and the rights of humanity. (applause)

The peoples of the world are tired and done with governments that exploit their peoples. (applause) And they are determined to have, by one process or another, that concerted order of conciliation and debate and conference which is set up in that great document which we know as the Covenant of the League of Nations.

For the heart of that document is not Article X, or the right to withdraw, or any other things you have been talking about.

The heart of that document is that every great fighting nation in the world—for Germany at present is not a great fighting nation (laughter)—every great fighting nation in the world solemnly engages that it will never resort to war without first having done one or the other of two things—either submitted the matter in dispute to arbitration, in which case it agrees to abide by the verdict, or, if it does not choose to submit it to arbitration, submit it to the examination and discussion of the Council of the League of Nations, before whom it promises to lay all the documents, to whom it promises to disclose all the pertinent facts, by whom it agrees all the documents and facts shall be published and laid before the opinion of the world. They agree that six months shall be allowed for the examination of those documents and facts by the Council of the League and then, if they are dissatisfied with the final arbitration, they will still not resort to war until three months after the verdict has been rendered. So that they all agree that there shall be nine months of deliberate discussion and frank weighing of the merits of the case before the whole jury of mankind before they will go to war. (applause)

And if any one of them disregards that promise and refuses to submit the question in dispute either to arbitration or to discussion, or goes to war within less than nine months, then there is an automatic penalty that is applied, more effective, I beg leave to say, than war itself, namely, the application of an absolute boycott. The nation that disregards that, we all agree, shall be isolated; shall be denied the right to ship out goods or ship them in, to exchange telegraph messages or messages by mail, to have any dealings of any kind with the citizens of the other members of the League. (applause)

First, the pressure of opinion and then the compelling pressure of economic necessity—those are the great bulwarks of peace. You say they are not sufficient? I put this proposition to you. You want insurance against war. Wouldn't you rather have 10 per cent insurance than none? If you could get 20 per cent insurance, wouldn't you be delighted? If you got 50 per cent insurance, wouldn't you think it ideal? Why, my fellow citizens, if you examine the provisions of this document, I think you will agree we will have 98 per cent insurance.

And that is what we promised to mothers and wives and sweethearts of these men that they should have—insurance against the terrible danger of losing those who were dear to them, slain on the battlefield because of the unhallowed plots of an autocratic government. Autocratic governments are excluded henceforth from respectable society. (applause) It is provided in the Covenant of the League of Nations that only self-governing peoples shall be admitted to its membership. And the reason that Germany is for the time being excluded is that we want to wait and see whether she really has changed permanently her form of constitution and her habit of government. If she has changed her mind in reality, if her people have taken charge of their own affairs and will prove it to us, they are entitled to come into respectable society and join the League of Nations. Until then, they are on probation. (laughter) And you see the way some of them talk, you would think the probation had to be rather long, because they don't seem to have repented of their essential purposes.

Now, offset against this, my fellow citizens, some of the things that are being said about the Covenant and the League and about the treaty. I want to begin with one of the essential objections which is made to this treaty, for I have come here disposed to business. I don't want to indulge in generalities. I don't want to dwell more than it is proper to dwell upon the great ideal purposes that lie behind this peace and this Covenant. I want to contrast some of the things that have been said with the real facts. (applause) There is nothing that is formidable in this world in public affairs except facts. Talk doesn't matter.

As I was saying the other night, if you suspect an acquaintance of yours of being a fool, encourage him to hire a hall. (laughter) Your fellow citizens will then know whether your judgment of him was right or wrong, and it won't be you that convinces them, it will be he who does the convincing. Because the best way to dissipate nonsense is to expose it to the open air. It is volatile. It is a volatile thing, whereas facts and proof are concrete things.

If I may tell a rather trivial story, when I was Governor of New Jersey, I got rather reluctant support for a certain measure of reform from a member of the Senate of the state who, I think, if he had been left to his own devices, would probably have not voted for the measure, but to whom a committee of fellow townsmen came and, so to speak, personally conducted his vote. After they had successfully conducted it, they solemnly brought him to my office to be congratulated. It was a great strain upon my gravity, but I pulled as straight a face as I could and thanked him and congratulated him. Then, tipping a very heavy wink indeed, he said, "Governor, they never get me if I see them coming first." And I have adopted that same motto. I never will let them get me if I see them coming first. (applause) The danger for some of the gentlemen we are thinking about tonight, but not mentioning, (laughter) is that the facts are coming, and they don't see them. (laughter) And my prediction is that the facts are going to get them and make a very comfortable meal off of them.

Let's take up some of these things, to grow serious again. In the first place, there is that very complex question of the cession of the rights which Germany formerly enjoyed in the Shantung Province in China, and which the treaty transfers to Japan.

The only way in which to clear this matter up is to know what lies back of it. Let me recall some circumstances which probably most of you have forgotten. I will have to go back to the year 1898, for it was in March of that year that the cessions which formerly belonged to Germany were transferred to her by the government of China. It had happened so that two German missionaries had been murdered. The central Government at Peking had done everything in its power to quiet the local disturbances and to allay the local prejudice against foreigners which led to the murder, and had been unable to do so. And the German government held them responsible, nevertheless, for the murder of the missionaries.

But it was not the missionaries that the German government was interested in. That was a pretext. Oh, my fellow citizens, how often have we made Christianity an excuse for wrong! How often! How often in attempting to protect what was sacred have we done what was tragically wrong! And that was what Germany did. She insisted that, because this thing had happened, for which the Peking government could not really with justice be held responsible, a very large and important part of one of the richest provinces in China should be ceded to them for sovereign control for a period of ninety-nine years; not only that, but they should have the right to penetrate the province with a railway and have the right to exploit any ores that lay within thirty miles on either side of the railway. And all this for ninety-nine years!

And they forced the Peking government to say that they did it in gratitude to the German government for certain services which she was supposed to have rendered but never did render. That was the beginning.

I don't know whether any of the gentlemen who are criticizing the present Shantung settlement were in public affairs at that time or not, but I will tell you what happened, so far as this government was concerned. One of the most enlightened of our Presidents was at the head of the government at that time—William McKinley, (applause) a man who loved his fellow men and believed in justice. And associated with him was one of our greatest statesmen—John Hay. (applause) The state of international law was such at that time that they did not feel at liberty to make even a protest against those concessions to Germany. Neither did they make any protest when, immediately following that, similar concessions were made to Russia, to Great Britain and France. It was almost immediately after that that China granted to Russia the right of possession and control of Port Arthur and a part of the region of Talien-Wan. Then England, although she had similar rights elsewhere in China, got a similar concession of Weihaiwei. And then France insisted that she must have a port, and got it for ninety-nine years.[3] And not against one of those did the government of the United States make any protest whatever. They only insisted that the door should not be shut in any of those regions against the trade of the United States. (applause)

You have heard of Mr. Hay's policy of the open door. That was his policy of the open door—not the open door to the rights of China, but the door to the goods of America.

I want you to understand, my fellow countrymen, I am not criticizing this because, until we adopt the Covenant of the League of Nations, it is an unfriendly act for any government to interfere in the affairs of another unless its own interests are immediately concerned. And the only thing Mr. McKinley and Mr. Hay were at liberty to do was to call attention to the fact that the trade of the United States might be unfavorably affected and insist that in no circumstances should this be done, a promise which was more or less kept.

Following that came the war between Russia and Japan. At the close of that war Japan got Port Arthur and the rights which Russia enjoyed in China, just as she is now getting Shantung and the rights which our recently defeated enemy had in China—an exactly identical operation. That peace that gave her Port Arthur was concluded, as you know, on the territory of the United States—at Portsmouth, New Hampshire. Nobody directed a protest against that. Japan had beaten Russia. Port Arthur did not at that time belong to China; it belonged for the period of the lease to Russia. And Japan was ceded what Japan had taken by the well-recognized processes of war.

[3] Kwangchowan.

Very well, at the opening of this war, Japan took Kiaochow and supplanted Germany in the Shantung Province. Now, all the processes were repeated, but repeated with a new sanction. In the meantime, after this present war began, England and France, not at the same time, but successively, feeling that it was essential that they should have the assistance of Japan in the Pacific, agreed that if Japan would go into the war and take whatever Germany had in the Pacific, she should retain everything north of the Equator which had belonged to Germany. And that treaty now stands. That treaty absolutely binds Great Britain and France. Great Britain and France cannot in honor, having offered Japan this inducement to enter the war and to continue her operations, consent to an elimination of the Shantung provision from the present treaty.

Very well, let us put these gentlemen to the test who are objecting to the Shantung settlement. Are they ready to fight Great Britain, France, and Japan, who will have to stand together, in order to get this province back for China? I know that they are not. Their interest in China is not the interest of assisting China, but of defeating the treaty.

They know beforehand that a modification of the treaty in that respect cannot be obtained, and they are insisting on what they know is impossible. But if they ratify the treaty and accept the Covenant of the League of Nations, they do put themselves in a position to assist China. (applause) They put themselves in that position for the very first time in the history of international engagements. They change the whole face of international affairs, because, after you have read the much debated Article X of the Covenant, I advise you to read Article XI. Article XI says it shall be the right of any member of the League to call attention at any time to anything, anywhere, that threatens to disturb the peace of the world or the good understanding between nations upon which the peace of the world depends. (applause)

That in itself constitutes a revolution in international relationships. Anything that affects the peace of any part of the world is the business of every nation. A nation doesn't have simply to insist that its trade shall not be interfered with; it has the right to insist that the rights of mankind shall not be interfered with. (applause)

And not only that, but back of this provision with regard to Shantung lies, as everybody knows, or ought to know, a very honorable promise which was made by the government of Japan in my presence in Paris, namely, that, just as soon as possible after the ratification of this treaty, they will return to China all sovereign rights in the province of Shantung. (applause) Great Britain has not promised to return Weihaiwei; France has not promised to return her port. Japan has promised to relinquish all the sovereign rights which were acquired by Germany for the remaining seventy-eight of the ninety-nine years of the lease, and to retain only what other governments have in many other parts of China, namely, the right to build and operate the railway under a corporation and to exploit the mines in the immediate neighborhood of that railway. In other words, she retains only the rights of economic concessionaires.

Personally, I am frank to say that I think all these nations have invaded some of the essential rights of China by going too far in the concessions which they have demanded, (applause) but that is an old story now, and we are beginning a new story. And in the new story, we all have the right to talk about what they have been doing and to convince them, by the pressure of the public opinion of the world, that a different course of action would be just and right. (applause) I am for helping China and not turning away from the only way in which I can help her. Those are the facts about Shantung. Doesn't the thing look a little different? (cries of "Yes" and applause)

Another thing that is giving some of our fellow countrymen pangs of some sort—(laughter) pangs of jealousy, perhaps—(applause) is that, as they put it, Great Britain has six votes in the League and we have only one. Well, our one vote, it happens, counts just as heavily as if every one of our states were represented and we had forty-eight, because it happens, though these gentlemen have overlooked it, that the Assembly is not an independent voting body. Great Britain has only one representative and one vote in the Council of the League of Nations, which originates all actions. And its six votes are in the Assembly, which is a debating and not an executive body. (applause) And in every matter in which the Assembly can vote along with the Council, it is necessary that all the nations represented on the Council should concur in the affirmative votes to make it valid. So that in every vote, no matter how many votes for it in the Assembly, in every vote in order for it to become valid, it is necessary that the United States should vote aye. So that, so far as I am concerned, as I have said before, I would rather be one and count six than six and count one. (laughter and applause)

Inasmuch as the Assembly is a debating body, that is the place where this exposure that I have talked about to the open air is to occur. It would not be wise for anybody to go into the Assembly with purposes that will not bear exposure, because that is the great cooling process of the world, that is the great place where gases are to be burned off. I ask you, in debating the affairs of mankind, would it have been fair to give Panama a vote, as she will have, Cuba a vote, both of them very much under the influence of the

United States, and not give a vote to the Dominion of Canada; to that great energetic republic in South Africa; to that place from which so many liberal ideas and liberal actions have come, that stout little Commonwealth of Australia? When I was in Paris, the men I could not tell apart, except by their hats, were the Americans and the Australians. They both had the swing of fellows who say, "The gang is all here, what do we care?" Could we deny a vote to that other little self-governing nation, for it practically is such in everything but its foreign affairs, New Zealand, or to those toiling—I was about to say uncounted—millions in India? Would you want to deprive these great communities of a voice in the debate? My fellow citizens, it is a proposition which has never been stated, because to state it answers it.

But they cannot outvote us. If we, as I said a minute ago, had forty-eight votes in the Assembly, they would not count any more than our one, because they would have to be combined, and it is easier to combine one than to combine forty-eight. The vote of the United States is potential to prevent anything that the United States does not care to approve. All this nonsense about six votes and one vote can be dismissed, and you can sleep with perfect quiet. In order that I may not be said to have misled you, I must say that there is one matter upon which the Assembly can vote, and which it can decide by a two-thirds majority without the concurrence of all the states represented in the Council, and that is the admission of new members to the League.

Then, there is that passion that some gentlemen have conceived, that we should never live with anybody else. You can call it the policy of isolation or the policy of taking care of yourself, or you can give any name you choose to what is thoroughly impossible and selfish. I say it is impossible, my fellow citizens. When men tell you that we are, by going into the League of Nations, reversing the policy of the United States, they have not thought the thing out. The statement is not true. The facts of the world have changed. It is impossible for the United States to be isolated. It is impossible for the United States to play a lone hand, because it has gone partners with all the rest of the world with regard to every great interest that it is connected with.

What are you going to do? Give up your foreign markets? Give up your influence in the affairs of other nations and arm yourselves to the teeth and double your taxes and be ready to spring instead of ready to cooperate? We are tied into the rest of the world by kinship, by sympathy, by interest in every great enterprise of human affairs. The United States has become the economic center, the financial center of the world. Our economic engagements run everywhere, into every part of the globe. Our assistance is essential to the establishment of normal conditions throughout the world. Our advice is constantly sought. Our standards of labor are being extended to all parts of the world, just so far as they can be extended. America is the producing center for all the ideas that are going to fecundate the great future. (applause)

You can no more separate this from the rest of the world than you can take all the tender roots of a great tree out of the earth and expect that tree to live. All the tendrils of our life—economic, social, and every other kind—are interlaced in and are inextricable with similar tendrils of mankind. And the only question which these gentlemen can ask us to answer is this—shall we exercise our influence in the world, which can henceforth be a profound and controlling influence, at a great advantage or at an intolerable disadvantage?

That is the only question you can ask. As I put it the other night, you have got this choice: you have got to be either provincials— little Americans—or big Americans—statesmen. You either have to be ostriches with your heads in the sand or eagles. (cries of "eagles") I doubt if the comparison, with the head in the sand, is a good one, because I suppose even an ostrich can think in the sand. What he does not know is that people are looking at the rest of him.

And our choice is in the bird kingdom either ostriches or eagles, and in my mind in the past the eagle has been misused. You know it was the double-headed eagle that represented Austria. You have heard of the eagles of Germany. But the only proper symbol of the eagle is the symbol for which we use it—as the bird of liberty and justice and peace. (applause)

Because I want to put it as a business proposition, if I am compelled to come down as low as that, for I don't like in debating the great traditions of a free people to bring it down to dollars and cents. But if anybody wants to bring it down to that, reason it out on that line, is it easier to trade with a man who suspects and dislikes you or with one who trusts you? Is it easier to trade with a man with a grouch or a man who opens his mind and his purse to you and treats you like a partner and a friend?

There is nothing which can more certainly put a drop of acid into every relationship we have in the world than if we now desert our former associates in this war. (applause) And that is exactly what we should be doing, and that is exactly what, unwisely and too soon, the German leaders have apprised us that they want us to do.

No part of the world has been so pleased by our present hesitation as the leaders of Germany, because their hope from the first has been that, sooner or later, we would fall out with our associates. Their hope was to divide us before the fighting stopped, and now their hope is to divide us after the fighting. You remember reading that a former German Privy Councillor, I think it was, said, in an interview the other day, that these debates in the Senate looked to him like the dawn of a new day. A new day for the world? No, a new day for the hopes of Germany. Because he saw what anybody can see who lifts his eyes and looks into the future—two isolated nations—one isolated nation now on probation, and then two—the other a nation infinitely trusted, infinitely believed in, that had given magnificent proof of its mettle and trustworthiness, now drawing selfishly and suspiciously apart and saying: "You may deceive us, you may draw us into broils, you may get us into trouble. We will take care of ourselves. We will trade with you, and we will trade on you."

Why, the choice is inconceivable. America is no quitter, (applause and cries of "No! No!")

And least of all is she a quitter in a great moral enterprise where her conscience is involved. And the only immortality in or about America is her conscience. America is not going to be great or immortal because she has immense wealth. Other great nations had immense wealth and went down in decay and disgrace, because they had nothing else. America is great because of the ideas she has conceived. America is great because of the purposes she has set herself to achieve. America is great because she has seen visions that other nations have not seen. And the one enterprise that does engage the steadfast loyalty and support of the United States is an enterprise for the liberty of mankind. (applause)

How can we make the purpose evident? I was saying in another place tonight that my dear father had once taught me that there was no use trying to reason out of a man what reason did not put in him. And yet here tonight I am trying to apply the remedy of reason. We must look about, gentlemen, and find some other remedy, because remedies in these matters are always homeopathic— like must cure like. And we must be made to see the great impulses of the nation in such fashion that they will not dare resist. I do not mean by any threat or political disaster.

Why, my fellow citizens, may I indulge in a confidence? I have had men politically disposed say to me: "As a Democrat, this is all to the good. These leaders of the Republican party in Washington are going to ruin the party." And they seem to think I will be pleased. I don't want to see the great Republican party misrepresented and misled. I don't want to see any advantage reaped by the party I am a member of because another great party has been misrepresented. Because I believe in the loyalty and Americanism and high ideals of my fellow citizens who are Republicans just as much as I believe in those things in the Democrats. It seems almost absurd to say that; of course I do. But when we get to the borders of the United States, we are neither Republicans nor Democrats. It is our privilege to scrap inside the family just as much as we please, (laughter) but it is our duty as a nation, in those great matters of international concern which distinguish us, to subordinate all such differences and to be a united family and all speak with one voice what we all know to be the high conception of American manhood and womanhood.

And there is a tender side to this great subject. Have these gentlemen no hearts? Do they forget the sons that are dead in France? Do they forget the great sacrifice this nation has made? Why, my friends, we did not go to France to fight for anything specially for America. We did not send men 3,000 miles away to defend our own territory. We did not take up the gage that Germany had thrown down to us because America was being specially injured. We sent those men over there because we saw that free people everywhere were in danger, and we had always been, and always will be, the champions of right and of liberty. (applause)

That is the glory of these men that sit here. The hardest thing I had to do, and many of you had to do, was to continue to wear civilian clothes during the war and not don the uniform, and not to risk something besides reputation—risk life and everything. Because we knew that an altar had been erected upon which that sacrifice could be made more gloriously than upon any other altar that had ever been lifted among mankind. And we desired to offer ourselves as a sacrifice for humanity. (applause) And that is what we shall do, my fellow countrymen. All the mists will pass away. A number of halls are being hired. (laughter) All the gases are being burnt off. And when you come down, after the gases have passed away, to the solid metal of which this nation is made, it will shine as lustrously and bright as it has ever shone throughout the history of the nation we love and the nation we will always consecrate ourselves to redeem. (applause)[4]

Printed in *Addresses of President Wilson*, with many corrections from the nearly complete text in the *Los Angeles Sunday Times*, Sept. 21, 1919.
[4] There is a WWT outline of this speech in WP, DLC.

To Mary Allen Hulbert

My dear Friend,   Hotel Alexandria Los Angeles 20 Sept., 1919.

We are here and all day to-morrow (or almost all) is our own, and I am writing for Edith and myself both to beg that you will lunch with us here at this hotel tomorrow at one o'clock.[1]

I had a little talk with Allan[2] in Washington a few weeks ago, as perhaps you know, and was so relieved to learn that you had entirely recovered from the accident to your foot.

We shall look forward with so much pleasure to seeing you.
Cordially and faithfully Yrs.,   Woodrow Wilson

WWTLS (WP, DLC).
  [1] There are, basically, two primary accounts of Wilson's last meeting with Mary Allen Hulbert on September 21.
  Edith Bolling Wilson, *My Memoir* (Indianapolis and New York, 1938), p. 281, has a very brief comment on the meeting, which reads as follows: "Mrs. Peck [Mary Allen Hulbert], whom my husband had known in Bermuda many years before, was to have lunch with us. Because of the work scandalmongers had done to make an intrigue of that friendship, I was glad to receive her, and show my disdain for such slander. She came—a faded, sweet-looking woman who was absorbed in an only son. She told many stories of her struggle to maintain herself and help him get his start. So wrapped up was she in her own problems that I am sure she forgot how fast time was flying, and had I not coveted every moment of it I would have enjoyed her. Presently some men came for an official conference. When my husband left the room to meet them Mrs. Peck said she would wait until he was through. Poor woman, weighed down with her own problems, of course she did not understand. Darkness had fallen when she finally rose to go."
  Mary Allen Hulbert, *The Story of Mrs. Peck: An Autobiography by Mary Allen Hulbert* (New York, 1933), pp. 267-77, provides a more detailed account. Mrs. Hulbert recalled that she had responded to Wilson's invitation with a note saying that she was unable to be at the Wilsons' hotel at the appointed time. Wilson later telephoned and said, as she remembered it: "How jolly to hear your voice. You *must* come to us tomorrow, for while we will be interrupted by occasional delegations, we can have practically an entire afternoon together. Can you arrange it at half past one?"
  Mrs. Hulbert agreed to the revised schedule and appeared at the Hotel Alexandria at the appointed time. "As we approached the Presidential suite," she wrote, "the door was flung wide, my coat taken by an attentive valet, and Mrs. Wilson stood there to greet me. Almost instantly Mr. Wilson joined us, and we went in to luncheon—four of us, for Admiral Grayson was of the party. It was a simple, homelike luncheon, and the chat was gracefully diverted from subjects disturbing to digestion. We talked, I think, of churches—how the President went to the Presbyterian Church, accompanied by Mrs. Wilson, and that she, in turn, attended her own church—Protestant Episcopal—accompanied by the President. I devoted some time to singing the California climate song and telling my old friend how well I thought he was looking—as fit as possible, in fact. Really, I was surprised and delighted that there should be so little evidence of the strain of those terrible years of war. . . .
  "Luncheon over, we went into the reception room of the suite. A delegation was announced almost at once, making it necessary for Mrs. Wilson and me to retire to an adjoining room, where, a little later, was staged the last talk I ever had with my old friend. All through the long afternoon we talked, save for occasional interrupting delegations or for the appearance of those who were, as Admiral Grayson expressed *sotto voce*: 'Converts, sir.' And, on one occasion, Admiral Grayson came in to ask Mrs. Wilson if she would receive a group of representative women. She said, firmly:
  " 'No, no. We will receive no one this afternoon. We have kept it free for Mrs. Hulbert'. . . .
  "Mrs. Wilson was not in the least as I had expected to find her from her photograph, the official likeness issued at the time of her engagement to Mr. Wilson. She was much more junoesque, but handsome, with a charming smile that revealed her strong, white teeth. She was, without question, a woman of strong character. She played well that

most difficult rôle of being the third party to the reunion of two old friends endeavoring to relive the incidents of years in a single afternoon.

"We sat in triangular formation—Mrs. Wilson and the President a little apart, and I at the apex. We had finished with generalities before we came into this room. And then Mr. Wilson at once asked me to tell him all that had befallen me since our last meeting in Washington on Memorial Day, 1915. I protested! 'Why go over the rough road now so finally behind us?'

"But he insisted that he wanted to hear *everything*. So I began slowly to give my recital of that weary time. I tried to make him realize that it was all over and not to be looked upon too seriously. What had happened had happened. He kept very still. Occasionally he bowed his head and nodded. . . . Mrs. Wilson said nothing.

"All through that afternoon we talked. We talked not wholly of matters concerning me, but about them—the Wilsons—and about the nation. I told him how I was approached by that alleged 'representative of the Republican party' who said that a member of the Wilson cabinet and his wife were ready to testify against the President if there were impeachment proceedings. I told him of the man who had come to me in Los Angeles bearing a letter from a member of his official family—the man who had said that 'Wilson and McAdoo were worrying' about me. And, as I talked, the President kept murmuring:

" 'So and So did that? Why did So and So do that?'

"My answer was always the same, 'That is for you to discover. I have neither the desire nor the power to learn. I merely present it as it came to me. You are in a position to learn the truth; I am not.' The President of the United States smiled wanly, but was silent.

"We laughed over some of the tales of iniquity thrown about both us—Woodrow Wilson and me—as a garment. But, 'God,' cried Woodrow Wilson at last, 'to think that you should have suffered because of me!'. . . .

"I replied, 'It is all over now and you will notice, please, that I am very well and certainly not downhearted. It is finished, so far as I am concerned. Now *you* know the truth and you should be able to scotch the lies. Let us talk now about you—the League of Nations—these fourteen points I have heard so much about. And why, please, all this venomous personal animosity?'

"Instantly the man changed. The Woodrow Wilson crying in the political wilderness appeared. 'That's just it. That's just it. Venomous personal animosity! If *I* had nothing to do with the League of Nations, it would go through like that!'

"And he made a swift gesture. 'But,' he went on, 'they all failed me—Lloyd George, Clemenceau, Orlando—all of them, all of them!'. . . ."

Mrs. Hulbert recalled that they spoke briefly of D'Annunzio's seizure of Fiume and that she had asked Wilson what the poet "was trying to do in Fiume." "And I was to be disappointed once more," she wrote, "for the President did not tell me. Instead he said, vehemently: 'Bah! He is behaving like an ass.' "

She wrote of their parting as follows:

"As I prepared to leave, the President laid his hand on his wife's shoulder and said to her:

" 'Isn't there something we can do?'

"She made no reply, for I broke in, saying, 'Not for me; not for my sake. I am quite all right.'

"Mrs. Wilson turned away, disappearing into another room to tell the valet to fetch my wrap. Woodrow Wilson came close to me and said again:

" 'Mary, is there nothing we can do?'

" 'Not for me,' I repeated, 'I am all right. But you can help Allen, if you wish. He is in New York, nearer you.'

"The President took out a memorandum book. 'Give me his address,' he said quickly. He closed the book. I turned to leave him.

"Mrs. Wilson went with me to the elevators. She bade me a kindly farewell. . . . The elevator quickly dropped me out of the life of my friend Woodrow Wilson—forever. The sun was low on the foothills as the jolting street car bore me back to Hollywood."

The only other recollection of the meeting which adds anything at all to the above quotations is found in Jonathan Daniels, *The End of Innocence* (Philadelphia and New York, 1954), pp. 292-93. Daniels, a son of Josephus Daniels, based his brief account on those of Mary Hulbert and Edith Wilson. However, he did add the following anecdote: "At the luncheon, Mrs. Peck wrote later, conversation was 'gracefully diverted from subjects disturbing to digestion.' That was not the story that she told to a North Carolina friend of hers who afterward brought [Josephus] Daniels into some awkward and abashed negotiations with Mrs. Peck for Wilson's letters to her. She told that friend, who told me, that at the luncheon Wilson spoke of how deeply he regretted the pain which must have been caused her by the gossip of his political enemies. Mrs. Peck said that Mrs. Wilson spoke then. Apparently she meant to be amusing in a strained situation. 'Where there's so much smoke, there must be some fire.' The 'faded, sweet-looking' Mrs. Peck burst out in anger with one of the ridiculous canards in a continental whispering against the Wilsons which attended the loud, open League debate."

[2] Mrs. Hulbert's son, Allen Schoolcraft Hulbert.

To William Phillips

[Los Angeles, Sept. 20, 1919]

Mr. Phillips, from the President.[1]

I fully approve of your proposals with regard to the Czechoslovak forces in Siberia and with regard to furnishing such supplies as are available to to [sic] forces under Kolchak and authorize you to show this telegram to the Secretary of the Treasury, the Secretary of War, and the Chairman of the Shipping Board.

[Woodrow Wilson][2]

WWT telegram (WP, DLC).
[1] Wilson was replying to W. Phillips to WW, Sept. 19, 1919 (second and third telegrams of that date).
[2] This was sent as WW to WP, Sept. 20, 1919, T telegram (SDR, RG 59, 861.00/5245, DNA).

From Edward Mandell House

Washington, D. C., Sept. 20 [1919]

I am forwarding for your information the following telegram just received from Colonel House, through the American Embassy at Paris:

"RUSH. 1410, September 19, 10 P.M. Strictly Confidential. [For the President][1] From Colonel House. I have been going over the situation here with Polk and find that, aside from pending business with which I have not been in touch, there are five present [principal] problems:

First: Italy, which depends so entirely upon your decision that it needs virtually no negotiation at this end.

Second: Roumania, which is being handled by the Supreme Council in conjunction with the Allied Mission at Budapest.

Third: The Hungarian treaty, and recognition of a Hungarian Government. The treaty is ready and the only question is therefore one of (?) a responsible government is formed to receive the document.

Fourth: The Russian situation, which in the opinion[s] of all of us is a matter which should be handled through the Foreign Offices, since no decision is possible here, with the heads of the governments no longer sitting.

Fifth: The Turkish treaty. I have talked with George, who feels that nothing can be done with this until it is known whether the United States will take mandates. The others are of the same opinion; and even after that is determined, a different and more technical delegation will be required. In our opinion it will not be necessary to keep more than one Commissioner here to carry on negotiations, particularly since you have certain definite policies which can be laid down, and there are few difficult boundary questions.

With regard to mandates Types B and C, our good offices for the French reservations concerning black armies in Togoland and the Cameroon[s] are quite finished. The French, as you know, though never opposing the principle of mandates over ex-Turkish territories, think it inexpedient to draft any general Type A mandate at this time, believing that each mandate of the A Class will be radically different from the others, and must depend upon the size and character of the territories, as they shall be arranged by the Supreme Council. There is a certain logic in this, and at all events the French will not yield the point. Therefore Lord Milner believes that no further action should be taken on mandates until the time of the Turkish treaty, which may not be until the turn of the year.

The British have let their plenipotentiaries go, and have only Eyre Crowe here, with the rank of an Ambassador. The Italian Government, now that Tittoni is away, have Scialoga, a man of no particular distinction; the Japanese are represented by their Ambassador. So that under the circumstances the presence of four American Commissioners seems not only unnecessary, but may lead to criticism in the United States.

Polk will report to the Department in a few days certain plans he has in mind for winding up the work of the Commission as soon as the Hungarian and the Bulgarian treaties are completed. Inasmuch as I shall doubtless be called eventually [to testify] before the Senate Committee, it seems advisable that I should give my testimony when it will be helpful. I am sailing between the first and tenth of October.

I have shown this to Polk and he agrees. Edward House"
                                                    William Phillips.

T telegram (WP, DLC).
    [1] Corrections and additions from the copy sent from the State Department: W. Phillips to WW, Sept. 20, 1919, T telegram (SDR, RG 59, 763.72119/6830, DNA).

From William Phillips

[Washington] 1919, Sept. 20.

In accordance with your instructions,[1] I called upon Senator Williams today and discussed with him the Armenian situation. He asked me to tell you he had come to the conclusion that the part of his bill recommending the use of the armed forces of the United States for Armenia should be stricken out, and this for two reasons:

First, because of the apparent willingness of the French to send forces to Armenia; and second, because of the decided feeling in the Foreign Relations Committee against the use of American forces for this purpose.

His bill would therefore authorize the suspension of the present restrictions against foreign armies recruiting from among their Nationals resident in the United States, as well as from persons desiring to enlist in the foreign armies, so far as these restrictions would affect the Armenian army, and at the same time authorize the immediate dispatch of arms and ammunition to Armenia from this country. The Senator told me that the sub-committee would summon me in a few days, and in the circumstances I should be grateful if you would indicate how far you wish them to go in support of Senator Williams' proposition.   William Phillips.

T telegram (WP, DLC).
[1] WW to WP, Sept. 16, 1919.

From the Diary of Dr. Grayson

Sunday, September 21, 1919.

The President went to church in the morning, although I had tried to keep him in bed. He insisted, however, that he was well enough to go to divine service.[1] After the church services, he took a short ride and returned to the hotel, where during the afternoon he saw a committee of the League to Enforce Peace,[2] and also received the members of the reception committee.[3]

Los Angeles was left at 7:00 o'clock that night after a two day stay that according to most of the men who knew the situation was one of the warmest demonstrations in the city's history. The President was greatly cheered by his reception and by the evident endorsement of his position by the people with whom he had come into contact. As a matter of fact, practically all of the newspapers had editorially endorsed his position.

[1] The Wilsons worshiped at St. Paul's Protestant Episcopal Procathedral. The Very Rev. Dr. William MacCormack, Dean of the Procathedral, presided and preached.

² Wilson met with a combined committee from the Los Angeles and Orange County branches of the League to Enforce Peace, William Miller Bowen, a lawyer of Los Angeles, chairman. For a report of the meeting, see the *Los Angeles Times*, Sept. 22, 1919, Part II, p. 1.

³ That is, the committee to greet the Wilsons on their arrival and to look after the local arrangements for their visit. Its members, with brief identifications of those not previously mentioned, were Mayor Snyder and his wife, May Ross Snyder; Frances Louise Taft (Mrs. William Aloysius) Edwards, sister of William Howard Taft and wife of a noted surgeon; George Smith Patton, lawyer and businessman of Los Angeles, active in Democratic party politics, father of then Col. George Smith Patton, Jr., U.S.A.; Harry Chandler, real estate magnate, president and publisher of the *Los Angeles Times*; Thomas Edward Gibbon, lawyer of Los Angeles; Ione Virginia Hill (Mrs. Josiah Evans) Cowles; Henry Stewart McKee; John Donnan Fredericks, lawyer of Los Angeles; and Edward Augustus Dickson, editor of the Los Angeles *Evening Express*.

To Frank Lyon Polk

[Los Angeles, Sept. 21, 1919]

For Polk through State Department.

Your cable conveying Tittoni's message received.¹ I am amazed and deeply distressed that Lloyd George and Clemenceau should now talk of Fiume passing under the sovereignty of Italy. That is the one point upon which they were firm when I was in consultation with them. I can of course in no circumstances consent to Italian sovereignty over Fiume in any form whatever. I am surprised and disappointed at Tittoni's rejection of our last proposals which were merely modifications of his own. I understood that I was accepting his second solution with regard to A free state of Fiume with the single addition of a plebescite. If it will help I am willing to accept his second solution without provision for a plebescite, leaving the whole future of the free state to the League of Nations provided it is understood that his proposal with regard to the protection of the Italianity of the corpus separatum of Fiume means only that it shall have the same degree of autonomy that it had under Hungary and no more. Please express to Tittoni my appreciation of the friendly spirit that prompted his message, my warm desire to serve Italy in any way that is consistent with the principles we have adopted, and the uselessness of continuing these attempts at a middle course. The mandate over Albania is a big price to pay for Italy's acquiescence but for lack of a better practicable solution for Albania I am willing to accept it.

[Woodrow Wilson]²

WWT MS (WP, DLC).
¹ W. Phillips to WW, Sept. 18, 1919 (telegram).
² This was sent in code as WW to WP, Sept. 21, 1919, T telegram (WP, DLC), and received in Washington as WW to WP, Sept. 21, 1919, T telegram (SDR, RG 59, 763.72119/6864, DNA).

To William Byron Colver

Los Angeles, Calif. 21 August [Sept.], 1919

Thank you for your telegram.[1] I approve of your sending to the Senate the original report, the Hoover reply, and the Commission's memorandum.   Woodrow Wilson

T telegram (WP, DLC).
[1] W. B. Colver to WW, Sept. 19, 1919.

From Upton Beall Sinclair

Dear Mr President: Pasadena California Sept 21st, 1919.

The attached petition for Amnesty[1] was adopted unanimously by a mass-meeting of two thousand people last Friday night, and I was commissioned to present it to you.

When I learned that this meeting was to be held, I stepped in amd [and] literally took it away from those who had started it. I insisted that it should be a loyal meeting: that the speakers should consist of those who had supported the government during the war. I insisted that something might be gained by appealing to you in this way; and I was ridiculed by the radicals. I acted as chairman of the meeting, and for the first time in my life I had trouble in controlling a radical audience. There was a murmur of distrust and bitterness all the time.

So, if now I come to bother a man as busy as yourself, it is not because I am lacking in good taste and personal self-respect. It is because I realize so keenly the dangers of this situation. I dont want to have to admit that I failed utterly, and to be made ridiculous for my persistent faith in you. It is not any question of myself personally, either way, but because I know how the bitterness is growing, down below the surface over which you move. And I am hoping that you will give me some sign, some hint that you do care about this matter. So it is that I am waiting at your door, and will wait till you either send me away, or grant me a few minutes.[2]

Very sincerely yours,   Upton Sinclair

TLS (WP, DLC).
[1] "PETITION FOR POLITICAL AMNESTY," printed petition (undated and without signatures) calling on Wilson to grant immediate amnesty to "all conscientious objectors and all others now in prison or awaiting trial because of their opinions." The Editors have found no news report of the "mass-meeting" of September 19 in the Los Angeles Times or elsewhere.
[2] There is no evidence that Wilson saw Sinclair at this time.

From the Diary of Dr. Grayson

Monday, September 22, 1919.

The first stop of the day came at Sacramento, where a crowd of 15,000 people had gathered in the train-shed to greet the President as he passed through. Assenting to the urgent entreaties of a number of business men of the city, the President agreed to make a five-minute talk from the rear platform of the MAYFLOWER. The crowd was most enthusiastic in its welcome, and it required the utmost effort to keep some of them who wanted to grasp his hand from actually injuring him in their enthusiasm.

The President made a very brief talk, emphasizing the fact that the great majority of those he saw at the station and along the roadside were children, and he repeated his hope that the Treaty would be ratified so that the necessity of sacrificing these children at the altar of war would be removed.

Leaving Sacramento the train proceeded to Reno, Nevada, which was reached at 8:00 o'clock that night. In Reno the President was greeted by a typical mining crowd and his welcome was all that could be desired. He spoke in a theatre[1] which had been fitted up so that his voice was carried to all of the other theatres in the city, the result being that he talked to five audiences instead of one, although he did not know that until after he had concluded his address. The President reverted at Reno back to his original strictures on radicalism, and also emphasized again the justice of the Shantung pact. The stay in Reno was cut short and he was there for only two hours.

At 10:00 o'clock that night the party started for Salt Lake City.

[1] The Rialto Theater, which held 1,900 persons. For this and other details of Wilson's visit to Reno, see Loren B. Chan, "Fighting for the League: President Wilson in Nevada, 1919," *Nevada Historical Society Quarterly*, XXII (Summer 1979), 115-27.

Remarks in Sacramento

September 22, 1919.

My fellow countrymen: I am overjoyed at this sincere greeting. It gives me great pleasure, indeed, to see and hear you. Not so much that I am personally gratified, but because I feel that you voice approval of that great Covenant designed to make peace permanent in the world. The Covenant is a movement to make for the betterment of the world. It is the first great combination of the power of the world. We must go ahead, and it is through this agency that we will progress. We simply cannot go back. We cannot retire into the past from which we have dragged ourselves. It is impossible in these circumstances for me to attempt a speech, but I can't let the occasion go by without telling you how strong it makes my heart that you should have given me so extraordinary and delightful a welcome as this. It is the more delightful to me because I believe that it is not only a desire to welcome me, but a desire to show your interest in and your support of the great cause I have come out to advocate.

The happy circumstance of this journey is that I have not come out to advocate anything personal to myself, and I have not come out to seek the fortunes of any man or group of men, but to seek the safety and guarantee of peace everywhere. We undertook a great war for a definite purpose.

That definite purpose is carried out in a great treaty. I have brought the treaty back, and we must not much longer hesitate to ratify it, because that treaty is a guarantee of peace; it is the guarantee of permanent peace, for all the great fighting nations of the world are combined in it to maintain a just settlement. So that, without this treaty, without the Covenant of the League of Nations which it contains, we would simply sink back into that slough of despond in which mankind was before this war began, with the strain of war and of terror constantly over them. We cannot go back. We will not go back.

It is more than a guarantee of peace. It is a guarantee of justice. For example, it affords the only hope of China and the hope of the restoration to her, not only of the sovereignty of Shantung, but of the sovereignty which other nations as well have taken away from her.

It affords the only expectation, in a similar case—for Belgium—that, by the pressure, the assembled, the irresistible pressure of public opinion throughout the world, its rights will be protected against aggression, that, by the combined force of the nations, right must be done to all. It is the first combination of the power of the world to see that justice shall reign everywhere. We cannot turn away from such an arrangement, and I am sure, my fellow countrymen, not only from this great outpouring here, but from the great outpourings I have seen everywhere in this country, the heart of America is right and that her purpose is irresistible.

I thank you sincerely for your welcome.

Printed in the *Sacramento Bee*, Sept. 22, 1919, with corrections from the incomplete text in *Addresses of President Wilson*.

An Address in Reno

September 22, 1919.

Governor Boyle, Mr. Chairman,[1] my fellow countrymen: A charmed circle has been drawn around me here, and I have been asked to stand within it. I think it has something to do with the apparatus in front.

The Governor and your chairman have both alluded to the fact that it does not often happen that the President comes to Nevada. Speaking for this President, I beg to say that it was not because I didn't want to come to Nevada more than once, because from the first, when I have studied the movements of the history of this great country, nothing has fascinated me so much or seemed so characteristic of that history as the movement to the frontier, the constant spirit of adventure, the constant action forward.

A wit in the East recently said, explaining the fact that we were able to train a great army so rapidly, that it was so much easier to train an American because you had to train him to go only one way. (applause) And that is and has been true of America and of the movement of population. It has always been one way. Never has there been any returning tide, always an advancing tide. And at the front of the advancing tide have always been the most adventurous spirits, the most originative spirits, the men who were ready to go anywhere and to take up any fortune to advance the things that they believed in and desired.

Therefore, it is with a sense of exhilaration that I find myself in this community, which your Governor has described as still a frontier community. You are a characteristic part of this great country which we all love.

And it is the more delightful to look at your individual aspect, because the subject that I have come to speak about is a forward-looking subject. Some of the critics of the League of Nations have their eyes over their shoulders; they are looking backward. I think that is the reason they are stumbling all the time. They are always striking their feet against obstacles which others avoid and which do not lie in the real path of the progress of civilization.

Their power to divert, or pervert, the view of this whole thing has made it necessary for me repeatedly on this journey to take the liberty that I am going to take with you tonight—of telling you just what kind of a treaty this is. Very few of them have been at pains to do that. Very few of them have given their audiences or the

---

[1] Emmet Derby Boyle, Democrat, and Charles S. Chandler, Republican state assemblyman and lawyer of Ely, who introduced Wilson. Chandler's brief remarks are quoted in Chan, "Fighting for the League," pp. 118-19.

country at large any conception of what this great document contains or of what its origin and purposes are. Therefore, I want, if you will be patient with me, to set the stage for the treaty, to let you see just what it was that was meant to be accomplished, and just what it was that was accomplished.

Perhaps I can illustrate best by recalling some history. Something over a hundred years ago, the last so-called peace conference sat in Vienna—back in the far year 1815, if I remember correctly. It was made up, as the recent conference in Paris was, of the leading statesmen of Europe. America was not then drawn into that general family and was not represented at that conference, and practically every government represented at Vienna at that time, except the government of Great Britain, was a government like the recent government of Germany, where a small coterie of autocrats were able to determine the fortunes of their people without consulting them, were able to use their people as puppets and pawns in the game of ambition which was being played all over the stage of Europe. But just before that conference, there had been many signs that there was a breaking up of that old order, there had been some very ominous signs, indeed.

It was not then so long ago that, though there were but 3,000,000 people subject to the crown of Great Britain in America, they had thrown off allegiance to that crown successfully and defied the power of the British Empire on the ground that nobody at a distance had a right to govern them, and that nobody had a right to govern them whom they did not choose to be their government, founding their government upon the principle that all just government rests upon the consent of the governed.

And there had followed, as you remember, that whirlwind of passion that we know as the French Revolution, when all the foundations of French government, not only, but of French society, had been shaken and disturbed—a great rebellion of a great suffering population against an intolerable authority that had laid all the taxes on the poor and none of them on the rich, that had used the people as servants, that had made the boys and men of France play upon the battlefield as if they were chessmen upon a board.

France revolted, and then the spirit spread, and the conference of Vienna was intended to check the revolutionary spirit of the time. Those men met in order to concert methods by which they could make monarchs and monarchies safe, not only in Europe, but throughout the world.

The British representatives at that conference were alarmed, because they heard it whispered that European governments, European monarchies, particularly those of the center of Europe—those of Austria and Germany—for Austria was then stronger than Germany—were purposing to extend their power to the western hemisphere, to the Americas. And the Prime Minister of Great Britain suggested to Mr. Rush, the Minister of the United States at the Court of Great Britain, that he put it in the ear of Mr. Monroe, who was then President, that this thing was afoot and it might be profitable to say something about it.

Thereupon, Mr. Monroe uttered his famous Monroe Doctrine, saying that any European power that sought either to colonize this western hemisphere or to interfere with its political institutions, or to extend monarchical institutions to it, would be regarded as having done an unfriendly act to the United States. And since then no power has dared interfere with the self-determination of the Americas.

That is the famous Monroe Doctrine. We love it, because it was the first effective dam built up against the tide of autocratic power. (applause) The men who constituted the Congress of Vienna, while they thought they were building of adamant, were building of cardboard. What they threw up looked like battlements, but presently were blown down by the very breath of insurgent people, for all over Europe the middle of the last century there spread, spread irresistibly, the spirit of revolution. Government after government was changed in its character. People said: "It is not only in America that men want to govern themselves, it is not only in France that men mean to throw off this intolerable yoke. All men are of the same temper and of the same make and same rights."

So the time of revolution could not be stopped by the conclusions of the Congress of Vienna, until it came about, my fellow citizens, that there was only one stronghold left for that sort of power—and that was at Berlin.

In the year 1914 that power sought to make reconquest of Europe and the world. It was nothing less than the reassertion of that old, ugly thing which the hearts of men everywhere always revolt against—the claim of a few men to determine the fortunes of all men, the ambition of little groups of rulers to dominate the world, the plots and intrigues of military staffs and men, who did not confide in their fellow citizens what it was that was their ultimate purpose.

So the fire burned in Europe, until it spread and spread like a great forest conflagration, and every free nation was at last aroused, saw the danger, saw the fearful sparks blowing over, carried by the winds of passion and likely to lodge in their own dear countries and destroy their own fair homes. And at last the chief champion and spokesman of liberty, beloved America, got into the war, (applause) and said: "We see the dark plot now. We promised at our birth to be the champions of humanity, and we have never made a promise yet that we will not redeem." I know how the tides of war were going when our men began to get over there in force, and I think it is nothing less than true to say that America saved the world.

Then a new congress of peace met to complete the work that the Congress of Vienna tried to stop and resist. At the very front of this treaty of peace, my fellow citizens, is the Covenant of the League of Nations. And at the heart of that lies this principle—that no nation shall be a member of that league which is not a self-governing and free nation; that no autocratic power may have any part in the partnership; that no power like Germany—such as Germany was—shall ever take part in its councils.

Germany has changed her constitution, as you know—has made it a democratic constitution, at any rate in form—and she is excluded for the time being from the League of Nations only in order that she may go through a period of probation to show that she means what she professes; to demonstrate that she actually does intend permanently to alter the character of her constitution and put into the hands of her people what was once concentrated as authority in Wilhelmstrasse in Berlin. If she can prove her change of heart and the permanency of her change of institutions, then she can come into respectable society. (applause) But if she cannot, she is excluded forever. At last the cycle is completed, and the free peoples who were resisted at Vienna have come into their own.

There was not a single statesman at Paris who did not know that he was the servant, and not the master, of his people. There was not one of them who did not know that the whole spirit of the times had changed, and that they were there to see that people were liberated, not dominated; that people were put in charge of their own territories and their own affairs. The chief business of the congress was to carry out that great purpose, and, at last, in the Covenant of the League of Nations, the Monroe Doctrine became the doctrine of the world. Not only may no European power impair the territorial integrity or interfere with the political independence of any state in the Americas, but no power anywhere may impair the territorial integrity or invade the political independence of another power. The principle that Mr. Canning suggested to Mr. Monroe has now been vindicated by its adoption by the representatives of mankind.

When I hear gentlemen ask the question, "Is the Monroe Doctrine sufficiently safeguarded in the Covenant of the League of Nations?", I can only say that it is, if I understand the English lan-

guage. It says in plain English that nothing in that Covenant shall
be interpreted as affecting the validity of the Monroe Doctrine.
Could anything be plainer than that? And when you add to that
that the principle of the Monroe Doctrine is applied to the whole
world, then surely I am at liberty to say that the heart of the document is the Monroe Doctrine itself.

We have at last vindicated the policy of America, because all
through that treaty, and you will presently see all through the Austrian treaty, all through the Bulgarian treaty, all through the Turkish treaty, all through the separate treaty we must make with Hungary, because she is separated from Austria, runs the same
principle, not only that no government can impose its sovereignty
on unwilling people, but that governments which have imposed
their sovereignty upon unwilling people must withdraw it.

All the regions that were unwillingly subject to Germany, subject to Austria-Hungary, and subject to Turkey are now released
from that sovereignty. And the principle is everywhere adopted
that territories belong to the people that live on them, and that they
can set up any sort of government they please, and that nobody
dare interfere with their self-determination and autonomy. I conceive this to be the greatest charter—nay, it is the first charter—
ever adopted of human liberty. It sets the world free everywhere
from autocracy, from imposed authority, from authority not chosen
and accepted by the people who obey it.

By the same token, it removes the grounds of ambition. My fellow citizens, we never undertake anything that we do not see
through. This treaty was not written, essentially speaking, at Paris.
It was written at Château-Thierry and in Belleau Wood and in the
Argonne. Our men did not fight over there for the purpose of coming back and letting the same thing happen again. They did not
come back with any fear in their hearts that their public men
would go back on them and not see the thing through. They went
over there expecting that the business would be finished. And it
shall be finished.

Nothing of that sort shall happen again, because America is
going to see it through. And what she is going to see through is
this, what is contained in Article X of the Covenant of the League.
Article X is the heart of the enterprise. Article X is the test of the
honor and courage and endurance of the world. Article X says that
every member of the League, and that means every great fighting
power in the world, Germany for the time being not being a great
fighting power, solemnly engages to respect and preserve as
against external aggression the territorial integrity and existing political independence of the other members of the League.

If you do that, you have absolutely stopped ambitious and aggressive war. There is one thing you have not stopped, and that I, for my part, do not desire to stop. And I think I am authorized to speak for a great many of my colleagues, if not all of my colleagues at Paris, that they do not wish to stop it. It does not stop the right of revolution. It does not stop the choice of self-determination. No nation promises to protect any government against the wishes and actions of its own people or of any portion of its own people. Why, how could America join in a promise like that? She threw off the yoke of a government. Shall she prevent any other people from throwing off the yoke that they are unwilling to bear? She never will, and no other government ever will, under this Covenant. But, as against external aggression, as against ambition, as against the desire to dominate from without, we all stand together in a common pledge, and that pledge is essential to the peace of the world.

I said that our people were trained to go only one way, that our soldiers were trained to go only one way, and that America will never turn back upon the path of emancipation upon which she has set out.(applause) Because not once, but several times, German orders were picked up, or discovered during the fighting, the purport of which was to certain commanders: "Don't let the Americans capture such and such a post, because if they ever get there, you can never get them out." (applause) They had got other troops out, temporarily at any rate, but they could not get the Americans out. The Americans were under the impression that they had come there to stay.

And I am under that impression about American political purposes. I am under the impression that we have come to the place where we have got in order to stay, and that some gentlemen are going to find that, no matter how anxious they are to know that the door is open and that they can get out any time they want to, they will be allowed to get out by themselves. We are going to stay in. We are going to see this thing finished, because, my fellow citizens, that is the only possibility of peace; and the world not only desires peace but it must have it.

Are our affairs entirely in order? Isn't the rest of the world aflame? Have you any conception of the restlessness, of the insubordinate restlessness, of the great populations of Europe and of great portions of Asia? Do you suppose that these people are going to resume any sort of normal life unless their rulers can give them adequate and ample guarantees of the future?

And do you realize—I wonder if America does realize—that the rest of the world deems America indispensable to the guarantee? (applause) For a reason of which we ought to be very proud. They see that America has no designs on any other country in the world. They keep in mind—they keep in mind more than you realize— what happened at the end of the Spanish-American War. There were many cynical smiles on the other side of the water when we said that we were going to liberate Cuba and then let her have charge of her own affairs. They said: "Ah, that is a very common subterfuge. Just watch. America is not going to let that rich island, with its great sugar plantations and its undeveloped agricultural wealth, get out of its grip again." And all Europe stood at amaze when, without delay or hesitation, we redeemed our promise and gave Cuba the liberty we had won for her. (applause) They know that we have no imperialistic purposes.

They know that we do not desire to profit at the expense of other peoples. And they know our power, they know our wealth, they know our indomitable spirit. And, when we put our names to the bond, then Europe will begin to be quiet, then men will begin to seek the peaceful solutions of days of normal industry and normal life, then men will take hope again, then men will cease to think of the revolutionary things they can do and begin to think of the constructive things they can do, will realize that disorder profits nobody and that order can at last be had upon terms of liberty and peace and justice.

Then the reaction will come on our own people, because, do you think, my fellow citizens, does any body of Americans think, that none of this restlessness, this unhappy feeling, has reached America? Do you find everybody about you content with our present industrial order? Do you hear no intimations of radical change? Do you learn of no organizations the object of which is nothing less than to overturn the government itself?

We are a self-possessed nation. We know the value of order. We mean to maintain it. We will not permit any minority of any sort to dominate us. (applause) But it is rather important for America, as well as for the rest of the world, that this infection should not be everywhere in the air, and that men everywhere should begin to look life and its facts in the face and come to calm counsels and purposes that will bring order and happiness and prosperity again.

If you could see the stopped, the arrested factories over there, the untilled fields, the restless crowds in the cities with nothing to do, some of them, you would realize that they are waiting for something. They are waiting for peace, and not only for peace but for the assurance that peace will last. And they cannot get that assurance if America withholds her might and her power and all the freshness of her strength from the assurance. So that there is a deep sense in which what your chairman said just now is profoundly true. We are the hope of humanity, and I, for one, have not the slightest doubt that we shall fulfill that hope.

Yet, in order to reassure you about some of the things about which you have been diligently misinformed, I want to speak of one or two details. I have set the stage now, and I have not half described the treaty. It not only fulfills the hopes of mankind by giving territories to the people that belong to them and assuring them that nobody shall take it from them, but it goes into many details.

It rearranges, for example, the great waterways of Europe, so that no one nation can control them, so that the currents of European life through the currents of its commerce may run free and unhampered and undominated. It embodies a great charter for labor by setting up a permanent international organization in connection with the League of Nations, which shall periodically bring the best counsels of the world to bear upon the problem of raising the levels and conditions of labor for men, women, and children. It goes further than that. We did not give Germany back her colonies, but we did not give them to anybody else. We put them in trust in the League of Nations, said that we would assign their government to certain powers, but assign them as trustees, responsible to the League, making annual reports to the League and holding the power under mandates which prescribe the methods by which they should administer those territories for the benefit of the people living in them, whether they were developed or undeveloped people. So that we put the same safeguards, and as adequate safeguards, around the poor, naked fellows in the jungles of Africa that we have around those peoples almost ready to assume the rights of self-government in some parts of the Turkish Empire, as, for example, in Armenia. It is a great charter of liberty and of safety, but let me come to one or two details.

It sticks in the craw of a great many persons that in the constitution of the League of Nations, as it is said, Great Britain has been given six votes and the United States only one. That would be very interesting if true, but it does not happen to be true. That is to say, it is not true in this sense—that the one American vote counts as much as the British six. In the first place, they haven't got six votes in the Council of the League, which is the only body that originates action, but in the Assembly of the League, which is the debating and not the voting body. Every time the Assembly participates in any active resolution of the League, that resolution must be concurred in by all the nations represented on the Council, which makes the affirmative vote of the United States in every instance necessary. The six votes of the British Empire cannot do anything to which the United States does not consent. Now—I am mistaken—there is one thing they can do. By a two-thirds vote, they can admit new members to the League. But I do not think that is a formidable privilege, since almost everybody is going to be in the League to begin with, and since the only large power that is not in the League enjoys, if I may use that word, a universal prejudice against it, which makes its early admission, at least, unlikely. But aside from admission of any members, which requires a two-thirds vote—in which the six British votes won't cut a very large figure—every affirmative vote that leads to action requires the assent of the United States. And, as I have frequently said, I think it is very much more important to be one and count six than to be six and count one.

So much for this bugaboo, for it is nothing else but a bugaboo. Bugaboos have been very much in fashion in the debates of those who have been opposing this League. The whole energy of that body is in the Council of the League, for whose every action in the way of formulating policy or directing energetic measures a unanimous vote is necessary. That may sometimes, I am afraid, impede the action of the League. But, at any rate, it makes the sovereignty and the sovereign choice of every nation that is a member of that League absolutely safe.

And pray do not deceive yourselves. The United States is not the only government that is jealous of its sovereignty. Every other government, big or little or middle sized that had to be dealt with in Paris, was just as jealous of its sovereignty as the United States. The only difference between some of them and us is that we could take care of our sovereignty, and they couldn't take care of theirs. But it has been a matter of principle with the United States to maintain that, in respect of rights, there was and should be no difference between a weak state and a strong state. Our contention has always been, in international affairs, that we should deal with them upon the principle of the absolute equality of independent sovereignty, and that is the basis of the organization of the League. Human society has not moved fast enough yet or far enough yet, my fellow citizens, for any part of that principle of sovereignty to be relinquished, by any one of the chief participants, at any rate. So that we have, at any rate, an absolute control over all the actions and measures of the League.

Then there is another matter, that lies outside of the League of Nations, that I find my fellow citizens, in this part of the continent, particularly, are deeply interested in. That is the matter of the cession of certain German rights in Shantung Province in China to Japan. I think that it is worthwhile to make that matter pretty clear, and I will have to ask you to be patient while I make a brief historical review in order to make it clear.

In the first place, remember that it does not take anything from China, it takes it from Germany, and I do not find that there is any very great jealousy about taking things from Germany. In 1898, China granted to Germany, for a period of ninety-nine years, certain very important rights around Kiaochow Bay, in the rich and ancient Province of Shantung, together with the right to penetrate the interior with a railway and exploit such ores as might be found in that province for thirty miles on either side of the railway.

We are thinking so much about that cession to Germany that we have forgotten that practically all of the great European powers had exacted similar cessions of China previously. They already had their foothold of control in China; they already had their control of railways; they already had their exclusive concessions over mines. Germany was doing an outrageous thing, I take the liberty of saying, as the others had done outrageous things, but it was not the first. At least, it had been done before. China lay rich and undeveloped, and the rest of the world was covetous, and it had made bargains with China, generally to China's disadvantage, which enabled the world to go in and exploit her riches. I am not now going to discuss the merits of that question, because it has no merits. The whole thing was bad, but it was not unprecedented. Germany obliged China to give her what China had given others previously. Immediately thereafter, China was obliged, because she had done this thing, to make fresh concessions to Great Britain of a similar sort, to make fresh concessions to France, to make concessions of a similar kind to Russia. It was then that she gave Russia Port Arthur and Talien-Wan.

Now, remember what followed. The government of the United States did not make any kind of protest against any of these cessions. We had at that time one of the most public-spirited and humane men in the executive chair at Washington that have ever graced that chair—I mean William McKinley—(applause) and his Secretary of State was a man whom we have all always delighted to praise, Mr. John Hay. But they made no protest against the cession to Germany, or to Russia, or to Great Britain, or to France. The only thing they insisted on was that none of those powers should close the door of commerce to the goods of the United States in those territories which they were taking from China. They took no interest, I mean so far as what they did was concerned, in the liberties and rights of China. They were interested only in the rights of the merchants of the United States.

I want to hasten to add that I do not say this even to imply criticism on those gentlemen, because, as international law stood then, it would have been an unfriendly act for them to protest in any one of these cases. Until this treaty was written in Paris it was not even proposed that it should be the privilege of anybody to protest in any such case if his own rights were not directly affected. Then, some time after that, followed the war between Russia and Japan. You remember where that war was brought to a close—by delegates of the two powers sitting at Portsmouth, New Hampshire, at the invitation of Mr. Roosevelt, who was then President. In that treaty, Port Arthur—China's Port Arthur, ceded to Russia—was ceded to Japan, and the government of the United States, though the discussions were occurring on its own territory, made no suggestion even to the contrary.

And now, the treaty in Paris does the same thing with regard to the German rights in China. It cedes them to the victorious power, I mean to the power that took them by force of arms, the power which was in the Pacific victorious in this war, namely, to Japan, and there is no precedent which would warrant our making a protest. Not only that, but, in the meantime, since this war began, Great Britain and France entered into solemn covenants of treaty with Japan that, if she would come into the war and continue her operations against Germany in the Pacific, they would lend their whole influence and power to the cession to Japan of everything that Germany had in the Pacific, whether on the mainland or in the islands north of the Equator. So that if we were to reject this provision in the treaty, Great Britain and France would not in honor be at liberty to reject it, and we would have to devise means to do what, let me say with all solemnity only war could do, force them to break their promise to Japan.

Well, you say, "Then, is it just all an ugly, hopeless business?" No, it is not, not if we adopt the League of Nations. Because the government of the United States was not bound by these treaties, the government of the United States was at liberty to get anything out of the bad business that it could get by persuasion and argument. And it was upon the instance of the government of the United States that Japan promised to return to China what none of these other powers has yet promised to return—all rights of sovereignty that China had granted Germany over any portion of the province of Shantung—the greatest concession in that matter that has ever been made by any power that has interested itself in the exploits of China—and to retain only what corporations out of many countries have long enjoyed in China—the right to run the railroad and extend its line to certain points and to continue to work the mines that have already been opened.

Not only that, but I said a minute ago that Mr. Hay and Mr. McKinley were not at liberty to protest. Turn to the League of Nations and see what will be the situation then. Japan is a member of the League of Nations, all these other powers that have exploited China are members, and they solemnly promise to respect and preserve the territorial integrity and existing political independence of China. Not only that, but in the next article, the international law of the world is revolutionized. It is there provided that it is the friendly right of any member of the League at any time to call attention to anything, anywhere, that is likely to disturb the peace of the world or the good understanding between nations upon which the peace of the world depends. If we had had the Covenant at that time, Mr. McKinley could, and I venture to say would, have said to Germany: "This is directly none of our business, for we are seeking no competitive enterprise of that sort in China, but this is an invasion of the territorial integrity of China. We have promised, and you have promised, to preserve and respect that integrity, and if you do not keep that promise it will destroy the good understanding which exists between the peaceful nations of the world. It will be an invasion, a violation of the essential principles of peace and of justice." Do you suppose for one moment that, if the matter had been put in that aspect—with the attention of the world called to it by the greater power of the United States—Germany would have persisted in that enterprise?

How had she begun it? She had made the excuse of the death of two German missionaries at the hands of irresponsible mobs in certain provinces of China an excuse for taking this valuable part of China's territory. Ah, my fellow citizens, it makes anybody who regards himself as a Christian blush to think what Christian nations have done in the name of protecting Christianity! But it cannot be done any more under the League of Nations.

It cannot be done without being cited to the bar of mankind, and if Germany had been cited to the bar of mankind before she began her recent tragical enterprise, she never would have undertaken it. You cannot expose such matters to the cool discussion of the world without disclosing all their ugliness, their illegitimacy, their brutality. This treaty sets up, puts in operation, so to say, puts into commission the moral force of the world. Our choice with regard to Shantung, therefore, is to keep out of the treaty—for we cannot change it in that respect—or go in and be an effective friend of China. I, for one, am ready to do anything or to cooperate in anything in my power to be a friend, and a helpful friend, to that great, thoughtful, ancient, interesting, helpless people, in capacity, in imagination, in industry, in numbers one of the greatest peoples in the world and entitled to the wealth that lies underneath their feet and all about them in that land which they have not as yet known how to bring to its development.

There are other things that have troubled the opponents of the League. One thing is they want to be sure they can get out. That does not interest me very much. If I go into a thing, my first thought is not how I can get out. My first thought is not how I can scuttle, but how I can help, how I can be effective in the game, how I can make the influence of America tell for the guidance and salvation of the world, not how I can keep out of trouble. I want to get into any kind of trouble that will help liberate mankind. I do not want always to be thinking about my skin or my pocketbook or my friendships. It is just as comfortable to die quietly in your bed, never having done anything worth anything, as to die as some of those fellows that we shall always love, when we remember them, died upon the field of freedom. Is there any choice? Do you think anybody outside the family is going to be interested in any souvenir of you after you are dead? They are going to be interested in souvenirs of the boys in khaki, whether they are of their family or not. They are going to touch with reverence any sword or musket or rapid-fire gun or cannon that was fired for liberty upon the fields of France.

I am not thinking of sitting by the door and keeping my hand on the knob, but if you want to do that, you can get out any time you want to. There is absolutely nothing in the Covenant to prevent you. I was present at its formulation, and I know what I am talking about, besides being able to understand the English language. It not only meant this, but said it, that any nation can, upon two years' notice, withdraw at any time, provided that, at the time it withdraws, it has fulfilled its international obligations and its obligations under the Covenant. But it does not make anybody judge as to whether it has fulfilled those obligations, except the nation that withdraws.

The only thing that can ever keep you in the League is being ashamed to get out. You can get out whenever you want to after two years' notice, and the only risk you run is having the rest of the world think you ought not to have got out.

I, for my part, am not very sensitive about that, because I have a memory. I have read the history of the United States. We are in the habit of keeping our international obligations, and I do not believe that there will ever come a time when any just question can be raised as to whether we have fulfilled them or not. Therefore, I am not afraid to go before the jury of mankind at any time on the record of the United States with regard to the fulfillment of its international obligations. And when these gentlemen who are criticizing it once feel, if they ever should feel, the impulse of courage instead of the impulse of cowardice, they will realize how much better it feels. Your blood is at least warm and comfortable, and the red corpuscles are in command when you have got some spunk in you. But when you have not, when you are afraid somebody is going to put over something on you, you are furtive and go about looking out for things, and your blood is cold, and you shiver when you turn a dark corner. That is not a picture of the United States. When I think of these great frontier communities, I fancy I can hear the confident tread, tread, tread of the great hosts that crossed this continent. They were not afraid of what they were going to find in the next canyon. They were not looking over their shoulders to see if the trail was clear behind them. They were making a trail in front of them, and they had not the least notion of going back. They were going to stay there, even if they had to change their names. I know you will do what I am sure all the rest of our fellow countrymen are doing—clear the deck of these criticisms that really have nothing in them, and look at the thing in its large aspect, in its majesty. Particularly, look at it as a fulfillment of the destiny of the United States, for it is nothing less. At last, after this long century and more of blood and terror, the world has come to the vision that that little body of 3,000,000 people, strung along the Atlantic Coast of this continent, had in that far year 1776. Men in Europe laughed at them, at this little handful of dreamers, this little body of men who talked dogmatically about liberty. And since then that fire which they started on that coast has consumed every autocratic government in the world, every civilized autocratic government. And now at last the flame has leaped to Berlin, and there is the funeral pyre of the German Empire.

Printed in *Addresses of President Wilson*, with a few additions and minor corrections from the complete text in the Reno *Nevada State Journal*, Sept. 23, 1919.

Newton Diehl Baker to Joseph Patrick Tumulty[1]

Washington DC 1919 Sep 22

At close of war we had about perfected self controlled aerial bombs which could fly more than a hundred miles and land practically at a point for which they were aimed carrying no pilot but immense quantities of high explosives[2] Stop The effect of this would have been to destroy a city substantially a hundred miles within enemy lines by a number of such bombs Stop Our discoveries of new and terrible gases and modes of distributing them all foreshadows that the next war would be so fearful in its effects upon civilian population and in destroying communities as to pass any precedent in history   Baker.

T telegram (WP, DLC).
    [1] This telegram was prompted by JPT to NDB, Sept. 21, 1919, Hw draft telegram (WP, DLC), which read as follows: "You recently made a speech describe [describing] the possible horrors of a future war, by the use of new instrumentalities of death &c. Can you send me a summary of this speech for use on our Trip." The Editors have been unable to find any report or text of Baker's speech.
    [2] Baker here refers to two projects, initiated in 1917 and still in the early testing stages at the time of the Armistice, to develop an "aerial torpedo" or "flying bomb." It was actually a small, propeller-driven airplane launched from rails or a catapult and directed to its target by an inertial guidance system, developed by Elmer Ambrose Sperry, which was also the ancestor of modern automatic pilot systems. The earlier, more complex aircraft was under development for the navy by a company headed by Sperry and his son, Lawrence, and was designed to carry 1,000 pounds of explosives up to seventy-five miles. A simpler, lighter, and much cheaper aircraft was being developed for the army by a team headed by Charles Franklin Kettering at the Dayton Wright Airplane Company. It was intended to carry 200 pounds of explosives for about ninety miles. In tests held in 1918 and 1919, prototypes of both flying bombs made wildly erratic flights, most of them finally crashing due to imperfections in the guidance systems. See Thomas Parke Hughes, *Elmer Sperry: Inventor and Engineer* (Baltimore and London, 1971), pp. 262-73, and Stuart W. Leslie, *Boss Kettering* (New York, 1983), pp. 80-87.

From Albert Sidney Burleson

For the President: The White House, Sept. 22, 1919

Referring to my former telegram.[1] Steps have been taken to enlist the active interest of cotton producers to press prompt and favorable action on the treaty. It has been brought to their attention that Europe needs our cotton and would buy liberally if she were in a position to pay for it, but that for the present she cannot command money in order to avert the calamity that will fall on both sides of the Atlantic unless she shall be supplied with raw material necessary to set her industries going; that it is absolutely necessary that liberal credits shall be open on that side of the Atlantic against which our exports of cotton can be charged until the spinners of Europe have time to reconvert them and reimburse themselves; that these credits cannot be arranged until the Peace Treaty is ratified and the League of Nations becomes a fact; that bankers realize, if the League is rejected, a condition of international chaos may supervene in which fresh international antagonism will be aroused, social unrest aggravated, and property rights throughout Europe jeopardized as seriously as they are today in Russia; that the ports of the world are still more or less closed by the restrictions that the various governments have found it necessary to impose, pending the formal ending of the war; that merchants who have the capital necessary for the extensions of the credit they would be glad to grant, provided reasonable security were provided, are deterred from taking risks because of the present unsatisfactory and uncertain conditions; that during the war it was possible to market the cotton crop because our government was willing to loan billions of dollars to our Allies; that further government credits are out of the question; that indeed our government would not be justified, if inclined, to extend them, until its permanent relationship to the borrowing powers are defined in an agreement and ratified by the Senate; that this continued delay threatens to find expression in a serious decline of cotton unless it is cured. We hope for good results from this.

I beg to direct your attention to another situation. Memphis is Senator McKellar's[2] home, and he is strong for the League without amendments and without reservations. Senator Shields[3] voted in committee for three reservations: Monroe Doctrine, domestic questions, and right to withdraw. He did not vote on Article X and will probably vote against an amendment of it. Previously he had declared himself in favor of Pi[t]tman's reservations.[4] He did not commit himself as to language in reservations for which he voted. He voted against all amendments. May I suggest that if you mention either Senator at Memphis, that you avoid any expression of criticism of Senator Shields. It might prove helpful if you would say a word about your high estimate of his character and ability as a lawyer, and your hope that he will stand firm against interfering with Section X, firm against every amendment, and speak kindly but regretfully of his position on reservations and hope that when all is ironed out, he will be in accord with all supporters of the League. It is most important that we get him to vote with us on Article X and against amendments, and we believe statement from you along these lines will produce results. If you feel that you cannot take this attitude, think it wise not to mention either Senator.

Underwood, Hitchcock, and McKellar know of this telegram and approve same. The situation in the Senate is improving. The effect of the speeches is beginning to be felt here.   Burleson

T telegram (WP, DLC).
    [1] ASB to WW, Sept. 13, 1919.
    [2] That is, Kenneth Douglas McKellar.
    [3] That is, John Knight Shields, the other senator from Tennessee. Wilson was scheduled to speak in Memphis on September 27.
    [4] For which, see the news report printed at Aug. 21, 1919, Vol. 62.

From William Phillips

Washington DC Sept 22 1919

Representative of the League to Enforce Peace[1] reports that the following reservation has been agreed upon by the mild reservationists with Senator Lodge and will be made public within two or three days. "The United States assumes no obligation under the provisions of Article X to preserve the territorial integrity or political independence of any other country or to interfere in controversies between other nations whether members of the League or not or to employ the military and naval forces of the United States under any article of the treaty for any purpose unless in any particular case the Congress, which under the Constitution has the sole power to declare war or authorize the employment of the military and naval forces of the United States, shall by act or joint resolution so declare."   William Phillips[2]

T telegram (WP, DLC).
[1] Harry Norris Rickey, director of the Washington office of the League to Enforce Peace.
[2] This was sent as WP to WW, Sept. 22, 1919, T telegram (SDR, RG 59, 763.72119/6914B, DNA).

Breckinridge Long to Joseph Patrick Tumulty

Washington, D. C., Sept. 22, 1919

Am reliably informed that the following Senators: Lenroot, McNary, McCumber, Nelson, Colt, and Kellogg, have agreed with Lodge as follows:

"The United States assumes no obligation under the provisions of Article X to preserve the territorial integrity (etc? etc.)

(this was also received in message from Mr. Phillips)

My informant advises that Lodge has accepted; also that those six Senators have agreed to stick together on all questions, and are opposed to all amendments. Consequently they hold the balance of power in the Senate. Taft has been requested to come to Washington immediately to induce a few other milder reservationists to join them.

Forster has left for the day, and everyone here has gone, so, deeming this important, I send it direct to you. The text as quoted above changes the committee report only by substituting the last phrase for the words "shall otherwise specifically determine" which appeared in the former agreement. Each of the above six are opposed to any amendments and practically assure defeat of all of them, with the possible exception of the voting strength amendment, which it is feared Walsh of Massachusetts and maybe one or two other Democrats will vote for.   Breckinridge Long

T telegram (WP, DLC).

Guy Mason[1] to Joseph Patrick Tumulty

Washington. Sept. 22, 1919

Mild reservationists and Lodge have gotten together. Victory for Lodge. Some Democrats joined McCumber in the deal. Strong action by the President necessary to beat this coalition.

Guy Mason

T telegram (WP, DLC).
    [1] Lawyer and member of the staff of the Washington office of the League to Enforce Peace.

Rudolph Forster to Joseph Patrick Tumulty

[The White House, Sept. 22, 1919]

Rickey brings me for the President reservation agreed to by McCumber, Kellogg, McNary, Lenroot, Colt, and Nelson, and accepted by Lodge, which is practically same as in McCormick's message.[1] Rickey feels that Republican Senators, with the exception of Johnson, Knox, and Brandegee, are nearer agreement today than ever on final form of reservations they will fight for. Will not send in full unless you so advise.   Forster.

T telegram (WP, DLC).
    [1] V. C. McCormick to WW, Sept. 18, 1919.

From William Phillips

Washington DC Sep 22 1919

Butler[1] British representative who will be Secretary General of the Labor Conference reports that there is some idea in Europe of attempting to postpone meeting as some powers in Europe think the conference would be a failure without United States representation. Butler is very strongly opposed to delay which he thinks would have an unfortunate and perhaps disastrous effect and asks if you would be willing to say that he could cable Drummond that in event of the United States ratification being delayed you would ask Congress for authority to have United States represented. Butler thinks such statement would end all talk of delay and would be very helpful. The matter is called to your attention because of the necessity of Butlers cabling this week in order to prevent efforts for postponement   William Phillips

T telegram (WP, DLC).
  [1] Harold Beresford Butler, Principal Assistant Secretary in the Ministry of Labor and a technical expert on labor questions in the British delegation to the Paris Peace Conference.

From the Diary of Dr. Grayson

Tuesday, September 23, 1919.

A halt was made at Ogden and the President and party were taken in automobiles for a trip through Bingham Canyon. No formal addresses were made here and the welcome was entirely of an informal character.[1]

Salt Lake City was reached at 4:30 in the afternoon and the usual automobile parade took place. The President was suffering very serious fatigue as a result of his exertions; in fact, the entire party was beginning to show the strain under which everyone was. The trip was far too strenuous and calculated to exhaust every possible bit of vitality that the President had. I was becoming more and more apprehensive of the results but was doing everything I possibly could to secure rest for the President whenever that was possible. However, his constantly recurring headaches, coupled with the fact that the irritation in his throat brought coughing spells that interfered greatly with his rest, caused me great concern.

After the automobile procession through the main streets, the President went back to his hotel and rested until 7:30 when he addressed an audience that filled every corner of the Mormon Temple.

The meeting in the Tabernacle was interesting in the extreme.[2] It was plain that among the audience were a number of people who were hostile to the President's program, but he was cheered with every courtesy. The Shantung settlement again formed the chief topic of his address, as it had been a subject of the deepest controversy throughout Utah.

Immediately after his night address the President returned to his train and the start was made for Cheyenne.

  [1] Wilson and his party were in Ogden for approximately one hour, from about 2:30 to 3:30 p.m. The Wilsons held an impromptu reception at which Wilson made the remarks printed below.
  [2] The police estimated the audience for Wilson's address in the Mormon Tabernacle at 12,000 persons. *Ogden*, Utah, *Examiner*, Sept. 24, 1919.

Joseph Patrick Tumulty to Rudolph Forster

[Ogden, Utah,] 23 September 1919.

Received your message conveying information from Rickey also received message from Guy Mason along same lines. President desires you to show to Hitchcock copy of your telegram to me conveying Rickey information and ask Hitchcock what present status of League situation is and what his advice to the President on League would be.

Who are the Democrats who joined McCumber in the deal?

J P Tumulty[1]

T telegram (WP, DLC).
[1] The received copy of this telegram is in EBR, RG 130, White House Staff Files, 1900-1935, DNA. Wilson's train arrived in Ogden at 2:30 p.m., and this telegram was sent at 2:54 p.m. The plain meaning of Wilson's message was that, now that the mild reservationists and Lodge had agreed on a reservation to Article X, Wilson needed Hitchcock's advice on what to do. One can only speculate on the reasons why Wilson, a short time later in Ogden, labeled opponents of the League as disloyal pro-Germans and why, an hour or so later in Salt Lake City, he declared war on the mild reservationists on the issue of the compromise reservation to Article X; again erred egregiously in saying that any reservation was tantamount to an amendment and would require renegotiation of the treaty, not only with the Allies but with Germany as well; and then went on to say that of course only Congress could authorize use of the military forces of the United States in the execution of obligations under Article X.

To the People of Utah[1]

[Sept. 23, 1919]

It is with the greatest pleasure that I find myself in the great state of Utah, and I regret that it is not possible for me to remain in Ogden long enough to express to its citizens the sense of privilege I feel in coming into contact with them, and the confidence I feel that, in common with all forward-looking Americans, they accept with enthusiasm the guarantees of peace we are now seeking to confirm.

May I not take the liberty of expressing the greatest interest in the good fortune of Ogden and northern Utah, and my hope that prosperity of the most substantial kind may continue to crown the efforts of its citizens.

Printed in the *Ogden, Utah, Standard*, Sept. 23, 1919.
[1] The following statement was given out by Tumulty upon the arrival of the presidential party at Ogden. *Ogden, Utah, Examiner*, Sept. 24, 1919.

Remarks in Ogden, Utah

September 23, 1919.

I cannot make a real speech in the circumstances, but it would be ungracious of me if I did not say how delightful I have felt the welcome of Ogden to be, and how refreshing it is to me to come into contact with you, my fellow citizens, in this part of the world which I wish I knew much better. You will understand that the theme that I have most at heart needs a lot of sea room to turn in, and I would despair of making any adequate remarks about so great a matter as the treaty of peace or the League of Nations. But I do find this, my fellow countrymen, that the thing is very near the heart of the people. There are some men in public life who do not seem to be in touch with the heart of the people, but those who are know how that heart throbs deep and strong for this great enterprise of humanity, for it is nothing less than that. We must set our purposes in a very definite way to assist the judgment of public men.

I do not mean in any way to coerce the judgment of public men, but to enlighten and assist that judgment, for I am convinced, after crossing the continent, that there is no sort of doubt that 80 percent of the people of the United States are for the League of Nations, and that the chief opposition outside legislative halls comes from the very disquieting element that we had to deal with before and during the war. All the elements that tended toward disloyalty are against the League, and for a very good reason. If this League is not adopted, we will serve Germany's purpose, because we will be dissociated from the nations with whom we cooperated in defeating Germany. Nothing is so gratifying, we now learn by cable, to public opinion in Germany as the possibility of their doing now what they could not do by arms—separating us in feeling when they could not separate us in fact. I, for my part, am in to see this thing through, because these men who fought the battles on the fields of France are not now going to be betrayed by the rest of us. We are going to see that the thing they fought for is accomplished, and it does not make any difference how long the fight or how difficult the fight, it is going to be won, and triumphantly won.

Printed in *Addresses of President Wilson.*

An Address in the Tabernacle in Salt Lake City

[[September 23, 1919]]

Governor Bamberger, President Grant,[1] my fellow countrymen: It is indeed inspiring to stand before this great audience, yet I feel that I have come to present a theme which deserves the greatest of all audiences. I must admit to a very considerable degree of unaffected diffidence in presenting this theme, because the theme is so much bigger than any man's capacity to present it adequately. It is a theme which must engage the enthusiastic support of every lover of humanity, every man who professes Christian convictions, because we are now as a nation asked to make what I cannot help characterizing as the most critical decision we have ever made in the history of America.

We sent our boys across the sea to defeat the purposes of Germany. We engaged that, if they would defeat the purposes of Germany, we would complete what they had begun and make such arrangements of international concert as would make it impossible for any such attempt ever to be made again. The question, therefore, is, shall we see it through, or shall we now, at this most critical juncture of the whole transaction, turn away from our associates in the war and decline to complete and fulfill our sacred promises to mankind?

I have now crossed the continent, my fellow countrymen, and am on my way cast again, and I feel qualified to render testimony as to the attitude of this great nation towards the Covenant of the League. And I say, without the slightest hesitation, that an overwhelming majority of our fellow countrymen purposes that this Covenant shall be adopted. One by one, the objections to it have melted away. One by one, it has become evident that the objections urged against it were without sufficient foundation. One by one, it has become impossible to support them as objections, and at last we come to the point of critical choice as to the very heart of the whole matter.

For, my fellow citizens, you know it troubled some of our public men because they were afraid that it was not perfectly clear that we could withdraw from this arrangement whenever we wanted. There is no justification for doubt in any part of the language of the Covenant on that point. The United States is at liberty to withdraw at any time upon two years' notice, the only restriction being when it withdraws it shall have fulfilled its international obliga-

[1] Simon Bamberger, Democratic Governor of Utah, who introduced Wilson; and Heber Jeddy Grant, banker and business entrepreneur of Salt Lake City and seventh President of the Church of Jesus Christ of Latter-day Saints, who gave the invocation.

tions and its obligations under the Covenant of the League. But it is left to its own conscience and to no other tribunal. It has to determine whether those obligations have been fulfilled or not. And I, for one, am not afraid of the judgment of mankind with regard to it. The United States never has failed to fulfill its international obligations. It never will fail. I am ready to go to the great jury of humanity upon that matter at any time that we should withdraw from this arrangement.

But I am not one of those, when I go into a great enterprise, think first of how I am going to get out of it. I think first of how I am going to stay in it, with what power of influences I am going to promote the objects of the great concert and association which is being formed. And that is the temper of America.

I was quoting the other night the jest of an American wit who, commenting upon the extraordinary rapidity with which we had trained an army, said that it was easier to train an army in America than anywhere else in less time, because you had to train them to go only one way. And they showed the effect of the training. They went only one way, and the issues that we are debating were really decided at Château-Thierry, Belleau Wood, and in the Argonne. So that we are now put to the test by these men who fought, as they were put to the test by those of us who ordered them to the field of battle. And the United States, the people of the United States, have the same training as their army. They do not look back, they go only one way.

The doubt as to whether some superior authority to our own Congress could intervene in matters of domestic policy is removed. The language of the Covenant expressly excludes the authorities of the League from taking any action or expressing any judgment with regard to domestic policies like immigration, like naturalization, like the tariff, like all of those things which have lain at the center so often of our political action.

Nobody doubts any longer that the Covenant gives explicit, unqualified recognition to the Monroe Doctrine. Indeed, it does more than that. It adopts the principle of the Monroe Doctrine as the principle of the world. The principle of the Monroe Doctrine is that no nation has the right to interfere with the affairs or to impose its own will in any way upon another nation. President Monroe said to the governments of Europe that any attempt of that sort on the part of any government of Europe would be regarded as an act unfriendly to the United States. The Covenant of the League endorses that. The Covenant of the League says that nothing in that document shall be construed as affecting the validity of the Monroe Doctrine, which says that if any power seeks to impose its will upon any American state in North America, Central America, or South America, it now acknowledges the right of the government of the United States to take the initiative.

So that the forces of objection being driven out of one post after another are now centering upon the heart of the League itself. I have come here tonight, my fellow countrymen, to discuss that critical matter that you constantly see in the newspapers, that we call reservations. I want you to have a very clear idea of what is meant by reservations.

Reservations are to all intents and purposes equivalent to amendments. I can say, I believe with confidence, that it is the judgment of the people of the United States that neither the treaty nor the Covenant should be amended. Very well, then, look at the character of reservations. What does a reservation mean? It means a stipulation that this particular government insists upon interpreting its attitude to that Covenant in a special way; it insists upon interpreting it in a way in which other nations do not interpret it. This thing, when we ratify it, is a contract. You cannot alter so much as the words of a contract without the consent of the other parties. Any reservation that we have will have to be carried to all the other signatories, Germany included. We shall have to get the consent of Germany, among the rest, to read this Covenant in some special way in which we prefer to read it in their interests, or in the interests of the safety of America. That, to my mind, is one of the most unacceptable things that could happen. To reopen the question of the meaning of this clearly written treaty is to reopen negotiations with Germany. And I don't believe that any part of the world is in the temper to do that. (applause) And in order to bring this matter, to put this matter, in such a shape as will lend itself to a concrete elucidation, let me read you what I understand is a proposed form of reservation:

"The United States assumes no obligation under the provisions of Article X to preserve the territorial integrity or political independence of any other country or to interfere in controversies between other nations, whether members of the League or not, or to employ military and naval forces of the United States under any article for any purpose, unless, in any particular case, Congress, which under the Constitution has the sole power to declare war or authorize the employment of military and naval forces of the United States, shall by act or joint resolution so declare."

Now, my fellow citizens (applause)—now wait a minute. You want to applaud that? Wait until you understand the meaning of it, and if you have a knife in your hands with which you intend to cut out the heart of this Covenant, applaud. But, if you want this

Covenant to have a heart in it, and want it to have a purpose in it, want it to be something subscribed to by a red-blooded nation, withhold your applause. Understand this thing before you form your sentiment with regard to it.

This is a rejection of the Covenant. (applause) This is an absolute refusal to carry any part of the same responsibility that the other members of the League carry. Does the United States want to be in on that special footing? (Cries of "No! No!") Does the United States want to say to the nations with whom it stood in this great struggle, "We have seen you through on the battlefield, but now we are done. (Cries of "No!") We are not intending to stand by you?"

Why, my fellow citizens, Article X is an engagement on the part of the great fighting nations of the world, because all the great fighting nations are going to be members of the League, that they will observe, respect, and preserve as against external aggression the territorial integrity and the existing political independence of the other members of the League. That is cutting into the heart of all war.

Every war of any consequence that you can cite originated in an attempt to seize the territory or interfere with the political independence of some other nation. We went into this war with the sacred promise that we regarded all nations as having the same rights, whether they were weak or strong, and unless we engage to sustain the weak, we have guaranteed that the strong will prevail, we have guaranteed that any imperialistic enterprise may revive, we have guaranteed that there is no barrier to the ambition of nations that have the power to dominate, we have abdicated the whole position of right and substituted the principle of might.

This is the heart of the Covenant, and what are these gentlemen afraid of? Nothing can be done under that article of the treaty without the consent of the United States. (applause) I challenge them to draw any other deduction from the provisions of the Covenant itself. In every case where the League takes action, the unanimous vote of the Council of the League is necessary. The United States is a permanent member of the Council of the League. Its affirmative vote is in every case necessary for every affirmative, or for that matter, every negative, action. (applause)

Let us go into particulars therefore. These gentlemen say, "We don't want the United States drawn into every little European squabble." Why of course we don't, and under the League of Nations, it is entirely within our choice of whether we will or not. The processes of the action of the League are certain to be this. When trouble arises in the Balkans, when somebody sets up a fire somewhere in Central Europe among those little nations, which are for the time being looking upon each other with a good deal of jealousy and suspicion, because the passions of the world have not yet cooled—whenever that happens, the Council of the League will confer as to the best methods of putting out the fire.

If you want to put out a fire in Utah, you don't send to Oklahoma for the fire engine. If you want to put out a fire in the Balkans, if you want to stamp out the smoldering flames in some part of Central Europe, you don't send to the United States for troops. The Council of the League selects the powers which are most ready, most available, most suitable, and selects them at their own consent, so that the United States would in no such circumstance conceivable be drawn in unless the flames spread to the world.

And would they then be left to themselves if they were not members of the League? You have seen the fire spread to the world once. Do you wish it to spread again? If you saw human liberty imperiled, would you wait to be a member of the League to go in? (cries of "No! No!")

Why, my fellow citizens, the whole thing goes directly to the conscience of the United States. If the fight is big enough to draw the United States in, I predict that they will be drawn in anyhow. And if it is not big enough to bring them in, it is inevitable that they can go in or stay out according to the decisions of the Council, which are dependent upon their own votes.

Why are these gentlemen afraid? There is no force to oblige the United States to do anything except moral force. Is any man, any proud American, afraid of moral force? Is any man afraid that the United States will resist the duress of duty? Why, I am so intensely conscious of the great conscience of this nation. I so see the inevitableness, as well as the dignity and the greatness—such declarations as President Grant has made—of aligning all the great organized moral forces of the world on the same side. It is inconceivable that they should be on different sides.

So that there is no necessity for the last part of this reservation. Everybody in the whole United States, and I say that advisedly, almost every public man, every statesman, in the world knows that, in order for the United States to go to war, it is necessary for Congress to act. They don't have to be told that, but that is not what this resolution says. This resolution says the United States assumes no obligation under the provision of Article X to preserve the territorial integrity or political independence of any other country—washes its hands of the whole business; says, "We don't want advice to create the presumption that we will do the right thing. We don't want to be committed to any more trouble." But when we say that, every time a case arises, that Congress will independently check it up and determine whether there is any moral obligation, and, after determining that, determine whether it will feel the moral obligation of any act, it is an absolute withdrawal from the moral obligations of Article X. And that is why I say that it would be a rejection of the Covenant and thereby a rejection of the treaty, for the treaty cannot be executed without the Covenant.

So I appeal, and I appeal with confidence, my fellow country-men, to the men whose judgment I am told has approved of res-ervations of this sort. I appeal to them to look into the matter again. I know some of the gentlemen who are anxious to have a reserva-tion of that sort. I know them to be high-minded, patriotic Ameri-cans. I know them to be men of mature judgment in that respect, and I respect them as much as I respect any man. But they have not looked into the matter. Are they willing to ask the rest of the world to go into this Covenant and to let the United States assume none of its obligations, and let us have all of the advantages and none of the responsibilities? Are they willing that our America should ask for special exemption, should seek special privileges, should ask to go into the arrangement and depend upon any judg-ment but its own judgment?

I confidently believe, my fellow citizens, that they will do no such a thing. That is not an interpretation of the Covenant. I have been trying to interpret it to you. That is a rejection of the Cove-nant, and, if that is adopted, the whole treaty falls to the ground. My fellow citizens, we must realize that a great and final choice is upon the people. Either we are going to guarantee civilization or we are going to abandon it. I use the word with perhaps the admis-sion that it may carry a slight exaggeration, but nevertheless ad-visedly, when I say abandon civilization, for what is the present condition of civilization? Everywhere, even in the United States, there is antagonism towards our process of government. We feel the evil influence on this side of the Atlantic, and on the other side of the Atlantic every public man knows that it is knocking at the door of his government.

While this unrest is assuming this menacing form, rebelling against authority, it cuts roads of force through the regular pro-cesses of government. The world is waiting on America. And while I say it with entire respect for the representatives of other govern-ments, I say it with knowledge: the government of the United States is the only government in the world that the rest of the world is waiting on. The government of the United States speaks for the people of the United States, and it is devoted to the service of a great people. And the world knows that the people can always apply this covenant of right, knows that nobody dares invade the public judgment of the people of the United States, and knows that the public judgment is on the side of right and justice for the people. It has seen the United States do what no other nation ever did. When we fought the war with Spain, there were many cynical smiles on the other side of the water when we professed a disinterested purpose, when we said we were going to win freedom for Cuba and then present it to her. They said: "Ah, yes—under the control of the United States. They will never let go of that rich island which they can exploit so much to their own advantage." When we kept that promise and proved our absolute disinterestedness, notwithstanding the fact that we had beaten Spain until she had to accept anything that we tendered, we paid her twenty millions of dollars for something that we could have taken, namely, the Philippine Islands, all the world stood at amaze and said: "Is it true, after all, that this people believes and means what it says? Is it true, after all, that this is a great altruistic force in the world?"

Now look what has happened, my fellow citizens. Poland, Bohemia, Armenia, Yugoslavia—there are kinsmen, I dare say, of these people in this audience—they could, none of them, have won their independence any more than Cuba could have won theirs. They were under an authority that is as reckless in the acts of its force, that is as regardless of the rights of people and of humanity, as the Spanish government ever was in the government of the Philippines by a force of might.

These people have been liberated, and now the world is waiting to see whether the United States will join in saying that it means what it fought for and guarantee their freedom and say: "What we have given to you, no man can take away." This is our final heroic test of character. And I for one have not the slightest doubt as to what the result of the test is going to be, because I know that at heart this people loves freedom and right and justice more than it loves money and material prosperity or any of the things that anybody can get but nobody can keep unless they have elevation of spirit enough to see the horizons of the destiny of man.

Instead of wishing to ask to stand aside, get the benefits of the League, but share none of its burdens or responsibilities, I for my part want to go in and accept what is offered to us—the leadership of the world. A leadership of what sort, my fellow citizens? Not a leadership that leads men along the lines by which great nations can profit out of weak nations, not an exploiting power, but a liberating power, a power to show the world that, when America was born, it was indeed a finger pointed towards those lands in which men might deploy some of these days and live in perfect freedom, look each other in the eyes as equals, see that no man was put upon, that no people were forced to accept authority which was not of their own choice, and that, out of the general generous impulse of the human genius and the human spirit, we were lifted along the levels of civilization to days when there should be wars no more, but men should govern themselves in peace. And now the world offers it to us.

It is inconceivable that we should reject it. It is inconceivable to demand that we put any condition upon accepting it, particularly— for I speak this with a certain hurt pride, my fellow citizens, as an American—particularly when we are so safeguarded that the world under the Covenant cannot do a thing that we do not consent to being done. Other nations, other governments, were just as jealous of their sovereignty as we have been, and this guarantees the sovereignty of all the members of this great union of nations. There is only one nation for the time being excluded, and that is Germany. And Germany is excluded only in order that she may go through a period of probation, only in order that she may prove to the world that she has made a real permanent change in her constitution, and that hereafter, not Wilhelmstrasse, but the votes of the German people, will determine the policy of the German government.

If I may say so without even by implication involving great public men whom I entirely respect, I want to say that the only popular clamor, that, after all the various reservations, the only popular clamor back of the impulse to reject any part of this treaty proceeds from exactly the same source that the pro-German propaganda proceeded from. I ask the honorable and enlightened men who I believe thoughtlessly favor reservations such as I have read to reflect upon that and examine into the truth of it, and to reflect upon this proposition that, by holding off from this League, they serve the purposes of Germany, for what Germany has sought throughout the war was, first, to prevent our going in, then to separate us in interest and purpose from the other governments with which we were associated.

Now, shall we, by the vote of the United States Senate, do for Germany what she could not do with her arms? We shall be doing it, whether we intend it or not. I exculpate the men I am thinking of entirely from the purpose of doing it. It would be unworthy of me to suggest such a purpose. But I do suggest, I do state with confidence, that that is the only end that would be gained, because Germany is isolated from the other nations. She desires nothing so much as that we should be isolated, because she knows that the same kind of suspicion, the same kind of hostility, the same kind of unfriendliness—that subtle poison that permeates every trouble that comes between nations—will center on the United States, as well as upon Germany. Her isolation will be broken; she will have a comrade, whether that nation wants to be her comrade or not, and what the lads did on the field of France will be undone. We will allow Germany to do in 1919 what she failed to do in 1918!

It would be unworthy of me, my fellow citizens, in the responsible position in which you have put me, if I were to overstate any of these things. I have searched my conscience with regard to them. I believe I am telling you the sober truth, and I am telling you what I get, not by intuition—I know no more than you do about it—but through those many voices that inevitably reach the government and do not always reach you. From overseas we know what the leading men of Germany are thinking and saying, and they are praying that the United States may stand off from the League.

I call upon you, therefore, my fellow citizens, to look at this thing in a new aspect, to look upon it, not with calculations of interest, not with fear of responsibility, but with a consciousness of the great moral issues which the United States must now decide and which, having decided, it cannot reverse. If we keep out of this League now, we can never enter it except alongside of Germany. We can either go in now or come in later with our recent enemies, and to adopt a reservation such as I have read, which explicitly renounces responsibility under the central engagement of the Covenant, is to do nothing less than that.

I hope that in order to strengthen this impression on your minds you will take pains to read the treaty of peace. You need not read all of it—a lot of it is technical and you can skip that. But I want you to get a picture of what is in this great document. It is much too narrow a view of it to think of it as a treaty of peace with Germany. It is that, but it is very much more than a treaty of peace with Germany. It is a treaty in which an attempt is made to set up the rights of peoples everywhere very explicitly. The lines of this treaty are going to be projected—have been projected—into the treaty with Austria, into the treaty with Bulgaria, into the treaty with Hungary, into the treaty with Turkey.

Everywhere the same principle is adopted—that the men who wrote the treaties at Versailles were not at liberty to give the property of anybody else to anybody else. And it is the first great international agreement in the history of civilization that was not based on the opposite principle. Every other great international arrangement has been a division of spoils. And this is an absolute renunciation of spoils, even with regard to the helpless parts of the world, even with regard to those poor benighted people in Africa, over whom Germany had exercised a selfish authority which exploited them and did not help them. Even they are not handed over to anybody else. The principle of annexation—the principle of extending sovereignty to territories that are not occupied by your own people—is rejected in this treaty. And all of those regions are put under the trust of the League of Nations, to be administered for the benefit of their inhabitants—the greatest humane arrangement that has ever been attempted. And the rules are laid down in the Covenant itself which prevent the selfish exploitation of these helpless people by the agents of the League who will exercise authority over them during the period of their development.

Then see how free course is given to our sympathies. I believe that there is no region in the world towards which the sympathies of the United States have gone out so abundantly as to the poor people of Armenia, those people infinitely terrified, infinitely persecuted. We have poured out money to relieve their distress. And at every turn we have known that every dollar we spent upon them might be rendered useless by the cruel authority over them. Then, under pretense of not being able to control its own affairs in those parts of the empire, the Turkish government might say that it was unable to restrain the horrible massacres which have made that country a graveyard.

Very well, Armenia is one of the regions that is to be under trust of the League of Nations. Armenia is to be redeemed. The Turk is to be forbidden to exercise his authority there. And Christian people are not only allowed to aid Armenia, but they are to be allowed to control Armenia. So that at last this great people, struggling through night after night of terror, knowing not when they would see their land stained with blood, are now given a promise of safety, a promise of justice, a possibility that they may come out into a time when they can enjoy their rights as free people that they never dreamed they would be able to exercise.

What great humane impulses of the human heart are expressed in this treaty! And we would be recreant to every humane obligation if we did not lend our whole force, if necessary make our utmost sacrifice, to maintain its provisions. We are approaching the time in the discussions of the Senate when it will be determined what we are going to say about it. And I am here making this public appeal to you and, through you, to gentlemen who have favored such utterances as I have read to you, now to take a second thought in the matter and realize that what they are after is already accomplished. The United States cannot be drawn into anything it doesn't wish to be drawn into, but the United States ought not to put itself in the position of saying: "You need not expect of us that we assume the same moral obligations that you assume. You need not expect of us that we will respect and preserve the territorial integrity and political independence of other nations."

And let me remove another misapprehension about that clause, my fellow citizens. Almost every time it is quoted, the words "external aggression" are left out. There was not a member of that conference with whom I conferred who wanted to put the least restraint upon the right of self-determination by any portion of the human family, who wished to put the slightest obstacle in the way of throwing off the yoke of any government if that yoke should become intolerable.

This does not guarantee any government against an attempt on the part of its own subjects to throw off its authority. The United States could not keep its countenance and make a promise like that, because it began by doing that very thing. The glory of the United States is that, when we were a little body of 3,000,000 people strung along the Atlantic Coast, we threw off the power of a great empire because it was not a power chosen or consented to by ourselves. We hold to that principle. We never will guarantee any government against the exercise of that right. No suggestion was made in the conference that we should. We merely ourselves promise to respect the territorial integrity and existing political independence of other members of the League and to assist in preserving them against external aggression.

And if we do not do that, the taproot of war is still sunk deep into the fertile soil of the human family. I am for cutting the taproot off. I am for making an insurance against war, and I am prudent enough to take 10 per cent insurance if I cannot get any more. I would be very pleased to get 25 per cent insurance. I would be delighted to get 50 per cent. And here, in conscience, I believe we are getting 98 per cent.

No body of men can give you absolutely 100 per cent insurance against war, any more than they could give you 100 per cent insurance against losing your temper. You cannot insure men against human passions, but notice what this Covenant does. It provides nine months as a minimum for the cooling off of human passions. It is pretty hard to be crazy mad for nine months. If you stay crazy mad, or crazy anything else, for nine months, it will be wise to segregate you from your fellow citizens. And the heart of this Covenant, to which very few opponents have ventured to draw attention, is this—that every great fighting nation in the world engages never to go to war without first having done one or the other of two things—without having either submitted the point in controversy to arbitration, in which case it promises absolutely to abide by the verdict or, having submitted it to the Council of the League of Nations, not for decision, but for a discussion, agreeing to lay all the documents and all the pertinent facts before the Council, agreeing that the Council shall publish the documents and the facts to mankind; that it will give six months to the Council for a consideration of the matter, that, even if it does not accept the result, it won't go to war for three months after the opinion is rendered. So that you have nine months in which to accomplish all the gentle work of mediation, all the sane work of discussion, all the quieting work of a full comprehension of what the result of bringing the matter to the issue of war would be upon the nations immediately concerned and upon the nations of the world.

And in Article XI, which follows Article X, it is made the right of any member of the League to call attention to anything, anywhere, which is likely to affect the peace of the world or the good understanding between nations upon which the peace of the world depends. So that, as the storm begins to gather, you can call the attention of the world to it, and the cleansing, purifying, cooling process of public opinion will at once begin to operate.

When Shantung Province, or a very important part of it, or Kiaochow Bay, was ceded by China to Germany in March 1898, the government of the United States uttered not a single protest. One of the most enlightened and humane men that has ever sat in the executive chair was President William McKinley. One of the ablest Secretaries of State in the long list of distinguished men who have occupied that office was associated with him as Secretary of State, the Honorable John Hay. They made not a single intimation of protest? Why? Because under international law as it was, and as it is until this Covenant is adopted, it would have been a hostile act for them to do any such thing unless they could show that the material or political interests of the United States were directly affected. And so the only ground which they insisted upon was that Germany should not close Shantung Province to the trade of the United States. They could not lift a little finger to help China. They could only try to help the trade of the United States.

Immediately after that concession, China made similar concessions to England, to Russia, and France. Again no protest, only insistence that the door should be kept open to our goods—not to our moral ideas, not to our sympathy with China, not to our sense of right violated, but to our merchandise. You don't hear anything about the concessions out there to Great Britain or to France, because, unhappily, neither they, nor the concession to Germany, were unprecedented. Poor China had done the like, not once, but many times before.

What happened after? In the treaty between Japan and Russia, after the Japanese-Russian war, a treaty signed on our own territory—in Portsmouth, New Hampshire—Port Arthur, the Chinese territory ceded to Russia, was transferred to Japan. Here were our own people sitting about, here was our own government that had invited these gentlemen to sit at Portsmouth. Did they object to Port Arthur being handed over—not handed back to China, but handed over to Japan?

I am not going to stop, my fellow citizens, to discuss the Shantung provision in all its aspects, but what I want to call your attention to is that, just so soon as this Covenant is signed, rather ratified, every nation in the world will have the right to speak out for China. (applause) I want to say very frankly, and I ought to add that representatives of these great nations themselves admit, that Great Britain, France, and the other powers which have insisted upon similar concessions in China will be put in a position where they will have to reconsider.

This is the only way to serve and redeem China, (applause) unless it be you want to start a war for the purpose. At the beginning of the war, during the war, Great Britain and France engaged by solemn treaty with Japan that, if she would come in the war and continue in the war, she could have, provided she in the meantime took it by force of arms, what Germany had in China. Those are treaties already in force. They are not waiting for ratification. France and England cannot withdraw from those obligations. And it will serve China not one iota if we should dissent from the Shantung arrangement. But, being parties to that arrangement, we can insist, if it is necessary to insist, upon the promise of Japan—the promise which the other governments have not matched—that she will return to China immediately all sovereign rights within the province of Shantung. (applause) Under the operations of Article XI and of Article X, it will be impossible for any nation to make any further inroads either upon the territorial integrity or the political independence of China.

And I, for one, want to say that my heart goes out to that great people, that learned people, that accomplished people, that honest people, hundreds of millions strong but never adequately organized for the exercise of force, therefore always at the mercy of anyone who has effective armies or navies, always subject to demands, never in position unassisted by the world to insist upon its own rights.

There is a test—an acid test. Are you willing to go into the great adventure of liberating hundreds of millions of human beings from a threat of foreign power? If you are timid, I can assure you you can do it without a drop of human blood. If you are squeamish about fighting, I will tell you that you won't have to fight.

The only force that outlasts all others and is finally triumphant is the moral judgment of mankind. (applause) Why is it that, when a man tells a lie about you, you don't wince? But when he tells the truth about you, if it is not creditable, then you wince? The only thing you are afraid of is the truth. The only thing you dare not face is the truth. The only thing that will get you sooner or later, no matter how you sneak or dodge, is the truth; the only thing that will conquer nations is the truth. (applause)

No nation is going to look the calm judgment of mankind in the face for nine months and then go to war. (applause) You can illustrate the great by the little. I dare say you have taken time to cool off sometimes. I know I have. It is very useful for a person, particularly with a Scotch disposition like my own, to withdraw from human society when he is mad all through and just think about the situation and reflect upon the consequences of making a conspicuous ass of himself. (applause) It is for that reason I have always said that if you have an acquaintance whom you suspect of being a fool, encourage him to hire a hall. There is nothing that tests a man's good sense like exposure to air.

And so we are applying this great healing sanitary influence to the affairs of nations and of men. And we can apply it only by the processes of peace which are offered to us after a conference, which I can testify was taken part in in the knowledge and in the spirit that never obtained before in any such conference; that we were not at liberty to work out the policy and ambitions of any government, and that our single duty and our single opportunity was to put the peoples of the world in possession of their own affairs. (applause)

And so, as much of the case, my fellow citizens, as I can lay before you on a single occasion—as much of this varied and diversified theme—is laid before you, and I ask your assistance to redeem the reputation of the United States. I ask you to make felt everywhere that it is useful to make it felt, not by way of threat, not by way of menace of any kind, but by way of compelling judgment, that the thing for us to do is to redeem the promises of America made in the solemn presence of mankind when we entered this war. (applause) For I see a happy vision before the world, my fellow countrymen. Every previous international conference was based upon the authority of governments. This, for the first time, was based upon the authority of peoples. It is, therefore, the triumphant establishment of the principle of democracy throughout the world, but only the establishment of the principle of political democracy. What the world now insists upon is the establishment of industrial democracy, is the establishment of such relationships between those who direct labor and those who perform labor as shall make a real community of interest, as shall make a real community of purpose, and shall lift the whole level of industrial achievement above bargain and sale into a great method of cooperation by which men, purposing the same thing, justly organizing the same thing, may bring about a state of happiness and of prosperity such as the world has never known before. We want to be friends of each other as well as friends of mankind. We want America to be a body of brethren. Then you may be sure that its leadership will bring the same sort of comradeship and intimacy of spirit and purity of purpose to the counsel and achievements of mankind.

Printed in the Salt Lake City *Salt Lake Tribune*, Sept. 24, 1919, with one major correction from the text in *Addresses of President Wilson*.

To Lyon Gardiner Tyler

My dear Dr. Tyler: Ogden, Utah, 23 September, 1919

I know you will understand my long delay in replying to your letter of August 30th.[1] It came just upon the eve of my trip through the country, and I have been obliged to turn aside from all personal matters in order to concentrate my attention upon the great business that I have been attempting to discuss with the country.

I need hardly tell you how deeply honored I feel by the action of the Board of Visitors of William and Mary College in conferring upon me the degree of Doctor of Laws, upon the nomination of the Faculty of the College, and that it gives me a sense of deep gratification to accept the honor. I beg that you will convey to the Board of Visitors and the members of the Faculty my deep sense of appreciation of this distinction conferred by an institution connected from the first with the highest traditions of the country.

Cordially and sincerely yours,   [Woodrow Wilson]

CCL (WP, DLC).
    [1] Printed at that date in Vol. 62.

Two Telegrams to William Phillips

Ogden, Utah, 23 September, 1919

With regard to the date of the International Labor Conference,[1] that is entirely in our hands and can be postponed only by us. I beg that you will give every assurance that we will lend our cooperation in the most effective way, whether we can at the time of the meeting actually participate officially or not.   Woodrow Wilson

¹ See W. Phillips to WW, Sept. 22, 1919 (second telegram of that date).

Ogden, Utah, 23 September, 1919

I greatly regret that Senator Williams has concluded to omit the authorization for sending troops to Armenia.¹ I believe that it is of immediate humane necessity to take energetic action and that the very existence of the Armenian people depends upon it. I would greatly appreciate his urgent assistance in this matter.

Woodrow Wilson

T telegrams (WP, DLC).
¹ See W. Phillips to WW, Sept. 20, 1919.

From Francesco Saverio Nitti

Washington [Sept. 23, 1919].

The following urgent message has just been received for you from Jay, American Embassy, Rome:

"3174 Sept. 23, 1 a.m. Very Confidential. The Prime Minister requested me late tonight to send following urgent personal appeal from him to the President. Italian Government has ordered telegraph line cleared for this message, which should reach you tomorrow morning and be rushed to the President. Message follows:

" 'When answering my message,¹ you were good enough to renew the assurances of your most warm friendship for Italy.² You know that I never doubted it, but not on this account was I less profoundly grateful for the sincere and profound sympathy of your message. You wanted, moreover, to add the expression of your most lively desire to render us a friendly service.

" 'You know the situation today. Italy, whose sacrifices you wished to recall in your speech at Tacoma as so superior in proportion to those of the Allies, is now, after too many months of waiting, profoundly desolate (?) [shaken].³ Italy, who wished spontaneously to rush to fight for human liberty, runs now the risk of becoming a spreading sore of agitation in Europe. Everything can be calmed by the recognition of Fiume to us, with the most ample security for the port and the railway, which would be entrusted [one would entrust] to the League of Nations.

" 'I appeal with all the more faith to you for your immediate word, because I know that you, although you have [again having]

expressed a different judgment, cannot but wish to weigh the new and tragic elements which have intervened.

" 'Immediate word of yours can guarantee security and order in Italy and, with Italy, in Europe.

" 'I respectfully implore your immediate word of deliverance, which may today save the country which has given so much of itself to the common cause.'

"Opening of Parliament has been today postponed by royal decree till Saturday. Press announces this is probably to give time for receipt of President's decision about Fiume.

"King has called a Crown Council for Thursday at Quirinal Palace, of leading members [statesmen] of all parties and principal generals and admirals."   William Phillips.

T telegram (WP, DLC).
    ¹ F. S. Nitti to WW, Aug. 31, 1919, Vol. 62.
    ² WW to F. S. Nitti, Sept. 3, 1919, Vol. 62.
    ³ Additions and corrections from P. A. Jay to RL, Sept. 23, 1919, T telegram (SDR, RG 59, 763.72119/6900, DNA).

From Frank Lyon Polk

Washington. Sept. 23, 1919

Following has just been received from Mr. Polk in regard to the Italian situation:

"4314 Sept 22, 12 P.M. Confidential. For the President and the Secretary of State. The French papers today announce that Tittoni told the Italian press that I had expressed my adhesion to the Clemenceau-Lloyd George Plan; namely, Fiume proper for the Italians; docks, railroads and port for the Jugo-Slavs. I have given out a statement at once denying this report. I have already warned the Italian delegation that I did not like their statements, and I will take up this particular statement with them immediately.

Had a long talk with Vesnitch this afternoon. He was disturbed over the reports that Lloyd George and Clemenceau were disposed to give Fiume to the Italians and wanted to know our position. I told him the facts.

News from Fiume, Zara, and Cattaro shows signs of unrest, and I think it probable that there will be difficulties between the two factions. I feel that Lloyd George and Clemenceau are anxious for Italians to ratify the treaty and that they were therefore willing to make this concession to Italy. The fact that the treaty is not ratified is becoming embarrassing to both the British and the French. Questions such as Silesia, the further disarming of Germany, and other questions constantly come up and the Council finds itself unable to act until after the treaty is ratified by three powers. They fear the Senate will not ratify for some time and therefore ratification by Italy necessary. Polk"   William Phillips.[1]

T telegram (WP, DLC).
[1] This was sent as FLP to WW, Sept. 23, 1919, T telegram (SDR, RG 59, 763.72119/6893, DNA). There is also a copy of Polk's original telegram in WP, DLC.

From William Phillips

Washington DC Sep 23 1919

My telegram Sept 20 concerning Armenia. Telegram just received from Polk[1] would indicate French plan agreed to by British on the 15th instant consists merely of sending about twelve thousand men to occupy places like Marash, Urfa, Malatia, in Cilicia and southern Armenia evacuated by the British thus carrying out the provisions of the Sykes Picot Agreement of 1916.[2] Clemenceau declines to send French troops to Russian Armenia via Batoum where the British withdrawal will be completed in about ten days. Malatia is more than three hundred miles from Erivan. Distance and small number of French troops would make it practically impossible for them to prevent the invasion or massacring of Armenians in Russian Armenia. These troops will probably be unable to help even northern and eastern Turkish Armenia.

The fact that the French are not sending troops to Russian Armenia removes the first reason why Senator Williams was thinking of striking out the part of his bill recommending the despatch of American troops and strengthens your position contained in your telegraphic instruction received on the 17th instant.[3]

Polk points out rightly that sending volunteers, ammunition et cetera can be assured only if the railway from Batoum to Erivan be held by American troops.

I have informed Senator Williams of Polks telegram and will act when summoned by the subcommittee in conformity with the instructions which you may give me.

In this connection and without prejudice to any action we may decide to take, may I submit to your consideration the advisability of you making a direct urgent appeal, in view of the most serious and critical situation, to Lloyd George and Clemenceau, the former to suspend the withdrawal of British troops, the latter to send French troops to Russian Armenia.   William Phillips

T telegram (WP, DLC).
[1] FLP to SecState, No. 4312, Sept. 22, 1919, T telegram (SDR, RG 59, 860J.01/90, DNA).
[2] About which, see n. 7 to the minutes of a meeting of the Council of Ten printed at

Feb. 6, 1919, Vol. 54, and the minutes of a meeting of the Council of Four printed at March 20, 1919, Vol. 56.
³ WW to W. Phillips, Sept. 16, 1919.

From the Diary of Dr. Grayson

Wednesday, September 24, 1919.

During the entire morning and until 4:00 o'clock in the afternoon the train ran over the Union Pacific Railroad through the mountains, with only halts for the changing of engines. The President remained in his stateroom for a good part of the day endeavoring to get some rest. He was suffering a great deal and his nervous condition was apparent.

At Cheyenne the party was greeted by a reception committee, headed by Governor [Carey] of Wyoming,¹ and an escort had been provided, made up of the entire 15th Cavalry, which was stationed at Fort D. A. Russell, just outside of the city limits. The meeting in Cheyenne was held in the local theatre,² and an orchestra made up entirely of women played a number of patriotic airs before the President spoke. The President's address followed closely the lines of his previous day's talk.

After the meeting ended the President was taken for a ride out through the grounds of Fort Russell and was shown the camp where the alien enemies had been interned during the war.

Cheyenne was left at 7:00 o'clock that night and a quick run was made to Denver, which was reached at 11:00 o'clock. Despite the lateness of the hour a large crowd was in the streets waiting to cheer the President on his arrival.

¹ Robert Davis Carey, Republican.
² The Denver *Rocky Mountain News*, Sept. 25, 1919, reported that the Princess Theater in Cheyenne had 1,500 seats.

An Address in the Princess Theater in Cheyenne

[[September 24, 1919]]

Governor Carey, my fellow countrymen: It is with genuine satisfaction that I find myself in this great state, which I have only too seldom visited, with a body of the citizens of this state in order that I may make clear some of the matters which have emerged in the discussion in the midst of which we now find ourselves. Governor Carey is quite right in saying that no document ever drew upon it more widespread discussion than the great treaty of peace with which your representatives returned from Paris.

And it is not to be wondered at, my fellow citizens, because that treaty is a unique document. It is the most remarkable document, I venture to say, in human history, because in it is recorded a complete reversal of the processes of government which had gone on throughout practically the whole history of mankind.

The example that we set in 1776, which some statesmen in Europe affected to disregard and others presumed to ridicule, nevertheless set fires going in the hearts of men which no influence was able to quench. And, one after another, the governments of the world have yielded to the influences of democracy. No man has been able to stay the tide, and there came a day when there was only one bulwark standing against it. That was in Berlin and Vienna—standing in the only territory which had not been conquered by the liberal forces of the opinion of the world, continued to hold fast, where there was planted a pair of governments that could use their people as they pleased, as pawns and instruments in a game of ambition, send them to the battlefield without condescending to explain to them why they were sent, send them to the battlefield to work out a dominion over free peoples on the part of a government that had never been liberalized and made free.

The world did not realize that it had come to the final grapple of principle. It was only by slow degree that we realized that we had any part in the war. We started the forces in 1776, as I have said, that made this war inevitable. But we were a long time realizing that, after all, that was what was at issue. We had been accustomed to regarding Europe as a field of intriguing, of rival ambitions, and of attempts to establish an empire. And at first we merely got the impression that this was one of the usual European wars, to which, unhappily, mankind had become only too accustomed.

You know how unwilling we were to go into it. I can speak for myself. I made every effort to keep this country out of the war, until it came to my conscience, as it came to yours, that after all it was our war, that the ambition of these central empires was directed against nothing less than the liberty of the world, and that if we were indeed what we had always professed to be—champions of the liberty of the world—it was not within our choice to keep out of the great enterprise.

And we went in just in time. I can testify, my fellow countrymen, that the hope of Europe had sunk very low when the American troops began to throng overseas. I can testify that they had begun to fear that the terror would be realized and that the German power would be established. At first they were incredulous that our men could come in force enough to assist them. At first they thought that it was only a moral encouragement they could get from seeing that gallant emblem of the Stars and Stripes upon their fields. Presently they realized that the tide was real, that here came men by the thousands, by the hundreds of thousands, by the millions; that there was no end to the force which would now be asserted to rescue the free peoples of the world from the terror of autocracy. And America had the infinite privilege of fulfilling her destiny and saving the world. I do not hesitate to say, as a sober interpretation of history, that American soldiers saved the liberties of the world.

I want to remind you of all this, my fellow citizens, because it is pertinent to the discussion that is now going on. We saved the liberties of the world, and we must stand by the liberties of the world. We cannot draw back.

You remember what happened in that fateful battle in which our men first took part. You remember how the French lines had been beaten and separated and broken at Château-Thierry, and you remember how the gates seemed to open for the advancement of the Germans upon Paris. And then a body of men, a little body of men—American soldiers and American marines—against the protests of French officers, against the command of the remote commanders, nevertheless dared to fill that breach, stopped that advance, turned the Germans back, and never allowed them to turn their faces forward again. They were advised to go back, and they asked the naive American question: "What did we come over here for? We did not come over here to go back; we came here to go forward." And they never went in any other direction. The men who went to Château-Thierry, the men who went into Belleau Wood, the men who did what no other troops had been able to do in the Argonne, never thought of turning back, they never thought of any *reservations* on their service. They never thought of saying, "We are going to do this much of the job and then scuttle and leave you to do the rest." And I am here, I am on this journey, to help this nation, if I can by my counsel, to fulfill and complete the task which the men who died upon the battlefields of France began. And I am not going to turn back any more than they did. I am going to keep my face just as they kept their face—forward towards the enemy.

My friends—I use the words advisedly—the only organized forces outside—I mean outside of congressional halls—the only organized forces in this country against this treaty are the forces of hyphenated Americans. I beg you to observe that I say the only organized forces, because I would not include many individuals whom I know in any such characterization. But I do repeat that it is the pro-German forces, and the other forces that showed their hyphen during the war, that are now organized against this treaty. And we can please nobody in America except these people by rejecting it or qualifying it in our acceptance of it.

I want you to recall the circumstances of this great war, lest we forget. We must not forget to redeem absolutely and without qualification the promises of America in this great enterprise. I have crossed the continent now, my friends, and am a part of my way back. I can testify to the sentiment of the American people. It is unmistakable. The overwhelming majority of them demand the ratification of this treaty. And they demand it because, whether they have analyzed it or not, they have a consciousness of what it is that we are fighting for.

We said that this was a people's war—I have explained to you that it was, though you did not need the explanation—and we said that it must be a people's peace. It is a people's peace. I challenge any man to find a contradiction to that statement in the terms of the great document with which I returned from Paris. It is so much of a people's peace that, in every portion of its settlement, every thought of aggrandizement—of territorial or political aggrandizement—on the part of the great powers was brushed aside, brushed aside by their own representatives. They declined to take the colonies of Germany in sovereignty and said they would consent and demand that they be administered in trust by a concert of the nations through the instrumentality of a league of nations. They did not claim a single piece of territory. On the contrary, every territory that had been under the dominion of the Central Powers, unjustly and against its own consent, is by that treaty, and the treaties which accompany it, absolutely turned over in fee simple to the people who live in it.

The principle is adopted without qualification upon which America was founded—that all just government proceeds from the consent of the governed. No nation that could be reached by the conclusions of this conference was obliged to accept the authority of a government by which it did not wish to be controlled. It is a peace of liberation. It is a peace in which the rights of peoples are realized, and, when objection is made to the treaty, is any objection made to the substance of the treaty? There is only one thing in the substance of the treaty that has been debated seriously, and that is the arrangement by which Japan gets the rights that Germany had in Shantung Province in China. I wish I had the time to go through the story of that fully. It was an unavoidable settlement, and nothing can be done for China without the League of Nations.

Perhaps you will bear with me if I take time to tell you what I am talking about. You know that China has been the common prey of the great European powers. Perhaps I should apologize to the representatives of those powers for using such a word, but I think they would admit that the word is justified. Nation after nation has demanded rights, semisovereign rights, and concessions with regard to mines and railways and every other resource that China could put at their disposition. And China has never been able to say "No." A great, learned, patient, diligent people, numbering hundreds of millions, has had no organized force with which to resist, and has yielded again and again and again to unjust demands.

One of these demands was made upon her in March 1898, by Germany—unjustly made. I will not go into the particulars, but I could justify that word "unjustly" made. A concession was demanded of her of the control of the whole district around Kiaochow Bay, one of the open doors to the trade and resources of China. She was obliged to yield to Germany practically sovereign control over that great region by the sea, and, into the interior of the province, Germany was privileged to extend a railway and to exploit all the deposits of ore that might be found for thirty miles on either side of the railway which she was to build.

And the government of the United States at that time, presided over by one of the most enlightened and beloved of our Presidents—I mean William McKinley—and the Department of State, guided by that able and high-minded man, John Hay, did not make the slightest protest. Why? Not because they would not if they could have aided China, but because under international law as it then stood, no nation had the right to protest against anything that other nations did that did not directly affect its own rights. And Mr. McKinley and Mr. Hay did insist that, if Germany took control of Kiaochow Bay, she should not close those approaches to China against the trade of the United States.

How pitiful, when you go into the court of right, you cannot protect China, you can only protect your own merchandise! You cannot say, "You have done a great wrong to these people." You have got to say, "We yield to the wrong, but we insist that you should admit our goods to be sold in those markets!" Pitiful, but nevertheless it was international law. All nations acted in that way at that time. Immediately following these concessions to Germany, Russia insisted upon a concession and got Port Arthur and other territories. England insisted, though she had had similar concessions in the past, upon an additional concession and got Weihaiwei.

France came into the game and got a port and its territory lying behind it for the same period of time that Germany had got her concession, namely, ninety-nine years.

Then came the war between Russia and Japan, and what happened? In a treaty signed on our own sacred territory, at Portsmouth in New Hampshire, Japan was allowed to take from Russia what had belonged to China—the concession of Port Arthur and of Talien-Wan, the territory in that neighborhood. The treaty was written under the auspices, so to say, of our own public opinion. But the government of the United States was not at liberty to protest and did not protest and acquiesced in the very thing which is being done in this treaty.

What is being done in this treaty is not that Shantung is being taken from China. China did not have it. It is being taken from Germany, just as Port Arthur was not taken from China but taken from Russia and transferred to Japan.

And in the meantime, before we got into the war, Great Britain and France had entered into solemn covenant by treaty with Japan that, if she would take what Germany had in Shantung by force of arms, and also the islands lying north of the Equator, which had been under German dominion in the Pacific, she could keep them when the peace came and its settlements were made. They were bound by a treaty of which we knew nothing, but which, notwithstanding our ignorance of it, bound them as much as any treaty binds. And this war was fought to maintain the sacredness of treaties. Great Britain and France, therefore, cannot consent to a change of the treaty in respect of the cession of Shantung, and we have no precedent in our history which permits us even to protest against it until we become members of the League of Nations.

I want this point to sink in, my fellow countrymen. The League of Nations changes the international law of the world with regard to matters of this sort. You have heard a great deal about Article X of the Covenant of the League, and I will speak of it presently, but read Article XI in conjunction with Article X. Every member of the League, in Article X, agrees never to impair the territorial integrity of any other member of the League or to interfere with its existing political independence.

Both of those things were done in all these concessions. There was a very serious impairment of the territorial integrity of China in every one of them, and a very serious interference with the political independence of that great but helpless kingdom. And Article X stops that for good and all. Then, in Article XI, it is provided that it shall be the friendly right of any member of the League at any time to call attention to anything, anywhere, that is likely to disturb the peace of the world or the good understanding between nations upon which the peace of the world depends. So that the ban would have been lifted from Mr. McKinley and Mr. Roosevelt in the matter of these things if we had the Covenant of the League. They could have gone in and said: "Here is your promise to preserve the territorial integrity and political independence of this great people. We have the friendly right to protest. We have the right to call your attention to the fact that this will breed wars and not peace, and that you have not the right to do this thing." Henceforth, for the first time, we shall have the opportunity to play effective friends to the great people of China, and I, for one, feel my pulses quicken and my heart rejoice at such a prospect. We, a free people, have hitherto been dumb in the presence of the invasion of the freedom of other free peoples, and now restraint is taken away. I say it is taken away, for we will be members of the Covenant. Restraint is taken away, and, the men that we profess to be, can speak out in the interest of free people everywhere.

But that is not all. America, as I have said, was not bound by the agreements of Great Britain and France, on the one hand, and Japan on the other. We were free to insist upon a prospect of a different settlement. And, at the instance of the United States, Japan has already promised that she will relinquish to China, immediately after the ratification of this treaty, all the sovereign rights that Germany had in Shantung Province—the only promise of that kind ever made, the only relinquishment of that sort ever achieved—and that she will retain only what foreign corporations have all over China—unfortunately, but as a matter of fact—the right to run the railroad and the right to work the mines under the usual conditions of Chinese sovereignty and as economic concessionaires, with no political rights or military power of any kind. It is really an emancipation of China, so far as that province is concerned, from what is imposed upon her by other nations in other provinces equally rich and equally important to the independence of China herself. So that inside the League of Nations we now have a foothold by which we can play the friend to China.

And the alternative? If you insist upon cutting out the Shantung arrangement, that merely severs us from the treaty. It does not give Shantung back to China. The only way you can give Shantung back to China is by arms in your hands, armed ships and armed men sent against Japan and France and Great Britain. A fratricidal strife, in view of what we have gone through! We have just redeemed France. We cannot with arms in our hands insist that France break a covenant, however ill-judged, however unjust. We cannot as her brothers in arms commit any such atrocious act against the fraternity of free people.

So much for Shantung. Nobody can get that provision out of that treaty and do China any service whatever, and all such professions of friendship for China are empty noise, for the gentlemen who make those professions know that what they propose will be not of the slightest service to her.

That is the only point of serious criticism with regard to the substance of the treaty. All the rest refers to the Covenant of the League of Nations. With regard to that, my fellow citizens, I have this to say. Without the Covenant of the League of Nations, that treaty cannot be executed. Without the adherence of the United States to that Covenant, the Covenant cannot be made effective.

To state it another way, the maintenance of the peace of the world, and the execution of the treaty, depend upon the whole-hearted participation of the people of the United States. I am not stating it as a matter of power, I am not stating it with the thought that the United States has greater material wealth and greater physical power than any other nation. The point that I want you to get is a very profound point. The point is that the United States is the only nation of the world that has sufficient moral force with the rest of the world. It is the only nation which has proved its disin-terestedness. It is the only nation which is not suspected by the other nations of the world of ulterior purposes. There is not a province in Europe in which American troops would not at this moment be welcomed with open arms, because the population would know that they had come as friends and would go as soon as their errand was fulfilled.

I have had delegations come to me, delegations from countries where disorder made the presence of troops necessary, and beg me to order American troops there. They said: "We trust them; we want them. They are our friends." And all the world, provided we do not betray them by rejecting this treaty, will continue to regard us as their friends and follow us as their friends and serve us as their friends. It is the noblest opportunity ever offered to a great people, and we will not turn away from it.

We are coming now to the grapple, because one question at a time is being cleared away. We are presently going to have a show-down, a showdown on a very definite issue, and I want to bring your minds to that definite issue.

A number of objections have been made to the Covenant of the League of Nations, but they have been disposed of in candid minds. The first was the question whether we could withdraw when we pleased. That is no longer a question in the mind of anybody who has studied the language and real meaning of the Covenant. We can withdraw, upon two years' notice, when we please. I state that with absolutely no qualification. Then there was the question as to whether it interfered with self-determination; that is to say, whether there was anything in the guarantee of Article X about territorial integrity and political independence which would interfere with the assertion of the right of great populations anywhere to change their governments, to throw off the yoke of sovereignties which they did not desire to live under. There is absolutely no such restraint. I was present and can testify that when Article X was debated, the most significant words in it were the words "against external aggression." We do not guarantee any government against anything that may happen within its own borders or within its own sovereignty. We merely say that we will not impair its territorial integrity or interfere with its political independence, and we will not countenance other nations outside of it making prey of it in the one way or the other.

Every man who sat around that table—and at the table where the conference on the League of Nations sat there were fourteen free peoples represented—every man around that table believed in the sacred right of self-determination, would not have dared to go back and face his own people if he had done or said anything that stood in the way of it. That is out of the way.

There was some doubt as to whether the Monroe Doctrine was properly recognized, though I do not see how anybody who could read the English language could have raised the doubt. The Covenant says that nothing contained in it shall be construed as affecting the validity of the Monroe Doctrine, so that, by a sudden turn in the whole judgment of the world, the Monroe Doctrine was accepted by all the great powers of the world. I know what their first impressions were about it. I know the history of their change of mind, and I know the heartiness and unanimity of the conclusion. Nothing can henceforth embarrass the policy of the United States in applying the Monroe Doctrine according to her own judgment.

But there was apprehension that some kind of a supergovernment had been set up which could some day interfere in our domestic affairs, say that our immigration laws were too rigorous and wrong; that our laws of naturalization were too strict and severe; that our tariff policy did not suit the rest of the world. The Covenant expressly excludes interference with domestic questions, expressly states that it shall not be the right of any authority of the League to interfere in matters of that sort. That matter is cleared away by anybody who can understand the clauses in question.

What remains, my fellow citizens, is the heart of the whole Covenant. Anybody who proposes to cut out Article X proposes to cut all the supports from under the peace and security of the world. And we must face the question in that light, we must draw the issue as sharply as that, we must see it through as distinctly as that.

But I want to utter another preface to that part of the discussion, since you are so very gracious and patient with me. The constitution of the League of Nations is not often enough explained. It is made up of two bodies. One, a comparatively large body, which is called the Assembly. The Assembly does not vote, except on a very few matters. The Assembly is not an originative body. The Assembly is, so to say, the court of the public opinion of the world. It is where you can broach questions, but not decide them. It is where you can debate anything that affects the peace of the world, but not determine upon a course of action upon anything that affects the peace of the world. The whole direction of the action of the League is vested in another body known as the Council. And nothing in the form of an active measure—no policy, no recommendation with regard to the action of the governments composing the League—can proceed except upon a unanimous vote of the Council. Mark you, a *unanimous* vote of the Council. In brief, inasmuch as the United States of America is to be a permanent member of the Council of the League, the League can take no step whatever without the consent of the United States of America.

My fellow citizens, think of the significance of that in view of the debates you have been listening to. There is not a single active step that the League can take unless we vote aye. The whole matter is—in that negative sense, in the ability to stop any action—in our hands. I am some time inclined to think that that weakens the League, that it has not freedom of action enough, notwithstanding that I share with all of my fellow countrymen a very great jealousy with regard to setting up any power that could tell us to do anything. But no such power is set up. And whenever a question of any kind with regard to active policy—and there are only three or four of them—is referred to the Assembly for its vote, its vote in the affirmative must include the representatives of all the nations which are represented on the Council. So that in the Assembly, as in the Council, any single nation that is a member of the Council has a veto upon active conclusions. That is my comment upon what you have been told about Great Britain having six votes and our having one. I am perfectly content with the arrangement, since our one offsets the British six. I do not want to be a repeater. If any one vote goes, I do not want to repeat it five times.

And isn't it just that in this debating body, from which, without the unanimous concurrence of the Council no active proceeding can originate, isn't it just that these votes should have been given to the self-governing powers of the British Empire? I am ready to maintain that position. Isn't it just that those stout little republics out in the Pacific—of New Zealand and Australia—should be able to stand up in the councils of the world and say something? Do you not know how Australia has led the free peoples of the world in many matters that have led to social and industrial reform? It is one of the most enlightened communities in the world and absolutely free to choose its own way of life independent of the British authority, except in matters of foreign relationship.

Do you not think that it is natural that that stout little body of men whom we so long watched with admiration in their contest with the British Crown in South Africa should have the right to stand up and talk before the world? They talked once with their arms, and, if I may judge by my contact with them, they can talk with their minds. They know what the interests of South Africa are, and they are independent in their control of the interests of South Africa. Why, two of the most impressive and influential men I met in Paris were representatives of South Africa, both of them members of the British peace delegation in Paris, and yet both of them generals who had made the British generals take notice through many months of their power to fight—the men whom Great Britain had fought and beaten and felt obliged to hand over their own government to, and say, "It is yours and not ours." They were men who spoke counsel, who spoke frank counsel.

And take our neighbor on the north. Do you not think Canada is entitled to a speaking part? I have pointed out to you that her voting part is offset, but do you not think she is entitled to a speaking part? Do you not think that that fine Dominion has been a very good neighbor? Do you not think she is a good deal more like the United States than she is like Great Britain? Do you not feel that probably you think alike?

When I was in Paris, the only way I could tell Australian troops from American troops on the streets was by their hats. They looked to me like Americans, and the Canadians did too. They walked like Americans; they had a sort of walk as if the ground under them belonged to them, at any rate for the time being. And I expected to hear them break out, "Hail, hail, the gang's all here, what do we care?" Just men who were born into a freedom of will and a freedom of action, and who are our natural partners in discussing the interests of free people.

And the only other vote given to the British Empire is given to that hitherto voiceless mass of humanity that lives in that region of romance and pity that we know as India. I am willing that India should stand up in the councils of the world and say something. I am willing that speaking parts should be assigned to these self-governing, self-respecting, energetic portions of the great body of humanity.

So I take leave to say that the deck is cleared of these bugaboos, of the fear that we cannot get out. I am not interested in getting out. I am interested in getting in. But we can get out. The door is not locked. You can sit on the edge of your chair and scuttle any time you want to. There are so many who are interested first of all in knowing that they are not in for anything that can possibly impose anything on them. Well, we are not in for anything that we do not want to continue to carry. We can help them in the matters of self-determination, as we never helped before. The six votes of the British Empire are offset by our own, if we choose to offset them. I dare say we shall often agree with them. But if we do not, they cannot do anything that we do not consent to. The Monroe Doctrine is taken care of. There is no danger of interference with domestic questions.

Well, what remains? Nothing except Article X, and that is the heart of the whole Covenant.

Let me repeat Article X. I do not know that I can do it literally, but I can come very near. Under Article X, every member of the League engages to respect and preserve as against external aggression the territorial integrity and existing political independence of the other members of the League. That cuts at the taproot of war. The wars of the past have been leveled against the liberties of people and against the territories of those who could not defend them. And if you do not cut at that taproot that upas tree is going to grow again. And I tell you, my fellow countrymen, that if you do not cut it up now, it will be harder to cut it up next time.

The next time will come; it will come while this generation is living. The children that crowd about our car as we move from station to station will be sacrificed upon the altar of that war. And it will be the last war. Humanity will never suffer another, if humanity survives.

My fellow countrymen, do you realize that, at the end of the war that has just closed, new instruments of destruction had been invented and were about to be used that exceeded in terrible force and destructive power any that had been used before in this war?

Why, you have heard with wonder of those great cannon from which the Germans sent shells seventy miles into Paris. Just before the war closed, shells had been invented that could be made to steer themselves and carry immense bodies of explosives a hundred miles into the interior of countries, no matter how great the serried ranks of their soldiers were at the border. And this war will be child's play as compared with another war. You have got to cut the root of the upas tree now or betray all future generations.

And we cannot without our vote in the Council, even in support of Article X, be drawn into wars that we do not wish to be drawn into. The second sentence of Article X is that the Council shall advise as to the method of fulfilling this guarantee, that the Council, which must vote by unanimous vote, must advise—cannot direct—what is to be done for the maintenance of the honor of its members and for the maintenance of the peace of the world. Is there anything that can frighten a man or a woman or a child, with just thought or red blood, in those provisions? And yet listen. I understand that this reservation is under consideration. I ask your very attentive ear:

"The United States assumes no obligation under the provisions of Article X to preserve the territorial integrity or political independence of any other country or to interfere in controversies between other nations, whether members of the League or not, or to employ the military and naval forces of the United States under any article of the treaty for any purpose, unless, in any particular case, the Congress, which under the Constitution has the sole power to declare war or authorize the employment of the military and naval forces of the United States, shall by act or joint resolution so declare."

In other words, my fellow countrymen, what this proposes is this. That we should make no general promise, but leave the nations associated with us to guess in each instance what we were going to consider ourselves bound to do, and what we were not going to consider ourselves bound to do. It is as if you said: "We will not join the league definitely, but we will join it occasionally. We will not promise anything, but from time to time we may cooperate. We will not assume any obligations."

Observe, my fellow citizens, as I have repeatedly said to you and cannot say too often, the Council of the League cannot oblige us to take military action without the consent of Congress. There is no possibility of that. But this reservation proposes that we should not acknowledge any moral obligation in the matter; that we should stand off and say: "We will see, from time to time. Consult us when you get into trouble, and then we will have a debate. And, after two or three months, we will tell you what we are going to do." The thing is unworthy and ridiculous, and I want to say distinctly that, as I read this, it would change the entire meaning of the treaty and exempt the United States from all responsibility for the preservation of peace. It means the rejection of the treaty, my fellow countrymen, nothing less. It means that the United States would take from under the structure its very foundations and support.

Now, I happen to know that there are some men in favor of that reservation who do not in the least degree realize its meaning—men whom I greatly respect, men who have just as much ardor to carry out the promises of the United States as I have, and I am not indicting their purpose. But I am calling their attention to the fact that, if any such reservation as that should be adopted, I would be obliged as the Executive of the United States to regard it as a rejection of the treaty. I ask them, therefore, to consider this matter very carefully.

For I want you to realize, and I hope they realize, what the rejection of the treaty means—two isolated and suspected people—the people of Germany and the people of the United States. Germany is not admitted to respectable company yet. She is not permitted to enter the League until such time as she shall have proved to the satisfaction of the world that her change of government and change of heart is real and permanent. Then she can be admitted.

Now, her dearest desire, feeling her isolation, knowing all the consequences that would result, economic and social, her dearest desire is to see the United States also cut off its association with the gallant peoples with whom side by side we fought this war. I am not making this statement by conjecture. We get it directly from the mouths of authoritative persons in Germany that their dearest hope is that America will now accomplish by the rejection of the treaty what Germany was not able to accomplish by her arms.

She tried to separate us from the rest of the world. She tried to antagonize the rest of the world against the United States, and she failed so long as American armies were in the field. Shall we fail now that only American voters are in the field?

The issue is final. We cannot avoid it. We have got to make it now, and, once made, there can be no turning back. We either go in with the other free peoples of the world to guarantee the peace of the world now, or we stay out and, on some dark and disastrous day, we seek admission to the League of Nations along with Germany.

The rejection of this treaty, my fellow citizens, means the necessity of negotiating a separate treaty with Germany. That separate treaty between Germany and the United States could not alter any sentence of this treaty. It could not affect the validity of any sentence of this treaty. It would simply be the government of the United States going, hat in hand, to the assembly at Weimar and saying: "May it please you, we have dissociated ourselves from those who were your enemies. We have come to you asking if you will consent to terms of amity and peace which will dissociate us, both of us, from the comradeship of arms and liberty." There is no other interpretation. There is no other issue. That is the issue, and every American must face it.

But I talk, my fellow citizens, as if I doubted what the decision would be. I happen to have been born and bred in America. There is not anything in me that is not American. I dare say that I inherit a certain stubbornness from an ancient stock from which I am remotely derived; but, then, all of you are derived, more or less remotely, from other stocks. You remember the exclamation of the Irishman who said, when he was called a foreigner, "You say we are furriners; I'd like to know who sittled this kintry but furriners!"

We were all foreigners once, but we have undergone a climatic change, and the marvel of America is its solidarity, is its homogeneity in the midst of its variety. The marvel about America is that, no matter what a man's stock and origin, you can always tell that he is an American the minute he begins to express an opinion. He may look sometimes like a foreigner, but tap him, and you will find that the contents is American. And, having been bred in that way myself, I do not have to conjecture what the judgment of America is going to be about a great question like this. I know beforehand, and I am only sorry for the men who do not know. If I did not know the law of custom and of honor against betting on a certainty, I would like to bet with them. But it would not be fair; I would be taking advantage of them.

If I may close with a word, not of jest, but of solemnity, I want to say, my fellow citizens, that there can be no exaggerating the importance of this peace and the importance of its immediate ratification, because the world will not and cannot settle down to normal conditions, either in America or anywhere else, until it knows what the future is going to be. If it must know that the future is going to be one of disorder and of rivalry and of the old contests of power, let it know it at once, so it can make its arrangements and its calculations and lay its taxes and recruit its armies and build its ships for the next great fight. But if, on the other hand, it can be told that it will have an insurance against war, that a great body of powerful nations has entered into a solemn covenant to substitute arbitration and discussion for war—for that is the heart of the Covenant—that all the great fighting peoples of the world have engaged to forego war and substitute arbitration and discussion—if it can know that the minds will be quieted, the disorders will presently cease, then men will know that we have the opportunity to do that great, that transcendent duty that lies ahead of us—sit quietly down in council chamber and work out the proper reforms of our own industrial and economic life.

They have got to be worked out. If this treaty is not ratified, they will be worked out in disorder, I mean throughout the world. I am not now intimating, for I do not think that disorder will shake the foundations of our own affairs. But it will shake the foundations of the world, and these inevitable, indispensable reforms will be worked out amongst disorder and suspicion and hatred and violence, whereas if we can have the healing influences of assured peace, they will be worked out in amity and quiet and by the judgment of men rather than by the passions of men. God send that day may come, and come soon! Above all, may God grant that it may come under the leadership of America!

Printed in the *Laramie*, Wyo., *Boomerang*, Sept. 25, 1919, with two sentences added from the text in *Addresses of President Wilson.*

From Gilbert Monell Hitchcock

Washington, D. C., September 24, 1919

For the President. Confidential. The situation has not materially changed since you left here. We have gained some tactical advantage by postponing consideration of the Johnson amendment[1] till after the other amendments are voted on. The Fall amendments[2] are set for consideration Friday. They will be beaten by substantial majorities. So also Shantung Amendment[3] will be beaten. Then probably next week vote should come on Johnson amendment. Vote on this will be closer but it will be defeated.[4] Thereafter we will consider various amendments that may be offered, and last of all the question of reservations will be reached. In reference to this, is still open, although it is true that McCumber, representing five or six Republicans, had many interviews with Lodge and has consented to reservation as quoted in Rickey's message. I am told the matter is not final, and that even in this form Lodge may not get assent of such Senators as Borah. My advice is against discussing reservations until you get back to Washington. Matter will probably still be open then. If Borah and Johnson believe that you might accept this amendment, they are not likely to assent to it. They want the issue in next Presidential campaign.

G. M. Hitchcock.

T telegram (WP, DLC).
  [1] About which, see n. 2 to the news report printed at Sept. 2, 1919, Vol. 62.
  [2] Senator Albert B. Fall was the author of thirty-five of the amendments to the text of the Treaty of Versailles reported by the Senate Foreign Relations Committee on September 10. See R. Forster to JPT, Sept. 5, 1919, n. 3. All of his amendments were designed to eliminate the participation of the United States in the various commissions to be established under the treaty to carry out its provisions. *New York Times*, Oct. 3, 1919.
  [3] About which, see n. 1 to the extract from Lansing's Desk Diary printed at Aug. 25, 1919, Vol. 62.
  [4] The Senate rejected all of the Fall amendments on October 2, the Shantung amendment on October 16, and the Johnson amendment on October 27. See the *New York Times*, Oct. 3, 17, and 28, 1919. For a detailed discussion of all these amendments and their fate, together with full citations to the relevant source material, see Lloyd E. Ambrosius, *Woodrow Wilson and the American Diplomatic Tradition: The Treaty Fight in Perspective* (Cambridge and New York, 1987), pp. 173, 189-97.

Rudolph Forster to Joseph Patrick Tumulty

The White House, Sept. 24, 1919

Mason says that Senators referred to[1] are Ashurst, Smith of Georgia, Shields, Walsh of Massachusetts, and Thomas. Has heard that Trammel also is for the reservation, but cannot run this down. Says that Shields and Walsh are not so far committed, and that they can be changed; that dissatisfaction over patronage questions have influenced them.

Cochran tells me that Pit[t]man and Harrison have advised him that Smith and Trammel are both wavering, but that they might be held in line if sufficient pressure from their States can be brought to bear.   Forster.

T telegram (WP, DLC).
  [1] See JPT to R. Forster, Sept. 23, 1919.

William Joseph Hamilton Cochran to Joseph Patrick Tumulty

The White House Sept 24 1919

Following from Cochran. Putoz Hofmo (Senator Hitchcock) is not the least disturbed by claims of the opposition they will pass the Kikku (Johnson) amendment. He said tonight he did not believe there would be more than three defections on our side. He told newspapermen this afternoon that the outcome of yesterdays action in the Putoh (Senate) was satisfactory to treaty supporters. The effort to postpone consideration of the Gyfyr (Fall) amendments was defeated and the purpose accomplished of having a definite day set for their consideration. Although he sought to have the vote today the net result was that Friday was agreed on. We have the votes to defeat these amendments and the effect should be good. Kikku (Johnson) whose return here is still an unsolved mystery is not satisfied with the maneuvering of Lycek (Lodge) and may kick up a fuss in the effort to have his amendment taken up first so as to sustain his excuse that he came back to be present when it is voted on. As things now stand his amendment may not be taken up for a week. When asked by newspapermen yesterday why he returned without going to his home state Kikku (Johnson) started to tell "in confidence" and then said he had better not "as it might cause some embarrassment." He didnt explain who would be embarrassed. It is the subject of comment that Lycek (Lodge) wired Kikku (Johnson) to return the day after valued Hibco (Hays) came to Washington and conferred with Lycek (Lodge) Kugru (Knox) Colba (Brandegee) and others. One explanation is that Hibco (Hays) had heard from Republican leaders where Kikku (Johnson) had spoken that he wasnt doing the party any good. Another explanation—and this by friends of Kikku (Johnson)—is that Kikku (Johnson) was getting too much personal publicity which old guarders thought might enhance his presidential aspirations. The latter sounds fishy.   Forster

T telegram (WP, DLC).

To Peter Augustus Jay

[Cheyenne, Wyo.] 24 September, 1919

Please transmit the following message to Mr. Jay at the American Embassy, Rome, in reply to Mr. Jay's message of September 23:

"Please express to Mr. Nitti my very cordial appreciation of his message and say to him that I have searched my heart and my conscience both repeatedly in the matter of Fiume, and have always been forced to the conclusion, from the first time that I conferred about it with Signor Orlando and Baron Sonnino, that I could not consistently with the principles upon which the rest of the treaty settlements are drawn, acquiesce in the extension of Italian sovereignty to Fiume. The question being one of principle, the form or degree of the sovereignty becomes a matter of comparative indifference, and I am obliged to maintain the position which my colleagues frankly stated to Mr. Tittoni on his arrival in Paris. To take any other course would in my judgment be to precipitate war in the Balkans and bring about a state of affairs in which it would be impossible for the United States to play any sincere part in guaranteeing peace or the permanency of settlements."

Please also acknowledge and express my appreciation of Mr. Polk's message No. 4314, Sept. 22.   Woodrow Wilson[1]

T telegram (WP, DLC).
 [1] The telegram received at the State Department is WW to P. A. Jay, Sept. 24, 1919, T telegram (SDR, RG 59, 763.72119/6925, DNA). The telegram sent to Jay is WW to P. A. Jay, Sept. 25, 1919, T telegram (SDR, RG 59, 763.72119/6900, DNA).

From William Phillips

Washington. Sept. 24, 1919

In connection with telegrams on the Italian situation forwarded you yesterday, following summary of official despatches regarding Fiume is sent for your information:

Majority of troops stationed at Fiume joined the insurgent troops: Italian General[1] in command lost control and declared there was graver matter than defense of Fiume on his hands, which was interpreted as referring to possible revolution in Italy. General Badoglio,[2] for the Government, offered to D'Annunzio volunteers pardon if they returned to duty within five days, otherwise to be treated as deserters. Information from Allied sources states situation much more serious than Government alleges, and large bodies of Italian troops have gone over to the movement. This contradicts official version.

Italian Government instituted rigorous land and sea blockade, to starve rebellious troops. Shedding of Italian blood might precipitate crisis in case of accident; extreme wing, Nationalist Party, desirous to bring it about. New military society, Trieste, has organized committees to raise funds and send supplies to Fiume army. British and French troops withdrew from Fiume September 14th. British left for Malta on the 17th, and French troops remained to guard supplies. Admiral Andrews[3] states Italian military authorities not supporting government policy in connection with Fiume. Little or no discipline on Italian battleship at Fiume. Italian general commanding troops sent to blockade city, declares situation may last for months, and his troops would take no real action.

French attitude of keeping back troops on shore after frequent advice from Italians to withdraw, complicates situation, which is further involved by fact that French General[4] also commands the Servian troops at Fiume. Admiral Andrews requested representations be made French government to move French supplies, troops, and ships outside harbor. When asked by French Admiral[5] if he would assist the French if attacked, replied his instructions did not contemplate rendering such assistance. If French garrison persists in remaining on shore, with French war vessels at wharves, grave danger of conflicts, on account of Italian unfriendly feeling towards French.

Reported that D'Annunzio has seized the telegraph lines out of Fiume. American consul[6] is on board Pittsburgh,[7] and fears present conditions will continue for some time. It is stated D'Annunzio has complete understanding with Croatians, who were first to welcome him, has promised to uphold Croatian Republic, and to redraw Croatian frontiers. Has 10,000 troops, limiting volunteers to that number.

Nitti's position stated to be very precarious. King has given him full power, but states that he will personally intervene, if drop of blood is shed. Important feature of D'Annunzio's movement is connection with coming elections, November 26th, when soldier candidates will be put up against all except Nationalist deputies. Giolitti[8] said to be awaiting his time to take action present Nationalist movement, and declares Italy has right to entire Adriatic, compensation. Italian Socialist party and Federation of Labor have issued anti-militarist appeal, which is adding a certain amount of strength to the Government. Nevertheless, in Government circles considerable apprehension of possible coup by some dissatisfied army commander.   William Phillips[9]

T telegram (WP, DLC).
    [1] Gen. Vittorio Emanuele Pittaluga, who commanded the Italian troops in Fiume at the time of D'Annunzio's coup.
    [2] Gen. Pietro Badoglio, Deputy Chief of Staff, who had been dispatched to Fiume by Premier Nitti to resolve the situation created by the coup.
    [3] That is, Rear Adm. Philip Andrews, commander of United States naval forces in the eastern Mediterranean.
    [4] Gen. Joseph Jean Michel Savy.
    [5] Probably Vice Adm. Ferdinand Jean Jacques de Bon, who became commander of the French Mediterranean squadron in May 1919.
    [6] Wilbur Keblinger, the American consul at Fiume.
    [7] That is, the cruiser Pittsburgh, Adm. Andrews' flagship.
    [8] That is, Giovanni Giolitti.
    [9] This was sent as W. Phillips to WW, Sept. 24, 1919, T telegram (SDR, RG 59, 763.72119/6900, DNA).

A News Report

[Sept. 25, 1919]

Wilson Dropped Greatness
And Showed His Weariness

There are times when a great man drops his greatness, and is just man. This happened to the president of the United States yesterday when, following his speech, he again took his seat in the automobile that was awaiting him.

President Wilson dropped the expression that was on his face throughout the speech, and a look of almost inexpressible weariness—the weariness of a nation—passed over his countenance.

Getting into his automobile, he looked around, and demanded: "Where is my overcoat?"

It was handed to him—held for him to put on, and with a courteous "Thank you," the president sank down on the seat cushion, and relaxed for a moment, whereupon the utter weariness showed plainly in deep lines around his eyes.

Printed in the Cheyenne *Wyoming State Tribune*, Sept. 25, 1919.

From the Diary of Dr. Grayson

Thursday, September 25, 1919.

The big auditorium and convention hall, in which William Jennings Bryan was nominated for the Presidency in 1908, was packed when the President reached it,[1] despite the fact that his address was at 10:00 o'clock in the morning. He had had a very trying night but his nerve was still working overtime and he carried the audience right off its feet at the start by a patriotic appeal that soon had the majority of the women using their handkerchiefs. The President again defended the League of Nations Covenant and declared that it was certain to prevent war.

He left Denver at 11:00 o'clock, and the train proceeded to Pueblo, where he had a two hours' stay scheduled. A steel strike was in progress in Pueblo but this had no effect and the President's reception was cordial in the extreme.

Before proceeding to the new city auditorium,[2] which he was to open with an inaugural address, the President and his party were taken to the Pueblo State Fair Grounds and driven around the race track so that the big crowd in attendance on the fair could have an opportunity to see the Chief Executive.

Returning to the hall the President delivered an address that was remarkable because of the fact that he was practically at the limit of his physical powers.

The President directed his remarks in his Pueblo speech to the women and children in the audience, as well as to the men. He related again the incident where a mother had approached him and had shaken hands with him, and, after saying—"God bless you, Mr. President"—had practically collapsed and turned away in tears. The President said that he had inquired as to the cause of this woman's emotion and was told that she was a mother who had sacrificed her sons for the nation's welfare. The President said that it was hard to realize that she had called for a blessing upon him when he had been compelled as Commander-in-Chief of the Armies of the United States to send them overseas to fight, and in this way had sacrificed the mother's sons. The President also said that he had been very greatly touched by the thousands of children that he had seen everywhere waving flags and cheering him. He very dramatically made it plain to the audience that he was willing to sacrifice his own life if by doing so he would be able to prevent the sacrifice of these children in war later on. The President carried his audience with him, and although he had planned to make only a very brief speech, he discussed every ramification of the Treaty and explained very carefully again to these people just why he believed the Treaty must be ratified if wars were to be prevented in the future and if America was to be kept from sacrificing most of her youth to preserve the institutions of the country.

Leaving the hall the President went directly back to the train. He was very tired and was suffering when he entered the car. I was concerned as to the best method of restoring him so that he could continue the trip, there being now only five set addresses scheduled. I asked the President whether in his opinion it would be of benefit to him if he could get out and stretch his legs by taking a walk, and he told me that he thought this probably would fill the bill and be a very great benefit to him. In consequence, we stopped the special train some twenty miles outside of Pueblo, and the President, Mrs. Wilson and myself went for a walk. We walked across the table-land and on up the country road directly away from the train. We stepped along at as brisk a pace as was possible without tiring the President too much.

The first person to recognize the President was an elderly farmer, who was driving along the road in a small automobile. The farmer recognized the President and stopped his car. He asked to have the honor of shaking hands with the President, and after this was done presented him with a head of cabbage and some apples, expressing the hope that the cabbage could be used for dinner that night.[3]

We walked for the better part of an hour. En route back to the train, the President saw a soldier in a private's uniform sitting in a chair on the porch of a house some distance back of the road. He was very plainly ill. The President climbed over the fence and went over and shook hands with him. The boy's father, mother and brothers came out while the President was talking to him, and all were very much touched with the consideration which the President had shown in stopping to express sympathy for the sick youth.

We returned to the private car just about one hour after leaving it, bringing with us the apples and the cabbage. The start was then resumed for Wichita, Kansas, where the President was scheduled to make an address the following morning.

That night at dinner the President said that he felt certain the walk had done him good, as his appetite seemed to have returned, and he had more of a desire to eat than he had had for several days past. All day, Thursday, the President had such a splitting headache, as he expressed it, "that he could hardly see."

From the time that we had reached Montana the President had been suffering from asthmatic attacks, which had very seriously interfered with his rest. He found it impossible to sleep while lying down and would choke up and cough during the night, being unable to breathe. Frequently I was summoned to him during the night to give him necessary aid and to assist him in breathing. All I could do, however, was to give him temporary relief, which would not last for more than two hours at a time, and the result was that it was necessary for him to sleep a good part of the time sitting up, propped up with pillows in a chair. He was so considerate that frequently when the attack would recur, instead of sending for me, the President himself would get up, prop himself up in a chair, and remain there. This was just another example of the consideration that he has always shown for every one.

The President was very desirous of retiring and endeavor to get some rest, but the information had come back to the train that great crowds had gathered at all of the stations along the road, and that the people were very anxious at least to catch a glimpse of the President as he sped through. In consequence, he remained up and at the first stop—Rocky Ford, Colorado—the crowd numbered fully 5,000 people. They surged about the car and shouted and cried for the President to come out and shake hands with them. I did my best to persuade the President to remain inside of the car until just before the train would pull out. The stop at Rocky Ford was a ten-minute one, it being a junction point where engines had to be changed and the cars re-iced. Secretary Tumulty and a number of the others on the train were very anxious that the President should spend the entire time on the platform shaking hands with the people. They said that a number of people in the crowd had declared that they had voted for the President but that if he would not come out and show himself and shake hands with them, they would never vote for him again. I made it very plain that the President was after all merely made of flesh and blood and nerves that had stood as much of a strain as a human being possibly could and that it would be very unwise were he to attempt to shake hands with all of the crowd that was there. Just before the train pulled out the President came out on the platform and grasped the hands of those who were closest to the rear end of the train. Then as the train moved out he stood there and waved his hand to the people as they stood lined up on either side of the tracks. After leaving here the President retired to his room.

¹ Various newspaper reports estimated Wilson's audience at the Denver Auditorium at anywhere from 11,000 to 15,000 persons. The figure of 12,000 persons in the Denver *Rocky Mountain News*, Sept. 26, 1919, is probably approximately correct.

² The *Pueblo*, Colo., *Chieftain*, Sept. 26, 1919, reported that the crowd in the auditorium numbered more than 3,000 persons.

³ For what seems to be a rather fanciful account of this incident, see the *Denver Post*, Sept. 26, 1919.

An Address in the Denver Auditorium

[[September 25, 1919]]

Mr. Chairman,¹ my fellow countrymen: I always feel a thrill of pride standing before a great company of my fellow citizens to speak of this great document which we shall always know as the Treaty of Versailles. I am proud to speak for it, because, for the first time in the history of international consultation, men have turned away from the ambitions of governments and sought to advance the fortunes of peoples. They have turned away from all those old plans of domination and sought to lay anew the foundations for the liberty of mankind. I say without hesitation that this is a great document of liberation. It is a new charter for the liberty of men.

And as we advanced from week to week and from month to month in the debate of this great document, I think a great many things we talked about at first have cleared away. A great many difficulties which were at first discovered, or which, unfortunately were not discovered, have been removed. Because, as a matter of

¹ Sebastian Harrison White, lawyer, Democrat, former Justice of the Supreme Court of Colorado, and chairman of the Colorado branch of the League to Enforce Peace.

fact, the center and heart of this document is that great instrument which is placed at the beginning of it—the Covenant of the League of Nations.

I think everybody now understands that you cannot work this treaty without that Covenant. Everybody certainly understands you have no insurance for the continuation of this treaty without the Covenant of the League of Nations. But you will notice that, with this single exception of the provision in regard to the transfer from the German Empire of the Shantung Province to Japan, practically nothing in the body of the treaty has seemed to constitute any great obstacle to its adoption. All the controversies, all the talk, has centered on the League of Nations, and I am glad to see the issue centered. I am glad to see the issue clearly drawn, for now all we have to decide is shall we stand by the settlements of liberty, or shall we not?

And I want, just by way of introduction, to call your attention and point out what is not often enough explained to audiences in this country—the actual constitution of the League of Nations. It is very simply constituted. It consists of two bodies—a Council and an Assembly. The Assembly is the numerous body. In it every self-governing state that has a vote on the League is represented, and not only the self-governing independent states, but the self-governing colonies and the Dominions, such as Canada, New Zealand, Australia, and South Africa. They are all represented in the Assembly.

And it is in the Assembly that the combined representation of the several members of the British Empire are assigned six votes. And you are constantly being told that Great Britain has six votes and we have one.

I want you to appreciate the full significance of that. They have six votes in the Assembly, and the Assembly doesn't vote. So that bubble is exploded. There are several matters in which the vote of the Assembly must cooperate with the vote of the Council, but in every such a case a unanimous vote of the Council is necessary. Inasmuch as the United States is a permanent member of the Council, her vote is necessary to every active policy of the League. And therefore the single vote of the United States always counts six, so far as the votes of the British Empire are concerned. And, if it is a mere question of pride, I would rather be one and count six than six and count six.

And that affords emphasis to the point I wish to keep distinctly in mind with regard to reservations and all the qualifications of ratification which are being discussed. No action can be undertaken by the League without the assenting vote of the United

States. I cannot understand the anxiety of some gentlemen for fear something is going to be put over on them. I cannot understand why, having read the Covenant of the League and examined its constitution, they are not satisfied with the fact that every active policy of the League must be concurred in by a unanimous vote of the Council, which means that the affirmative vote of the United States is in every instance necessary.

And, that being the case, it becomes sheer nonsense, my fellow citizens, to talk about a supergovernment being set up over the United States. It becomes sheer nonsense to say that any authority is constituted which can move our armies to other parts of the world. It cannot interfere with our domestic questions. It cannot direct our international policy, even, in any matter in which we do not consent to be directed. We are under our own direction, just as much under the Covenant of the League of Nations as we are now.

Of course, I do not mean to say that we do not agree, so to say, to pool our moral issues. We do that in acquiescing in the Covenant of the League and do attempt to adopt certain fundamental moral principles of right and justice, which, I dare say, we do not need to promise to live up to, but which we are certainly proud to promise to live up to. We are not turning any corner, and we do not intend to change our course of government or our standards of government. And it is American standards of government that are set up in the Covenant of the League of Nations.

And what is the Covenant for? To hear most of the debate, you would think it was an ingenious contrivance for subtle interference with the affairs of the United States. On the contrary, it is one of the most solemn covenants ever entered into by all the great fighting powers of the world—that they will never resort to war again without first having either submitted the question at issue to arbitration and undertaken to abide by the verdict of the arbitrators, or submitted it to discussion by the Council of the League of Nations, laying all the documents, all the facts, before that Council, consenting that that Council should lay all those documents and all those facts before the world; to allow six months for that discussion, and, even if they are not satisfied with the opinion—for it is only an opinion in that case, rendered by the Council—they agree not to go to war for three months after the opinion has been rendered—nine months' submission to the moral judgment of the world. And in my judgment, that is an almost complete assurance against war.

If any such covenants as that had existed in 1914, Germany never would have gone to war. And one thing that Germany could not afford to do, and knew that she could not afford to do, was to submit her case to the public opinion of the world. We have now abundant proof of what would have happened, because it was the moral judgment of the world that combined the world against Germany.

We were a long time, my fellow citizens, seeing that we belonged in the war, but just so soon as the real issues of it became apparent, we knew that we belonged there. And we did an unprecedented thing—we threw the whole power of a great nation into a quarrel with the origination of which it had had absolutely nothing to do.

I think there is nothing that appeals to the imagination more in the history of men than those convoyed fleets crossing the ocean with millions of American soldiers aboard—those crusaders, those men that loved liberty enough to leave their home and fight for it upon distant fields of battle, those men who swung out into the open as if in fulfillment of the long prophecy of American history. There is nothing finer in the records of public action than the united support of the American people behind this great war.

And I ask your close observation to the principal events, my fellow countrymen. Out of doors, that is to say, out of the legislative halls, there is no organized opposition to this treaty except among the people who tried to defeat the purposes of this government in the war. Hyphen is the knife that is being stuck into this document.

The issue is clearly drawn, because, inasmuch as we are masters of our own participation in the action of the League of Nations, why do we need reservations? If we cannot be obliged to do anything that we do not ourselves favor, why qualify our acceptance of a perfectly safe agreement? The only object, my fellow citizens, is to give the United States exceptional advantages in the League of Nations, to exempt it from the obligations which the other members assume, or to put a special interpretation upon the duties of the United States under the Covenant, which interpretation is not applicable to the duties of the other members of the Covenant.

And, for my part, I say it is unworthy of the United States to ask for any special privileges of this kind. I am for going into a body of equals or staying out. Why, that is the very principle we have been fighting for and have been proud to fight for—that the rights of the weaker nations were just as sacred as the rights of the greater nations. That is what this treaty was drawn to establish.

You must think of this treaty along the lines of those that run out into the Austrian, the Bulgarian, and the Turkish treaties. In every one of these the principle is to liberate people who have been living under a sovereignty that is alien, unwelcome, and a burden to those who have lived under them. We have induced them to adopt the American principle that all government is derived from the consent of the governed.

All down through the center of Europe and the heart of Asia has gone this process of liberty, taking the alien yoke off the necks of suffering peoples and putting forth the American principle that you cannot impose on anybody a sovereignty that is not of his own choice. If the result of these great liberations are not guaranteed, they will fall like a house of cards.

What was the program of the Pan-Germans? From Bremen to Baghdad. That is the very portion of the country over which these liberations have been extended. It goes into effect in countries that have long been under Prussian domination. If we now merely set them up and leave them in their own weakness to take care of themselves, German intrigue will accomplish whatever it can accomplish. And we will have abandoned the people whom we liberated. The thing is inconceivable. The thing is impossible.

We have therefore come to the straight-cut line—adoption or rejection. Qualifying the adoption is not adoption. It is perfectly legitimate, I will admit, to say in what sense we understand certain articles. They are all perfectly obvious, so far as I can see, but if you want to make the obvious more obvious, I see no objection. If by a multiplicity of words you can make simple words speak more plainly, I think that it is simply a rhetorical exercise, nothing more.

Qualification means asking for special privileges for the United States, and we cannot ask that. We must either go in or stay out. If we go in what do we get? I am not confining our views to ourselves alone. America has joined the world; she did not stop to calculate the loss or the advantages or disadvantages. But she went in on one great principle—a willingness to serve mankind while serving herself. What we gain in this treaty is, first of all, the substitution of arbitration and discussion for war. If we got nothing else, it was worth the whole game to get that.

My fellow countrymen, we fought this war in order that there might not be another like it. I am under bond, I am under bonds to my fellow citizens of every sort, and I am particularly under bond to the mothers of this country, to the wives of this country, and to the sweethearts of this country to see to it that their sons and husbands and sweethearts never have to make the supreme sacrifice again. When I passed your state Capitol square this morning, I saw thousands of children there to greet me. And I felt a lump in my throat. And, I thought, these are the little people I am arguing for. These are my clients. These girls who stayed at home suffered more than those who died. For them the tears at home are more bitter than the agonies on the battlefield. So I will not turn away from the straight path I have set for myself—to redeem the promise I have made.

You may ask if this is absolute insurance against war? Certainly not. Nobody can give absolute insurance against human passions. But if you can get a little insurance against a catastrophe, is it not better than getting none at all? Let us assume that it is only 25 per cent insurance against war. Can any humane man reject that insurance? Let us suppose it is 50 per cent insurance against war. My friends, in my calm judgment it is 98 per cent insurance against war. That is what I went over to Europe to get. That is what I got. And that is what I brought back.

Stop for a moment to think of the next war, if there should be one. I do not hesitate to say that the war we have just been through, though it was fought through with terror of every kind, is not to be compared with the one we would have to face next time. There were instruments possessing methods of destruction inconceivable, which were just ready for use when the war ended— great projectiles which guided themselves, capable of one hundred miles or more, and bursting tons of explosives on helpless cities, something which the Germans, who bombarded Paris from a great distance, could not conceive. What they used were toys as compared with what would be used in the next war.

I ask any soldier if he wants to go through any hell like that again. That is what the next war would be. And that is what would be the destruction of mankind. And I am for any kind of insurance against it and the barbarous reversal of civilization.

And consequently it means disarmament. Think of the economic burden and the restriction of liberty in professional and mechanical lines in the maintenance of great armies, not only in the United States, but in Germany, Italy, France, and Great Britain. If the United States should stand off, we would have to have the biggest army in the world. There would be nobody else to take care of our fortunes. We would have to look out for ourselves.

When I hear gentlemen say, "We will be independent, and we are able to look out for ourselves," I say, consult your fellow citizens. It will have to mean universal conscription, taxes such as we have never seen, concentration of authority in the governmental activities and for the uses of these terrible instruments.

You cannot conduct a war or command an army by a debating society. You cannot determine the war in community centers. The commander in chief is going to have to have a staff like the German staff. You will have to center it in the commander in chief of the army and navy. America will never consent to any such thing.

Then, if we have this great treaty, we have what the world never had before—a court of public opinion of the world. I do not think you can exaggerate the significance of that. International law has been up to this time a sort of international code of manners. You could not mention to any other government anything that concerned it unless you could prove that your own interests were immediately involved. Unless you could prove that it was your own material interest that was involved, it was impolite to speak of it. There might be something brooding that threatened the peace of the entire world, but unless the interests of the United States were involved, we could not allude to it for a minute.

I am going to allude for a moment to a matter so interesting that I wish I could develop it. This cession in which China gave to Germany the Shantung Province in 1898 was an iniquitous thing at the outset. But our great President, William McKinley, and our great Secretary of State, John Hay, did not protest. It was an outrageous invasion of the rights of China. It was an invasion of the rights of China that they did not protest, but they asked that Germany, after she got what did not belong to her, would please not close the door against the trade of the United States.

I am not saying this by way of criticism. That is all, under international manners, that they had the right to ask. International law has been the principle of minding your own business, particularly when something outrageous was up. And Article XI of the League of Nations makes matters of that sort everybody's business. Under Article XI, any member of the League can at any time call attention to anything, anywhere, which is likely to affect the interests of the world, the least nation as well as the biggest. Panama, to take one of our near neighbors—can stand up and challenge the right of any nation of the world to do a thing which threatens the peace of the world. It does not have to be the big nation to do it.

The voice of the world is at last released. The conscience of the world is at last given a forum, and the rights of nations under this treaty are given a place to be heard. If there are nations that wish to exercise the power of self-determination, but are not represented by this treaty, they can come in, they can point out their demands and show how it affects their interest and the quiet of the world. They can point out their demands, and, on account of the good understanding between nations, there is a forum here for the rights of mankind which was never before dreamed of, and in that forum any representative has the right to speak his full mind.

If that is not a wholesale moral clearinghouse, I wish somebody would suggest a better. There have been a great many things unspoken that ought to have been spoken. There have been nations and multitudes that had nobody to speak for them in any court of conscience anywhere, and now they are given a hearing. And all forward-looking men now see a way in which they may look forward to a real progressive civilization.

There is another matter which I am sure will interest a great many within the sound of my voice. If we do not have this treaty of peace, labor will continue to be not what it ought to be—a human function, but a purchasable commodity throughout the world. There is incorporated in the articles of this great treaty a Magna Carta of labor. There is set up a means of periodical examination of the conditions of labor all over the world, protecting the labor of women and children that have not the physical endurance to endure the burden put on them. And it is the duty of the nations of the world to study the methods of labor and raise the scale of human labor.

You know what that means. We have not done our full duty in regard to the amelioration of the conditions of labor in America, but the conditions here are better than anywhere else. And we now have an opportunity to exercise our full influence to raise the standard everywhere to the levels we have tried to raise in this country, and also as between those who employ labor and those who labor. The heart of the world has never got into this business. The conscience of the world has never been released along these lines in regard to the improvement of the conditions of labor. And, more than that, unless we find some method such as I have been alluding to, we will not have released the real energy of labor. Men are not going to work and produce what they should produce if they feel they are not justly treated. And if you want to realize the real wealth of this country, then bring about the human relationship between employers and employees which will make them co-laborers and partners and fellow workers. All that is open to us under and through the instrumentality of the League of Nations and under this great treaty. And still we debate whether we should ratify it or not.

There is a great deal of pleasure in talking, I admit. And some men, even some men I don't agree with, I admit, talk very well, indeed. It is a pleasure to hear them when they are honest; it is a pleasure to be instructed by them when they know what they are talking about. But we have reached the stage now when all the things that need to be debated have been debated, and all the doubts are cleared up. They are cleared up just as thoroughly as the English language can clear them. The people of the United

States are no longer susceptible to being misled as to what is in this Covenant, and they now have this exceedingly interesting choice to make.

I have said it a great many times, my fellow countrymen, but I must say it again, because it is a pleasant thing to testify to—the fundamental thing that I discovered on the other side of the water was that all the great peoples of the world are looking to America for leadership. There can be no mistaking that. The evidences were too overwhelming, the evidences were too profoundly significant, because what underlay them was this: we are the only nation which so far has not laid itself open to suspicion of ulterior motives. We are the only nation which has not made it evident that, when we go to anybody's assistance, we mean to stay there longer than we are welcome.

Day after day I received delegations in Paris asking—what? Credits from the United States? No. Merchandise from the United States? Yes, if possible, but that was not the chief point. Asking that I send American troops to take the place of other troops, because they told us: "We will welcome them with open arms as friends, should they come, for their sakes and not for anything that America can possibly in the future have in mind." What an extraordinary tribute to the principles of the United States! What an extraordinary tribute to the sincerity of the people of the United States! I never was so proud in my life as when these evidences began to accumulate. I had been proud always of being an American, but I never before realized fully what it meant. It meant to stand at the front of the moral forces of the world.

And so, my fellow citizens, I think we must come to sober and immediate conclusions. There is no turning aside from the straight line. We must now either accept this arrangement or reject it. If we accept it, there is no danger either to our safety or to our honor. If we reject it, we will meet with suspicion, with distrust, with dislike, with disillusionments everywhere in the world.

This treaty has to be carried out. In order to carry this treaty out, it is necessary to reconstruct Europe economically and industrially. If we do not participate in that reconstruction, we will be shut out from it, and, by consequence, the markets of Europe will be shut to us. The combinations of European governments are ready to be formed to exclude us wherever it is possible to exclude us. If you want to come to the hard and underlying basis of material interests, the United States will everywhere trade at overwhelming disadvantage just so soon as we have forfeited, and deservingly forfeited, the confidence of the world.

I ask merchants: "Who are good customers, friends or enemies?

Who are good customers, those who open their doors to you, or those who have made some private arrangement elsewhere which makes it impossible to trade with you?" I have heard Europe spoken of as bankrupt. There may be some difficulties in paying the public debts, but there are going to be no insuperable difficulties to rebeginning the economic and industrial life of Europe. The men are there, the materials are there, the energy is there, and the hope is there. They are ready for the great enterprises of the future, and it is for us to choose whether we will enter those great enterprises upon a footing of advantage and of honor or upon a footing of disadvantage and distrust.

Therefore, from every point of view, I challenge the opponents of this treaty to show cause why it should not be ratified. I challenge them to show cause why there should be any hesitation in ratifying it. I do not understand the delay. I do not understand covert processes of opposition. It is time we knew where we shall stand, for observe, my fellow citizens, the negotiation of treaties rests with the Executive of the United States. When the Senate has acted, it will be up to me to determine whether its action constitutes an adoption or rejection. And I beg the gentlemen who are responsible for the action of the United States Senate to make it perfectly clear whether it is an adoption or a rejection. I do not wish to draw doubtful conclusions. I do not wish to do injustice to the processes of any honest mind. But when that treaty is acted upon, I must know whether it means that we have ratified it or rejected it, and I feel confident that I am speaking for the people of the United States.

When it is election time, my fellow citizens, a man ought to be doubtful of what the meaning of his intercourse with his fellow citizen is, because it is easy for applause to go to the head, it is easy for applause to seem to mean more than it is. It is easy for assurances of individual support to be given a wider implication than can properly be given them. But I thank God that, on this occasion, the whole issue has nothing to do with me. I didn't carry any purpose of my own to Paris. I didn't carry any purpose that I did not know from the action of public opinion in the United States was the purpose of the United States.

It was not the purpose of a party. It was not the purpose of any section of our fellow citizens. It was a purpose subscribed to by American public opinion and formally adopted by the governments with which we had to deal on the other side. And we came back with a document embodying the principles insisted upon at the outset and carried by the American delegation to Paris.

And therefore I think that I have the right to say that I have the support of the people of the United States. The issue is so big that it transcends all party and personal interests.

I must admit to you, with apologies to Judge White, that I was a little embarrassed by Judge White's introduction. I knew perfectly well it would be embarrassing after that introduction to stand up here and allow you to look at the "Great Man." If I might tell a very trifling story, my feeling was that of a very unsophisticated old country woman who went into a sideshow at a circus and saw, or thought that she saw, a man read a newspaper through a two-inch board. She said: "Let me out of here. This is no place for me to be with these thin things on." I felt that my disguise of greatness was painfully thin, but, happily, that has nothing to do with it.

I was a spokesman; I was an instrument. (A woman's voice in the audience: "You were a chosen spokesman.") I did not speak any privately conceived idea of my own. I merely tried to absorb the influences of public opinion in the United States, and that, my fellow citizens, is the function of all of us. We ought not, in a great crisis like this, to follow any private opinion. We ought not to follow any private purpose. We ought, above all things else, to forget that we ever divide ourselves into parties when we vote. We are all democrats because we believe in a people's government, and what I plead for is nothing less than a people's peace.

Printed in the *Denver Post*, Sept. 25, 1919, with some corrections from the incomplete texts in the Denver *Rocky Mountain News*, Sept. 26, 1919, and in *Addresses of President Wilson*.

An Address in the City Auditorium in Pueblo, Colorado

September 25, 1919.

Mr. Chairman[1] and fellow citizens: It is with a great deal of genuine pleasure that I find myself in Pueblo, and I feel it a compliment that I should be permitted to be the first speaker in this beautiful hall. One of the advantages of this hall, as I look about, is that you are not too far away from me, because there is nothing so reassuring to men who are trying to express the public sentiment as getting into real personal contact with their fellow citizens.

I have gained a renewed impression as I have crossed the continent this time of the homogeneity of this great people to whom we belong. They come from many stocks, but they are all of one kind. They come from many origins, but they are all shot through with the same principles and desire the same righteous and honest

[1] Alva Adams, businessman of Pueblo, Democratic Governor of Colorado, 1887-1889, 1897-1899, 1905.

things. So I have received a more inspiring impression this time of the public opinion of the United States than it was ever my privilege to receive before.

The chief pleasure of my trip has been that it has nothing to do with my personal fortunes, that it has nothing to do with my personal reputation, that it has nothing to do with anything except the great principles uttered by Americans of all sorts and of all parties which we are now trying to realize at this crisis of the affairs of the world.

But there have been unpleasant impressions as well as pleasant impressions, my fellow citizens, as I have crossed the continent. I have perceived more and more that men have been busy creating an absolutely false impression of what the treaty of peace and the Covenant of the League of Nations contain and mean. I find, moreover, that there is an organized propaganda against the League of Nations and against the treaty proceeding from exactly the same sources that the organized propaganda proceeded from which threatened this country here and there with disloyalty. And I want to say—I cannot say it too often—any man who carries a hyphen about with him carries a dagger that he is ready to plunge into the vitals of this republic whenever he gets the chance. (applause) If I can catch any man with a hyphen in this great contest, I will know that I have caught an enemy of the republic. My fellow citizens, it is only certain bodies of foreign sympathies, certain bodies of sympathy with foreign nations that are organized against this great document, which the American representatives have brought back from Paris. Therefore, it is in order to clear away the mists, in order to remove misapprehensions, in order to do away with false impressions that have clustered around this great subject, that I want to tell you a few simple things about these essential things—the treaty and the Covenant of the League of Nations.

Don't think of this treaty of peace as merely a settlement with Germany. It is that. It is a very severe settlement with Germany, but there is not anything in it that she did not earn. (applause) Indeed, she earned more than she can ever be able to pay for, and the punishment exacted of her is not a punishment greater than she can bear. And it is absolutely necessary in order that no other nation may ever plot such a thing against humanity and civilization.

But the treaty is so much more than that. It is not merely a settlement with Germany; it is a readjustment of those great injustices which underlay the whole structure of European and Asiatic societies. Of course this is only the first of several treaties. They are all constructed on the same plan. The Austrian treaty follows the same lines. The treaty with Hungary follows the same lines. The treaty with Bulgaria follows the same lines. The treaty with Turkey, when it is formulated, will follow the same lines.

What are those lines? They are based on the principle that every government dealt with in this great settlement is put in the hands of the people and taken out of the hands of coteries and sovereigns who had no right to rule over the people. (applause) It is a people's treaty, that accomplishes by a great sweep of practical justice the liberation of men who never could have liberated themselves. And the power of the most powerful nations has been devoted, not to their aggrandizement, but to the liberation of people whom they could have put under their control if they had chosen to do so. Not one foot of territory is demanded by the conquerors, not one single item of submission to their authority is demanded by them. The men who sat around that table in Paris knew that the time had come when the people were no longer going to consent to live under masters, but were going to live their lives as they chose to live and under such governments as they chose to erect. That is the fundamental principle of this great settlement.

And we did not stop with that. We added a great international charter for the rights of labor. (applause) Reject this treaty, impair it, and this is the consequence to the laboring men of the world— there is no international tribunal which can bring the moral judgments of the world to bear upon the great labor questions of the day. What we need to do with regard to the labor questions of the day, my fellow countrymen, is to lift them into the light, is to lift them out of the haze and distraction of passion, of hostility, into the calm spaces where men look at things without passion. The more men you get into a great discussion the more you exclude passion. Just so soon as the calm judgment of the world is directed upon the question of justice to labor, labor is going to have a forum such as it never was supplied with before. And men everywhere are going to see that the problem of labor is nothing more nor less than the problem of the elevation of humanity. (applause) We must see that all the questions which have disturbed the world, all the questions which have eaten into the confidence of men toward their governments, all the questions which have disturbed the processes of industry, shall be brought out where men of all points of view, men of all attitudes of mind, men of all kinds of experience, may contribute their part to the settlement of the great questions which we must settle and cannot ignore.

But at the front of this great treaty is put the Covenant of the League of Nations. It will also be at the front of the Austrian treaty and the Hungarian treaty and the Bulgarian treaty and the treaty with Turkey. Every one of them will contain the Covenant of the League of Nations, because you cannot work any of them without the Covenant of the League of Nations. Unless you get the united, concerted purpose and power of the great governments of the world behind this settlement, it will fall down like a house of cards.

There is only one power to put behind the liberation of mankind, and that is the power of mankind. It is the power of the united moral forces of the world. And in the Covenant of the League of Nations, the moral forces of the world are mobilized. For what purpose? Reflect, my fellow citizens, that the membership of this great League is going to include all the great fighting nations of the world, as well as the weak ones. It is not for the present going to include Germany, but for the time being Germany is not a great fighting country. (applause) But all the nations that have power that can be mobilized are going to be members of this League, including the United States. And what do they unite for? They enter into a solemn promise to one another that they will never use their power against one another for aggression; that they never will impair the territorial integrity of a neighbor; that they will never interfere with the political independence of a neighbor; that they will abide by the principle that great populations are entitled to determine their own destiny and that they will not interfere with that destiny; and that, no matter what differences arise amongst them, they will never resort to war without first having done one or other of two things—either submitting the matter of controversy to arbitration, in which case they agree to abide by the result without question, or, having submitted it to the consideration of the Council of the League of Nations, laying before that Council all the documents, all the facts, agreeing that the Council can publish the documents and the facts to the whole world. You understand that there are six months allowed for the mature consideration of these facts by the Council, and, at the expiration of these six months, even if they are not then ready to accept the advice of the Council with regard to the settlement of the dispute, they will still not go to war for another three months.

In other words, they consent, no matter what happens, to submit every matter of difference between them to the judgment of mankind. And, just so certainly as they do that, my fellow citizens, war will be in the far background, war will be pushed out of that foreground of terror in which it has kept the world for generation after generation, and men will know that there will be a calm time of deliberate counsel.

The most dangerous thing for a bad cause is to expose it to the opinion of the world. The most certain way that you can prove that a man is mistaken is by letting all his neighbors know what he thinks, by letting all his neighbors discuss what he thinks, and, if he is in the wrong, you will notice that he will stay at home, he will not walk on the streets. He will be afraid of the eyes of his neighbors. He will be afraid of their judgment of his character. He will know that his cause is lost unless he can sustain it by the arguments of right and of justice. The same law that applies to individuals applies to nations.

But you say, "We have heard that we might be at a disadvantage in the League of Nations." Well, whoever told you that either was deliberately falsifying or he had not read the Covenant of the League of Nations. I leave him the choice. I want to give you a very simple account of the organization of the League of Nations and let you judge for yourselves. It is a very simple organization. The power of the League, or rather the activities of the League, lie in two bodies. There is the Council, which consists of one representative from each of the Principal Allied and Associated Powers—that is to say, the United States, Great Britain, France, Italy, and Japan, along with four other representatives of the smaller powers chosen out of the general body of the membership of the League. The Council is the source of every active policy of the League, and no active policy of the League can be adopted without a unanimous vote of the Council. That is explicitly stated in the Covenant itself.

Does it not evidently follow that the League of Nations can adopt no policy whatever without the consent of the United States? The affirmative vote of the representative of the United States is necessary in every case.

Now, you have heard of six votes belonging to the British Empire. Those six votes are not in the Council. They are in the Assembly, and the interesting thing is that the Assembly does not vote. (applause) I must qualify that statement a little, but essentially it is absolutely true. In every matter in which the Assembly is given a vote—and there are only four or five—its vote does not count unless concurred in by the representatives of all the nations represented on the Council. So that there is no validity to any vote of the Assembly unless in that vote also the representative of the United States concurs. That one vote of the United States is as big as the six votes of the British Empire. (applause) I am not jealous for advantage, my fellow citizens, but I think that is a perfectly safe situation. There isn't validity in a vote, either by the Council or the Assembly, in which we do not concur. So much for the statements about the six votes of the British Empire.

Look at it in another aspect. The Assembly is the talking body.

The Assembly was created in order that anybody that purposed anything wrong would be subjected to the awkward circumstance that everybody could talk about it. This is the great assembly in which all the things that are likely to disturb the peace of the world or the good understanding between nations are to be exposed to the general view. And I want to ask you if you think it was unjust, unjust to the United States, that speaking parts should be assigned to the several portions of the British Empire? Do you think it unjust that there should be some spokesman in debate for that fine little stout republic down in the Pacific, New Zealand? Do you think it unjust that Australia should be allowed to stand up and take part in the debate—Australia, from which we have learned some of the most useful progressive policies of modern time, a little nation only five million in a great continent, but counting for several times five in its activities and in its interest in liberal reform.

Do you think it unjust that that little republic down in South Africa, whose gallant resistance to being subjected to any outside authority at all we admired for so many months, and whose fortunes we followed with such interest, should have a speaking part? Great Britain obliged South Africa to submit to her sovereignty, but she immediately after that felt that it was convenient and right to hand the whole self-government of that colony over to the very men whom she had beaten.

The representatives of South Africa in Paris were two of the most distinguished generals of the Boer army, two of the most intelligent men I ever met, two men that could talk sober counsel and wise advice along with the best statesmen in Europe. To exclude General Botha and General Smuts from the right to stand up in the parliament of the world and say something concerning the affairs of mankind would be absurd.

And what about Canada? Is not Canada a good neighbor? I ask you, is not Canada more likely to agree with the United States than with Great Britain? Canada has a speaking part. And then, for the first time in the history of the world, that great voiceless multitude, that throng hundreds of millions strong in India, has a voice among the nations of the world. And I want to testify that some of the wisest and most dignified figures in the peace conference at Paris came from India, men who seemed to carry in their minds an older wisdom than the rest of us had, whose traditions ran back into so many of the unhappy fortunes of mankind that they seemed very useful counselors as to how some ray of hope and some prospect of happiness could be opened to its people. I, for my part, have no jealousy whatever of those five speaking parts in the Assembly. Those speaking parts cannot translate themselves into five votes that can in any matter override the voice and purpose of the United States.

Let us sweep aside all this language of jealousy. Let us be big enough to know the facts and to welcome the facts, because the facts are based upon the principle that America has always fought for, namely, the equality of self-governing peoples, whether they were big or little—not counting men, but counting rights, not counting representation, but counting the purpose of that representation.

When you hear an opinion quoted you do not count the number of persons who hold it; you ask, "Who said that?" You weigh opinions, you do not count them. And the beauty of all democracies is that every voice can be heard, every voice can have its effect, every voice can contribute to the general judgment that is finally arrived at. That is the object of democracy. Let us accept what America has always fought for, and accept it with pride—that America showed the way and made the proposal. I do not mean that America made the proposal in this particular instance. I mean that the principle was an American principle, proposed by America.

When you come to the heart of the Covenant, my fellow citizens, you will find it in Article X, and I am very much interested to know that the other things have been blown away like bubbles. There is nothing in the other contentions with regard to the League of Nations, but there is something in Article X that you ought to realize and ought to accept or reject. Article X is the heart of the whole matter.

What is Article X? I never am certain that I can from memory give a literal repetition of its language, but I am sure that I can give an exact interpretation of its meaning. Article X provides that every member of the League covenants to respect and preserve the territorial integrity and existing political independence of every other member of the League as against external aggression.

Not against internal disturbance. There was not a man at that table who did not admit the sacredness of the right of self-determination, the sacredness of the right of any body of people to say that they would not continue to live under the government they were then living under. And under Article XI of the Covenant, they are given the privilege to say whether they will live under it or not. For following Article X is Article XI, which makes it the right of any member of the League at any time to call attention to anything, anywhere, that is likely to disturb the peace of the world or the good understanding between nations upon which the peace of the world depends. I want to give you an illustration of what that would mean.

You have heard a great deal—something that was true and a great deal that was false—about that provision of the treaty which hands over to Japan the rights which Germany enjoyed in the province of Shantung in China. In the first place, Germany did not enjoy any rights there that other nations had not already claimed. For my part, my judgment, my moral judgment, is against the whole set of concessions. They were all of them unjust to China, they ought never to have been exacted, they were all exacted by duress from a great body of thoughtful and ancient and helpless people. There never was any right in any of them. Thank God, America never asked for any, never dreamed of asking for any.

But when Germany got this concession in 1898, the government of the United States made no protest whatsoever. That was not because the government of the United States was not in the hands of high-minded and conscientious men. It was. William McKinley was President and John Hay was Secretary of State—as safe hands to leave the honor of the United States in as any that you can cite. They made no protest because the state of international law at that time was that it was none of their business unless they could show that the interests of the United States were affected, and the only thing that they could show with regard to the interests of the United States was that Germany might close the doors of Shantung Province against the trade of the United States. They, therefore, demanded and obtained promises that we could continue to sell merchandise in Shantung. And what good that would be for the independence of China, it is very difficult to see.

Immediately following that concession to Germany, there was a concession to Russia of the same sort—of Port Arthur, and Port Arthur was handed over subsequently to Japan on the very territory of the United States. Don't you remember that, when Russia and Japan got into war with one another, the war was brought to a conclusion by a treaty written at Portsmouth, New Hampshire? And in that treaty, without the slightest intimation from any authoritative sources in America that the government of the United States had any objection, Port Arthur, Chinese territory, was turned over to Japan.

I want you distinctly to understand that there is no thought of criticism in my mind. I am expounding to you a state of international law. Now, read Article X and XI. You will see that international law is revolutionized by putting morals into it. Article X says that no member of the League, and that includes all these nations that have done these things unjustly to China, shall impair the territorial integrity or the political independence of any other member of the League. China is going to be a member of the League. Article XI says that any member of the League can call attention to anything that is likely to disturb the peace of the world or the good understanding between nations, and China is for the first time in the history of mankind afforded a standing before the jury of the world.

I, for my part, have a profound sympathy for China, and I am proud to have taken part in an arrangement which promises the protection of the world to the rights of China. The whole atmosphere of the world is changed by a thing like that, my fellow citizens. The whole international practice of the world is revolutionized.

But, you will say, "What is the second sentence of Article X? That is what gives very disturbing thoughts." The second sentence is that the Council of the League shall advise what steps, if any, are necessary to carry out the guarantee of the first sentence, namely, that the members will respect and preserve the territorial integrity and political independence of the other members. I do not know any other meaning for the word "advise" except "advise." The Council advises, and it cannot advise without the vote of the United States. Why gentlemen should fear that the Congress of the United States would be advised to do something that it did not want to do, I frankly cannot imagine, because they cannot even be advised to do anything unless their own representative has participated in the advice.

It may be that that will impair somewhat the vigor of the League, but, nevertheless, the fact is so—that we are not obliged to take any advice except our own, which to any man who wants to go his own course is a very satisfactory state of affairs. Every man regards his own advice as best, and I dare say every man mixes his own advice with some thought of his own interest. Whether we use it wisely or unwisely, we can use the vote of the United States to make impossible drawing the United States into any enterprise that she does not care to be drawn into.

Yet Article X strikes at the taproot of war. Article X is a statement that the very things that have always been sought in imperialistic wars are henceforth forgone by every ambitious nation in the world.

I would have felt very lonely, my fellow countrymen, and I would have felt very much disturbed if, sitting at the peace table in Paris, I had supposed that I was expounding my own ideas. Whether you believe it or not, I know the relative size of my own ideas; I know how they stand related in bulk and proportion to the moral judgments of my fellow countrymen. And I proposed nothing whatever at the peace table at Paris that I had not sufficiently certain knowledge embodied the moral judgment of the citizens of the United States. I had gone over there with, so to say, explicit instructions.

Don't you remember that we laid down fourteen points which should contain the principles of the settlement? They were not my points. In every one of them I was conscientiously trying to read the thought of the people of the United States. And, after I uttered those points, I had every assurance given me that could be given me that they did speak the moral judgment of the United States and not my single judgment. Then, when it came to that critical period just a little less than a year ago, when it was evident that the war was coming to its critical end, all the nations engaged in the war accepted those fourteen principles explicitly as the basis of the Armistice and the basis of the peace.

In those circumstances, I crossed the ocean under bond to my own people and to the other governments with which I was dealing. The whole specification of the method of settlement was written down and accepted beforehand, and we were architects building on those specifications. It reassures me and fortifies my position to find how, before I went over, men whose judgment the United States has often trusted were of exactly the same opinion that I went abroad to express. Here is something I want to read from Theodore Roosevelt:

"The one effective move for obtaining peace is by an agreement among all the great powers in which each should pledge itself not only to abide by the decisions of a common tribunal, but to back its decisions by force. The great civilized nations should combine by solemn agreement in a great world league for the peace of righteousness; a court should be established. A changed and amplified Hague Court would meet the requirements, composed of representatives from each nation, whose representatives are sworn to act as judges in each case and not in a representative capacity." Now, there is Article X. He goes on and says this: "The nations should agree on certain rights that should not be questioned, such as territorial integrity, their right to deal with their domestic affairs, and with such matters as whom they should admit to citizenship. All such guarantee each of their number in possession of these rights."[2]

Now, the other specification is in the Covenant. The Covenant in another portion guarantees to the members the independent control of their domestic question. There is not a leg for these gentlemen to stand on when they say that the interests of the

[2] Theodore Roosevelt, "Theodore Roosevelt Writes on Helping the Cause of World Peace," *New York Times*, Oct. 18, 1914, Sect. 5, p. 1.

United States are not safeguarded in the very points where we are most sensitive. You do not need to be told again that the Covenant expressly says that nothing in this Covenant shall be construed as affecting the validity of the Monroe Doctrine, for example. You could not be more explicit than that.

And every point of interest is covered, partly for one very interesting reason. This is not the first time that the Foreign Relations Committee of the Senate of the United States has read and considered this Covenant. I brought it to this country in March last in a tentative, provisional form, in practically the form that it now has, with the exception of certain additions which I shall mention immediately. I asked the foreign relations committees of both houses to come to the White House, and we spent a long evening in the frankest discussion of every portion that they wished to discuss. They made certain specific suggestions as to what should be contained in this document when it was to be revised. I carried those suggestions to Paris, and every one of them was adopted.

What more could I have done? What more could have been obtained? The very matters upon which these gentlemen were most concerned were the right of withdrawal, which is now expressly stated; the safeguarding of the Monroe Doctrine, which is now accomplished; the exclusion from action by the League of domestic questions, which is now accomplished. All along the line, every suggestion of the United States was adopted after the Covenant had been drawn up in its first form and had been published for the criticism of the world. There is a very true sense in which I can say this is a tested American document.

I am dwelling upon these points, my fellow citizens, in spite of the fact that I dare say to most of you they are perfectly well known, because, in order to meet the present situation, we have got to know what we are dealing with. We are not dealing with the kind of document which this is represented by some gentlemen to be. And, inasmuch as we are dealing with a document simon-pure in respect of the very principles we have professed and lived up to, we have got to do one or other of two things—we have got to adopt it or reject it. There is no middle course. You cannot go in on a special-privilege basis of your own. I take it that you are too proud to ask to be exempted from responsibilities which the other members of the League will carry. We go in upon equal terms or we do not go in at all. And if we do not go in, my fellow citizens, think of the tragedy of that result—the only sufficient guarantee of the peace of the world withheld! Ourselves drawn apart with that dangerous pride, which means that we shall be ready to take care of ourselves. And that means that we shall maintain great standing armies and an irresistible navy; that means we shall have the organization of a military nation; that means we shall have a general staff, with the kind of power that the General Staff of Germany had, to mobilize this great manhood of the nation when it pleases, all the energy of our young men drawn into the thought and preparation for war.

What of our pledges to the men that lie dead in France? We said that they went over there, not to prove the prowess of America or her readiness for another war, but to see to it that there never was such a war again.

It always seems to make it difficult for me to say anything, my fellow citizens, when I think of my clients in this case. My clients are the children; my clients are the next generation. They do not know what promises and bonds I undertook when I ordered the armies of the United States to the soil of France, but I know. And I intend to redeem my pledges to the children; they shall not be sent upon a similar errand.

Again and again, my fellow citizens, mothers who lost their sons in France have come to me and, taking my hand, have shed tears upon it, not only that, but they have added, "God bless you, Mr. President!" Why, my fellow citizens, should they pray God to bless me? I advised the Congress of the United States to create the situation that led to the death of their sons. I ordered their sons overseas. I consented to their sons being put in the most difficult parts of the battle line, where death was certain, as in the impenetrable difficulties of the forest of Argonne.

Why should they weep upon my hand and call down the blessings of God upon me? Because they believe that their boys died for something that vastly transcends any of the immediate and palpable objects of the war. They believe, and they rightly believe, that their sons saved the liberty of the world. They believe that, wrapped up with the liberty of the world, is the continuous protection of that liberty by the concerted powers of all civilized people. They believe that this sacrifice was made in order that other sons should not be called upon for a similar gift—the gift of life, the gift of all that died.

And, if we did not see this thing through, if we fulfilled the dearest present wish of Germany and now dissociated ourselves from those alongside whom we fought in the war, would not something of the halo go away from the gun over the mantelpiece, or the sword? Would not the old uniform lose something of its significance? These men were crusaders. They were not going forth to prove the might of the United States. They were going forth to prove the might of justice and right. And all the world accepted them as crusaders, and their transcendent achievement has made all the world believe in America as it believes in no other nation organized in the modern world. There seems to me to stand between us and the rejection or qualification of this treaty the serried ranks of those boys in khaki—not only those boys who came home, but those dear ghosts that still deploy upon the fields of France.

My friends, on last Decoration Day, I went to a beautiful hillside near Paris, where was located the cemetery of Suresnes, a cemetery given over to the burial of the American dead. Behind me on the slopes was rank upon rank of living American soldiers. And, lying before me upon the levels of the plain, was rank upon rank of departed American soldiers. Right by the side of the stand where I spoke, there was a little group of French women who had adopted these boys—they were mothers to these dear boys—putting flowers every day upon those graves, taking them as their own sons, their own beloved, because they had died to save France. France was free, and the world was free because America had come! I wish that some men in public life who are now opposing the settlement for which these men died could visit such a spot as that. I wish that that feeling which came to me could penetrate their hearts. I wish that they could feel the moral obligation that rests upon us not to go back on those boys, but to see the thing through, to see it through to the end and make good their redemption of the world. For nothing less depends upon us, nothing less than the liberation and salvation of the world.

You will say, "Is the League an absolute guarantee against war?" No, I do not know any absolute guarantee against the errors of human judgment or the violence of human passion. But I tell you this: with a cooling space of nine months for human passion, not much of it will keep hot.

I had a couple of friends who were in the habit of losing their tempers, and, when they lost their tempers, they were in the habit of using very unparliamentary language. Some of their friends induced them to make a promise that they never swear inside the town limits. When the impulse next came upon them, they took a streetcar to go out of town to swear, and by the time they got out of town, they did not want to swear. They came back convinced that they were just what they were—a couple of unspeakable fools, and the habit of losing their tempers and of swearing suffered great inroads upon it by that experience.

Now, illustrating the great by the small, that is true of the passions of nations. It is true of the passions of men, however you combine them. Give them space to cool off. I ask you this: if this is not an absolute insurance against war, do you want no insurance at all? Do you want nothing? Do you want not only no probability that war will not recur, but the probability that it will recur? The arrangements of justice do not stand of themselves, my fellow citizens. The arrangements of this treaty are just, but they need the support of the combined power of the great nations of the world. (applause) And they will have that support.

Now that the mists of this great question have cleared away, I believe that men will see the truth, eye to eye and face to face. There is one thing that the American people always rise to and extend their hand to, and that is the truth of justice and of liberty and of peace. We have accepted that truth, and we are going to be led by it, and it is going to lead us, and, through us, the world, out into pastures of quietness and peace such as the world never dreamed of before. (applause)

Printed in *Addresses of President Wilson*, with a few minor corrections from the complete text in the *Pueblo, Colo., Chieftain*, Sept. 26, 1919.

A Description of Wilson at Work

[Sept. 25, 1919]
PRESIDENT ALWAYS PATIENT, NO MATTER HOW HE'S RUSHED, DECLARES HIS STENOGRAPHER
(By A. W. Stone[1])

The tremendous executive ability and capacity for work possessed by President Wilson never interferes in the least with his good nature and geniality.

This is vouched for by Gilbert F. Close, the president's private stenographer, who is at the head of a corps of three stenographic experts accompanying the executive on the present tour of the United States.

"The president dictates dozens of letters every day of the trip," declared Mr. Close. "Sometimes they run literally into the hundreds.[2] Often he is obliged to get rid of a large volume of correspondence early in the mornings. He arises, usually, at 7 o'clock, and calls for me as soon as he is dressed. Between that time and 8 o'clock, when he takes breakfast, I take down letters as rapidly as I can make the pencil fly. He later resumes the work as soon as he gets aboard his car, the Mayflower, after his day's speechmaking.

"But the president never becomes impatient, no matter how much he may be rushed with work.

"He never walks the floor, dictating in the nervous fashion characteristic of many men of large affairs. Instead, he sits quietly in a chair—usually a deeply upholstered one—taking letter after letter and note after note from the pile on the table before him, the stream of words flowing smoothly from his lips, almost without cessation.

"His command of diction is marvelous. Seldom does he have to correct himself. Apparently the right and most expressive words come to his mind automatically. Never is it necessary to make a change after the letter is finished.

"The president is not a rapid dictator. But he never loses time between sentences, paragraphs or letters. His mind works with the precision of a machine. He is never verbose—always extraordinarily brief. But there is never the slightest hint of brusqueness in his letters, for he possesses the rare faculty of brevity coupled with polish and courtesy.

"The president's big, white teeth gleam continually as he talks. Frequently he smiles in sympathy with a humorous reference in a letter.

"And his native courtesy extends to the stenographer as well as to the person to whom he is writing.

" 'That was a little tedious, wasn't it?' he sometimes remarks at the conclusion of a particularly exacting session of work.

"If one characteristic more than another crops out in the dictation of the presidential correspondence, it is the wonderful faculty of concentration which is his.

"With the weight of a world's responsibilities on his shoulders, he has no time for reflection during the tremendous rush of work. His capacity for execution is extraordinary. This is in part due, I believe, to the excellent physical trim in which he keeps himself, of course, but it is no less due to his high mentality and ability to grasp details.

"His mind is that of a jurist in its power to weigh all parts of a proposition and to determine the relative value of each. He discards the non-essential with uncanny accuracy, selecting the wheat from the chaff as readily and as speedily as an old-fashioned fanning mill.

"It is true that he receives for personal attention only such matters as cannot be handled by his corps of secretaries, headed by Joseph P. Tumulty, but even this means more work than three ordinary men could attend to.

"The president seldom has time to rest and enjoy the scenery as his special train speeds over the country. He sleeps only about six hours out of twenty-four. Perhaps two hours are spent at meals; the balance of the time is spent at work either in public speaking, receptions, or dictating speeches and correspondence."

Printed in the *Denver Post*, Sept. 25, 1919.
    [1] Albert W. Stone, a reporter for the *Denver Post*.
    [2] A gross exaggeration. We have printed everything but a few routine letters.

Joseph Patrick Tumulty to Rudolph Forster

Pueblo, Colo., Sept. 25, 1919.

Please get in touch with State Department and find out when the King of Belgium is to arrive at Hoboken. The President wishes to leave for New York to reach there the night before the day of the King's arrival. Please arrange for accommodations for the President at the Waldorf. The President understands that the State Department is making the arrangements for the reception of the King and is handling the details of his visit in New York and Washington, including his trip from New York to Washington. He assumes that the King and Queen will travel in a separate car. He is perfectly agreeable to having the King's car the last coach on the train from New York to Washington. Please advise as early as possible when the President will have to leave Washington for New York in order to be there as indicated. Please advise Moran.[1] Please make no arrangements for me at the Waldorf. I expect to stay at Knickerbocker.   J. P. Tumulty.

T telegram (WP, DLC).
    [1] That is, William Herman Moran, chief of the Secret Service.

From Peter Augustus Jay

[Washington, Sept. 25, 1919]

The following telegram has been received from the American Embassy, Rome, dated September 23.

"I have had early today a long private audience with one of the most important members of the Government in order to obtain his views of the situation. He does not wish to be quoted as speaking either for himself or for the Italian government, and I send this therefore as the impression which has been given to me of the Italian Government's views and fears in regard to the situation. Indeed His Excellency said in substance:

"The Government cannot state this [these things,][1] opinion[s] even to you or to any [and in front] of the Allies, as [well as] before our own people we must maintain the attitude at least of confidence. It is the opinion of the government that this is the most critical (?) [difficult] hour in the history of Italy, not excepting the hour of her decision to come into the war. The gravity of the situation is shown by the extreme measure taken by the Government of assembling a Crown Council of all the leading statesmen, independent of party, as well as military and naval chiefs. Only precedent for such an act in an emergency is the royal consultation of 1849 before Italy was a kingdom.

"Nitti's point of view is that he wants the king to have the opinion of all competent leaders, as he feels hesitation (?) [a delicacy] about guiding Italian policy [going on] without such a consultation. He thinks his policy is best, but if the others do not agree with him, he is willing to retire. At present he feels it is not a question of men but of saving the country. It is a matter for the fighting forces. The government sees with regret the greatest peril [It is in the fighting forces the Government sees the greatest peril.]. It fears it cannot hold off the army any longer, while already the Navy has practically gone over to D'Annunzio, and it is feared that perhaps half the population would rise in favor of Italian claims and the liberation of Italian brothers in the Adriatic. The people are already wearied by war and do not desire to be remobilized, but there are still two million soldiers under arms who would follow [it is said] their officers. Against this militarist movement would be the Socialists and labor organizations, which represent roughly the other half of the population, and they would do their best to prevent the movement of troops by destroying means of communication. The result, it is of course feared by the Government, would be civil disruption, if not civil war. Indeed, the nearest parallel my informant found was the situation which led to the Civil War in the United States. This disaster of armed civil disruption the Government feels may be precipitated at any moment on sudden news of further killing of Italians in the Adriatic by Serbs being made public. It does not believe it would then be able any longer to hold the army, as the Serbs have nothing to lose and all to gain by bringing about such a disaster. The Government fears the situation may be brought to a head at any moment, and if civil disruption breaks out in Italy and law and order goes by the board, it fears anarchy will spread within a week to France and later to England.

"The nation, my informant intimated, believes rightly or wrongly that only from Mr. Wilson can come the word of deliverance which will save Italy from civil war and European civilization from the dangers of anarchy.

"My own personal opinion is that the situation is becoming rapidly extremely serious, and while I can hardly believe that half the population is ready to risk everything for Fiume, I believe a sufficiently large proportion of the people either hold or can be induced to hold such views, and that there is an evident possibility they may be able to throw the country into a state of practical disruption which may even lead to a new form of government, if not anarchy. American Mission informed. Jay"

Also following telegram same source, September 24th.

"Although Embassy has no definite official news this morning, there is no doubt the D'Annunzio movement is taking stronger hold on people, while Government is gradually losing control of army. The Navy, including high ranking officers, as already reported, is completely out of hand. Today's papers have conspicuous headings, asking whether war is to be the consequence of D'Annunzio's reported advance into Dalmatia.[2] Press calls attention to inevitable diplomatic complications which would be caused by invasion of Dalmatia and consequent defiance of Peace Conference, but even conservative opinion agrees it would be better than having internal anarchy. Press confirms what I heard yesterday, that the situation is gravest in history of modern Italy. Tremendous importance is attached to hitherto unprecedented Crown Council to be held by King tomorrow. Up till this morning both King, Nitti, and Under-Secretary of State[3] were anxiously awaiting President's reply. I hear that last evening Tittoni told a friend he feared President's reply, even if (assenting to ?) [favorable to] decisions of Paris Conference, might be too late, as D'Annunzio had ruined everything by his action and was now preparing to seize by force all Italian popular claims across the Adriatic. Tittoni further told my informant that this placed him in an extremely embarrassing position and that he felt he ought to resign, but Nitti kept him from doing so in order not to smash the cabinet, as there was in sight no other political group capable of handling the situation. There is persistent rumor, which however I cannot believe, that the King may either voluntarily resign or be forced by circumstances to abdicate, in order to preserve Italy from anarchy, thus acting upon the conspicuous precedent set by his ancestor, Charles Albert in 1849 at Novara.[4] American Mission informed. Jay."

William Phillips.

T telegram (WP, DLC).

[1] Corrections and additions from W. Phillips to WW, Sept. 25, 1919, T telegram (SDR, RG 59, 763.72119/6927, DNA).

[2] It was widely rumored, both in Italy and elsewhere, that D'Annunzio would soon follow his seizure of Fiume with an invasion of Dalmatia. However, as it turned out, it was not until November 14 that he made a very brief incursion into the city of Zara. He returned to Fiume on November 15, leaving three companies of troops in Zara as a symbol of his presence in Dalmatia. See the *New York Times*, Nov. 16 and 17, 1919, and Leeden, *The First Duce: D'Annunzio at Fiume*, pp. 88, 124-27.

[3] Carlo Sforza.

[4] Charles Albert of Savoy, King of Sardinia from 1831 to 1849, had abdicated on March 23, 1849, after his defeat by Austrian forces at the battle of Novara. He was succeeded by his son, Vittorio Emanuele II, who in 1861 became the first King of a united Italy.

From Carter Glass

Washington DC Sept 25 1919

Czecho Slovak Republic has applied through American Mission and Department of State for additional loan from United States of twelve million dollars to repatriate Czekho Slovak troops now in Siberia. Department of State urges military and political importance of return of these troops. Your approval is therefore requested of establishment of credit for this purpose in favor Czecko Slovak Republic up to twelve million dollars. If you approve establishment of credit Treasury will discuss with treasurers of Great Britain and France the proportions to be borne by them of the necessary advances to extent of such participation by them. Advances made by our Treasury will be reduced below amount for which your approval is requested.[1]   Carter Glass

T telegram (WP, DLC).
    [1] Wilson's reply was as follows: "Entirely approve loan to Czecho-Slovak Republic under conditions named in your telegram of today." WW to C. Glass, Sept. 25, 1919, T telegram (WP, DLC).

From the Diary of Dr. Grayson

Friday, September 26, 1919.

This morning at two o'clock I was awakened from my sleep and told that the President was suffering very much. I went at once to the private car and found him unable to sleep and in a highly nervous condition, the muscles of his face were twitching, and he was extremely nauseated. The strain of the trip had at last taken its toll from him and he was very seriously ill. He had a very bad asthmatic attack—the worst that he had had on the trip. For a few minutes it looked as if he could hardly get his breath. I was obliged to give him every possible care and attention. His condition was such that I did not feel that he ought to continue the trip. Although I was reluctant to do so, I felt that it was my duty to suggest to him that he call the trip off and that we return to Washington. He begged me not to make any such suggestion. He said that he realized fully that his enemies would take advantage of any abandonment of the trip at present to call him a quitter, and he declared that he wanted to finish out the work that he had started, no matter what it might cost him. He told me that he wanted to continue and he hoped that he would be stronger and better before we reached Wichita. The President told me that if I were to tell him that I was going to call the trip off, it would do more harm than good. He said: "Why, if you were to tell me that, I certainly would not be able to sleep at all tonight." I did everything possible and finally I was able to get him asleep.

As soon as he had fallen into a slumber, I went back into the other car and told Secretary Tumulty that the trip must be called off. I told him that the President's physical condition was such that it was utterly out of the question for him to attend any meeting at Wichita. I then had him send for the train officials and told them that the train was not to be run into the station at Wichita but was to be halted in the yards outside the city. They were not told at that time that the trip was off, that being a matter that was kept between Mrs. Wilson, Secretary Tumulty and myself.

I then waited until the President woke up. As soon as I found that he was awake I went to his state-room to break the news to him that the trip was to be abandoned. I looked in through the door expecting to find him in bed, but instead I found him up and shaving. Abandoning the trip was the farthest thing from his thoughts at that particular moment. I told him that it was my judgment that he could not make any additional speeches at this time; that to do so might prove fatal. He rebelled and said that he wanted to go on, and again repeated that if he were to abandon the trip his enemies would take advantage of it to say that he had quit. I was insistent, however, and I told him that he owed it to the country, as well as to Mrs. Wilson and his children to stop now before very serious developments should occur. I made it very plain to the President that his physical strength was completely exhausted, and that he was not in any way in shape to make another speech. He finally consented and said: "If you feel that way about it, I will surrender."

As soon as I had secured the President's consent to call the trip off I went out and got Secretary Tumulty and brought him back, telling him definitely that the President had agreed that there should be no further meetings. The President said to Secretary Tumulty: "I don't seem to realize it, but I seem to have gone to pieces. The Doctor is right. I am not in condition to go on. I have never been in a condition like this, and I just feel as if I am going to pieces." The President looked out of the window and he was almost overcome by his emotions. He choked and big tears fell from his eyes as he turned away.

The President told Secretary Tumulty that he had planned to answer Senator Capper, of Kansas, who had declared that the Shantung settlement was the greatest crime of a century. The President was anxious to tell the people of Wichita what the situation was that Senator Capper had so glibly denounced. He asked Secretary Tumulty, therefore, to give to the press a copy of his address dealing with the Shantung problem which was a part of his Los Angeles speech. This was done, as the President was not in condition to prepare a new and more detailed statement.

Immediately on leaving the President, Secretary Tumulty went to his car and sent for a stenographer. A statement which placed the responsibility for the calling off of the trip upon me was immediately prepared and issued. This statement simply recited the fact that I did not believe the President could continue. It is as follows:

"The President has exerted himself so constantly and has been under such a strain during the last year and has so spent himself without reserve on this trip that it has brought on a nervous reaction in his digestive organs.

"Doctor Grayson therefore insists upon the cancellation of his remaining appointments and his immediate return to Washington, notwithstanding the President's earnest desire to complete his engagements."

The train was now lying on a siding in the yards in North Wichita. The newspaper correspondents hurried to telephones and into the city to send news of the sudden ending of the trip throughout the world. Meanwhile, the President remained secluded in his car and every effort was made to keep the constantly gathering crowd from making a noise and disturbing him. One of the members of the party was sent into Wichita to notify the local committee that the trip had been abandoned. He returned shortly afterwards with the chairman and some of the officials of the committee. Abandonment of the trip was a very grievous disappointment to the city of Wichita. Fully 25,000 people had come into the city from the surrounding country to see, if they could not hear, the President. The streets of the city were jammed and the city auditorium had been filled since eight o'clock with a crowd that taxed its resources. The committee sent word to the people that the President was sick and could not speak.

Meanwhile, every arrangement was being made for an immediate and speedy return to Washington. The railroad officials were busily engaged in routing the train through, so that we could get back to the White House as soon as possible. Questions as to where the President would be taken came up, but I declined to consider any suggestion, believing that when I could get him back into the White House he would be far better off than he would be anywhere else, and in Washington I would have available anything that I might require or any specialists for consultation that I might consider necessary.

While we were waiting a telegram from the committee at Oklahoma City saying that there was deep sorrow there that the President would not be able to keep his engagement to make a speech there that night. The telegram said that fully 100,000 people had gathered in the city to cheer the President.

At 11:00 o'clock in the morning the train started back for Washington via Kansas City and St. Louis. The President was secluded in his state-room in the Private Car MAYFLOWER and I remained in constant attendance upon him on the homeward trip.

The news of the collapse and of the abandonment of the trip created a sensation throughout the United States and there was deep sorrow for the most part among those who had watched the hard fight that the President had made in carrying his side of the Treaty controversy to the people themselves.

All along the railroad en route to Kansas City crowds gathered but they were very respectful and there was no cheering or noise of any kind. We arrived at Kansas City at 5:00 o'clock in the afternoon and remained there for an hour while the re-routing of the schedule was being perfected.

Although the President was in his drawing room greatly nauseated and suffering severely, the opposition newspapers refused to accept the fact that he was the very sick man that he really was. For instance, the New York SUN, which had been consistently unfair and which had made misrepresentations about every meeting that the President had addressed on the entire trip, notwithstanding the fact that it had a representative on board the special train, carried a story declaring that the President was not sick. It quoted one of the negro cooks on the car as saying that the President had eaten a very hearty meal for a sick man although as a matter of honest fact he had hardly eaten anything at all. The spirit of the opposition newspapers was very bitter and unfair, not only this day but until after we got back to Washington.

To Jessie Woodrow Wilson Sayre

[Wichita, Kan.] 26 September, 1919

Returning to Washington. Nothing to be alarmed about. Love from all of us.   Woodrow Wilson[1]

T telegram (WP, DLC).
[1] Wilson sent the same telegram, *mutatis mutandis*, to Margaret Wilson.

Two Telegrams from Joseph Patrick Tumulty to Rudolph Forster

Wichita, Kansas, Sept. 26, 1919.

On account of illness the President is returning to Washington at once via Kansas City and St Louis, arriving Washington Sunday morning 8 o'clock. Hold all mail.   J. P. Tumulty.

Newton, Kansas, September 26, 1919.

Present plan is to arrive Washington one o'clock Sunday afternoon. Please notify all concerned. In addition to our baggage wagon, have three quartermaster trucks meet train with men to handle baggage.   J. P. Tumulty.

T telegrams (WP, DLC).

A News Report

[Sept. 26, 1919]

PRESIDENT IS ILL AND CANCELS HIS TOUR

Wichita, Kan., Sept. 26.—President Wilson Friday canceled the remainder of his tour under orders from Admiral Cary T. Grayson, the president's physician, and will return to Washington direct from Wichita. Admiral Grayson gave illness and physical exhaustion as the reason for his action.

Altho there was said there was nothing critical about the president's condition, Dr. Grayson, his physician, declared a nervous reaction affecting his digestive organs made suspension of his trip imperative.

Mr. Wilson was ill most of Thursday night and the decision to return at once to the capital was reached just before his train arrived in Wichita. The president himself wanted to continue his speaking program, but Dr. Grayson would not permit it.

The president's address which was to have been delivered at the Forum building Friday morning was canceled.

The presidential train did not pull into the station at Wichita where a large crowd was waiting to welcome the president. Altho he wanted at least to greet the people here, Dr. Grayson would not permit him to leave his private car.

Secretary Tumulty issued the following statement:

The president has exerted himself so constantly and has been under such a strain during the last year and has so spent himself without reserve on this trip that it has brought on a nervous re-action in his digestive organs.

Dr. Grayson, therefore, insists upon the cancellation of his re-maining appointments and his immediate return to Washington, notwithstanding the president's earnest desire to complete his engagements.

Leaving Wichita at 11 o'clock Friday after a stop of about two hours, the presidential special will reach Washington Sunday morning. It will go by way of Kansas City and St. Louis.

Altho outwardly the president had appeared to be standing well the hard ordeal of more than three weeks of travel and speechmak-ing, it became known Friday that for some days he had suffered from headache. He also has been much fatigued by the confine-ment of his special train, interrupted only by brief stops which have been spent mostly in riding thru crowds and speaking to au-diences so large as to require all his exertion to make his voice heard.

Mr. Wilson has made nearly forty speeches since he left Wash-ington on Sept. 3, and has spent all but about half a dozen nights on the train. Five addresses remained on his uncompleted sched-ule. After the two Friday, he was to have spoken in Little Rock and Memphis Saturday and in Louisville Monday morning, returning to Washington on Tuesday.

It was declared by members of the president's party that one of the ordeals which seemed to be most trying on his nerves has been the automobile parades thru the cities he has visited. He has trav-eled many miles standing in his car and waving his hat in response to the cheers of welcome. This feature of the trip also apparently has been very tiring to Mrs. Wilson also, who has accompanied him wherever he went, and who during the last few days has shown evidences of being anxious for the strain to end.

To avoid the crowds, the president has made several minor shifts in his schedule. At San Diego, Calif., last Friday, he went aboard his train immediately after the informal dinner given in his honor instead of remaining for the night, and when he reached Los An-geles the next day he tried in vain to slip quietly to his hotel for a Sunday's rest.

Later in the day, at Los Angeles, he arranged to take the air in a brief automobile ride by sending out personally and hiring a taxi-cab instead of using the conspicuous flag-draped car that had been provided for his use.

In a number of other cases since then the president has tried to curtail his program and has seized every opportunity to get a mo-ment's relaxation. His train was stopped for more than an hour

Thursday after leaving Pueblo, Colo., while Mr. and Mrs. Wilson took a long walk down a dusty country road by the Arkansas river.

The details of the president's indisposition were not revealed, but it was indicated that he had a slight touch of indigestion. Dr. Grayson thought it would pass away quickly if Mr. Wilson remained quietly in bed, but said he would insist upon absolute rest.

Altho the presidential special was due to reach Wichita at 7 o'clock Friday morning, the arrival was delayed until 9, as has been the case in all cities where an earlier arrival had been scheduled. Shortly before 9 the train was sidetracked on the outskirts of the city and it was a half hour later that the decision to suspend the trip was announced in Secretary Tumulty's statement.

Assistant Secretary Brahaney went by motor to the Wichita station, a mile away, to tell the local reception committee that the president could not leave the train. On the way the streets were lined by thousands who had gathered along the route of the scheduled automobile ride in the business section.

Later the following statement was issued from the train:
"To the People of Wichita:

"It is with sincere regret that I am unable to meet the fine people of Wichita and Kansas, to lay before them all the facts regarding the treaty of peace and the League of Nations. I know with what candor they would desire to treat this important matter, and I am confident what their judgment of the facts would be. It is a real disappointment to me that I must leave Kansas without having the pleasure of again coming into personal contact with them.

"WOODROW WILSON."

Just before the train left Wichita it was said the president was feeling better and was sitting up.

Printed in the *Denver Post*, Sept. 26, 1919.

Two Telegrams from Frank Lyon Polk

[Washington, Sept. 26, 1919]

September 26, 1 P.M. Following telegram in regard to the Adriatic situation has just been received from Mr. Polk:

"Very Urgent. 4355. [September 25, 10 p.m.][1] Confidential. For the President and Secretary of State. Information from Italy shows extremely serious situation. Italians in Paris say that the calling of the Crown Council probably means that Nitti feels that the only person who could [can] save the situation is the King.

Italians here frankly admit that there is a revolution on in Italy, and whole situation is beyond government's control. I have received many reports from the Adriatic, and Admiral Andrews has asked for instructions as to what course he should pursue in Spalato. The American Commission here takes the position that the American force has been sent to Spalato for the purpose of maintaining order, and that they should carry out their instructions unless another course is taken by the President or the Supreme Council. In view of this position, I brought the matter up at the Supreme Council this morning, stating that we had reason to fear that the Italians would attempt same movement in Spalato that they had successfully carried on in Fiume; that our forces were there for the purpose of keeping order, and that I wished to know what the view of the Council was on the subject. The Italian representative, Scialoja, immediately read a note from Tittoni to the French, urging that the French maintain order in Cattaro. It is anticipated [apparent] that the Italians are thoroughly alive to the danger of the situation. I told the Council that in our opinion no Italian ships should be permitted to go to Spalato, and that the American forces would see that order was kept, even if force were necessary. This met with the approval of the Council. I also pointed out that if this were not done, the 2,000 Jugo-Slavs in Spalato would be uneasy, [undoubtedly] call for reinforcements, and war would be on between the Jugo-Slavs and the Italians. I said that as long as we could keep order in Spalato, we would use all our influence to keep the Serbs quiet.

Please inform me immediately what your views are as to the course our Naval officers [force] should follow in Spalato. In the meantime we have recommended to Admiral Knapp that he increase the American force at that port as much as he can."

William Phillips.

[1] Corrections and additions from W. Phillips to WW, Sept. 26, 1919, T telegram (SDR, RG 59, 763.72119/6935, DNA).

[Washington, Sept. 26, 1919]

September 26, 2 P.M. Following telegram has just been received from Mr. Polk in regard to the Adriatic situation:

"4354. [September 26, 9 a.m.][1] Strictly Confidential. For the President and Secretary of State. I read your 3195[2] to Scialoja (this cable conveyed your reply to Tittoni's message). He was tremendously depressed and said he did not know what the outcome in Italy would be. I impressed upon him that I had discussed the question of fleets with him, and we were not considering in any way any of the other questions in connection with the Adriatic settlement. Tittoni had asked me to communicate only with Scialoja and to keep your answer secret. Scialoja asked that I tell no one for the present, as this news would complicate the situation hopelessly for them. He said he would telegraph Tittoni immediately and let me know how the matter should be treated. Under the circumstances I told him it was only reasonable to grant his request.

Clemenceau has been busy in the Chamber of Deputies, and I will tell him tomorrow morning when I see him. I have refused to discuss the matter with the mission [newspapermen][3] here, and they do not know the answer has been received."

William Phillips.

T telegrams (WP, DLC).
    [1] This addition from the copy in the State Department: WP to WW, Sept. 26, 1919, T telegram (SDR, RG 59, 763.72119/6943, DNA).
    [2] WW to FLP, Sept. 21, 1919.
    [3] This correction from the copy in the A.C.N.P. files: FLP to WP, Sept. 26, 1919, T telegram (SDR, RG 256, 186.3411/855a, DNA).

Rudolph Forster to Joseph Patrick Tumulty

The White House, Sept 26 1919

King and Queen of Belgium will arrive Hoboken Friday October third in afternoon. Hour not yet definitely determined. Depending on tide, probably twelve thirty or four thirty. Will arrange for the Presidents leaving Washington on Thursday second stopping at Waldorf Thursday night and going by special ferry to Hoboken Friday. Train to be at dock for return trip. Will the President wish to leave Washington early enough to dine in New York. Will arrange for following party at Waldorf unless you advise of additions. The President Mrs Wilson Admiral Grayson Mr Close Secret Service operatives messenger maid. State Department will arrange for trip from Hoboken to Washington. Forster

T telegram (WP, DLC).

From the Diary of Dr. Grayson

Saturday, September 27, 1919.

The first stop of the special was made at St. Louis at 3:00 o'clock in the morning. A large batch of telegrams from every section of the United States was put on board here. These telegrams were from men and women of every shade of political opinion and they all united in expressing their deep sorrow and regret over the illness of the President. When Indianapolis was reached several cablegrams were put on board which had been forwarded from the

White House at Washington. Among them were messages from King George of England and Premier Clemenceau of France, both expressing their deepest sorrow and sympathy and their earnest wish for the President's speedy recovery.

During the run across Indiana and Ohio large crowds were in evidence at all of the stations through which the train passed. The crowds were most respective in their demeanor and it was plain that they were deeply touched over the President's illness.

Arriving at Pittsburgh that night additional messages of sorrow and expressions of hope that the President would soon recover were received.

I kept the President closely secluded in his room and did everything that I possibly could to relieve his suffering. His spells of coughing, which had been in evidence all through the trip beginning shortly after we had left Washington, were very hard to check, inasmuch as it was impossible to use internal remedies because of the resisting condition of the President's stomach.

Two News Reports

[Sept. 27, 1919]

WILSON VERY ILL, CONDITION CAUSE OF REAL ANXIETY

On Board President Wilson's Special Train, Sept. 27.—Just before the presidential special reached Indianapolis late in the forenoon, Dr. Cary T. Grayson, Mr. Wilson's personal physician, issued the following bulletin:

"The president's condition is about the same. He has had a fairly restful night.   GRAYSON."

(By John Edwin Nevin.)

On Board President Wilson's Special Train En Route to Washington, Sept. 27.—Secluded in his private car Mayflower and being given every possible attention, President Wilson today was en route to the White House. He is a sick man. Just how sick may not be completely determined for several days. But his condition is sufficiently grave to cause both Mrs. Wilson, his devoted wife, and Admiral Grayson, his personal physician, material concern.

Admiral Grayson, who has been ensconced in one of the other cars of the train, spent Friday night on the private car Mayflower. He made the change so that he would be close to his patient should there be any great need of his services. Mrs. Wilson remained in complete charge of the nursing of the president, however.

The president has attempted too much. That is the plain, honest fact of the case. He has stirred his none too sturdy and vigorous physique far beyond its normal capacity. The inevitable result is that he must now have absolute and complete rest and quiet for days and probably weeks.

He has had some rest during the last twenty-four hours and there were, Saturday morning, certain evidences that the rest was having a beneficial effect. But until he can get back to the White House, where he can have complete seclusion, it will be impossible for him to get the nursing and absence from motion that is so necessary in cases of nervous exhaustion. The train is being run at a moderate schedule in order that there shall be a minimum of jarring to the chief executive. And in his stateroom in his private car he is propped up and sustained by pillows and made as comfortable as is possible under the circumstances.

The president's condition is not alarming. Admiral Grayson has made that very plain to offset wild rumors that he has suffered a complete nervous breakdown. But the doctor, who knows the president's physical condition better than any other living person, very frankly says that only complete rest for some time will restore his distinguished patient sufficiently for him to resume charge of the perplexing affairs that now confront the nation.

Plans for the president to confer with the senators leading the fight for the confirmation of the treaty of Versailles have been abandoned. So have all suggestions for his and Mrs. Wilson's participation in the welcome of King Albert of Belgium and Queen Elizabeth, when they reach New York on next Friday afternoon. In fact, every official function and engagement that had been made or suggested for the president for the coming two or three weeks has been called off. He is to have absolute rest and quiet.

For the present Mr. Wilson will remain at the White House. It is entirely possible that later on he will go to some secluded spot where he can get light exercise in the open air and be free from all interference. But for the next few days, after he reaches Washington, it is the intention of Admiral Grayson to keep his patient in the White House, where everything that may be needed for his comfort or his care will be close at hand and available at instant notice.
. . .

When the special train reached Terre Haute, Ind., at 8:50 o'clock Saturday morning, the president still was resting in his state room. Mrs. Wilson was at his bedside. Admiral Grayson still was in the president's car and sent out word that there was nothing as yet to be added to Friday night's official announcement.

Printed in the *Denver Post*, Sept. 27, 1919.

PUSH RESERVATION WILSON SCOUTED
Republicans Now Favor Compromise Which, the
President Said, "Knifes the Treaty."

Washington, Sept. 27.—Opposition in the Senate to the unqualified acceptance of the League of Nations covenant as a part of the
Versailles treaty, has become focussed within the last week, it developed today, upon an effort for compromise upon the identical
reservation touching Article X., relating to the guarantee of territorial integrity of members of the League, which President Wilson,
in his Salt Lake City speech,[1] asserted would be a "knife-thrust at
the treaty."

This particular reservation, denounced so bitterly by the President, was drafted as a substitute for the drastic one reported out by
the Foreign Relations Committee majority and now before the Senate.[2] It was discussed by "mild reservationists" and leaders of the
Republican forces advocating the committee reservation, with the
view of reaching a definite compromise.

As explained by Republican leaders in the Senate today, the reservation, much milder than that urged by the committee majority,
met with the general support of the "mild reservationists," and received tentatively the approval of Senator Lodge as leader of the
conservative forces. After it became evident that it might become
the basis of effective compromise, it was communicated to the
President through the agency of the League to Enforce Peace,[3] of
which former President Taft is the head.

President Wilson was informed by the official of the League to
Enforce Peace who sent it to him that the reservation was being
considered as the basis of compromise and that there was an appreciable sentiment for it in the Senate.

That the President would bitterly oppose the acceptance of the
reservation became vividly evident in his Salt Lake City speech,
where he read the reservation, and proceeded to tell his audience
that it would "knife the treaty."

Senator McCumber of North Dakota, a leader of the "mild reservationists," revealed today that he had had a copy of the reservation for some days before it was telegraphed to the President,
and that he had discussed it with Senator Lodge, together with
others of the conservative leaders, as well as his confreres in the
"mild reservation" group.

The reservation, Mr. McCumber said, had been drawn with the
distinct purpose of effecting a compromise on the stringent reservation projected by the Foreign Relations Committee majority,
which, he said, many Senators regard as virtually putting the

United States out of all participation in disputes involving territorial integrity of League members.

The committee reservation, Mr. McCumber pointed out, assumed the blunt attitude that the United States would not accept any of the decrees of the League as to disputes over territorial integrity, or other controversies between nations in the League, "except by action of Congress." The assumption conveyed, Mr. McCumber said, was that the United States would decline to concern itself to act under any treaty obligation unless it saw fit.

In a reservation of his own, now before the Senate as a substitute,[4] Mr. McCumber went on to say, the authority of Congress was emphasized as necessary to "adopt the suggestions" of the League as to participation in any dispute under Article X. While reserving to Congress the authority to act in the disposition of its soldiers in a foreign conflict, Mr. McCumber said, the reservation did not convey any hint that the United States arbitrarily would hold itself aloof from the League edicts.

The resolution offered as a compromise, Mr. McCumber said, was even milder than his own. While he preferred the one he had drafted, he would favor the compromise if it appeared to command the support of a majority of Senators. At the time the reservation was telegraphed to the President, Mr. McCumber said, it appeared likely that the compromise would be effected. Since that time the situation, so far as he could discern it, had not changed.

This compromise reservation as discussed by the Republican leaders and telegraphed to the President is as follows:

The United States assumes no obligations under the provisions of Article X. to preserve the territorial integrity of any other country or to interfere in controversies between other nations, whether members of the League or not, or to employ the military or naval forces of the United States under any article of the treaty for any purpose, unless in any particular case the Congress, which under the Constitution has the sole power to declare war or authorize the employment of the military and naval forces, shall by act or joint resolution so declare.

How far the projected compromise reservation would command support of Democratic Senators has not been indicated. Senator Hitchcock, acting minority leader, said tonight that he did not know of any Democrats having agreed to support it. He knew of its having been wired to the President by an official of the League to Enforce Peace. The fact that the President immediately had opposed it, Mr. Hitchcock said, might be taken as an index of the attitude the bulk of Democratic Senators would assume.

It has been clearly brought out in these weeks of discussion over the treaty that the proponents of the treaty in the Democratic ranks of the Senate would oppose any reservations, on the ground that they would throw the treaty back to the principal signatories, if not the Peace Conference, said Mr. Hitchcock. It makes no difference whether it is the reservation of the majority of the Foreign Relations Committee or any compromise that would, in effect, be an amendment to the treaty. All will be opposed by those who want the treaty ratified without dangerous change.

Senator Lodge's acceptance of the proposed compromise, it was stated today, was entirely tentative. If Mr. Lodge found that later on, the majority of the Republican Senators would not accept it, he would insist upon the committee amendment. But the chances of agreement on the substitute reservation were declared by several leaders to be extremely favorable. On the three other reservations offered by the majority of the Foreign Relations Committee, it is understood there is absolutely accord. These embrace the withdrawal clause, the Monroe Doctrine, and purely domestic questions, such as tariff and immigration. . . .

Printed in the *New York Times*, Sept. 28, 1919.

[1] Printed at Sept. 23, 1919.

[2] That is, the so-called Lodge reservation to Article X, for which, see R. Forster to JPT, Sept. 5, 1919, n. 3.

[3] See W. Phillips to WW, Sept. 22, 1919 (first telegram of that date).

[4] McCumber had read into the *Congressional Record* on September 5 six reservations to the Versailles Treaty which were intended to serve as a substitute for those adopted by the Senate Foreign Relations Committee on the preceding day (for the text of which, see the footnote cited in n. 2 above). McCumber's reservation on Article X read as follows:

"2. That no obligation rests upon the United States under article 10, unless and until the council of the league of nations shall advise, and that the advice and suggestions of the council as to the means of carrying the said obligations into effect are only advisory, and that any undertaking under the provisions of article 10, the execution of which may require the use of American military or naval forces, or economic measures, can, under the Constitution, be carried out only by the action of the Congress, and that failure of the Congress to adopt the suggestions of the council of the league, or to provide such military or naval forces, or economic measures shall not constitute a violation of the treaty." *Cong. Record*, 66th Cong., 1st sess., p. 4903.

McCumber also included his reservations in his minority report, printed as Part 3 of 66th Cong., 1st sess., *Senate Report No. 176*. However, the version of his reservation on Article X printed therein omitted the first clause as quoted above and began as follows: "That the suggestions of the council. . . ." *Ibid.*, p. 9.

Joseph Patrick Tumulty to Rudolph Forster

Richmond, Ind., Sept. 27, 1919.

Revised schedule calls for arrival Washington eight o'clock Sunday morning. If the President wishes to rest we may park car outside and not come in station until hour or two later. Better be prepared, however, with motors and trucks meet train at eight o'clock. Notify Moran. President had fairly good night and was still in bed

when we left Indianapolis at ten o'clock. Please tell Pollock at Olds-
mobile to have Brahany's car at White House Offices tomorrow
morning. Tell White House be prepared to serve breakfast.

J. P. Tumulty.

T telegram (WP, DLC).

Two Telegrams to William Phillips

[Columbus, Ohio] 27 September, 1919

With regard to the Adriatic,[1] Polk is entirely right about Spalato,
and Knapp should send reinforcements there as promptly and in
as strong force as possible. I hope that Polk will advise the associated governments to act in similar manner wherever it is possible
to assist in the maintenance of order and the prevention of force in
the Adriatic ports.   Woodrow Wilson[2]

[1] Wilson was replying to FLP to WW, Sept. 26, 1919 (first telegram of that date).
[2] The received copy of this telegram is WW to WP, Sept. 27, 1919, T telegram (SDR,
RG 59, 763.72119/6976, DNA). It was transmitted as WP to FLP, No. 3273, Sept. 27,
1919, T telegram (SDR, RG 256, 186.3411/861, DNA).

[En route] 27 September, 1919

In regard to the King of the Belgians, the doctor so strongly advises my taking a complete rest for the present that I would be very
much obliged if you would communicate with the King at sea and
find whether it is entirely agreeable to him to take his trip through
the country before coming to Washington. If he is willing, I hope
that it will be possible to make arrangements for his trip to be taken
directly from New York after his landing, and I hope that it can be
arranged to have him met at New York by the highest officials of
the State and War Departments and full military honors shown
him there.   Woodrow Wilson

T telegrams (WP, DLC).

From the Diary of Dr. Grayson

Sunday, September 28, 1919.

The President had a very restless night. In fact, from the time
we left Wichita the night journey had been exceedingly trying so
far as he was concerned. Last night we found that the train was
running so fast that the private car, placed as it was on the very
rear end, swung from side to side and rocked and made it exceedingly uncomfortable for the President. I sent for the railroad offi-

cials and told them that this had to be stopped, and that the schedule had to be cut down so that the train would run smoothly. I insisted that this course be followed so that the President would not sustain discomfiture even if we did not reach Washington until hours after the original time that they had set. They did fairly well, but this morning they again started to run fast and I again ordered them to slacken the speed. Leaving Harrisburg on the York Branch, en route to Washington, the train again began to run at an unwarranted rate of speed, and I sent for the railroad officials and told them flatly that they were not to exceed twenty-five miles an hour until Washington was reached. This time I got action!

The first town of any size was at Baltimore, but the officials had made arrangements to permit no one to get to the platform and no crowd had to be contended with.

Washington was reached soon after 11:00 o'clock. The President was up and dressed and was able to walk to the waiting automobile without assistance. He said good-bye to the engineer and the conductor and to all of the train officials before leaving the station, and, as he walked down the platform, he waved his hand in farewell to the newspaper men and the other members of the party who were standing alongside of the train watching him.

There was a crowd of 1500 people gathered in the concourse and outside of the Union Station, and they cheered the President as he emerged through the iron-grilled doors of the train-shed. He waved his hand and took his hat off in response to the cheers.

Entering the waiting automobile, the President was driven directly to the White House, and I proceeded to put him to bed at once. After resting for a short time the President arose at about 3:00 o'clock and went for a two-hour motor ride through the parks. It was a bright sunshiny day and he slept most of the time in the automobile.

Now that we were back in the White House, where it was possible to see that no one interfered with him at all, I took steps to put into effect the rest cure which I had planned and which I realized was the only thing which would restore him again to health. It was commenced immediately upon our return from the drive and strictly adhered to. The one thing that I was most insistent on was that he should not be bothered with any matters of official character, and especially that no question of controversy should be brought to his attention. Suggestions which might make necessary conferences with Cabinet officials or other public men were vetoed by me. It was to be complete rest, not partial rest, and nothing was to be allowed to interfere with the President's restoration to health if possible.

To William Phillips

My dear Mr. Phillips: The White House, 28 September, 1919

Will you not be kind enough to have the following sent to Mr. Jay, our Chargé at Rome:

"Instructions from the President: Do not allow yourself to be, or even to seem to be, impressed by what is being said to you by members of the Italian Government with regard to the present crisis. It is all part of a desperate endeavor to get me to yield to claims which, if allowed, would destroy the peace of Europe. You cannot make the impression too definite and final that I cannot and will not yield; that they must work out their crisis for themselves. With a little decision and courage they could have stopped this agitation long ago, but they fomented it rather than checked it. I have been dealing with the whole thing at close range for nine months and know that the only course to be pursued is one of absolute firmness in which the whole responsibility is put upon the Italian Government and they are given no possible excuse for unloading it on anybody else."

Cordially and sincerely yours,   the President[1]

T telegram (SDR, RG 59, 763.72119/7040, DNA).
    [1] This was sent as W. Phillips to FLP, No. 3275, September 28, 1919, T telegram (SDR, RG 59, 763.72119/7040, DNA).

Newton Diehl Baker to Edith Bolling Galt Wilson

My dear Mrs Wilson   [Washington] September 28, 1919

If anything comes to the White House in the next few days which you think I could do and so save the President having to give it attention while he should be resting, will you please feel free to send it to me or to send for me without hesitation day or night.

I tried a trip about one third as strenuous as his and I know that he will need rest to get back to his old self

Faithfully yours,   Newton D. Baker

ALS (EBW Papers, DLC).

From Albert Sidney Burleson

My dear Mr. President: Washington September 29, 1919

Just a line to express the earnest hope that you will now take a well earned rest. If you will only do this, I am confident in a very short time you will again be thoroughly on your feet.

The situation in the Senate is constantly improving. It is firmly believed by those who are in the best position to know that the Administration forces have the votes to defeat all amendments and reservations. I still feel sure that you can win the fight *"clean cut"* if you continue to stand firm. Senators Ashurst and Smith, of Georgia, are again in line against all amendments, and Senator Underwood says that if there is no wavering on our part now that in the end you will be asked to define just what you would consent to in the way of "mild reservations or interpretations."

May God preserve you.

Faithfully yours,   A. S. Burleson

TLS (WP, DLC).

From James Watson Gerard

New York, September 29, 1919.

Congratulations on the success of your tour and sincere hope for a speedy recovery. Please stop drinking coffee and substitute milk, you will find your nerves improve very quickly.

James W. Gerard.

T telegram (WP, DLC).

From Cleveland Hoadley Dodge

Dear President   New York Sept. 29th 1919

Hard luck! How in thunder you stood it as long as you did no one can tell. Anyhow, I pray God you may soon be all right again and in position to take it a little more easy, & get some health giving golf. I hear from many sides good reactions from your trip & if it has only scotched you for a bit, it was well worth while

À Dios—with lots of love from us all

Ever affly   Cleveland H Dodge

Don't bother to answer this

ALS (WP, DLC).

From Albert, King of the Belgians

S.S. GEORGE WASHINGTON, Radio, Cape Race, N. F.,
Sept. 29, 1919

The Queen and I greatly regret to hear of your illness and wish you a speedy recovery. We thank you for the tour you have planned

for us and we look forward to our meeting in Washington on our
return.   Albert.

T radiogram (WP, DLC).

From Edward Mandell House

Paris, September 29, 1919.
We are greatly distressed to hear of your illness. Our love and
good wishes are always with you.   Edward House.

T telegram (WP, DLC).

Frank Lyon Polk to William Phillips

Paris, September 29th, 1919.
4427, Confidential. For Phillips from Polk. Please cable me, to be
deciphered by me, exact situation in regard to President health.
Also whether he is able to attend to business. Absolutely necessary
to have the most accurate information possible for my guidance.
American Mission.

T telegram (SDR, RG 59, 811.001W69/662, DNA).

A News Report

[*Sept. 30, 1919*]
Wilson Sleeping Better and Improving;
Allowed to Give a Little Time to Work
Washington, Sept. 30.—President Wilson seems to be getting
better. His motor ride yesterday afternoon was beneficial and he
took another ride today. The air was not as chilly as it was yesterday and the sun was shining brightly.
At 10.30 o'clock tonight Real Admiral Grayson issued the following bulletin from the White House:
The President spent a fairly comfortable day and is improving.
This morning's bulletin issued by Rear Admiral Cary T. Grayson,
the President's physician, said that "the President had a good
night's rest, and is improving." There is every reason to believe that
Admiral Grayson is not concealing anything in regard to the President's condition. No specialist has been called in and the rest
treatment prescribed by Admiral Grayson seems to be all that is
required.

Although the President has been told that he must not attempt to undertake any official duties, he was permitted last night to talk with Secretary Tumulty over the telephone concerning the situation in the Senate with respect to the Versailles Treaty. The ban against official conferences and other engagements is still in force, however, and there is no indication when it will be lifted.

Whether the President will leave Washington for a rest is something about which no statement is forthcoming from the White House.

Printed in the *New York Times*, Oct. 1, 1919.

From Edward Mandell House

Dear Governor: Paris. September 30, 1919.

I am enclosing a copy of a letter from Herron[1] which came to me this morning. Strangely enough, Herron writes me several times a week and is not deterred by my brief acknowledgments without comment.

We are counting on sailing early next week and this letter will precede me by only a few days. I am sure it is the best thing to do. Polk, White and Bliss concur in this opinion.

As a matter of fact, the Crillon should be closed and everything reduced here to a minimum in order to avoid the criticism which is already rife.

U [*sic*] I am glad to see by the papers this morning that you were able to go driving yesterday. I sincerely hope that your attack will be short lived.   Affectionately yours,   E. M. House

TLS (WP, DLC).
    [1] G. D. Herron to EMH, Sept. 28, 1919, TCL (WP, DLC). The significant portion of this brief letter reads as follows: "Let me beg you to urge the President to yield on the question of Fiume. He can do so without loss to himself; he would gain rather. If he does not, Italy will break into civil war; the Balkans will instantly be aflame; and, in less than three months, the whole of Europe will be burning—this time to ashes. And upon the President will fall all the blame, all the curses."

William Phillips to Frank Lyon Polk

                              Washington, September 30, 1919.

3291 For Polk from Phillips. To be deciphered by Mr. Polk personally. Your 4427, September 29. Grayson tells me President is suffering from nervous exhaustion which has produced several complications. His digestion is completely upset. He is suffering from an attack of asthma and finds great difficulty in sleeping. He cannot consider any work whatsoever this week. Grayson thinks by next week he can do little work. Today he is much better than he has been and Grayson feels encouraged.

T telegram (SDR, RG 59, 811.001W69/662, DNA).

A News Report

[*Oct. 1, 1919*]

President is Again Jaded
After Another Restless Night

Washington, Oct. 1.—No important change in the condition of President Wilson was noted in today's White House bulletins, though it was said his progress toward recovery was not so apparent as it had been yesterday. The bulletin issued at 1 P.M. read:

The President had a restless night and consequently is feeling somewhat jaded today.

Throughout the day the President felt the effects of his restless night. In the morning, however, he was able to get some sleep, and in the afternoon he took an automobile ride, to his apparent benefit. Tonight's bulletin recorded no change.

Printed in the *New York Times*, Oct. 2, 1919.

Cary Travers Grayson to Harry Augustus Garfield

Personal.

Dear Doctor Garfield: The White House October 1, 1919.

I wish to thank you very much for your kind note. I appreciate most deeply your generous interest.

The President is suffering from nervous exhaustion, complicated by asthmatic attacks—which followed an attack of influenza in Paris. These attacks have been intermittent and became more aggravated while traveling on the train, interfering considerably with his sleep and rest. The strain was too much for any one made of flesh and blood, as you say, to stand. In addition to the nervous energy required, the enormous and enthusiastic crowds sapped a great deal of his vitality. Even at places where the train did not stop hundreds and thousands of people would gather to greet him, and he conscientiously tried at least to wave his hand to them. This lasted anywhere from six in the morning until one to two A.M. With the nervous and physical exhaustion, his stomach refused to perform its functions, and I felt it absolutely necessary to persuade him, against his wishes, to call off the remaining part of the trip. His case, naturally, is one that will not run along perfectly smooth, but I think he is progressing as satisfactorily as could be expected in the circumstances. His appetite, for instance, is slowly improving, and but for the troublesome asthmatic attacks he would not experience a great deal of difficulty in the return of his ability to sleep. I am insisting on rest and quiet and the diversion of his mind from official matters. I notice as his strength is beginning to come back a desire on his part to get back to his official duties—which is a very good sign, but I fear a difficult one for me to handle.

I am having Dr. de Schweinitz,[1] of Philadelphia, an eye specialist who has examined him twice a year for the last five or six years, see him tomorrow. I am also having Dr. Dercum,[2] of Philadelphia, a nerve specialist, see him Friday.

I had much pleasure in telling the President of your letter and it cheered him immensely. He asked me to give you his best love.

With kindest regards to both Mrs. Garfield[3] and yourself, believe me, Yours sincerely, Cary T. Grayson

TLS (H. A. Garfield Papers, DLC).
[1] George Edmund de Schweinitz, M.D., distinguished ophthalmologist of Philadelphia, one of Wilson's physicians since 1906.
[2] Francis Xavier Dercum, M.D., Ph.D. (1856-1931), pioneer neurologist, Professor of Nervous and Mental Diseases, Jefferson Medical College.
[3] Belle Hartford Mason (Mrs. Harry A.) Garfield.

Robert Lansing to Frank Lyon Polk

My dear Frank: Washington October 1, 1919.

Here I am back in my office feeling very fit and ready to take up the work from which I have been relieved for nearly a month. Never have Mrs. Lansing and I so enjoyed a holiday. The weather was splendid. The peaceful life, most restful. We both are well and have a measure of energy stored away.

The distressing thing at the present time is the illness of the President and his inability to take part in public affairs. As far as I can learn—though the whole matter is shrouded in secrecy for some reason—the President just avoided a complete nervous collapse. Of course I have not seen him and have gained no personal impression of his condition, but I believe from what I can learn that it is more mental than physical, though of course it is often difficult to differentiate between the effects. There prevails a general feeling in Washington that the President's intense advocacy of the Covenant which has become a veritable obsession with him has caused an abnormal mental state which excludes everything else from his thoughts, and that the only possible way for him to regain normality is to put the subject out of his mind. Whether he will be able to do this is a question as he seems to be possessed of a sort of monomania concerning the League. My belief is that Grayson is endeavoring to clear his mind of this burden. I have not seen Grayson but have talked with Tumulty, who seems to be only vaguely informed of the situation.

Meanwhile the treaty debate in the Senate continues with the usual political claptrap and oratorical fireworks. The President, as you know, insists on ratification without reservations or amendments, and Hitchcock is leading the fight on that plan. Personally I believe that there will be reservations and that ratification without them cannot be obtained. What the President will do in the event reservations go through is a problem. His back is up and his jaw set against any compromise. The politic course would seem to be to accept reservations, but have them so worded that they amount only to interpretations. An uncompromising attitude will get us nowhere. If reservations should pass and the President should withdraw the treaty because of them, he would be charged with preventing an immediate restoration of peace. As "peace" is the most potent argument for speedy ratification, we would lose it as an asset and be put on the defensive by being forced to explain the withdrawal. I think that to be placed in that position would be extremely unfortunate. Anyone who delays having the treaty go into effect will be severely blamed. I find many Republicans feel that their Senators are playing mighty poor politics in delaying ratification. If the President should withdraw the treaty, he will be the one to catch it.

Since I wrote you and while I was at Henderson the contemptible Bullitt made his exhibition of Bolshevik good faith by repeating in garbled form a confidential interview with me. In view of the fact that it was founded on a measure of truth, that is, enough truth so that I would have to explain my statements as quoted by the little traitor, I could not flatly deny his testimony. Rather than make such an explanation I determined the best course was to make no comment. All I did to offset the impression made was to declare in a speech which I made a week after the hearing that the treaty should be ratified without delay and without change unless national sovereignty was affected and that the treaty did not do that. Ignoring the Bullitt statement has worked out as I thought it would. For a week, as long as there was a possibility of my commenting, it was played up by the opposition press, but now it is apparently dead.

October 4th.

Since I began this letter I have had to go to New York to receive Belgian royalty and there have been developments in regard to the President's condition, which have changed my views as to his illness and imposed new responsibilities on me.

The press will tell you that the President is a very sick man. I had a long talk yesterday with Grayson and Tumulty and feel much discouraged. The President's mind is clear and acute, but he is physically much shattered. I think his state is dangerous and may become critical at any time. He is confined to his bed and can do no business of any sort. As Grayson admitted in reply to my questions that it would be weeks and probably months before the President could resume his duties, if he recovers at all, I said that the possibility of the Vice-President assuming the Presidency would have to be considered, since the work of the Government would have to go on. With this in mind I have called a meeting of the Cabinet for Monday (the 6th) to discuss the matter and to determine the action that should be taken. I also telegraphed to you that you cannot expect personal views of the President on any subject at present.

Grayson is keeping up on the fact that the President has reserve powers and has "come back" in the past with unexpected strength. Nevertheless the Admiral looks haggard and worn, and makes no effort to disguise his anxiety. He indicated that it might be days before the crisis is passed and before he can tell what the outcome will be. The gravity of the situation cannot be overestimated.

This breakdown is the result of the President's western trip on top of his continuous work for the past year. He was physically unable to endure the strain, and called upon his body to do more than it was able. I did everything that I could to dissuade him from going as I could see no political benefit and felt he could do more efficient work here. He *would* go, however, and this is the result.

As I am very busy I can write no more but will keep you advised.

With affectionate regard, my dear Frank,

Faithfully yours,   Robert Lansing.

TLS (F. L. Polk Papers, CtY).

Joseph Patrick Tumulty to Edith Bolling Galt Wilson

My dear Mrs Wilson   The White House Oct 2nd 1919

Please do not think me unfeeling and lacking in sympathy for our dear and wonderful Chief.[1]

Only the desire to leave you free to devote your wholehearted love and care to him, has kept me reluctantly away. The feeling I have that I can render no service to him whom I deeply love as I did my own dear father makes my heart heavy, indeed.

My little girls tomorrow morning are offering their communion for him. God will not desert us in this critical hour of need. Please let the President know that we all think of him every minute of the day and that my poor, humble prayers are lifted up each day for his early recovery.   Sincerely, your friend,   Tumulty

ALS (WP, DLC).

[1] Wilson had just suffered a stroke, which resulted in a complete paralysis of the left side of his body. For a description of this event, see Edwin A. Weinstein, *Woodrow Wilson: A Medical and Psychological Biography* (Princeton, N. J., 1981), p. 357, and the essay by Dr. Park printed as Appendix II in this volume.

The reader will find in the balance of this volume news reports, diary entries, and memoranda of various kinds by contemporaries relating to Wilson's stroke and illness to November 5, 1919. The entry from the Diary of Ray Stannard Baker, printed at November 5, 1919, which records a long conversation between Baker and Dr. Grayson, is revealing, particularly about Wilson's condition during July and August and on the western tour in September. It confirms what Dr. Park and we have said in Volume 62, that Wilson was a very sick man during that period, even before he undertook his speaking tour.

Only three firsthand witnesses have left accounts of Wilson's illness from mid-July through early November 1919.

Mrs. Wilson's *My Memoir*, pp. 272-96, is with some exceptions a straightforward account, which says that Wilson suffered a stroke which paralyzed the left side of his body.

Dr. Grayson's account in *Woodrow Wilson: An Intimate Memoir* (New York, 1960), pp. 94-100, 108-10, is brief and for the most part anecdotal and uninformative. Grayson says that Wilson suffered a thrombosis, or clot, in an artery in the brain, but that there was no rupture. To newspapermen, he always insisted that Wilson suffered from "nervous fatigue," "nervous prostration," etc., and he consistently refused to say that Wilson had suffered a stroke (except in the exclamation quoted by Irwin Hood Hoover in the extract from his memoir).

We have printed the third firsthand account in the portion of Hoover's draft of a memoir as Appendix I in this volume. Hoover, Head Usher of the White House, had served Wilson faithfully since March 4, 1913, and was devoted to him, as Wilson was to Hoover. To us, Hoover's account has the ring of truth. He wrote about Wilson and the White House scene only to the degree that he had personally witnessed them. For example, he knew that Wilson was not performing normally during the six weeks before he set out upon the western tour; but he did not understand the causes of Wilson's abnormal behavior, and he did not attempt to explain them. He thought that Wilson had suffered his stroke on the western tour in Wichita, because he read accounts of Wilson's breakdown sent from that city. He wrote what he did about Tumulty's alleged isolation because he did not know the degree to which Tumulty, who was not in the White House but in the Executive Offices, was in communication with Mrs. Wilson and her husband. Hoover impresses us as an intelligent and sturdily honest witness. Hoover's memoir was written soon after Wilson's death. He published a revised version of the extract that we print in his *Forty-Two Years in the White House* (Boston and New York, 1934), pp. 99-106.

Much new evidence, including Dr. Grayson and Dr. Dercum's reports, on Wilson's stroke will be printed in Vol. 64

Peter Augustus Jay to Robert Lansing

Rome, October 2nd 1919.

Urgent. 3204. Personal for Secretary of State or Phillips.

Please telegraph me in conformity with personal information true condition of the President's health. I sincerely trust newspaper reports are exaggerated.

Also instruct me regarding above for official use with Italian Government stating specially whether President is unable personally to attend to current matters. I have been repeatedly explaining in view of President's recent personal instructions to me that further appeals to him about Fiume are useless and this should close matter. Jay

T telegram (SDR, RG 59, 811.001W69/670, DNA).

From the Desk Diary of Robert Lansing

Thursday Oct 2 [1919]

Telephoned Grayson who reported President's condition bad. Telephoned Kirk[1] to get in touch with Long[2] and have him tell the King[3] impossible for him to see Prest even if he came to Washington.

Hw bound diary (R. Lansing Papers, DLC).
[1] That is, Alexander Comstock Kirk, now Lansing's private secretary.
[2] That is, Breckinridge Long.
[3] That is, Albert.

Two News Reports

[Oct. 3, 1919]

"VERY SICK MAN," SAYS GRAYSON
OF PRESIDENT IN LATE NIGHT BULLETIN
by ALBERT FOX.

President Wilson's condition has taken a decidedly unfavorable turn and precautionary measures have at once been taken to guard against a complete nervous breakdown. Dr. F. X. Dercum, one of the leading neurologists of the country, has been summoned from Philadelphia and with four other specialists is assisting Rear Admiral Cary T. Grayson, the President's personal physician, on the case.

Former Secretary of the Treasury W. G. McAdoo, the President's son-in-law, has arrived from the West, and his daughter, Mrs. McAdoo, is on the way here.

After a two-hour consultation at the President's bedside between Dr. Dercum; Rear Admiral E. R. Stitt,[1] head of the Naval Medical School; Capt. John B. Dennis,[2] director of the Naval Dispensary; Dr. Sterling Ruffin,[3] Mrs. Wilson's family physician, and Admiral Grayson, the following bulletin was issued by the latter:

"10.00 p.m.—The President is a very sick man. His condition is less favorable today and he has remained in bed throughout the day.

"After consultation with Doctor F. X. Dercum, of Philadelphia; Doctors Sterling Ruffin and E. R. Stitt, of Washington, in which all agreed as to his condition, it was determined that absolute rest is essential for some time.   GRAYSON."

Admiral Grayson remained at the White House after the bulletin was announced. Heretofore, he has gone home immediately after announcing the President's condition.

Shortly after the bulletin was issued Mr. McAdoo entered the White House. He said that he had read the bulletin but had no further information than what it contained.

Dr. Grayson's diagnosis of the case was concurred in unanimously by the specialists. At 11 o'clock yesterday morning, Dr. Grayson issued the following bulletin:

"The President had a fairly good night but his condition is not at all good this morning."

Immediately after posting the bulletin, it became known that Dr. Grayson had summoned Dr. Dercum. It developed too that Dr. Grayson had been in consultation during the week with Rear Admiral Stitt and Capt. Dennis but until yesterday had not thought it necessary for them to see the President. Dr. George de Schweinitz, an eye specialist who has treated the President before, has been summoned for reasons not yet explained, excepting that nervous disorders are often intimately connected with or caused by eye trouble.

Dr. Dercum reached Washington in response to a hurry call about 4 o'clock and went direct to the White House where, with the other specialists, he was conducted to the President's bedroom.

For the first time since the President's illness he has been obliged to stay in bed and it was very evident that Dr. Grayson was much worried over his patient's condition, though this does not necessarily mean, it is explained, that there is immediate cause for alarm.

The President, despite the unfavorable turn in his condition, did not want to have specialists called and it took considerable persuasion on the part of Dr. Grayson to convince him that this step was wise.

Only after Dr. Grayson had said that he himself needed relief from the strain did the President finally consent.

As a matter of fact the strain on Dr. Grayson has been very severe for the President's physician has been obliged to be with him day and night.

There were some indications Wednesday that the President was not responding to treatment as it had been hoped. His physical condition had improved so far as the stomach trouble was concerned, but his exhausted nerves still kept him in a jaded and unfavorable state.

The suggestion of Dr. Grayson that the President spend part of the day in the White House grounds, getting the benefit of the open air, did not appeal to the President, and signs of exhaustion were otherwise manifest.

The President's illness is diagnosed as "nervous exhaustion," but the danger is that the present attack of neurosthenia[4] may develop into nervous prostration, in which case it would be many months before the President would be able to resume his duties.

At present, the specialists are fighting to prevent this and Dr. Grayson, who has kept the President in trim by the closest study and the greatest care, is said to be confident that the President's reserve stamina and will power will carry him through the crisis.

But there is no doubt that the President's condition is such as to give much concern.

Dr. Grayson shows this plainly and no effort is made by Secretary Tumulty or others at the White House to minimize their anxiety.

One natural cause for deep concern is the fact that the President is now more than 62 years old. He has not been of robust physical condition, it is admitted, and only through following the careful course of training prescribed by Dr. Grayson has he kept in trim.

The intestinal trouble, from which he has frequently suffered, is accentuated by the frayed nerves and there is consequently fear of complications on this account.

It is understood that all matters of international or national interest will have to be dropped by the President for the time being. It is regarded as of paramount importance to relieve his mind of worry and strain. Even under favorable conditions, it cannot be predicted at present how long it will be before the President can resume his official duties.

Printed in the *Washington Post*, Oct. 3, 1919.
    [1] Edward Rhodes Stitt, M.D., a specialist in tropical diseases.
    [2] John Benjamin Dennis, M.D.
    [3] Professor of Medicine at George Washington University.
    [4] About neurasthenia, see Dr. Park's essay printed as Appendix II.

Found Wilson Cheerful, Dr. Dercum Announces

[*Oct. 3, 1919*]

Philadelphia, Oct. 3.—Dr. Francis X. Dercum, noted neurologist, who examined President Wilson said today the President's condition is grave but that he is in a cheerful frame of mind.

Dr. Dercum returned to his home, 1719 Walnut Street, last night, after spending an hour and a half at the President's bedside in the White House, yesterday. "We merely confirmed Dr. Grayson's diagnosis," he said, "made previously, and found the President very much in need of rest. He is very cheerful and takes an interest in what is going on. This is an encouraging indication."

The President, according to Dr. Dercum, realizes that he is a sick man and is making an effort to stop chafing under the restraint that compels him to relinquish temporarily the helm of the administration. By nature, said the neurologist, he is a "hard man to handle," from the viewpoint of a physician.

"The President is not the type of man to be warned by his symptoms," said Dr. Dercum. "This led him to overtax his strength, when he should have been husbanding it after the strain of the peace conference."

Dr. Dercum added he would not return to Washington unless summoned.

Dr. George E. de Schweinitz, the ophthalmologist, of 1705 Walnut Street, will be called on for consultation some time this week, according to Dr. Grayson. Dr. de Schweinitz has been oculist for the President and his family for many years.

The medical history of the White House is intimately linked with the lives of Philadelphia specialists. Physicians and surgeons of this city have frequently been called to the capital and elsewhere for consultation on illnesses of Presidents of the United States, from George Washington to the present day.

Dr. J. Chalmers Da Costa was hurriedly summoned to Paris during the peace conference to examine the President. . . .[1]

Printed in the *Washington Post*, Oct. 4, 1919.

[1] John Chalmers Da Costa, M.D. of Philadelphia, pioneer alienist, distinguished anatomist and surgeon, in 1919 Gross Professor of Surgery at the Jefferson Medical College.

The report that Dr. Da Costa had been hurriedly summoned to Paris to examine Wilson could only have come from Da Costa himself. Moreover, there are several references in his personal file in the archives of Thomas Jefferson University to the fact that he treated Wilson in Paris.

Dr. Grayson, in the entry from his diary printed at April 24, 1919, Vol. 58, says that Da Costa called at Wilson's residence on that day to pay his respects. Da Costa had just arrived in France on *U.S.S. George Washington*. According to Grayson, Da Costa, who was then a lieutenant commander in the Naval Medical Corps, said that he was chagrined by stories to the effect that he had been hurriedly summoned to Paris in connection with Wilson's health. Again, according to Grayson, Da Costa said that he had come in accordance with routine orders.

There does not seem to be much doubt that Grayson had called Da Costa to Paris for consultation and that Da Costa did indeed examine Wilson in connection with the immediate background or perhaps the occurrence of what we think was the small stroke that Wilson suffered in late April 1919. About this illness, see the appendixes printed in Vol. 58.

From the Desk Diary of Robert Lansing

Friday Oct 3 [1919]

Conferred with Tumulty and Grayson in Cabinet room. Tumulty pointed to left side significantly. Discussed V.P. acting as Prest.[1] Decided to call Cabinet meeting Monday. P.M.G.[2] phoned me about Shantung amendment[3] and Italian ratification[4] There for an hour. . . .

Secy Baker. Told him of serious situation of Prest. Approves Cabinet meeting. . . .

Hood[5] on precedents as to V.P. acting as Prest. None. . . .

Called meeting of Cabinet for Monday at 11 am. Left at 4:50

[1] Tumulty later described this episode as follows:
"A few days after the President returned from the West and lay seriously ill at the White House, with physicians and nurses gathered about his bed, Mr. Lansing sought a private audience with me in the Cabinet Room. He informed me that he had called diplomatically to suggest that in view of the incapacity of the President we should arrange to call in the Vice-President to act in his stead as soon as possible, reading to me from a book which he had brought from the State Department, which I afterwards learned was 'Jefferson's Manual,' the following clause of the United States Constitution:
" 'In case of the removal of the President from office, or his death, resignation, or inability to discharge the powers and duties of the said office, the same shall devolve upon the Vice President.'
"Upon reading this, I coldly turned to Mr. Lansing and said, 'Mr. Lansing, the Constitution is not a dead letter with the White House. I have read the Constitution and do not find myself in need of any tutoring at your hands of the provision you have just read.' When I asked Mr. Lansing the question as to who should certify to the disability of the President, he intimated that that would be a job for either Doctor Grayson or myself. I immediately grasped the full significance of what he intimated and said: 'You may rest assured that while Woodrow Wilson is lying in the White House on the broad of his back I will not be a party to ousting him. He has been too kind, too loyal, and too wonderful to me to receive such treatment at my hands.' Just as I uttered this statement Doctor Grayson appeared in the Cabinet Room and I turned to him and said: 'And I am sure that Doctor Grayson will never certify to his disability. Will you, Grayson?' Doctor Grayson left no doubt in Mr. Lansing's mind that he would not do as Mr. Lansing suggested. I then notified Mr. Lansing that if anybody outside of the White House circle attempted to certify to the President's disability, that Grayson and I would stand together and repudiate it. I added that if the President were in a condition to know of this episode he would, in my opinion, take decisive measures. That ended the interview.
"It is unnecessary to say that no further attempt was made by Mr. Lansing to institute ouster proceedings against his chief." Tumulty, *Woodrow Wilson as I Know Him,* pp. 443-44.
Lansing's account of his meeting with Tumulty and Grayson follows:
"On Friday, the 3d, I went over to the Executive Offices at 11:30 a.m. and conferred in the Cabinet Room with Tumulty and Grayson for an hour as to the President's condition, his present disability and the possible necessity of the Vice President's acting. We decided that it was not advisable to call a Cabinet meeting immediately as it would unduly alarm the nation but that it would be wise to call one on the following Monday."
"RECORD OF THE CABINET MEETINGS HELD DURING THE PRESIDENT'S ILLNESS," T MS dated Feb. 23, 1920 (R. Lansing Papers, DLC).
"Jefferson's Manual" was Thomas Jefferson, *A Manual of Parliamentary Practice. For*

the Use of the Senate of the United States (Washington, 1801). There were many later, often greatly expanded editions of this work, some of which included the text of the Constitution. Tumulty's final statement seems to be correct. Also, there is no evidence to indicate that Lansing, either on this occasion or later, had any sort of coup in mind. He was simply doing what he himself and Tumulty said, namely, suggesting that it was necessary to have someone in the White House who could make decisions. Lansing's suggestion should be viewed in the larger context of his own immediate situation. He was being bombarded with urgent and important requests for answers to specific questions, none of which he felt he was able to answer without specific authorization from the President. His difficulties in this regard will become evident in the documents that follow.

² That is, Postmaster General.

³ About which, see n. 1 to the extract from the Lansing Desk Diary printed at Aug. 25, 1919, Vol. 62, and G. M. Hitchcock to WW, Sept. 24, 1919, n. 4.

⁴ Probably a reference to speculation as to whether Italy would soon ratify the peace treaties. As it turned out, King Vittorio Emanuele III issued a decree on October 6 in which he approved the treaties of peace with Germany and Austria. It was announced on that date also that the King would submit the treaties to the new Italian Parliament when it met in December. *New York Times*, Oct. 9, 1919.

⁵ Edwin Milton Hood, dean of the Washington press corps, a representative of the Associated Press who reported extensively on the Department of State and knew most of its leading figures well.

From the Diary of Josephus Daniels

October Friday 3 1919

The news of the serious illness of the President fell like a pall on all hearts. Could not work. Baker said he feared the worst. Joe Tumulty in tears. "We must all pray" he said.

Hw bound diary (J. Daniels Papers, DLC).

Elisabeth, Queen of the Belgians, to Edith Bolling Galt Wilson

My dear Mrs. Wilson,   New York Oct. 3d, 1919

The news of the President's illness has caused me the deepest pain and it has detracted greatly from the pleasure I have felt from the wonderful reception being accorded us.

I beg you to send me any news you have on the President's condition and I will follow the progress he makes with interest & with the sincere hope of a rapid recovery.

Thanking you for your so kind letter and beautiful flowers I remain, dear Mrs. Wilson,   Yours sincerely   Elisabeth

ALS (WP, DLC).

From Désiré Félicien François Joseph Cardinal Mercier

Springfield, Mass., Oct. 3, 1919.

Accept my sympathy. I pray for your prompt recovery.

Cardinal Mercier.

T telegram (WP, DLC).

Two News Reports

[Oct. 4, 1919]

PRESIDENT IS IMPROVED SLIGHTLY, LATE REPORT BY DR. GRAYSON SAYS

By ALBERT W. FOX.

President Wilson's condition continues grave and virtually unchanged, though a slight improvement was recorded by Admiral Grayson in the 10 o'clock bulletin issued last night. The slight change for the better came at the end of a day of deep concern and brought some relief, though the crisis has by no means passed.

The nervous exhaustion from which the President is suffering cannot yet be said to be yielding to treatment but the President himself is understood to now fully appreciate his condition and to show signs of willingness to completely relax and place himself in the hands of his physicians.

Until yesterday the President's desire to fight against the complete abandonment of his cares and worries has been a difficult factor in the case, but Admiral Grayson is said now to have succeeded in persuading the President that absolute rest and relaxation are of the most pressing importance.

The President's physical condition remains about as it was Thursday with pulse normal, no temperature and heart action good. He experienced yesterday some difficulty in articulation but this has not been a matter of much concern.

Trained nurses have now been in attendance to assist Mrs. Wilson and Miss Margaret Wilson, who have been showing every devotion. Mrs. McAdoo, the President's daughter, arrived during the afternoon and Mrs. Francis B. Sayre, the President's other daughter arrived during the evening. Joseph R. Wilson, the President's brother, has arrived from Baltimore.

The anxiety which the nation and the entire world feel over the President's illness was in constant evidence here, now that it is beginning to be realized how critical the President's condition may become.

There is no immediate fear, but there is always the possibility of complications, and the battle which Admiral Grayson and the specialists are now waging is to decide whether or not the President has a good chance to fully recover within a reasonable time or whether complete nervous breakdown necessitates months of enforced complete rest.

Now that the extent of the drain upon the President's vitality resulting from his intense and prolonged activities is apparent, it is realized that it was only the skill and devotion of his physician, Edmund [Admiral] Cary T. Grayson, who has been his constant attendant since he first set sail for Europe, that prevented an earlier breaking down.

It may be several days before Admiral Grayson can say that the crisis is past, and in the meantime the most stringent measures to guarantee absolute rest and relaxation will be enforced.

Not even Mr. McAdoo, the President's son-in-law, was permitted to see him yesterday afternoon. Mr. McAdoo, who arrived here from the West Thursday, expected to leave for New York yesterday evening, but decided to remain over until today.

The morning bulletin given out by Admiral Grayson was delayed until 12:10 owing to a lengthy consultation held between Admiral Grayson, Admiral Stitt and Dr. Sterling Ruffin.

Dr. Francis X. Dercum, the world famous authority on nervous troubles, was consulted over the long-distance telephone. He will remain in Philadelphia unless summoned.

Supplementing the bulletin, which said simply that the President's condition was unchanged, Admiral Grayson said that the President's mind was alert and clear, that his physical condition was fairly good and that he was able to take some nourishment.

Printed in the *Washington Post*, Oct. 4, 1919.

[*Oct. 4, 1919*]

MORE ENCOURAGING DAY
Good Night's Sleep Preceded,
Bettering the President's Condition

Washington, Oct. 4.—President Wilson's condition improved today. Bulletins issued this forenoon and at 10:30 o'clock this evening stated that he had not only held his ground but had gained to some extent.

The President slept most of the day, following a night of natural sleep, and this pleased his physicians very much. Mr. Wilson also retained his light nourishment better today than during the recent days.

Admiral Grayson, the President's physician, described his patient tonight as more calm. He was gratified by the fact that, although the excessive humidity bothered the President during the day, he was able to maintain the improvement of the last twenty-four hours.

Although there has been this improvement no attempt is made to conceal the fact that the President is still a very sick man. Fluctuations in his condition should not be necessarily regarded as alarming, it is stated at the White House. For this reason the bulletins sent out are framed in a conservative wording. Every effort is made not to over-emphasize a very slight improvement as a sign that the President will be in excellent health within a few days. It was said tonight that he was still "skating on thin ice."

Dr. Grayson continues to show by his demeanor that the President is improving. Tonight he was even more cheerful than after he left the forenoon conference, and walked out of the White House with Bernard M. Baruch, who had called to present his sympathies. The doctor looks a different man from two days ago, when his face showed his keen anxiety.

Dr. Francis Dercum, neurologist, came from Philadelphia today to attend the forenoon conference, and Dr. George De Schweinitz, President Wilson's longtime eye specialist, examined the President's eyes, with the result that he pronounced them in the same condition as six months ago.[1]

Rear Admiral E. R. Stitt and Dr. Sterling Ruffin also participated in the conference. Drs. Dercum and De Schweinitz returned to Philadelphia this afternoon.

Printed in the *New York Times*, Oct. 5, 1919.
  [1] The reason for De Schweinitz's trip to Paris in April 1919 ("six months ago") comes out in the second news report printed at October 12, 1919.
  The reporter who wrote that story obviously talked to Dr. Da Costa, and Da Costa may well have examined Wilson to determine if he had had a cerebrovascular accident. The "well known surgeon" quoted in this report was obviously Da Costa. Da Costa, in his remarks, was referring to De Schweinitz. Da Costa was a surgeon, not an ophthalmologist, and De Schweinitz was an ophthalmologist, not a surgeon.
  The reference to the "trouble which had previously caused a retinal hemorrhage" was to the cerebrovascular accident (which we have called a stroke) of May 28, 1906, which had caused a retinal hemorrhage in Wilson's left eye and in fact had caused him to lose all but peripheral vision in that eye. About this attack in 1906, see WW to J. D. Greene, May 30, 1906, n. 1, Vol. 16.
  Da Costa obviously knew about Wilson's history of cerebrovascular disease. The "oculist" called to treat Wilson in April 1919 could only have been De Schweinitz.
  All this would appear to be conclusive new evidence that Wilson suffered a cerebrovascular accident in late April 1919, undoubtedly a small stroke.

From the Diary of Josephus Daniels

October Saturday 4 1919

President seemed better. No temperature said Grayson But I'll show my temper if you keep me in this bed much longer

From the Desk Diary of Robert Lansing

Saturday Oct 4 [1919]

Left at 12:50 Had a long talk with Secy Lane at the Club on the situation and the necessity of having an Executive to do business. Talked also of leaving the Cabinet as he intends to do.[1]

[1] Actually, Lane did not resign until March 1, 1920, when he became vice-president of the Pan-American Petroleum Co.

From the Diary of Josephus Daniels

October Sunday 5 1919

Went to Ex. Office to see Tumulty. He was full of indignation because Post sent Fox to report condition of President.[1] Ed Mc-Lean[2] always said he was ready to do anything, but never did anything decent.

Grayson came in—he said WW had comfortable night, slept naturally, wished food this morning & wished stenographer so he could dictate a few letters. Grayson told him he ought not to work on Sunday. Feels better abt WW but says we are not out of the woods.

Received reply from Mrs WW to my note Hoped people would pray spontaneously for her "dear husband."

[1] Obviously, Tumulty and probably Grayson and Mrs. Wilson also had been very upset by Fox's report printed at October 3 on account of the degree to which it revealed the seriousness of Wilson's condition.
[2] Edward Beale McLean, publisher of the *Washington Post* and *Cincinnati Enquirer*.

A News Report

[Oct. 6, 1919]

WILSON HAS GOOD DAY
Appetite Improving, Sleeping Better, Grayson Says.
SEEMS ON ROAD TO RECOVERY

The favorable trend of President Wilson's condition continued yesterday and there were indications that those attending him thought he might be definitely on the road to recovery.

After the best night's sleep he has had since he was taken ill ten days ago, the President was in such good spirits that Rear Admiral Cary T. Grayson, his personal physician, had difficulty in persuading him to remain in bed. The physician insisted on this point, however, and indicated he had no intention of permitting the patient to get on his feet until the change in his condition was more decisive.

Although the day's bulletin did not record any marked improvement, it contained details of the President's general condition which Dr. Grayson seemed to regard as hopeful signs. It was issued at 11 a.m. and said:

"The President had a very good night and if there is any change in his condition it is favorable. His appetite is improving and he is sleeping better.   GRAYSON."

Dr. Grayson did not have anything to say beyond what was put in his bulletin but it was apparent that there was a more cheerful feeling around the White House. Rear Admiral E. R. Stitt and Dr. Sterling Ruffin, who had been called into consultation several days ago, saw the President yesterday morning, and remained at the White House for an hour. They left at 11 o'clock, after having been in consultation with Dr. Grayson for some time.

That Mr. Wilson was able to eat and sleep with more regularity was considered particularly promising, since these are the two most important requisites for cure of the complications which followed his attack of nervous exhaustion. His digestive organs have been sensitive for years and his respiratory system, weakened by an attack of influenza last spring, is said to have interfered during his present illness with his ability to sleep soundly.

For the first time since he became ill the President now has rested easily for two consecutive nights and the result was reflected as soon as he awoke this morning in a desire to get back to his desk. When Dr. Grayson forbade that, Mr. Wilson is said to have asked that a stenographer be called so he could dictate some letters, but his physician headed off the request by reminding the President that it was Sunday and he was a good Presbyterian.

His physicians said he finally accepted the inevitable cheerfully, saying he would try to be a good patient. It was declared his mind was very alert, and that he chatted and joked with members of his family about his illness, seeming dissatisfied only with his confinement.

Printed in the *Washington Post*, Oct. 6, 1919.

Joseph Patrick Tumulty to William Bauchop Wilson, with Enclosure

Dear Mr. Secretary: [The White House] 6 October 1919.

The President wishes you to read the attached word of greeting at the opening of the labor conference this afternoon.[1]

Sincerely yours,   [J. P. Tumulty]

CCL (WP, DLC).
[1] As the news report printed at Oct. 7, 1919, reveals, Wilson did not dictate the Enclosure. Tumulty undoubtedly did so.
The "labor conference" was the Industrial Conference, about which see WW to S. Gompers, Sept. 3, 1919, Vol. 62; and B. M. Baruch to C. T. Grayson, Sept. 9, 1919, and the extract from the Grayson Diary printed at Sept. 16, 1919, n. 1.

E N C L O S U R E

6 October, 1919.

It is a matter of the deepest regret that I cannot meet with you at the opening of your conference from which I expect so much of hope will come to the country. I venture to suggest that it is the expectation of the people that you will make a searching investigation into those ways and means by which peace and harmony have been secured in a large number of our industries, that these methods may be extended more universally. This work must be carried on in the confidence that there is a way by which thinking, reasonable men may be brought to an agreement so that every party may know that it is given that consideration which it deserves because of the service which it renders to the public. For we are all parts of a larger system. The nation's interests are paramount at all times and if we look for that policy which will carry us forward upon lines of fair dealing, this conference cannot fail and the value of democracy will again be made manifest.

CC MS (WP, DLC).

From the Desk Diary of Robert Lansing

Monday Oct 6 [1919]

Cabinet meeting 11-12:45. All members present. Grayson gave us report on Prest's condition which is encouraging. Discussed estimates also Industrial Conference.

From the Diary of Josephus Daniels

October Monday 6 1919

Attended Cabinet called by Lansing. He said important matters needed attention and if the President would not be able soon to attend to the public business we ought to consider what steps to take. Should the V.P. be called upon. He thought so. Referred to the Constitutional provision "in case of the inability of the President." What constitutes "inability" & who is to decide it. Garfield was shot early in July, said Houston & no "inability" was said to exist. L said "Wayne MacVeagh[1] ran the government." No decisions & nothing but discussion

Grayson came before Cabinet & said President was better but no business should come before him now. His condition encouraging but we are not out of the woods. President wanted to know why meeting of Cabinet was held—did *not* like it.

[1] That is, (Isaac) Wayne MacVeagh, who was Attorney General in the Garfield cabinet. Grayson's account of this meeting is printed as an addendum in Vol. 64.

Pietro Cardinal Gasparri to Joseph Patrick Tumulty

Roma (Received Oct. 6, 1919)

The Holy Father[1] is most anxious about condition health President Wilson. His Holiness wishes and prays speedy recovery, and would be grateful to be kept informed about course illness illustrious patient.   Cardinal Gasparri.

T telegram (J. P. Tumulty Papers, DLC).
[1] That is, Pope Benedict XV.

A News Report

[Oct. 7, 1919]

WILSON STILL GAINS
May Be Allowed to Do Little
Work Later in Week.

President Wilson continued his progress toward recovery yesterday, his physicians reporting that cumulative effects of several comfortable days and nights slowly was making itself felt in a gain of strength. He was kept in bed, however, and it was emphasized that he still was far from being a well man.

Last night's bulletin said:

"The President had a fairly comfortable day with a slight improvement."

The morning bulletin was brief, but expressed optimism on the part of the physicians. It was signed by Rear Admiral Stitt, head of the naval medical school here, and Dr. Sterling Ruffin, of Washington, in addition to Rear Admiral Cary T. Grayson, the President's personal physician, and said:

"The improvement in the President's condition noted yesterday (Sunday) has continued. He had a satisfactory night."

There was no indication that the President would be permitted to resume the duties of his office at any time soon although it was said he might be able to give attention to some official matters later in the week.

At a cabinet meeting at the White House, over which Secretary Lansing presided, Dr. Grayson advised that none but the most pressing business be referred to the President. Afterward Secretary Tumulty announced that a session around the cabinet table had revealed little in various departments that required immediate attention. . . .

Amplifying the bulletins, Dr. Grayson said the President again insisted upon attending to public matters he considered pressing. The President particularly desired to write a message to the industrial conference to have been read at the opening session yesterday.

Dr. Grayson said he was not yet ready for the President to do any work and would continue to insist that he have absolute quiet and rest and keep his mind away from official matters. The physician fears that any excessive activity on the part of the President might cause a reaction.

While a spirit of optimism pervades the White House because of the continued improvement in the President's condition, Dr. Grayson said he did not want to be too optimistic and would continue to watch his patient carefully. He also said the President was proving "a good patient."

Printed in the *Washington Post*, Oct. 7, 1919.

To Josephus Daniels

The White House 7 October, 1919.

Memorandum from the President to the Secretary of the Navy:

If the Congress should ask questions concerning the employment of our Navy forces in the Adriatic or Mediterranean, please refer the questions to me at once, informing Congress you have done so by my direction, and that the replies will be forthcoming in due course unless indeed the Executive should find it was not compatible with the public interest to convey to the Congress at this time the particular information desired.[1]

T MS (J. Daniels Papers, DLC).
[1] This was a copy of an EBWhw MS (WP, DLC), dictated by Wilson.

From the Diary of Josephus Daniels

October Tuesday 7 1919

Had telephone from Mrs WW that she was sending Mr Wagner[1] with a message dictated by the President to her. It read: . . .

I wrote what I had done & she replied. She said WW had not signed the note because Dr G did not wish any business brought to him. "Thank you for your personal word of rejoicing with us over the President's improvement."

[1] That is, Charles C. Wagner, White House stenographer.

Josephus Daniels to Edith Bolling Galt Wilson

My Dear Mrs. Wilson: Washington. Oct. 7. 1919.

I am in receipt of the message and will act accordingly. On the last of September the Senate passed a resolution calling on the Secretary of the Navy for information.[1] In response I sent a communication of which the enclosed is a copy.[2] You will observe I express no opinion or give no information as to the authority under which the action was taken, confining myself to Admiral Knapp's plain report. I am sure this would be in accordance with the President's wishes.

Secretary Lansing has written a statement, which he forwarded to the White House some days ago, giving the facts according to the Navy officers of conditions at Spalato, Trau and places on the Dalmatian Coast. This gives the President all the information in both the State and Navy Departments. My own judgment is that, in view of my communication which gave all the facts to the Senate, there is no necessity of any other letter going to the Senate at this time. The answer to the resolution addressed to the President may well await his recovery.

It is heartening to know he has better days and we all hope and pray for steady restoration to his perfect health and strength. We are with you always in love and thought.

Sincerely your friend, Josephus Daniels

ALS (WP, DLC).

¹ S. Res. 195, introduced by Philander C. Knox on September 26, 1919, and approved by the Senate on the same date, requested Daniels to inform it whether American marines had been landed at Trau on or about September 25 to compel Italian forces to evacuate the town, as stated in an Associated Press dispatch published in the *Washington Post*, Sept. 26, 1919. The resolution quoted the news report in full. *Cong. Record*, 66th Cong., 1st sess., pp. 5936-37.

² JD to President of Senate, Oct. 1, 1919, CCL (WP, DLC). In this letter, Daniels quoted H. S. Knapp to JD, Sept. 30, 1919, a telegram which explained in detail the incident referred to in n. 1 above. Knapp revealed that, on September 23, three truck loads of Italian soldiers commanded by an Italian captain had crossed the line dividing the Italian and Serbian zones of occupation and surprised and captured the small Serbian garrison at Trau. The Italian regional command notified Capt. David French Boyd, senior American naval officer in the area, that the raid was unwarranted and unauthorized and requested him to repel the raiders. Boyd and members of his staff persuaded the intruders to leave and the regional commander of the Serbian forces to refrain from a counterattack. Boyd subsequently found it necessary to land "a small guard" from *U.S.S. Olympia* to protect an Italian army captain and three soldiers stranded by the breakdown of their truck. The Italian Admiral, Enrico Millo di Casalgiate, formally thanked Boyd for his action. Knapp believed that Boyd's prompt action had prevented "open warfare" between the Italian and Serbian occupation forces.

Edith Bolling Galt Wilson to Josephus Daniels

Copy

My dear Mr. Secretary: The White House Oct. 7, 1919

I am in receipt of your letter with enclosure of the communication sent to the Senate on the last of September in respons to the Resolution calling for "Information"—namely the Report of Adml. Knapp In view of the fact that this had already been done before you received the Memorandum dictated by the President to me this morning and taken to you in person by Mr. Wagner—

I will not submit the matter to the President at present, as the Drs insist all business shall be kept from him—and as it is "finished business" so far as your files are concerned.

I will hold the Report & am sending you this by way of receipt & explanation.

Thank you for your personal word of rejoicing with us over the Presidents improvement, & with warm regards, believe me
                              Faithfully   Edith Bolling Wilson

ALS (WP, DLC).

From the Diary of Breckinridge Long

Tuesday, October 7, 1919

After suggesting to the Secretary the possible inadvisability of the visit of the Prince of Wales as planned, he agreed. This afternoon I talked to Admiral Grayson at the White House and he said the President is still in grave danger and will be for some days, possibly weeks, to come and that by the date of the intended arrival of the Prince he will probably not be well enough to have him at the White House as a guest and may not be able even to see him. His blood pressure is getting back to normal but he is very weak and some of his veins are very thin and Grayson fears even the least irritation and worry. He has even taken the newspapers from him and is keeping him absolutely quiet and fears it may be two months before he will be well again tho' he feels he can soon decide official business of a routine nature if it is put up to him in writing.

I reported this to Mr. Lansing and he thought I should see Lindsay[1] at the Brit Embassy, which I did, and told him the truth about the Pres't as per a memo. I will dictate in the morning, for I feel it was a very important and delicate conversation and should be of record at the Department. Lindsay and I thought Lord Grey should talk to Mr. Lansing about it and we probably will arrange a talk between them tomorrow. (N.B.—Mrs. Wilson declined to sign a cable to Queen Mary suggesting he do not come over after Mr. Lansing has requested he do not be changed and withdrew the request—so he comes).

Hw bound diary (B. Long Papers, DLC).
  [1] That is, Ronald Charles Lindsay.

From the Diary of Josephus Daniels

October Wednesday 8 1919

Baker had cable from Gen Graves indicating that Cossacks would attack American soldiers protecting R.R. in Siberia & J would aid them, covertly at first, actively if necessary.[1] "Important if true." Lansing & Baker asked me to come over. WW had sent NDB to K City to give explicit instructions to G what he should do & what he should not do.[2] Original purpose in sending our troops into Siberia was to protect RR & bring out Checko-Slovaks We brought out a number, but balance are beyond the Ural Mts the main backbone of Kolchak's army. They cannot get to RR & K cannot consent for them to leave now. Lenin & Trotsky might give permission for them to return through Russia for then they would have K. at their mercy. Many people must starve in Siberia. Many more will starve if we come out & the RRs are closed. Are Js playing game to get control of all Siberia bordering the Pacific

Could the A navy whip J. navy? asked Baker. Yes, but we must have bases and supplies & they are wanting & we would require time. WW hesitates to withdraw & leaving starving people to their fate.

Baker to see Grayson. Otherwise to hold another conference. "Government cannot stop functioning because President is sick" said Lansing.

¹ W. S. Graves to the Adjutant General, No. 493, Oct. 7, 1919, T telegram (SDR, RG 59, 861.00/5472, DNA).
² See W. Wiseman to A. C. Murray, Sept. 14, 1918, n. 2, Vol. 51.

William Phillips to Peter Augustus Jay

Washington, October 9, 1919.

Your 3204, October 2nd.

For Jay from Phillips. CONFIDENTIAL FOR YOUR INFORMATION AND GUIDANCE. President is seriously ill and Grayson does not expect him to be able to handle any business for a minimum of at least six weeks. The condition of nervous exhaustion has certain definite complications which have been causing uneasiness.

FOR THE ITALIAN GOVERNMENT, you may say that Grayson has announced that the President is a very sick man but during the last two or three days there has been a continual improvement.

T telegram (SDR, RG 59, 811.001W69/670, DNA).

From the Diary of Josephus Daniels

October Friday 10 1919

As to Cossacks & Japs, matter was taken up with WW by Grayson. WW said "Tell Lansing to insist upon immediate answer to note."¹

¹ The note (to the Japanese government) is printed as an Enclosure with RL to WW, Aug. 30, 1919, Vol. 62. Lansing's note to Tokyo in response to Wilson's instructions is RL to R. S. Morris, Oct. 10, 1919, T telegram (SDR, RG 59, 861.77/1128, DNA). It is printed in FR 1919, Russia, pp. 586-87.

Three News Reports

[Oct. 11, 1919]

WILSON IS IMPROVED

President Wilson continued to gain strength yesterday and his physicians announced that his appetite, one of the troublesome elements in his illness, had been restored to a satisfactory state. He was kept in his room again during the day and was permitted to see no one except the physicians and members of his family. He talked over several matters of public business, however, with Rear Admiral Grayson, his personal physician, who gave him some detailed information he had asked for.

The President now has been on the mend for a week and his physicians seemed much encouraged at his progress, though they predicted that his recovery will continue to be very slow.

Despite the progress the President is making toward complete recovery, the physicians will insist on a long period of absolute rest and quiet. Dr. Grayson said it would not be safe to do other than follow this course of treatment.

Dr. Francis X. Dercum, Philadelphia neurologist, is expected to see the President again today, and Dr. Grayson said he intended to have Dr. Dercum come from Philadelphia about once a week until the President has recovered entirely. A talking machine has been placed in the President's room, and he is entertained at intervals with music.

Mrs. Wilson also continues to read light prose and poetry to him.

Printed in the *Washington Post*, Oct. 11, 1919.

[*Oct. 11, 1919*]

PRESIDENT NEEDS LONG REST
Physicians Dispel Hope of
Early Resumption of His Duties.

Washington, Oct. 11. (Associated Press.)—Hope that President Wilson soon might regain his normal health and resume fully the duties of his office was swept away today by his physicians, who announced it would be impossible for him to leave his bed "for an extended period." The physicians' announcement brought home to officials the possible effect of the President's illness on public affairs, and renewed discussion of what expedient might be adopted should the press of executive business reach a point demanding more attention that he could give it.

The disposition on all sides seems to be to refrain from raising the question of the President's disability to act under the Constitution, but officials are known to have considered it as one of the possibilities of the situation.

The Constitution provides that in case of the President's "disability," the Vice President shall act as Chief Executive, but there is no precedent for such a transfer of authority and official opinion is divided as to how it might be brought about should the necessity arise.

The physicians' announcement was not taken to mean that Mr.

Wilson would be prohibited from sitting up in bed, and it was considered entirely possible he might be permitted to sign a few important bills and orders each day as his progress continues. That will be a matter, however, which those attending him must decide as time goes on, and the disposition of officials seems to be to let any question of his disability solve itself as specific cases arise.

Although the accumulation of executive business is said not to be great, measures now ready for Executive action include the Prohibition Enforcement bill[1] and important amendments to the food control act.[2] It is agreed on all sides that mere failure to sign a legislative measure would not constitute disability, since bills passed by Congress become laws automatically if the President fails to act within ten days after they reach him. The view of some Administration officials is that measures known to have Mr. Wilson's approval could be legally written on the statute books under this provision while those known to be unacceptable could be held up by Administration leaders in the Senate and House.

In any consideration of the question of disability, it is pointed out that most of the sweeping powers vested in the Executive as war expedients still are in the hands of the President alone. Consequently, although by common agreement each member of the Cabinet is conducting his duties as if he were President, so far as his particular department is concerned, it is suggested that cases might arise under war legislation in which any department head would be powerless.

Who could declare a President's disability is known to present something of a puzzle to the legal advisers of the Government. The Constitution is silent on the point, and in the absence of an exact precedent a number of divergent opinions have been advanced informally. In some quarters it is held that the decision could be properly made by the Cabinet, because it would be in a position to judge if the functioning of a Chief Executive really were necessary in the public interest. In every case of the death of a President, it is said, it has been the Cabinet which has notified the Vice President of his succession to the presidency.

What might be the result should the Cabinet disagree as to a President's disability, and whether the decision would have to be unanimous or by a majority vote, admittedly presents another complication.

In the opinion of some, it would require a resolution of Congress to make valid a transfer of executive authority because of disability. It is argued that once the point is raised formally, the question is thrown into Congress just as it is in case of a deadlock in the Electoral College. It also is urged by some that the whole matter would be one for determination by the Supreme Court on the hypothesis that it would be a judicial question solely. It is pointed out that the Supreme Court undoubtedly would have the final decision in the matter should a law signed by a Vice President, acting as President, be challenged on its constitutionality.

All the discussion of the subject by officials has been, it is emphasized, purely academic. Vice President Marshall, although he has made no public expression on the subject, is understood to be entirely opposed to having the point raised in the present instance unless absolutely necessary to the interest of the nation, and the President's friends feel that he would be much hurt if any steps were taken to relieve him temporarily of his responsibilities.

[1] This was H.R. 6810, introduced by Andrew John Volstead, Republican of Minnesota, on June 27, 1919. Wilson's veto message is printed at Oct. 27, 1919.

[2] H.R. 8624, introduced by Gilbert Nelson Haugen, Republican of Iowa, on August 21. It amended Sect. 1 of the Food Control Act of 1917 to include wearing apparel and containers for foods, feeds, and fertilizers in the list of "necessaries" covered by the original Act. A new Title II providing for a Rent Commission of the District of Columbia to control rents in the district was also added. Wilson approved this bill on October 22, 1919.

[Oct. 11, 1919]

REPORTS WILSON SUFFERED SHOCK

Manchester, N. H., Oct. 11.—In a letter to a Manchester friend, received today, Senator George H. Moses says that President Wilson "may live," and adds, "but he will not be any material force or factor in anything."

Senator Moses writes of the President:

"The President is a very sick man. He suffered some kind of a cerebral lesion, either during his speech at Pueblo or immediately thereafter, and one of the readily discernible results is a slight facial paralysis.

"His condition is such that while this lesion is healing, he is absolutely unable to undergo any experience which requires concentration of mind and the consequent suffusion of blood in the brain, the pressure of which would be likely to reopen this lesion, or to cause new ones with a probable fatal result.

"Of course, he may get well—that is, he may live, but if he does he will not be any material force or factor in anything.

"One of the interesting rumors here is that Colonel House is coming home to try to impress on the President that he should abdicate for a few months and call Marshall to be Acting President.[1]

"Physicians here describe the cerebral lesion, when followed by paralysis, as a shock or rupture of the cerebral arteries. It might take the form of apoplexy and is sometimes called cerebral hemorrhage."

Printed in the *New York Times*, Oct. 12, 1919.

¹ House was ill on his arrival at Hoboken on October 12 and hence had little to say to the waiting reporters. However, the *New York Times* and New York *World*, Oct. 13, 1919, noted that, when asked if he intended to advise Wilson to turn over his duties to Marshall, House laughed aloud but made no other reply.

Two News Reports

[*Oct. 12, 1919*]

RUMOR BUSY ABOUT WILSON
Speculation on Nature of Illness
Is Increased by Moses Letter.
GRAYSON'S COMMENT SCANT

Washington, Oct. 12.—Dr. Grayson declined today to comment on the exact nature of President Wilson's condition, speculation about which has been greatly increased by the publication of the letter of Senator Moses of New Hampshire to one of his constituents. Tonight Dr. Grayson issued the usual bulletin without granting the usual interview to newspapermen, and at his home, later, it was stated that the doctor had returned to the White House and was to spend the night there.

The fact that Dr. Grayson had decided to spend the night at the White House aroused interest. Late tonight inquirers there found no evidences of activity. When the President first returned, Dr. Grayson spent every night there. Since then he has been at the White House off and on at nights. It was impossible to learn whether his staying there tonight had any special significance.

Pressed for a statement this morning as to the character of the President's illness and for comment on Senator Moses's letter, Dr. Grayson asked whether "Senator Moses is a physician." When told that he was not, Dr. Grayson remarked that "Senator Moses must have information that I do not possess."

Dr. Grayson was asked whether the President had suffered a cerebral lesion or hemorrhage, and said he would not at this moment comment on any of the reports circulated as to the President's condition, explaining that he and the other attending physicians had agreed on a policy of not answering questions based on current reports.

In response to another question, based on the letter of Senator Moses, Dr. Grayson remarked that it would not do to attach "too much credibility to long-distance diagnosis."

Senator Moses, when reached late tonight, admitted that he wrote the letter as printed in THE NEW YORK TIMES this morning.

"Certainly I admit it," said Senator Moses. "I have no reason for denying it. I have had more than half a dozen letters from inquiring constituents of mine in New Hampshire asking for information as to the real condition of the President. I have answered these letters, in the light of my best information, in the same way.

"Other Senators have had similar inquiries from constituents. I do not recall just now to whom it was I wrote this particular letter, but in all the letters I wrote, in reply to constituents, I said the same thing.

"I do not pretend to have any straight line on the White House. In these letters I have merely given my constituents a statement of the facts as I understand them in the light of the best evidence that I have been able to obtain here."

The effect of the publication of the Moses letter, containing the statement that the President had suffered a cerebral lesion, and that "while he may get well, he will not be any material force or factor in anything," has been a more insistent feeling throughout Congressional circles in Washington that the situation has reached a point where some definite official statement should be issued to the country disclosing the exact nature of the President's illness.

More than thirty bulletins have now been issued dealing with the progress of the President's condition from day to day. In none of them is there any statement as to the nature of the President's illness more definite than that contained in one of the earlier bulletins which stated that the President was ill from "nervous exhaustion." Persistent efforts have been made to ascertain from the White House something more definite about the President's case. Dr. Grayson has steadily refused to say what is the matter with the President, and he and the other attending physicians have decided to stand by the announcements made in the brief official bulletins which are issued twice daily at the White House. It was pointed out tonight that in none of these bulletins had there been any technical statement of the case, no announcement as to the pulse, temperature and blood pressure of the patient, and that for the most part the bulletins had not contained more than two brief sentences.

In the absence of any official statement of a definite character regarding the President's illness, rumor and gossip have run wild in Washington and all sorts of stories have been current for more than a week. Some of these have been brought to the attention of Dr. Grayson, who has either denied them informally or refrained from commenting.

Senator Hitchcock, who is the Democratic leader in the Senate and has made visits to the White House during the past week,[1] was asked by THE NEW YORK TIMES correspondent tonight whether he possessed any information in corroboration of the statements contained in the Moses letter. After the text of the letter, as published, was read to Senator Hitchcock, he said:

"That does not conform to what information I have about the President's illness. I should call those statements a very gross exaggeration of the President's condition. I happen to know that the President has reached some important decisions while he was in bed. He has had submitted to him some important matters on which he has passed. I doubt if he could have done so if his case was as represented in the letter attributed to Senator Moses."

When Senator Hitchcock was asked about the character of the decisions that had been reached by the President on the matters submitted to him, he said that naturally he could not say anything as to that.

The statement in the Moses letter that the President had suffered some kind of a cerebral lesion and that one of the readily discernible results was a slight facial paralysis, was a repetition of a story that has been current everywhere in Washington during the last week. It is the story that has been given the most credence in Senatorial cloak-room gossip, and the one that has survived more persistently than any other explanation of the President's illness, in the absence of an official denial.

Some of the stories told in Washington are regarded as without any real foundation, others are considered ridiculous and have not persisted, but the statement that the President has had a cerebral lesion or a slight blood-leakage from one of the blood vessels in the brain continues to be circulated by men in and out of public life who profess to have their information from some one in a position to know. This story has been brought to the attention of Dr. Grayson, and he has consistently declined to authorize official denial or comment upon it.

It is known, though, that the one thing the President's physicians have been trying to guard against is the snapping of a blood vessel in the President's head.

This much has been informally admitted to the correspondent of THE NEW YORK TIMES by one of the attending physicians.

"What we have been afraid of," this physician stated last Monday night, "is that something might snap, and for that reason the treat-

[1] Although Hitchcock might have visited Tumulty in the Executive Offices, there is no record in the Head Usher's diary of any visit by him to the White House proper.

ment prescribed for the President is absolute rest, both mental and physical."

Whether this fear has been based on absolute knowledge that there had already been a slight cerebral leakage or on knowledge that the President's condition of nervous exhaustion was such that a strong flow of blood to the brain might cause such a snapping of an artery, is something that no one connected with the case has been ready to state. However, fear that there might be such a snapping, resulting in paralysis, is undoubtedly entertained by the physicians and explains the statement in yesterday's bulletin in which all four physicians joined, that the President's condition "is such as to necessitate his remaining in bed for an extended period."

The statement attributed to Senator Moses that "one of the readily discernible results is a slight facial paralysis" was also a repetition of the statement that has been given wide circulation here that the President has experienced some difficulty in properly using the muscles of the lower part of his face. Nothing is learned to confirm the statement that there has been any kind of paralysis of the muscles of the face, but it is known from an authoritative source that while the President was touring the West there was a twitching of the muscles of one cheek while he was speaking, that this was noticeable at Pueblo and while he was being hurried home by special train from Wichita. Even before the President's trip West Dr. Grayson had at times noticed such a twitching, and whenever it occurred it was always regarded as an index to the physician that the President was overstraining himself physically.

A prominent Democratic Senator, who did not care to be quoted, made the statement tonight that he had learned definitely that Secretary Tumulty had not seen the President from the time of his return until Friday, Oct. 10. That was the day the President had made a request for certain information from the Director General of Railroads, which Mr. Tumulty had been sent to obtain.

[*Oct. 12, 1919*]

HAD SLIGHT RETINAL LESION.
Reason for Dr. Da Costa's Trip to
Paris to See Wilson.

Philadelphia, Oct. 12.—It became known here today that Dr. J. Chalmers Da Costa's trip to Paris, while President Wilson was attending the Peace Conference, was for the purpose of examining the President for trouble which had previously caused a retinal hemorrhage.

A well known surgeon here said today:

"It has, of course, been known for over a year that long before he went to Paris the President did have a slight retinal lesion, with slight hemorrhage of the retinal surface that soon cleared up, but, naturally, called for an expert oculist to examine his eye and his general condition and his tendencies. Since then he has gone through more exhausting labors than almost any other man in the world.

"When he succumbed to the exhaustion of this train trip west, it was the most prudent thing in the world to call in an opthalmologist in addition to the medical men and the nerve specialist, since an examination of the retinal surface would indicate whether or not there was a congestion or hemorrhage there, and, consequently, whether there was more than a localized congestion that led to the attack that brought about the cancellation of the trip.

"Apparently the eye examination was favorable and the indications are that the local congestion will yield and is yielding to treatment readily and that the President, as the phrase goes, will fully recover, but, of course, slowly and will be precluded from undertaking in the future the exhausting activities which have brought about his present condition."

Printed in the *New York Times*, Oct. 13, 1919.

Two News Reports

[*Oct. 13, 1919*]

President's Condition Is "About the Same,"
Says the Latest White House Bulletin

Washington, Oct. 13.—The following bulletin on President Wilson's condition was issued at the White House tonight:

White House, Oct. 13, 10 P.M.—The President's condition is about the same.   GRAYSON.

The morning bulletin read:

White House, Oct. 13, 12:15 P.M.—The President's condition remains much the same as for the last several days. His temperature, with the exception of one day, pulse and respiration rate, heart action and blood pressure are normal, and have been so since the onset of his illness. His kidneys are functioning normally.   GRAYSON,
                                                                      RUFFIN,
                                                                      STITT.

[*Oct. 13, 1919*]

WILSON'S MIND IS 'CLEAR' AND HE CAN ACT, BUT GRAYSON SAYS CURE REQUIRES TIME; SENATORS DISCUSS DISABILITY, WON'T ACT

Washington, Oct. 13.—The outstanding development of the past twenty-four hours in connection with President Wilson's condition is the declaration by Dr. Grayson, the President's physician, that his mind is as "clear as a bell," and that there is nothing in his condition that renders it impossible for him to act; but that it is considered best for him to continue the absolute rest cure, mental and physical, which has been prescribed, and to keep business from him as long as possible, except on very important or absolutely urgent matters.

"In a pinch," said Dr. Grayson tonight, "the President would be able to sign measures or to act, but for the present we are following the policy, which has been the treatment from the beginning, of keeping business away from the President as long as possible."

Dr. Grayson said that the President's condition was about the same as it had been during the last four days. When he was informed that a proposal to obtain certain information from the President, relative to the treaty, had been under consideration today by the Senate Foreign Relations Committee, which, however, had not acted on the proposal, Dr. Grayson said that if such a request were to come from the committee at this time he would pay no attention to it, but continue to devote all his time and efforts toward the effort to bring about the speediest possible restoration of the President to good health.

"We will continue to insist that the President should have rest and quiet and nursing, and that the element of time should be devoted to this treatment. I will try to keep business away from the President. I may be over-cautious in this matter, but I would rather err on the side of caution than to fail to be cautious in such a case.

"If it is absolutely necessary for some matter to be brought to the President's attention, he could attend to it, and that would be a different matter. But in my treatment of the case, in association with physicians who have been in attendance upon the President, I have forgotten all about politics and am thinking only of the President's health.

"The President's mind is as clear as it ever was. The only question is whether the treatment prescribed for him is to have a fair chance."

It was evident from Dr. Grayson's informal talk with the newspapermen that he was satisfied with the progress that had been made by the President, but that the physician's determination to have his rest cure treatment carried out was fixed.

"If we were to let up in our measure of caution," said Dr. Grayson, "we might regret it. It might be easy for me to let up in insisting that business be kept away from him, and easy to become too optimistic, but when I have the care of the President's life in my hands I consider it my duty to take no chances whatever."

Dr. Grayson issued a bulletin on the President's condition tonight, but had been considering the advisability of refraining from issuing bulletins twice daily. He pointed out that all the bulletins the last few days had been very much the same because the President's condition remained about the same, and it was not necessary to issue bulletins twice daily, but at the request of members of the press he issued a bulletin tonight, despite the fact that he felt that there was nothing new to be said.

Dr. Grayson gave fullest assurances today and tonight that if any material change occurred in the President's condition he would make the fact known. He asserted positively that nothing would be kept from the public if the President's illness should take a critical turn. He has, in fact, made arrangements under which representatives of the press will be notified in any such contingency.

Dr. Grayson today stood firm in his refusal to take official notice of the statements contained in the letter of Senator Moses of New Hampshire, or to discuss any of the current reports.

"We do not consider it proper," he said, "to pay any attention to these reports, but will stand on the official bulletins. If I were to pay attention to all these reports, I would have you newspapermen running your legs off trying to obtain comment from me."

The three physicians who have regularly attended Mr. Wilson agreed in the morning bulletin that the President's temperature—except on one day—pulse, rate of respiration, heart action, and blood pressure are normal and have been so since the onset of his illness, and that his kidneys are functioning normally. The morning bulletin was longer and more precise than usual and had a very good effect. More bulletins of this character, it is believed, would go a long way toward doing away with a number of reports that have been in circulation during the last week, especially in the last two days.

That the President has been able to transact some business was learned from Senator Hitchcock of Nebraska, who is in charge of the treaty fight on the floor of the House, who asserted that the President has within the past four days transacted some important business. Senator Hitchcock told the representative of THE NEW YORK TIMES that he was aware that the President had acted on at least two important matters within that period. What these matters were Senator Hitchcock, of course, would not say, and nothing was ascertainable at the White House as to their character. But it can be stated that they were important enough to be brought to the President's attention, and that if they had not been of that character they would not have been laid before him.

These facts demonstrate that when necessary, the President can also act on other matters. So far as the signing of bills is concerned, it is declared also at the White House that the President is fully able to do this, and to attach his signature understandingly, but that bills have not been presented to him yet for the reason that those awaiting his signature can still be held away from him for several days. These bills are the prohibition enforcement measure, the amendments "putting teeth into" the food control law, and the bill to curb rent profiteering in the District of Columbia.

Printed in the *New York Times*, Oct. 14, 1919.

Robert Lansing to Frank Lyon Polk

Washington, October 14, 1919.

Strictly CONFIDENTIAL for Polk. Hitchcocks personal estimate is that Shantung amendment[1] will be defeated by about 8 votes and that Johnson amendment[2] regarding six to one vote of Great Britain will probably be defeated by about the same vote though it may possibly be closer.

The President is doing as well as could be expected. Provided there are no complications and his physicians are able to prevent him from giving attention to public affairs he will probably recover his strength in time. It will, however, be several weeks before he can attend to matters other than the most urgent. Every precaution is necessary and no chances can be taken, as there might be a relapse. I am seeking his advice about nothing, because his health is the first consideration. This will indicate to you that his condition is still serious though not alarming. Lansing

TS and Hw telegram (SDR, RG 59, 811.001W69/807g, DNA).
[1] About which, see n. 1 to the extract from the Lansing Desk Diary printed at Aug. 25, 1919, Vol. 62.
[2] About which, see the news report printed at Sept. 2, 1919, and n. 2 thereto, *ibid*.

A News Report

[Oct. 15, 1919]

SPENT RESTLESS DAY
But Wilson's Condition Improved Last Night, Grayson Reports.
ANOTHER SPECIALIST CALLED

Due to an unimportant but irritating new complication,[1] President Wilson spent a restless and uncomfortable day, but his condition last night was described by his personal physician, Rear Admiral Grayson, as improved. The general condition of Mr. Wilson was described as favorable, Rear Admiral Grayson, his personal physician, and Drs. Stitt and Ruffin, the consulting physicians, noting in the bulletin during the day that his temperature, pulse, respiration, heart action and blood pressure were normal.

In connection with issuance of the night bulletin, Dr. Grayson announced that Dr. H. A. Fowler, a Washington specialist,[2] had been called in for consultation, and through his efforts it had been able to reduce the swelling of the prostate gland, which, it was stated, had interfered with the rest of the President Monday night.

The bulletin from the White House read:

"10 p.m., White House.—The President has had a restless and uncomfortable day, but he is better tonight.   GRAYSON."

The earlier bulletin was as follows:

"White House, 12:15 p.m.—The President did not have a restful night last night. His restlessness was caused by a swelling of the prostate gland, a condition from which he has suffered in the past and which has been intensified more or less by his lying in bed. His general condition, however, is good. As noted yesterday, his temperature, pulse, respiration, heart action and blood pressure are normal.   GRAYSON,

                                                            "RUFFIN,

                                                            "STITT."

While announcement that the President's rest was being interfered with by a swollen prostate gland, it was emphasized by Dr. Grayson that such was not uncommon and was of little importance save as it caused some discomfort. The new element entering into the President's illness, it was stated, was of the nonoperative type.

Reports that Congress might adjourn pending the President's recovery were met at the White House with the statement that such a step was absolutely unnecessary and would be opposed vigorously by the executive.

It was reiterated yesterday that the President's condition was such as to allow him to act on any important legislative matter that might demand his attention.

Printed in the *Washington Post*, Oct. 15, 1919.
[1] Wilson was beginning to suffer from a urinary obstruction caused by an enlargement of the prostate gland, which made it difficult for him to void.
[2] Harry Atwood Fowler, M.D., a urologist of Washington.

William Cox Redfield to Joseph Patrick Tumulty, with Enclosure

My dear Mr. Tumulty: [Washington] October 15, 1919.

I enclose a personal note to the President which I should be glad to have delivered to him whenever it may seem right. It informs him of my intention to remain throughout this month and to leave Washington on November 1, and suggests the appointment of Mr. Sweet[1] as my successor in view of his intimate knowledge of the work of the Department. Let me say to you that there can be no interruption of the work in any event because not only Mr. Sweet but also Mr. Thurman, Dr. Stratton and Mr. Rogers[2] have been authorized to sign as Acting Secretary in my absence.

Very truly yours,   William C Redfield

TLS (WP, DLC).
[1] Edwin Forrest Sweet, Assistant Secretary of Commerce.
[2] Albert Lee Thurman, Solicitor of the Department of Commerce; Samuel Wesley Stratton, Director of the National Bureau of Standards; and Samuel Lyle Rogers, Director of the Bureau of the Census.

E N C L O S U R E

From William Cox Redfield

My dear Mr. President   [Washington] Octr. 15. 1919

As promised in my last note[1] I shall remain in charge here until the close of the month. My house here is rented to the Serbian Legation from Nov. first and I have secured a house in Brooklyn from that day. We expect to leave Washington on the morning of Saturday, Nov. 1.

It would gratify me greatly if Mr. Sweet could be appointed my successor for the brief time that remains. He is wise in counsel and sound in doctrine. He has the Department work at his finger's end. There is no special call for initiative or driving power. The work is well organized and manned. The estimates to carry us till June 30, 1921 are in. I believe Mr. Sweet can handle the work in its present shape as well as anyone and better than most. I deeply regret the illness which has distressed you and hope the progress toward strength now reported may continue and quicken.

Not being sure that I shall be able to see you before leaving may I send a word of personal affection and confidence

Yours cordially   William C. Redfield

ALS (WP, DLC).
    ¹ WCR to WW, Aug. 30, 1919, Vol. 62.

A News Report

[Oct. 16, 1919]

GOOD DAY FOR WILSON
President's Condition Satisfactory,
Bulletin Says.
WHITE HOUSE OPTIMISTIC

Absence of any new complication in President Wilson's illness brought from his bedside late yesterday the assurance that he is "getting better." Elimination of the recent annoyance caused by a slightly enlarged gland has removed the only outstanding obstacle to his convalescence, and about the White House there was manifested a decided atmosphere of optimism.

His condition in the day was summarized in the following bulletin:

"10:30 p.m., White House. The President has had a satisfactory day.   GRAYSON."

"11:55 a.m., White House. The President had a good night's rest, enjoyed his breakfast, and aside from a slight headache, continues to make improvement. The condition which caused the restlessness of Monday night, and about which Dr. Fowler was consulted, gave no trouble during the night.

"GRAYSON,
"RUFFIN,
"STITT."

With the exception of the news furnished him by Mrs. Wilson the President has learned very little of national and international developments, although he is given daily a general summary of events.

The President has at times expressed a keen desire for more comprehensive reports and has asked Rear Admiral Grayson, his personal physician, for news, but always Dr. Grayson has succeeded in keeping away from his patient information that might prove trying to his nerves with the reminder that as a physician he has been too busy to keep in touch with government subjects.

The President's appetite is reported to be as good as expected and a recurrence of the glandular trouble is not anticipated. Only a moderate rate of recovery is looked for and indications official and otherwise are that the improvement announced yesterday may be continued.

Printed in the *Washington Post*, Oct. 16, 1919.

Margaret Woodrow Wilson to Edith Gittings Reid[1]

Dearest Mrs. Reid,   The White House [c. Oct. 16, 1919]

Please, *please* forgive my not writing to you sooner. I can hardly forgive myself for I know that you do truly love my wonderful Father and so must have been deeply concerned about him all this time.

He is really better now, and we are all much happier than we were a week ago. Of course he still has to lie very quiet, can hardly do much besides sleep—but we are hoping that because of his wonderful ability he will recuperate much more quickly than ordinary persons with nervous exhaustion. I *know* that he will for I believe that he is the devil's annointed.

We do not talk with him much, but the other day I told him that I had heard from you and that you were saving funny stories to tell him. As soon as they think it well to read to him I shall read him your letter,[2] for I know that it will comfort him.

I wonder if you could write me some little lines of "human interest" stories, as Mr. Tumulty calls them. His mind seems to revert, as he lies there, to people he used to know, and he asks me if I have heard anything lately about so and so and so and so. Edith and I felt like perfect "gumps" yesterday for he kept asking us for news—not about big things but little, and since we both of us have had but one thought for two weeks our minds were entirely blank. It was then that I told him that you were saving up stories. Perhaps you could write me (dictate to a stenographer) some of the stories you had in mind. He seems to be hungering and thirsting for some of the "fun in the world."

Can you give me news about his old Baltimore friends—who's been married and who has babies and so forth?

One would think that I sat down to write this letter with only the thought of getting use out of you. I would be perfectly capable of writing with that one thought since it is for Father, but as a matter of fact it occurred to me after I began writing.

Don't worry about him, for the papers are really getting the truth about him, that is the official bulletins are. Most of the rest of the stuff written about him is entirely made up.

He smiled with pleasure when I spoke of you, a shadow of his real smile, for he is so weak, but none the less from the heart.

Thank you so much for your letter to me. I'm afraid that it will be impossible to have Doctor Thayer,[3] as already there are three doctors hovering around. I wish he could

With my love and admiration, as ever,

Faithfully yours,   Margaret W. Wilson

When he can see any one besides Edith and me, I know that he will ask to see you M.W.W.

TCL (WC, NjP).
[1] Mrs. Harry Fielding Reid, Wilson's old friend and correspondent of Baltimore.
[2] It is missing.
[3] William Sydney Thayer, M.D., Professor of Medicine at the Johns Hopkins University Medical School.

Three News Reports

[Oct. 17, 1919]

WILSON TOLD OF VOTE
Grayson Allows Him to Hear
Shantung Clause Is Beaten.
DAY "FAIRLY SATISFACTORY"

Further indication of the steady improvement in the condition of President Wilson, who yesterday entered the fourth week of his illness, was given last night in the statement by White House officials that the vote on the Shantung amendment to the peace treaty was imparted to him within a few minutes after the Senate roll call.

The President, earlier in the day, it was learned, was advised that an important vote in the Senate peace treaty controversy was near. As the news did not seem to worry him, Rear Admiral Grayson, his personal physician, gave permission for the sending of the vote to the sick room when recorded.

Secretary Tumulty received the news of the vote at the White House immediately after announcement by the Senate tellers and sent it to the President's room, where it was given to him by his nurse, Mrs. Wilson having left his bedside for a few minutes.

The bulletin issued at the White House at 10:15 o'clock last night said:

"The President had a fairly satisfactory day.   GRAYSON."

The day bulletin read:

"The White House, 11:55 a.m.—The discomfort which the President suffered for two days has been relieved to a very great

extent. He had a good night. His temperature, pulse, respiration and kidney function continue normal.   GRAYSON,
                                                                "RUFFIN,"
                                                                "STITT."

The day bulletin was supported by unofficial reports throughout the afternoon, although there was no disposition to create an impression that a radical improvement could be noted for some time.

Affairs demanding Mr. Wilson's attention are still being shoved into other channels, as was the prohibition enforcement act, which was sent yesterday to the Attorney General for consideration before executive action is taken.

Printed in the *Washington Post*, Oct. 17, 1919.

[*Oct. 17, 1919*]

PRESIDENT IMPROVES AFTER A SETBACK;
DR. YOUNG, GLAND SPECIALIST, CALLED IN

Washington, Oct. 17.—Concern over the condition of President Wilson was renewed today with a return of the swelling of the prostate gland, which developed several days ago and has served to check the general improvement of his condition during the last two weeks.

Tonight this gland development was reported as being so definitely improved that an operation would not be necessary, for the present at least; but the fact that an operation might have been required today is a sufficient indication of the apprehension that was entertained by the physicians this morning.

The text of tonight's bulletin read:

White House, Oct. 17, 10 P.M. The President's prostatic gland swelling, referred to in previous bulletins, is definitely improved and causing little discomfort, so that the treatment has been simplified. The kidneys are functioning normally and the heart action is excellent. The temperature, pulse and blood pressure remain normal.   GRAYSON,
                                          YOUNG,
                                          RUFFIN,
                                          STITT,
                                          FOWLER.

The morning bulletin was:

White House, Oct. 17, 12:15 P.M. The President passed a comfortable night, and is feeling well this morning. His temperature, pulse, and respiration rates are normal. The prostatic condition is not as satisfactory as yesterday, and is checking general improvement of the past two weeks.   GRAYSON,

                                                                RUFFIN,

                                                                STITT.

When the prostatic swelling reappeared this morning in more aggravated form than on Wednesday it was decided to call in Dr. Hugh Hampton Young, Clinical Professor of Urology in the Johns Hopkins Medical School, Baltimore, who is regarded as this country's leading authority on all ailments relating to the prostate gland. Dr. Young reached the White House at 3 o'clock and went into immediate consultation with Rear Admiral Cary T. Grayson, the President's physician, and Drs. Stitt, Ruffin, and Fowler.[1]

Tonight the President's condition had been relieved by [without] artificial means, without the use of instruments and without an operation, and Dr. Young left Washington for Baltimore at 9 o'clock. He will return to Washington tomorrow, and Dr. F. X. Dercum of Philadelphia, the eminent neurologist, who has been in consultation in the case, will probably also have another look at the President tomorrow.

Before the arrival of Dr. Young, it had been feared that an operation for prostate gland swelling would be necessary. This operation is one of the most difficult that is attempted and is usually undertaken only as a last resort. However, about the time Dr. Young reached the White House the gland swelling had improved and, after a very careful examination of the patient, Dr. Young decided that it would not be necessary, for the present, to operate.

Dr. Young also made a careful examination of the President's kidney conditions, and after visiting the White House went to the naval laboratory to conduct certain tests. Following this he returned to Baltimore with the understanding that he would return tomorrow afternoon.

The President's three physicians who visited him this morning—Drs. Grayson, Stitt, and Ruffin—felt some apprehension over the gland condition, and decided that it would be better to summon Dr. Young, who is a specialist with an international reputation, before the gland trouble went too far, as it might introduce a complication by affecting the President's kidneys.

The report was current throughout Washington late in the afternoon and until the time when the night bulletin was issued at 10 o'clock that an operation had been performed on the President. This rumor vanished as soon as Dr. Grayson authorized the statement that no operation had been necessary, and that none was for the present considered necessary.

Dr. Young is the specialist who operated upon David R. Francis, the American Ambassador to Russia, for an enlargement of the prostate gland. He also operated on the late "Diamond Jim" Brady[2] when the latter found it necessary to try to obtain a newly built-up stomach.

He is the eighth physician who has been called in to consider the President's case since Mr. Wilson's return from the West. Besides Dr. Grayson, who has general charge of the distinguished patient, the others called have been Dr. Ruffin, a general practitioner; Rear Admiral Stitt, in charge of the Naval Hospital, who is an authority on the blood; Dr. Dercum of Philadelphia, a brain and nerve specialist; Dr. Fowler, who was called in on Wednesday as a specialist in urology; Captain John B. Dennis of the Naval Dispensary, who was called in once early in the case; Dr. de Schweinitz of Philadelphia, an eye specialist, and finally Dr. Young.

It is understood that the examination made by Dr. Young indicated that the President's kidneys had not been involved in any new complication. The complication resulting from the gland swelling had the effect of checking the improvement that had been evident, slow, but steady, during the greater part of last week and early this week.

It can be stated that the President has not yet reached the point where he can be considered out of danger and the indications now are that the extended period during which his doctors declared last Saturday he would have to remain in bed will extend into weeks if not into months, even though he receives the best of care and attention and is restricted to absolute rest. . . .

The statement was made tonight that the real nature of the disease from which the President has been suffering is "fatigue neurosis." This is declared to be a functional rather than an organic trouble, and the President is said to have shown signs of it before he went on his Western trip. At one time, it is said to have affected the nerves of one of his arms and to have been responsible for a twitching of the muscles of his face, while on his trip.

[1] At least one of the attending physicians, perhaps Dr. Fowler, had advised an operation to place a catheter, through a median line abdominal incision, into Wilson's bladder as the only way to save his life. At this point, Dr. Grayson called in Dr. Young, who, on a basis of British experience in treating wounded soldiers during the war by a similar operation, had concluded that it was much safer to rely upon nature taking its course than to run the risk of a high probability of mortality due to the operation. Dr. Young says that he told Grayson that an operation would probably be fatal and that Wilson would probably void naturally in due time. According to Young, Grayson did follow his advice and Wilson voided naturally a few hours later. Hugh H. Young, *Hugh Young, A Surgeon's Autobiography* (New York, 1940), pp. 399-401.

Mrs. Wilson's account of this episode is probably inaccurate. She says that Dr. Young recommended an operation but that Grayson told her that it would be fatal and that she made the decision not to operate. Edith Bolling Wilson, *My Memoir*, p. 291.

As will be seen, although Wilson did manage to void on October 17, he had difficulty for about a week in urinating, and Dr. Young was called back to the White House several times.
² James Buchanan Brady.

[*Oct. 17, 1919*]

DR. H. H. YOUNG TELLS OF WILSON JESTING

Baltimore. Oct. 17.—Dr. Hugh H. Young, on his return late tonight from Washington, said:

"I found the President much better than I had expected from previous impressions which I had got from the public press. He was quite tranquil and comfortable and his general condition was excellent.

"The prostate gland swelling, which has been referred to in the bulletins, was very definitely improved, so that the treatment could be simplified. His cheerfulness and brightness showed that he was distinctly better than for the past few days.

"As an evidence of his alertness, I may mention an amusing incident that occurred. Admiral Grayson remarked to him that he needed a barber. I remarked: 'Why not have the doctor shave you, as they did in olden times, when the surgeons were all barbers?' Whereupon the President quickly remarked: 'They are still barbarous.' "

Dr. Young would not give any indication as to whether an operation would be necessary.

Printed in the *New York Times*, Oct. 18, 1919.

Edith Bolling Galt Wilson to Loulie Hunter House

My dear Mrs. House: The White House Oct. 17, 1919

I am delighted to know through you¹ of the Colonels' improvement and hope with all my heart it is steady and permanent and that the X Ray will furnish no new cause for anxiety.²

Thank you for your sympathy and concern for the President. We feel he is gaining a little every day but every nerve had been crying out for weeks before he gave up, and therefore we cannot expect miracles in a rapid restoration.

When he is better I will tell him of your letter and the Col.s message,³ but as we keep every thing from him (which it is not important to have his advise about, & which would annoy or distress him, I have not yet told him of the Col's illness or that he has left Paris⁴—for I knew how anxious he was that he remain there for the time.

I know how good it is to be back again in your own home, and hope the cloud of the illness will soon lift. Affectionate greetings to you both—from Edith B. Wilson.

ALS (E. M. House Papers, CtY).
    [1] Mrs. House's letter to Mrs. Wilson is missing.
    [2] House began his voyage home from France on October 6 and arrived at Hoboken on October 12. He had to be assisted down the gangway. He spoke to waiting reporters briefly and explained his illness as follows: "I was attacked in Paris with a recurrence of the gravel [kidney stones] from which I suffered a year ago, and for the last eight days I have had a fever, which left me today." *New York Times*, Oct. 13, 1919. His physician, Dr. Albert Richard Lamb, issued a bulletin on October 13 which stated that House had suffered on the voyage from an attack of "renal colic." *Ibid.*, Oct. 14, 1919. House confirmed this diagnosis in his diary (T MS, CtY) entry for October 21, 1919, and noted also that he was just then out of bed and beginning to receive callers.
    [3] EMH to WW, Sept. 29, 1919.
    [4] See EMH to WW, Sept. 30, 1919.

A News Report

[Oct. 19, 1919]

WILSON HAS BEST DAY
Specialists Now Hold Operation
Will Not Be Necessary.

President Wilson passed the best day he has known since his present illness began, Rear Admiral Cary T. Grayson, his physician, said last night. No operation will be necessary to relieve the swelling of the prostate gland, which has complicated the case, and the President is making slow but satisfactory progress toward recovery from his nervous exhaustion.

This was the conclusion reached by six attending physicians after a consultation late yesterday which lasted more than an hour and a half. Their optimistic views were reflected in the bulletin issued at 10 p.m. The day's bulletins were:

"Ten p.m.—The President has had a comfortable day. He is taking abundant nourishment and is somewhat stronger. The improvement in the prostatic condition has been maintained very satisfactorily, and no change in the simple treatment employed is contemplated.

GRAYSON,
"DERCUM,
"YOUNG,
"FOWLER,
"RUFFIN,
"STITT."

"Eleven twenty a.m.—The President rested well last night. There is no material change to note in his general condition. No new symptoms have developed.

GRAYSON,
"RUFFIN,
"STITT."

The decision that no operation was necessary was made by Dr. Hugh Young, the Baltimore specialist, while Dr. F. X. Dercum, of Philadelphia, saw signs of improvement in the President's nervous condition. All of the doctors were agreed that he was making progress toward recovery.

The program of complete rest from official cares prescribed by Dr. Grayson and his associates will continue to be enforced, it was stated. There is no intention of referring to the President any matter not absolutely requiring the exercise of his official powers.

Dr. Grayson indicated that he would not favor referring any bill to the President for signature at present, unless it was one on which he desired to exercise his veto power. Otherwise measures would be allowed to go upon the statute books at the expiration of the ten day period provided by the constitution.

The prohibition enforcement bill is now awaiting presidential action. The impression prevailed tonight that it would be allowed to become effective without Mr. Wilson's signature.

Printed in the *Washington Post*, Oct. 19, 1919.

Franklin Knight Lane to Joseph Patrick Tumulty, with Enclosure

Dear Joe   Washington [Oct. 20, 1919]

Here is a letter to the President & a suggested letter from him to us.

Please scrutinize the latter carefully.

I should have whatever reply the President makes by 11 o'clock altho' I dont believe we will get to the breaking point this morning. And I think it should only be used if one side or the other actually threatens to go out. The Employers wont go I'm sure. The Employees talk of it.   F.K.L.

ALI (WP, DLC).

E N C L O S U R E

From Franklin Knight Lane

My dear Mr. President: Washington October 19, 1919.

I am sorry to annoy you, but I must. This Industrial Conference is likely to end tomorrow or very soon after without doing anything. The elements have come to an impasse. They cannot agree as to collective bargaining.

The Labor people say that unless we can recognize this right we can get nowhere. The Employers say that they are not yet ready to give up dealing with their men as individuals. The Public Group is most liberal, siding strongly on this matter with the Labor Group.

The latter thrust the steel strike to the front at the beginning of the conference, thereby throwing consternation into both other groups. It was a bit of audacious labor politics, fine strategy from a labor standpoint, if the conference had not been in session, but demoralizing to the whole movement of the conference as a creative body, because it forced the conference to consider the matter of settling a strike before it had time to consider the cause of strikes. We came to the end while still at the beginning.

Action on a resolution calling on strikers and strikees to get back to pre-strike conditions was deferred by the conference to await action on a resolution—on collective bargaining,—and there we are, with some of the delegates angry and pretty nearly every one disgusted.

I am trying today to gather the scattered elements together and make a last appeal. Heretofore I have not participated, but as a last hope I think I should. And so I turn to you for a word that will help. Won't you please send me a line saying that this conference must not break up, that it must take up more than one phase of the labor problem and try to frame a program before it rests its fate on any one plank, and that the country will have a sense of outrage, of being greviously [grievously] wronged if any group in the conference does not attempt seriously and wisely to accommodate itself to the need of the day which is for adjustment; that we cannot have industrial war without raising a cynical smile on the lip of every red revolutionist the world round, that these are the ones who have been saying that industrial peace must be the product of revolution resulting in the overthrow of the autocrats of capital, that destruction must precede construction—and to give these people hope, confidence and assurance is to wring our hands in despair and confess defeat for the processes of evolutionary democracy.

I enclose a suggested letter.

Cordially yours,   Franklin K. Lane

TLS (WP, DLC).

To the Industrial Conference

[[The White House, Oct. 20, 1919]]

To the Ladies and Gentlemen of the Industrial Conference:

I am advised by your Chairman that you have come to a situation which appears to threaten the life of your conference, and because of that I am presuming to address a word of very solemn appeal to you as Americans. It is not for me to assess the blame for the present condition.

I do not speak in a spirit of criticism of any individual or of any group. But having called this conference, I feel that my temporary indisposition should not bar the way to a frank expression of the seriousness of the position in which this country will be placed should you adjourn without having convinced the American people that you had exhausted your resourcefulness and your patience in an effort to come to some common agreement.

At a time when the nations of the world are endeavoring to find a way to avoid international war, are we to confess that there is no method to be found for carrying on industry except in the spirit and with the very method of war? Must suspicion and hatred and force rule us in civil life? Are our industrial leaders and our industrial workers to live together without faith in each other, constantly struggling for advantage over each other, doing naught but what is compelled?

My friends, this would be an intolerable outlook, a prospect unworthy of the large things done by this people in the mastering of this continent—indeed, it would be an invitation to national disaster. From such a possibility my mind turns away, for my confidence is abiding that in this land we have learned how to accept the general judgment upon matters that affect the public weal. And this is the very heart and soul of democracy.

It is my understanding that you have divided upon one portion only of a possible large program which has not fully been developed. Before a severance is effected, based upon present differences, I believe you should stand together for the development of that full program touching the many questions within the broad scope of your investigations.

It was in my mind when this conference was called that you would concern yourselves with the discovery of those methods by which a measurable co-operation within industry may have been secured and if new machinery needs to be designed by which a minimum of conflict between employers and employes may reasonably be hoped for, that we should make an effort to secure its adoption.

It cannot be expected that at every step all parties will agree upon each proposition or method suggested. It is to be expected, however, that as a whole a plan or program can be agreed upon which will advance further the productive capacity of America through the establishment of a surer and heartier co-operation between all the elements engaged in industry. The public expects not less than that you shall have that one end in view and stay together until the way is found leading to that end or until it is revealed that the men who work and the men who manage American industry are so set upon divergent paths that all efforts at co-operation are doomed to failure.

I renew my appeal with full comprehension of the almost incomparable importance of your tasks to this and to other peoples, and with full faith in the high patriotism and good faith of each other that you push your task to a happy conclusion.

(Signed) Woodrow Wilson.[1]

Printed in the *New York Times*, Oct. 23, 1919.
[1] This letter was read to the conference on October 22. Gompers then introduced a final resolution approving in principle collective bargaining. The members representing the public voted in favor of it; those representing employers voted against it. Thereupon, the labor members, led by their chief, walked out of the meeting room. *New York Times*, Oct. 23, 1919.
It is impossible to know whether Tumulty showed Lane's draft of the letter to the conference to Wilson before he, Tumulty, sent it. There is no draft of it or any EBWhw memorandum concerning it in the Wilson, Tumulty, or Edith B. Wilson papers in DLC.

From the Diary of Colonel House

October 21, 1919.

The President's condition is such that no one is seeing him outside of his physician and Mrs. Wilson. Both Burleson and Lansing have been here to see me. Burleson came at the request of Secretary Baker. The entire Cabinet are greatly exercised over the President's inability to transact executive business. Lansing clearly desires the Cabinet to proceed independently. Burleson and Baker are more considerate of the President's sensibilities. Lansing told me that he had called one or two Cabinet meetings already and he understood the President was displeased. He indicated, however, that he intended to continue to call them because he thought it the proper thing to do. He was anxious that I see Mrs. Wilson and persuade her that it would be wise to allow him, Lansing, to act for the President during his disability. It is a question whether the Cabinet shall go ahead or whether the Vice President shall be called in. Of the two it seems to me that the President would prefer the Cabinet acting, although, if I were in his place, I should do the reverse and allow Marshall to act. I should take a complete rest until I recovered.

There is much discussion in Washington and elsewhere as to whether the President has suffered a stroke. McAdoo, who has seen him, declares Grayson says he has not had one. On the other hand, when the President became so much worse after he returned to Washington, Tumulty told Lansing the President had had a stroke which affected his left side.[1] However, Tumulty has only seen the President once and that within the last few days, and he may or may not have gotten his information from Grayson.

T MS (E. M. House Papers, CtY).
  [1] See Lansing's memorandum printed at Nov. 5, 1919.

From the Diary of Henry Fountain Ashurst

October 21, 1919.

At the Senate I was informed that Senator Hitchcock, Democrat leading the fight for Treaty Ratification, had gone to the White House, to inform Dr. Grayson, who in turn is to tell W.W. that the Treaty cannot be ratified without vital reservations. A good move, but it comes too late. Such information should have been conveyed to W.W. sixty days ago.

Leading Democratic Senators counted noses today and found 49 Republicans and 6 Democrats for Reservations whilst the Democrats have but 41 votes to oppose the 55, so the Democratic Senators are now "framing reservations" but the Republicans will defeat every Democratic proposal. They will then vote for their own Reservations and go to the elections pointing to the fact that the Republican Senators "Americanized the Treaty."

T MS (AzU).

A News Report

[Oct. 22, 1919]

President, Better, Signs Four Bills
After Having One of His Best Nights

Washington, Oct. 22.—President Wilson had a comfortable day today, following what was described by his physicians as "one of the best nights since his illness began." The fatigue from which the President suffered last night after attending to the sending of his letter to Secretary Lane, to be read to the National Industrial Conference, is declared to have disappeared and he awoke in good condition this morning. During the day he signed four bills[1] and attended to other business.[2] Dr. Grayson, the attending physician, is still urging, however, that the President refrain as much as possible from doing any work.

Tonight's bulletin read:

White House, Oct. 22, 10 P.M.—The President has had a comfortable day.   GRAYSON.

The morning bulletin was as follows:

White House, Oct. 22, 11:10 A.M.—The President had one of the best nights since his illness began. His temperature, pulse, and respiration rates continue normal. His digestion is more satisfactory.   GRAYSON,

RUFFIN,

STITT.

Dr. Hugh Hampton Young, of Baltimore, and Dr. Harry A. Fowler, of Washington, were again at the White House today. Dr. Grayson said the prostatic trouble had not returned but that both these physicians would be asked to check up on the case from time to time.

Dr. Grayson said tonight that the President was "mending gradually," but that he was still to be regarded as a bed patient and there had been no change in the program of treatment.

While the President signed four bills today, and attended to some other matters of business, this is not to be interpreted as meaning that Dr. Grayson and the physicians have relaxed their plan for keeping work away from the President as long as possible. The President has been rather insistent that he should do some work, and the contest between the President and his physicians over the rule against transaction of business has been resumed. It has reached the point again where today it was considered wise not to stand in his way too persistently.

Printed in the *New York Times*, Oct. 23, 1919.

[1] See n. 2 to the second news report printed at Oct. 11, 1919. For the other three bills, all of minor importance, see 41 *Statutes at Large* 293-97.

[2] Wilson remitted the sentences of two army prisoners and signed extradition papers for Augustine Spinozzi, then being held in France at the request of United States law officers. *Washington Post*, Oct. 23, 1919.

Edward Mandell House to Edith Bolling Galt Wilson

Dear Mrs. Wilson: New York City. October 22, 1919.

I was deeply concerned to read what you had to say in your letter to Mrs. House regarding the President.[1] The fact that you have not told him of my return indicates that he is either much sicker than

I had thought, or that he laid more stress upon my remaining abroad than seemed to me possible.

At the end of August or the first of September, when he asked me not to come home for the moment[2] I replied that I would gladly stay until after the first of October,[3] which was the time he indicated as being desirable for me to remain. In another cable and in two letters[4] I told him that I would sail sometime between the first and tenth, and not having received a reply I took it for granted that he was convinced as I was that it was best for me to be here.

I take it that for some reason he has not read these letters or cables. There was no difference of opinion as to what was best for me to do with those in Paris to whom I talked, like Wallace,[5] Polk and the other Commissioners, and I concluded that I had convinced the President also.

My work was entirely finished and there had begun to be unpleasant comment regarding my continued presence. As I wrote the President, in my opinion, the Commission ought to be either entirely broken up or continued with one man in charge. The British have only one man, and he is of second or third rate importance— Sir Eric [Eyre] Crowe.

I was so unhappy and uneasy about the President's condition before I left that I should have come in any event even if there had been no understanding.

The doctors advise my keeping quiet for sometime but if you feel that I can be of any service whatever I shall be glad to come to Washington whenever you indicate.

I am sure you know how deeply distressed I am, and how willingly I would do anything in my power to serve either the President or you.   Your friend always,   E M House

TLS (WP, DLC).
    [1] EBW to Loulie H. House, Oct. 17, 1919.
    [2] See WW to EMH, Aug. 28, 1919, Vol. 62.
    [3] EMH to WW, Aug. 31, 1919, *ibid*.
    [4] EMH to WW, Sept. 3, 1919, *ibid*,; EMH to WW, Sept. 15, 1919; and EMH to WW, Sept. 20, 1919.
    [5] That is, Hugh Campbell Wallace.

From Robert Lansing, with Enclosure

Washington October 22, 1919.

MEMORANDUM TO BE READ TO THE PRESIDENT

The imminence of the capture of Petrograd from the Bolsheviki[1] has raised the question of the feeding of the population.

For this purpose the Russian Embassy desires to buy 29,000

tons of wheat flour, value estimated at $3,700,000, from the United States Grain Corporation.

The Cabinet discussed the matter Tuesday and was of the opinion that everything possible should be done to effect this transaction.

The Grain Corporation is prepared to furnish the flour but does not feel that it can do so on a credit basis without your express authority. A letter to Mr. Barnes embodying this authority, prepared in the State Department and approved by Mr. Lansing, is attached for your signature.

T MS (WP, DLC).
    ¹ The anti-Bolshevik Russian Northwestern Army, commanded by Gen. Nikolai Nikolaevich Yudenich, about October 1 had begun a drive to capture Petrograd. By October 21, advance units had penetrated the outskirts of the city. However, the larger defending Red Army, under the personal command of Leon Trotsky, took the offensive. The Northwestern Army was driven into retreat and in mid-November was stricken by an epidemic of spotted typhus. By the end of that month, Yudenich's army, decimated by enemy action, desertions, and disease, had virtually ceased to exist. See William Henry Chamberlin, *The Russian Revolution, 1917-1921* (2 vols., New York, 1935), II, 271-75; George Stewart, *The White Armies of Russia: A Chronicle of Counter-Revolution and Allied Intervention* (New York, 1933), pp. 230-35; and Richard H. Ullman, *Britain and the Russian Civil War, November 1918-February 1920* (Princeton, N. J., 1968), pp. 281-86.

E N C L O S U R E

My dear Mr. Barnes: [The White House] 22 October, 1919.

It has been brought to my attention that the Russian Ambassador at Washington, Mr. Boris Bakhmeteff, has made application to the Grain Corporation to purchase, on a partial credit basis, 29,000 tons of wheat flour with a view to shipping 20,000 tons for the relief of the civilian population of Petrograd and such adjoining regions as may be freed from Bolshevik control, and the remainder to Archangel for the relief, under similar conditions, of the civilian population of northern Russia. I understand that Mr. Bakhmeteff desires to enter into a contract with you on behalf of the Russian Embassy.

I consider it of the utmost importance and urgency that food be made available for the civilian population of the regions in question. It is the announced policy of this Government to relieve in every possible way the material distress of the Russian people. It is considered, moreover, that economic relief of this character is the most effective means of limiting the spread of Bolshevism and of protecting, thereby, the Government of the United States from the dangers of subversive propaganda.

Pursuant to the authority conferred upon me by Act of Congress approved March 4, 1919, I hereby direct and authorize you to sell to the Russian Embassy, on credit or otherwise, the wheat flour mentioned above on such terms as you may, in your discretion, determine.

I am, my dear Mr. Barnes,

Very sincerely yours,   Woodrow Wilson[1]

TLS (Letterpress Books, WP, DLC).
  [1] This letter was retyped in the White House, and Wilson signed it.

A News Report

[*Oct. 23, 1919*]

President Maintains His Improvement;
"Dry" Enforcement Bill Awaits His Action

Washington, Oct. 23.—No new symptoms or complications have developed in the President's illness, and his physicians appear to be satisfied with the progress he has made during the last few days. The night bulletin read:

White House, Oct. 23, 10:20 P.M. The President is satisfactorily maintaining the improvement which he has recently made.

GRAYSON.

The morning bulletin read:

White House, Oct. 23, 12 o'clock. The President is making as satisfactory progress as is possible in the circumstances. No new symptoms have developed.   GRAYSON,

RUFFIN,

STITT.

No action was taken by the President during the day on the bill for the enforcement of national and wartime prohibition. The bill, accompanied by an opinion by Attorney General Palmer as to its constitutionality, is at the White House but has not been laid before the President. There is no indication that the President will veto the bill. He has until Oct. 28 to sign it or permit it to become law without his signature.

The President was again in touch with the affairs of the Industrial Conference during the day. Secretary Tumulty made a report to him of the latest development in the conference. Following this the President sent a message in writing to Secretary Lane through Secretary Tumulty regarding the work of the conference. After that the President's physicians insisted that he do no more work during the day, and the President spent the afternoon resting.

While the President has been more active today and yesterday in attending to matters in connection with the Industrial Conference, it was made plain at the White House that his physicians are insisting as much as possible on adherence to their program of refraining from official work as much as possible.

Printed in the *New York Times*, Oct. 24, 1919.

Joseph Patrick Tumulty to Franklin Knight Lane

Dear Mr. Secretary: The White House October 23, 1919

I have learned that there seems to be a misunderstanding as to what the President desires of the public group in the labor and capital conference. The President realizes the peculiar situation which now confronts the conference by reason of the withdrawal of the labor group, and so the idea of an elaborate industrial program, I am sure, was not in his thought.

In order that the matter may be cleared up, I desire to say that the President wished the public group to make a report to him containing advice and suggestions as to what that group thought it possible and wise for it to do in the present industrial situation.

Sincerely yours,   J P Tumulty

TLS (WP, DLC).

Franklin Knight Lane to Joseph Patrick Tumulty, with Enclosure

Dear Joe—   Washington [Oct. 23, 1919]

I still think that this is the wise course—say good bye to the Employers and invite the Public to go on. Am waiting at the office for reply.   F.K.L.

ALI (WP, DLC).

E N C L O S U R E

Dear Mr. Lane: October 23, 1919.

It has been with a distinct shock that I have learned of the withdrawal from your conference of the Labor group, for it had been my expectation that the conference would continue in full exercise of its functions until a program making for industrial peace had been secured.

This withdrawal, however, should not in my opinion lead to the abandonment of the work of supreme importance which the conference has undertaken, although it may properly require that its character be somewhat altered.

Employers and employees not being able to agree upon a wise plan of procedure, the burden of attempting to suggest such a plan must fall upon the public, therefore, I would suggest that the conference continue with the Public group alone, giving to the country the benefit of its council.

There is a work to be done in the determination of humane industrial policies and in the devising of machinery for their execution, which is distinctly the Public's duty in that it transcends the interests of either Capital or Labor, for the Public bears the burden of the quarrels which arise from the indifferences or the arrogances of either side.

I beg that you express to the members of the Employers group my appreciation of their offer to remain in the conference and my deep regret that this effort at constructive industrial statesmanship through the cooperative effort of the three groups should have been given a temporary check.

Cordially yours,

T MS (WP, DLC).

Edith Bolling Galt Wilson to Edward Mandell House

My dear Col. House   The White House Oct. 23/1919

Your letter has just come & I am sorry if mine to Mrs. House has caused you unhappiness.

I really do not know whether the letters & cables you speak of ever reached the President for we were moving so fast that he had almost no time except that which he had to devote to the preparation of his speeches, for he made 2 or 3 every day & tried to adapt them to the locality and particular need of the audiences he addressed.

And when we did get home Dr. Grayson forbid his looking at the vast accumulation here.

I am happy to say that his progress goes on from day to day although, as I wrote Mrs. House, it necessarily must be slow, and not knowing anything of your coming home can do him no harm. While should he still have the conviction (that I knew he did have some time ago) about your remaining in Paris, it might have caused him to worry. So that is the reason I decided not to volunteer the information.

Needless to say had he asked the question I would have told him the truth. But in the circumstances I feel sure you will agree with my judgment.

I am so glad to hear you are feeling stronger and hope you will go slow and not over tax your strength

Thank you for your offer to be of service. I know of nothing now, for the best cure seems to be rest and freedom from everything.

I am writing with many interruptions, so please pardon repetitions.

With the hope for your speedy recovery believe me always,

Edith Bolling Wilson

ALS (E. M. House Papers, CtY).

Cary Travers Grayson to Gilbert Monell Hitchcock

My dear Senator: The White House October 23, 1919.

I read your kind letter to the President[1] and it was most comforting to him and I think did him a lot of good. He asked me especially to tell you how deeply he appreciated your message and how grateful he is to you for it.

With warm regards, believe me,

Sincerely yours, Cary T. Grayson

TLS (G. M. Hitchcock Papers, DLC).

[1] Hitchcock's letter is missing. He obviously left it with Grayson when he saw him on October 21, about which meeting see the extract from the Ashurst Diary printed at that date.

Joseph Patrick Tumulty to William Bauchop Wilson

My dear Mr. Secretary: The White House 24 October 1919.

The President desires me to say that he has been watching with the deepest interest your efforts to bring about an adjustment of the impending strike in the bituminous coal fields of the country and was glad to have your report[1] of the status of the negotiations now being carried on under your direction.

He requests me to convey the following message to you:

"I have been watching with deep and sincere interest your efforts to bring about a just settlement of the differences between the operators and the coal miners in the bituminous coal fields of the country. It is to be hoped that the good judgment that has been exercised by both operators and miners in years gone by in the adjustment of their differences will again prevail in the present crisis. All organized society is dependent upon the maintenance of its fuel supply for the continuance of its existence. The Government has appealed with success to other classes of workers to postpone similar questions until a reasonable adjustment could be arrived at. With the parties to this controversy rests the responsibility of seeing that the fuel supply of the nation is maintained. At this time, when the whole world is in need of more supplies, it would be a cruel neglect of our high duty to humanity to fail them.

"I have read with interest the suggestion made by you that the wage scale committees of the operators and miners go into conference without reservation for the purpose of negotiating an agreement as though no demands had been made or rejected, having due regard to the interests of their respective groups. I am in accord with that suggestion. No body of men knows better the details, intricacies and technicalities of mining than do the miners and operators. No body of men can work out the details of a wage scale on a more equitable basis. Their judgment would undoubtedly be based upon the sum total of knowledge of the industry. Whatever their differences may be, no matter how widely divergent their viewpoints may be from each other, it is a duty that they owe to society to make an earnest effort to negotiate those differences and to keep the mines of our country in operation. After all, the public interest in this vital matter is the paramount consideration of the Government and admits of no other action than that of consideration of a peaceful settlement of the matter as suggested by you. If for any reason the miners and operators fail to come to a mutual understanding, the interests of the public are of such vital importance in connection with the production of coal that it is incumbent upon them to refer the matters in dispute to a board of arbitration for determination, and to continue the operation of the mines, pending the decision of the board."[2]

Sincerely yours,   J. P. Tumulty

TCL (J. P. Tumulty Papers, DLC).

[1] W. B. Wilson's report is missing; however, it consisted of a narrative of the meetings that he had held with representatives of the United Mine Workers of America and the coal operators on October 21, 22, and 23 to avert the nationwide strike of bituminous miners scheduled for November 1. About these conferences, see the *New York Times*, Oct. 15, 18, 22, 23, and 24, 1919. For the background of the strike, see WBW to WW, Sept. 5, 1919 (second letter of that date), and its Enclosures.

[2] The *New York Times*, Oct. 25, 1919, reported that Wilson dictated this message to Tumulty at the request of Secretary Wilson, and that the letter was delivered to him at 4 p.m. on October 24. This may or may not have happened. Tumulty's letter to W. B. Wilson was printed, *inter alia*, in the *New York Times*, Oct. 25, 1919.

Joseph Patrick Tumulty to Walker Downer Hines

Personal

Dear Mr. Hines: The White House. October 24, 1919.

What do you think of the enclosed as our next step?

Sincerely yours   Tumulty

TL (J. P. Tumulty Papers, DLC).

Walker Downer Hines to Joseph Patrick Tumulty, with Enclosure

Dear Mr. Tumulty: Washington October 24, 1919

Replying to your note of today, I inclose the draft accompanying it with the following suggestions:

It occurs to me that at "A" on page 1, it would be wise to include a brief summary of the appeal which the President has made for a renewed discussion of the whole subject and for calling off of the strike, and the fact (upon which I suppose this last step will be based) that the miners' organization has declined to adopt such suggestion.

I also again raise the question whether it would not be wise at the point I have marked "B" on page 3, to insert the following paragraph which Mr. Clagett[1] called to your attention this morning:

"Subjects of this character are largely questions of degree. When a movement reaches the point where it appears to involve practically the entire productive capacity of the country with respect to one of the most vital necessities of daily domestic and industrial life and when the movement is asserted in the circumstances I have stated and at a time and in a manner calculated to involve the maximum of danger to the public welfare in the critical period now confronting the country, and before it has actually emerged from a state of war, beyond all question the public interest in the matter becomes the paramount consideration and admits of no other action than that which I am now taking and proposing to take."

It occurs to me that the inclusion of this last mentioned paragraph will emphasize the important point that the action now taken is not in any sense a precedent for cases of less serious degree.

I presume the President has satisfied himself, or will do so, by communication with the Attorney General, as to the correctness of the position that the proposed strike is illegal. I believe this is the case under the Lever Act, but, of course, the Attorney General would be the proper officer of the Government to give an authoritative opinion on this legal question.

Sincerely yours,   Walker D Hines

TLS (J. P. Tumulty Papers, DLC).
¹ Maurice Brice Clagett, Assistant to the Director General of Railroads.

E N C L O S U R E

No I

On September 23, 1919, the convention of the United Mine Workers of America at Cleveland, Ohio, adopted a proposal declaring that all contracts in the bituminous field shall be declared as having automatically expired November 1, 1919, and making various demands including a 60% increase in wages and the adoption of a six-hour work day for five days of the week, and providing that, in the event a satisfactory wage agreement should not be secured for the central competitive field before November 1, 1919, (to replace the agreement then in effect,) the national officials should be authorized and instructed to call a general strike of all bituminous miners and mine workers throughout the United States, effective November 1, 1919.

A   The officers of the organization are now proposing to make the strike effective November 1st. This constitutes one of the gravest steps that has ever been proposed in this country affecting the economic welfare and the domestic comfort and health of the people. This step is taken to abrogate an agreement as to wages which was made with the sanction of the United States Fuel Administration and which was to run during the continuance of the war, but not beyond April 1, 1920. The step is taken to enforce conditions which would seriously increase the cost of living to all the people in the country and to all the industries in the country. This strike is attempted at a time when the Government is making the most earnest effort to reduce the cost of living and has appealed with success to other classes of workers to postpone similar questions until a reasonable opportunity has been afforded for dealing with the cost of living. It is recognized that the strike, if successful, will practically shut off the country's supply of its principal fuel at a time when interference with that supply is calculated to create a fuel famine for the approaching winter. All interests alike in America will be affected by a strike of this character, and the victims of it will be not the rich only, but the poor and the needy as well— those least able to provide in advance a fuel supply for domestic use. It will involve the shutting down of countless industries and the throwing out of employment of a large part of the workers of the country. The strike also involves the danger of hampering, and in many cases stopping, the operation of railroads, electric light and gas plants, street railway lines and other public utilities, and the shipping to and from this country, and also threatens to prevent our aiding the allied countries with the supplies of coal which they so seriously need. The country is confronted with this prospect at a time when we are not only engaged in the most earnest effort to restore normal industrial and economic processes which have been dislocated by the war, but when the war itself is still a fact, when the world is still in suspense as to negotiations for peace, when our troops are still being transported and when their means of transport is in urgent need of coal.

From whatever angle the subject may be viewed it is apparent that such a strike in such circumstances would represent the most far-reaching and injurious combination ever presented in this country for the purpose of limiting production and distribution of one of the most essential necessaries of life and for the purpose indirectly of limiting the production and distribution of all other necessaries of life. A strike under these circumstances is unthinkable.

This step has apparently been taken without any vote upon the specific proposition by the individual members of the United Mine Workers of America throughout the United States. I cannot believe that any right of any American worker needs for its protection the taking of this step at the time and in the manner now proposed, and I am convinced that when the time and manner are considered the step constitutes a fundamental attack, which is wrong both morally and legally, upon the rights of society and upon the welfare of our country. I feel convinced that individual members of the United Mine Workers of America would not upon full consideration vote in favor of such a strike under these conditions.

B   I have noted with great concern the unfortunately distorted views which are now being disseminated in condemnation of the just rights of labor, and I cannot escape the conclusion that the greatest wrong that could be done to the righteous cause of labor is being done by the unlawful proposal of this strike.

In all of these circumstances I solemnly request both the national and the local officers and also the individual members of the United Mine Workers of America to reconsider the action taken by their convention in September and at once to recall all orders looking to a strike on November 1st, and to take whatever steps may be necessary to prevent any stoppage of work.

It is time for plain speaking. These matters with which we now deal touch not only the welfare of a class but vitally concern the well-being, the comfort, and the very life of all the people. In this matter the public interest is paramount, and I feel it my duty to declare that any attempt to carry out the purposes of this strike and thus to paralyze the industry of the country with the consequent suffering and distress of all our people would be considered a grave moral and legal wrong against the Government and people of the United States. I feel it my duty, also, to warn all persons concerned that ways and means will be found to protect the interests of the nation in any emergency that may arise out of this unhappy business.

I further hold myself in readiness at the request of either or both sides to appoint at once a tribunal to investigate all the facts with a view to aiding in the earliest possible orderly elucidation of the questions at issue between the coal operators and the coal miners, to the end that the just rights, not only of those interests but also of the general public, may be fully developed at the earliest possible date.

CC MS (J. P. Tumulty Papers, DLC).

From the Diary of Josephus Daniels

October Saturday 25 1919

Cabinet met at 11 o'clock. Lansing sick. Glass presided. Called on Wilson to give result of negotiations on coal strike. He believed operators wanted a strike, feeling that coal men had presented demands greater than public sentiment would approve. Miners passed resolution to strike without vote of workers before negotiating unless they were given 5 day week & 6 hours per day & 60% increase in wages. Wilson thought miners did not expect to obtain all this. Crux of situation that miners had made contract for certain wages as long as the war lasted. They claimed the war was over & they were not bound. Operators claimed they were bound until peace treaty was signed even if war conditions were ended. Glass presented paper "that has been handed me" (Tumulty handed it to him) & suggestion of which WW should sign. Discussed generally and changes were made. Appointed Palmer Lane & Wilson to redraft & bring to Cabinet at meeting at 4 o'clock. Discussed & made a few verbal changes and then it was type-written (each member of Cabinet had copy) & when all had approved we sent for Grayson who took it to the President. He brought it back approved, but we suggested that he return & get the President to sign it. He did so & given to the press

A Statement[1]

The White House October 25, 1919

On September 23, 1919, the convention of the United Mine Workers of America at Cleveland, Ohio, adopted a proposal declaring that all contracts in the bituminous field shall be declared as having automatically expired November 1, 1919, and making various demands including a 60% increase in wages and the adoption of a six-hour work day and a five-day week; and providing that, in the event a satisfactory wage agreement should not be secured for the central competitive field before November 1, 1919, the national officials should be authorized and instructed to call a general strike of all bituminous miners and mine workers throughout the United States, effective November 1, 1919.

Pursuant to these instructions, the officers of the organization have issued a call to make the strike effective November 1st. This is one of the gravest steps ever proposed in this country affecting the economic welfare and the domestic comfort and health of the people. It is proposed to abrogate an agreement as to wages which was made with the sanction of the United States Fuel Administration and which was to run during the continuance of the war, but not beyond April 1, 1920. This strike is proposed at a time when the Government is making the most earnest effort to reduce the cost of living and has appealed with success to other classes of workers to postpone similar disputes until a reasonable opportunity has been afforded for dealing with the cost of living. It is recognized that the strike would practically shut off the country's supply of its principal fuel at a time when interference with that supply is calculated to create a disastrous fuel famine. All interests would be affected alike by a strike of this character, and its victims would be not the rich only, but the poor and the needy as well,—those least able to provide in advance a fuel supply for domestic use. It would involve the shutting down of countless industries and the throwing out of employment of a large part of the workers of the country. It would involve stopping the operation of railroads, electric light and gas plants, street railway lines and other public utilities, and the shipping to and from this country, thus preventing our giving aid to the allied countries with supplies which they so seriously need. The country is confronted with this prospect at a time when the war itself is still a fact, when the world is still in suspense as to negotiations for peace, when our troops are still being transported and when their means of transport is in urgent need of fuel.

From whatever angle the subject may be viewed, it is apparent that such a strike in such circumstances would be the most far-reaching plan ever presented in this country to limit the facilities of production and distribution of a necessity of life and thus indirectly to restrict the production and distribution of all the necessaries of life. A strike under these circumstances is not only unjustifiable, it is unlawful.

The action proposed has apparently been taken without any vote upon the specific proposition by the individual members of the United Mine Workers of America throughout the United States, an almost unprecedented proceeding. I cannot believe that any right of any American worker needs for its protection the taking of this extraordinary step, and I am convinced that when the time and manner are considered, it constitutes a fundamental attack, which is wrong both morally and legally, upon the rights of society and upon the welfare of our country. I feel convinced that individual members of the United Mine Workers would not vote, upon full consideration, in favor of such a strike under these conditions.

When a movement reaches the point where it appears to involve practically the entire productive capacity of the country with respect to one of the most vital necessities of daily domestic and industrial life and when the movement is asserted in the circumstances I have stated and at a time and in a manner calculated to involve the maximum of danger to the public welfare in this critical hour of our country's life, the public interest becomes the paramount consideration.

In these circumstances I solemnly request both the national and the local officers and also the individual members of the United Mine Workers of America to recall all orders looking to a strike on November 1st, and to take whatever steps may be necessary to prevent any stoppage of work.

It is time for plain speaking. These matters with which we now deal, touch not only the welfare of a class, but vitally concern the well-being, the comfort and the very life of all the people. I feel it my duty in the public interest to declare that any attempt to carry out the purposes of this strike and thus to paralyze the industry of the country with the consequent suffering and distress of all our people, must be considered a grave moral and legal wrong against the Government and the people of the United States. I can do nothing less than to say that the law will be enforced, and means will be found to protect the interests of the nation in any emergency that may arise out of this unhappy business.

I express no opinion on the merits of the controversy. I have already suggested a plan by which a settlement may be reached,[2] and I hold myself in readiness at the request of either or both sides to appoint at once a tribunal to investigate all the facts with a view to aiding in the earliest possible orderly settlement of the questions at issue between the coal operators and the coal miners, to the end that the just rights, not only of those interests but also of the general public, may be fully protected.[3]

T MS (WP, DLC).
[1] This was published, for example, in the *New York Times*, Oct. 26, 1919.
[2] That is, the plan outlined in JPT to WBW, Oct. 24, 1919.
[3] This was published, not over Wilson's name, but as "A Statement by the President." There is no evidence that Wilson saw it before it was issued.

A Veto Message

The White House,
To the House of Representatives: *October 27, 1919*

I am returning, without my signature, H.R. 6810, "An act to prohibit intoxicating beverages, and to regulate the manufacture, production, use, and sale of high-proof spirits for other than beverage purposes, and to insure an ample supply of alcohol and promote its use in scientific research and in the development of fuel, dye, and other lawful industries."

The subject matter treated in this measure deals with two distinct phases of the prohibition legislation. One part of the act under consideration seeks to enforce war-time prohibition. The other provides for the enforcement which was made necessary by the adoption of the constitutional amendment. I object to and can not approve that part of this legislation with reference to war-time prohibition. It has to do with the enforcement of an act which was passed by reason of the emergencies of the war and whose objects have been satisfied in the demobilization of the Army and Navy, and whose repeal I have already sought at the hands of Congress. Where the purposes of particular legislation arising out of war emergency have been satisfied, sound public policy makes clear the reason and necessity for repeal.

It will not be difficult for Congress in considering this important matter to separate these two questions and effectively to legislate regarding them, making the proper distinction between temporary causes which arose out of war-time emergencies and those like the constitutional amendment of prohibition which is now part of the fundamental law of the country. In all matters having to do with the personal habits and customs of large numbers of our people we must be certain that the established processes of legal change are followed. In no other way can the salutary object sought to be accomplished by great reforms of this character be made satisfactory and permanent.   Woodrow Wilson.[1]

Printed in 66th Cong., 1st sess., House of Representatives, Doc. No. 282 (Washington, 1919).
¹ This veto was overridden by a vote of 175 to fifty-five in the House on October 27 and sixty-five to twenty in the Senate on October 28. *Cong. Record*, 66th Cong., 1st sess., pp. 7610-11, 7633-34. For the text of the Volstead Act, see 41 *Statutes at Large* 305.
Tumulty wrote this message, and David F. Houston went over it and made suggestions for changes, which Tumulty made on the T draft in the J. P. Tumulty Papers, DLC. See also John M. Blum, *Joe Tumulty and the Wilson Era* (Boston, 1951), p. 313, n. 3. According to Daniels, he, Palmer, Glass, and Redfield thought that the veto was a "big mistake & indefensible." Daniels Diary, Oct. 27, 1919. Insofar as we know, Wilson never knew about the veto message.

Joseph Patrick Tumulty to Edith Bolling Galt Wilson

Dear Mrs. Wilson: The White House 27 October 1919.

Secretary Houston called to see me this morning to say that he had been in conference with representatives of the International Labor Conference who expressed a desire to consult him with reference to the appointment of a chairman of this Conference. They said their desire was to select Mr. Taft but they would not do it if his selection were not acceptable to the President. I diplomatically conveyed to Secretary Houston what I thought the President's attitude was toward Mr. Taft. Secretary Houston said another man who had been suggested was Mr. Herbert Hoover.

At an opportune moment, will you kindly take this matter up with the President and let me know what he thinks?

Sincerely yours,   [J P Tumulty]

CCL (J. P. Tumulty Papers, DLC).

A News Report

[*Oct. 30, 1919*]

BELGIAN ROYALTIES SEE THE PRESIDENT

Washington, Oct. 30.—King Albert and Queen Elizabeth of the Belgians and their son, Prince Leopold, were received informally by President Wilson in his sickroom at the White House late this afternoon. The circumstances surrounding this historic meeting between the constitutional heads of the two nations were very striking and impressive, and the scene will probably linger long in the minds of the few who were with the President.

It was not thought when the King, Queen, and Prince came to Washington on Monday that the President would be able to see them personally. Consequently no such plans were embraced in the schedule of their visit to Washington, and it was only planned that Mrs. Wilson should tender them an informal tea at the White House at 4:45 o'clock this afternoon, on the eve of the departure of the royal party from Washington for Newport News, from which port they will sail for home.

President Wilson was aware of the plans for this informal reception by Mrs. Wilson to the King, Queen, and Prince, and feeling that he was strong enough to receive the King the President expressed a desire to see him personally. Rear Admiral Cary T. Grayson, the President's physician, did not feel like interposing an objection and assented to the arrangement for the visit of King Albert to the President, which finally resulted in the President seeing also Queen Elizabeth and the Prince. King Albert was in the President's sickroom ten minutes. Queen Elizabeth was there five minutes, and during a part of her visit to the President's room the Prince was also present.

While the King was with the President, the latter presented him with a specially bound set of Mr. Wilson's "History of the American People." The President autographed the first volume of the set before handing it to the King. The King had the five volumes of this set with him when he left the White House after this afternoon's historic meeting.

When the royal party arrived at the White House, at 4:45 o'clock, in two automobiles, they had made a record run from the Catholic University of America, where the King had been decorated. They were late leaving the University, and the chauffeurs had to speed their cars for what they were worth, in order to enable the royal party to be prompt for their engagement at the White House. Probably 10,000 persons, including a flood of Government clerks from the neighboring departments, were crowded around the White House fences when the royal party arrived.

On entering the White House the King, Queen, and Prince were first received by Mrs. Wilson, Mrs. Sayre, and Miss Margaret Wilson.

Admiral Grayson was with the President at the time of their arrival. After the President learned of the arrival of the visitors he asked Admiral Grayson to bring King Albert up for a brief, informal visit. The King stepped into the White House elevator, and operated it himself by pressing an electric button. Dr. Grayson met the King on his arrival on the second floor, and escorted him into the President's sickroom.

The greeting between the King and the President was very cordial and wholly informal. The President extended his hand when the King entered. King Albert advanced and shook the President's hand. The President, sitting half-way up in bed, asked the King to be seated, and the royal visitor sat in a chair at the right side of the President's bed. Dr. Grayson remained while the King was there. The ruler, aware that he was visiting an ill man, did not care to remain too long, but indicated to Dr. Grayson he would like to remain with the President just as long as the physician would permit him to do so.

The President first told the King how glad he was of the opportunity to see the King personally before the latter left the country, saying how happy he was to renew an acquaintance begun in Europe, and regretted that he had not had opportunity while in Europe to see more of the Belgian ruler. The President expressed regret also that he was compelled by the state of his health to be on his back, instead of his feet, while receiving the King.

There was nothing formal or official about the meeting between the President and the King. Formality was brushed aside, and they met as man to man. Dr. Grayson, who was present, stated tonight that the evidences of genuine friendship exhibited during the meeting between the two men was rather impressive.

The President told the King he hoped that he, the Queen, and members of their party had enjoyed their visit to the country, and that they were pleased with the reception that had been given them by the American people. The King replied that he was unable to find words adequately to express the appreciation of himself and the Queen for the splendid manner in which they had been received everywhere they had gone in this country. The King spoke in praise of the American people and of the development of this country since he was here twenty-one years ago.

Then the King told the President how sorry he felt about his illness, saying the President was greatly loved by the Belgian people, who were distressed to learn of his illness. "For myself," said the King, "I hope that your ideas and ideals will be carried out. My feeling is that they will be."

The President thanked the King and then their conversation for nearly ten minutes branched off into many subjects. The President wanted to know about conditions in Belgium, whether the King had recently visited England, about Lloyd George, about Premier Clemenceau, and conditions in France. During this conversation the President paid very fine tributes to both Lloyd George and Clemenceau.

In saying farewell to the President the King expressed a strong hope that the President would soon be restored to health, and thanked the President for the opportunity of being allowed to visit him. While the King was with the President the visitor several times turned to Dr. Grayson and asked whether he was overstaying his time.

"I hope," said the King to Dr. Grayson, "you will tell me when to go, but also hope you won't tell me to go soon."

The President told the King he was also anxious to see and chat with the Queen. When the King went to rejoin the party down-stairs, he conveyed to the Queen the President's oral request for a moment's talk with her. Mrs. Wilson and the Queen then went to the second story. Dr. Grayson was present when they reached the President's room. The Queen was very much pleased over this un-expected visit to the President. The meeting was wholly demo-cratic and informal, and the cheerful manner of the Queen, while she was present, had a very good effect on the President.

While the President was chatting with the Queen and Mrs. Wil-son, he suddenly realized that he was wearing over his shoulders a very old gray sweater which he has had since he first entered the White House and to which he is much attached. He apologized for being forced to wear a sweater on such an occasion.

"This old gray sweater," said the President, "is not very much on looks, but it has certainly rendered me splendid service." He placed his hand affectionately on the old piece of wearing apparel.

During his talk with the Queen the President inquired about the Prince, saying he would like also to see the young man very much. The Queen replied that the boy was downstairs with the King and would feel honored to meet the President.

The President inquired whether there was anything to interfere with his seeing the boy. The Queen turned toward Dr. Grayson and indicated that the physician was possibly the only obstacle. Dr. Grayson's heart melted and he went downstairs for the boy. The President talked with the Prince several minutes. The Prince, who is a manly and modest young fellow, was rather embarrassed in the presence of the President, but acquitted himself well. The Presi-dent asked the boy about his school in England, told the boy he looked like the King, his father, and then added:

"Your father is every inch a man. I hope you will be worthy of your sire, and believe that you will be."

It is learned that the boy made a very fine impression on the President.

While the Queen was conversing with the President, she sat on a chair at the left hand side of the President's bed, across from where the King sat. After five minutes' conversation with the Pres-ident, the Queen, accompanied by Mrs. Wilson and the Prince, re-joined the King, who had been entertained on the lower floor by

Mrs. Sayre and Miss Wilson, and the royal party soon afterwards left the White House. No attachés or aides were with the royal party when they went to the White House.[1]

Printed in the *New York Times*, Oct. 31, 1919.
[1] Edith B. Wilson, *My Memoir*, pp. 292-95, is a good account of the royal family's visit to the White House.

From the Desk Diary of Robert Lansing

Thursday Oct 30 [1919]

Cabinet meeting 11-12:40. Coal strike. Fuel administration's Legal remedies. Dr. Garfield and Hines and Tumulty present. Hitchcock phoned me and I pointed out danger of our claiming American primacy in re League of Nations. . . .

At reception tonight Long told me that Grayson told him that Prest demanded immediate recall of Major Stuart of British Embassy.[1] I saw Sir Wm. Tyrrell[2] and told him what Grayson said

[1] Maj. Charles Kennedy Craufurd-Stuart, Lord Grey's private secretary. He had also served as Lord Reading's private secretary during his ambassadorship in the United States in 1918 and 1919. It had been reported to Wilson, by a person or persons unknown, that Craufurd-Stuart had made disparaging remarks about either Wilson, Mrs. Wilson, or both (accounts differ on this point), at one or more social gatherings during both his earlier and current sojourns in America. The Major maintained both then and later that he had done no such thing.

The demand for Craufurd-Stuart's recall led to a lengthy correspondence between Lansing, Grey, the British Foreign Office, and John W. Davis, the American Ambassador in London. The upshot was that Grey threatened to resign his mission to the United States rather than give up the services of Craufurd-Stuart, and Lansing ultimately acquiesced in the Major's remaining in the United States as a purely private member of Grey's household. See George Egerton, "Diplomacy, Scandal and Military Intelligence: The Craufurd-Stuart Affair and Anglo-American Relations, 918–1920," *Intelligence and National Security*, II (Oct. 1987), 110–34.

[2] That is, Sir William (George) Tyrrell, who also had accompanied Lord Grey to the United States as his secretary.

From Robert Lansing

My dear Mr. President: Washington October 31, 1919.

You will recall that we discussed the matter of the reorganization of European transportation as provided for in the Peace Treaty. You expressed general approval of the plan for our participation as suggested by Mr. Henry White and Mr. Herbert Hoover. The substance of their suggestion was that an American of considerable experience, preferably a railway president, should be appointed to represent us on the commissions dealing with cession of rolling stock and reorganization of German railways, and also to act as arbitrator in connection with the cession of river boats and material.

Mr. Polk has on several occasions wired me urging that we take immediate action toward carrying out this plan. He emphasizes the chaotic conditions which exist, both on the railways and rivers in central and southeastern Europe. The feeling of the Allies is that our failure to appoint the arbitrator, which the Treaty calls upon us to designate, is resulting in an unnecessary prolongation of these chaotic conditions, and that our delay in appointing a representative on the railway commissions is holding up the commencement of their work, and thus making it impossible for the land transportation systems to resume their normal functioning as soon as the Treaty comes into force.

The Secretary of War has consented to detail Colonel Kelly,[1] of the Engineers, to make a preliminary survey of the situation on the Danube River, but even this does not relieve matters much as Colonel Kelly will hardly know what subjects his survey should cover until the entire situation has been mapped out by our arbitrator.

In view of your approval of our participation in these matters, and in view of their urgency in order to rehabilitate transportation in central Europe, I beg leave to suggest for your consideration the advisability of immediately designating an American of suitable qualifications who could proceed to Europe in the near future to familiarize himself with the general situation in order that when the Treaty is ratified he may be immediately appointed as our official representative to carry out the Treaty provisions regarding transportation. Such an unofficial appointment would not, in my opinion, amount to a disregard of the Senate's expressed wishes regarding our participation in the Peace Treaty prior to ratification, especially as we will be expected to appoint an arbitrator whether or not we ratify the Treaty. Such an unofficial appointment would go far to relieve the uncertainty surrounding our intentions regarding participation in the rehabilitation of the European transportation systems, and would convince the nations immediately affected that we will not neglect their interests in the matter. This in itself will undoubtedly restore confidence, and thus have an immediately beneficial effect upon the railways and rivers in question.

If you should consider it advisable to name an unofficial representative at the present time, I would suggest to you the name of Mr. Fairfax Harrison,[2] or Mr. Daniel Willard,[3] as a suitable representative to undertake this work.   √

Faithfully yours,   Robert Lansing

Approved[4]

TLS (WP, DLC).
  ¹ William Kelly.
  ² President of the Southern Railway Co.
  ³ WW's or EBW's underlining. Willard was president of the Baltimore and Ohio Railroad Co.
  ⁴ EBWhw. This letter was an enclosure with R. Forster to EBW, Nov. 4, 1919, TLS (WP, DLC): "Mr. Tumulty asks if you will not be good enough to read the attached letter and present it to the President if and when you think wise."

Alexander Mitchell Palmer to Roland Sletor Morris

Washington, November 3, 1919.

Personal and confidential for the Ambassador from the Attorney General:

Quote: Answering your message nineteenth have conveyed to Mrs. Wilson your sympathy which is much appreciated. Alarming rumors concerning President's condition quite unfounded. Physically weak but in every other respect in splendid shape. Doctors report him rapidly improving. He transacts public business daily. I had a personal conference with him Thursday for thirty minutes on serious coal strike situation.¹ Hope you will get home for a vacation this winter. Best regards from all. Palmer Unquote.

Lansing

TS telegram (SDR, RG 59, 811.001W69/782a, DNA).
  ¹ Palmer conferred with Wilson, in the presence of Dr. Grayson, at 4 p.m. on October 30 for about twenty minutes. He was the first cabinet member to see Wilson since his stroke of October 2. "I went over the whole situation with the President," Palmer told reporters as he emerged from the White House, "and the President gave his approval to what has been done up to this time. He also made certain suggestions of his own which I cannot discuss at this time." New York Times, Oct. 31, 1919. For Palmer's action following this meeting, see n. 1 to the extract from the Daniels Diary printed at Nov. 4, 1919.

A News Report

[Nov. 4, 1919]

PRESIDENT INTERESTED
IN ELECTION RETURNS

Washington, Nov. 4.—President Wilson's condition has so much improved tonight that election returns were given him as they came in during the early part of the night. The President was especially interested in the returns from his home state of New Jersey.

President Wilson today signed the urgent deficiency appropriation bill, carrying $2,300,000 for enforcement of wartime prohibition and the food and fuel control act. The measure also provides $6,000,000 for the Alaskan railroad.

For the first time since he has been in the White House, President Wilson was unable to go to his home in Princeton, N. J., to cast his ballot.

Printed in the *New York Times*, Nov. 5, 1919.

Joseph Patrick Tumulty to Edith Bolling Galt Wilson, with Enclosures

Dear Mrs. Wilson: The White House [Nov. 4, 1919].

Will you please convey this message to the President when you feel an opportune moment has arrived? Tumulty

All the names checked are approved by the President including Brandeis, & he will be glad for you to follow your suggestion as to seeing the Justice in person.[1]

TLS (WP, DLC).
[1] EBWhw.

E N C L O S U R E 1

From Joseph Patrick Tumulty

Dear Governor: The White House 4 November, 1919

I am submitting the list of names suggested for the New Capital and Labor Conference. If I were making the selection, I would select Governor Glynn[1] instead of Ray Stannard Baker. Ray Stannard Baker is writing the most complimentary articles about you, appearing in various newspapers throughout the country,[2] and his selection might be embarrassing to Baker himself. Ex-Governor Glynn stands well with the country.

I am also sending a letter from Secretary Daniels suggesting that Brandeis be asked to preside over this conference. I think this is a suggestion that ought to be well considered. It would be an admirable thing if it could be done. If you feel like acting upon it, would you not be willing to ask me to see Brandeis and urge his acceptance of it? Cordially, J. P. Tumulty

P.S. Since dictating the above, I am in receipt of another letter from Secretary Daniels, attached.

TLS (WP, DLC).
[1] That is, Martin Henry Glynn, former Governor of New York.
[2] This was a series of six articles on Wilson's activities at the Paris Peace Conference which were released biweekly by the United Feature Syndicate of New York. They were published, for example, in eight installments in the *Springfield*, Mass., *Republican*, Oct.

24, 25, 28, and 31 and Nov. 4, 7, 11, and 14, 1919. They were reprinted in book form as *What Wilson Did at Paris* (Garden City, N. Y., 1919).

E N C L O S U R E   I I

From Josephus Daniels

Dear Mr. President: The White House Nov. 3, 1919.

Upon looking over the list of names suggested to you I find that without intention of ignoring so large an element of our population it happens there is no Roman Catholic in the list. I do not believe in considering a man's religious faith, but in our country where so large a proportion of our skilled and unskilled workers are Catholic it would be regarded an intentional omission if not one was in the list.

It would seem wise to appoint ex-Governor Martin H. Glynn, of New York, and Mr. Kelley,[1] of Montana, or other like men of affairs when making up your commission.

In the present unrest, will you permit me to say that I feel it of the utmost importance that the appointment of this body should be made at once?

We are all heartened by news of your steady improvement.

Sincerely yours   Josephus Daniels

ALS (WP, DLC).
[1] Cornelius Francis Kelley, president of the Anaconda Copper Mining Co.

E N C L O S U R E   I I I

Josephus Daniels to Joseph Patrick Tumulty

Dear Joseph: Washington. Nov. 3, 1919.

Ordinarily I know that the President does not like to appoint a Supreme Court Justice to other duties, but in the present emergency I believe in naming the new Industrial Board he would be wise to name Justice Brandeis. Please call this to his attention before the appointments are made. I believe the commission or board should be named soon.   Sincerely   Josephus Daniels

ALS (WP, DLC).

ENCLOSURE   IV

From Franklin Knight Lane

My dear Mr. President: Washington October 31, 1919.

In accordance with the unanimous desire of the Cabinet I beg to submit to you the names of the men whom it is suggested might in your pleasure form a new industrial conference.

√ Secretary William B. Wilson √   1
~~Ex President William H. Taft, or ex Attorney~~
General George W. √ Wickersham √√   2
√ Ex-Attorney-General Thomas W. Gregory √   3
√ Herbert Hoover √   4
Owen D. Young, Vice President of the General   5
Electric Co. of New York
~~Ray Stannard Baker~~, or ex-Governor Glynn √√   6
√ W. O. Thompson, President of the Ohio State √   7
University
√ Ex-Secretary of Commerce Oscar S. Straus √   8
√ Ex-Governor Henry C. Stuart of Virginia √   9
√ Richard Hooker, Editor of the Springfield √   10
Republican
√ George T. Slade, former Vice President of the √   11
Northern Pacific Railway Co.
√ H. J. Waters, Agricultural Editor of the √   12
Kansas City Star
√ Stanley King, formerly of the War Department √   13
√ Ex-Governor Samuel W. McCall of Massachusetts √   14
√ Professor Frank W. Taussig of Harvard √   15
√ Henry M. Robinson of Pasadena, Calif., formerly   16
of the Shipping Board, √
√ Julius Rosenwald.[1] √   17

These names are given to you in the way of suggestion with the expectation that you will add to or take from the list. It was the suggestion of Mr. Baruch's group,[2] I believe, that fifteen be the approximate size of the new conference. We have omitted all members of the former conference, as those with whom we spoke seemed to think this the wise course, and most of them do not wish to participate. I enclose a suggested letter that you may possibly care to send to those whom you may see fit to appoint as members of this conference.

Cordially and faithfully yours,   Franklin K. Lane

TLS (WP, DLC).
[1] Those persons on this list not already prominently identified in this series were

Henry Carter Stuart, George Theron Slade, and Henry Jackson Waters. Numbering and check marks seem to be WWhw.
² That is, the public members of the Industrial Conference.

E N C L O S U R E   V

Dear Mr.

In accordance with the suggestion given me by the Public Group of the recent Industrial Conference, I am calling a new body together to carry on this vitally important work, and I trust you will give me the pleasure of naming you as one of its members.

Guided by the experience of the last conference I have thought it advisable that in this new body there should be no recognition of distinctive groups, but that all of the new representatives should have concern that our industries may be conducted with such regard for justice and fair dealing that the workman will feel himself induced to put forth his best effort that the employer will have an encouraging profit, and that the public will not suffer at the hands of either class. It is my hope that this conference may lay the foundation for the development of standards and machinery within our industries by which these results may be attained.

It is not expected that you will deal directly with any condition which exists today, but that you may be fortunate enough to find such ways as will avoid the repetition of these deplorable conditions.

The conference will meet at a place to be hereafter designated in this city on the 15th of November next.

TC MS (WP, DLC).

From the Diary of Josephus Daniels

November Tuesday 4 1919

Wrote to President that in naming Industrial Commission Brandeis ought to head it—that in the list of names suggested by the Cabinet there was no Catholic & that would be taken as a discrimination & lose the force of any finding.

President sent me word to please see Brandeis. He expressed deep regret that Palmer had asked an injunction¹ and thought in present situation no Commission should be appointed & he did not think he could do any public service. The miners had an excellent case, but it was so poorly handled and they placed themselves in the wrong & were not properly understood.

Sympathy must go with justice

¹ A. Mitchell Palmer had issued a lengthy public statement on October 29 in which he said that the proposed strike of the coal miners was illegal under the terms of the Lever Food and Fuel Control Act of 1917 (about which, see the index references under "Lever bill" in Vol. 52 of this series) and that he would take all necessary actions to enforce that act in the event of a strike. *New York Times*, Oct. 30, 1919. As has been noted, Palmer conferred with Wilson on October 30.

At Palmer's request, Albert Barnes Anderson, judge of the Federal District Court in Indianapolis, on October 31 issued a temporary restraining order which forbade the leaders of the United Mine Workers of America to take any action to put the strike into effect. However, the rank and file of the workers began the strike as scheduled at midnight on that date. *Ibid.*, Nov. 1, 1919. During the week that followed, Gompers and other labor leaders argued passionately that the restraining order should be withdrawn by the court. However, following a second hearing on November 8, Judge Anderson issued a permanent injunction, which ordered the leaders of the U. M. W. to rescind their strike order of October 15 by no later than 6 p.m. on November 11. The judge stated that the right to strike was not at issue. The Lever Act, which forbade anyone from interfering with the production of necessaries, was constitutional and still in force. Hence, the question at issue was simply that of the enforcement of the law. *Ibid.*, Nov. 9, 1919. Gompers and many union officials denounced the injunction and threatened to defy its enforcement. However, John L. Lewis, acting president of the U. M. W., announced on November 11 that he would obey the injunction. *Ibid.*, Nov. 12, 1919. This did not bring the strike to an end since most of the miners remained off the job.

Joseph Patrick Tumulty to Robert Lansing

My dear Mr. Secretary: The White House November 4, 1919.

Referring to your letter of October 31st concerning the reorganization of European transportation as provided for in the Peace Treaty, the President approves the appointment of Mr. Daniel Willard as our unofficial representative on the work in question, as you suggest.¹   Sincerely yours,   J P Tumulty

TLS (SDR, RG 59, 763.72119/7617, DNA).
¹ As a result of the above letter, Lansing wrote to Willard on November 17 to request him to serve as the "unofficial representative," pending the approval of the peace treaty by the Senate. Lansing explained that there would be a "main commission for consultative purposes only." There would be four subcommissions which would make "authoritative decisions," one each to deal with German railways in the territories ceded to Belgium, Poland, Czechoslovakia, and Denmark. The presidents of the main commission and of the four subcommissions were all to be Americans. Willard was to hold all five of these presidencies after the Senate had approved the peace treaty. Lansing hoped that Willard would be able to proceed immediately to Paris to familiarize himself with his new duties, although he admitted that the matter of Willard's compensation could not be arranged until after the Senate had approved the treaty. RL to D. Willard, Nov. 17, 1919, CCL (SDR, RG 59, 763.72119/7617, DNA).

A Thanksgiving Proclamation¹

[Nov. 4, 1919]

The Season of the year has again arrived when the people of the United States are accustomed to unite in giving thanks to Almighty God for the blessings which He has conferred upon our country during the twelve months that have passed. A year ago our people poured out their hearts in praise and thanksgiving that through divine aid the right was victorious and peace had come to the nations which had so courageously struggled in defense of human liberty and justice. Now that the stern task is ended and the fruits of achievement are ours, we look forward with confidence to the dawn of an era where the sacrifices of the nations will find recompense in a world at peace.

But to attain the consummation of the great work to which the American people devoted their manhood and the vast resources of their country they should, as they give thanks to God, reconsecrate themselves to those principles of right which triumphed through His merciful goodness. Our gratitude can find no more perfect expression than to bulwark with loyalty and patriotism those principles for which the free peoples of the earth fought and died.

During the past year we have had much to make us grateful. In spite of the confusion in our economic life resulting from the war we have prospered. Our harvests have been plentiful, and of our abundance we have been able to render succor to less favored nations. Our democracy remains unshaken in a world torn with political and social unrest. Our traditional ideals are still our guides in the path of progress and civilization.

These great blessings, vouchsafed to us, for which we devoutly give thanks, should arouse us to a fuller sense of our duty to ourselves and to mankind to see to it that nothing that we may do shall mar the completeness of the victory which we helped to win. No selfish purpose animated us in becoming participants in the world war, and with a like spirit of unselfishness we should strive to aid by our example and by our cooperation in realizing the enduring welfare of all peoples and in bringing into being a world ruled by friendship and good will.

WHEREFORE, I, Woodrow Wilson, President of the United States of America, hereby designate Thursday, the twenty-seventh day of November next, for observance as a day of thanksgiving and prayer by my fellow-countrymen, inviting them to cease on that day from their ordinary tasks and to unite in their homes and in their several places of worship in ascribing praise and thanksgiving to God the Author of all blessings and the Master of our destinies.

In WITNESS WHEREOF, I have hereunto set my hand and caused the seal of the United States to be affixed.

DONE in the District of Columbia this 5th day of November, in the year of our Lord, one thousand nine hundred and nineteen, and of the independence of the United States the one hundred and forty-fourth.

(SEAL.)   Woodrow Wilson

By the President:
 Robert Lansing,
 Secretary of State.

Printed copy (WP, DLC).
 [1] About the authorship of this proclamation, see Lansing's memorandum on the state of Wilson's health printed at November 5, 1919.

To Calvin Coolidge

[The White House] November 5, 1919.

I congratulate you upon your election as a victory for law and order.[1] When that is the issue all Americans stand together.[2]

Woodrow Wilson

T telegram (Letterpress Books, WP, DLC).
 [1] Coolidge had been reelected Governor of Massachusetts on November 4 by a vote of 317,774 to 192,673 for his Democratic opponent, Richard Henry Long. Tumulty had submitted a draft of this telegram to Wilson. Wilson returned it with his revisions in the handwriting of EBW. The second sentence of the telegram sent was Wilson's.
 [2] Coolidge replied to Wilson's telegram on November 5 as follows: "I deeply appreciate your telegram of congratulation. I trust the election here will aid in the upholding of the laws of America in particular and strengthen the hand of righteous authority everywhere." *New York Times*, Nov. 6, 1919.

To Edward Irving Edwards

[The White House] November 5, 1919.

Please accept my hearty congratulations on your election.[1]

Woodrow Wilson

T telegram (Letterpress Books, WP, DLC).
 [1] Edwards, a Democrat and banker of Jersey City, had been elected Governor of New Jersey on November 4, defeating his Republican opponent, Newton Albert Kendall Bugbee, by a vote of 217,486 to 202,976.

Joseph Patrick Tumulty to Edith Bolling Galt Wilson, with Enclosure

Dear Mrs. Wilson: The White House, November 5, 1919.

When you think an opportune time has arrived, will you not be good enough to present the attached letter to the President from Secretary Lansing?   Faithfully yours,   J. P. Tumulty

TLS (WP, DLC).

ENCLOSURE

From Robert Lansing

Dear Mr. President: Washington November 4, 1919.

It seems desirable to accord recognition to the present provisional government of Costa Rica which has been established by the following events: Tinoco, after depositing the Government in Juan Bautista Quiros, left his country and in departing took with him most of his waning power and influence. Mr. Juan Bautista Quiros, upon advice of the most notable persons of Costa Rica, turned over the Government of that country to Francisco Aguilar Barquero, Second Designado of the regime of Alfredo Gonzales which Tinoco displaced. Thus Aguilar Barquero, upon accepting the provisional presidency, might be regarded as having reestablished the constitutional succession of the Gonzales administration. Aguilar Barquero did more, for after annulling the Tinoco constitution, he placed in vigor the constitution of 1871 under which he called for Presidential elections to be held in December next, and removed the Tinoco adherents, thereby obliterating whatever vestige of Tinoco influence might have remained in the Government.

The acts of the Aguilar Barquero government seem to have met with the approval of the majority of Costa Ricans.[1]

I have the honor, therefore, to recommend that recognition be accorded the present provisional government of Aguilar Barquero; that Castro Quesada who is now here with a letter asking that he be so regarded, be accepted as the provisional diplomatic representative of that government whose President should be informed that we will be pleased to receive a new Costa Rican Minister at Washington. In this connection I should like also discreetly to insinuate that the new proposed Minister should be some person other than Castro Quesada.

In view of your great sympathy for the Costa Ricans and your desire to lend a helping hand to struggling constitutional governments I feel that you would like personally to pass upon this proposed action.   Faithfully yours,   Robert Lansing.

TLS (WP, DLC).
    [1] On the refusal of Wilson to recognize the regime of Federico Tinoco Granadas since the latter's seizure of power in Costa Rica on January 27, 1917, see the index references to "Costa Rica" in Vols. 52-54 of this series.
    As a result of ever-increasing opposition, both within Costa Rica and from neighboring Central American countries, Tinoco, on August 1, 1919, had asked the permission of the Costa Rican Congress to leave the country because of illness but did not mention resignation from the presidency. His brother and close political adviser, Joaquín Tinoco Granadas, resigned his position of Designado (President Designate) on August 9, and the Congress chose Juan Bautista Quirós to replace him. Joaquín Tinoco was assassinated on August 10 and Federico Tinoco fled the country on August 12. Quirós became Acting President on the same date. *FR 1919*, I, 848-51 *passim*.

Lansing, on August 30, instructed Benjamin Franklin Chase, the American Consul at San José, to make it known that the United States would not recognize Quirós' government. "The governmental power," Lansing continued, "should be deposited in the hands of Francisco [Aguilar] Barquero, successor to the executive power under the Alfredo Gonzalez [Flores] régime. Barquero should hold free and open elections for president at earliest possible date. Were this done, it would appear that the necessary legal formalities had been complied with to constitute a legitimate government worthy of recognition by the Government of the United States." *Ibid.*, p. 857.

Following the receipt of Lansing's message, Quirós and Barquero and their advisers agreed that Barquero should become Acting President and Quirós Minister of War. Barquero took power on September 2 or 3. *Ibid.*, pp. 858-59. See also Dana G. Munro, *Intervention and Dollar Diplomacy in the Caribbean, 1900-1921* (Princeton, N. J., 1964), pp. 442-44.

Edith Bolling Galt Wilson to Robert Lansing

The White House [c. Nov. 5, 1919].

The President says it is impossible for him to take up such matters[1] until he is stronger & can study them.

So if an answer must be made, the Sec. of State can say he (the Sec.) cannot act without the President's consent & that the P. directs the matter be held in obeyance until he can act

AL (WP, DLC).
  [1] Wilson was responding to RL to WW, Nov. 4, 1919, CCL (SDR, RG 59, 763.72119/7644a, DNA). Lansing enclosed in his letter copies of the most significant recent diplomatic correspondence between himself, Polk, and Tittoni on the Adriatic question. Lansing summarized the situation in some detail. In mid-October, Tittoni had submitted new proposals, based upon Wilson's most recent statements on the subject (for which, see W. Phillips to WW, Sept. 11, 1919; JPT to WP, Sept. 13, 1919; and WW to FLP, Sept. 21, 1919), but including additional points, which Lansing stated as follows: "1) the further concession of a strip of coast land in Istria from Fianona to Volosca to insure continuity of boundary between Italy and the corpus separatum of Fiume; 2) a special statute [status?] for Fiume beyond its autonomous privileges under Hungary; 3) that diplomatic representation at Zara be given Italy; [and] 4) that the Island of Lagosta be given [to] Italy." Lansing had refused to accept these proposals and had so cabled Polk.
  However, Lansing soon learned that Polk, strongly supported by Clemenceau and Lloyd George, was, in Lansing's words, "inclined to make certain concessions." Polk had requested authority to use his own judgment on five points, again as paraphrased by Lansing: "1) conceding to Italy the strip of eastern coast of Istria including Volosca; 2) demilitarizing the Dalmatian mainland coast as far south as the Raguza region; 3) increasing Italian territory around Valona; 4) making Zara a free city without either Italian or Jugoslav sovereignty, the government of the city and its international relations to be under the control of the League of Nations; [and] 5) allowing either Italy or Jugoslavia, instead of Jugoslavia alone, to improve the Boyana River in Albania."
  Lansing now proposed to send a dispatch to Polk in which, he said, "I refuse to authorize the concessions suggested in points (1) and (2), but, while not recommending them, am willing to leave to Polk's discretion the concessions suggested under points (3), (4), and (5), since I regard them as flexible details of which the basic principles have already been secured."

From Josephus Daniels

My Dear Mr. President: Washington. Nov. 5. 1919.

Last night I conveyed your message to Justice Brandeis and had a long talk with him. He is strongly of the opinion that in the present militant attitude of employees and employers, accentuated by the injunction, he could not have opportunity to do any real constructive work and he feels quite as strongly that in the present tense condition no body that could be named would be able to study and present plans that would lead us out of the present bog. The miners had a good case, in his opinion, but it was handled so badly that they put themselves in the wrong.

At the meeting of the cabinet, when the Industrial Committee or Board was suggested, I think all of us felt that the sooner you named the commission the better. I confess that I am shaken in that opinion by the position of Justice Brandeis. The injunction hearing is to be held on Saturday and everything seems to be standing still until that is settled. It might be well to delay the appointment of your board until then if you think there is weight in the strong feeling of the Justice. If you desire I will take the matter up with him again. Command me in any way

It makes us happy to learn of your steady gain.

                    Devotedly your friend,   Josephus Daniels

ALS (WP, DLC).

A Memorandum by Robert Lansing

                                        November 5, 1919.

THE PRESIDENT'S STATE OF HEALTH.

Yesterday I sent over to the White House a Thanksgiving Proclamation which I had drafted on the evening of the 3rd. Today it was returned to me signed by the President and also his signed authorization to affix to it the Great Seal of the United States.

The Proclamation, as drafted, was not changed in a single word. This fact caused me much concern as to the physical condition of the President, since it showed either that he was not permitted to read the document or that, if he did read it, he was not in a mental state to do so critically. In either case decided weakness was shown, because I cannot conceive of the President, if he was able to review a proclamation of this sort, permitting it being issued to the people without putting into it some of his own phrases and so impressing it with his personality.

But even more than this failure to pass upon the wording of the

Proclamation his signatures were shocking manifestations of his serious physical state. Instead of his firm and plain writing the signature attached to the Proclamation was almost illegible. Without knowing the name intended to be written "Woodrow" could not have been deciphered. "Wilson" was better written, but was very shaky and uneven, while the flourish at the end looked quite unnatural. The signature on the authorization was better, but that too was evidently written by a man whose nerves or muscles were with difficulty controlled. Both signatures were written with a lead pencil and did not appear to be done hastily.

I was surprised and distressed by these proofs of the President's condition, because though I knew that he had been threatened with, if he had not actually suffered, a slight stroke, I had assumed from the repeated assurances of the physicians that he was almost normal. I know now that he is still a very sick man, and that his convalescence will take much time. If he is really better than he was, and I am sure that he is, he must have been critically ill, if not very near death.

After seeing this Proclamation with its pitiful signature I feel more alarmed as to the outcome of the President's illness than I have at any time except on the Wednesday[1] after his return to Washington when Tumulty by motions indicated partial paralysis of the left side. If he has only progressed thus far toward recovery during the last month I cannot see how he can really conduct the Government for months to come.

T MS (R. Lansing Papers, DLC).
[1] October 1, 1919.

From the Diary of Ray Stannard Baker

Washington, Nov. 5 [1919].

I lunched at the White House with Mrs. Wilson at 1:30. I had a hard time getting through the gates, for the President has been ill & has had no visitors. Mrs. MacAdoo, Mrs. Sayre & Miss Margaret Wilson, the President's daughters, were there: and Admiral and Mrs. Grayson. They were all very warm in their commendations of the Wilson articles. Mrs. Wilson looks worn & tired after her long vigil, but remains irrepressibly cheerful. Grayson told me he did not see how they could have gotten along without her. She has been up all hours of the night with the President & has never faltered in her attention.

The western trip must have been a terrible affair, as she & Admiral Grayson told me about it. The President was ill when he started & went against the express & urgent advice of his physician. The President felt that he *must* do all he could to inform the American people of the League of Nations & try to the limit of his ability to get it adopted by public opinion. From the first he had no appetite & could not digest what he did eat because he was under such nervous strain. The Doctor had to feed him liquid & pre-digested foods during the day & night. Soon he could not sleep. The western altitudes affected him: but he would not give up. In Montana the hot dry weather & the dust caused an affection [infection] of the throat & he developed a kind of asthma. The Doctor repeatedly sprayed out his nose & throat: often having to do it in the middle of the night. In Washington he began to have terrible headaches—so blinding, that when he got up to speak he would see double. Yet he would not give in. At several functions in California—one a dinner in which those present smoked inordinately, he suffered frightfully—but made a wonderful speech. He never complained, he never scorned his condition—and he refused the beseeching requests of Dr Grayson to stop & rest. Coming east one day the doctor saw a curious drag or looseness at the left side of his mouth—a sign of danger that could no longer be obscured & he & Mrs. Wilson took things into their own hands & called off the trip. No one knows yet how serious the attack was or what the President has been through. I spent the entire afternoon talking with Grayson & he went into every phase of the case & read me his secret report—the substance of which I will not even put down here. He asked my judgment as to what he had done & I told him I thought he was absolutely right in doing what he did. It was a stupendous responsibility he had to assume; but he has both wisdom & courage—a fine, brave, simple man if ever there was one. He has never lost his head & his struggle with the other doctors when they were all for operation in the prostate difficulty was a notable affair. In this he was supported by Mrs. Wilson.

The President will be much longer in getting up & about than anyone knows—& he may never get up. The Doctor has invented & had built a kind of chair back, with arms, for use by the President in his bed. He has also a new wheel-chair in which, presently, he hopes the President may be able to get about. The President is undeniably better, but the doctor is guarding him closely, keeping everyone away—& preventing, as much as possible, any business coming to his attention. This is hard to do because the President's mind is exceedingly acute, as good as ever it was, & he chafes at the inactivity. I did not see him myself. I am sure I could have seen him if I had asked—but, of course, would not. Not even the secretaries & others in the White House know what the real trouble is.

The President has never lost his sense of humor: nor ever failed, even at his worst, to have a witty response. When one of the doctors was pounding him by tapping with one finger the President asked: "Why are you knocking? I'm at home." They were taking a sample of his blood. "That's what the Senate has been trying to do to me!" he remarked.

Mrs. Wilson is a woman of much stronger character than people realize. She has no great education. (Yesterday she spoke of the "decīsive vote of California," shortening the i and then said, "I mean decīsive—Mr. Wilson is always correcting me!["]) but real natural gifts & having common sense. She conducted herself in the highest places in Europe with perfect ease & grace. She watches the President's interests as only a woman of great power could do. Grayson told me this story of her in Paris. Col. House was trying to get the President to write a commendatory letter to Wickham Steed of *The Times*[1] (and blaming him for having written to Frank Simonds).[2] He told Mrs. Wilson that Steed was a good man to cultivate—that he (House) could make him write anything he liked, and urged that the President commend him. Mrs. Wilson opened a drawer at her side & took out an article that Steed had written not long before telling what a great man the Colonel was, how he was slowly leading the President & how hard it was to get the President informed upon European affairs. It was a glorification of the Colonel and a snidely detraction of the President. She handed him this article. "I suppose," she said, "he wrote that for you." The Colonel flushed & was much confused: and never afterwards came to see Mrs. Wilson.[3] The Colonel's stock has fallen to zero. He is no longer a factor. He tried at Paris to conciliate away everything that the President stood for.

Once in the Council of Four Clemenceau accused Wilson of pro-Germanism.[4] W. very angry: could not eat his luncheon. Made a great speech in the afternoon[5] in reply on the situation in Europe, saying he was not for an easy peace but a just peace & painting a picture of what Europe would be like if an unjust peace were imposed upon Germany. Clemenceau got up & came over to him with tears in his eyes & said: "I agree with you, Mr. President: I agree with you." Lloyd George echoed, "And I too."

Mrs. Wilson told me that the President wanted to appoint me on the new industrial council of 15 but held back, fearing he would be charged with rewarding me for writing these articles. I'm glad he did not appoint me. I think I can be of more use in the same field at my own calling.

I dined with the amiable Sweets.[6] Dr. Stratton[7] was there.

One of the first things that Admiral Grayson did when he became the President's physician (he told me) was to stop the use of coal-tar medicines[8] which the President had been taking for headache &c. Also the President had used a stomach "bath" to treat indigestion: & that also was discontinued.[9]

The plain fact is that the President has a 600 horse-power motor in a frail, light, delicate chassis. A great, powerful driving will directed by an intellect so ambitious to achieve that no physical body could bear the strain for long at a time—especially if the hills are high and rugged, as they were at Paris. So he keeps breaking down: Dr. Grayson, the clever mechanician always at his side to watch the machine.

The President is almost the only man I ever knew who really over-works. Most people over-eat, over-drink, over-loaf—few really over-work.

Hw MS (R. S. Baker Papers, DLC).

[1] That is, Henry Wickham Steed, editor of the London *Times*.

[2] WW to F. H. Simonds, March 26, 1919, CCL (WP, DLC), which read as follows: "I must not allow the rush of these days to prevent my turning aside at least for a moment to express my very deep appreciation of the fine support you are giving to the things that are worth while in this great settlement we are trying to effect. Your approval and support are of the greatest service and I do not want to wait any longer to let you know that I am sincerely grateful." About Simonds, see JPT to WW, March 30, 1919 (second telegram of that date), n. 1, Vol. 56.

[3] For a detailed discussion of this meeting between Mrs. Wilson and Colonel House, see n. 2 to the extract from the Grayson Diary printed at April 21, 1919, Vol. 57, as well as the other accounts cited therein.

[4] About this incident, see the extracts from the diaries of Colonel House and V. C. McCormick, as well as the memorandum by Lansing printed at March 28, 1919, Vol. 56.

[5] See the minutes of the Council of Four printed at March 28, 1919, 4 p.m., *ibid.*

[6] Edwin Forrest Sweet and Sophia Fuller Sweet.

[7] That is, Samuel Wesley Stratton.

[8] Aspirin and other such analgesics.

[9] About Wilson and his stomach pump, see Weinstein, *Woodrow Wilson: A Medical and Psychological Biography*, pp. 126, 146, and 149.

ADDENDA

To Catharine Milligan McLane[1]

My dear Madam,   Bryn Mawr, Pa., 19 March, 1888

It gives me great pleasure to answer the questions contained in your letter of March 17th, which reached me this morning; it would give me greater pleasure if I could answer them satisfactorily. Unhappily there is,—so far as I know,—nowhere any expanded treatment in English either of the functions of the communal orphan councillors or of the detailed operation of the Poor Relief Ward Committee system. In volume 46 of the *Contemporary Review* (1884), p. 769 there is an article by Prof. Gneist on the Government of Berlin which contains the same outline of the government of the city that I gave. My description was based largely upon this article, as the latest complete statement of the scheme of city government in Prussia since the reforms of '72 and '76. But it contains no more particulars on the special points you mention than I gave. The work of Ward Committees is so largely within their own discretion, is so flexible, that I imagine it would hardly bear exact outlining.

Prof Gneist's distinctively *administrative* works have not, I am sorry to say, been translated. His "History of the English Constitution," however (2 vols.), and his "English Parliament" (one vol.) have been; and in these works may be found, incidentally, many of the more important of his conclusions concerning English administrative development. Together they contain a very adequate outline of his characteristic contributions to English governmental history. The 'History' was published (in this country) in New York, 1886, the sketch of the Parliament, N. Y., 1887. Regretting that I have been unable to tell you more,

                    Very truly Yrs.,   *Woodrow Wilson.*

ALS (WC, NjP).
  [1] Wilson was replying to Catharine M. McLane to WW, March 17, 1888, Vol. 5.

To Charles Warren[1]

My dear Sir,   Princeton, New Jersey, 15 January, 1900.

I am sincerely obliged to you for your kind letter of the thirteenth. It gratifies me very deeply that you should keep in mind your desire to have me address the Reform Club.

But it would seem as if I were never to be allowed to enjoy the privilege of becoming its guest. This time it is not a trip abroad that stands in the way but a congested calendar. I have already promised so many speeches for this season that I dare not promise more. If I did I should be obliged to neglect literary work of the first importance (to me) and endanger a serious miscarriage in trying to fulfil my obligations to several publishers.

Allow me again to express my very deep appreciation and my very sincere regret.

Very sincerely Yours,   Woodrow Wilson

TLS (MHi).
[1] Lawyer of Boston; later a prolific writer on American constitutional history; Assistant Attorney General of the United States, 1914-1918.

To John Carver Palfrey[1]

My dear Sir: Princeton, New Jersey. 14 Feb[r]uary, 1903.

I consider it a real honor that the Massachusetts Reform Club should invite me to speak before them on so interesting and important a matter, and should add to the compliment by leaving it to my suggestion at what date their dinner should be held; and I need hardly assure you that both the occasion and the subject make the strongest appeal to my interest. But I am sorry to say that the recent death of my father has put me sadly out of spirits for everything which does not seem to come to me directly as a matter of official duty. I am trying, in spite of my distress, to meet the alumni at their dinners; but I feel that other engagements of that kind must be postponed until another season.

I know that you will appreciate my feeling in this matter; and I beg that you will express to the Committee of the Club my very sincere appreciation and regret.

Very sincerely yours,   Woodrow Wilson

TLS (MHi).
[1] Of Boston; engineer, soldier, military historian.

An Announcement

The White House [c. Dec. 4, 1915].

It was announced at the White House to-day that the marriage of Mrs. Galt and the President will take place on Saturday the eighteenth of December. As previously stated, the ceremony will be performed at Mrs. Galt's home, No. 1308 Twentieth Street, N.W. The only guests will be Mrs. Galt's mother, her brothers and sisters, the President's brother and sister, his daughters, and the members of his immediate household. No invitations will be issued.

WWT MS (J. P. Tumulty Papers, DLC).

To Joseph Patrick Tumulty

Dear Tumulty: [The White House, c. Jan. 15, 1918]

Mr. James M. Beck[1] expressed some hesitation about coming with the committee which Creel has organized and which is coming to see me on Monday afternoon, because he was afraid he was not sufficiently *persona grata* at the White House. I think his criticism and his whole attitude before we went into the war were abominable and inexcusable, but I "ain't harboring no ill will" just now and I hope that you will have the intimation conveyed to him through Mr. Creel or otherwise that he will be welcomed.

                                                    The President.

TL (J. P. Tumulty Papers, DLC).
[1] About James Montgomery Beck, see G. Creel to WW, Jan. 15, 1918, n. 1, Vol. 45.

From Joseph Patrick Tumulty

Dear Governor: [The White House, c. Jan. 19, 1918]

The newspaper men asked me this morning what the attitude of the administration was towards the proposed super-cabinet.[1] I hedged as much as I could, but I asked if it was not the same proposition that came up some months ago advocated by Senator Weeks, in a new disguise,—if it was not the same kind of a commission that had harassed Mr. Lincoln. I think we ought to let our attitude be known unofficially for the guidance of men who wish to help us. If we do nothing at this time to let it be known, it would seem that our opposition to this kind of legislation had been silenced by the furore over the fuel order. In other words, we ought to show by our attitude that the tantrums on the Hill are making no impression on us whatever.   The Secretary.

TL (J. P. Tumulty Papers, DLC).
[1] About this, see n. 1 to G. F. Peabody to WW, Jan. 19, 1918, Vol. 46.

To Joseph Patrick Tumulty

Dear Tumulty: [The White House, c. Jan. 19, 1918]

Of course, I am opposed to the idea of a "super-cabinet" and regard it as nothing more nor less than a renewal of the perpetual
effort of the Republicans to force representation in the administration. Republicans of the finest sort and of the finest capacity are
working for and with the administration on all hands and there is
no need whatever for a change at the head of the administering
departments. I am utterly opposed to anything of the sort and will
never consent to it. You will know how to create the impression on
the minds of the newspapermen that I regard it as merely a partisan effort to hamper and embarrass the administration.

                                             The President.

TL (J. P. Tumulty Papers, DLC).

Notes of Conversations with Wilson
by William Emmanuel Rappard[1]

                                             [Nov. 20, 1918]

I have just come from the White House. After a moment's talk
at the gate to the grounds, I was admitted about 4:40, and I was
immediately ushered into the lobby, where I found myself alone.
Then, almost at once, a secretary asked me to go into a nearby and
much better furnished and more comfortable room, where the
President was waiting for me. Blue jacket with two American decorations.

Impression: carrying himself as well as the previous year[2] but
more cheerful and even more forthcoming. Laughing at times
gently, at times almost boisterously, especially in alluding to narrow-minded foreign governments: Franco-Italian hatred, Lloyd
George's political fluctuations, character of Spanish neutrality,
"*disciplining Germany.*" I am trying to reproduce course conversation.

I follow my plan. He recalls to me with warmth last meeting. I:
even more important, since this year it is a matter of general political interests. White House, public opinion in Switzerland, enthusiasm for America and himself in Switzerland, in Europe, among
the neutrals as well as among the Allies and belligerents. Negligible influence of the elections. We all look to him and fear only one
thing, that he might become "practical." "*I'm not going to relax in
the least. I'm going over to Europe because the Allied governments
don't want me to.*" (Laughter.) In order to prevent the discussion

from taking a troublesome course and in order not to be obliged to ask the Allies constantly to reverse regrettable decisions. Also to say a few plain truths, especially to England, on the freedom of the seas. *"I want to tell Lloyd George certain things I can't write to him. I'll tell him: Are you going to grant the freedom of the seas? If not, are you prepared to enter into a race with us to see who will have the larger navy, you or we?"*

I lay stress upon the power of public opinion, which makes him all-powerful and which allows him to go over the head of the Allied governments. *"I know it, and I know how jealous they are. I'm stubborn but one has to be worldly wise."* Had proposed Switzerland as conference seat but is inclined not to make dispute.

I speak to him of Swiss participation. Does not believe it. Switzerland will not be admitted, without doubt, but neither Spain (one does not know the motives of her policy), nor South American republics. He hopes to do in Paris what he had tried to do without success some years ago with South and Central America: to extend Monroe Doctrine so as to make it a principle of mutual protection. *"Not a big-brother affair, but a real partnership."*

He brings me back to the subject of "practical," he tells me: The solutions cannot be ideal, and I know that *"everybody will be disgusted with me,"* although I will try to do the impossible in order to be just. But excessive pretensions: Poland, which wishes to take over purely German regions, which is not content with Danzig as a free port with assured access, but would like ownership. The same with Czechoslovaks and Yugoslavs.

In Paris, the Allies alone will deliberate in subcommissions. But how to begin cooperation neutrals? Advantages:

(1) necessity to have their advice on questions which concern them;

(2) disinterested support Wilson policy.

Wilson: "We will consult them when their interests come into play." I: "But national dignity. Not criminals whom one summons to the bar when it pleases the judges." Wilson: "No, but suitors whom one calls in order to protect their interests." I: "Then your advice would be for them to confine themselves to being vigilant." Wilson: *"Vigilant and intimate."* I: "How 'intimate' if they are not admitted?" Wilson: "All that will be known. As for myself, I will not at all promise to keep the secret on the object of deliberations." I: "But if public, *'vigilant'* suffices. How and with whom to be *'intimate'* into the bargain?"

—*"Well, Mr. House, my alter ego, will always be ready to hear any suggestions."*

I try to show Wilson that this method is contrary to true league interests and American interests, for he will always have support of the neutrals. And I come back to admission request. *"Well, if you asked to be consulted every time a question concerning your interests came up, How would that do?"* I: "That would make us a species of protectorates of the Allies." —"Then," Wilson says, "my advice would be to postpone all decision until I have had the time to put myself in a position to understand the psychology of those whom I am going to try to persuade in Paris. But don't ask only me, but all the Allies." I: "On the method of procedure, yes. But we prefer to ask you, yourself, because we know you [to be] the most disinterested." Wilson: *"Yes, but the Allies are getting a bit jealous. I had to tell the Germans to address us all as the people over there resented it. They think I want to run it all."* I: *"But you are, I hope."* Wilson: *"I hope so too, but it would be unwise to let them feel it too obviously."*

I explain to him neutrality question. "If you form league without us and if you should accept us later, we will have had nothing to say about its formation. Now, we, like all the other neutrals of Europe, will have particular claims. Neutrality has saved us. Would it still be possible?" Wilson: "If you remain outside, you will always have our support in case of aggression." I: "But our tradition, our popular desire, is not to remain outside. And if we enter, will we still have the benefit of our neutrality?" Wilson: "Yes, why would that not be possible?" I: "And in case economic blockade?" Wilson: "We would provision you." I: "But we depend as much on Germany as Germany on us." Wilson: "There will be less of that after the war than before." I: "Problem remains unresolved." Wilson: "We will talk about that again in Paris." I: "You will be further from Switzerland in Paris than in Washington." Wilson: "In one sense, yes, but we will remember Switzerland for we stand by her."

Remainder conversation about sanctions. Rather obscure. Wishes disarmament but not international police. *"The question of the command would break up the Conference immediately."* Collective action—economic and military—yes. But promised, obligatory? Doubtful.

The end of the conversation a little hurried, because the next visitor had been waiting for twenty minutes.

To my question: "In the absence of international police force, don't you fear that disarmament will collide with rivalries and mutual suspicions?" —*"I'm sure of it. France and Italy, for instance, have no use for each other. It will be a long rocky road."*

Could not part conference relative League of Nations take place outside Paris, in Switzerland, for example?

Wilson: "I have not thought of it, but not impossible."

I open Borgeaud packages which he accepts with thanks.

Excuses himself for not being able to keep me longer. On offer service in Europe: *"Thank you. Yes. We'll get in touch in Paris."*

General impression: extraordinary candor. *"Thinking aloud"*— *"Between you and me"* (on rivalries among Allies). But, in spite of firm will, seems to me all the same to have been a little manipulated by Allies in affair exclusion of the neutrals. In order to obtain Swiss participation, if that is still possible, it would require a very intense diplomatic work.

Very cordial personal good will and really intimate tone.

If neutrals are admitted, it will in any case be only following decision to be taken at Paris and only for part conference which will follow settlement war—not in 1918. As for Germany, can be admitted to the League of Nations only later. *"Not on probation, a term offensive. But postponed."*

"Economic policy of League not necessarily free trade. But no discrimination among members."

"Through my cable to Lloyd George[3] I tied him up in his speech."

On Bolshevism in Switzerland, reassured but *"Trouble from all the people you've been obliged to be hospitable to."*

The suspicions in Mexico explain themselves in a certain measure by the affair of the annexation of Texas, *"a somewhat dark spot in our national history."*

William F. Rappard, "Woodrow Wilson, la Suisse et Genève," in *Centenaire Woodrow Wilson, 1856-1956* (Geneva, n.d.), pp. 51-54.

1 Text in English in the following printed in italics.

2 Rappard, a member of a special commission sent by the Swiss Federal Council to the United States, had talked to Wilson at the White House on November 1, 1917. They talked mainly about Swiss neutrality and American support for it, the difficulties of getting supplies through to Switzerland, and the possibilities of a future league of nations. What struck him above all, Rappard afterwards wrote, in what Wilson said about a future international regime was its tone, which betrayed an ardent conviction and even an internal exultation. Rappard quotes Wilson's words as follows:

"The constitution of a league of nations, he tells me, is, in my eyes, a matter of moral persuasion more than of legal organization. I have never worked for the formation of a league of peoples with the intention of favoring one of the groups of belligerents at the expense of the other, but only for the good of all peaceful humanity. When men of good will, whatever be their country, have understood their true common interest, the most formidable obstacles which bar the road to the establishment of a new international order will be surmounted. This is why my most fervent desire is that this war result in a peace in which justice be imposed on all. When we can finally come to negotiations, it will be with the firm will to ask nothing for ourselves and to do everything to prevent anything whatsoever unjust from being gained."

Rappard later wrote that he had been struck by Wilson's physical condition—by the vitality flowing from his body which, in spite of his sixty-two years, still had the appearance of youth, almost of adolescence. Rappard was also impressed by Wilson's vivacity, penetration of thought, the strength of his jaw and chin, his frankness, the impeccable preciseness of his speech, etc. Rappard, "Woodrow Wilson," pp. 31-39.

3 WW to D. Lloyd George, Nov. 14, 1918, and the note thereto, Vol. 53.

[Feb. 12, 1919][1]

This evening at 8 o'clock, Hôtel Murat. From 8:00 to 8:50 conversation tête-à-tête with Himself. Setting: French gendarmes notified. Soldiers present arms. Monumental entry. Ushered into pretty room. President arrives in a moment in dinner jacket, American flag and precious stones in buttonhole. Tone cordial and confiding. Sometimes gay but in general serious. Subjects: Switzerland and League of Nations with neutrality. Had never thought of neutrality. Plan, which I acknowledged having seen, envisages obligatory economic sanctions, optional military. All the same, it would be necessary to ask exemption from five leading powers on entering. Perhaps in exchange services in peacetime. Seat: favorable to Geneva. Perhaps French should ask it for them. The Hague, English opposed. Himself, Wilson, not of opinion on justice English suspicions. Not on monarchical land. Suggests Switzerland offer site with privilege extraterritoriality. Would perhaps facilitate exemption (*sanctions*). Procedure: envisage soliciting admission when League founded. Offer beforehand perhaps advisable.

I say: We had been rather far apart: reason demanded prudence. Above all, scruple American Constitution.

About Rhine [River]: Unaware of French intentions. But indignant. Always the same, always selfish. I to undertake to see on his behalf Lansing and White (confidence in his knowledge of diplomatic customs). Wants representation. But do not counsel with head foreign affairs, for does not like to summon to the bar above all ministers of rank superior to those who hear them and must judge them.

Wishes still to remind duties toward neutrals before leaving. Believes that we ourselves are the only ones to be agitated on subject participation. Has no air of reproaching us.

New states admitted if "*self-governing*." Will perhaps go to Geneva, if other neutrals only not so jealous. The Spaniards want his visit at all costs. Does not wish to go there.

Remainder of conversation about France. Heartbroken. "*Petty*." "*Stupid*." "*Insane*." "*Obsession*." Asks me if national opinions always with him. I only know too much to reply. Press evidently very bad. Yes, but not free country, as bureaucratic as Prussia. Takes paper from pocket and reads orders given to press by French government: 1) Republicans in U. S.; 2) exaggerate Russian disorder; 3) excite fear of Germany.

"How they have tormented me with devastated regions." Now that I have seen Rheims, say that it is not enough. Say I am without heart (*bowels*). Wish to starve Germany, then make her pay.

Would like international army against Germany. Wilson: but Poland, Bohemia, Hungary, Yugoslavia are also threatened! On annexations, Wilson will be inexorable. *"Rather be stoned in the streets than give in."*

Valentine Thomson and Trocadéro affair.[2] Clemenceau prevented womens' demonstration. Wants to prevent contact with public opinion.

General impression: Vigor, now and then a little fatigue. True disappointment and irritation against France. Sympathy for Geneva. *"Perhaps my presbyterianism?"*

Recommends to retenir [keep in mind?]:

1) Nondiplomatic representation;
2) Offer site like District of Columbia;
3) See Lansing and White on Rhine.

Very high praise International Red Cross and perhaps trip to Geneva on this subject.

Printed in Rappard, "Woodrow Wilson," pp. 55-56.

[1] Rappard's report of this conversation is W. E. Rappard to H. Sulzer, Feb. 13, 1919, Vol. 55.

[2] About which, see G. F. Close to W. C. Bullitt, Jan. 15, 1919; W. C. Bullitt to G. F. Close, Jan. 18, 1919; and the extract from the Diary of Edith Benham printed at Jan. 27, 1919, Vol. 54.

APPENDIX I

From a Memoir by Irwin Hood Hoover[1]

THE FACTS ABOUT PRESIDENT WILSON'S ILLNESS

[undated]

He returned to America, arriving in Washington, midnight of July 8/1919. The rest and diversion on the boat had apparently done him a lot of good. He seemed quite his normal self again. He seemed to feel he had left many of his troubles behind. He was looking to the future with a feeling of satisfaction and confidence. I am sure he did not sufficiently measure what he was going up against or if he did, he felt the complete master of the situation. His every disposition gave evidence that such was the case and his conversation of the future took him back to Geneva as the Head of the League of Nations in all the power and prominence that position would give to him. On one occassion the writer was asked if he would like to go back to Geneva.[2] This in view of the fact of having just finished being with him, night and day during all the time of his stay in Europe and even closer than ever, in Paris.

During this time, his return from Europe and the start of his so-called Western trip lasting about six weeks he went about the even tenor of his usual ways. He motored a great deal, went for golf several times, attended the theaters and saw a number of daily visitors. Still it was evident that those about him and and even himself was making an effort to conserve his health. He had several notable appointments during this time, especially the one with the Foreign Relations Committee of the Senate. To those of us who just looked on and listened, the President was not at his best at that meeting. In fact all thru this period he manifested an over anxiety toward his guests. He had one short spell of sickness during this time which left him confined to his room for a couple of days.[3]

But what appealed to us the more was that he refrained from going to the Executive Office during this time. Most of his appointments were made in the White House proper and it was noticed

[1] We have printed the first part of this draft memoir, which covers Hoover's memory of Wilson from his first acquaintance with him through the Paris Peace Conference, in n. 1 to the House Diary printed at June 23, 1919, Vol. 61.

[2] Hoover may have misremembered in recollecting Wilson's talk about going back to Geneva, but, on the other hand, Wilson might have been thinking about his stay there with Ellen Axson Wilson on September 9-10, 1903. See Vol. 14, pp. 540-41. There is no reason to doubt Hoover's statement that Wilson thought that he would go to Geneva as the United States member of the Council of the League of Nations.

[3] Here Hoover was, without knowing the cause of it, referring to Wilson's illness on July 19, 1919, about which see Dr. Park's essay printed as an Appendix in Vol. 62 and the index references in that volume to "Woodrow Wilson—Health."

that he was doing a lot of resting, retiring to his room from time to time during the day, shutting himself off from all the world.

In the meantime by his orders, arrangements had been made for his Western trip and on the evening of Sept 3/1919, he left the White House for the station to join the others who were to accompany him. He returned to Washington on the morning of Sept 28/19 after his collapse or whatever it was that overtook him out in Wichita, Kansas.

Upon his return he appeared none the worse than when he left. True he looked a little peaked and seemed to have lost some of his spirit. His face was a little more florid than usual but there was apparently, nothing alarming in his condition. Only those of us who knew could help but remember the days in Paris, not so long passed and of the suspicion of the French servants and of the moving of the furnishings in the palace where we lived.

He took up his daily routine, went motoring &c, stayed a little close to his private quarters but otherwise left no impression but what after a little rest he would come around alright as he had done after his illness in Paris.

Thus the days went on, four in number, until Thursday, Oct 2/19 when the crash came.

The story of this, his last and lasting illness is tragic. It is curious how it is told. It looses none of its tragedy. The whole truth of coarse as before stated can be told by only one person in all the world. That, Mrs. Woodrow Wilson, the second. Especially all that is known of the climax must come from her. Whether she will ever tell the world just what happened I doubt and those of us who attempt it must be given credit for honesty of purpose in narrating the facts as they came to us and make due allowance for most unusual and startling circumstances that were existent at the time.

At exactly ten minutes before nine oclock on this memorable day, (I noted the time in writing the same day) my telephone on the desk in the Ushers room at the White House rang, and Mrs. Wilsons voice said, "Please get Dr. Grayson, the President is very sick" The telephone used was a private one that did not go thru the general telephone switchboard. Mrs. Wilson had come all the way out to the end of the upper hall to use this particular 'phone instead of the regular 'phone right in the room they occupied. I reasoned at the time that it was done to avoid publicity, for their had been talk of the operators on the switchboard listening in and diseminating talk that would occur from time to time.

I immediately called Dr. Grayson at his home, repeated the message as Mrs. Wilson had given it to me and ordered one of the White House automobiles to go for him trying to appreciate the emergency. I then went up stairs to see if there was anything I could do. Upon reaching the upper floor, I saw that all doors were closed; so I was helpless in the premises in so far as being of any assistance at the time. The servants were about but none of them had heard Mrs. Wilson 'phone and knew nothing of the President being sick. I waited up there until Dr. Grayson came which was but a few minutes at most. A little after nine I should say. Dr. Grayson attempted to walk right in but the door was locked. He knocked gently and upon being opened he entered. I continued on to wait in the outer hall. In about ten minutes Dr. Grayson came out and with raised arms, said "My God the President is paralized, send for Dr. Stitt and the nurse," mentioning the name of the latter, the same one who had been in attendance upon the first Mrs. Wilson and who was with her when she died.

The remark of Dr. Grayson made an indellible impression on my mind. "Paralized" what a fate for such a great man. I am free to say I never heard the word mentioned thereafter in connection with the Presidents condition, by those who were in a position to know the truth. Here, Dr. Grayson returned to the Presidents room, there was not much excitement. The second Doctor and nurse arrived and were shown to the room. The employes about the place began to get wise of the President being very ill but could find out nothing. Other doctors were sent for during the day and the best that could be learned was that the President was resting quietly. Dr. Dircum and Dr. Davis of Phila were sent for the first arriving a little after noon. Dr. Ruffin, Mrs. Wilson's personal physician was also sent for. There were doctors everywhere. A consultation of them all together was held about four oclock. An aire of secrecy had come over things during the day. Those outside the room could find out nothing, including family and employes. It was during this time the beginning of the deception practiced on the American people had its inception. Never was a conspiracy so pointedly and so artistically formed. After events but bore out this conclusion to the mind of all in a position to observe and have any interest in the fate of the patient. It was my privilege to go in the room in the late afternoon. Some rearrangement of the furnishings of the room had to be made and the domestic attendents on the floor were not looked upon with favor for this purpose. So, Dr. Grayson, the nurse and myself did the job.

The President layed stretched out on the large Lincoln bed. He looked as if dead. There was not a sign of life. His face bore a long cut about the temple from which the signs of blood were still evident. His nose also bore a long cut lengthwise. This too looked red and raw. There was no bandage. He was just gone as far as one could judge from appearances, especially when one had been told as I had that he was paralized.

Soon after I made confidential inquiry as to how and when it all happened. I was told and know it to be right that he had went to the bath upon arising in the morning and was sitting on the stool when the affliction overcame him. That he tumbled over on the floor, striking his head on the sharp plumbing of the bath tub in his fall. That, Mrs. Wilson hearing groans from the bath went in and found him in an unconscious condition. She dragged him to the bed in the room ajourning [adjoining] and came out in the hall to call over the 'phone for the doctor as before mentioned.

For the next three or four days the White House was like a hospital. There were all kinds of medical aparatus and more doctors and more nurses. Day and night this went on.

All the while the only answer one could get from their inquiry as to his condition was that it "showed signs of improvement." No details, no explanations, it seemed as if all had become clamlike.

This condition just seemed to go on indefinately. It was perhaps three weeks or more before an change seemed to come over things. I had been in and out of the room many times during this period and I saw very little change. He just lay helpless. True, he had been taking nourishment but the working the doctors had been doing on him had just about sapped his remaining vitality. All his natural functions had to be artifically helped and relieved and he appeared just as helpless as one could possibly be and live.

Still he lived and what a triumph that was and what an incentive to those most interested, personally, materially and otherwise. And he lived on but oh what a wreck of his former self. He did grow better but that does not say much. I was with him every day at some time for some purpose and saw him, even unto the end, at his private residence. There was never a moment during all that time when he was but a shadow of his former self. He had changed from a giant to a pigmy in every wise that one would rate in a fair reckoning. He was physically, almost incapicated, mentally but a guisser compared to the normal understanding of his great mind. Could articulate but indistinctly and think but feebly. It was so sad that those of us about him, who almost universally admired him would turn our head away when he came along or we went near to him.

Going back a little to about the time when it seemed there was a little confidence restored as to his life being spared it is interesting to note the doings of and about an incapicitated President of the United States. During his early illness everything in the way of business came to a standstill. But there came a time when something had to be done. This time sort of crawled on gradually. For at least a month or more not one word was mentioned to him about the business of the office and he was so sick he did not take the initative to inquire. No secretary, no official, no stenographer, no one with business had seen him even. He was lifted out of bed and placed in a comfortable chair for a short while each day. He gradually seemed to kind of get used to his helpless condition. At times Mrs. Wilson would read to him. Finally when it could no longer be delayed some matters of importance requiring his signature were read to him and with a pencil, his hand steadied and pointed, he would sign where the hand had been placed. I saw many of these signatures and they were but mere scribbles compared to his normal signature. All a sort of a mechanical process which even seemed to exhaust him withal.

This orignal stroke or whatever it was simply put the President out of business, mentally & physically for at least a month. At the end of that time he could be lifted from the bed, placed in a chair beside the bed and chair and man moved to another part of the room. After a few days of this an invalid rolling chair was tried but it soon proved a failure. He could not sit upright. It was evident that more rigid braces for the poor old deformed body was necessary. The writer suggested one of the single person rolling chairs like the ones used on the board walk at Atlantic City. This was agreed too and arrangements were made to hire one from a dealer at Atlantic City. The arrangement orignally was to hire it for $5.00 per week but as time went on and it was seen that the chair was to be a pernament affair in the daily doings of the President, the chair was bought outright. Upon arrival we changed the foot rest part of it, making it to stand out straight on a line with the seat thereby avoiding the necessity of the bending of the legs when he was placed in it. This chair was used every time the President got out of bed for the remaining days at the White House. The writer has pushed this chair day after day during the entire time. Even his few journeys out of the house in it, he would be rolled to the elevator and practically carried the rest of the way to the automobile in waiting. His several trips to the theater were pitiful. I accompanied him and with much assistance could but akwardly get him into the boxes, always being driven to the rear entrance of the play houses.

If there was ever a man in bad shape he was. There was no comparison with the President that went to Paris and before. He was changed in every way and every one about him recognized and understood it to be so. He could not talk plain, mumbled more than he articulated, was helpless and looked awful. Everybody tried to help him realizing he was so dependent for everything. The stories in the papers from day to day may have been true in their way but never was deception so universally practiced in the White House as it was in those statements being given out from time to time. And the strange part to me was that the President in his feeble way, entered into the scheme. He permitted himself to be cama-flouged like on occassions of his socalled Cabinet Meetings[4] and his meeting of the Congressional Committee from the Senate.[5] At all of the Cabinet meetings held he would be rolled into the Cabi-net room in his old chair and fixed up prior to the coming of the Cabinet members. He sat there during all the meetings as one in a trance, the Cabinet members doing all the talking. He would have agreed to about anything they said for the thought of ending the meeting was the paramount one in his mind if there were any thoughts there at all. The Cabinet members would not tell what was in their minds or there would have been a different arrange-ment brought about.

Likewise when the Senate Committee came the great cama-flouge took place. He had been sitting up in his rolling chair but when the time came for the committee to arrive he was put to bed. The room was darkened, only one light on the bed side table left burning. He was propped up with pillows and covered over en-tirely, except his head and right arm. It was quite impossible for one coming in from a well lighted part of the house to see any thing to satisfaction. Mrs. Wilson stood at the foot of the bed, the nurse on the side of the bed, Dr. Grayson in the doorway, which was left open, and me behind Grayson. There visit was very short, seem-ingly nothing but salutations being indulged in. They made no ef-fort to cross examine or inquire beyond his feelings and his condi-tion and he went thru with this so well, everyone was happy afterwards that there had been nothing more serious happen.

So it went thru the Fall and into the Winter. On sunshine days he would be wheeled out into the south grounds for an hour or so. If there were some papers or matters pending these would be read to him at this time. But only those that Mrs. Wilson thought should be read to him. These would reach her thru Grayson. To him they had come mostly from Tumulty or some other official who had en-trance to Graysons good graces. He would tell Mrs Wilson what had been said about the matter and she would tell the President.

[4] Cabinet meetings are known to have been held on April 14, 20, and 27; May 4, 11, 18, and 25; June 1, 8, and 15; July 20; August 3, 10, 17, 24, and 31; September 14, 21, and 28; October 5 and 12; November 9, 16, 23, and 30; December 14 and 28, 1920; January 11, 18, and 25; February 1 and 15; and March 1, 1921.

[5] That is, Wilson's conversation with Senators Fall and Hitchcock on December 5, 1919.

Likewise the word would be passed back thru the same channels of some decision the President had made.

But even of this there was but very little. Tumulty tried so hard to get to the President during all this time of months but he was kept away as if he was a leper.[6] No doubt, Grayson would have let him in for they sort of worked together but Mrs Wilson would not do so and so Grayson could not insist. Not for a minute for the truth of the matter was, that Grayson himself did not have much to say in affairs. He could reach Mrs Wilson but dare not go beyond. He could get one to see Mrs Wilson but there his influence stopped. He was blamed for a lot he didn't do along that line for the truth of the matter was that in affairs of that kind, Graysons status was not so high with Mrs Wilson, especially in view of the fact that she knew he was working in a measure with Tumulty.

Tumulty was loyal to the choar [core], there was no position he would not have taken in the premises for the Presidents best interest, real or imagined. He never gave up even in the light of the akward position he was occupying. In the matter of the Presidents message to Congress,[7] it was Tumulty and Swem with the help of the Cabinet members who prepared that document which went as a composition of the President. This Swem, a fine young fellow, smart and understanding. Even when the President was well [he] played such a large part in his corespondence and the preparation of all his papers. Thus it became easy when the necessity arose for him to prepare additional papers and get them approved some how and send them forth as originals.

Hw MS (I. H. Hoover Papers, DLC).

[6] Here, Hoover was writing without complete knowledge. It is impossible to know whether, where, and how often Tumulty saw Wilson between October 2 and mid-November. The statement in the first news report printed at October 12 to the effect that Tumulty saw Wilson on October 10 may or may not be correct. The first meeting that we can be reasonably sure about occurred on November 20. See RL to WW, Nov. 21, 1919, printed as an enclosure with RL to JPT, Nov. 21, 1919. Beginning in early December, Tumulty resumed his role as chief adviser to Wilson and saw him frequently. Meanwhile, as documents in this volume have revealed, Tumulty, both on his own and in conjunction with various administration leaders, conducted the domestic business of the Executive branch. For example, as we have seen, Tumulty wrote Wilson's message vetoing the Volstead bill and, in cooperation with Hines and members of the cabinet, the statement on the coal strike attributed to Wilson.

[7] Wilson's Annual Message printed at Dec. 2, 1919.

APPENDIX II

WOODROW WILSON'S STROKE OF
OCTOBER 2, 1919
BY BERT E. PARK, M.D., M.A.

Woodrow Wilson was seriously ill when he embarked upon his western speaking tour on September 3, 1919, a fact of which only his physician, Dr. Cary T. Grayson, and a handful of close associates were aware.[1] Wilson had long suffered from untreated malignant hypertension, the effects of which can be described as follows:

He suffered from chronic elevations of blood pressure, which affect the body in several ways. Forced to pump blood against sustained resistance in peripheral blood vessels, the heart eventually enlarges and then fails. The kidneys become incompetent filters through which toxic wastes are excreted, a reflection of progressive vascular damage in this and virtually every other organ in the body—among them, the eyes, with resultant retinal hemorrhages and exudates, and the brain, leading to premature atherosclerosis, blockage, or even rupture of small vessels within its depths.

Enough patients have been followed through the years to divide the progression of untreated hypertension into three states. During the first three to six years of sustained blood-pressure elevations, the patient remains asymptomatic. Once hypertension reaches an accelerated phase, retinal hemorrhages result, and headaches become pervasive. Over the next two to four years, signs of cardiac and renal insufficiency appear, and strokes occur. By then, the disease has reached a "malignant," or fulminant, stage.[2]

Even if we ignore a series of minor strokes that appear to have affected Wilson's right arm at the turn of the century, his first retinal hemorrhage in 1906 is a matter of record and represents prima facie evidence of the presence of accelerated hypertension. Moreover, its occurrence at Wilson's relatively young age of forty-nine attests to the severity of his underlying condition. That thirteen further years of this untreated disorder would lead to disastrous consequences should come as no surprise.

Long before entering public office, Wilson had been plagued by incessant headaches; by 1913, he was taking so many medicines for them that Dr. Grayson felt compelled to streamline his therapeutic regimen.[3] Yet hypertension continued its inexorable pro-

[1] Bert E. Park, "Wilson's Neurologic Illness during the Summer of 1919," printed as an Appendix in Vol. 62; R. S. Baker Diary, printed at Nov. 5, 1919; I. H. Hoover memoir, printed as Appendix I in this volume.
[2] Adams, R. D., and Victor, M., *Principles of Neurology*, 4th edn. (New York: McGraw Hill, 1989), p. 677.
[3] Baker Diary, printed at Nov. 5, 1919. Grayson, Cary T., *Woodrow Wilson: An Intimate Memoir* (New York: Holt, Rinehart and Winston, 1960), pp. 2-3.

gression. By 1916, Wilson's kidneys showed signs of malfunctioning. It was only a matter of time before his heart would begin to fail, which became manifest while he was still in Paris during the spring of 1919. This was followed by at least one further stroke and a host of intermittent cognitive disturbances during the summer, the most notable of which was his performance before the Senate Foreign Relations Committee on August 19, 1919.[4]

If such developments were lost on most of Wilson's contemporaries, hypertension's physical manifestations could no longer be ignored once the tour began. Grayson himself alludes in his diary to Wilson's headaches on at least nine separate occasions, the last of which, just prior to the President's collapse, he describes as being so "splitting" that Wilson "could hardly see."[5] Moreover, Grayson had despaired over Wilson's fatigue for so long that, by September 25, even the newspaper correspondents were taking notice.[6] Added to this list of symptoms in Grayson's diary were eight separate references to "congestion," nightly coughing spells, and "asthmatic attacks" that prevented Wilson from sleeping.[7] On September 26, these telltale signs of congestive heart failure reached crisis proportions; indeed, Grayson's diary entry just the day before includes a classic description of that condition.[8]

Despite the inroads that long-standing hypertension makes on the thought processes of its victims—and which Wilson had transiently manifested before undertaking the speaking tour—a superficial reading of his speeches might suggest that he remained an effective speaker to the very end. Speaking extemporaneously from brief outlines, Wilson incorporated a variety of themes in well-constructed arguments in his earlier speeches. As one measure of his adaptability, he approached similar points from differing perspectives and rarely fell back on stock phrases or trite clichés to embellish his points. All of this was testimony to his will power, endurance, and genius, which even physiologic adversity could not completely compromise. Even so, Wilson's physical deterioration ultimately took a noticeable toll toward the end of the western tour. Many of his later speeches were uncharacteristically repetitive, rambling, and poorly constructed. Moreover, a disdain for weighing new facts and a perceptible rigidity in his thinking became apparent as the tour dragged on.

That disaster impended was intimated by two reports which alluded to at least two separate stroke warnings before the Presi-

---

[4] A transcript of which is printed at that date in Vol. 62; see also my essay, cited above.
[5] Grayson Diary, printed at Sept. 25, 1919.
[6] See the news report printed at Sept. 25, 1919.
[7] See, for example, the Grayson Diary, printed at Sept. 23 and 27, 1919.
[8] *Ibid.*, Sept. 25, 1919.

dent's overt breakdown occurred. At one point on the trip, Grayson noticed "a curious drag or looseness of the left side" of Wilson's mouth, which he recognized as a "sign of danger that could no longer be obscured." A later news release alluded to a "fatigue neurosis," which at one point on the tour was said to "have affected the nerves of one of his arms and to have been responsible for a twitching of the muscles of his face."[9]

All observers were in error in at least one respect: Wilson's left-sided facial twitch was a chronic affliction that was unrelated to temporary decreases of blood to the brain. As has been outlined in some detail in a previous study,[10] this "nervous tic" was a classic manifestation of what neurologists today call "hemifacial spasm." This is caused by a blood vessel compressing the facial nerve as it exits from the brain stem and is related neither to vascular insufficiency nor hypertension. Yet the "looseness" of his mouth was a different matter entirely, which would become all too obvious once the fateful stroke occurred on October 2.

This is the way matters stood in the early morning hours of September 26, when Wilson's first collapse occurred after his speech the evening before in Pueblo, Colorado. Whether or not an overt stroke warning (a "transient ischemic attack") resulted is unclear, as the data is somewhat contradictory. Whereas Grayson found his patient out of sorts and in a "highly nervous condition," he did not mention the transient paralysis of Wilson's left arm to which both Mrs. Wilson and Joseph P. Tumulty later alluded.[11] Either way, the cumulative strain on his heart, and an apparent acceleration of his hypertension, were such that Wilson himself believed that he "had gone to pieces." For one thing, he was unable to sleep, having experienced the "worst asthmatic attack" of the entire trip. For another thing, he was suffering from a severe headache and intractable nausea. Although Grayson ascribed these symptoms to a "nervous reaction in his digestive organs,"[12] the evidence suggests an exacerbation of Wilson's heart failure under the duress of an acute hypertensive crisis. The latter not only gives rise to headache and nausea; focal deficits such as a transient paralysis may also occur. As a consequence, the patient becomes anxious and agitated, just as Wilson did.

Wilson's first breakdown on September 26, then, was not a

[9] Baker Diary, printed at Nov. 5, 1919; second news report printed at Oct. 17, 1919.
[10] Park, B. E., *The Impact of Illness on World Leaders* (Philadelphia: University of Pennsylvania Press, 1986), p. 11.
[11] Grayson Diary, printed at Sept. 26, 1919; and Weinstein, E. A., *Woodrow Wilson: A Medical and Psychological Biography* (Princeton: Princeton University Press, 1980), p. 355.
[12] Grayson Diary, printed at Sept. 26, 1919.

stroke; rather, at this point Wilson's blood pressure was simply running out of control. This may induce swelling of the blood vessels and the optic nerve that any eye specialist can readily diagnose by examining the retina, just as Dr. George Edmund de Schweinitz did two weeks later, when he described a "local congestion" in the eye similar to the findings he had uncovered while Wilson was ill in Paris.[13] This condition, known as "papilledema," takes a number of weeks to resolve. That De Schweinitz documented such congestion well into the second week of Wilson's illness in September and October is confirmatory physical evidence that Wilson's hypertension had reached a crescendo at the end of the western tour.

Dr. Grayson recognized this convergence of symptoms as a portentous development. Therefore his ministrations to the President, and the appropriate restrictions he placed on him, reflect well on Grayson as a physician.

But it was left to Ray Stannard Baker and Irwin Hood Hoover to reveal for posterity that Wilson had in fact suffered a severe stroke, which paralyzed his left side, on October 2 after returning to Washington. Despite the speculations of Senator Moses and others to that effect in the press, the furthest that Grayson's medical bulletins ever went was to describe Wilson's collapse as "nervous exhaustion," a condition he later upgraded to a "functional," not organic, "fatigue neurosis."[14]

However, to suggest that medical knowledge at the time precluded arriving at a definitive diagnosis, or that Grayson may have believed that exhaustion alone was the real culprit is hard to believe in view of the fact that Grayson knew that Wilson had suffered a devastating paralysis.[15] It is significant that he refused to comment on Moses' assertion.[16]

One might assume that, as a general practitioner, Grayson was merely adhering to the diagnosis of "nervous exhaustion" (i.e., "neurasthenia") rendered by his neurologic consultant, Dr. Francis X. Dercum. To conclude otherwise, then, requires examining the data in some detail in relation to what was known of both neurasthenia and stroke at the time and Grayson's refusal to affirm publicly any diagnosis other than the former.

Textbooks of Grayson's day defined neurasthenia and stroke as two distinctly different entities.[17] Not only were strokes recognized

---

[13] See the second news report printed at Oct. 12, 1919.
[14] See the first news report printed at Oct. 3, 1919, and the second news report printed at Oct. 17, 1919.
[15] See the Hoover memoir, printed as Appendix I in this volume.
[16] See the first news report printed at Oct. 12, 1919.
[17] See, for example, *A Text-Book of Medicine*, R. L. Cecil, ed. (Philadelphia and Lon-

to be caused by structural lesions of the brain on the basis of thrombosis or embolism, but strokes involving the carotid, middle cerebral, and perforating arteries were already so explicitly described in the literature of that time that even the general practitioner was expected to know the difference between them and neurasthenia. The only instance in which confusion might arise between stroke and neurasthenia was when "brain softening" due to a thrombosis failed to give rise to focal symptoms such as a paralysis. Those rare occurrences, interestingly enough, occasionally appeared "under the guise of *neurasthenia*." Yet the constancy of symptoms and signs of vascular disease elsewhere, "especially in the retina," were said to "readily clarify the diagnosis."[18]

Neurasthenia, on the other hand, was described by textbooks of the day as a "functional neurosis of fatigue," or "pathological fatigue," brought on, in large measure, by overwork and worry, alcohol poisoning, "excessive sexual indulgence," etc., particularly among urban dwellers. It was expected "to yield readily to very simple treatments of the nerves," including enforced bed rest and dietary modification, particularly the ingestion of milk. No other disorder was said to have produced "such a multiplicity of symptoms . . . of the subjective physical type," among them tremor, fatigue, indigestion, palpitations, headaches, and insomnia.[19] No wonder Grayson proposed just such a diagnosis to explain Wilson's collapse in late September 1919; after all, his patient initially had most of the symptoms described.

Yet to diagnose a devastating paralysis as resulting from neurasthenia six days later ignored the wisdom embodied in virtually every general medical textbook of that time, which precluded the diagnosis of neurasthenia if an underlying structural lesion of the brain was present. Indeed, Dercum denied that he himself had made the diagnosis of neurasthenia after examining Wilson on October 3. He took great pains instead to emphasize that he had "merely confirmed Dr. Grayson's diagnosis," and not the other way around.[20] This was the only instance in which he publicly commented on Wilson's illness. As perhaps the most esteemed neurologist of his day, Dercum could not have failed to recognize that Wilson was now paralyzed; he obviously knew the difference between a stroke and neurasthenia.

---

don: W. B. Saunders Co., 1927), pp. 1308-1309 and 1419-24. Medical textbooks as a rule reflect the thinking and practice of medicine over the preceding decade. The 1927 edition would, therefore, represent medical thought on strokes and neurasthenia as of 1919.

[18] *Ibid.*, p. 1309.
[19] *Ibid.*, pp. 1419-26.
[20] See the second news report printed at Oct. 3, 1919.

Dr. Young, unwittingly, it would seem, revealed the truth, at least partially, in an interview with a reporter for the Baltimore *Sun* printed in that newspaper on February 10, 1920. "As you know," Dr. Young said, "in October last we diagnosed the President's illness as a thrombosis, (clot in a blood vessel), which affected his left arm and leg."

It now seems beyond doubt that the diagnoses that could account for Wilson's left-sided paralysis include the following: (1) a hypertension-related occlusion or bursting of a small perforating vessel deep within the right side of the brain, where the tracts controlling motor function converge; (2) an occlusion of the carotid artery or its major intracranial branch, the middle cerebral artery, which supplies the overlying cortex of the right side of the brain; or (3) a blood clot under the brain cover, known as a "subdural hematoma," which resulted from the blow sustained during Wilson's fall from the toilet on the morning of his stroke.

The second diagnosis seems the most plausible, and for the following reasons. As for a clot overlying the brain, it would be unlikely that such profound deficits would evolve so rapidly after the fall. Typically, in such cases paralysis and an altered level of consciousness occur slowly over time, as pressure on the brain accumulates. As for the possibility of an occlusion or rupture of a deeply seated vessel in the brain, previous essays in this series have already proposed that just such events had occurred in Wilson's past medical history.[21] Yet, as a rule, these are neither as long lasting nor as devastating as Wilson's final stroke proved to be. For the remainder of his life, he had profound weakness of his left arm and leg, along with the loss of his entire left-sided field of vision. This combination of deficits can only occur in large-vessel occlusions, such as a thrombosis of the carotid or middle cerebral arteries. It is often preceded by transient stroke warnings, two of which appear in the record shortly before Wilson's stroke of October 2 occurred.

The issue of presidential disability warrants some further comment. That Wilson was disabled for at least the first month of his illness in the constitutional sense, such that he was unable to carry out the duties of the office, the documents in this volume make clear. It was not until October 13 that he was able to perform any but the most rudimentary duties, and another two weeks before he was well enough to meet with a cabinet member.[22] Even then, his performance from that point on was minimal at best; witness Lan-

[21] See the Appendixes to Volumes 58 and 62.
[22] See the second news report printed at Oct. 13, 1919, and A. M. Palmer to R. S. Morris, Nov. 3, 1919.

sing's comments on November 5 regarding the Thanksgiving Day Proclamation, which he cited as evidence that Wilson was still unable to handle the duties of his office.[23]

As was said in the essay on Wilson's health during the summer of 1919 in Volume 62, impairment can be quantitated on the basis of specific criteria outlined by the American Medical Association's *Guides to the Evaluation of Permanent Impairment*.[24] Using these criteria, as was said in the essay just mentioned, Wilson would have been certified as being from 15 to 45 per cent impaired even before he embarked on the western tour. These same criteria can now be used to quantify the progression of Wilson's impairment following his stroke in early October.

With regard to disturbances in complex and integrated functions, not only was Wilson unable to perform at a level even approaching "most activities of daily living as well as before onset"; he was forbidden to do so. That equates by today's standards with at least 15 per cent impairment. Taking the next criterion of emotional disturbance, Grayson's notation of his patient's "nervous anxiety," and Wilson's own poignant surmise that he "had gone to pieces," far exceeds the lowest level of compromise defined as "mild to moderate emotional disturbance under stress." That represents an additional 15 per cent impairment. Third, for the first three to four weeks at least after his stroke, Wilson alternated between fitful sleep and varying levels of consciousness, more than adequate impairment to equate with a 5 to 15 per cent deficiency. Finally, his documented hemifacial spasm, variable speech disturbances, and overt paralysis fit that category defined as "neurologic disturbances" to the letter. This is not even to mention his congestive heart failure and underlying hypertension, both with their own assigned percentages of impairment. Most important of all, percentages from separate categories are *additive* in computing impairment, attesting to the conclusion that Wilson would be defined today during the first month of his illness at a level well above 50 per cent impairment of the whole person.[25]

Wilson's disability had obvious consequences for immediate events. If he had taken the League's critics to task during the speaking tour, he did so with all of the decorum and propriety that befitted his office. After his collapse, he heaped vengeance upon them. That extended to some of his subordinates, as Lansing would soon discover. Yet making speeches before succumbing to

[23] See Lansing's memorandum printed at Nov. 5, 1919.
[24] American Medical Association, *Guides to the Evaluation of Permanent Impairment*, 2nd edn. (Chicago: American Medical Association, 1984), x.
[25] *Ibid.*, p. 63.

illness was one thing; formulating policy with decisive action after suffering a stroke was quite another. As fate would have it, delicate political and diplomatic questions came to a head on or about the very day that Wilson broke down in Colorado. With the Italian government threatened by dissolution, members of the American commission in Paris were urgently in need of further instructions from their President. At home, opposition in the Senate to an unqualified acceptance of the League Covenant, revolving in particular around Article X, solidified within the same week. Although Wilson acted with dispatch to address both problems, this would be the last such activity his associates would see until January, at the earliest. Now, others such as Tumulty and Lansing, began to act in Wilson's stead, whether that applied to the pending Industrial Conference, the nationwide coal strike, a deteriorating situation in Russia, or simply running cabinet meetings.

To summarize, Wilson's underlying hypertension and congestive heart failure had no appreciable impact on the speaking tour itself, except insofar as they accounted for an occasional ineffective speech, until they led to the trip's abrupt termination. Nor would Wilson's stroke five days later have been prevented had Grayson acted any differently; given the natural history of the disease, a cerebrovascular collapse was long overdue. Equally certain, Wilson was seriously disabled, both in a medical and constitutional sense, despite Grayson's and other doctors' assertions to the contrary. Following on the heels of previous physiologic insults to his brain, neither Wilson's thought processes nor his conduct in office would ever be the same again. Insofar as this would have a dramatic impact on the most important political struggle Wilson ever faced, that story remains to be told. It constitutes the heart of Volume 64 of *The Papers*.

INDEX

NOTE ON THE INDEX

THE alphabetically arranged analytical table of contents at the front of the volume eliminates duplication, in both contents and index, of references to certain documents, such as letters. Letters are listed in the contents alphabetically by name, and chronologically within each name by page. The subject matter of all letters is, of course, indexed. The Editorial Notes and Wilson's writings are listed in the contents chronologically by page. In addition, the subject matter of both categories is indexed. The index covers all references to books and articles mentioned in text or notes. Footnotes are indexed. Page references to footnotes which place a comma between the page number and "n" cite both text and footnote, thus: "418,n1." On the other hand, absence of the comma indicates reference to the footnote only, thus: "59n1"—the page number denoting where the footnote appears.

The index supplies the fullest known form of names and, for the Wilson and Axson families, relationships as far down as cousins. Persons referred to by nicknames or shortened forms of names can be identified by reference to entries for these forms of the names.

All entries consisting of page numbers only and which refer to concepts, issues, and opinions (such as democracy, the tariff, money trust, leadership, and labor problems), are references to Wilson's speeches and writings.

Four cumulative contents-index volumes are now in print: Volume 13, which covers Volumes 1-12, Volume 26, which covers Volumes 14-25, Volume 39, which covers Volumes 27-38, and Volume 52, which covers Volumes 40-49 and 51.

INDEX

Adamic, Louis, 238n1, 273n2
Adams, Alva, 500,n1
Addresses of President Wilson, 19n, 42n, 117n, 131n, 138n, 148n, 162n2, 180n, 197n, 221n, 234n, 252n, 388n, 407n, 418n, 427n, 441n, 448n, 463n, 484n, 513n
Adee, Alvey Augustus, 58,n1
Adrianople, Turkey, 236
Adriatic question, 91-92; Clemenceau and Lloyd George's recommendations, 204-206; Polk on prospects of final settlement, 204-10; Vittorio Emanuele appeals to WW for settlement of, 270, 297-98; WW's terms for settlement, 270-71; Fiume is obstacle in settlement of, 393; Polk on severe crisis, 524-25, 525-26; WW on reinforcements for Spalato, 532; WW on not yielding his position on, 534; and U.S. naval forces, 556-57, 557n,2; Italian troops in Trau, 557,n1,2; WW unable to address issue, EBW tells Lansing to hold decision, 617,n1; *see also* Fiume
African Methodist Episcopal Zion Church (Washington, D.C.), 268n1
aircraft: torpedo and bombing tests and projects, 441-42,n1,2
Alaskan Railroad, 608
Albania: and Adriatic question, 206, 208, 209, 270, 364
Albert, King of the Belgians, 21, 119, 166, 259, 515, 526, 542; wishes to bestow honors on WW and other officials, 307-308; WW cannot accept proposed decoration by, 392; WW's illness causes change in plans, 528, 532, 543; get-well wishes to WW, 535-36; received by WW, 602-606
Albona (now Labin, Yugoslavia), 205, 298
Allen, Ben Farwell, 275-76,n4
Alsace-Lorraine, 132
Amalgamated Association of Iron, Steel, and Tin Workers, 30n1
Ambrosius, Lloyd E., 482n3
American Commission on Irish Independence, 118n2
American Committee for the Independence of Armenia, 304n1
American Federation of Labor, 30n1; and Washington, D.C., police situation, 149-50; and Boston police strike, 167,n6, 267; and police, 295
American Indians, 168
American Mercury, 238n1
American Revolution, 26, 429
Anaconda Copper Mining Company, 610n1
Anderson, Albert Barnes, 612n1
Anderson, Mary, 56-57, 58-59
Andrews, Philip, 485,n3, 486n7, 525
Armenia: WW on, 71, 458; issue of U.S. troops to, 304, 423, 464, 466
Armour, Norman, 307,n1, 308
arms limitation: *see* disarmament

Army (U.S.): *see* United States Army
Ashurst, Henry Fountain, 118,n3, 483, 535, 586
Asia Minor, 60
"'Assassin' of Wilson" (Adamic), 238n1, 273n2
Assling railroad, 206
Assling Triangle, 206, 208
Associated Business Men's Clubs of San Francisco, 340,n1
Associated Press, 52n4, 547n5
Associated Women's Clubs of San Francisco: Grayson on WW's address to, 308-309; WW's notes for address to, 309-10; WW's address to, 311-22
Atlantic Monthly, 387n4
Australia: WW on, 477, 505
Austria, 20, 24; and International Labor Conference, 62, 91; *see also* Paris Peace Conference—*Austrian treaty*
Austria-Hungary: WW on, 10; war costs, 221, 243, 349; battle deaths, 222, 243, 349
Azerbaijan, 157, 348

Badoglio, Pietro, 485,n2
Baker, George Luis, 275,n3, 284n1
Baker, Newton Diehl, 164, 223, 274, 361, 421, 548, 585; on Pomerene's concern over reservationists' strategy, 296; suggested resolution honoring Foch, 301; on horrors of next war and aircraft bombing projects, 441-42,n1,2; offers to help EBW to lessen WW's work load, 534; and Siberian situation, 559, 560
Baker, Ray Stannard, 6; on WW's health, 539n1, 619-22, 642; and second Industrial Conference appointments, 609, 621
Bakhmet'ev, Boris Aleksandrovich, 394,n2, 589
Balfour, Arthur James: and Thrace, 60, 120; and International Labor Conference, 62; and Adriatic question, 91, 92, 207, 208-209, 210; desire to ajourn Council of the Heads of Delegations, 306; WW declines rectorship offered by University of Glasgow, 395-96
Balkans, The, 61, 188, 485, 537n1
Baltimore and Ohio Railroad Company, 607n1
Baltimore *Sun*, 275n4, 643
Bamberger, Simon, 449,n1
Barnes, Julius Howland: and flour to Russia, 589-90
Barnum, Gertrude, 57,n4
Barquero, Francisco Aguilar, 616,n1
Bartlett, Louis, 350,n2
Bartlett, Ruhl Jacob, 223n1
Baruch, Bernard Mannes, 551; and steel strike situation, 53, 149, 300, 301; on police crisis in Washington, D.C., and labor, 149-50; appointed to Industrial Conferences, 300,n1, 336, 611

Beck, James Montgomery: WW on, 625

Belgium, 232; WW on, 21-22, 45-46, 242-43, 258-59, 427; King Albert wishes to bestow honors on WW and other officials, 307-308; war costs, 349; plans for Albert's visit to U.S., 515, 526, 532; King, Queen, and Prince visit WW in his sickroom, 602-606

Belleau Wood, Battle of, WW on, 432, 450, 469

Benedict XV, Pope: get-well wishes from, 555

Berkeley, California: WW's address in, 350-52; photograph of WW in, *illustration section*

Berkeley Daily Gazette, 350n2, 352n

Billings, Montana: WW's arrival and reception in, 168; WW's address in, 170-80

Billings, Mont.., Gazette, 162n, 163n, 168n2, 180n

Bingham, Robert, 256-57,n3

Bingham School (North Carolina), 256n3

Bismarck, North Dakota: WW's arrival and activities in, 152-53; WW's address in, 153-62; photograph of WW in, *illustration section*

Bismarck Daily Tribune, 162n

Blacks: *see* Negroes

Bliss, Tasker Howard, 91, 537; and Bullitt testimony, 337n1

Blum, John Morton, 601n1

Bohemia, 10, 11, 24, 82, 186

Bolsheviks and Bolshevism, 394, 588-89,n1; WW on, 73, 134, 214; *see also* Russia

Bonar Law, Andrew, 306, 307

Bonsor, William T., 303

Borah, William Edgar, 210, 223n1; and reservations, 296, 482-83

Bosnia, Yugoslavia, 372

Boss Kettering (Leslie), 441n2

Boston police strike, 167,n6,7, 265, 267, 302; WW learns of and comments on, 169, 196, 211, 216

"Boston Police Strike of 1919" (Lyons), 167n6

Botha, Louis: WW on, 286, 287, 477, 505

Bowen, William Miller, 423n2

Boxer Rebellion, 329

Boyana River, 210

Boyd, David French, 557n2

Boyle, Emmet Derby, 53, 54, 428,n1

Bradfute, Oscar Edwin: appointed to first Industrial Conference, 300,n1

Brady, James Buchanan ("Diamond Jim"), 579,n2

Brahany, Thomas W., 302,n2, 524, 532

Brandegee, Frank Bosworth, 445, 484; and Bullitt testimony, 337n1

Brandeis, Louis Dembitz: suggested for second Industrial Conference appointment, 609; on postponing appointments to second Industrial Conference, 618

Brazil, 232

Brewster, Thomas T., 56,n5

Britain: *see* Great Britain

Britain and the Russian Civil War, November 1918-February 1920 (Ullman), 588n1

Brody, David, 30n1

Brookings, Robert Somers: appointed to first Industrial Conference, 300,n1

Brotherhood of Electrical Workers, 29n2

Brown, William Cornelius, 268,n1

Brownlow, Louis: and police situation in Washington, 150,n1, 264-65, 295, 302

Bryan "cooling-off" treaties, 66,n7, 67

Budziszewski, Cora, 250,n2

Bugbee, Newton Albert Kendall, 615n1

Bulgaria: and Thrace, 61, 121, 122, 151,n4, 236, 305; war costs, 221, 243, 349; *see also* Paris Peace Conference—*Bulgarian treaty*

Bullard, Robert Lee, 362,n1

Bullitt, William Christian: testimony before Foreign Relations Committee impeaches Lansing's loyalty to WW, and Lansing's explanation to WW, 337-38,n1; Lansing on statement on treaty by, 541

Bullitt Mission to Russia: Testimony Before the Committee on Foreign Relations, United States Senate (Bullitt), 337n1

Burgess, Ward: appointed to first Industrial Conference, 300,n1

Burleson, Albert Sidney, 585; on strategy for treaty ratification, 266; on progress of enlisting cotton producers to support treaty, 442-43; on position of Tennessee's senators on treaty, 443; offers get-well wishes and informs WW of improving Senate situation, 534-35

Burnquist, Joseph Alfred Arner, 122,n1, 124, 125,n2, 126, 128, 131,n1

Burton, Theodore Elijah, 228,n2

Butler, Harold Beresford, 445-46,n1

Cabinet (U.S.): *see* Wilson, Woodrow—*Cabinet*

California, University of (Berkeley), 340n3; WW speaks in Greek Theater at, 340n1

Callaway, Fuller Earle: appointed to first Industrial Conference, 300,n1

Calvin Coolidge: The Quiet President (McCoy), 167n6

Cameroons, The, 422

Campbell, James Edwin, 7,n1

Canada: WW on, 232, 477-78, 505

Canning, George, 192,n2, 430, 431

Capper, Arthur: WW wishes to answer on Shantung settlement, 519

Carey, Robert Davis, 467,n1

Carlyle, Thomas, 12

Carranza, Venustiano, 165

Casalgiate, Enrico Millo di, 557n1

Casey, Michael, 269

Catholic Church: *see* Roman Catholic Church

Catholic University of America, 603

Cattaro (now Kotor, Yugoslavia), 206, 465, 525

Cecil, Lord Robert (Edgar Algernon Robert Gascoyne-): WW on, 286, 287

Cellere, Count Vincenzo Macchi di, 298n1

Central Presbyterian Church of Des Moines, 92,n1

Chadbourne, Thomas Lincoln, Jr.: appointed to first Industrial Conference, 300,n1

Chamberlin, William Henry, 588n1

Chan, Loren B., 426n1, 428n1

Chandler, Charles S., 428,n1

Chandler, Harry, 423,n3

Charles Albert of Savoy, King of Sardinia, 514,n4

Chase, Benjamin Franklin, 616n1

Chase, Stuart, 389n2

Chase, Perley Morse & Co., 389n2

Château Thierry, Battle of: WW on, 432, 450, 469

Cherso (now Cres, Yugoslavia), 205, 207

Cheyenne, Wyoming, 446; WW's arrival and address in, 467, 467-82

Cheyenne *Wyoming State Tribune*, 487

Chicago *Evening Post*, 399

Chicago Federation of Labor, 30n1

China: WW on historical background of Shantung settlement, 314-17, 436-40; WW on treaty as hope for, 427, 461-62; *see also* Shantung settlement

Christmas: Its Unfinished Business (Crothers), 387,n4

Cincinnati Enquirer, 552n2

City in Terror, 1919: The Boston Police Strike (Russell), 167n6

Civil War (U.S.): WW on, 145-46, 172, 234

Clagett, Maurice Brice, 595,n1

Clemenceau, Georges, 120, 306, 343, 527; and Constantinople issue, 60, 61; on Adriatic question and Fiume, 204-206, 208, 209, 210, 364, 393, 424, 465, 526, 617n1; House on growing enthusiasm for League of Nations by, 271-72; on Paris Peace Conference, 299; and issue of French ships contracted for in U.S., 366-69; issue of troops to Armenia, 466; WW on, 604; Baker on anecdote about WW and, 621

Cleveland *Plain Dealer*, 275

Close, Gilbert Fairchild, 526; on WW's work habits, 513-14

coal: WW on situation in Europe, 156

coal industry: strike threat creates crisis situation, 54-55, 55, 56, 593-94, 595-97; WW's statement on proposed strike, 599-601; Palmer meets with WW on, 608,n1; restraining order against strike, 612,n1; Brandeis on injunction, 618

Coal Operators Association, 56n5

Cochran, William Joseph Hamilton, 151,n3; on situation in Senate and Foreign Relations Committee on treaty reservations, 198, 483, 483-84

Coeur d'Alene, Idaho: WW's arrival and activities in, 210-11; WW's address in, 212-21

Coeur d'Alene Evening Press, 210n1

Coffman, Noah Beery, 241,n1

collective bargaining: and first Industrial Conference stalemate, 582-83, 584n1

Colt, LeBaron Bradford: and reservations, 150, 296, 444, 445

Columbus, Ohio: WW's arrival in, 3; WW's address in, 7-18

Columbus *Ohio State Journal*, 3n5, 18n

Colver, William Byron, 301, 425; on differences with Food Administration, 389-91

Commission on the League of Nations: WW explains efforts of, 285-86

Congress (U.S.): *see* United States Congress

Congressional Record, 66th Cong., 1st sess., 3n4, 52n3, 198n1,3,4, 304n1, 389n, 531n4, 557n1, 601n1

Congress of Vienna, 429

conscientious objectors: Sinclair and petition for amnesty, 425,n1

Consolidated Coal Company (Baltimore), 56n2

Constantine I (of Greece), 61

Constantinople, 59n2, 60-62, 121, 236, 337n1; WW on, 34-35, 188, 342

Constitution (U.S.): *see* United States Constitution

Coolidge, Archibald Cary, 209

Coolidge, Calvin: and Boston police strike, 167n6, 169; WW's election congratulations and Coolidge's response, 615,n1

Cossacks, 559, 560

Costa Rica: Lansing recommends recognizing, 616; political situation in, 616n1

cost of living, 46, 125-29, 596, 599; Hines on, 119; WW addresses Minnesota legislature on, 123

cotton: Burleson on treaty support by producers of, 442-43

cotton situation: Burleson on, 266

Cottrell (or Cotterell), C. R., 273n2

Council of Four: WW on, 99, 343; Bullitt on, 337n1

Council of the Heads of Delegations, 61,n2; and Rumania, 119-20,n2,3; and adjournment issue, 299, 306, 391, 422, 537

Council of the League of Nations, 260, 328-29, 414

Council of Ten: Bullitt on, 337n1

Cowgill, James S., 63,n1

Cowles, Ione Virginia Hill (Mrs. Josiah Evans), 407n1, 423,n3

Craufurd-Stuart, Charles Kennedy, 606,n1

Creel, George, 625

Croatians: and Fiume, 486

Crothers, Samuel McChord, 387,n4

Crowe, Sir Eyre, 307, 422, 588

Cuba: WW on Spanish-American War and, 184, 434, 455

Curtis, Edwin Upton, 167n6

Curzon, George Nathaniel, 1st Marquess of Kedleston, 306

Czechoslovakia, 188; and Czech troops in Russia: request and approval of repatriation loan, 394, 394-95, 421, 518

Da Costa, John Chalmers, 546,n1, 551n1; visit to WW in Paris, 546,n1, 551n1, 567-68

Dairen, China: see Talien-wan
Dalmatia, 206, 208, 365; and D'Annunzio incursion, 517,n2
Daniels, Jonathan, 419n1
Daniels, Josephus, 239, 419n1, 556-57, 598; on WW's health, 548, 552, 555, 557; on Cabinet meeting, 555, 598; on U.S. naval forces to Trau and Adriatic region, 556-57, 557; on Siberian situation and Cossacks, 559, 560; on threatened coal strike, 598; and WW's veto of Volstead bill, 601n1; on appointment suggestions for second Industrial Conference, 609, 610, 612; on Brandeis' suggestion of postponing appointments to second Industrial Conference, 618
D'Annunzio, Gabriele: occupation of Fiume, 298,n2, 364-65, 419n1, 486, 516-17; incursion into Dalmatia, 517,n2
Davie, John Leslie, 352n1
Davis, David J., 29-30,n1
Davis, David William, 210-11, 212
Davis, Edward Parker, 166, 167, 634
Davis, Ellen Duane (Mrs. Edward Parker), 166
Davis, John William, 606n1
Davis, Nellie Johnson (Mrs. David William), 211,n3
Davis, Norman Hezekiah, 268
Dawes, Charles Gates: appointed to first Industrial Conference, 300,n1
Dayton Wright Airplane Company, 441n2
Deák, Francis, 61n2
De Bon, Ferdinand Jean Jacques, 485-86,n5
Debs, Eugene Victor, 238n1, 273n2
Declaration of Independence: WW on, 360
Dedeagatch (now Alexandroupolis, Greece), 121, 236, 305
Democratic National Committee, 151n3
Democratic party, 26, 228; outlook for ratification of Versailles Treaty, 151; and League to Enforce Peace's prediction on treaty ratification, 235; WW on, 417-18; and reservations to Article X, 444-45, 530-31; and reservation issue in Senate, 586
Denikin, Anton Ivanovich, 394
Dennis, John Benjamin, 544,n2, 579
Dennison, Ohio, 3,n2
Denver, Colorado: WW's arrival in, 467; WW's address in, 487,n1, 490-500
Denver Post, 489n3, 500n, 515n, 524n
Denver Rocky Mountain News, 467n2, 487n1, 500n
Dercum, Francis Xavier, 539,n2, 543, 544, 546, 550, 551, 561, 578, 579, 581, 582, 634, 642
De Schweinitz, George: see Schweinitz, George de
Des Moines, Iowa: Grayson on WW's arrival and speech in, 65-66; WW's address in, 76-88; WW attends church in, 92
Des Moines Sunday Register, 88n
Dickson, Edward Augustus, 423,n3
Dietz, Leonora Antoinette Cooke (Mrs. Gould Price), 94,n1

Diplomacy, Scandal and Military Intelligence (Egerton), 606n1
disarmament: WW on, 68-69, 83, 136, 160, 260-61, 495; and Naval Appropriations Act of 1916, 169-70, 178, 219
District of Columbia: see Washington, D.C.
District of Columbia, Committee on (House of Reps.), 265
District of Columbia, Committee on (Senate): and police strike, 295, 302
Dodd, William Edward, 6
Dodecanese Islands, 392
Dodge, Cleveland Hoadley: get-well wishes to WW, 535
Drummond, Sir (James) Eric, 59, 445
Duncan, James A., 273n2
Dunne, Edward Fitzsimons, 118,n2
Durand, Walter Y., 389n2

Edge, Walter Evans, 203
Edge bill on foreign banking, 203
Education and Labor, Committee on (Senate), 30n1
Edward Albert Christian George Andrew Patrick David, Prince of Wales, 297,n1, 559
Edwards, Edward Irving: WW's election congratulations to, 615,n1
Edwards, Frances Louise Taft (Mrs. William Aloysius), 423,n3
Egerton, George, 606n1
Eliot, Charles William: appointed to first Industrial Conference, 300,n1
Elisabeth (Elisabeth Valerie), Queen of the Belgians, 21, 119, 166, 515, 526, 535-36, 542; WW's welcoming of canceled, 528; thanks EBW for flowers, sends WW get-well wishes, 548; received by WW, 602-606
Elliott, Edward Graham, 340n3
Elliott, Margaret Randolph Axson (Mrs. Edward Graham), sister of EAW, 340n3
Elmer Sperry: Inventor and Engineer (Hughes), 441n2
Endicott, Henry Bradford: appointed to first Industrial Conference, 300,n1
End of Innocence (Jonathan Daniels), 419n1
England: see Great Britain
Evans, Edward J., 29-30,n2

Fairweather, Tom Patterson, 65n4
Fall, Albert Bacon: and Bullitt testimony, 337n1; and amendments to treaty, 482,n2,4; meeting with WW during his illness, 637,n5
Fall amendments, 482,n2,4, 483-84
Farmers' Nonpartisan League: see Nonpartisan League
Fassett, Charles Marvin, 224,n1
Federal Trade Commission: and steel prices, 89-90, 301; and differences with Food Administration, 389-91, 425
Federal Trade Commission Act, 89
Feiss, Paul Louis: appointed to first Industrial Conference, 300,n1

Field, W. K., 56,n3
Fighting for the League (Chan), 428n1
Finance, Committee on (Senate), 203n3
First Duce: D'Annunzio at Fiume (Ledeen), 298n2, 517n2
Fitzgerald, Cecil Bernard, 254,n1
Fitzpatrick, John: on steel strike situation, 29-30,n1, 148-49, 164
Fiume, 91-92, 306-307, 617n1; WW's position on, 270, 424, 484-85, 543; invasion of by D'Annunzio, 298-99,n2, 364-66, 485; ongoing negotiations over, 364-66; Clemenceau urges WW to agree to Adriatic settlement, 393; Nitti's plea for, 464-65; Britain and France advocate Italy be given, 465-66; crisis in Italy over, 485-86, 516-17; Herron on WW yielding position on, 537,n1; and WW's health, 543
Foch, Ferdinand: suggested resolution honoring, 301n1,2
Food Administration: differences with Federal Trade Commission, 389, 390
Food Control Act of 1917: *see* Lever Food and Fuel Control Act
Food Control Act of 1919, 562n2, 571, 608
Foreign Affairs, Committee on (House of Reps.): WW on meeting with, 287, 288, 319, 326, 376, 510
Foreign Relations, Committee on (Senate): majority report on treaty, 52,n3; WW on meeting with, 86, 103, 247, 287, 288, 319, 326, 376, 510; and Irish situation, 118,n2; minority report on treaty, 198,n1; House on appearing before, 299; Bullitt's testimony before, 337-38,n1; and Armenia, 423; and Fall amendments, 482n2; and Article X, 529, 530n4, 531; I. H. Hoover on WW's meeting with, 632; and WW's health, 640
Forster, Rudolph, 51-52, 92, 117, 118, 198, 268, 295, 392, 444, 445, 447, 483, 522; on misinterpretation of WW's remarks on secret treaties, 93; on outlook for treaty ratification, 150-51; on Naval Appropriations Act and arbitration statement, 169-70; on plans for arrival of Albert, 526
Fort, John Franklin, 391,n6
Fort Abraham Lincoln (North Dakota), 152,n2
Fort Russell (Wyoming), 467
Forty-Two Years in the White House (I. H. Hoover), 539n1
Foster, William Zebulon, 29-30,n1, 149
Fourteen Points: mentioned, 222; WW on, 509
Fowler, Harry Atwood, 572,n2, 578,n1, 579, 581, 587
Fox, Albert W.: reports on WW's health, 543-45, 549-50, 552,n2
France: and Constantinople, 59n2; WW on French people, 132; and Shantung settlement, 193, 413, 438; war costs, 221, 243, 349; battle deaths, 222, 243, 349; and Czech troops in Russia, 394, 395; WW on business interests of, 397; and military sit-

uation in Fiume, 485-86; Rappard on WW's views of, 631; *see also* France and the United States, and under the names of spokesmen for, such as Clemenceau, Georges
France and the United States: controversy over ships ordered by France and not delivered, 366-69
Francis, David Rowland, 579
Francis Ferdinand, Archduke of Austria, 19-20,n1, 108, 187, 245, 359-60, 372-73
Frazier, Lynn Joseph, 153,n1
Fredericks, John Donnan, 423,n3
freedom of the seas: WW on, 384, 627
French Revolution, 12-13, 429
Fresno, Calif., Republican, 309n3
Fuel Administration (U.S.), 56n1, 596, 599

Gage, Lyman Judson, 370,n2, 383, 386
Gallagher, Andrew J., 269, 302-303
Gardner, Frederick Dozier, 31,n1, 33, 43
Garfield, Belle Hartford Mason (Mrs. Harry Augustus), 539,n3
Garfield, Harry Augustus, 54, 606; on coal situation, 54, 55, 56; receives detailed account of WW's condition, 538-39
Garfield, James Abram, 196, 555
Gary, Elbert Henry: and steel strike situation, 30n1, 66, 149; appointed to first Industrial Conference, 300,n1
Gasparri, Pietro Cardinal, 555
Gay, Edwin Francis: appointed to first Industrial Conference, 300,n1
Geneva, Switzerland: and League of Nations, 630, 631, 632,n1
George V (of Great Britain), 527
George Washington University, 544n3
Gerard, James Watson: get-well wishes to WW, 535
German propaganda in the United States: WW on resurgence of, 110, 143-44, 215, 292, 321, 333, 334, 385, 401, 456-57, 469-70, 501; WW on League of Nations opponents and, 447n1, 448
Germany: WW on rehabilitation of, 36-37; and International Labor Conference, 62, 91; battle deaths, 221, 243, 349; war costs, 221, 243, 349; and lifting of blockade, 266,n1; and China and Shantung settlement, 411-13, 437, 471, 507
Gibbon, Thomas Edward, 423,n3
Gibson, Hugh Simons, 82,n2
Giolitti, Giovanni, 486,n8
Glasgow, William Anderson, Jr., 390n4
Glasgow, University of: WW unable to accept rectorship of, 395-96
Glass, Carter, 421; on international financial situation and U.S. Treasury's position, 200-204, 336; on loan request for repatriation of Czech troops, 518; and WW's veto of Volstead bill, 601n1
Glynn, Martin Henry, 609,n1, 610, 611
Gneist, Rudolf von, 623
Gompers, Samuel, 52, 65, 148, 265; on steel industry and threatened strike, 29-30,n1,

Gompers, Samuel (*cont.*)
163; and Washington, D.C., police situation, 149-50; and threatened coal strike, 612n1
Gonzáles Flores, Alfredo, 616,n1
Goodrich, James Putnam, 4,n6
Gould, Ashley Mulgrave, 264-65,n1
Grain Corporation (U.S.): and flour to Russia, 588-90
Grant, Heber Jeddy, 449,n1
Grant, Ulysses Simpson, 453
Graves, William Sidney, 559
Grayson, Alice Gertrude (Altrude) Gordon (Mrs. Cary Travers), 619
Grayson, Cary Travers, 53, 149, 300, 419n1, 467, 526, 543, 544, 581, 593, 598, 606; WW's activities and speeches in Columbus, Ohio, and Indianapolis, 3-5; in St. Louis, 31-33; in Kansas City and Des Moines, 62-66; on tour in Omaha and Sioux Falls, 93-96; insists WW conserve his strength, 96; in Minnesota, 122-24; in Bismarck, 152-53; in Billings and Helena, 168-69; in Idaho and Spokane, 210-11; in Tacoma and Seattle, 236-40, 273; in Portland, 274-76; on WW's arrival, activities, and speeches in Oakland and San Francisco, 308-10, 340; notices first signs of break in WW, 338n4; on first test of "voice phone" by WW, 369-70; in San Diego, 369-70; in Los Angeles, 396-97, 423; in Sacramento and Reno, 426; concern over WW's health, 446, 488-90; in Ogden and Salt Lake City, 446; in Cheyenne, 467; in Denver and Pueblo, 487-90; WW's illness causes trip cancellation, 518-20; press statement on trip cancellation, 520; return to Washington, 526-27, 527-28, 532-33; bulletin on WW's health, 527; emphatic about strict rest for WW, 533; on WW's health, 537-38, 538-39, 542, 552,n1; and question of WW's disability, 547,n1; skill and devotion prevented earlier breakdown of WW's health, 550; on WW's improved condition, 552-53; reports to Cabinet on WW's health, 554, 555; more health bulletins issued, 568, 572, 574, 576-77, 577-78, 587, 590; on WW's mental condition and ability to work, but rest cure is priority, 569-71; R. S. Baker on, 620; reaction to WW's stroke, 634; Park on role of during WW's illness, 639-46; refuses to comment on report of a stroke, 642
Great Britain: and Constantinople, 59n2; and Shantung settlement, 193, 413, 438; war costs, 221, 243, 349; battle deaths, 222, 243, 349; WW on League of Nations Commission representatives from, 286; honors bestowed on Foch, 301n1; wishes to adjourn Council of Heads of Delegations, 306, 391; WW on voting power in League of Nations, 231-32, 309-10, 320-21, 328-29, 377-78, 414-15, 435-36, 476-77, 491-92, 504-505; and issue of ships ordered by France from U.S., 367-69; and Czech

troops in Russia, 394, 395; WW on business interests of, 397; troops withdrawn from Fiume, 485; *see also* Great Britain and the United States, and under the names of spokesmen for, such as Lloyd George, David
Great Britain and the United States: WW to receive the Prince of Wales, 297,n1; and Craufurd-Stuart affair, 606n1
Great Northern Railway, 124n5
Greece: and Thrace, 59n2, 60-62, 121-22, 305, 391-92
Gregory, Thomas Watt: and second Industrial Conference, 611
Grey, Edward, 1st Viscount Grey of Fallodon, 559; and Craufurd-Stuart affair, 606n1
Guides to the Evaluation of Permanent Impairment (American Medical Association), 644

Hague, The, 630
Hale, Reuben Brooks, 341,n1
Hamilton, Edward H., 309n2
Hannon, William, 29-30,n1, 149
Hanson, Ole, 238n1
Hapsburgs: WW on, 358
Harding, Warren Gamaliel: and Bullitt testimony, 337n1
Harding, William Lloyd, 65n4
Harrison, Fairfax, 607,n2
Harrison, Byron Patton (Pat), 483
Hart, Louis Folwell, 241,n1
Harvard University, 300n1
Haugen, Gilbert Nelson, 562n2
Hawkins, John Russell, 268,n1
Hay, John, 315, 330, 331, 332, 412, 437, 439, 460, 471, 496, 507
Hays, Will H. (William Harrison), 150, 484
Hearst, William Randolph, 167n7
Hearst newspapers, 398
Helena, Montana: WW's reception in, 168-69,n5; WW's address in, 180-97; address mentioned, 265, 267
Helena, Mont., Daily Independent, 169n5, 197n
Herford, Oliver, 350
Herron, George Davis: on Fiume, 537,n1
Hill, James Jerome, 124n5
Hill, Louis Warren, 124,n5
Hines, Walker Downer: on steel prices, 88-91, 118-19, 300-301; and coal strike, 595-96, 606
History of the American People (Wilson): WW presents set to Albert, 603
Hitchcock, Gilbert Monell, 6, 106, 117, 118, 296, 443, 593, 606; and Foreign Relations Committee's minority report, 198,n1; and Armenia, 304n1; and Bullitt's testimony, 337; on reservations, 363, 482-83, 483, 541, 586; WW seeks advice from on Article X and reservations, 447,n1; predicts defeat of Johnson and Shantung amendments, 482, 571; and compromise reservation on Article X, 530-31; on WW's

health, 566,n1, 570-71; meeting with WW during his illness, 637,n5
Hodgson, Laurence Curran, 124,n6, 138,n1, 139
Hohenzollerns, The: WW on, 358
Holmes, Oliver Wendell, Sr., 252
Hood, Edwin Milton, 547,n5
Hooker, Richard: and second Industrial Conference, 611
Hoover, Herbert Clark, 44, 389-90, 606; Leffingwell on financial projections of, 267-68; and International Labor Conference, 602; and second Industrial Conference, 611
Hoover, Irwin Hood, 642; on WW's health, 539n1, 632-38
House, Edward Mandell: and League of Nations and treaty ratification, 59; on Clemenceau's growing enthusiasm for League of Nations, 271-72; on adjourning Council of Heads of Delegations and returning to U.S., 299-300, 537; and Bullitt testimony, 337n1; on five remaining principal problems, 421-22; get-well wishes to WW, 536; ill upon arrival from Paris, 563n1, 580-81,n2; on WW's health, 563,n1, 585-86; friction with EBW, 587-88, 592-93, 621; R. S. Baker on falling out between WW and, 621; WW on, 627
House, Loulie Hunter (Mrs. Edward Mandell), 580-81, 592
Houston, David Franklin, 555, 601n1; and International Labor Conference, 602
Hovannisian, Richard G., 304n1
Hughes, Charles Evans, 223n1
Hughes, Thomas Parke, 441n2
Hugh Young, A Surgeon's Autobiography (Young), 578n
Hulbert, Allen Schoolcraft, 419,n2, 419n1
Hulbert, Mary Allen: last meeting with WW, 419,n1
Hungary, 24, 82; see also Paris Peace Conference—Hungarian treaty
Hungary at the Paris Peace Conference: The Diplomatic History of the Treaty of Trianon (Deák), 61n2
Hurley, Edward Nash, 421; and France's ships, 366, 367, 367-68

Idria (now Idrija, Yugoslavia), 297
India: WW on, 478, 505
Indianapolis, Indiana: WW's arrival and activities in, 3-4; WW's address in, 19-29
Indianapolis News, 3n5, 29n
Indians, American: see American Indians
Industrial Board of the Department of Commerce, 88,n1
Industrial Conference (first): and steel strike situation, 149,n2, 163; and police situation, 150, 265, 295; WW on, 176, 273n2; request for Negro representation at, 268; WW announces appointments to, 300,n1; WW urges Baruch to accept appointment to, 336; WW's message to, 554,n1; Lane on problems at, 582-83, 583-84, 591-92;

WW's interest in during his illness, 590, 591, 591-92; withdrawal of labor from, 591-92
Industrial Conference (second): appointment suggestions, 609-12; and R. S. Baker, 609, 621; Brandeis suggests postponing appointments to, 618
Industrial Workers of the World (I.W.W.): and WW's tour of Seattle, 238,n1; and Negroes, 268
Interallied Military Mission (Budapest), 61,n2
International Congress of Working Women (proposed), 57, 58-59
International Labor Conference: and National Women's Trade Union League, 57, 58-59; issue of admission of German and Austrian delegates, 62, 91; WW on, 14, 78, 99, 147, 261-62, 357, 373, 435, 502; concern over possible postponement of, 445-46, 463-64; suggestions for chairman of, 602
Intervention and Dollar Diplomacy in the Caribbean, 1900-1921 (Munro), 616n1
Investigation of Strike in Steel Industries: Hearings Before the Committee on Education and Labor, United States Senate, Sixty-Sixth Congress, First Session, 30n1
Ireland: issue of representatives not being heard at Paris Peace Conference, 118,n2, 269, 304, 310; WW on, 304; and Article X, 389,n1
Irish Americans, 389
Irish Race Convention, 389
iron industry, 29-30
Irvine, Benjamin Franklin, 283,n1
Istria, 206, 270-71, 298, 617n1
Italy: WW on, 11-12, 259; WW on economy of, 156; war costs, 221, 243, 349; battle deaths, 222, 243, 349; and occupation of Fiume, 298-99,n2; Polk on situation in, 364-66; Fiume situation causes crisis in, 464-65, 485-86, 515-17; Britain and France anxious treaty be ratified by, 465-66; WW on not yielding his position on, 534; King approves peace treaty with Germany and Austria, 547n4; and invasion of Trau, 557n2; information to be given on WW's health, 560; see also Adriatic question; Fiume; Italy and the United States; and under the names of the spokesmen for, such as Tittoni, Tommaso; Vittorio Emanuele III
Italy and the United States: and crisis in Spalato, 524-25, 532
I.W.W.: see Industrial Workers of the World

Jackson, Charles Samuel, 275,n2, 277, 282
James, George Roosa: appointed to first Industrial Conference, 300,n1
Japan: war costs, 349; and Russia and Cossacks, 559, 560; see also Shantung settlement
Japanese-Russian War: see Russo-Japanese War

Jay, Peter Augustus, 270, 297, 484-85; meets with Vittorio Emanuele on Fiume crisis, 297-98; on crisis in Italy over Fiume, 515-17; requests and receives information on WW's health, 543, 560
Jefferson, Thomas, 547n1
Jefferson Medical College, 539n2, 546n1
Joe Tumulty and the Wilson Era (Blum), 601n1
Johns Hopkins Medical School, 576n3, 578
Johnson, Douglas Wilson, 59n2, 270, 365; on Thrace and Greece, 61-62; and Adriatic question, 91, 92, 207,n2, 209, 210
Johnson, Hiram Warren, 223n1, 309n3, 340, 371, 445; WW answers allegations of, 309, 310; speech attacking League of Nations and Versailles Treaty, 398,n1, 399; and reservations, 482-83n4, 484
Johnson, Jackson, 32,n3, 33
Johnson amendment, 482, 483, 484, 571
Jones, Thomas Davies: appointed to first Industrial Conference, 300,n1
Jones, William Carey, 350,n1
Joseph, Archduke of Austria, 61n2
Jusserand, Jean Jules, 366

Kansas City, Missouri: Grayson on WW's arrival and address in, 63-64; WW's address in, 66-75
Kansas City Star, 63n2, 75n, 223n2
Karger, Gustav J., 51,n1, 150
Keblinger, Wilbur, 486,n6
Kelley, Cornelius Francis, 610n1
Kellogg, Frank Billings: and treaty reservations, 151, 296, 363, 444, 445
Kelly, William, 607,n1
Kenyon, William Squire, 198,n4
Kerr, Philip, 306
Kettering, Charles Franklin, 441n2
Kiaochow, China, 84, 413, 471
Kiaochow Bay, 330
Kiel, Henry William, 31,n1, 33
King, Stanley: and second Industrial Conference, 611
Kingdom of the Serbs, Croats and Slovenes: *see* Yugoslavia
Kipps, Jack, 238n1, 273n2
Kirk, Alexander Comstock, 543,n1
Kittrell College, 268n1
Knapp, Harry Shepard, 525, 532, 557,n2, 558
Knox, Philander Chase, 223n1, 445, 484, 557,n1; on Versailles Treaty, 3,n4; and Bullitt testimony, 337,n1
Kolchak, Aleksandr Vasil'evich, 394, 421, 559
Kwangchowan, China, 412,n3

labor: WW on treaty and, 14-15, 78, 87, 99, 110, 176, 246, 261-62, 356, 357, 373, 497, 502; suggestions for volunteer speakers, bureau for interpretation of WW's position, 53, 54; and Women's Trade Union League, 56-57; and steel strike, 65-66; WW on relationship between capital and, 127-28, 146-47, 244; request for Negro representation at Industrial Conference, 268; WW meets with labor leaders in Seattle, 273,n2; leaders wish to meet with WW in San Francisco, 296-97, 302-303; WW answers San Francisco leaders with memorandum, 303-304; WW's message to first Industrial Conference, 554,n1; and coal strike, 593-94, 595-98, 599-601; *see also* Industrial Conference, first and second; International Labor Conference; labor unions; strikes; Wilson, Woodrow: WESTERN TOUR—THEMES
Labor, Department of, 54
Labor in Crisis: The Steel Strike of 1919 (Brody), 30n1
labor unions: and steel strike, 29-30,n1, 148-49; and police situation, 265, 295, 296; San Francisco Labor Council's resolutions and questions, 268-70; *see also* strikes
Lagosta (now Lastovo, Yugoslavia), 91, 208, 617n1
Lamb, Albert Richard, 580n1
Lamb, Charles, 347
Lamont, Florence Haskell Corliss (Mrs. Thomas William), 165
Lamont, Thomas William, 165, 388
Landon, Archer A.: appointed to first Industrial Conference, 300,n1
Lane, Franklin Knight, 552,n1, 590, 598; on problems at first Industrial Conference, 582-83, 583-84, 591-92; appointment suggestions for second Industrial Conference, 611
Lansing, Eleanor Foster (Mrs. Robert), 540
Lansing, Robert, 60, 119-20, 120-22, 391, 543, 552, 559; and Bullitt testimony, 337-38,n1, 338n4, 541; Tumulty on resignation plans for, 337n4; concern over WW's leadership ability, 540-42, 542, 547,n1, 560; on Senate fight over reservations, 541; and Cabinet meetings, 554, 555, 556; and Adriatic question, 557; on WW's health, 571; House on desire to proceed independently of WW by, 585; on Russia's wish to buy flour from U.S., 588-89; on appointment to transportation commission outlined in peace treaty, 606-607; and Craufurd-Stuart incident, 606n1; recommends recognition of Costa Rican government, 616; informed by EBW that WW unable to address Adriatic question, 617; on Thanksgiving Proclamation as indicator of WW's poor health, 618-19; role during WW's illness, 645
Laramie, Wyo., Boomerang, 482n
Law, Andrew Bonar, 306, 307
Lawrence, David, 238n1, 265
League of Nations: Foreign Relations Committee's reservations concerning, 52n3; WW advocates treaty ratification before start of, 59; Rumanian situation, 119n2; and Senate reservations to Article X, 150-51, 392, 444, 444-45, 445, 447n1; and Senate Foreign Relations Committee's mi-

nority report on reservations, 198n1; and Fiume, 205, 207, 364, 423, 464; Wickersham's position changes, 223n1; WW on one weakness of, 232; WW on meaning of, 255-64; House on Clemenceau's growing enthusiasm for, 271-72; WW's memorandum answers San Francisco Labor Council's questions on, 302-303, 303-304; WW on difference between Assembly of and Council of, 328-29; and Bullitt testimony before Foreign Relations Committee, 337-38,n1; and Article X and Ireland, 389,n1; H. W. Johnson on, 398,n1; effort to compromise Article X, 529-31,n4; Lansing on WW's monomania concerning, 541; Rappard's notes of conversation with WW on, 627-31; see also Versailles Treaty, and Wilson, Woodrow: WESTERN TOUR—THEMES
"League of Nations" (T. Roosevelt), 223n2
League to Enforce Peace, 94,n3, 223n1, 241n1, 375, 386, 423,n2, 444,n1, 445n1, 490n1, 529; prediction on treaty ratification, 235; WW on, 289
League to Enforce Peace (Bartlett), 223n1
Ledeen, Michael Arthur, 298n2, 517n2
Leffingwell, Russell Cornell, 165, 267-68
Lenin, V. I. (Vladimir Il'ich Ul'ianov), 559
Lenroot, Irvine Luther: and treaty reservation, 151, 363
Leopold (Prince of Belgium): visits WW in his sickroom, 602-606
Leslie, Stuart W., 441n2
Lever Food and Fuel Control Act of 1917, 562,n2, 612n1
Lewis, John Llewellyn: and coal strike, 612n1
Liberty Loan Acts, 200, 201
Liberty Loans: WW on, 251
limitation of armaments: see disarmament
Lincoln, Abraham, 625
Lindsay, Ronald Charles, 297,n1, 559
Link, Arthur Stanley, 66n7
Lissa (now Vis, Yugoslavia), 206, 208
Little Rock, Arkansas, 523
Lloyd George, David, 343, 422; on Adriatic question and Fiume, 204-206, 207, 209, 364, 393, 424, 465, 617n1; and Council of the Heads of Delegations, 299, 306; issue of troops to Armenia, 466; WW on, 604; Baker on anecdote about WW and, 621
Lodge, Henry Cabot, 118, 223n1, 296, 333,n3, 380; and reservation on Article X, 150, 235, 363, 444, 444-45, 445, 447n1; WW supports his own position with quotations from, 285, 371, 375; and Bullitt testimony, 337,n1; and situation in Senate regarding amendments to treaty, 482, 484; and compromise reservation to Article X, 529,n2, 531
London, Treaty of (1915): and Adriatic question, 209
London Times, 621,n1
Long, Breckinridge, 93, 543,n2, 558-59, 606; on WW's reaction to Bullitt testimony, 338n4; on situation in Senate on

reservations and Article X, 444-45
Long, Richard Henry, 615n1
Longley, Harry Sherman, 76n1
Los Angeles, California: WW's arrival and activities in, 396-97, 423, 523; WW's speeches in, 400-407, 407-18
Los Angeles Evening Express, 423,n3
Los Angeles Examiner, 398
Los Angeles Sunday Times, 400n1, 407n,n2, 418n
Los Angeles Times, 398n1, 423n2,3
Louisville, Kentucky, 523
Lussin (Lussino, now Losinj, Yugoslavia), 206
Lyons, Richard L., 167n6

McAdoo, Eleanor Randolph Wilson (Mrs. William Gibbs), daughter of WW and EAW, 167, 543, 619; arrives at White House, 549
McAdoo, William Gibbs: at White House during WW's illness, 543, 544, 550; and WW's health, 586
McCall, Samuel Walker: and second Industrial Conference, 611
MacCormack, William, 423,n1
McCormick, Vance Criswell: congratulates WW on effect of tour, 117; on League to Enforce Peace's prediction on treaty ratification, 235; and treaty reservations, 363, 392
McCoy, Donald R., 167n6
McCumber, Porter James: and treaty reservations, 150, 296, 363, 444, 445, 447, 482; on compromise reservation to Article X, 529-30,n4
McGlachlin, Edward Fenton, Jr., 274,n2, 361,n1, 361-62
McGuire, Michael J., 269, 296-97
McKean, Frank Chalmers, 92n1
McKee, Henry Stewart, 400n1, 423,n3
McKellar, Kenneth Douglas, 443,n2
McKelvie, Samuel Roy, 94
McKinley, William: and China and open-door policy, 211, 315, 330, 332, 397, 412, 437, 439, 460, 471, 473, 496, 507; WW on League of Nations and, 370; extracts from last speech of, 398, 398-99, 407
McLane, Catharine Milligan, 623
McLean, Edward Beale, 552,n2
McNab, Gavin, 309, 340; appointed to first Industrial Conference, 300,n1
McNary, Charles Linza, 150; and reservations on Article X, 444-45
MacVeagh, (Isaac) Wayne, 555,n1
Mains, Lillian, 168,n4
Mains, William Lee, 168,n3, 170
Malatia, Turkish Armenia, 466
Mandan, North Dakota: WW's remarks in, 162, 163
mandates (trusteeships): House on, 422; WW on: see Wilson, Woodrow: WESTERN TOUR—THEMES
Manual of Parliamentary Practice. For the

Manual of Parliamentary Practice (cont).
	Use of the Senate of the United States (Jefferson), 547n1
Mapes, Carl Edgar, 265,n7
March, Peyton Conway, 361
Marshall, Thomas Riley, 117, 265, 542, 555, 563n1, 563, 585, 586
Mary, Queen (Victoria Mary of Teck), consort of George V, 559
Mason, Guy, 445,n1, 447, 483
Massachusetts: gubernatorial election of 1920, 615,n1
Matthews, Mark Allison, 273n1
Mayflower, U.S.S., 119
Medora, North Dakota, 153,n4
Memphis, Tennessee, 443, 523
Mercier, Désiré Félicien François Joseph, Cardinal Mercier, 166, 197; get-well wishes, 549
Meredith, Edwin Thomas: appointed to first Industrial Conference, 300,n1
Metropolitan, 223,n2
Mexico, 165; WW on, 195
Meyers, J. Edward, 131,n1
Mills College, 352n1
Milner, Alfred, 1st Viscount Milner, 299, 307, 422
Minneapolis, Minnesota: WW's reception in, 123-24,n3; WW's address in, 123-24,n1, 131-38
Minneapolis Journal, 113n, 148n
Minneapolis Morning Tribune, 123n3,4
Missouri River, 152
Monroe, James, 192, 430, 450
Monroe Doctrine: Foreign Relations Committee's reservation concerning, 52n3; Rappard on WW's hope to extend, 627; WW on: *see* Wilson, Woodrow: WESTERN TOUR—THEMES
Montenegro, 210
Mooney, Tom, 273n2
Moran, William Herman, 515,n1, 531
Morris, Roland Sletor, 395, 608
Moses, George Higgins: on WW's health, 563-64, 564-67, 570, 642
Mott, Sara Maude Robinson (Mrs. Ernest J.), 311,n1
Munro, Dana Gardner, 616n1
Murdock, Victor, 391,n6
Murray, Robert K., 167n6
Myers, Henry Lee, 197, 265
Myers Resolution, 265, 295
My Memoir (Edith B. Wilson), 419n1, 539n1, 578n1, 606n1

National Coal Association, 56
National Committee for Organizing Iron and Steel Workers, 30n1
National Industrial Conference: *see* Industrial Conferences
National Race Congress, 268,n1
National Women's Trade Union League, 56-57, 58-59
Naval Affairs Committee (House of Reps.), 160,n2

Naval Appropriation Act of 1916, 160n2, 164, 169-70, 261
naval appropriation bill of 1917, 164, 177-78
naval appropriation bill of 1918, 160,n2, 164, 177-78
naval appropriation bill of 1919, 160n2, 164, 177-78
Negroes: and unorganized labor, 268
Nelson, Knute: and reservations on Article X, 150, 444, 445
Nevada Historical Quarterly, 426n1
Nevin, John Edwin: on WW's health and return trip to Washington, 527-28
New, Harry Stewart, 5; and Bullitt testimony, 337n1
Newark, Ohio, 3,n2
New England Quarterly, 167n6
New Jersey: WW's interest in election in, 608, 615,n1
newspapers: Los Angeles papers endorse WW's position, 423; opposition papers on trip cancellation, 521; *see also* under the names of the individual newspapers, such as *New York Times; Springfield,* Mass., *Republican*
New York *Evening Post,* 238n1
New York Herald, 273n2
New York *Sun,* 521
New York Times, 3n4, 18n, 52n3, 75n, 97n, 118n3, 138n, 148n, 152n1, 163n, 165n, 180n, 197n, 198n2,3,4, 211n6, 223n1, 238n1, 254n2, 273n2, 275n4, 283n1, 300n1, 309n2, 333n3, 337n1, 376, 482n2,4, 517n2, 531n, 537n, 538n, 547n4, 551n, 564n,n1, 565, 568n, 580n, 581n2, 585n,n1 587n, 591n, 593n1, 594n2, 599n1, 606n, 608n1, 609n, 612n1, 615n2
New York Tribune, 165, 223n1, 238n1, 273n2, 309n2
New York *World,* 3n3,5, 267, 273n2, 309n2, 370n2, 564n1
New Zealand, 477, 505
Nitti, Francesco Saverio, 210, 486, 516, 517, 524; protests against occupation of Fiume, 298-99; plea to WW regarding Fiume, 464-65; WW answers on Fiume, 485-86
Nolan, William Ignatius, 125,n1
Nonpartisan League, 95, 152, 153n1
Norris, George William, 94, 106, 197, 390,n1; accuses WW of erroneous statement, 93
North Dakota, U.S.S., 153,n4
Novara, Battle of, 517,n4

Oakland, California: WW's activities in, 308; WW's address in, 340,n3, 352-61
Oakland Tribune, 340n1, 361n
O'Connell, John A., 268-70, 303
Ogden, Utah: WW's activities in, 446, 447,n1; WW's remarks in, 447, 448
Ogden, Utah, *Examiner,* 446n2, 447n
Ogden, Utah, *Standard,* 447n
Ohio Farm Bureau Federation, 300n1

Ohio State University, 7n1
Oklahoma City, Oklahoma: and WW's trip cancellation, 520-21
Olcott, Ben Wilson, 275n1, 283n1
Olympia, U.S.S., 557n2
Omaha, Nebraska: Grayson on WW's reception in, 93-94; WW's address in, 97-107
Omaha *World-Herald,* 107n
open-door policy: WW on, 412, 437, 460, 507
Oregon, U.S.S., 239
Oregon Historical Quarterly, 276n5
Orlando, Vittorio Emanuele, 343
Owen, Robert Latham, 203
Oxnard, California, 369

Page, Florence Lathrop Field (Mrs. Thomas Nelson), 382-83,n2
Page, Thomas Nelson, 382-83,n1
Palfrey, John Carver, 624,n1
Palmer, Alexander Mitchell: and Volstead bill, 590, 601n1; and coal strike, 598, 608,n1, 612n1; on rumors about WW's health, 608
Pan-American Petroleum Company, 552n1
Paris Peace Conference: and Senate Foreign Relations Committee's minority report on reservations, 198n1; WW on, 341
  Austrian treaty, 13, 82, 111, 372, 457, 493-94, 501-502; Vittorio Emanuele III gives royal assent to, 547n4
  Bulgarian treaty, 151,n4, 166, 299, 306, 372, 432, 457, 493-94, 502, 502-503
  Hungarian treaty, 299, 306, 307, 372, 421, 432, 457, 502, 502 503
  Turkish treaty, 299, 372, 422, 432, 457, 493-94, 502, 502-503
  Versailles treaty: see Versailles Treaty
Park, Bert Edwin, 539n1; analysis of WW's medical history and stroke of Oct. 2, 1919, 639-46
Parker, Frank, 362,n1
Parsons, B. A., 66,n1
Pasco, Washington, 211n6
Patterson, James R., 275n4
Patton, George Smith, 423,n3
Patton, George Smith, Jr., 423n3
Payne, John Barton, 366, 367, 368-69
Peek Committee: *see* Industrial Board of the Department of Commerce
Pelagosa Islands (now Pelagruz Islands, Yugoslavia), 206, 208
Perley Morse & Co., 389n2
Permanent Court of International Justice (proposed), 261
Pershing, John Joseph, 117; and welcoming parade, 274n2; WW regrets he's unable to welcome, 295
Peters, Andrew James, 167n6, 169
Petigru, James Louis, 252,n4
Petition for Political Amnesty, 425,n1
Petrograd, Russia: and flour, 588-90,n1
Philadelphia *Public Ledger,* 275n4
Philippine Islands, 74, 383, 384, 455
Phillips, William, 119, 119-20, 166, 204,

235-36, 271-72, 297, 304, 369, 392, 392-93, 560; and International Labor Conference, 62, 445-46, 463-64; on Fiume and Adriatic question, 91-92, 270, 364-66, 485-86, 532, 534; on Thrace, 151, 305; on occupation of Fiume, 298-99; on Russian situation and needed aid, 394, 421; on troops to Armenia, 423, 464, 466; on reservation concerning Article X, 444; on WW's health, 537-38
Pierson, George Washington, 168n3, 170
Pittaluga, Vittorio Emanuele, 485,n1
Pittman, Key, 483; on public opinion in Washington and ratification prospects, 117-18; and Foreign Relations Committee's minority report on reservations, 198,n1
Pittsburgh, U.S.S., 486,n7
Pittsburgh Coal Company, 56
Poland: WW on, 10-11, 13-14, 24-25, 82, 98, 186, 250, 372
Pola (now Pula, Yugoslavia), 298
Polish Americans: Cora Budziszewski in Tacoma, 250,n2
Polk, Frank Lyon, 59, 151, 166, 421, 422, 537, 571, 588, 607; and Thrace, 60-62, 120-22, 235-36, 305; and Adriatic question, 91-92, 204-10, 270, 617n1; on Rumanian situation, 119,n2,3; concern over adjourning Council of Heads of Delegations, 299, 306, 391; on pressure from Britain and France regarding Fiume, 424, 465-66; and troops to Armenia, 466; on severe Italian crisis, 524-25; and Italy and Spalato, 532; inquires about WW's health, 536; receives word on WW's health, 537-38
Pomerene, Atlee: on treaty reservations, 198,n1, 198,n3, 296
Port Arthur, China, 314, 315, 323, 330, 412, 437, 438, 461, 471, 472, 507
Portland, Oregon: WW's activities in, 274-76; newsmen in automobile accident, 275-76, 277; WW's addresses in, 277-83, 283-94
Portland *Morning Oregonian,* 283n
Portland *Oregon Daily Journal,* 275, 283n1, 294n
Portsmouth, Treaty of (1905), 438, 461, 472, 507
prices and price-fixing: and coal, 55; and steel, 88-91, 118-19, 301
Princeton University, 340n3
Prince of Wales: *see* Edward Albert Christian George Andrew Patrick David
progressivism: WW on, 127, 216
prohibition enforcement bill: *see* Volstead bill
public opinion in the United States: WW on treaty and, 388, 448, 449, 470, 499, 500
Public Papers of Woodrow Wilson (Baker and Dodd), 6
Pueblo, Colorado: Grayson on WW's arrival and activities in, 487-88; WW's address in, 500-515
Pueblo, Colo., Chieftain, 487n2, 513n

Quesada, Castro, 616
Quirós, Juan Bautista, 616,n1

race riots: WW on, 196
railroad crisis of 1916, 251,n1
railroad situation, 54; W. B. Wilson on nationwide campaign to interpret WW's statement to railroad shopmen, 53, 54; WW on, 78
Rappard, William Emmanuel: notes of conversation with WW in Nov. 1918, 626-31
Rathdrum, Idaho, 210n1
Reardon, Timothy A., 269
Red Cross organizations: WW on Versailles Treaty and, 262, 357
Redfield, William Cox, 52,n4; on his resignation and suggestions for successor, 573-74; and WW's veto of Volstead bill, 601n1
Red Scare: A Study in National Hysteria, 1919-1920 (Murray), 167n6
Reed, James Alexander, 64, 167,n5,7
Reid, Edith Gittings (Mrs. Henry Fielding), 575-76,n1
Reinhardt, Aurelia Isabel Henry (Mrs. George Frederick), 352,n1
Reno, Nevada: Grayson on WW's arrival and activities in, 426; WW's address in, 428-41
reparation: WW on, 9, 36, 44, 171-72
Reparation Commission: WW on, 36-37, 44
Republican party, 26; and situation in Senate regarding reservations, 150, 235, 363, 445, 482, 529, 531, 541, 586; WW on nonpartisan character of treaty, 222, 228-29, 247, 248, 257, 288, 386, 417-18; Tumulty on answering criticism of, 399-400; and proposed super cabinet, 626
Republican party in Indiana, 4
Republican party in Missouri, 32
Republic of Armenia (Hovannisian), 304n1
Reynolds, Stanley Meade, 275,n4
Richmond, Indiana: 3n5; WW's remarks in, 18-19
Rickey, Harry Norris, 444,n1, 445, 447
Riddell, Crockett Morgan, 241,n1
Robins, Margaret Dreier (Mrs. Raymond), 56,n2
Robinson, Henry Mauris: and second Industrial Conference, 611
Rockefeller, John Davison, Jr.: appointed to first Industrial Conference, 300,n1
Rocky Ford, Colorado, 489-90
Rogers, Samuel Lyle, 573,n2
Rolph, James, Jr., 308,n1, 323,n1
Roman Catholic Church: and labor, 610, 612
Roosevelt, Theodore, 94, 438, 473; in North Dakota, 153,n3; and League of Nations, 223,n2; WW quotes from, 371, 376; on international court, 509
Roosevelt in the Kansas City Star: War-Time Editorials by Theodore Roosevelt, with an Introduction by Ralph Stout, 223n2
Root, Elihu, 223n1
Rosenthal, B. B., 269

Rosenwald, Julius: and second Industrial Conference, 611
Roumania: see Rumania
Rowell, Chester Harvey, 309,n3, 323,n1
Ruffin, Sterling, 544,n3, 550, 551, 553, 556, 578, 579, 634; bulletins on WW's health, 568, 574, 577, 578, 579, 581, 587, 590
Rumania, 24, 61, 82, 119-20,n2,3, 306, 421
Rush, Richard, 430
Russell, Charles Edward: appointed to first Industrial Conference, 300,n1
Russell, Francis, 167n6
Russia: WW on, 70, 76-77, 95-96, 134, 145, 152, 161-62, 174-75, 214, 216, 245, 263; battle deaths, 221, 243, 349; war costs, 221, 243, 349; and China, 314, 330, 437, 438; and Bullitt's testimony before Foreign Relations Committee, 337,n3; need for aid, 394; House on, 421-22; issue of troops to Armenia, 466; U.S. to send grain to, 588-90,n1
Murmansk and Archangel, intervention in: and flour from U.S., 589
Siberia, intervention in, 394; loan request and repatriation of Czech troops, 394-95, 421, 518; Daniels on, 559-60
Russian Revolution, 1917-1921 (Chamberlin), 588n1
Russo-Japanese War, 315, 330, 412, 438, 472, 507
Ryan, Michael J., 118n2

Sacramento, California: WW's arrival and activities in, 426; WW's remarks in, 426-27
Sacramento Bee, 427n
St. Joseph, Missouri, 64
St. Louis, Missouri: speeches in mentioned, 32; WW's address to Chamber of Commerce in, 33-42, 45, 198,n1; WW's address in Coliseum, 43-51; Norris criticizes WW's address in, 93
St. Louis Chamber of Commerce: WW's address to, 33-42; address mentioned, 32, 45
St. Louis Globe-Democrat, 42n, 51n
St. Louis Post-Dispatch, 18n, 29n, 32n, 42n, 51n, 52n4
St. Louis Republic, 151n3
St. Paul, Minnesota: WW kept waiting by Governor, 122, 124; WW's reception and activities in, 122-23, 124,n4; WW's addresses in, 125-31, 138-48; photograph, illustration section
Salt Lake City, Utah: WW's activities in, 446, 447,n1; WW's address in, 446,n2, 449-63; WW's address mentioned, 529
Salt Lake City Salt Lake Tribune, 463n
San Diego, California: WW's arrival and activities in, 369-70, 523; WW's addresses in, 371-82, 382-88; photograph of WW in, illustration section
San Diego Evening Tribune, 382n, 388n
San Francisco, California: WW's activities in, 308-10, 340; Grayson on WW's address in Civic Auditorium, 309-10,n2; WW's address to Associated Women's Clubs of,

311-22; notes for address in Civic Auditorium, 322-23; WW's address in Civic Auditorium, 323-36; WW's luncheon address in, 341-50; photograph of WW in, *illustration section*

San Francisco Chronicle, 336n, 350n

San Francisco Examiner, 309n2, 322n, 336n, 350n

San Francisco Labor Council, 268-70; requests meeting with WW, 296-97, 302-303; WW's memorandum answers questions posed by, 303-304

Santa Catalina Island, 370

Savy, Joseph Jean Michel, 485,n4

Sayre, Jessie Woodrow Wilson (Mrs. Francis Bowes), daughter of WW and EAW, 619; shares family news and thanks WW for birthday gift, 166-67; notified of WW's cancelled trip, 521; arrives at White House, 549; and visit of Belgian royalty, 603, 606

Sayre, Woodrow Wilson, grandson of WW: Jessie on resemblance to WW, 167,n4

Scheller-Steinwartz, Robert Richard von, 254,n2, 333-34,n2

Schneidermann, Rose, 56

Schweinitz, George Edmund de, 539,n1, 544, 551,n1, 579, 641

Scialoja, Vittorio, 393, 525, 525-26; House on, 422

Seattle, Washington: Grayson on WW's arrival and activities in, 237-40, 273; WW attends First Presbyterian Church of, 273,n1; WW's remarks and address in, 253-54, 254-64; WW meets with labor leaders, 273,n2

Seattle Post-Intelligencer, 210n1,2, 211n5, 234n, 264n, 273n1

Seattle Times, 398

Seibold, Louis, 3n3, 370n2

Serbia: WW on start of war and, 20, 24, 109, 187-88, 245-46, 259, 360, 372-73

Sforza, Count Carlo, 517,n3

Shantung amendment: rejected by Senate, 482,n4; Hitchcock's prediction concerning, 482, 571; result of Senate vote on brought to WW's bedside, 576

Shantung settlement: WW on, 28, 40, 83-84, 94-95, 104-105, 123-24, 193-94, 237, 314-17, 329-32, 411-13, 436-40, 460-61, 470-74, 496, 507; Norris accuses WW of erroneous statement on, 93, 94; WW's concern over Capper's opposition to, 519-20

Sherman, Lawrence Yates, 295,n1

Shields, John Knight: and treaty reservations, 198,n1, 443,n3, 483

Shiloh Baptist Church (Washington, D.C.), 268n1

Shotwell, James Thomson, 58

Siberia: *see* Russia, Siberia, intervention in

Sibert, William Luther, 362,n1

Silesia, 306; *see also* Upper Silesia

Simmons, Furnifold McLendel: on treaty reservations, 118, 198,n3

Simonds, Frank Herbert, 621,n2

Sinclair, Upton Beall: on conscientious objectors, 425,n1

Sioux Falls, South Dakota: WW's arrival in, 95; WW's address in, 107-17

Sioux Falls Daily Argus-Leader, 117n

Slade, George Theron, 611

Small, Robert T., 275-76,n4

Smith, Hoke, 483, 535

Smith, James Ellwood, 43,n1

Smith, Marcus Aurelius: and Foreign Relations Committee's minority report on reservations, 198,n1

Smuts, Jan Christiaan, 286, 287, 477; WW on, 505

Smyrna (now Izmir, Turkey), 61

Snyder, May Ross (Mrs. Meredith Pinxton), 423,n3

Snyder, Meredith Pinxton, 407n1, 423,n3

"Something Desperate In His Face": Woodrow Wilson in Portland at the "Very Crisis of his Career" (Trow), 276n5

South Africa, 477, 505

Southern Railway Company, 607n1

Spain, 232

Spalato (now Split, Yugoslavia), 525, 532, 557

Spanish-American War: WW on, 434, 455

Spargo, John: appointed to first Industrial Conference, 300,n1

Spencer, Selden Palmer, 296

Sperry, Elmer Ambrose, 441n2

Sperry, Lawrence, 441n2

Spinozzi, Augustine, 587,n2

Spokane, Washington: WW's arrival in, 211,n5,6; WW's address in, 224-34

Spokane Spokesman Review, 221n4, 234n

Springfield, Mass., Republican, 609n2, 611

standard of living, 15

State, Department of: and National Women's Trade Union League, 57, 58-59

Steed, Henry Wickham, 621,n1

steel industry: and strike, 29-30,n1, 52, 65, 148, 149, 163, 583; and steel rail prices and disclosure issue, 88-91, 118-19, 300, 301; and breakup of first Industrial Conference, 582-83

Stephens, William Dennison, 308,n1

Stewart, George, 588n1

Stewart, Samuel Vernon, 169,n6, 180

Stewart, Stella Baker (Mrs. Samuel Vernon), 169,n7

Stitt, Edward Rhodes, 544,n1, 550, 551, 553, 556, 568, 574, 577, 578, 579, 581, 587, 590, 634

Stone, Albert W., 513-14,n1

Story of Mrs. Peck: An Autobiography by Mary Allen Hulbert, 419n1

Stratton, Samuel Wesley, 573,n2, 621

Straus, Oscar Solomon: and second Industrial Conference, 611

strikes: steel, 29-30,n1, 52, 65, 148-49, 163, 583; Boston police, 167,n6,7; bituminous coal, 593-94, 595-98, 599-601

Stuart, Henry Carter, 611

Summerall, Charles Pelot, 362,n1

Supreme Court (U.S.): *see* United States Supreme Court
Supreme Council of the Principal Allied and Associated Powers: *see* Council of Four
Suresnes Cemetery: WW on his remarks at, 181, 197, 512
Swanson, Claude Augustus: and Foreign Relations Committee's minority report on reservations, 198,n1
Sweet, Edwin Forrest, 573,n1, 621
Sweet, Louis Dennison: appointed to Industrial Conference, 300,n1
Sweet, Sophia Fuller (Mrs. Edwin Forrest), 621
Swem, Charles Lee: and WW's western tour, 5-6, 97; I. H. Hoover on, 638
Switzerland: Rappard's notes on meeting with WW on League of Nations, neutrality and, 627-31
Sykes-Picot Agreement of 1916, 466

Tacoma, Washington: Grayson on WW's arrival and activities in, 236-37; WW's speeches in, 240-41, 241-52; photograph of WW in, *illustration section*
Tacoma Ledger, 241n, 250n2
Tacoma News Tribune, 252n
Taft, William Howard, 94, 444; WW praises for League of Nations work, 222, 248; his reservation on Article X, 363; and International Labor Conference, 602
Talien-wan (Dairen), China, 314,n3, 323, 330, 412, 437, 472
Tardieu, André Pierre Gabriel Amédée, 271, 305; on Adriatic question and Thrace, 60, 120-22, 208-209
Taussig, Frank William: and Industrial Conference, 611
Taylor, Henry Noble, 56,n4
Thanksgiving Proclamation, 613-15; as indicator of WW's illness, 618-19, 644
Thayer, William Sydney, 576,n3
Theodore Roosevelt Writes on Helping the Cause of World Peace (*New York Times*), 509,n2
Thomas, Charles Spalding, 483
Thompson, Samuel Huston, Jr., 391,n6
Thompson, William Oxley, 7,n1; and Industrial Conference, 611
Thrace, 59n2, 60-62, 120-22, 305; Phillips on deferring decision on, 151; Polk on, 235-36; WW's note to Vénisélos on settlement, 391-92
Thurman, Albert Lee, 573,n2
Tighe, M. F., 149
Tinoco Granadas, Féderico, 616,n1
Tinoco Granadas, Joaquín, 616n1
Tittoni, Tommaso, 62, 484; on Fiume and Adriatic question, 91-92, 270, 297, 364-66, 393, 424, 465, 517, 525, 526, 617n1
Titus, Louis: appointed to first Industrial Conference, 300,n1
Togoland, 422
Trammel, Park, 483
Trau (now Trogir, Yugoslavia), 557n1,2

Treasury (U.S.): WW on Glass' suggestions, 336
Treaty of Peace With Germany: Hearings Before the Committee on Foreign Relations United States Senate, 66th Cong. 1st sess., 118n2
Treaty of Versailles: *see* Versailles Treaty
Trieste, 298, 485
Trotsky, Leon (Leib or Lev Davydovich Bronstein), 559, 588n1
Trow, Clifford W., 276n5
trusteeships: *see* mandates
Tumulty, Joseph Patrick, 51, 52, 64, 91, 92, 117, 117-18, 150, 163, 165, 198, 221, 235, 264, 268, 296, 302, 369, 371, 444, 447, 483, 490, 514, 552,n1, 556, 582, 606, 625, 626; and proposed women's international labor conference, 58-59; on plans for California tour, 164; and steel strike, 164; strategy and ideas for WW's speeches, 164, 222-23, 397-99; on WW's reaction to Bullitt testimony, 338n4; on answering criticism of WW's opponents, 399-400; and possible horrors of next war, 441; plans for Albert's visit, 515; on trip cancellation, 519, 522-23; organizes WW's return to Washington, 522, 531-32; WW discusses treaty with via telephone, 537; prayers and sympathy on WW's illness, 539; on WW's health, 539n1, 542, 548, 586, 619; loyalty to WW indicates he will never certify WW is disabled, 547,n1, 638; on first Industrial Conference, 554,n1, 590, 591; WW's unavailability to during illness, 567, 638; and Shantung amendment vote, 576; and coal strike, 593-94, 595-98; and veto message of Volstead bill, 601n1; appointment suggestions for second Industrial Conference, 602, 609-12; and reorganization of European transportation, 613; messages to WW filter through EBW, 615; on proposed super cabinet, 625; I. H. Hoover on WW's illness and, 637, 638,n6; role during WW's illness, 638,n6, 645
Turkey, 49, 71, 74, 100, 236; Tardieu on Thrace and, 121, 122; war costs, 221, 243, 349; *see also* Paris Peace Conference—Turkish treaty
Tyler, Lyon Gardiner, 463
Tyrrell, Sir William (George), 606n1

Uglian (Ugliano, now Uljan, Yugoslavia), 91, 206, 207, 208
Ullman, Richard Henry, 588n1
Underwood, Oscar Wilder, 443, 535
Unie (now Unije, Yugoslavia), 206, 208
unions: *see* labor unions
United Mine Workers of America, 56n1, 593n1, 596, 597, 599, 600, 612n1
United Press, 58
United States: war casualties, 221-22, 223, 243, 349; war costs, 221, 243, 349
United States: European relief, credits and postwar reconstruction: WW on, 44-45,

499; Glass on Treasury and, 200-204; Leffingwell on Hoover's financial projections, 267-68; and transportation commissions, 606-607; transportation commissions appointments made, 613,n1; *see also* reparation

United States Army: WW on, 74-75, 81, 108, 293-94; battle injuries and deaths, 223, 243; WW's message to First Division, 274; First Division, 361-62; issue of troops to Armenia, 423

United States Congress: WW on war-declaration power of, 229, 346-47; and Pershing's welcome, 295; suggested resolution honoring Foch, 301,n1,2; and presidential disability, 562; I. H. Hoover on authorship of WW's message to, 638

House of Representatives: WW's veto message of Volstead bill and House vote on, 601,n1; *see also* under the names of individual committees, such as Foreign Affairs, Committee on

Senate: and WW's speeches on western tour, 6; and treaty reservations, 198,n1,2,3,4; predictions on treaty approval by, 235; and police situation, 295; and Armenia, 304,n1; and Federal Trade Commission and Hoover report, 425; reservations on Article X, 444, 444-45; rejection of various amendments to treaty, 482,n2,4; Shantung amendment defeated, 482,n4, 576; WW on rejection or ratification of treaty, 499; effort to compromise on Article X, 529-31; Burleson on improved situation in, 535; Hitchcock predictions on amendments, 571; reports of possible adjournment opposed by WW, 572; reservations needed for treaty ratification, 586; vote to override veto of Volstead bill, 601n1; *see also* under the names of specific senators, such as Hitchcock, Gilbert Monell; Lodge, Henry Cabot; and under the names of individual committees, such as Foreign Relations, Committee on

United States Constitution, 235; and issue of presidential disability, 547,n1, 561, 562

United States Fuel Administration: *see* Fuel Administration

United States Grain Corporation: *see* Grain Corporation

United States Navy: and forces in Adriatic, 556-57, 557,n2

United States Shipping Board: and France's ships, 366-69; and Czech troops in Russia, 395

United States Steel Corporation, 301, 66, 148, 149

United States Supreme Court: and presidential disability, 562-63

Upper Silesia: WW on, 13-14, 98, 186-87

Urbana, Ohio, 3n5

urgent deficiency appropriation bill, 608

Valona, Albania, 206, 209, 617n1

Van Kleek, Mary Abby, 57,n3

Vénisélos, Eleuthérios Kyrios, 60, 61, 166; WW's message to, 391

Versailles Treaty: Knox on, 3n4; WW's concern over delay in Senate action on, 17-18, 76-79, 155, 156, 255; WW advises reading French text if one cannot understand English, 48, 85, 103; Foreign Relations Committee reports treaty to Senate with four reservations, 52,n3; WW's ten principles of, 163; Foreign Relations Committee's minority report on reservations, 198,n1,2; Glass on effect of ratification delay on financial and economic situation, 203; Burleson's strategy for ratification, 266; Pomerene's concern over mild reservationists' strategy, 296; and Bullitt-Lansing exchange and controversy, 337-38, 541; public opinion in California on, 388; H. W. Johnson on, 398,n1; Burleson on cotton producers and, 442-43; Burleson on Tennessee's senators position on, 443; Britain and France anxious to have Italy ratify, 465-66; Hitchcock on amendment situation in Senate, 482-83, 571; Vittorio Emanuele III gives royal assent to, 547n4; reservations needed for ratification, 586; organization of transportation commissions as outlined in, 606-607, 613,n1; for WW's comments on *see* Wilson, Woodrow—WESTERN TOUR—THEMES; *see also* League of Nations

Vesnić (Vesnitch), Milenko R., 465

Vienna, Congress of (1815): *see* Congress of Vienna

Vittorio Emanuele II, 517,n4

Vittorio Emanuele III, 270, 382, 465, 486, 516, 517, 524, 547,n4; urges WW to accept Tittoni's proposals, 297-98

Volosca (now Opatija, Yugoslavia), 617n1

Volstead, Andrew John, 562n1

Volstead bill, 562,n1, 571, 582, 590, 608; WW's veto of, 601

Wagner, Charles C., 557,n1, 558

Waldron, John Milton, 268,n1

Wallace, Hugh Campbell, 588; suggests resolution honoring Foch, 301,n1

Walsh, David Ignatius, 445, 483

Walsh, Francis Patrick, 118,n2; on Article X and Ireland, 389

War Cabinet (U.S.) (super cabinet) (proposed), 625, 626

War Finance Corporation: Glass on financial situation and, 200, 203

Warren, Charles, 623-24,n1

Washington, George, 375, 406

Washington, D.C.: police situation in, 149-50, 150, 264-65, 295, 296; WW on threatened police strike in, 302; WW's arrival in from western tour, 533, photograph, *illustration section*; Rent Commission formed, 562n2, 571

Washington Herald, 265

Washington Post, 265, 273n2, 274n2, 545n,

Washington Post (cont).
  546n1, 550n, 553n, 556n, 557n1, 561n,
  573n, 575n, 577n, 582n, 587n2
Washington Star, 265
Washington Times, 265
Waters, Henry Jackson, 611
Watson, James Eli, 5
Wattles, Gurden Wallace, 94n3
Weaver, James Bellamy, 76,n1
Weeks, John Wingate, 625
Weihaiwei, China, 314, 323, 330, 412, 413,
  471-72
Weinstein, Edwin Alexander, 539n1
western Thrace: *see* Thrace
What Wilson Did at Paris (R. S. Baker),
  609n2
Wheelwright, Jere Hungerford, 56,n2
White, Henry, 91, 537, 606; and Bullitt tes-
  timony, 337n1
White, John Philip, 56,n1
White, Sebastian Harrison, 490,n1, 500
*White Armies of Russia: A Chronicle of
  Counter-Revolution and Allied Interven-
  tion* (Stewart), 588n1
Wichita, Kansas: WW cancels trip to, 520,
  522-23; WW's message to people of, 524
Wickersham, George Woodward: on League
  of Nations, 222-23,n1; WW on conversion
  of, 248; and second Industrial Conference,
  611
Wickersham Answers League Obstruction-
  ists (*New York Times*), 223n1
Wilde, Louis J., 370,n1, 371, 382
Willard, Daniel, 607,n3, 613,n1
William and Mary College: WW receives
  honorary degree from, 463
Williams, John Sharp: and Foreign Relations
  Committee's minority report, 198,n1; and
  troops to Armenia, 304,n1, 464, 466
Williams, Joyce Grigsby, 606n1
Wilson, Edith Bolling Galt (Mrs. Woodrow),
  165, 167, 526, 558, 559, 575, 578n1, 585,
  608; on western tour with WW, 4, 31, 32,
  63, 65, 94, 95, 96, 122, 168, 169, 239, 273,
  308, 382, 419; reception in Portland, 276;
  on meeting with Mrs. Hulbert, 419n1;
  Mrs. Hulbert on, 419n1; and decision to
  cancel remainder of trip, 519; trip exhausting for, 523; nurses WW on return to
  Washington, 527, 528; N. D. Baker offers
  to help lessen WW's work load, 534; and
  WW's stroke, 539n1; as WW's nurse, 549,
  619, 621; and WW's health, 552n1; and
  Adriatic crisis, 557, 558, 617; entertains
  WW by reading, 561, 636; furnishes WW
  with news, 574; informs Mrs. House of
  WW's condition, 580-81; House's concern
  about news of him being withheld from
  WW by, 587-88; on reasons for not telling
  WW of House's return from Paris, 592;
  and visit of Belgian royalty, 603, 605,
  606n1; and Craufurd-Stuart affair, 606n1;
  messages to WW filter through, 609, 615;
  on WW being unable to study Adriatic
  question at this time, 617; appears tired

and worn, 619; R. S. Baker on, 619, 621;
  and House, 621; marriage announcement
  to WW, 624-25; at time of WW's stroke,
  633-64; during WW's illness, 637, 637-38,
  638; influence during WW's illness, 638
Wilson, Ellen Louise Axson (Mrs. Woodrow), 632n1
Wilson, Joseph R., brother of WW: arrives at
  White House, 549
Wilson, Joseph Ruggles, father of WW, 417;
  WW on death of, 624
Wilson, Margaret Woodrow, daughter of WW
  and EAW, 549, 619; notified of WW's canceled trip, 521; and visit of Belgian royalty,
  603, 606; asks Mrs. Reid for human interest stories for WW, 575-76
Wilson, William Bauchop, 56, 554; on nationwide campaign to interpret WW's
  statement to railroad shopmen, 53, 54;
  compares railroad and coal situations, 54-
  55; on Women's Bureau, 56-57; and coal
  strike, 593, 598; and second Industrial
  Conference, 611

WOODROW WILSON

confident of acceptance of treaty, impatient
  with delay, 17-18; on his remarks at Sur-
  enes Cemetery, 181, 197; message to First
  Division, 274; regrets that he is unable to
  welcome Pershing, 295; to receive the
  Prince of Wales, 297,n1; memorandum
  answers San Francisco Labor Council's
  questions, 303-304; Albert wishes to bestow honors on WW and other officials,
  307-308; reaction to Bullitt testimony,
  338n4; on origins of the war, 359-60; first
  test of "voice phone," 369-70; cannot accept foreign decoration by Albert, 392; declines rectorship of University of Glasgow,
  395-96; Tumulty's strategy and suggestions for WW's speeches, 397-99; honorary degree from William and Mary College, 463; plans for Albert's arrival, 515,
  526; on Albert's visit, 532; to be informed
  of Senate vote on reservations, 586; visit
  from Belgian royalty, 602-606; presents
  Albert with set of *History of the American
  People*, 603; Thanksgiving Proclamation,
  613-15; sends election congratulations to
  Coolidge and Edwards, 615,n1; commit-
  ment to early literary work, 624; I. H. Hoover on authorship of WW's message to
  Congress, 638

APPEARANCE AND IMPRESSIONS

Jessie on resemblance of her new son to,
  167,n4; Mrs. Hulbert on, 419n1; "the
  weariness of a nation passed over his
  countenance," 487; at work, when dictating letters, 514; extraordinary concentration, 514; Rappard on, 626, 629, 630, 631;
  I. H. Hoover on, 633-35

Woodrow Wilson, cont.

APPOINTMENT SUGGESTIONS,
APPOINTMENTS AND RESIGNATIONS

Redfield's resignation and suggestions for his successor, 52,n4, 573-74,n1,2; Women's Bureau, 56,n1, 57,n4; request for Negro delegates to first Industrial Conferences, 268; and Industrial Conference, 300,n1, 336, 609-12; Tumulty suggests WW's illness prevented request for Lansing's resignation, 338n4; and Lane, 552,n1; and appointments for transportation commissions as designated by treaty, 606-607, 613,n1; Brandeis suggests postponing appointments to second Industrial Conference, 618

CABINET

Lansing calls meeting to consider WW's disability, 542; meetings of, 554, 556, 606; and WW's disability, 555, 562, 585-86; on grain for Russia, 589; on coal situation, 598; and second Industrial Conference appointments, 618; WW's attendance of during his illness, 637; and authorship of WW's message to Congress, 638

FAMILY AND PERSONAL LIFE

news from Jessie, 166-67; grandson's christening postponed, 167; Jessie on resemblance of her new son to, 167,n4; on his ancestors, 282; last meeting with Mrs. Hulbert, 419,n1; description of WW at work, 513-14, emotion on canceling trip, 519; daughters notified of trip cancellation, 521; family all arrive at White House during illness, 549, 550; Margaret asks Mrs. Reid for human interest stories to tell WW, 575-76; receives Belgian royalty in his sickroom, 602-606; announcement of marriage to EBG, 624-25; death of his father (1903) defers activities of, 624

HEALTH

Grayson on WW's poor condition at start of tour, 3; headaches, 3, 32, 152, 275, 340, 397, 446, 489, 523, 574, 620, 639, 640; Grayson on strain and fatigue of tour on, 64, 123, 211n5, 276; cold, 96; Grayson insists WW conserve his strength, 96; Grayson's concern over WW's needed rest, 237; alleged effect of I.W.W. "silent demonstration" in Seattle on, 238n1; cough and coughing spells, 275, 446, 527; Grayson refuses to permit WW to speak at fairgrounds in Oregon, 275; Grayson on needed rest to prevent breakdown, 309; first physical indication of break, 338n4; speaks at Berkeley reportedly against wishes of his physician, 340n1; Grayson's concern over damp weather's effect on, 370; fatigue, 397, 446; Grayson's continued concern over, 446, 488-90; nervous

Woodrow Wilson, cont.

condition apparent, 467; takes walk for an hour to stretch legs, 488-89; asthmatic attacks, 489, 539; face-muscle twitching, nauseated, seriously ill, "stroke warning," 518-19; Grayson insists on trip cancellation, 518-21; reasons given press for trip cancellation, 522, 523; news article on Grayson's plans for WW's rest on return to Washington, 527-28; fairly good night on train, 531; Grayson on WW's restless night and discomfort due to train speed, 532-33; Grayson emphatic about strict rest for WW, 533; rests upon return to White House, 533; get-well wishes, 534, 535, 535-36, 536, 548, 549, 580; news reports on improved condition, 536-37, 552-53; official bulletin on, 536; Polk inquires about, 536; Grayson's analysis of situation, 537-38; bulletins indicate no change, 538; Grayson gives Garfield account of WW's condition, 538-39; specialists called in, 539, 544-45, 546,n1, 551, 553, 634; suffers stroke, 539n1; Tumulty's grief, 539; Lansing on WW's condition and effect on running of government, 540-41, 542; Lansing calls Cabinet meeting to consider WW's disability, 542; news reports and bulletins on, 543-45; and nervous exhaustion (neurasthenia), 545, 642; illness during Paris Peace Conference, 546,n1, 551n1; continued news reports and bulletins on, 549-50, 550-51; "stroke" of 1906, 551n1; Grayson reports to Cabinet on, 554; bulletins report gains, 55-56; Long relays Grayson's report to Lansing on, 558-59; news reports continue, 560-61, 561-63, 563-64; unable to resume duties for some time, 560, 561; rumor of cerebral lesion, 563-64, 564-67; rumors starting, 564-67; rumor of slight facial paralysis, 566, 567; retinal lesion, 567-68; twitching of facial muscles (hemifacial spasm), 567, 579, 640-41, 641; more bulletins and news reports, 568, 572, 574-75, 576-77, 577, 577-78, 586-87, 590; Grayson on mental alertness of WW, but rest cure a priority, 569-71; Lansing on, 571; prostate gland affliction, 572,n1, 577-78, 578-79,n1, 580, 581-82, 620; upsetting news kept from, 580; health bulletins continue, 581; issue of who acts for WW during disability, 585; stroke rumors, 586; House concerned over information about himself being withheld from WW, 587-88; signs bills, but still required to rest, 587; improvement visible, 608; Palmer on rumors, 608; Lansing on Thanksgiving Proclamation as indication of WW's poor health, 618-19; Lansing on WW's signature as reflection of severe illness, 619; R. S. Baker on Grayson's and EBW's account of WW's health on western trip, 619-20; R. S. Baker on, 619-22, 622; Grayson on left facial drag or looseness, 620; R. S. Baker on secrecy concern-

Woodrow Wilson, cont.

ing, 620; Grayson stopped some early remedies, 622; had rest before western trip,
632-33; I. H. Hoover on, 632-38; I. H.
Hoover's account of day of stroke, 633; I.
H. Hoover on beginning of deception of
public regarding, 634, 635, 637; purchase
of special chair from Atlantic City, 636;
signature change, 636; hypertension, 639;
Park's analysis of WW's medical history
and stroke of Oct. 2, 1919, 639-46; eye
problem, 641; Park on presidential disability, 644-45

OPINIONS AND COMMENTS

This treaty is not merely meant to end this
single war. It is meant as a notice to every
government which in the future will attempt this thing that mankind will unite to
inflict the same punishment, 8-9; on revolution, 12-13; on secret treaties, 28, 39,
137, 261, 359; The greatest nationalist is
the man who wants his nation to be the
greatest nation, and the greatest nation is
the nation which penetrates to the heart of
its duty and mission among the nations of
the world, 33; The seed of war in the modern world is industrial and commercial rivalry, 45; on Bolshevism, 73; on isolation,
79; on "Germanism," 113; on idealism,
113, 189; on progressivism, 127, 216; on
ethnic diversity of America, 139-40, 280;
on hyphenated Americans, 140, 143, 320-
21, 469-70, 493, 501; In order to live tolerable lives, you must lift the fear of war
and the practice of war from the lives of
nations, 144; on radicalism, 177; on U.S.
decision to enter war, 181-82, 191, 213,
233-34, 293, 312, 347, 401, 430, 468; on
the world's confidence in America, 184; on
economic conditions, 189; on police
strikes, 196, 302; on one weakness of
League of Nations, 232; The choice that
we have to make now is whether we will
receive the influences of the rest of the
world and be affected by them, or dominate the influences of the world and lead
it, 279; The only thing in the world that is
unconquerable is the thought of men, 282;
The only thing that makes the world inhabitable is that it is sometimes ruled by
its purest spirits, 321-22; on Paris Peace
Conference, 341; The only effective force
in the world is the force of opinion, 345,
360; This treaty is nothing else than an organization of liberty and mercy for the
world, 357; Stop for a moment to think of
the next war, if there should be one. . . . I
ask any soldier if he wants to go through
any hell like that again. That is what the
next war would be. And that is what would
be the destruction of mankind. And I am
for any kind of insurance against it and the
barbarous reversal of civilization, 495; My
clients are the children; my clients are the

Woodrow Wilson, cont.

next generation. They do not know what
promises and bonds I undertook when I
ordered the armies of the United States to
the soil of France, but I know. And I intend to redeem my pledges to the children;
they shall not be sent upon a similar errand, 511

RECREATION

takes walk, 32; automobile rides, 92, 423,
523, 533, 536, 538; EBW reads to, 561,
636; "talking machine" entertains WW,
561; I. H. Hoover on period between return from Paris and western trip, 632; attends theater, 636

RELIGIOUS LIFE

282; attends church in Des Moines, 92; attends church in Seattle, 273; attends
church in Los Angeles, 423

WESTERN TOUR
(ACTIVITIES, EVENTS, SPEECHES)

first appearance, 3; preparation and delivery
of speeches, 6; address in Columbus,
Ohio, 7-18; remarks in Richmond, Indiana, 18-19; address in Indianapolis Coliseum, 19-29; addresses in St. Louis, 33-
42, 43-51; welcome in Kansas City, 63-64;
complains of heat in Kansas City Auditorium, 64n1; in St. Joseph, Missouri, 64-65;
arrival and activities in Des Moines, 65-66;
address in Kansas City, 66-75; address in
Des Moines, 76-88; wants only absolutely
urgent mail forwarded, 92, 120, 151; arrival in Sioux Falls, 95; rides on rear platform, 95; on train, 96-97; address in
Omaha, 97-107; address in Sioux Falls,
107-17; address in Minneapolis Armory,
123-24,n1, 131-38; address in St. Paul,
124, 138-48; address to joint session of
Minnesota legislature, 125-31; arrival and
address in Bismarck, 152-62; remarks in
Mandan, North Dakota, 162, 163; plans
for California tour, 164; reception and activities in Billings and Helena, 168-69; address in Billings, 170-80; address in Helena, 180-97; stay in Coeur d'Alene and
Spokane, 210-11; address in Cour d'Alene,
212-21; speech in Spokane, 224-34; activities in Tacoma and Seattle, 236-40;
I.W.W. "silent demonstration" in Seattle,
238,n1, 240; speeches in Tacoma, 240-41,
241-52; remarks and address in Seattle,
253-54, 254-64; meets with labor leaders
in Seattle, 273,n2; activities in Portland,
274-76; automobile accident, 275-76, 277;
addresses in Portland, 277-83, 283-94; arrival and activities in Oakland and San
Francisco, 308-10, 340; address to Associated Women's Clubs of San Francisco,
311-22; address in Civic Auditorium, 322-
23, 323-36; luncheon address in San Fran-

Woodrow Wilson, cont.

cisco, 341-50; address in Berkeley, 350-52; address in Oakland, 352-61; first test of microphone, 369-70; arrival and activities in San Diego, 369-70; addresses in San Diego, 371-82, 382-88; arrival and activities in Los Angeles, 396-97, 423; speeches in Los Angeles, 400-407, 407-18; arrival and activities in Sacramento, 426; remarks in Sacramento, 426-27; address in Reno, 428-41; activities and speeches in Ogden, Utah, and Salt Lake City, 446n2, 447, 448, 449-63; arrival and address in Cheyenne, 467, 467-82; arrival, activities and speeches in Denver and Pueblo, 487-88,n2, 490-500, 500-513; walk on Colorado plateau, 488-89; description and schedule of typical day, 513-14; cancellation of remaining speeches, 519-20, 522-24; sends message to people of Wichita, 522, 523, 524; on return trip to Washington, 526, 527, 531-32; back in Washington, 532-33; photographs of WW during tour, *illustration section*

WESTERN TOUR—THEMES

The end of American isolation, 36, 79, 112, 115, 138, 155-56, 173, 189, 215, 279, 291-92, 334, 401-402, 407, 415-17, 448, 456-57, 480
The treaty an American document, 66-67, 72, 77, 82, 98, 184-85, 281, 311, 342, 401
The treaty a nonpartisan document, 19, 26, 49-50, 97-106, 130-31, 221, 228-29, 247-48, 288-89, 374-75, 386, 417-18, 494, 499-500
The treaty a world settlement, 7, 72, 131-32, 154, 171, 184-85, 212, 225, 344, 351
The treaty a humane document, 15-16, 34, 97, 137, 173, 262, 351, 354, 356-57, 371-73, 380, 458
the Magna Carta of Labor, 14-15, 78-79, 99, 110, 127-28, 137, 146-47, 246, 261-62, 356, 373, 497, 502
the mandate (trustee) system a protection of indigenous peoples, 15-16, 111-12, 435, 458
the redemption of the rights of new and weak nations, 10-11, 24-25, 34-35, 187, 259, 291, 329, 335-36, 374, 379-80, 403
the protection of women and children, suppression of traffic in drugs, etc., 16, 137, 262, 357
The necessity of American leadership in League to prevent future wars, 9, 17-18, 28-29, 37, 47, 78-79, 107-108, 113, 115, 116-17, 134, 145-46, 155, 157-58, 160-62, 172, 179-80, 180-81, 217-18, 234, 248-49, 284, 292, 312, 334-35, 348, 350, 360-61, 382, 384, 386-87, 405-406, 410, 418, 433-34, 448, 469, 474, 478, 494-95, 498, 510-12
Defense of various provisions of the Covenant

Woodrow Wilson, cont.

the Monroe Doctrine, 49, 85-86, 103, 192-93, 230-31, 247-48, 287-88, 318-19, 322, 327, 376, 403, 429-30, 430, 431-32, 450-51, 475
the Shantung settlement, 28, 40, 83-84, 94-95, 104-105, 123-24, 193-94, 237, 314-17, 329-32, 411-13, 436-40, 460-61, 470-74, 496, 507
voting in the Assembly (six votes for the British Empire), 231-32, 309-10, 320-21, 328-29, 377-78, 414-15, 435-36, 476-78, 491-92, 504-506
the right of withdrawal, 102-103, 179, 190-91, 226-27, 288, 319-20, 326-27, 440-41, 449-50, 475
The League of Nations and collective security
Article X the heart of the covenant for peace, 22, 40-42, 84, 101, 158-59, 191-92, 214, 226, 227-29, 316-18, 331-32, 345, 403-404, 432-33, 451-52, 459-60, 475-76, 478-80, 506, 507-508, 509
Article XI and the peacekeeping machinery of the League (procedures for settlement of international disputes), 20-21, 23-24, 37-38, 48-49, 67-68, 86-87, 100, 109, 114-15, 135, 142-43, 158, 176, 194-95, 218, 245-46, 255-57, 345-47, 380-81, 386-87, 409, 482, 492, 494, 503; (boycotts), 23, 38-39, 49, 68, 87, 100, 135-36, 257-58, 346, 409-10
the League as insurance against future war, 101-102, 146-47, 175-76, 195, 225, 227-28, 359-60, 380-81, 409-10, 459-60, 481-82, 105, 512-13
On reservations and changes, 102-104, 105, 160, 171, 185, 219-20, 231, 262-63, 290, 291, 379, 392, 451-54, 479-80, 498, 510
Reservations to Article X, 158-59, 452-54, 478-80, 480-82; *see also* Article X the heart of the covenant for peace, above
Opponents of the League, 25-26, 29, 43, 72-73, 105, 228, 289, 325, 351, 352, 402-403, 408, 428-29, 449

End of Woodrow Wilson entry

Wilson: The New Freedom (Link), 66n7
"Wobblies": *see* Industrial Workers of the World
women: and labor unions and proposed international labor conference, 56-57, 58-59; WW on, 140
Women's Bureau (Department of Labor), 56-57
Woodrow Wilson: A Medical and Psychological Biography (Weinstein), 539n1
Woodrow Wilson: An Intimate Memoir (Grayson), 539n1
Woodrow Wilson and the American Diplomatic Tradition: The Treaty Fight in Perspective (Ambrosius), 482n4
Woodrow Wilson As I Know Him (Tumulty), 338n4, 547n1
Worden, Montana, 168,n1

World War: battle deaths and war costs, 221, 243-44, 349, 349-50; WW on start of, 372-73, 430-31

Young, Hugh Hampton, 578-79,n1, 580, 581, 582, 587, 643
Young, Owen D.: and second Industrial Conference, 611
Yudenich, Nikolai Nikolaevich, 588n1

Yugoslavia (Kingdom of the Serbs, Croats and Slovenes), 82, 188; and Adriatic question and Fiume, 205, 207-208, 209-10, 298, 365, 366, 465, 525

Zara (now Zadar, Yugoslavia), 91, 206, 207-208, 465, 617n1; and D'Annunzio invasion of, 517n2